AF323556

Blockchain Science
Distributed Ledger Technology

Roger Wattenhofer

Preface

Blockchain Birth

In 2008, an enigma only known as *Satoshi Nakamoto* published a paper titled *Bitcoin: A Peer-to-Peer Electronic Cash System*. Apart from a few early Bitcoin enthusiasts nobody expected a revolution.

Computer scientists working in the area of cryptocurrencies were not all that excited by Bitcoin, because cryptocurrencies had been around for decades already. In 1983, David Chaum proposed a cryptocurrency called *ecash*, later also known as *Digicash*. Other currencies such as *b-money* or *bit gold* followed, all long before Bitcoin.

For cryptocurrency researchers, Bitcoin was just another cryptocurrency. Indeed, all of Bitcoin's ingredients were already known. Proof-of-work? First suggested to fight email spam in 1993. Merkle trees? Patented in 1979. Public key cryptography? Discovered in the early 1970s. Data replication? Pretty surely the Babylonians did this already! What about the *blockchain*? This word is *not* even in Satoshis Bitcoin paper – but used much earlier in a 1997 cryptocurrency called *HashCash*.

Really, Bitcoin was just a clever combination of known techniques, and science usually does not care much about such combinations. However, not only was the combination clever, Satoshi also provided the Bitcoin software for download. While earlier cryptocurrencies were mostly of academic interest, everybody could be part of this wonderful new Bitcoin world. Everybody could participate, and become rich!

In the early years, Bitcoins had little value. In May 2010, two pizzas were exchanged for 10,000 Bitcoins. Around this time, the first Bitcoin exchanges started, and soon enough the cost of a

Bitcoin exploded. Within the next few years, the general public started to notice, and so did the scientific community.

In the mid-2010s, Bitcoin became a popular cocktail party topic. People were puzzled that it is feasible to transfer money by just exchanging large numbers. If large numbers represent money, why can one not spend the same Bitcoin twice? The ingredients of cryptocurrencies had been used long before Bitcoin, in every web browser and email client. But now these old ingredients became exciting again since they directly represented money. We got ourselves a genuine gold rush!

Blockchain Boom

Personally, I started working on cryptocurrencies and the Bitcoin blockchain in 2012. In the mid-2010s, I quite often found myself explaining Bitcoin and its techniques to colleagues and friends.

Such enthusiasm in my research was an unfamiliar experience for me, so eventually I decided to write this book. The first edition was published in January 2016, at the very same time my student Christian Decker successfully defended his PhD thesis – as far as I know he was the first Bitcoin/blockchain PhD student in the world!

After Christian graduated, I did not really plan to continue working in the area. I try to work on fresh and upcoming topics, and I expected the interest in blockchains might soon come to an end.

I was wrong. The price of a Bitcoin continued to surge, and people were more enthusiastic about cryptocurrencies and blockchains than ever before. Not surprisingly, the excitement for the topic and the price of a Bitcoin in USD are correlated. In January 2016, a Bitcoin was worth about USD 400, almost 100 times more than when I first looked into the subject in 2012. Certainly the interest in blockchains today is even bigger than in early 2016. We are in the blockchain era – the term blockchain is often mentioned together with other mega trends in computer science and information technology, such as machine learning or quantum computing.

Blockchain Basics

The interest of the scientific community in distributed ledgers (or "blockchains") is much older than even the first cryptocurrency. A sizeable amount of work in distributed systems and cryptography is about storing transactions securely. Many organizations and companies built distributed ledgers. For instance, in 1971 NASDAQ opened the first computerized stock market, which is basically a distributed ledger.

The Turing Award is recognized as the highest distinction in computer science, a "Nobel Prize of Computing". Thanks to Google, the award is also accompanied by a prize of USD 1 million.

Maybe surprisingly, a good number of Turing Awards can be linked to blockchains in one or another way. There is the 2002 Turing Award for Ronald Rivest, Adi Shamir and Leonard Adleman, the 2012 award for Silvio Micali and Shafi Goldwasser, or the 2015 award for Martin Hellman and Whitfield Diffie. These are the Turing Awards for cryptographic breakthroughs so far. Likewise, there have been Turing Awards for distributed computing, in particular 2008 for Barbara Liskov, 2013 for Leslie Lamport, and to some degree also the 2010 award for Leslie Valiant. In other words, in the last ten years roughly half of all Turing Awards can be linked to blockchains. This book is as least as much about these Turing Awards as it is about Bitcoin.

While almost all the scientific work of these "blockchain Turing Awards" was already developed in the 20th century, the awards were given in 2002, 2008, 2010, 2012, 2013 and 2015. In other words, not only is the general public electrified by blockchains, it seems that also the scientific community was electrified all along.

In summary, the blockchains have been around long before the term blockchain emerged. Various brilliant (Turing Award worthy!) concepts have existed before Satoshi's Bitcoin blockchain, each with its own advantages and disadvantages.

Blockchain Book

The idea of this book is to give a scientifically precise description of the most interesting approaches that have emerged, before Bitcoin and after. If you are interested in "blockchains", this book will help you to get a deep understanding of the topic. We will learn what is possible and what is not.

This book introduces the basic techniques when building fault-tolerant distributed systems. We will present different protocols and algorithms that allow for fault-tolerant operation, and we will discuss practical systems that implement these techniques. The focus is clearly on the fundamentals, we hardly ever will mention company names.

The book presents the main ideas independently from each other, each topic has its own chapter. Each chapter starts with an introductory story that motivates the content of the chapter. Algorithms, protocols and definitions are presented formally, so that we know precisely what we are talking about. Some insights are proved in theorems, so that we learn why the concepts or algorithms are correct, and what they can guarantee. Most of the other text is presented as remarks. These remarks discuss various informal thoughts, and often set the stage for the next idea. However, one will get the essence of this book without reading any remarks. Each chapter also discusses the history of the ideas presented in the chapter, in order to find the original research.

Third Edition

Apart from many minor improvements, this third edition of the book contains a lot more content. In particular, the third edition includes new chapters and sections on broadcast, shared coins, selfish mining, DAG-blockchains, payment hubs, proof-of-stake, strong consistency and logical time (Chapters 6, 11 and 12) In addition, the book features an appendix, discussing some of the underlying fundamentals such as game theory, physical clocks, and Markov chains (Chapters 14, 15 and 16).

Acknowledgements

Some colleagues have helped in writing and improving this book. Thanks go to Georg Bachmeier, Pascal Bissig, Philipp Brandes, Christian Decker, Manuel Eichelberger, Klaus-Tycho Förster, Arthur Gervais, Pankaj Khanchandani, Barbara Keller, Rik Melis, Darya Melnyk, Tejaswi Nadahalli, Peter Robinson, Jakub Sliwinski, Selma Steinhoff, Julian Steger, David Stolz, and Saravanan Vijayakumaran. Jinchuan Chen, Qiang Lin, Yunzhi Xue, and Qing Zhu translated this book into Simplified Chinese, and along the way found improvements to the English version as well. Thanks!

Roger Wattenhofer

Contents

III   Appendix   215

Chapter 1

Introduction

1.1 Why Distributed Systems?

Today's computing and information systems are inherently *distributed*. Many companies are operating on a global scale, with thousands or even millions of machines on all the continents. Data is stored in various data centers, computing tasks are performed on multiple machines. At the other end of the spectrum, also your mobile phone is a distributed system. Not only does it probably share some of your data with the cloud, the phone itself contains multiple processing and storage units. Your phone is a complicated distributed architecture.

Moreover, computers have come a long way. In the early 1970s, microchips featured a clock rate of roughly 1 MHz. Ten years later, in the early 1980s, you could get a computer with a clock rate of roughly 10 MHz. In the early 1990s, clock speed was around 100 MHz. In the early 2000s, the first 1 GHz processor was shipped to customers. In 2002 one could already buy a processor with a clock rate between 3 and 4 GHz. If you buy a new computer today, chances are that the clock rate is still between 3 and 4 GHz, since clock rates basically stopped increasing. Clock speed can apparently not go beyond a few GHz without running into physical issues such as overheating. Since 2003, computing architectures are mostly developing by the multi-core revolution. Computers are becoming more parallel, concurrent, and distributed.

Finally, data is more reliably stored on multiple geographically distributed machines. This way, the data can withstand regional disasters such as floods, fire, meteorites, or electromagnetic pulses, for instance triggered by solar superstorms. In addition, geographically distributed data is also safer from human attacks. Recently we learned that computer hardware is pretty insecure. Scary attacks exist, with scary names such as spectre, meltdown, rowhammer, memory deduplication. There are even attacks on hardware that is considered secure! If we store our data on multiple machines, it may be safe assuming hackers cannot attack all machines concurrently. Moreover, data and software replication also help availability, as computer systems do not need to be shut down for maintenance.

In summary, today almost all computer systems are distributed, for different reasons:

- Geography: Large organizations and companies are inherently geographically distributed, and a computer system needs to deal with this issue anyway.

- Parallelism: To speed up computation, we employ multicore processors or computing clusters.

- Reliability: Data is replicated on different machines to prevent data loss.

- Availability: Data is replicated on different machines to allow for access at any time, without bottlenecks, minimizing latency.

Even though distributed systems have many benefits, such as increased storage or computational power, they also introduce challenging *coordination* problems. Some say that going from one computer to two is a bit like having a second child. When you have one child and all cookies are gone from the cookie jar, you know who did it!

Coordination problems are so prevalent, they come with various flavors and names. Probably there is a term for every letter of the alphabet: agreement, blockchain, consensus, consistency, distributed ledger, event sourcing, fault tolerance, etc.

Coordination problems will happen quite often in a distributed system. Even though every single *node* (node is a general term for anything that computes, e.g. a computer, a multiprocessor core, a network switch, etc.) of a distributed system will only fail once every few years, with millions of nodes, you can expect a failure every minute. On the bright side, one may hope that a distributed system may have enough redundancy to tolerate node failures and continue to work correctly.

1.2 Book Overview

The central concept of this book will be introduced in Chapter 2. The research community originally called this concept *state replication*, see Definition 2.8, today the term blockchain is also popular. We achieve state replication if all nodes of a distributed system agree on a sequence of commands (or transactions), the same set of commands in the same order. State replication can be achieved using various algorithms, depending on the failures and attacks the distributed system must be able to tolerate.

In Chapter 2 we will motivate and introduce the basic definitions, and present Paxos, an algorithm that achieves state replication even though a minority of nodes in the system may crash. Paxos is one of the earliest "blockchain protocols, and still used in many distributed systems.

In Chapter 3 we will explain why Paxos may not make progress, and that indeed no deterministic protocol can solve state replication if we are unlucky. This is a theoretical insight with highly practical implications. However, on the positive side, we will also introduce a fast randomized consensus protocol that can solve state replication even if nodes crash.

In Chapter 4 we look beyond simple crash failures, and introduce protocols that work even in the presence of malicious behavior (some nodes in the system behave arbitrarily badly, as if they were controlled by an attacker), in synchronous and asynchronous systems. In addition, we will explore different definitions what could be considered when we say that a distributed system is "correct".

In Chapter 5 we introduce some basic cryptographic principles that will help us to implement various efficient protocols in the remaining chapters of the book. We do not tailor our description towards any specific cryptographic tool, but describe the basic mathematical foundations.

In Chapter 6, we study a basic technique called broadcast. In addition, we study so-called shared coins. In Chapter 3 we have already seen that randomness might help to solve state replication. So we need to get a better understanding how distributed randomness can be generated.

In Chapter 7 we use message authentication, a cryptographic primitive introduced in In Chapter 5. We first present a simple synchronous protocol, and then PBFT, a state of the art asynchronous protocol for implementing state replication if message authentication is available. Many popular permissioned blockchain protocols, e.g. the hyperledger fabric, are variants of PBFT.

In Chapter 8 we investigate scalability issues by studying so-called quorum systems. If a set of servers is no longer powerful enough, and adding more servers does not help, quorum systems may be an elegant solution.

So far, the focus was on so-called permissioned systems. A permissioned (or closed) system is a system where the nodes are known. The second part of the book is about permissionless (or open) systems, where the nodes are not known a priori. If the nodes of a system are not known, we need additional concepts such as proof-of-work.

In Chapter 9 we introduce weaker consistency concepts that have been popular among permissionless blockchain protocols. We discuss the Bitcoin blockchain protocol as a prime example of such a permissionless but only eventually consistent protocol. We also discuss payment channels and networks as a popular solution to drastically increase the throughput of a permissionless blockchain.

In Chapter 10 we dig a bit deeper and explain some of the fascinating details of Bitcoin, such as how the Bitcoin script is defined.

In Chapter 11 we study some recent developments that are prevalent in the world of permissionless blockchains. First, we look at the selfish mining problem of proof-of-work blockchains such as Bitcoin or Ethereum. Then we study blockchains beyond simple chains, where blocks are encouraged to have multiple parent blocks. Next we study smart contracts, and how they can help to build payment hubs. And Finally we briefly discuss proof-of-work alternatives such as proof-of-stake.

In Chapter 12 we study strong consistency and logical time, two important concepts when it comes to build asynchronous distributed systems.

Finally, in Chapter 13 we explore weaker consistency concepts, and present highly scalable distributed storage solutions.

The book also features an appendix, a few chapters that may help understanding some of the fundamentals of the main content.

In Appendix 14 we introduce the fundamental concepts of game theory. The classic failure models of distributed systems are crash failures (Chapter 2) and byzantine failures (Chapter 4), but a modern view must also contain selfishness. We used game theoretic arguments in some of the chapters, e.g. in Chapter 11.

In Appendix 15 we introduce to the area of physical clocks and clock synchronization. Having well-synchronized physical clocks (instead of just logical clocks as discussed in Chapter 12) becomes more and more popular in distributed systems.

In Appendix 16 we introduce the fundamental concepts of Markov chains, a concept that was used in the analysis of selfish mining in Chapter 11.

Chapter Notes

Many good textbooks have been written on the subject, e.g. [AW04, CGR11, CDKB11, Lyn96, Mul93, Ray13, TS01]. James Aspnes has written an excellent freely available script on distributed systems [Asp14]. Similarly to our book, these focus on large-scale distributed systems, and hence there is some overlap with our book. There are also some excellent textbooks focusing on small-scale multicore systems, e.g. [HS08].

While there are literally hundreds of blockchain books, almost all of them are different from this book. Some will discuss Bitcoin and other cryptocurrencies at length, but will ignore permissioned blockchains, even though they are much more relevant in practice. Others take a rather economic view, focussing on applications, not worrying about the technology at all. And most books will just tell the most entertaining stories. This book is very different, as it explains the concepts on an academic level.

Bibliography

[Asp14] James Aspnes. Notes on Theory of Distributed Systems, 2014.

[AW04] Hagit Attiya and Jennifer Welch. *Distributed Computing: Fundamentals, Simulations and Advanced Topics (2nd edition)*. John Wiley Interscience, March 2004.

[CDKB11] George Coulouris, Jean Dollimore, Tim Kindberg, and Gordon Blair. *Distributed Systems: Concepts and Design*. Addison-Wesley Publishing Company, USA, 5th edition, 2011.

[CGR11] Christian Cachin, Rachid Guerraoui, and Lus Rodrigues. *Introduction to Reliable and Secure Distributed Programming*. Springer Publishing Company, Incorporated, 2nd edition, 2011.

[HS08] Maurice Herlihy and Nir Shavit. *The Art of Multiprocessor Programming.* Morgan Kaufmann Publishers Inc., San Francisco, CA, USA, 2008.

[Lyn96] Nancy A. Lynch. *Distributed Algorithms.* Morgan Kaufmann Publishers Inc., San Francisco, CA, USA, 1996.

[Mul93] Sape Mullender, editor. *Distributed Systems (2nd Ed.).* ACM Press/Addison-Wesley Publishing Co., New York, NY, USA, 1993.

[Ray13] Michel Raynal. *Distributed Algorithms for Message-Passing Systems.* Springer Publishing Company, Incorporated, 2013.

[TS01] Andrew S. Tanenbaum and Maarten Van Steen. *Distributed Systems: Principles and Paradigms.* Prentice Hall PTR, Upper Saddle River, NJ, USA, 1st edition, 2001.

Part I

Permissioned Systems

Chapter 2

Fault-Tolerance & Paxos

How do you create a fault-tolerant distributed system? In this chapter we start out with simple questions, and, step by step, improve our solutions until we arrive at a system that works even under adverse circumstances, Paxos.

2.1   Client/Server

Definition 2.1 (node). *We call a single actor in the system **node**. In a computer network the computers are the nodes, in the classical client-server model both the server and the client are nodes, and so on. If not stated otherwise, the total number of nodes in the system is n.*

Model 2.2 (message passing). *In the **message passing model** we study distributed systems that consist of a set of nodes. Each node can perform local computations, and can send messages to every other node.*

Remarks:

- We start with two nodes, the smallest number of nodes in a distributed system. We have a *client* node that wants to "manipulate" data (e.g., store, update, ...) on a remote *server* node.

Algorithm 2.3 Naïve Client-Server Algorithm

1: Client sends commands one at a time to server

Model 2.4 (message loss). *In the message passing model with* **message loss***, for* **any** *specific message, it is not guaranteed that it will arrive safely at the receiver.*

Remarks:

- A related problem is message corruption, i.e., a message is received but the content of the message is corrupted. In practice, in contrast to message loss, message corruption can be handled quite well, e.g. by including additional information in the message, such as a checksum.

- Algorithm 2.3 does not work correctly if there is message loss, so we need a little improvement.

Algorithm 2.5 Client-Server Algorithm with Acknowledgments

1: Client sends commands one at a time to server
2: Server acknowledges every command
3: If the client does not receive an acknowledgment within a reasonable time, the client resends the command

---

Remarks:

- Sending commands "one at a time" means that when the client sent command c, the client does not send any new command c' until it received an acknowledgment for c.

- Since not only messages sent by the client can be lost, but also acknowledgments, the client might resend a message that was already received and executed on the server. To prevent multiple executions of the same command, one can add a *sequence number* to each message, allowing the receiver to identify duplicates.

- This simple algorithm is the basis of many reliable protocols, e.g. TCP.

- The algorithm can easily be extended to work with multiple servers: The client sends each command to every server, and once the client received an acknowledgment from each server, the command is considered to be executed successfully.

- What about multiple clients?

Model 2.6 (variable message delay). *In practice, messages might experience different transmission times, even if they are being sent between the same two nodes.*

Remarks:

- Throughout this chapter, we assume the variable message delay model.

Theorem 2.7. *If Algorithm 2.5 is used with multiple clients and multiple servers, the servers might see the commands in different order, leading to an inconsistent state.*

Proof. Assume we have two clients u_1 and u_2, and two servers s_1 and s_2. Both clients issue a command to update a variable x on the servers, initially $x = 0$. Client u_1 sends command $x = x + 1$ and client u_2 sends $x = 2 \cdot x$.

Let both clients send their message at the same time. With variable message delay, it can happen that s_1 receives the message from u_1 first, and s_2 receives the message from u_2 first.[1] Hence, s_1 computes $x = (0 + 1) \cdot 2 = 2$ and s_2 computes $x = (0 \cdot 2) + 1 = 1$.

$\square$

Definition 2.8 (state replication). *A set of nodes achieves **state replication**, if all nodes execute a (potentially infinite) sequence of commands $c_1, c_2, c_3, \ldots,$ in the same order.*

---

[1]For example, u_1 and s_1 are (geographically) located close to each other, and so are u_2 and s_2.

Remarks:

- State replication is a fundamental property for distributed systems.

- For people working in the financial tech industry, state replication is often synonymous with the term blockchain. The Bitcoin blockchain we will discuss in Chapter 9 is indeed one way to implement state replication. However, as we will see in all the other chapters, there are many alternative concepts that are worth knowing, with different properties.

- Since state replication is trivial with a single server, we can designate a single server as a *serializer*. By letting the serializer distribute the commands, we automatically order the requests and achieve state replication!

Algorithm 2.9 State Replication with a Serializer

1: Clients send commands one at a time to the serializer
2: Serializer forwards commands one at a time to all other servers

3: Once the serializer received all acknowledgments, it notifies the client about the success

---

Remarks:

- This idea is sometimes also referred to as *master-slave replication*.

- What about node failures? Our serializer is a single point of failure!

- Can we have a more *distributed* approach of solving state replication? Instead of directly establishing a consistent order of commands, we can use a different approach: We make sure that there is always at most one client sending a command; i.e., we use *mutual exclusion*, respectively *locking*.

Algorithm 2.10 Two-Phase Protocol

Phase 1

1: Client asks all servers for the lock

Phase 2

2: **if** client receives lock from every server **then**
3:    Client sends command reliably to each server, and gives the lock back
4: **else**
5:    Clients gives the received locks back
6:    Client waits, and then starts with Phase 1 again
7: **end if**

Remarks:

- This idea appears in many contexts and with different names, usually with slight variations, e.g. *two-phase locking (2PL)*.

- Another example is the *two-phase commit (2PC)* protocol, typically presented in a database environment. The first phase is called the *preparation* of a transaction, and in the second phase the transaction is either *committed* or *aborted*. The 2PC process is not started at the client but at a designated server node that is called the *coordinator*.

- It is often claimed that 2PL and 2PC provide better consistency guarantees than a simple serializer if nodes can *recover* after crashing. In particular, alive nodes might be kept consistent with crashed nodes, for transactions that started while the crashed node was still running. This benefit was even improved in a protocol that uses an additional phase (3PC).

- The problem with 2PC or 3PC is that they are not well-defined if exceptions happen.

- Does Algorithm 2.10 really handle node crashes well? No! In fact, it is even worse than the simple serializer approach (Algorithm 2.9): Instead of needing one available node, Algorithm 2.10 requires *all* servers to be responsive!

- Does Algorithm 2.10 also work if we only get the lock from a subset of servers? Is a majority of servers enough?

- What if two or more clients concurrently try to acquire a majority of locks? Do clients have to abandon their already acquired locks, in order not to run into a deadlock? How? And what if they crash before they can release the locks?

- Bad news: It seems we need a slightly more complicated concept.

- Good news: We postpone the complexity of achieving state replication and first show how to execute a single command only.

2.2   Paxos

Definition 2.11 (ticket). *A **ticket** is a weaker form of a lock, with the following properties:*

- **Reissuable:** *A server can issue a ticket, even if previously issued tickets have not yet been returned.*

- **Ticket expiration:** *If a client sends a message to a server using a previously acquired ticket t, the server will only accept t, if t is the most recently issued ticket.*

Remarks:

- There is no problem with crashes: If a client crashes while holding a ticket, the remaining clients are not affected, as servers can simply issue new tickets.

- Tickets can be implemented with a counter: Each time a ticket is requested, the counter is increased. When a client tries to use a ticket, the server can determine if the ticket is expired.

- What can we do with tickets? Can we simply replace the locks in Algorithm 2.10 with tickets? We need to add at least one additional phase, as only the client knows if a majority of the tickets have been valid in Phase 2.

Algorithm 2.12 Naïve Ticket Protocol

Phase 1

1: Client asks all servers for a ticket

Phase 2

2: **if** a majority of the servers replied **then**
3:    Client sends command together with ticket to each server
4:    Server stores command only if ticket is still valid, and replies to client
5: **else**
6:    Client waits, and then starts with Phase 1 again
7: **end if**

Phase 3

8: **if** client hears a positive answer from a majority of the servers **then**
9:    Client tells servers to execute the stored command
10: **else**
11:    Client waits, and then starts with Phase 1 again
12: **end if**

Remarks:

- There are problems with this algorithm: Let u_1 be the first client that successfully stores its command c_1 on a majority of the servers. Assume that u_1 becomes very slow just before it can notify the servers (Line 9), and a client u_2 updates the stored command in some servers to c_2. Afterwards, u_1 tells the servers to execute the command. Now some servers will execute c_1 and others c_2!

- How can this problem be fixed? We know that every client u_2 that updates the stored command after u_1 must have used a newer ticket than u_1. As u_1's ticket was accepted in Phase 2, it follows that u_2 must have acquired its ticket after u_1 already stored its value in the respective server.

- Idea: What if a server, instead of only handing out tickets in Phase 1, also notifies clients about its currently stored command? Then, u_2 learns that u_1 already stored c_1 and instead of trying to store c_2, u_2 could support u_1 by also storing c_1. As both clients try to store and execute the same command, the order in which they proceed is no longer a problem.

- But what if not all servers have the same command stored, and u_2 learns multiple stored commands in Phase 1. What command should u_2 support?

- Observe that it is always safe to support the most recently stored command. As long as there is no majority, clients can support any command. However, once there is a majority, clients need to support this value.

- So, in order to determine which command was stored most recently, servers can remember the ticket number that was used to store the command, and afterwards tell this number to clients in Phase 1.

- If every server uses its own ticket numbers, the newest ticket does not necessarily have the largest number. This problem can be solved if clients suggest the ticket numbers themselves!

Algorithm 2.13 Paxos

Client (Proposer)	**Server (Acceptor)**

Initialization ....

c $\triangleleft$ *command to execute*	$T_{\max} = 0$ $\triangleleft$ *largest issued ticket*
$t = 0$ $\triangleleft$ *ticket number to try*	
	$C = \perp$ $\triangleleft$ *stored command*
	$T_{\text{store}} = 0$ $\triangleleft$ *ticket used to store C*

Phase 1 ....

1: $t = t + 1$
2: Ask all servers for ticket t

      3: **if** $t > T_{\max}$ **then**
      4:     $T_{\max} = t$
      5:     Answer with ok(T_{store}, C)
      6: **end if**

Phase 2 ....

7: **if** a majority answers ok **then**
8:     Pick $(T_{\text{store}},\ C)$ with largest T_{store}
9:     **if** $T_{\text{store}} > 0$ **then**
10:         $c = C$
11:     **end if**
12:     Send **propose**(t, c) to same majority
13: **end if**

      14: **if** $t = T_{\max}$ **then**
      15:     $C = c$
      16:     $T_{\text{store}} = t$
      17:     Answer success
      18: **end if**

Phase 3 ....

19: **if** a majority answers success **then**
20:     Send **execute**(c) to every server
21: **end if**

Remarks:

- Unlike previously mentioned algorithms, there is no step where a client explicitly decides to start a new attempt and jumps back to Phase 1. Note that this is not necessary, as a client can decide to abort the current attempt and start a new one *at any point* in the algorithm. This has the advantage that we do not need to be careful about selecting "good" values for timeouts, as correctness is independent of the decisions when to start new attempts.

- The performance can be improved by letting the servers

send negative replies in phases 1 and 2 if the ticket expired.

- The contention between different clients can be alleviated by randomizing the waiting times between consecutive attempts.

Lemma 2.14. *We call a message* propose(t,c) *sent by clients on Line 12 a **proposal for (t,c)**. A proposal for (t,c) is **chosen**, if it is stored by a majority of servers (Line 15). For every issued* propose(t',c') *with $t' > t$ holds that $c' = c$, if there was a chosen* propose(t,c).

Proof. Observe that there can be at most one proposal for every ticket number τ since clients only send a proposal if they received a majority of the tickets for τ (Line 7). Hence, every proposal is uniquely identified by its ticket number τ.

Assume that there is at least one propose(t',c') with $t' > t$ and $c' \neq c$; of such proposals, consider the proposal with the smallest ticket number t'. Since both this proposal and also the propose(t,c) have been sent to a majority of the servers, we can denote by S the non-empty intersection of servers that have been involved in both proposals. Recall that since propose(t,c) has been chosen, this means that that at least one server $s \in S$ must have stored command c; thus, when the command was stored, the ticket number t was still valid. Hence, s must have received the request for ticket t' *after* it already stored propose(t,c), as the request for ticket t' invalidates ticket t.

Therefore, the client that sent propose(t',c') must have learned from s that a client already stored propose(t,c). Since a client adapts its proposal to the command that is stored with the highest ticket number so far (Line 8), the client must have proposed c as well. There is only one possibility that would lead to the client not adapting c: If the client received the information from a server that some client stored propose(t^*,c^*), with $c^* \neq c$ and $t^* > t$. In this case, a client must have sent propose(t^*,c^*) with $t < t^* < t'$, but this contradicts the assumption that t' is the smallest ticket number of a proposal issued after t. $\qquad\Box$

Theorem 2.15. *If a command c is executed by some servers, all servers (eventually) execute c.*

Proof. From Lemma 2.14 we know that once a proposal for c is chosen, every subsequent proposal is for c. As there is exactly one first **propose**(t,c) that is chosen, it follows that all successful proposals will be for the command c. Thus, only proposals for a single command c can be chosen, and since clients only tell servers to execute a command, when it is chosen (Line 20), each client will eventually tell every server to execute c. □

Remarks:

- If the client with the first successful proposal does not crash, it will directly tell every server to execute c.

- However, if the client crashes before notifying any of the servers, the servers will execute the command only once the next client is successful. Once a server received a request to execute c, it can inform every client that arrives later that there is already a chosen command, so that the client does not waste time with the proposal process.

- Note that Paxos cannot make progress if half (or more) of the servers crash, as clients cannot achieve a majority anymore.

- The original description of Paxos uses three roles: Proposers, acceptors and learners. Learners have a trivial role: They do nothing, they just learn from other nodes which command was chosen.

- We assigned every node only one role. In some scenarios, it might be useful to allow a node to have multiple roles. For example in a peer-to-peer scenario nodes need to act as both client and server.

- Clients (Proposers) must be trusted to follow the protocol strictly. However, this is in many scenarios not a reasonable assumption. In such scenarios, the role of the proposer can be executed by a set of servers, and clients need to contact proposers, to propose values in their name.

- So far, we only discussed how a set of nodes can reach decision for a single command with the help of Paxos. We call such a single decision an *instance* of Paxos.

- For state replication as in Definition 2.8, we need to be able to execute multiple commands, we can extend each instance with an instance number, that is sent around with every message. Once the 1st command is chosen, any client can decide to start a new instance and compete for the 2nd command. If a server did not realize that the 1st instance already came to a decision, the server can ask other servers about the decisions to catch up.

Chapter Notes

Two-phase protocols have been around for a long time, and it is unclear if there is a single source of this idea. One of the earlier descriptions of this concept can found in the book of Gray [Gra78].

Leslie Lamport introduced Paxos in 1989. But why is it called Paxos? Lamport described the algorithm as the solution to a problem of the parliament of a fictitious Greek society on the island Paxos. He even liked this idea so much, that he gave some lectures in the persona of an Indiana-Jones-style archaeologist! When the paper was submitted, many readers were so distracted by the descriptions of the activities of the legislators, they did not understand the meaning and purpose of the algorithm. The paper was rejected. But Lamport refused to rewrite the paper, and he later wrote that he *"was quite annoyed at how humorless everyone working in the field seemed to be"*. A few years later, when the need for a protocol like Paxos arose again, Lamport simply took the paper out of the drawer and gave it to his colleagues. They liked it. So Lamport decided to submit the paper (in basically unaltered form!) again, 8 years after he wrote it – and it got accepted! But as this paper [Lam98] is admittedly hard to read, he had mercy, and later wrote a simpler description of Paxos [Lam01].

Leslie Lamport is an eminent scholar when it comes to understanding distributed systems, and we will learn some of his contributions in almost every chapter. Not suprisingly, Lamport has won the 2013 Turing Award for his fundamental contributions to the "theory and practice of distributed and concurrent systems, notably the invention of concepts such as causality and logical clocks, safety and liveness, replicated state machines, and sequential consistency" [Mal13]. One can add arbitrarily to this official citation, for instance Lamports popular LaTeX typesetting system, based on Donald Knuths TeX.

Bibliography

[Gra78] James N Gray. *Notes on data base operating systems.* Springer, 1978.

[Lam98] Leslie Lamport. The part-time parliament. *ACM Transactions on Computer Systems (TOCS)*, 16(2):133–169, 1998.

[Lam01] Leslie Lamport. Paxos made simple. *ACM Sigact News*, 32(4):18–25, 2001.

[Mal13] Dahlia Malkhi. Leslie Lamport. ACM webpage, 2013.

Chapter 3

Consensus

3.1 Two Friends

Alice wants to arrange dinner with Bob, and since both of them are very reluctant to use the "call" functionality of their phones, she sends a text message suggesting to meet for dinner at 6pm. However, texting is unreliable, and Alice cannot be sure that the message arrives at Bob's phone, hence she will only go to the meeting point if she receives a confirmation message from Bob. But Bob cannot be sure that his confirmation message is received; if the confirmation is lost, Alice cannot determine if Bob did not even receive her suggestion, or if Bob's confirmation was lost. Therefore, Bob demands a confirmation message from Alice, to be sure that she will be there. But as this message can also be lost...

You can see that such a message exchange continues forever, if both Alice and Bob want to be sure that the other person will come to the meeting point!

Remarks:

- Such a protocol cannot terminate: Assume that there are protocols which lead to agreement, and P is one of the protocols which require the least number of messages. As the last confirmation might be lost and the protocol still needs to guarantee agreement, we can simply decide to always omit the last message. This gives us a new protocol P' which requires less messages than P, contradicting the assumption that P required the minimal amount of messages.

- Can Alice and Bob use Paxos?

3.2   Consensus

In Chapter 2 we studied a problem that we vaguely called agreement. We will now introduce a formally specified variant of this problem, called *consensus*.

Definition 3.1 (consensus). *There are n nodes, of which at most f might crash, i.e., at least $n - f$ nodes are* **correct**. *Node i starts with an input value v_i. The nodes must decide for one of those values, satisfying the following properties:*

- **Agreement** *All correct nodes decide for the same value.*

- **Termination** *All correct nodes terminate in finite time.*

- **Validity** *The decision value must be the input value of a node.*

Remarks:

- We assume that every node can send messages to every other node, and that we have reliable links, i.e., a message that is sent will be received.

- There is no broadcast medium. If a node wants to send a message to multiple nodes, it needs to send multiple individual messages. If a node crashes while broadcasting, not all nodes may receive the broadcasted message. Later we will call this best-effort broadcast.

- Does Paxos satisfy all three criteria? If you study Paxos carefully, you will notice that Paxos does not guarantee termination. For example, the system can be stuck forever if two clients continuously request tickets, and neither of them ever manages to acquire a majority.

3.3 Impossibility of Consensus

Model 3.2 (asynchronous). *In the **asynchronous model**, algorithms are event based ("upon receiving message ..., do ... "). Nodes do not have access to a synchronized wall-clock. A message sent from one node to another will arrive in a finite but unbounded time.*

Remarks:

- The asynchronous time model is a widely used formalization of the variable message delay model (Model 2.6).

Definition 3.3 (asynchronous runtime). *For algorithms in the asynchronous model, the **runtime** is the number of time units from the start of the execution to its completion in the worst case (every legal input, every execution scenario), assuming that each message has a delay of **at most** one time unit.*

Remarks:

- The maximum delay cannot be used in the algorithm design, i.e., the algorithm must work independent of the actual delay.

- Asynchronous algorithms can be thought of as systems, where local computation is significantly faster than message delays, and thus can be done in no time. Nodes are only active once an event occurs (a message arrives), and then they perform their actions "immediately".

- We will show now that crash failures in the asynchronous model can be quite harsh. In particular there is no deterministic fault-tolerant consensus algorithm in the asynchronous model, not even for binary input.

Definition 3.4 (configuration). *We say that a system is fully defined (at any point during the execution) by its **configuration** C. The configuration includes the state of every node, and all messages that are in transit (sent but not yet received).*

Definition 3.5 (univalent). *We call a configuration C **univalent**, if the decision value is determined independently of what happens afterwards.*

Remarks:

- We call a configuration that is univalent for value v v-valent.

- Note that a configuration can be univalent, even though no single node is aware of this. For example, the configuration in which all nodes start with value 0 is 0-valent (due to the validity requirement).

- As we restricted the input values to be binary, the decision value of any consensus algorithm will also be binary (due to the validity requirement).

Definition 3.6 (bivalent). *A configuration C is called **bivalent** if the nodes might decide for 0 or 1.*

Remarks:

- The decision value depends on the order in which messages are received or on crash events. I.e., the decision is not yet made.

- We call the initial configuration of an algorithm C_0. When nodes are in C_0, all of them executed their initialization code and possibly, based on their input values, sent some messages. These initial messages are also included in C_0. In other words, in C_0 the nodes are now waiting for the first message to arrive.

Lemma 3.7. *There is at least one selection of input values V such that the according initial configuration C_0 is bivalent, if $f \geq 1$.*

Proof. As explained in the previous remark, C_0 only depends on the input values of the nodes. Let $V = [v_0, v_1, \ldots, v_{n-1}]$ denote the array of input values, where v_i is the input value of node i.

We construct $n + 1$ arrays $V_0, V_1, \ldots, V_n$, where the index i in V_i denotes the position in the array up to which all input values are 1. So, $V_0 = [0, 0, 0, \ldots, 0]$, $V_1 = [1, 0, 0, \ldots, 0]$, and so on, up to $V_n = [1, 1, 1, \ldots, 1]$.

Note that the configuration corresponding to V_0 must be 0-valent so that the validity requirement is satisfied. Analogously, the configuration corresponding to V_n must be 1-valent. Assume that all initial configurations with starting values V_i are univalent. Therefore, there must be at least one index b, such that the configuration corresponding to V_{b-1} is 0-valent, and configuration corresponding to V_b is 1-valent. Observe that only the input value of the bth node differs from V_{b-1} to V_b.

Since we assumed that the algorithm can tolerate at least one failure, i.e., $f \geq 1$, we look at the following execution: All nodes except b start with their initial value according to V_{b-1} respectively V_b. Node b is "extremely slow"; i.e., all messages sent by b are scheduled in such a way, that all other nodes must assume that b crashed, in order to satisfy the termination requirement. Since the nodes cannot determine the value of b, and we assumed that all initial configurations are univalent, they will decide for a value v independent of the initial value of b. Since V_{b-1} is 0-valent, v must be 0. However we know that V_b is 1-valent, thus v must be 1. Since v cannot be both 0 and 1, we have a contradiction.

$\square$

Definition 3.8 (transition). *A **transition** from configuration C to a following configuration C_τ is characterized by an event $\tau = (u, m)$, i.e., node u receiving message m.*

Remarks:

- Transitions are the formally defined version of the "events" in the asynchronous model we described before.

- A transition $\tau = (u, m)$ is only applicable to C, if m was still in transit in C.

- C_τ differs from C as follows: m is no longer in transit, u has possibly a different state (as u can update its state based on m), and there are (potentially) new messages in transit, sent by u.

Definition 3.9 (configuration tree). *The **configuration tree** is a directed tree of configurations. Its root is the configuration C_0 which is fully characterized by the input values V. The edges of the tree are the transitions; every configuration has all applicable transitions as outgoing edges.*

Remarks:

- For any algorithm, there is exactly *one* configuration tree for every selection of input values.

- Leaves are configurations where the execution of the algorithm terminated. Note that we use termination in the sense that the system as a whole terminated, i.e., there will not be any transition anymore.

- Every path from the root to a leaf is one possible asynchronous execution of the algorithm.

- Leaves must be univalent, or the algorithm terminates without agreement.

- If a node u crashes when the system is in C, all transitions $(u, *)$ are removed from C in the configuration tree.

Lemma 3.10. *Assume two transitions $\tau_1 = (u_1, m_1)$ and $\tau_2 = (u_2, m_2)$ for $u_1 \neq u_2$ are both applicable to C. Let $C_{\tau_1\tau_2}$ be the configuration that follows C by first applying transition τ_1 and then τ_2, and let $C_{\tau_2\tau_1}$ be defined analogously. It holds that $C_{\tau_1\tau_2} = C_{\tau_2\tau_1}$.*

Proof. Observe that τ_2 is applicable to C_{τ_1}, since m_2 is still in transit and τ_1 cannot change the state of u_2. With the same argument τ_1 is applicable to C_{τ_2}, and therefore both $C_{\tau_1\tau_2}$ and $C_{\tau_2\tau_1}$ are well-defined. Since the two transitions are completely independent of each other, meaning that they consume the same messages, lead to the same state transitions and to the same messages being sent, it follows that $C_{\tau_1\tau_2} = C_{\tau_2\tau_1}$. □

Definition 3.11 (critical configuration). *We say that a configuration C is **critical**, if C is bivalent, but all configurations that are direct children of C in the configuration tree are univalent.*

Remarks:

- Informally, C is critical, if it is the last moment in the execution where the decision is not yet clear. As soon as the next message is processed by any node, the decision will be determined.

Lemma 3.12. *If a system is in a bivalent configuration, it must reach a critical configuration within finite time, or it does not always solve consensus.*

Proof. Recall that there is at least one bivalent initial configuration (Lemma 3.7). Assuming that this configuration is not critical, there must be at least one bivalent following configuration; hence, the system may enter this configuration. But if this configuration is not critical as well, the system may afterwards progress into another bivalent configuration. As long as there is no critical configuration, an unfortunate scheduling (selection of transitions) can always lead the system into another bivalent configuration. The only way how an algorithm can *enforce* to arrive in a univalent configuration is by reaching a critical configuration.

Therefore we can conclude that a system which does not reach a critical configuration has at least one possible execution where it will terminate in a bivalent configuration (hence it terminates without agreement), or it will not terminate at all.

$\square$

Lemma 3.13. *If a configuration tree contains a critical configuration, crashing a single node can create a bivalent leaf; i.e., a crash prevents the algorithm from reaching agreement.*

Proof. Let C denote critical configuration in a configuration tree, and let T be the set of transitions applicable to C. Let $\tau_0 = (u_0, m_0) \in T$ and $\tau_1 = (u_1, m_1) \in T$ be two transitions, and let C_{τ_0} be 0-valent and C_{τ_1} be 1-valent. Note that T must contain these transitions, as C is a critical configuration.

Assume that $u_0 \neq u_1$. Using Lemma 3.10 we know that C has a following configuration $C_{\tau_0 \tau_1} = C_{\tau_1 \tau_0}$. Since this configuration follows C_{τ_0} it must be 0-valent. However, this configuration also follows C_{τ_1} and must hence be 1-valent. This is a contradiction and therefore $u_0 = u_1$ must hold.

Therefore we can pick one particular node u for which there is a transition $\tau = (u, m) \in T$ which leads to a 0-valent configuration. As shown before, all transitions in T which lead to a 1-valent configuration must also take place on u. Since C is critical, there must be at least one such transition. Applying the same argument again, it follows that all transitions in T that lead to a 0-valent configuration must take place on u as well, and since C is critical, there is no transition in T that leads to a bivalent configuration. Therefore *all* transitions applicable to C take place on the *same* node u!

If this node u crashes while the system is in C, *all transitions are removed*, and therefore the system is stuck in C, i.e., it terminates in C. But as C is critical, and therefore bivalent, the algorithm fails to reach an agreement.

$\square$

Theorem 3.14. *There is no deterministic algorithm which always achieves consensus in the asynchronous model, with $f > 0$.*

Proof. We assume that the input values are binary, as this is the easiest non-trivial possibility. From Lemma 3.7 we know that there must be at least one bivalent initial configuration C. Using Lemma 3.12 we know that if an algorithm solves consensus, all executions starting from the bivalent configuration C must reach a critical configuration. But if the algorithm reaches a critical configuration, a single crash can prevent agreement (Lemma 3.13). $\qquad\square$

Remarks:

- If $f = 0$, then each node can simply send its value to all others, wait for all values, and choose the minimum.

- But if a single node may crash, there is no deterministic solution to consensus in the asynchronous model.

- How can the situation be improved? For example by giving each node access to randomness, i.e., we allow each node to toss a coin.

3.4 Randomized Consensus

Algorithm 3.15 Randomized Consensus (Ben-Or)

1: $v_i \in \{0, 1\}$ $\lhd$ input bit
2: round $= 1$
3: decided $=$ false

4: Broadcast `myValue`$(v_i,$ round$)$

5: **while** true **do**

    Propose

6:     Wait until a majority of `myValue` messages of current round arrived
7:     **if** all messages contain the same value v **then**
8:        Broadcast `propose`$(v,$ round$)$
9:     **else**
10:       Broadcast `propose`$(\bot,$ round$)$
11:     **end if**

12:     **if** decided **then**
13:       Broadcast `myValue`$(v_i,$ round$+1)$
14:       Decide for v_i and terminate
15:     **end if**

    Vote

16:     Wait until a majority of `propose` messages of current round arrived
17:     **if** all messages propose the same value v **then**
18:       $v_i = v$
19:       decided $=$ true
20:     **else if** there is at least one proposal for v **then**
21:       $v_i = v$
22:     **else**
23:       Choose v_i randomly, with $Pr[v_i = 0] = Pr[v_i = 1] = 1/2$
24:     **end if**
25:     round $=$ round $+ 1$
26:     Broadcast `myValue`$(v_i,$ round$)$
27: **end while**

Remarks:

- The idea of Algorithm 3.15 is very simple: Either all nodes start with the same input bit, which makes consensus easy. Otherwise, nodes toss a coin until a large number of nodes get – by chance – the same outcome.

Lemma 3.16. *As long as no node sets **decided** to true, Algorithm 3.15 does not get stuck, independent of which nodes crash.*

Proof. The only two steps in the algorithm when a node waits are in Lines 6 and 16. Since a node only waits for a majority of the nodes to send a message, and since $f < n/2$, the node will always receive enough messages to continue, as long as no correct node set its value decided to true and terminates. $\square$

Lemma 3.17. *Algorithm 3.15 satisfies the validity requirement.*

Proof. Observe that the validity requirement of consensus, when restricted to binary input values, corresponds to: If all nodes start with v, then v must be chosen; otherwise, either 0 or 1 is acceptable, and the validity requirement is automatically satisfied.

Assume that all nodes start with v. In this case, all nodes propose v in the first round. As all nodes only hear proposals for v, all nodes decide for v (Line 17) and exit the loop in the following round. $\square$

Lemma 3.18. *Algorithm 3.15 satisfies the agreement requirement.*

Proof. Observe that proposals for both 0 and 1 cannot occur in the same round, as nodes only send a proposal for v, if they hear a *majority* for v in Line 8.

Let u be the first node that decides for a value v in round r. Hence, it received a majority of proposals for v in r (Line 17). Note that once a node receives a majority of proposals for a value, it will adapt this value and terminate in the next round. Since there cannot be a proposal for any other value in r, it follows that no node decides for a different value in r.

In Lemma 3.16 we only showed that nodes do not get stuck as long as no node decides, thus we need to be careful that no node gets stuck if u terminates.

Any node $u' \neq u$ can experience one of two scenarios: Either it also receives a majority for v in round r and decides, or it does not receive a majority. In the first case, the agreement requirement is directly satisfied, and also the node cannot get stuck. Let us study the latter case. Since u heard a majority of proposals for v, it follows that every node hears *at least one* proposal for v. Hence, all nodes set their value v_i to v in round r. Therefore, all nodes will broadcast v at the end of round r, and thus all nodes will propose v in round $r + 1$. The nodes that already decided in round r will terminate in $r + 1$ and send one additional `myValue` message (Line 13). All other nodes will receive a majority of proposals for v in $r + 1$, and will set decided to true in round $r + 1$, and also send a `myValue` message in round $r + 1$. Thus, in round $r + 2$ some nodes have already terminated, and others hear enough `myValue` messages to continue in Line 6. They send another `propose` and a `myValue` message and terminate in $r + 2$, deciding for the same value v. $\qquad\square$

Lemma 3.19. *Algorithm 3.15 satisfies the termination requirement, i.e., all nodes terminate in expected time $O(2^n)$.*

Proof. We know from the proof of Lemma 3.18 that once a node hears a majority of proposals for a value, all nodes will terminate at most two rounds later. Hence, we only need to show that a node receives a majority of proposals for the same value within expected time $O(2^n)$.

Assume that no node receives a majority of proposals for the same value. In such a round, some nodes may update their value to v based on a proposal (Line 20). As shown before, all nodes that update the value based on a proposal, adapt the same value v. The rest of the nodes choses 0 or 1 randomly. The probability that all nodes choose the same value v in one round is hence at least $1/2^n$. Therefore, the expected number of rounds is bounded by $O(2^n)$. As every round consists of two message exchanges, the asymptotic runtime of the algorithm is equal to the number of rounds. $\qquad\square$

Theorem 3.20. *Algorithm 3.15 achieves binary consensus with expected runtime $O(2^n)$ if up to $f < n/2$ nodes crash.*

Remarks:

- How good is a fault tolerance of $f < n/2$?

Theorem 3.21. *There is no consensus algorithm for the asynchronous model that tolerates $f \geq n/2$ many failures.*

Proof. Assume that there is an algorithm that can handle $f = n/2$ many failures. We partition the set of all nodes into two sets N, N' both containing $n/2$ many nodes. Let us look at three different selection of input values: In V_0 all nodes start with 0. In V_1 all nodes start with 1. In V_{half} all nodes in N start with 0, and all nodes in N' start with 1.

Assume that nodes start with V_{half}. Since the algorithm must solve consensus independent of the scheduling of the messages, we study the scenario where all messages sent from nodes in N to nodes in N' (or vice versa) are heavily delayed. Note that the nodes in N cannot determine if they started with V_0 or V_{half}. Analogously, the nodes in N' cannot determine if they started in V_1 or V_{half}. Hence, if the algorithm terminates before any message from the other set is received, N must decide for 0 and N' must decide for 1 (to satisfy the validity requirement, as they could have started with V_0 respectively V_1). Therefore, the algorithm would fail to reach agreement.

The only possibility to overcome this problem is to wait for at least one message sent from a node of the other set. However, as $f = n/2$ many nodes can crash, the entire other set could have crashed before they sent any message. In that case, the algorithm would wait forever and therefore not satisfy the termination requirement.

$\square$

Remarks:

- Algorithm 3.15 solves consensus with optimal fault-tolerance – but it is awfully slow. The problem is rooted in the individual coin tossing: If all nodes toss the same coin, they could terminate in a constant number of rounds.

- Can this problem be fixed by simply always choosing 1 at Line 22?!

- This cannot work: Such a change makes the algorithm deterministic, and therefore it cannot achieve consensus (Theorem 3.14). Simulating what happens by always choosing 1, one can see that it might happen that there is a majority for 0, but a minority with value 1 prevents the nodes from reaching agreement.

- Nevertheless, the algorithm can be improved by tossing a so-called *shared coin*. A shared coin is a random variable that is 0 for all nodes with constant probability, and 1 with constant probability. Of course, such a coin is not a magic device, but it is simply an algorithm. To improve the expected runtime of Algorithm 3.15, we replace Line 22 with a function call to the shared coin algorithm.

3.5 Shared Coin

Algorithm 3.22 Shared Coin (code for node u)

1: Choose local coin $c_u = 0$ with probability $1/n$, else $c_u = 1$
2: Broadcast $\texttt{myCoin}(c_u)$

3: Wait for $n - f$ coins and store them in the local coin set C_u
4: Broadcast $\texttt{mySet}(C_u)$

5: Wait for $n - f$ coin sets
6: **if** at least one coin is 0 among all coins in the coin sets **then**
7:     return 0
8: **else**
9:     return 1
10: **end if**

Remarks:

- Since at most f nodes crash, all nodes will always receive $n - f$ coins respectively coin sets in Lines 3 and 5. Therefore, all nodes make progress and termination is guaranteed.

- We show the correctness of the algorithm for $f < n/3$. To simplify the proof we assume that $n = 3f + 1$, i.e., we assume the worst case.

Lemma 3.23. *Let u be a node, and let W be the set of coins that u received in at least $f + 1$ different coin sets. It holds that $|W| \geq f + 1$.*

Proof. Let C be the multiset of coins received by u. Observe that u receives exactly $|C| = (n - f)^2$ many coins, as u waits for $n - f$ coin sets each containing $n - f$ coins.

Assume that the lemma does not hold. Then, at most f coins are in all $n - f$ coin sets, and all other coins $(n - f)$ are in at most f

coin sets. In other words, the total number of coins that u received is bounded by

$$|C| \leq f \cdot (n - f) + (n - f) \cdot f = 2f(n - f).$$

Our assumption was that $n > 3f$, i.e., $n - f > 2f$. Therefore $|C| \leq 2f(n - f) < (n - f)^2 = |C|$, which is a contradiction. $\quad\square$

Lemma 3.24. *All coins in W are seen by all correct nodes.*

Proof. Let $w \in W$ be such a coin. By definition of W we know that w is in at least $f + 1$ sets received by u. Since every other node also waits for $n - f$ sets before terminating, each node will receive at least one of these sets, and hence w must be seen by every node that terminates. $\quad\square$

Theorem 3.25. *If $f < n/3$ nodes crash, Algorithm 3.22 implements a shared coin.*

Proof. Let us first bound the probability that the algorithm returns 1 for all nodes. With probability $(1 - 1/n)^n \approx 1/e \approx 0.37$ all nodes chose their local coin equal to 1 (Line 1), and in that case 1 will be decided. This is only a lower bound on the probability that all nodes return 1, as there are also other scenarios based on message scheduling and crashes which lead to a global decision for 1. But a probability of 0.37 is good enough, so we do not need to consider these scenarios.

    With probability $1 - (1 - 1/n)^{|W|}$ there is at least one 0 in W. Using Lemma 3.23 we know that $|W| \geq f + 1 \approx n/3$, hence the probability is about $1 - (1 - 1/n)^{n/3} \approx 1 - (1/e)^{1/3} \approx 0.28$. We know that this 0 is seen by all nodes (Lemma 3.24), and hence everybody will decide 0. Thus Algorithm 3.22 implements a shared coin. $\quad\square$

Remarks:

- We only proved the worst case. By choosing f fairly small, it is clear that $f + 1 \not\approx n/3$. However, Lemma 3.23 can be proved for $|W| \geq n - 2f$. To prove this claim you need to substitute the expressions in the contradictory statement: At most $n - 2f - 1$ coins can be in all $n - f$ coin sets, and $n - (n - 2f - 1) = 2f + 1$ coins can be in at most f coin sets. The remainder of the proof is analogous, the only difference is that the math is not as neat. Using the modified Lemma we know that $|W| \geq n/3$, and therefore Theorem 3.25 also holds for *any* $f < n/3$.

- We implicitly assumed that message scheduling was random; if we need a 0 but the nodes that want to propose 0 are "slow", nobody is going to see these 0's, and we do not have progress. There exist more complicated protocols that solve this problem.

Theorem 3.26. *Plugging Algorithm 3.22 into Algorithm 3.15 we get a randomized consensus algorithm which terminates in a constant expected number of rounds tolerating up to $f < n/3$ crash failures.*

Chapter Notes

The problem of two friends arranging a meeting was presented and studied under many different names; nowadays, it is usually referred to as the *Two Generals Problem*. The impossibility proof was established in 1975 by Akkoyunlu et al. [AEH75].

The proof that there is no deterministic algorithm that always solves consensus is based on the proof of Fischer, Lynch and Paterson [FLP85], known as FLP, which they established in 1985. This result was awarded the 2001 PODC Influential Paper Award (now called Dijkstra Prize). The idea for the randomized consensus algorithm was originally presented by Ben-Or [Ben83]. The concept of a shared coin was introduced by Bracha [Bra87]. A shared coin that can withstand worst-case scheduling has been developed by Alistarh et al. [AAKS14]; this shared coin was inspired by earlier shared coin solutions in the shared memory model [Cha96].

Apart from randomization, there are other techniques to still get consensus. One possibility is to drop asynchrony and rely on time more, e.g. by assuming partial synchrony [DLS88] or timed asynchrony [CF98]. Another possibility is to add failure detectors [CT96].

Bibliography

[AAKS14] Dan Alistarh, James Aspnes, Valerie King, and Jared Saia. Communication-efficient randomized consensus. In *28th International Symposium of Distributed Computing (DISC), Austin, TX, USA, October 12-15, 2014*, pages 61–75, 2014.

[AEH75] EA Akkoyunlu, K Ekanadham, and RV Huber. Some constraints and tradeoffs in the design of network communications. In *ACM SIGOPS Operating Systems Review*, volume 9, pages 67–74. ACM, 1975.

[Ben83] Michael Ben-Or. Another advantage of free choice (extended abstract): Completely asynchronous agreement protocols. In *Proceedings of the second annual ACM symposium on Principles of distributed computing*, pages 27–30. ACM, 1983.

[Bra87] Gabriel Bracha. Asynchronous byzantine agreement protocols. *Information and Computation*, 75(2):130–143, 1987.

[CF98] Flaviu Cristian and Christof Fetzer. The timed asynchronous distributed system model. In *Digest of Papers: FTCS-28, The Twenty-Eigth Annual International Symposium on Fault-Tolerant Computing, Munich, Germany, June 23-25, 1998*, pages 140–149, 1998.

[Cha96] Tushar Deepak Chandra. Polylog randomized wait-free consensus. In *Proceedings of the Fifteenth Annual ACM Symposium on Principles of Distributed Computing, Philadelphia, Pennsylvania, USA*, pages 166–175, 1996.

[CT96] Tushar Deepak Chandra and Sam Toueg. Unreliable failure detectors for reliable distributed systems. *J. ACM*, 43(2):225–267, 1996.

[DLS88] Cynthia Dwork, Nancy A. Lynch, and Larry J. Stockmeyer. Consensus in the presence of partial synchrony. *J. ACM*, 35(2):288–323, 1988.

[FLP85] Michael J. Fischer, Nancy A. Lynch, and Mike Paterson. Impossibility of Distributed Consensus with One Faulty Process. *J. ACM*, 32(2):374–382, 1985.

Chapter 4

Byzantine Agreement

In order to make flying safer, researchers studied possible failures of various sensors and machines used in airplanes. While trying to model the failures, they were confronted with the following problem: Failing machines did not just crash, instead they sometimes showed arbitrary behavior before stopping completely. With these insights researchers modeled failures as arbitrary failures, not restricted to any patterns.

Definition 4.1 (Byzantine). *A node which can have arbitrary behavior is called **byzantine**. This includes "anything imaginable", e.g., not sending any messages at all, or sending different and wrong messages to different neighbors, or lying about the input value.*

Remarks:

- Byzantine behavior also includes collusion, i.e., all byzantine nodes are being controlled by the same adversary.

- We assume that any two nodes communicate directly, and that no node can forge an incorrect sender address. This is a requirement, such that a single byzantine node cannot simply impersonate all nodes!

- We call non-byzantine nodes *correct* nodes.

Definition 4.2 (Byzantine Agreement). *Finding consensus as in Definition 3.1 in a system with byzantine nodes is called **byzantine***

agreement. *An algorithm is f-resilient if it still works correctly with f byzantine nodes.*

Remarks:

- As for consensus (Definition 3.1) we also need agreement, termination and validity. Agreement and termination are straight-forward, but what about validity?

4.1   Validity

Definition 4.3 (Any-Input Validity). *The decision value must be the input value of **any** node.*

Remarks:

- This is the validity definition we used for consensus, in Definition 3.1.

- Does this definition still make sense in the presence of byzantine nodes? What if byzantine nodes lie about their inputs?

- We would wish for a validity definition which differentiates between byzantine and correct inputs.

Definition 4.4 (Correct-Input Validity). *The decision value must be the input value of a **correct** node.*

Remarks:

- Unfortunately, implementing correct-input validity does not seem to be easy, as a byzantine node following the protocol but lying about its input value is indistinguishable from a correct node. Here is an alternative.

Definition 4.5 (All-Same Validity). *If **all** correct nodes start with the same input v, the decision value must be v.*

Remarks:

- If the decision values are binary, then correct-input validity is induced by all-same validity.

- If the input values are not binary, but for example from sensors that deliever values in $\mathbb{R}$, all-same validity is in most scenarios not really useful.

Definition 4.6 (Median Validity). *If the input values are orderable, e.g. $v \in \mathbb{R}$, byzantine outliers can be prevented by agreeing on a value close to the **median** of the correct input values – how close depends on the number of byzantine nodes f.*

Remarks:

- Is byzantine agreement possible? If yes, with what validity condition?

- Let us try to find an algorithm which tolerates 1 single byzantine node, first restricting to the so-called synchronous model.

Model 4.7 (synchronous). *In the **synchronous model**, nodes operate in synchronous rounds. In each round, each node may send a message to the other nodes, receive the messages sent by the other nodes, and do some local computation.*

Definition 4.8 (synchronous runtime). *For algorithms in the synchronous model, the **runtime** is simply the number of rounds from the start of the execution to its completion in the worst case (every legal input, every execution scenario).*

4.2 How Many Byzantine Nodes?

Remarks:

- Byzantine nodes may not follow the protocol and send syntactically incorrect messages. Such messages can easily be deteced and discarded. It is worse if byzantine nodes send syntactically correct messages, but with a bogus content, e.g., they send different messages to different nodes.

Algorithm 4.9 Byzantine Agreement with $f = 1$.

1: Code for node u, with input value x:

Round 1

2: Send $\texttt{tuple}(u, x)$ to all other nodes
3: Receive $\texttt{tuple}(v, y)$ from all other nodes v
4: Store all received $\texttt{tuple}(v, y)$ in a set S_u

Round 2

5: Send set S_u to all other nodes
6: Receive sets S_v from all nodes v
7: $T = $ set of $\texttt{tuple}(v, y)$ seen in at least two sets S_v, including own S_u
8: Let $\texttt{tuple}(v, y) \in T$ be the tuple with the smallest value y
9: Decide on value y

- Some of these mistakes cannot easily be detected: For example, if a byzantine node sends different values to different nodes in the first round; such values will be put into S_u. However, some mistakes can and must be detected: Observe that all nodes only relay information in Round 2, and do not say anything about their own value. So, if a byzantine node sends a set S_v which contains a $\texttt{tuple}(v, y)$, this tuple must be removed by u from S_v upon receiving it (Line 6).

- Recall that we assumed that nodes cannot forge their source address; thus, if a node receives $\texttt{tuple}(v, y)$ in Round 1, it is guaranteed that this message was sent by v.

Lemma 4.10. *If $n \geq 4$, all correct nodes have the same set T.*

Proof. With $f = 1$ and $n \geq 4$ we have at least 3 correct nodes. A correct node will see every correct value at least twice, once directly from another correct node, and once through the third correct node. So all correct values are in T. If the byzantine node sends the same value to at least 2 other (correct) nodes, all correct nodes will see the value twice, so all add it to set T. If the byzantine node sends all different values to the correct nodes, none of these values will end up in any set T. $\qquad\square$

Theorem 4.11. *Algorithm 4.9 reaches byzantine agreement if $n \geq$ 4.*

Proof. We need to show agreement, any-input validity and termination. With Lemma 4.10 we know that all correct nodes have the same set T, and therefore agree on the same minimum value. The nodes agree on a value proposed by any node, so any-input validity holds. Moreover, the algorithm terminates after two rounds. $\square$

Remarks:

- If $n > 4$ the byzantine node can put multiple values into T.

- Algorithm 4.9 only provides any-input agreement, which is questionable in the byzantine context. One can achieve all-same validity by choosing the smallest value that occurs at least twice, if a value appears at least twice.

- The idea of this algorithm can be generalized for any f and $n > 3f$. In the generalization, every node sends in every of $f + 1$ rounds all information it learned so far to all other nodes. In other words, message size increases exponentially with f.

- Does Algorithm 4.9 also work with $n = 3$?

Theorem 4.12. *Three nodes cannot reach byzantine agreement with all-same validity if one node among them is byzantine.*

Proof. We will assume that the three nodes satisfy all-same validity and show that they will violate the agreement condition under this assumption.

In order to achieve all-same validity, nodes have to deterministically decide for a value x if it is the input value of every correct node. Recall that a Byzantine node which follows the protocol is indistinguishable from a correct node. Assume a correct node sees that $n - f$ nodes including itself have an input value x. Then, by all-same validity, this correct node must deterministically decide for x.

In the case of three nodes ($n - f = 2$) a node has to decide on its own input value if another node has the same input value. Let us call the three nodes u, v and w. If correct node u has input 0 and correct node v has input 1, the byzantine node w can fool them by telling u that its value is 0 and simultaneously telling v that its value is 1. By all-same validity, this leads to u and v deciding on two different values, which violates the agreement condition. Even if u talks to v, and they figure out that they have different assumptions about w's value, u cannot distinguish whether w or v is byzantine. $\square$

Theorem 4.13. *A network with n nodes cannot reach byzantine agreement with $f \geq n/3$ byzantine nodes.*

Proof. Assume (for the sake of contradiction) that there exists an algorithm A that reaches byzantine agreement for n nodes with $f \geq \lceil n/3 \rceil$ byzantine nodes. We will show that A cannot satisfy all-same validity and agreement simultaneously.

Let us divide the n nodes into three groups of size $n/3$ (either $\lfloor n/3 \rfloor$ or $\lceil n/3 \rceil$, if n is not divisible by 3). Assume that one group of size $\lceil n/3 \rceil \geq n/3$ contains only Byzantine and the other two groups only correct nodes. Let one group of correct nodes start with input value 0 and the other with input value 1. As in Lemma 4.12, the group of Byzantine nodes supports the input value of each of the node, so each correct node observes at least $n - f$ nodes who support its own input value. Because of all-same validity, every correct node has to deterministically decide on its own input value. Since the two groups of correct nodes had different input values, the nodes will decide on different values respectively, thus violating the agreement property. $\square$

4.3 The King Algorithm

Lemma 4.15. *Algorithm 4.14 fulfills the all-same validity.*

Proof. If all correct nodes start with the same value, all correct nodes propose it in Round 2. All correct nodes will receive at least $n - f$ proposals, i.e., all correct nodes will stick with this value, and never change it to the king's value. This holds for all phases. $\square$

Lemma 4.16. *If a correct node proposes x, no other correct node proposes y, with $y \neq x$, if $n > 3f$.*

Proof. Assume (for the sake of contradiction) that a correct node proposes value x and another correct node proposes value y. Since a good node only proposes a value if it heard at least $n - f$ `value`

Algorithm 4.14 King Algorithm (for $f < n/3$)

1: $x = $ my input value
2: **for** phase $= 1$ to $f + 1$ **do**

   Round 1

3:   Broadcast `value`(x)

   Round 2

4:   **if** some `value`(y) received at least $n - f$ times **then**
5:     Broadcast `propose`(y)
6:   **end if**
7:   **if** some `propose`(z) received more than f times **then**
8:     $x = z$
9:   **end if**

   Round 3

10:   Let node v_i be the predefined king of this phase i
11:   The king v_i broadcasts its current value w
12:   **if** received strictly less than $n - f$ `propose`(y) **then**
13:     $x = w$
14:   **end if**
15: **end for**

---

messages, we know that both nodes must have received their value from at least $n - 2f$ distinct correct nodes (as at most f nodes can behave byzantine and send x to one node and y to the other one). Hence, there must be a total of at least $2(n - 2f) + f = 2n - 3f$ nodes in the system. Using $3f < n$, we have $2n - 3f > n$ nodes, a contradiction. $\qquad\square$

Lemma 4.17. *There is at least one phase with a correct king.*

Proof. There are $f + 1$ phases, each with a different king. As there are only f byzantine nodes, one king must be correct. $\qquad\square$

Lemma 4.18. *After a round with a correct king, the correct nodes will not change their values v anymore, if $n > 3f$.*

Proof. If all correct nodes change their values to the king's value, all correct nodes have the same value. If some correct node does not change its value to the king's value, it received a proposal at least $n - f$ times, therefore at least $n - 2f$ correct nodes broadcasted this proposal. Thus, all correct nodes received it at least $n - 2f > f$ times (using $n > 3f$), therefore all correct nodes set their value to the proposed value, including the correct king. Note that only one value can be proposed more than f times, which follows from Lemma 4.16. With Lemma 4.15, no node will change its value after this round. $\square$

Theorem 4.19. *Algorithm 4.14 solves byzantine agreement.*

Proof. The king algorithm reaches agreement as either all correct nodes start with the same value, or they agree on the same value latest after the phase where a correct node was king according to Lemmas 4.17 and 4.18. Because of Lemma 4.15 we know that they will stick with this value. Termination is guaranteed after $3(f + 1)$ rounds, and all-same validity is proved in Lemma 4.15. $\square$

Remarks:

- Algorithm 4.14 requires $f + 1$ predefined kings. We assume that the kings (and their order) are given. Finding the kings indeed would be a byzantine agreement task by itself, so this must be done before the execution of the King algorithm.

- Do algorithms exist which do not need predefined kings? Yes, see Section 4.5.

- Can we solve byzantine agreement (or at least consensus) in less than $f + 1$ rounds?

4.4   Lower Bound on Number of Rounds

Theorem 4.20. *A synchronous algorithm solving consensus in the presence of f crashing nodes needs at least $f + 1$ rounds, if nodes decide for the minimum seen value.*

Proof. Let us assume (for the sake of contradiction) that some algorithm A solves consensus in f rounds. Some node u_1 has the smallest input value x, but in the first round u_1 can send its information (including information about its value x) to only some other node u_2 before u_1 crashes. Unfortunately, in the second round, the only witness u_2 of x also sends x to exactly one other node u_3 before u_2 crashes. This will be repeated, so in round f only node u_{f+1} knows about the smallest value x. As the algorithm terminates in round f, node u_{f+1} will decide on value x, all other surviving (correct) nodes will decide on values larger than x. $\square$

Remarks:

- A general proof without the restriction to decide for the minimum value exists as well.

- Since byzantine nodes can also just crash, this lower bound also holds for byzantine agreement, so Algorithm 4.14 has an asymptotically optimal runtime.

- So far all our byzantine agreement algorithms assume the synchronous model. Can byzantine agreement be solved in the asynchronous model?

4.5 Asynchronous Byzantine Agreement

Algorithm 4.21 Asynchronous Byzantine Agreement (Ben-Or, for $f < n/10$)

1: $x_u \in \{0, 1\}$ $\triangleleft$ input bit
2: r = 1 $\triangleleft$ round
3: decided = false
4: Broadcast **propose**(x_u,r)
5: **repeat**
6:      Wait until $n - f$ **propose** messages of current round r arrived

7:      **if** at least $n/2 + 3f + 1$ **propose** messages contain same value x **then**
8:         $x_u = x$, decided = true
9:      **else if** at least $n/2 + f + 1$ **propose** messages contain same value x **then**
10:         $x_u = x$
11:      **else**
12:         choose x_u randomly, with $Pr[x_u = 0] = Pr[x_u = 1] = 1/2$
13:      **end if**
14:      r = r + 1
15:      Broadcast **propose**(x_u,r)
16: **until** decided (see Line 8)
17: decision = x_u

Lemma 4.22. *Let a correct node choose value x in Line 10, then no other correct node chooses value $y \neq x$ in Line 10.*

Proof. For the sake of contradiction, assume that both 0 and 1 are chosen in Line 10. This means that both 0 and 1 had been proposed by at least $n/2 + 1$ out of $n - f$ correct nodes. In other words, we have a total of at least $2 \cdot n/2 + 2 = n + 2 > n - f$ correct nodes. Contradiction! $\qquad\square$

Theorem 4.23. *Algorithm 4.21 solves binary byzantine agreement as in Definition 4.2 for up to $f < n/10$ byzantine nodes.*

Proof. First note that it is not a problem to wait for $n - f$ propose messages in Line 6, since at most f nodes are byzantine. If all correct nodes have the same input value x, then all (except the f byzantine nodes) will propose the same value x. Thus, every node receives at least $n - 2f$ propose messages containing x. Observe that for $f < n/10$, we get $n - 2f > n/2 + 3f$ and the nodes will decide on x in the first round already. We have established all-same validity! If the correct nodes have different (binary) input values, the validity condition becomes trivial as any result is fine.

What about agreement? Let u be the first node to decide on value x (in Line 8). Due to asynchrony another node v received messages from a different subset of the nodes, however, at most f senders may be different. Taking into account that byzantine nodes may lie (send different propose messages to different nodes), f additional propose messages received by v may differ from those received by u. Since node u had at least $n/2 + 3f + 1$ propose messages with value x, node v has at least $n/2 + f + 1$ propose messages with value x. Hence every correct node will propose x in the next round, and then decide on x.

So we only need to worry about termination: We have already seen that as soon as one correct node terminates (Line 8) everybody terminates in the next round. So what are the chances that some node u terminates in Line 8? Well, we can hope that all correct nodes randomly propose the same value (in Line 12). Maybe there are some nodes not choosing randomly (entering Line 10 instead of 12), but according to Lemma 4.22 they will all propose the same.

Thus, at worst all $n - f$ correct nodes need to randomly choose the same bit, which happens with probability $2^{-(n-f)+1}$. If so, all correct nodes will send the same propose message, and the algorithm terminates. So the expected running time is exponential in the number of nodes n in the worst case. $\qquad\square$

Remarks:

- This Algorithm is a proof of concept that asynchronous byzantine agreement can be achieved. Unfortunately this algorithm is not useful in practice, because of its runtime.

- Note that for $f \in O(\sqrt{n})$, the probability for some node to terminate in Line 8 is greater than some positive constant. Thus, the Ben-Or algorithm terminates within expected constant number of rounds for small values of f.

Chapter Notes

The project which started the study of byzantine failures was called SIFT and was founded by NASA [WLG+78], and the research regarding byzantine agreement started to get significant attention with the results by Pease, Shostak, and Lamport [PSL80, LSP82]. In [PSL80] they presented the generalized version of Algorithm 4.9 and also showed that byzantine agreement is unsolvable for $n \leq 3f$. The algorithm presented in that paper is nowadays called *Exponential Information Gathering (EIG)*, due to the exponential size of the messages.

There are many algorithms for the byzantine agreement problem. For example the Queen Algorithm [BG89] which has a better runtime than the King algorithm [BGP89], but tolerates less failures. That byzantine agreement requires at least $f + 1$ many rounds was shown by Dolev and Strong [DS83], based on a more complicated proof from Fischer and Lynch [FL82].

While many algorithms for the synchronous model have been around for a long time, the asynchronous model is a lot harder. The only results were by Ben-Or and Bracha. Ben-Or [Ben83] was able to tolerate $f < n/5$. Bracha [BT85] improved this tolerance to $f < n/3$.

Nearly all developed algorithms only satisfy all-same validity. There are a few exceptions, e.g., correct-input validity [FG03], available if the initial values are from a finite domain, median validity [SW15, MW18, DGM+11] if the input values are orderable, or values inside the convex hull of all correct input values [VG13, MH13, MHVG15] if the input is multidimensional.

Before the term *byzantine* was coined, the terms Albanian Generals or Chinese Generals were used in order to describe malicious behavior. When the involved researchers met people from these countries they moved – for obvious reasons – to the historic term byzantine [LSP82].

Bibliography

[Ben83] Michael Ben-Or. Another advantage of free choice (extended abstract): Completely asynchronous agreement protocols. In *Proceedings of the second annual ACM symposium on Principles of distributed computing*, pages 27–30. ACM, 1983.

[BG89] Piotr Berman and Juan A Garay. *Asymptotically optimal distributed consensus*. Springer, 1989.

[BGP89] Piotr Berman, Juan A. Garay, and Kenneth J. Perry. Towards optimal distributed consensus (extended abstract). In *30th Annual Symposium on Foundations of Computer Science, Research Triangle Park, North Carolina, USA, 30 October - 1 November 1989*, pages 410–415, 1989.

[BT85] Gabriel Bracha and Sam Toueg. Asynchronous consensus and broadcast protocols. *Journal of the ACM (JACM)*, 32(4):824–840, 1985.

[DGM+11] Benjamin Doerr, Leslie Ann Goldberg, Lorenz Minder, Thomas Sauerwald, and Christian Scheideler. Stabilizing Consensus with the Power of Two Choices. In *Proceedings of the Twenty-third Annual ACM Symposium on Parallelism in Algorithms and Architectures*, SPAA, June 2011.

[DS83] Danny Dolev and H. Raymond Strong. Authenticated algorithms for byzantine agreement. *SIAM Journal on Computing*, 12(4):656–666, 1983.

[FG03] Matthias Fitzi and Juan A Garay. Efficient player-optimal protocols for strong and differential consensus. In *Proceedings of the twenty-second annual symposium on Principles of distributed computing*, pages 211–220. ACM, 2003.

[FL82] Michael J. Fischer and Nancy A. Lynch. A lower bound for the time to assure interactive consistency. 14(4):183–186, June 1982.

[LSP82] Leslie Lamport, Robert E. Shostak, and Marshall C. Pease. The byzantine generals problem. *ACM Trans. Program. Lang. Syst.*, 4(3):382–401, 1982.

[MH13] Hammurabi Mendes and Maurice Herlihy. Multidimensional Approximate Agreement in Byzantine Asynchronous Systems. In *Proceedings of the Forty-fifth Annual ACM Symposium on Theory of Computing*, STOC, June 2013.

[MHVG15] Hammurabi Mendes, Maurice Herlihy, Nitin Vaidya, and Vijay K. Garg. Multidimensional agreement in Byzantine systems. *Distributed Computing*, 28(6):423–441, January 2015.

[MW18] Darya Melnyk and Roger Wattenhofer. Byzantine Agreement with Interval Validity. In *37th Annual IEEE International Symposium on Reliable Distributed Systems (SRDS), Salvador, Bahia, Brazil*, October 2018.

[PSL80] Marshall C. Pease, Robert E. Shostak, and Leslie Lamport. Reaching agreement in the presence of faults. *J. ACM*, 27(2):228–234, 1980.

[SW15] David Stolz and Roger Wattenhofer. Byzantine Agreement with Median Validity. In *19th International Conference on Priniciples of Distributed Systems (OPODIS), Rennes, France*, 2015.

[VG13] Nitin H. Vaidya and Vijay K. Garg. Byzantine Vector Consensus in Complete Graphs. In *Proceedings of the 2013 ACM Symposium on Principles of Distributed Computing*, PODC, July 2013.

[WLG$^+$78] John H. Wensley, Leslie Lamport, Jack Goldberg, Milton W. Green, Karl N. Levitt, P. M. Melliar-Smith, Robert E. Shostak, and Charles B. Weinstock. Sift: Design and analysis of a fault-tolerant computer for aircraft control. In *Proceedings of the IEEE*, pages 1240–1255, 1978.

Chapter 5

Cryptography Basics

As we have seen in Section 4.5, state replication as introduced in Definition 2.8 can be solved by using randomization. It turns out, however, that cryptographic tools may simplify protocols considerably. Before we present these crypto-based protocols in the remainder of this book, we will briefly give an introduction to public-key cryptography in this chapter. We discuss some of the most important concepts such as encryption or digital signatures. Public-key cryptography is one of the biggest scientific achievements of the last century. Two people that never met before can establish a common secret in plain sight? Sounds like pure magic! The idea of this chapter is to reveal some of the tricks of this "crypto magic". This chapter is not tailored towards any particular application, rather we present the foundations in a vanilla way.

5.1   Key Exchange

How to agree on a common secret key in public, if you never met before?

Definition 5.1 (Primitive Root). *Let $p \in \mathbb{N}$ be a prime. $g \in \mathbb{N}$ is a primitive root of p if the following holds: For every $h \in \mathbb{N}$, with $1 \le h < p$, there is a $k \in \mathbb{N}$ s.t. $g^k = h \mod p$.*

Algorithm 5.2 Diffie-Hellman Key Exchange

Input: Publicly known prime p and a primitive root g of p.
Result: Alice and Bob agree on a common secret key.

1: Alice picks k_A, with $1 \leq k_A \leq p - 2$ and sends $g^{k_A} \mod p$ to Bob
2: Bob picks k_B, with $1 \leq k_B \leq p - 2$ and sends $g^{k_B} \mod p$ to Alice
3: Alice calculates $\left(g^{k_B}\right)^{k_A} \mod p = g^{k_B k_A} \mod p$
4: Bob calculates $\left(g^{k_A}\right)^{k_B} \mod p = g^{k_A k_B} \mod p$
5: Alice & Bob have a common secret key $g^{k_A k_B} \mod p = g^{k_B k_A} \mod p$

Remarks:

- Also, we will use k for keys, m for messages, p for primes, g for primitive roots, and c for ciphertext (encrypted messages). Generally speaking, an encryption algorithm encrypts a plain message m by applying a key k, resulting in ciphertext c.

- Small (not so secure) example for prime $p = 5$ and primitive root $g = 2$: $2^1 = 2 \mod 5$, $2^2 = 4 \mod 5$, $2^3 = 3 \mod 5$, $2^4 = 1 \mod 5$. One more primitive root for $p = 5$ exists. There are sophisticated methods to quickly find primitive roots, but they are beyond the material covered in this chapter.

- Algorithm 5.2 with $p = 5$ and $g = 2$: Alice picks $k_A = 2$ with $2^2 = 4 \mod 5$, and Bob picks $k_B = 3$ with $2^3 = 3 \mod 5$. Thus, Bob receives 4 and Alice receives 3. Then, Bob calculates $4^3 = 4 \mod 5$, and Alice calculates $3^2 = 4 \mod 5$. Hence, Alice and Bob have agreed on the common secret key of 4.

- How secure is Algorithm 5.2?

Definition 5.3 (Discrete Logarithm Problem). *Let $p \in \mathbb{N}$ be a prime, and let $g, a \in \mathbb{N}$ with $1 \leq g, a < p$. The discrete logarithm problem is defined as finding an $x \in \mathbb{N}$ with $g^x = a \mod p$.*

Remarks:

- Intuitively, the best approach to calculate the common secret key of Algorithm 5.2 from the publicly known p, g, g^{k_A}, g^{k_B} is to solve the discrete logarithm problem. This is also the best known attack.

- However, for some classes of primes there are better attacks, which is why one often resorts to so-called safe primes p, where $p' = (p-1)/2$ is also a prime.

- How to find big enough primes though? Deterministic methods are still too slow in practice. Thus, let's go probabilistic with the following primality test.

Algorithm 5.4 Probabilistic Primality Testing

Input: An odd number $p \in \mathbb{N}$.
Result: Is p a prime?

1: Let $j, r \in \mathbb{N}$ and j odd with $p - 1 = 2^r j$
2: Select $x \in \mathbb{N}$ uniformly at random, $1 \leq x < p$
3: Set $x_0 = x^j \mod p$
4: **if** $x_0 = 1$ or $x_0 = p - 1$ **then**
5:    Output "p is probably prime" and **stop**
6: **end if**
7: **for** $i = 1, \ldots r - 1$ **do**
8:    Set $x_i = x_{i-1}^2 \mod p$
9:    **if** $x_i = p - 1$ **then**
10:      Output "p is probably prime" and **stop**
11:    **end if**
12: **end for**
13: Output "p is not prime"

Lemma 5.5. *Algorithm 5.4 is correct with probability 75% if it outputs "p is probably prime", and 100% correct if it outputs "p is not prime".*

Corollary 5.6. *The runtime of Algorithm 5.4 is $O(r) \in O(\log p)$*

Remarks:

- The proof for the probabilistic correctness of the primality test in Algorithm 5.4 goes beyond the material covered in this chapter.

- Algorithm 5.4 is a Monte Carlo algorithm as its (fast) runtime is deterministic, but the output can be wrong with bounded probability. However, running the algorithm again on the same p, but with different x, produces an independent result, allowing to bound the error probability by $\frac{1}{4^r}$ in r runs.

- A simple method to find big primes is thus as follows: Pick a big random number p, with p being odd. Run Algorithm 5.4 until p is prime with the desired probability of $1 - \varepsilon$. If p is not prime, pick another p. According to the prime number theorem, the average distance between two primes of size at most n is just $\ln n$, i.e., there is a good chance to find a big prime.

- While it is easy to find big primes, the problem of factorization is believed to be hard: I.e., given some integer x, find the prime factors of x. Many cryptographic protocols rely on the (perceived) hardness of the factorization problem, most famously RSA.

Definition 5.7 (Man in the Middle Attack). *A man in the middle attack is defined as an attacker Eve deciphering or changing the messages between Alice and Bob, while Alice and Bob believe they are communicating directly with each other.*

Theorem 5.8. *The Diffie-Hellman Key Exchange from Algorithm 5.2 is vulnerable to a man in the middle attack.*

Proof. Assume that Eve can intercept and relay all messages between Alice and Bob. That alone does not make it a man in the middle attack, Eve needs to be able to decipher or change messages without Alice or Bob noticing. However, Eve can emulate Alice's and Bob's behavior to each other, by picking her own k'_A, k'_B, and then agreeing on common keys $g^{k_A k'_B}$, $g^{k_B k'_A}$ with Alice and Bob, respectively. Thus, Eve can relay all messages between Alice and Bob while deciphering and (possibly) changing them, while Alice and Bob believe they are securely communicating with each other. $\qquad\square$

Remarks:

- It is a bit like concurrently playing chess with two grandmasters: If you play white and black respectively, you can essentially let them play against each other by relaying their moves.

- How do we fix this? One idea is to personally meet in private first, exchange a common secret key $k_{A,B}$, and then use this key for secure communication. Now a man in the middle cannot change the key.

Definition 5.9 (Forward Secrecy). *A sequence of secured communication rounds has the property of forward secrecy, if discovering the secret key(s) of a single communication round does not reveal the content of past communication rounds.*

Remarks:

- So Alice and Bob cannot use the same secret key multiple times.

Algorithm 5.10 Diffie-Hellman Key Exchange with Forward Secrecy

---

Input: Alice's and Bob's common secret key $k_{A,B}$, and furthermore a prime p with a primitive root g for p.
Result: A Diffie-Hellman key exchange not vulnerable to a man in the middle attack, and with forward secrecy.

1: Bob picks a random number $1 \leq k_B \leq p - 2$ and sends Alice $g^{k_B} \mod p$ encrypted with $k_{A,B}$ as c_B as a challenge
2: Alice picks a random number $1 \leq k_A \leq p - 2$ and sends $g^{k_A} \mod p$ encrypted with $k_{A,B}$ as c_A to Bob as a challenge
3: Alice and Bob decrypt the respective messages, and Alice sends $g^{k_B} + 1$ encrypted with $k_{A,B}$ to Bob as a response (and Bob as well with $g^{k_A} + 1$)
4: If decryption yields $g^{k_A} + 1$ for Alice, and $g^{k_B} + 1$ for Bob, respectively, they accept the round key $g^{k_A k_B} \mod p$

Lemma 5.11. *Algorithm 5.10 has the property of forward secrecy and is not vulnerable to a man in the middle attack, if encryption with $k_{A,B}$ is secure.*

Proof. For a man in the middle attack, Eve needs to be able to decrypt and encrypt with $k_{A,B}$ to convince Alice and Bob that they directly communicated with each other, which is a contradiction to the security assumption. Regarding forward secrecy, if the attacker Eve gathers the secret key $g^{k_A k_B}$ of a communication round, she can decrypt the messages of this communication round. Even if Eve gains access to $k_{A,B}$, she cannot gain access to the keys generated in past communication rounds. $\square$

Remarks:

- Observe that forward secrecy only applies to communication rounds in the past. If Eve gains access to $k_{A,B}$, she can perform man in the middle attacks in future communication rounds.

- However, we have a new inconvenience: Alice and Bob need to agree on a secret key $k_{A,B}$ beforehand. Furthermore, with n participants, everyone needs $n-1$ different keys.

5.2   Public Key Cryptography

"Love all, trust a few." – William Shakespeare

Definition 5.12 (Public Key Cryptography). *A public key cryptography system uses two keys: A public key k_p, to be disseminated to everyone, and a secret (private) key k_s, only known to the owner. A message encrypted with the secret key can be decrypted with the corresponding public key. Analogously, a message encrypted with the public key can be decrypted with the corresponding secret key.*

Remarks:

- Popular public key cryptosystem include RSA and elliptic curve cryptography.

- With public key cryptography, we have reduced the number of keys – everyone just needs a secret and a public key.

- A conceptual way to think of public key cryptography is as follows: The secret key is a physical (secret) key that opens a specific type of padlock, and this type of padlock is freely available. The public key is a physical key too, freely available, but it opens only a (secret) specific type of padlock. If Alice wants to send Bob an encrypted message, she applies his public padlock to the message container, and only Bob can open it. Similarly, if Alice wants to authenticate her message to Bob, she locks the container with her secret padlock, and only Alice's public key can unlock it. Lastly, if Alice wants to ensure both encryption and authentication, she applies both her own secret padlock and Bob's public padlock to the message container.

- We will now extend the Diffie-Hellman algorithm to public key cryptography.

Algorithm 5.13 Elgamal Public Secret Key Generation

Input: Publicly known prime p and a primitive root g of p.
Result: Alice generates a public and a secret key

1: Alice picks random k_s with $1 \leq k_s \leq p - 2$ as her secret key
2: Alice calculates $k_p = g^{k_s} \mod p$ as her public key

Remarks:

- Alice can publish p, g, k_p, but should keep k_s to her own.

- We will now start with encryption, before covering authentication.

Algorithm 5.14 Elgamal Public Key Encryption and Decryption

Input: Alice and Bob know p, g, k_p, Alice knows k_s.
Result: Bob sends Alice an encrypted message, which she can decrypt.

1: Bob picks a message $1 \leq m \leq p-2$ and a random $1 \leq x \leq p-2$

2: Bob sends $g^x \mod p$ and $c = m \cdot k_p^x \mod p$ to Alice
3: Alice first calculates $y = (g^x)^{p-k_s-1} \mod p$
4: Alice then obtains $m = y \cdot c \mod p$

Theorem 5.15 (Fermat's little theorem). *Let p be a prime number. Then, for any $a \in \mathbb{N}$ holds: $a^p = a \mod p$. If a is not divisible by p, then $a^{p-1} = 1 \mod p$.*

Lemma 5.16. *Algorithm 5.14 is correct.*

Proof.

$$
\begin{aligned}
y \cdot c &= (g^x)^{p-k_s-1} \left(m \cdot k_p^x \right) \quad \mod p \\
&= (g^x)^{p-k_s-1} \left(m \cdot (g^{k_s})^x \right) \quad \mod p \quad (\text{using } k_p = g^{k_s} \mod p) \\
&= (g^x)^{p-k_s-1} m \cdot (g^x)^{k_s} \quad \mod p \\
&= m (g^x)^{p-1} \quad \mod p \\
&= m \quad \mod p \quad (\text{using Theorem 5.15}).
\end{aligned}
$$

$\square$

Remarks:

- We can now send someone an encrypted message using public key cryptography, but what about authentication?

- Again, we first need some number theoretic preliminaries.

Definition 5.17 (Greatest Common Divisor, gcd). *The greatest common divisor (gcd) of two integers i_1, i_2 is the largest integer that divides i_1 and i_2 without a remainder.*

Theorem 5.18. *Let p be a prime and i be an integer with $\gcd(i, p) = 1$. Let $a_1, a_2 \in \mathbb{N}$. If $a_1 = a_2 \mod (p-1)$, then $i^{a_1} = i^{a_2} \mod p$.*

Remarks:

- A multiplicative inverse modulo p (in this algorithm: $x^{-1} \mod p$), can be calculated using, e.g., the extended Euclidean algorithm.

Lemma 5.20. *Algorithm 5.19 is correct.*

Proof. With $d = (m - ak_s)x^{-1} \mod (p-1)$, it follows that:

$$ dx = m - ak_s \quad \mod (p-1) \Rightarrow m = dx + ak_s \quad \mod (p-1). $$

Using Theorem 5.18, we now obtain $g^{dx+ak_s} = g^m \mod p$. Hence,

$$ k_p^a a^d \quad \mod p = \left(g^{k_s} \right)^a (g^x)^d = g^{ak_s} g^{dx} \quad \mod p = g^m \quad \mod p. $$

$\square$

Algorithm 5.19 Elgamal Authentication

Input: Alice and Bob know p, g, k_p, Alice knows k_s.
Result: Alice signs a message $1 \leq m \leq p - 2$, which Bob authenticates.

1: Alice picks a random $1 \leq x \leq p - 1$, with $gcd(x, p - 1) = 1$
2: Alice calculates $a = g^x \mod p$ and $b = x^{-1} \mod (p - 1)$
3: Alice calculates $d = (m - ak_s)b \mod (p - 1)$
4: Alice sends the message m and the signature (a, d) to Bob
5: Bob checks if $1 \leq a \leq p - 1$, else he rejects
6: Bob accepts Alice's signature for m if $k_p^a a^d = g^m \mod p$

Remarks:

- The security of the Elgamal public key cryptography again depends on the hardness of the discrete logarithm problem.

- We can now authenticate a message using public key cryptography, e.g., we can check that the public key of Alice corresponds to Alice's secret key.

- However, we are back still at our old problem: How do I know that Alice's public key really belongs to Alice? Maybe Eve pretended to be Alice? To use a famous saying by Peter Steiner: *"On the Internet, nobody knows you're a dog"*.

- What can we do, unless we personally meet with everyone to exchange secret keys? The answer lies in trusting a few, in order to trust many: Let's say that you don't know Alice, but both Alice and you know Doris. If you trust Doris, then Doris can verify Alice's public key for you. In the future, you can ask Alice to vouch for her friends as well, etc.

- Trust is not limited to real persons though, especially since Alice and Doris are represented by their keys. Take a website like PayPal for example. How do you know that you give them your credit card information, and not some infamous Nigerian princess Eve? You probably don't know anybody who personally knows PayPal...

Definition 5.21 (Web of Trust). *Let $G = (V, E)$ be a graph, where an edge between two nodes u, v represents trust between u, v. For any two nodes u, w, we say u trusts w if there is a path from u to w in G.*

Remarks:

- Hence, if you want someone to authenticate themselves, you need to find a path in the Web of Trust to them.

- In practice, the Web of Trust is a bit more sophisticated, as you can assign various levels of trust – and you might only trust someone in short distance.

- The whole situation is a bit of a chicken and egg dilemma though. In the beginning, you don't trust anyone, and nobody trusts you. You may want to find some well-connected nodes and gain their trust. This is the motivation for certificate authorities.

Definition 5.22 (Certificate Authority, CA). *A certificate authority is a node in a web of trust that is trusted by many other nodes.*

Remarks:

- A main distinction between a CA (or nodes in general) and your real-life friends is that trust is not needed to be mutual, edges in the web of trust can also be directed. As such a node u might trust v, but v does not necessarily need to trust u.

- You will find trust for some certificate authorities pre-installed on your system/browser, known as root certificates. When you want to know if you can trust a node, the node can supply you with a path (chain of trust) from the CA. More specifically, you will be supplied with signatures which you can check (as you trust the CA).

- Again, one can implement various levels of trust, e.g., you might only trust short paths.

- Moreover, a CA might get compromised. This leads to the idea of key revocation, where one can check if a key for a signature has been compromised – the corresponding certificate can be generated by anyone holding the respective secret key. Another idea is to also generate expiration dates for keys.

- A totally different problem is that your own set of root certificates might be compromised, e.g., if malicious software adds new root certificates to one's device.

5.3 Secret Sharing & Bulk Encryption

"Three may keep a secret, if two of them are dead." – Benjamin Franklin

Definition 5.23 (Perfect Secrecy). *An encryption algorithm has perfect secrecy, if the encrypted message reveals no information to an attacker, except for the possible maximum length of the message.*

Definition 5.24 (Threshold Secret Sharing). *Let $t, n \in \mathbb{N}$ with $1 \leq t \leq n$. An algorithm that distributes a secret among n participants such that t participants need to collaborate to recover the secret is called a (t,n)-threshold secret sharing scheme.*

Algorithm 5.25 (n, n)-Threshold Secret Sharing

Input: A secret k, encoded in binary representation of length $l(k)$.
Secret distribution

1: Generate $n - 1$ random binary numbers k_i of length $l(k)$ and distribute them among $n - 1$ participants
2: Give participant n the value k_n as the result of *XOR* of k and $k_1, \ldots, k_{n-1}$, i.e., $k_n = k \oplus k_1 \oplus k_2 \oplus \cdots \oplus k_{n-1}$

Secret recovery

1: Collect all n values $k_1, \ldots, k_n$ and obtain $k = k_1 \oplus k_2 \oplus \cdots \oplus k_{n-1} \oplus k_n$

Theorem 5.26. *Algorithm 5.25 has perfect secrecy even if $n - 1$ participants collaborate.*

Proof. The theorem holds as applying the *XOR* operation $\oplus$ to a random bitstring and k results in a random bitstring. $\qquad\square$

Remarks:

- How can we achieve a (t, n)-threshold secret sharing scheme with perfect secrecy?

Algorithm 5.27 (t, n)-Threshold Secret Sharing

Input: A secret k, represented as a real number.

Secret distribution

1: Generate $t - 1$ random $a_1, \ldots, a_{t-1} \in \mathbb{R}$
2: Obtain a polynomial f of degree $t - 1$ with $f(x) = k + a_1 x + \cdots + a_{t-1} x^{t-1}$
3: Generate n distinct $x_1, \ldots, x_n \in \mathbb{R} \setminus 0$
4: Distribute $(x_1, f(x_1))$ to participant P_1, $\ldots$, $(x_n, f(x_n))$ to P_n

Secret recovery

1: Collect t pairs $(x_i, f(x_i))$ from at least t participants
2: Use Lagrange's interpolation formula to obtain $f(0) = k$

Remarks:

- With at most $t - 1$ pairs $(x_i, f(x_i))$, there are infinitely many possible polynomials with different values for $f(0)$.

- There are many other (t, n)-threshold secret sharing schemes, e.g., with intersecting hyperplanes.

- Note that in practice, a finite field of prime order instead of real numbers is used.

- We can now use the ideas in this section so far to develop a bulk encryption algorithm with perfect secrecy.

Definition 5.28 (Bulk Encryption Algorithm). *A bulk encryption algorithm can securely encrypt a message of any size.*

Algorithm 5.29 One-Time Pad

Input: A message m known to Alice, and a symmetric key k (as a random bitstring) of length $l(k)$ known by both Alice and Bob.

Encryption

1: Alice sends $c = m \oplus k$ to Bob

Decryption

1: Bob obtains m by $m = c \oplus k$

Corollary 5.30. *Algorithm 5.29 has perfect secrecy.*

Remarks:

- Note that Algorithm 5.29 has one big disadvantage – Alice and Bob need to agree on a large random number first! While this is feasible for, e.g., secret agents, it is quite impractical for everyday usage.

- One can use padding to also remove information about the length of the message, e.g., by adding random bits to the secret.

Definition 5.31 (Electronic Code Book, ECB). *Given a method to encrypt a block of x bits, ECB encrypts a message of length rx by splitting the message into r blocks of length x, encrypting each block separately.*

Remarks:

- Do we now have a secure method to easily encrypt a large message, if we can encrypt small blocks, each using the same one-time pad?

- Suppose you have two message blocks m_1, m_2 of the same length, encrypted with k, resulting in c_1, c_2. However, you can obtain $m_1 \oplus m_2 = c_1 \oplus c_2$, giving you information about m_1 and m_2.

Definition 5.32 (Cipher Block Chaining, CBC). *Given a method f to encrypt a block of x bits, CBC encrypts a message of length rx by splitting the message into r blocks of length x, $m_1, m_2, \ldots, m_r$, encrypting (the plaintext of) each block XORed with the previous encrypted block, i.e., $c_i = f(m_i \oplus c_{i-1})$. The first block c_0 is initialized randomly.*

Remarks:

- Are we secure now? Using the same technique as in the last remark, you can again get, e.g., $m_4 \oplus m_5$.

- CBC is still one of the standard techniques though when encrypting blocks successively, as more advanced algorithms are not susceptible to this simple attack for one-time pads. An example would be the advanced encryption standard (AES). Using AES with CBC is an example of a bulk encryption algorithm. The operation of AES is beyond the scope of this short chapter however.

5.4   Message Authentication & Passwords

I've been imitated so well I've heard people copy my mistakes. –
Jimi Hendrix

Definition 5.33 (Replay Attack). *In a replay attack a previously
valid message from Alice to Bob is sent again from an eavesdropper
Eve to Bob.*

Remarks:

- An easy way to prevent replay attacks is to include time
  stamps in messages. Bob can detect a replay attack, if
  the time stamp is too old or multiple messages with the
  same time stamp arrive. Another idea is to use *nonces*
  (numbers only used once), with the sender and receiver
  keeping track of the nonces used so far.

- Another issue is that an attacker could change an encrypted message without knowing the content

Definition 5.34 (Malleability). *If ciphertext c can be changed to
c' such that the receiver decrypts it into a different message m'
without noticing, the encryption algorithm is malleable.*

Remarks:

- The Elgamal encryption Algorithm 5.14 is malleable: An
  attacker can relay $c = m \cdot k_p^x \mod p$ as $z \cdot c$, resulting in
  a valid decryption of zm.

- Thus, we need a way to ensure that the messages cannot
  be changed by an attacker. A natural solution are one-
  way hash functions.

Definition 5.35 (One-Way Hash Function). *A hash function is a
function $h : U \to S$. A hash function is called one-way, if for a
given $z \in S$ it is computationally hard to find an element $x \in U$
with $h(x) = z$.*

Definition 5.36 (Collision Resistant Hash Function). *A hash function $h : U \to S$ is called collision resistant, if it is computationally
hard to find elements $x \neq y$, $x, y \in U$, with $h(x) = h(y) \in S$.*

Remarks:

- It can be shown that a collision resistant hash function is also a one-way hash function.

Theorem 5.37 (Example for a Collision Resistant Hash Function). *Let $p = 2q + 1$ be a safe prime, with primitive roots $g_1 \neq g_2$ of p. The hash function $h : \{0, \ldots, q - 1\} \times \{0, \ldots, q - 1\} \to \mathbb{Z} \setminus \{0\}$ with $h(x_1, x_2) = g_1^{x_1} g_2^{x_2} \mod p$ is a collision resistant hash function.*

Remarks:

- For a small example, let us pick $p = 5$ with primitive roots $g_1 = 2$ and $g_2 = 3$. We choose $x_1 = 3$ and $x_2 = 4$, obtaining the hash $h(3, 4) = 2^3 3^4 \mod 5 = 3 \mod 5$.

- Popular hash functions used in cryptography include the Secure Hash Algorithm (SHA) and the Message-Digest Algorithm (MD).

- It can be shown that finding a collision for the hash function described in Theorem 5.37 is equivalent to solving the discrete logarithm problem for $\log_{g_1} g_2$. Thus, the hash function is a collision resistant hash function, as we assume the discrete logarithm problem to be computationally hard.

- One might think that using a collision resistant hash function is good enough to store passwords for a service. E.g., store the hash of each password, and then compare it to the input of the user. Even if the hashes are leaked, an attacker Eve cannot recover the passwords – or can she?

- In practice, many users use short passwords, trading security for convenience. Eve can sample the hashes of common passwords such as *"password"*, revealing the passwords of all users using these simple passwords. To counter this attack, one uses a technique called *salting*: The service adds a random bitstring (the *salt*) to each password before storing the hash (or, less secure, but simpler, the username). Even if the salt is known for each user, Eve needs to attack the hash of each user individually.

- To make life for Eve even harder, it is good practice to use hash functions that provably need a lot of computation and memory to execute. However, there is still a trade off as the real user wants to log in fast as well.

- Many web services already offer secure two-factor authentication (e.g., via mobile phones) instead of just passwords or challenge-response systems. However, there is a trade-off between security and convenience.

- Are we resistant against malleability now, if we include a hash of the encrypted message? No: An attacker changing the message can change the hash as well, as the hash function is not assumed to be secret. How do we prevent the hash from being modified without being noticed? The answer are HMACs:

Definition 5.38 (Message Authentication Code, MAC). *A message authentication code is a bitstring that verifies that a message comes from the desired sender and was not changed until reaching the receiver.*

Definition 5.39 (Hash-Based Message Authentication Code, or HMAC). *A hash-based message authentication code is a MAC that uses a collision resistant hash function in combination with a secret key.*

Algorithm 5.40 Hash-Based Message Authentication Code Generation

---

Input: An encrypted message c, to be sent from Alice to Bob, the publicly known hash function h from Theorem 5.37, and a secret key $1 \leq k \leq c$ known to Alice and Bob.
Result: An HMAC for c, checkable by Bob.

1: Alice computes $h_A = h(k, h(k, c))$, and sends c, h_A to Bob
2: Bob computes $h_B = h(k, h(k, c))$, and checks if $h_A = h_B$

Remarks:

- In practice, if $k > c$, then k will be hashed to have a smaller size. Also, the key will be padded for extra security.

- If an attacker wants to change the message, he needs to change the HMAC too. To change the HMAC, he needs to know the secret key k

- Algorithm 5.40 can be also used with any other collision resistant hash function.

5.5 Transport Layer Security

Now we have all the key ingredients to understand network security.

Protocol 5.41 (Transport Layer Security, TLS). *TLS is a network protocol in which a client and a server exchange information in order to communicate in a secure way. Common features include a key exchange protocol (Section 5.1), the authentication of the server to the client (5.2), a bulk encryption algorithm (5.3), and a message authentication algorithm (5.4).*

Remarks:

- TLS is the successor of Secure Sockets Layer (SSL). However, sometimes in practice the term SSL includes (the newer) TLS as well.

- HTTPS (Hypertext Transfer Protocol Secure) is not a protocol on its own, but rather denotes the usage of HTTP via TLS or SSL.

- SSH (Secure Shell), even though close in name to SSL, is something different: It is a protocol to allow a client to remotely access a server, e.g., for a command-line interface.

Chapter Notes

The concept of one-way functions is surprisingly old. In 1874, William Stanley Jevons wrote: "Can the reader say what two numbers multiplied together will produce the number 8616460799? I think it unlikely that anyone but myself will ever know." [Jev74]. To spill the beans: $89681 \cdot 96079$. The Diffie-Hellman Key Exchange was published in the seminal paper [DH76], parallel unpublished work also existed from Ellis et al. at the British intelligence service GCHQ. For some works showing the hardness of breaking the

Diffie-Hellman key exchange, we refer to, e.g., [dB88], [Mau94], [Sho97]. For some more recommendations on how to choose the parameters of the Diffie-Hellman key exchange see RFC 3526 at `http://tools.ietf.org/html/rfc3526`. The currently fastest algorithms to solve the discrete logarithm problem still have non-practical runtime, e.g., [Adl79]. The idea of challenging the other party to return an encrypted version of one's random number incremented by one in Algorithm 5.10 is taken from the Kerberos protocol. The Elgamal cryptosystem was published by Elgamal in 1984 [Gam84], some years after RSA [RSA78]. The first deterministic polynomial primality test, by Agrawal, Kayal, and Saxena, was published in [MA04], with an improved runtime of $\tilde{O}(\log^6 p)$ available at `https://math.dartmouth.edu/~carlp/aks041411.pdf`. The Miller-Rabin primality test is from Rabin [Rab80] and Miller [Mil76]. For an introduction to number theory, we recommend, e.g., [SO85]. The idea for the web of trust was proposed by Zimmermann in 1992. For certificate chains and key revocation, we refer to RFC 5280 at `http://tools.ietf.org/html/rfc5280`. The Chaum-van-Heijst-Pfitzmann hash function described in Theorem 5.37 was published in [CvHP91] by Chaum et al., for the reduction to the discrete logarithm problem see, e.g., [Sti95]. However, the runtime of the Chaum-van-Heijst-Pfitzmann hash function is too high in practice, it is chosen in this chapter as it is easier to understand compared to other related work. The subsequently described HMAC Algorithm 5.40 is from RFC 2104 at `https://tools.ietf.org/html/rfc2104`, with further security updates in RFC 6151, cf. `https://tools.ietf.org/html/rfc6151`. The secret sharing variant discussed in this chapter is from Shamir [Sha79], Blakley developed similar work in parallel in 1979 [Bla79], and also discussed its relation to one-time pads [Bla80]. While CBC seems superior to ECB, there is one downside: Decryption of ECB can be parallelized, but the decryption of CBC has to be sequential. The in this context mentioned AES encryption is a symmetric key algorithm, based on the Rijndael cipher of Daemen and Rijmen. Details of the Advanced Encryption Standard can be found in `http://csrc.nist.gov/publications/fips/fips197/fips-197.pdf`. AES, with a key length of 128,192, or 256 bits, replaced DES (Data Encryption Standard), as its key length of just 56 was no longer secure enough against brute-force attacks. While this chapter was based on the discrete logarithm problem, other problems with similar characteristics exist. A simple alternative is the factorization problem. Many current systems such as Bitcoin use cryptography based on so-called elliptic curves. For a general overview of the topic of computer security, we recommend [PHS03] and [FS03]. Lastly, as a very general recommendation, we urge you not to implement your own cryptosystem unless you really know what you are doing – there is just too much that can easily be missed.

Bibliography

[Adl79] Leonard Adleman. A subexponential algorithm for the discrete logarithm problem with applications to cryptography. In *Proceedings of the 20th Annual Symposium on Foundations of Computer Science*, SFCS '79, pages 55–60, Washington, DC, USA, 1979. IEEE Computer Society.

[Bla79] G.R. Blakley. Safeguarding cryptographic keys. In *Proceedings of the 1979 AFIPS National Computer Conference*, pages 313–317, Monval, NJ, USA, 1979. AFIPS Press.

[Bla80] G. R. Blakley. One time pads are key safeguarding schemes, not cryptosystems fast key safeguarding schemes (threshold schemes) exist. In *Proceedings of the 1980 IEEE Symposium on Security and Privacy, Oakland, California, USA, April 14-16, 1980*, pages 108–113. IEEE Computer Society, 1980.

[CvHP91] David Chaum, Eugène van Heijst, and Birgit Pfitzmann. Cryptographically strong undeniable signatures, unconditionally secure for the signer. In Joan Feigenbaum, editor, *Advances in Cryptology - CRYPTO '91, 11th Annual International Cryptology Conference, Santa Barbara, California, USA, August 11-15, 1991, Proceedings*, volume 576 of *Lecture Notes in Computer Science*, pages 470–484. Springer, 1991.

[dB88] Bert den Boer. Diffie-hillman is as strong as discrete log for certain primes. In Shafi Goldwasser, editor, *Advances in Cryptology - CRYPTO '88, 8th Annual International Cryptology Conference, Santa Barbara, California, USA, August 21-25, 1988, Proceedings*, volume 403 of *Lecture Notes in Computer Science*, pages 530–539. Springer, 1988.

[DH76] Whitfield Diffie and Martin E. Hellman. New directions in cryptography. *IEEE Trans. Information Theory*, 22(6):644–654, 1976.

[FS03] Niels Ferguson and Bruce Schneier. *Practical cryptography*. Wiley, 2003.

[Gam84] Taher El Gamal. A public key cryptosystem and a signature scheme based on discrete logarithms. In G. R. Blakley and David Chaum, editors, *Advances in Cryptology, Proceedings of CRYPTO '84, Santa Barbara, California, USA, August 19-22, 1984, Proceedings*, volume 196 of *Lecture Notes in Computer Science*, pages 10–18. Springer, 1984.

[Jev74] William Stanley Jevons. *The Principles of Science: A Treatise on Logic and Scientific Method*. Macmillan & Co., 1874.

[MA04] Nitin Saxena Manindra Agrawal, Neeraj Kayal. PRIMES Is in P. *Annals of Mathematics*, 160(2):781–793, 2004.

[Mau94] Ueli M. Maurer. Towards the equivalence of breaking the diffie-hellman protocol and computing discrete algorithms. In Yvo Desmedt, editor, *Advances in Cryptology - CRYPTO '94, 14th Annual International Cryptology Conference, Santa Barbara, California, USA, August 21-25, 1994, Proceedings*, volume 839 of *Lecture Notes in Computer Science*, pages 271–281. Springer, 1994.

[Mil76] Gary L. Miller. Riemann's hypothesis and tests for primality. *J. Comput. Syst. Sci.*, 13(3):300–317, December 1976.

[PHS03] Josef Pieprzyk, Thomas Hardjono, and Jennifer Seberry. *Fundamentals of computer security*. Springer, 2003.

[Rab80] M.O. Rabin. Probabilistic algorithms for testing primality. *J. Number Theory*, 12:128 – 138, 1980.

[RSA78] R. L. Rivest, A. Shamir, and L. Adleman. A method for obtaining digital signatures and public-key cryptosystems. *Commun. ACM*, 21(2):120–126, February 1978.

[Sha79] Adi Shamir. How to share a secret. *Commun. ACM*, 22(11):612–613, 1979.

[Sho97] Victor Shoup. Lower bounds for discrete logarithms and related problems. In Walter Fumy, editor, *Advances in Cryptology - EUROCRYPT '97, International Conference on the Theory and Application of Cryptographic Techniques, Konstanz, Germany, May 11-15, 1997, Proceeding*, volume 1233 of *Lecture Notes in Computer Science*, pages 256–266. Springer, 1997.

[SO85] Winfried Scharlau and Hans Opolka. *From Fermat to Minkowski: lectures on the theory of numbers and its historical development.* Undergraduate Texts in Mathematics. Springer, New York, 1985.

[Sti95] Douglas R. Stinson. *Cryptography - theory and practice.* Discrete mathematics and its applications series. CRC Press, 1995.

Chapter 6

Broadcast & Shared Coins

In Chapter 4 we have developed a fast solution for synchronous byzantine agreement (Algorithm 4.14), yet our *asynchronous* byzantine agreement solution (Algorithm 4.21) is still awfully slow. Is there a fast asynchronous algorithm, possibly based on some advanced communication methods?

6.1 Random Oracle and Bitstring

Definition 6.1 (Random Oracle). *A random oracle is a trusted (non-byzantine) random source which can generate random values.*

Algorithm 6.2 Shared Coin with Magic Random Oracle

1: **return** c_i, where c_i is ith random bit by oracle

Remarks:

- Algorithm 6.2 as well as the following shared coin algorithms will for instance be called in Line 12 of Algorithm 4.21. So instead of every node throwing a local coin (and hoping that they all show the same), the nodes throw a *shared* coin. In other words, the value x_u in Line 12 of Algorithm 4.21 will be set to the return value of the shared coin subroutine.

- We have already seen a shared coin in Algorithm 3.22. This concept deserves a proper definition.

Definition 6.3 (Shared Coin). *A **shared coin** is a binary random variable shared among all nodes. It is 0 for all nodes with constant probability, and 1 for all nodes with constant probability. The shared coin is allowed to fail (be 0 for some nodes and 1 for other nodes) with constant probability.*

Theorem 6.4. *Algorithm 6.2 plugged into Algorithm 4.21 solves asynchronous byzantine agreement in expected constant number of rounds.*

Proof. If there is a large majority for one of the input values in the system, all nodes will decide within two rounds since Algorithm 4.21 satisfies all-same-validity; the shared coin is not even used.

If there is no significant majority for any of the input values at the beginning of algorithm 4.21, all correct nodes will run Algorithm 6.2. Therefore, they will set their new value to the bit given by the random oracle and terminate in the following round.

If neither of the above cases holds, some of the nodes see an $n/2 + f + 1$ majority for one of the input values, while other nodes rely on the oracle. With probability $1/2$, the value of the oracle will coincide with the deterministic majority value of the other nodes. Therefore, with probability $1/2$, the nodes will terminate in the following round. The expected number of rounds for termination in this case is 3. $\square$

Remarks:

- Unfortunately, random oracles are a bit like pink fluffy unicorns: they do not really exist in the real world. Can we fix that?

Definition 6.5 (Random Bitstring). *A **random bitstring** is a string of random binary values, known to all participating nodes when starting a protocol.*

Algorithm 6.6 Naive Shared Coin with Random Bitstring

1: **return** b_i, where b_i is ith bit in common random bitstring

---

Remarks:

- But is such a precomputed bitstring really random enough? We should be worried because of Theorem 3.14.

Theorem 6.7. *If the scheduling is worst-case, Algorithm 6.6 plugged into Algorithm 4.21 does not terminate.*

Proof. We start Algorithm 6.6 with the following input: $n/2+f+1$ nodes have input value 1, and $n/2-f-1$ nodes have input value 0. Assume w.l.o.g. that the first bit of the random bitstring is 0.

If the second random bit in the bitstring is also 0, then a worst-case scheduler will let $n/2+f+1$ nodes see all $n/2+f+1$ values 1, these will therefore deterministically choose the value 1 as their new value. Because of scheduling (or byzantine nodes), the remaining $n/2-f-1$ nodes receive strictly less than $n/2+f+1$ values 1 and therefore have to rely on the value of the shared coin, which is 0. The nodes will not come to a decision in this round. Moreover, we have created the very same distribution of values for the next round (which has also random bit 0).

If the second random bit in the bitstring is 1, then a worst-case scheduler can let $n/2-f-1$ nodes see all $n/2+f+1$ values 1, and therefore deterministically choose the value 1 as their new value. Because of scheduling (or byzantine nodes), the remaining $n/2+f+1$ nodes receive strictly less than $n/2+f+1$ values 1 and therefore have to rely on the value of the shared coin, which is 0. The nodes will not decide in this round. And we have created the symmetric situation for input value 1 that is coming in the next round.

So if the current and the next random bit are known, worst-case scheduling will keep the system in one of two symmetric states that never decide.

$\square$

Remarks:

- Theorem 6.7 shows that a worst-case scheduler cannot be allowed to know the random bits of the future.

- Note that in the proof of Theorem 6.7 we did not even use any byzantine nodes. Just bad scheduling was enough to prevent termination.

- Worst-case scheduling is an issue that we have not considered so far, in particular in Chapter 3 we implicitly assumed that message scheduling was random. What if scheduling is worst-case in Algorithm 3.22?

Lemma 6.8. *Algorithm 3.22 has exponential expected running time under worst-case scheduling.*

Proof. In Algorithm 3.22, worst-case scheduling may hide up to f rare zero coinflips. In order to receive a zero as the outcome of the shared coin, the nodes need to generate at least $f + 1$ zeros. The probability for this to happen is $(1/n)^{f+1}$, which is exponentially small for $f \in \Omega(n)$. In other words, with worst-case scheduling, with probability $1 - (1/n)^{f+1}$ the shared coin will be 1. The worst-case scheduler must make sure that some nodes will always deterministically go for 0, and the algorithm needs n^{f+1} rounds until it terminates. □

Remarks:

- With worst-case asynchrony, some of our previous results do not hold anymore. Can we at least solve asynchronous (assuming worst-case scheduling) *consensus* if we have crash failures?

- This is indeed possible, but we need to sharpen our tools first.

6.2   Shared Coin on a Blackboard

Definition 6.9 (Blackboard Model). *The **blackboard** is a trusted authority which supports two operations. A node can **write** its message to the blackboard and a node can **read** all the values that have been written to the blackboard so far.*

Remarks:

- We assume that the nodes cannot reconstruct the order in which the messages are written to the blackboard, since the system is asynchronous.

Algorithm 6.10 Crash-Resilient Shared Coin with Blackboard (for node u)

1: **while** true **do**
2:    Choose new local coin $c_u = +1$ with probability $1/2$, else $c_u = -1$
3:    Write c_u to the blackboard
4:    Set $C =$ Read all coinflips on the blackboard
5:    **if** $|C| \geq n^2$ **then**
6:       **return** sign(sum(C))
7:    **end if**
8: **end while**

Remarks:

- In Algorithm 6.10 the outcome of a coinflip is -1 or $+1$ instead of 0 or 1 because it simplifies the analysis, i.e., "$-1 \approx 0$".

- The *sign* function is used for the decision values. The sign function returns $+1$ if the sum of all coinflips in C is positive, and -1 if it is negative.

- The algorithm is unusual compared to other asynchronous algorithms we have dealt with so far. So far we often waited for $n - f$ messages from other nodes. In Algorithm 6.10, a single node can single-handedly generate all n^2 coinflips, without waiting.

- If a node does not need to wait for other nodes, we call the algorithm *wait-free*.

- Many similar definitions beyond wait-free exist: lock-free, deadlock-free, starvation-free, and generally non-blocking algorithms.

Theorem 6.11 (Central Limit Theorem). *Let $\{X_1, X_2, \ldots, X_N\}$ be a sequence of independent random variables with $Pr[X_i = -1] = Pr[X_i = 1] = 1/2$ for all $i = 1, \ldots, N$. Then for every real number z,*

$$\lim_{N \to \infty} Pr\left[\sum_{i=1}^{N} X_i \leq z\sqrt{N}\right] = \Phi(z) < \frac{1}{\sqrt{2\pi}} e^{-z^2/2},$$

where $\Phi(z)$ is the cumulative distribution function of the standard normal distribution evaluated at z.

Theorem 6.12. *Algorithm 6.10 implements a polynomial shared coin.*

Proof. Each node in the algorithm terminates once at least n^2 coinflips are written to the blackboard. Before terminating, nodes may write one additional coinflip. Therefore, every node decides after reading at least n^2 and at most $n^2 + n$ coinflips. The power of the adversary lies in the fact that it can prevent $n - 1$ nodes from writing their coinflips to the blackboard by delaying their writes. Here, we will consider an even stronger adversary that can hide up to n coinflips which were written on the blackboard.

We need to show that both outcomes for the shared coin ($+1$ or -1 in Line 6) will occur with constant probability, as in Definition 6.3. Let X be the sum of all coinflips that are visible to every node. Since some of the nodes might read n more values from the blackboard than others, the nodes cannot be prevented from deciding if $|X| > n$. By applying Theorem 6.11 with $N = n^2$ and $z = 1$, we get:

$$Pr(X < -n) = Pr(X > n) = 1 - Pr(X \leq n) = 1 - \Phi(1) > 0.15.$$

$\square$

Lemma 6.13. *Algorithm 6.10 uses n^2 coinflips, which is optimal in this model.*

Proof. The proof for showing quadratic lower bound makes use of configurations that are indistinguishable to all nodes, similar to Theorem 3.14. It requires involved stochastic methods and we therefore will only sketch the idea of where the n^2 comes from.

The basic idea follows from Theorem 6.11. The standard deviation of the sum of n^2 coinflips is n. The central limit theorem tells us that with constant probability the sum of the coinflips will be only a constant factor away from the standard deviation. As we showed in Theorem 6.12, this is large enough to disarm a worst-case scheduler. However, with much less than n^2 coinflips, a worst-case scheduler is still too powerful. If it sees a positive sum forming on the blackboard, it delays messages trying to write $+1$ in order to turn the sum temporarily negative, so the nodes finishing first see a negative sum, and the delayed nodes see a positive sum. $\square$

Remarks:

- Algorithm 6.10 cannot tolerate even one byzantine failure: assume the byzantine node generates all the n^2 coinflips in every round due to worst-case scheduling. Then this byzantine node can make sure that its coinflips always sum up to a value larger than n, thus making the outcome -1 impossible.

- In Algorithm 6.10, we assume that the blackboard is a trusted central authority. Like the random oracle of Definition 6.1, assuming a blackboard does not seem practical. However, fortunately, we can use advanced broadcast methods in order to implement something like a blackboard with just messages.

6.3   Broadcast Abstractions

Definition 6.14 (Accept). *A message received by a node v is called* ***accepted*** *if node v can consider this message for its computation.*

Definition 6.15 (Best-Effort Broadcast). ***Best-effort broadcast*** *ensures that a message that is sent from a correct node u to another correct node v will eventually be received and accepted by v.*

Remarks:

- Note that best-effort broadcast is equivalent to the simple broadcast primitive that we have used so far.

- Reliable broadcast is a stronger paradigm which implies that byzantine nodes cannot send different values to different nodes. Such behavior will be detected.

Definition 6.16 (Reliable Broadcast). ***Reliable broadcast*** *ensures that the nodes eventually agree on all accepted messages. That is, if a correct node v considers message m as accepted, then every other node will eventually consider message m as accepted.*

Algorithm 6.17 Asynchronous Reliable Broadcast (code for node u)

1: Broadcast own message $\mathtt{msg}(u)$
2: **if** received $\mathtt{msg}(v)$ from node v **then**
3:     Broadcast $\mathtt{echo}(u, \mathtt{msg}(v))$
4: **end if**
5: **if** received $\mathtt{echo}(w, \mathtt{msg}(v))$ from $n-2f$ nodes w but not $\mathtt{msg}(v)$ **then**
6:     Broadcast $\mathtt{echo}(u, \mathtt{msg}(v))$
7: **end if**
8: **if** received $\mathtt{echo}(w, \mathtt{msg}(v))$ from $n - f$ nodes w **then**
9:     Accept($\mathtt{msg}(v)$)
10: **end if**

Theorem 6.18. *Algorithm 6.17 satisfies the following properties:*

1. *If a correct node broadcasts a message reliably, it will eventually be accepted by every other correct node.*

2. *If a correct node has not broadcast a message, it will not be accepted by any other correct node.*

3. *If a correct node accepts a message, it will be eventually accepted by every correct node*

Proof. We start with the first property. Assume a correct node broadcasts a message $\mathtt{msg}(v)$, then every correct node will receive $\mathtt{msg}(v)$ eventually. In Line 3, every correct node (including the originator of the message) will echo the message and, eventually, every correct node will receive at least $n - f$ echoes, thus accepting $\mathtt{msg}(v)$.

The second property follows from byzantine nodes being unable to forge an incorrect sender address, see Definition 4.1.

The third property deals with a byzantine originator b. If a correct node accepted message $\mathtt{msg}(b)$, this node must have received at least $n - f$ echoes for this message in Line 8. Since at most f nodes are byzantine, at least $n-2f$ correct nodes have broadcast an echo message for $\mathtt{msg}(b)$. Therefore, every correct node will receive these $n - 2f$ echoes eventually and will broadcast an echo itself. Thus, all $n - f$ correct nodes will have broadcast an echo for $\mathtt{msg}(b)$ and every correct node will accept $\mathtt{msg}(b)$.

$\square$

Remarks:

- Algorithm 6.17 does not terminate. Only *eventually*, all messages by correct nodes will be accepted.

- The algorithm has a linear message overhead, since every node again broadcasts every message.

- Note that byzantine nodes can issue arbitrarily many messages. This may be a problem for protocols where each node is only allowed to send one message (per round). Can we fix this, for instance with sequence numbers?

Definition 6.19 (FIFO Reliable Broadcast). *The **FIFO (reliable) broadcast** defines an order in which the messages are accepted in the system. If a node u broadcasts message m_1 before m_2, then any node v will accept message m_1 before m_2.*

Algorithm 6.20 FIFO Reliable Broadcast (code for node u)

1: Broadcast own round r message $\mathtt{msg}(u, r)$
2: **if** received first message $\mathtt{msg}(v, r)$ from node v for round r **then**
3:    Broadcast $\mathtt{echo}(u, \mathrm{msg}(v, r))$
4: **end if**
5: **if** not echoed any $\mathtt{msg'}(v, r)$ before **then**
6:    **if** received $\mathtt{echo}(w, \mathrm{msg}(v, r))$ from $f + 1$ nodes w but not $\mathtt{msg}(v, r)$ **then**
7:       Broadcast $\mathtt{echo}(u, \mathrm{msg}(v, r))$
8:    **end if**
9: **end if**
10: **if** received $\mathtt{echo}(w, \mathrm{msg}(v, r))$ from $n - f$ nodes w **then**
11:    **if** accepted $\mathtt{msg}(v, r - 1)$ **then**
12:       Accept($\mathtt{msg}(v, r)$)
13:    **end if**
14: **end if**

Theorem 6.21. *Algorithm 6.20 satisfies the properties of Theorem 6.18. Additionally, Algorithm 6.20 makes sure that no two messages $\mathtt{msg}(v, r)$ and $\mathtt{msg'}(v, r)$ are accepted from the same node. It can tolerate $f < n/3$ Byzantine nodes or $f < n/2$ crash failures.*

Proof. Just as reliable broadcast, Algorithm 6.20 satisfies the first two properties of Theorem 6.18 by simply following the flow of messages of a correct node.

For the third property, assume again that some message originated from a byzantine node b. If a correct node accepted message $\mathtt{msg}(b)$, this node must have received at least $n - f$ echoes for this message in Line 10.

- Byzantine case: If at most f nodes are byzantine, at least $n - 2f > f + 1$ correct nodes have broadcast an echo message for $\mathtt{msg}(b)$.

- Crash-failure case: If at most f nodes can crash, at least $n - f > f + 1$ nodes have broadcast an echo message for $\mathtt{msg}(b)$.

In both cases, every correct node will receive these $f + 1$ echoes eventually and will broadcast an echo. Thus, all $n - f$ correct nodes will have broadcast an echo for $\mathtt{msg}(b)$ and every correct node will accept $\mathtt{msg}(b)$.

It remains to show that at most one message will be accepted from some node v in a round r.

- Byzantine case: Assume that some correct node u has accepted $\mathtt{msg}(v, r)$ in Line 12. Then, u has received $n - f$ echoes for this message, $n - 2f$ of which were the first echoes of the correct nodes. Assume for contradiction that another correct node accepts $\mathtt{msg'}(v, r)$. This node must have collected $n - f$ messages $\mathrm{echo}(w, \mathtt{msg'}(v, r))$. Since at least $n - 2f$ of these messages must be the first echo messages sent by correct nodes, we have $n - 2f + n - 2f = 2n - 4f > n - f$ (for $f < n/3$) echo messages sent by the correct nodes as their first echo. This is a contradiction.

- Crash-failure case: At least $n - 2f$ not crashed nodes must have echoed $\mathtt{msg}(v, r)$, while $n - f$ nodes have echoed $\mathtt{msg'}(v, r)$. In total $2n - 3f > n - f$ (for $f < n/2$) correct nodes must have echoed either of the messages, which is a contradiction.

$\square$

Definition 6.22 (Atomic Broadcast). *__Atomic broadcast__ makes sure that all messages are received in the same order by every node. That is, for any pair of nodes u, v, and for any two messages m_1 and m_2, node u receives m_1 before m_2 if and only if node v receives m_1 before m_2.*

Remarks:

- Definition 6.22 is equivalent to Definition 2.8, i.e., atomic broadcast = state replication.

- Now we have all the tools to finally solve asynchronous consensus.

6.4 Blackboard with Message Passing

Algorithm 6.23 Crash-Resilient Shared Coin (code for node u)

1: **while** true **do**
2:     Choose local coin $c_u = +1$ with probability $1/2$, else $c_u = -1$

3:     FIFO-broadcast $\text{coin}(c_u, r)$ to all nodes
4:     Save all received coins $\text{coin}(c_v, r)$ in a set C_u
5:     Wait until accepted own $\text{coin}(c_u)$
6:     Request C_v from $n - f$ nodes v, and add newly seen coins to C_u
7:     **if** $|C_u| \geq n^2$ **then**
8:         **return** $\text{sign}(\text{sum}(C_u))$
9:     **end if**
10: **end while**

Theorem 6.24. *Algorithm 6.23 solves asynchronous binary agreement for $f < n/2$ crash failures.*

Proof. The upper bound for the number of crash failures results from the upper bound in 6.21. The idea of this algorithm is to simulate the read and write operations from Algorithm 6.10.

Line 3 simulates a read operation: by accepting the own coinflip, a node verifies that $n - f$ correct nodes have received its most recent generated coinflip $\text{coin}(c_u, r)$. At least $n - 2f > 1$ of these nodes will never crash and the value therefore can be considered as stored on the blackboard. While a value is not accepted and therefore not stored, node u will not generate new coinflips. Therefore, at any point of the algorithm, there is at most n additional generated coinflips next to the accepted coins.

Line 6 of the algorithm corresponds to a read operation. A node reads a value by requesting C_v from at least $n - f$ nodes v.

Assume that for a coinflip $\mathtt{coin}(c_u, r)$, f nodes that participated in the FIFO broadcast of this message have crashed. When requesting $n - f$ sets of coinflips, there will be at least $(n - 2f) + (n - f) - (n - f) = n - 2f > 1$ sets among the requested ones containing $\mathtt{coin}(c_u, r)$. Therefore, a node will always read all values that were accepted so far.

This shows that the read and write operations are equivalent to the same operations in Algorithm 6.10. Assume now that some correct node has terminated after reading n^2 coinflips. Since each node reads the stored coinflips before generating a new one in the next round, there will be at most n additional coins accepted by any other node before termination. This setting is equivalent to Theorem 6.12 and the rest of the analysis is therefore analogous to the analysis in that theorem. $\square$

Remarks:

- So finally we can deal with worst-case crash failures *and* worst-case scheduling.

- But what about byzantine agreement? We need even more powerful methods!

6.5   Using Cryptography

We can use the cryptographic techniques from Chapter 5.

Algorithm 6.25 Preprocessing Step for Algorithm 6.26 (code for dealer d)

1: According to Algorithm 5.27, choose polynomial p of degree f
2: **for** $i = 1, \ldots, n$ **do**
3:      Choose coinflip c_i, where $c_i = 0$ with probability $1/2$, else $c_i = 1$
4:      Using Algorithm 5.27, generate n shares $(x_1^i, p(x_1^i)), \ldots, (x_n^i, p(x_n^i))$ for c_i
5: **end for**
6: Send shares $\mathtt{msg}(x_u^1, p(x_u^1))_d, \ldots, \mathtt{msg}(x_u^n, p(x_u^n))_d$ to node u

---

Algorithm 6.26 Shared Coin using Secret Sharing (ith iteration)

1: Request shares from at least $f + 1$ nodes
2: Using Algorithm 5.27, let c_i be the value reconstructed from the shares
3: **return** c_i

Theorem 6.27. *Algorithm 4.21 together with Algorithm 6.25 and Algorithm 6.26 solves asynchronous byzantine agreement for $f < n/3$ in expected 3 number of rounds.*

Proof. In Line 1 of Algorithm 6.26, the nodes collect shares from $f + 1$ nodes. Since a byzantine node cannot forge the signature of the dealer, it is restricted to either send its own share or decide to not send it at all. Therefore, each correct node will eventually be able to reconstruct secret c_i of round i correctly in Line 2 of the algorithm. The running time analysis follows then from the analysis of Theorem 6.4. $\qquad\square$

Remarks:

- In Algorithm 6.25 we assume that the dealer generates the random bitstring. This assumption is not necessary in general.

- We showed that cryptographic assumptions can speed up asynchronous byzantine agreement.

- Algorithm 4.21 can also be implemented in the synchronous setting.

- A randomized version of a synchronous byzantine agreement algorithm can improve on the lower bound of $t + 1$ rounds for the deterministic algorithms.

Definition 6.28 (Cryptographic Hash Function). *A hash function hash : $U \to S$ is called **cryptographic**, if for a given $z \in S$ it is computationally hard to find an element $x \in U$ with $hash(x) = z$.*

Remarks:

- Popular hash functions used in cryptography include the Secure Hash Algorithm (SHA) and the Message-Digest Algorithm (MD).

Algorithm 6.29 Simple Synchronous Byzantine Shared Coin (for node u)

1: Each node has a public key that is known to all nodes.
2: Let r be the current round of Algorithm 4.21
3: Broadcast $\mathbf{msg}(r)_u$, i.e., round number r signed by node u
4: Compute $h_v = \mathrm{hash}(\mathrm{msg}(r)_v)$ for all received messages $\mathbf{msg}(r)_v$

5: Let $h_{min} = \min_v h_v$
6: **return** least significant bit of h_{min}

Remarks:

- In Algorithm 6.29, Line 3 each node can verify the correctness of the signed message using the public key.

- Just as in Algorithm 4.9, the decision value is the minimum of all received values. While the minimum value is received by all nodes after 2 rounds there, we can only guarantee to receive the minimum with constant probability in this algorithm.

- Hashing helps to restrict byzantine power, since a byzantine node cannot compute the smallest hash.

Theorem 6.30. *Algorithm 6.29 plugged into Algorithm 4.21 solves synchronous byzantine agreement in expected 5 rounds for up to $f < n/10$ byzantine failures.*

Proof. With probability $1/3$ the minimum hash value is generated by a byzantine node. In such a case, we can assume that not all correct nodes will receive the byzantine value and thus, different nodes might compute different values for the shared coin.

With probability $2/3$, the shared coin will be from a correct node, and with probability $1/2$ the value of the shared coin will correspond to the value which was deterministically chosen by some of the correct nodes. Therefore, with probability $1/3$ the nodes will reach consensus in the next iteration of Algorithm 4.21. The expected number of rounds is:

$$1 + \sum_{i=0}^{\infty} 2 \cdot \left(\frac{2}{3}\right)^i = 5$$

$\square$

Chapter Notes

Asynchronous byzantine agreement is usually considered in one out of two communication models – shared memory or message passing. The first polynomial algorithm for the shared memory model that uses a shared coin was proposed by Aspnes and Herlihy [AH90] and required exchanging $O(n^4)$ messages in total. Algorithm 6.10 is also an implementation of the shared coin in the shared memory model and it requires exchanging $O(n^3)$ messages. This variant is due to Saks, Shavit and Woll [SSW91]. Bracha and Rachman [BR92] later reduced the number of messages exchanged to $O(n^2 \log n)$. The tight lower bound of $\Omega(n^2)$ on the number of coinflips was proposed by Attiya and Censor [AC08] and improved the first non-trivial lower bound of $\Omega(n^2/\log^2 n)$ by Aspnes [Asp98].

In the message passing model, the shared coin is usually implemented using reliable broadcast. Reliable broadcast was first proposed by Srikanth and Toueg [ST87] as a method to simulate authenticated broadcast. There is also another implementation which was proposed by Bracha [Bra87]. Today, a lot of variants of reliable broadcast exist, including FIFO broadcast [AAD05], which was considered in this chapter. A good overview over the broadcast routines is given by Cachin et al. [CGR14]. A possible way to reduce message complexity is by simulating the read and write commands [ABND95] as in Algorithm 6.23. The message complexity of this method is $O(n^3)$. Alistarh et al. [AAKS14] improved the number of exchanged messages to $O(n^2 \log^2 n)$ using a binary tree that restricts the number of communicating nodes according to the depth of the tree.

It remains an open question whether asynchronous byzantine agreement can be solved in the message passing model without cryptographic assumptions. If cryptographic assumptions are however used, byzantine agreement can be solved in expected constant number of rounds. Algorithm 6.25 presents the first implementation due to Rabin [Rab83] using threshold secret sharing. This algorithm relies on the fact that the dealer provides the random bitstring. Chor et al. [CGMA85] proposed the first algorithm where the nodes use verifiable secret sharing in order to generate random bits. Later work focuses on improving resilience [CR93] and practicability [CKS00]. Algorithm 6.29 by Micali [Mic18] shows that cryptographic assumptions can also help to improve the running time in the synchronous model.

Bibliography

[AAD05] Ittai Abraham, Yonatan Amit, and Danny Dolev. Optimal resilience asynchronous approximate agreement. In *Proceedings of the 8th International Conference on Principles of Distributed Systems*, OPODIS'04, pages 229–239, Berlin, Heidelberg, 2005. Springer-Verlag.

[AAKS14] Dan Alistarh, James Aspnes, Valerie King, and Jared Saia. Communication-efficient randomized consensus. In Fabian Kuhn, editor, *Distributed Computing*, pages 61–75, Berlin, Heidelberg, 2014. Springer Berlin Heidelberg.

[ABND95] Hagit Attiya, Amotz Bar-Noy, and Danny Dolev. Sharing memory robustly in message-passing systems. *J. ACM*, 42(1):124–142, January 1995.

[AC08] Hagit Attiya and Keren Censor. Tight bounds for asynchronous randomized consensus. *J. ACM*, 55(5):20:1–20:26, November 2008.

[AH90] James Aspnes and Maurice Herlihy. Fast randomized consensus using shared memory. *Journal of Algorithms*, 11(3):441 – 461, 1990.

[Asp98] James Aspnes. Lower bounds for distributed coin-flipping and randomized consensus. *J. ACM*, 45(3):415–450, May 1998.

[BR92] Gabriel Bracha and Ophir Rachman. Randomized consensus in expected $o(n^2 logn)$ operations. In *Proceedings of the 5th International Workshop on Distributed Algorithms*, WDAG '91, pages 143–150, Berlin, Heidelberg, 1992. Springer-Verlag.

[Bra87] Gabriel Bracha. Asynchronous byzantine agreement protocols. *Information and Computation*, 75(2):130 – 143, 1987.

[CGMA85] B. Chor, S. Goldwasser, S. Micali, and B. Awerbuch. Verifiable secret sharing and achieving simultaneity in the presence of faults. In *26th Annual Symposium on Foundations of Computer Science (sfcs 1985)*, pages 383–395, Oct 1985.

[CGR14] Christian Cachin, Rachid Guerraoui, and Lus Rodrigues. *Introduction to Reliable and Secure Distributed Programming*. Springer Publishing Company, Incorporated, 2nd edition, 2014.

[CKS00] Christian Cachin, Klaus Kursawe, and Victor Shoup. Random oracles in constantinople: Practical asynchronous byzantine agreement using cryptography. *Journal of Cryptology*, 18:219–246, 2000.

[CR93] Ran Canetti and Tal Rabin. Fast asynchronous byzantine agreement with optimal resilience. In *Proceedings of the Twenty-fifth Annual ACM Symposium on Theory of Computing*, STOC '93, pages 42–51, New York, NY, USA, 1993. ACM.

[Mic18] Silvio Micali. Byzantine agreement , made trivial. 2018.

[Rab83] M. O. Rabin. Randomized byzantine generals. In *24th Annual Symposium on Foundations of Computer Science (sfcs 1983)*, pages 403–409, Nov 1983.

[SSW91] Michael Saks, Nir Shavit, and Heather Woll. Optimal time randomized consensus – making resilient algorithms fast in practice. In *Proceedings of the Second Annual ACM-SIAM Symposium on Discrete Algorithms*, SODA '91, pages 351–362, Philadelphia, PA, USA, 1991. Society for Industrial and Applied Mathematics.

[ST87] T. K. Srikanth and S. Toueg. Optimal Clock Synchronization. *Journal of the ACM*, 34:626–645, 1987.

Chapter 7

Authenticated Agreement

In Section 6.5 we have already had a glimpse into the power of cryptography. In this Chapter we want to build a *practical* byzantine fault-tolerant system using cryptography. With cryptography, Byzantine lies may be detected easily.

7.1 Agreement with Authentication

Definition 7.1 (Signature). *Every node can **sign** its messages in a way that no other node can forge, thus nodes can reliably determine which node a signed message originated from. We denote a message* $\mathtt{msg}(x)$ *signed by node* u *with* $\mathtt{msg}(x)_u$.

Remarks:

- Algorithm 7.2 shows a synchronous agreement protocol for binary inputs relying on signatures. We assume there is a designated "primary" node p that all other nodes know. The goal is to decide on p's value.

Theorem 7.3. *Algorithm 7.2 can tolerate* $f < n$ *byzantine failures while terminating in* $f + 1$ *rounds.*

Proof. Assuming that the primary p is not byzantine and its input is 1, then p broadcasts $\mathtt{value}(1)_p$ in the first round, which will

---

Algorithm 7.2 Byzantine Agreement with Authentication

Code for primary p:

```
1: if input is 1 then
2:     broadcast value(1)_p
3:     decide 1 and terminate
4: else
5:     decide 0 and terminate
6: end if
```

Code for all other nodes v:

```
7:  for all rounds i ∈ {1, ..., f + 1} do
8:      S is the set of accepted messages value(1)_u.
9:      if |S| ≥ i and value(1)_p ∈ S then
10:         broadcast S ∪ {value(1)_v}
11:         decide 1 and terminate
12:     end if
13: end for
14: decide 0 and terminate
```

---

trigger all correct nodes to decide on 1. If p's input is 0, there is no signed message $\mathtt{value}(1)_p$, and no node can decide on 1. $\quad\square$

If primary p is byzantine, we need all correct nodes to decide on the same value for the algorithm to be correct.

Assume $i < f + 1$ is minimal among all rounds in which any correct node u decides on 1. In this case, u has a set S of at least i messages from other nodes for value 1 in round i, including one of p. Therefore, in round $i + 1 \leq f + 1$, all other correct nodes will receive S and u's message for value 1 and thus decide on 1 too.

Now assume that $i = f + 1$ is minimal among all rounds in which a correct node u decides for 1. Thus u must have received $f + 1$ messages for value 1, one of which must be from a correct node since there are only f byzantine nodes. In this case some other correct node u' must have decided on 1 in some round $j < i$, which contradicts i's minimality; hence this case cannot happen.

Finally, if no correct node decides on 1 by the end of round $f + 1$, then all correct nodes will decide on 0. $\quad\square$

Remarks:

- The algorithm only takes $f + 1$ rounds, which is optimal as described in Theorem 4.20.

- Using signatures, Algorithm 7.2 solves consensus for any number of failures! Does this contradict Theorem 4.12? Recall that in the proof of Theorem 4.12 we assumed that a byzantine node can distribute contradictory information about its own input. If messages are signed, correct nodes can detect such behavior – a node u signing two contradicting messages proves to all nodes that node u is byzantine.

- Does Algorithm 7.2 satisfy any of the validity conditions introduced in Section 4.1? No! A byzantine primary can dictate the decision value. Can we modify the algorithm such that the correct-input validity condition is satisfied? Yes! We can run the algorithm in parallel for $2f + 1$ primary nodes. Either 0 or 1 will occur at least $f + 1$ times, which means that one correct process had to have this value in the first place. In this case, we can only handle $f < \frac{n}{2}$ byzantine nodes.

- If the primary is a correct node, Algorithm 7.2 only needs two rounds! Can we make it work with arbitrary inputs? Also, relying on synchrony limits the practicality of the protocol. What if messages can be lost or the system is asynchronous?

7.2 Practical Byzantine Fault Tolerance

Practical Byzantine Fault Tolerance (PBFT) is one of the first and perhaps the most instructive protocol for achieving state replication among nodes as in Definition 2.8 with byzantine nodes in an asynchronous network. We present a very simple version of it without any optimizations.

Definition 7.4 (System Model). *There are $n = 3f + 1$ nodes and an unbounded number of clients. There are at most f byzantine nodes, and clients can be byzantine as well. The network is asynchronous, and messages have variable delay and can get lost. Clients send requests that correct nodes have to order to achieve state replication.*

The ideas behind PBFT can roughly be summarized as follows:

- Signatures guarantee that every node can determine which node/client generated any given message.

- At any given time, every node will consider one designated node to be the *primary* and the other nodes to be *backups*. Since we are in the variable delay model, requests can arrive at the nodes in different orders. While a primary remains in charge (this timespan corresponds to what is called a *view*), it thus has the function of a serializer (cf. Algorithm 2.9).

- If backups detect faulty behavior in the primary, they start a new view and the next node in round-robin order becomes primary. This is called a *view change*.

- After a view change, a correct new primary makes sure that no two correct nodes execute requests in different orders. Exchanging information will enable backups to determine if the new primary acts in a byzantine fashion.

Definition 7.5 (View). *A **view** is represented locally at each node i by a non-negative integer v (we say i **is in view** v) that is incremented by one whenever the node changes to a different view.*

Definition 7.6 (Primary; Backups). *A node that is in view v considers node v mod n to be the **primary** and all other nodes to be **backups**.*

Definition 7.7 (Sequence Number). *During a view, a node relies on the primary to pick consecutive integers as **sequence numbers** that function as indices in the global order (cf. Definition 2.8) for the requests that clients send.*

Remarks:

- All nodes start out in view 0 and can potentially be in different views (i.e. have different local values for v) at any given time.

- The protocol will guarantee that once a correct node has executed a request r with sequence number s, then no correct node will execute any $r' \neq r$ with sequence number s, not unlike Lemma 2.14.

- Correct primaries choose sequence numbers such that they are *dense*, i.e. if a correct primary proposed s as the sequence number for the last request, then it will use $s + 1$ for the next request that it proposes.

- Before a node can safely execute a request r with a sequence number s, it will wait until it knows that the decision to execute r with s has been reached and is widely known.

- Informally, nodes will collect confirmation messages by sets of at least $2f + 1$ nodes to guarantee that that information is sufficiently widely distributed.

Definition 7.8 (Accepted Messages). *A correct node that is in view v will only* **accept messages** *that it can authenticate, that follow the specification of the protocol, whose components can be validated in the same way, and that also belong to view v.*

Lemma 7.9 (2f+1 Quorum Intersection). *Let S_1 with $|S_1| \geq 2f+1$ and S_2 with $|S_2| \geq 2f + 1$ each be sets of nodes. Then there exists a correct node in $S_1 \cap S_2$.*

Proof. Let S_1, S_2 each be sets of at least $2f + 1$ nodes. There are $3f + 1$ nodes in total, thus due to the pigeonhole principle the intersection $S_1 \cap S_2$ contains at least $f + 1$ nodes. Since there are at most f faulty nodes, $S_1 \cap S_2$ contains at least 1 correct node. $\square$

7.3 PBFT: Agreement Protocol

First we describe how PBFT achieves agreement on a unique order of requests within a view.

Remarks:

- Figure 7.10 shows how the nodes come to an agreement on a sequence number for a client request. Informally, the protocal has these three steps:

  1. The primary sends a **pre-prepare**-message to all backups, informing them that he wants to execute that request with the sequence number specified in the message.

  2. Backups send **prepare**-messages to all nodes, informing them that they agree with that suggestion.

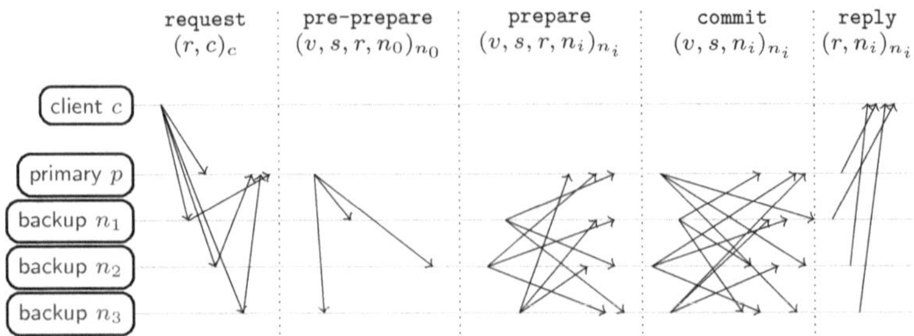

Figure 7.10: The agreement protocol used in PBFT for processing a client request, exemplified for a system with 4 nodes. Node n_0 is the primary in current view v. Time runs from left to right. Messages sent at the same time need not arrive at the same time. indexrequest

3. All nodes send `commit`-messages to all nodes, informing everyone that they have committed to execute the request with that sequence number. They execute the request and inform the client.

- Figure 7.10 shows that all nodes can start each phase at different times.

- To make sure byzantine nodes cannot force the execution of a request, every node waits for a certain number of `prepare`- and `commit`-messages with the correct content before executing the request.

- Definitions 7.11, 7.14, 7.16 specify the agreement protocol formally. Backups run Phases 1 and 2 concurrently.

Definition 7.11 (PBFT Agreement Protocol Phase 1; Pre-Prepared Primary). *In **phase 1** of the agreement protocol, the nodes execute Algorithm 7.12.*

Definition 7.13 (Faulty-Timer). *When backup b accepts request r in Algorithm 7.12 Line 4, b starts a local **faulty-timer** (if the timer is not already running) that will only stop once b executes r.*

Algorithm 7.12 PBFT Agreement Protocol: Phase 1

Code for primary p in view v:

1: accept **request**$(r, c)_c$ that originated from client c
2: pick next sequence number s
3: send **pre-prepare**$(v, s, r, p)_p$ to all backups

Code for backup b:

4: accept **request**$(r, c)_c$ from client c
5: relay **request**$(r, c)_c$ to primary p

Remarks:

- If the faulty-timer expires, the backup considers the primary faulty and triggers a view change. We explain the view change protocol in Section 7.4.

- We leave out the details regarding for what timespan to set the faulty-timer as they are an optimization with several trade-offs to consider; the interested reader is advised to consult [CL$^+$99].

Definition 7.14 (PBFT Agreement Protocol Phase 2; Pre-prepared Backups). *In phase 2 of the agreement protocol, every backup b executes Algorithm 7.15. Once it has sent the* **prepare**-*message, b has* **pre-prepared** *r for (v, s).*

Algorithm 7.15 PBFT Agreement Protocol: Phase 2

Code for backup b in view v:

1: accept **pre-prepare**$(v, s, r, p)_p$
2: **if** p is primary of view v and b has not yet accepted a **pre-prepare**-message for (v, s) and some $r' \neq r$ **then**
3:    send **prepare**$(v, s, r, b)_b$ to all nodes
4: **end if**

Definition 7.16 (PBFT Agreement Protocol Phase 3; Prepared-Certificate). *A node n_i that has pre-prepared a request executes Algorithm 7.17. It waits until it has collected $2f$* **prepare**-*messages (including n_i's own, if it is a backup) in Line 1. Together with the* **pre-prepare**-*message for (v, s, r), they form a* **prepared-certificate**.

Algorithm 7.17 PBFT Agreement Protocol: Phase 3

Code for node n_i that has pre-prepared r for (v, s):

1: wait until $2f$ **prepare**-messages matching (v, s, r) have been accepted (including n_i's own message, if it is a backup)
2: send $\mathtt{commit}(v, s, n_i)_{n_i}$ to all nodes
3: wait until $2f + 1$ **commit**-messages (including n_i's own) matching (v, s) have been accepted
4: execute request r once all requests with lower sequence numbers have been executed
5: send $\mathtt{reply}(r, n_i)_{n_i}$ to client

Remarks:

- Note that the agreement protocol can run for multiple requests in parallel. Since we are in the variable delay model and messages can arrive out of order, we thus have to wait in Algorithm 7.17 Line 4 until a request has been executed for all previous sequence numbers.

- The client only considers the request to have been processed once it received $f + 1$ **reply**-messages sent by the nodes in Algorithm 7.17 Line 5. Since a correct node only sends a **reply**-message once it executed the request, with $f + 1$ **reply**-messages the client can be certain that the request was executed by a correct node.

- We will see in Section 7.4 that PBFT guarantees that once a single correct node executed the request, then all correct nodes will never execute a different request with the same sequence number. Thus, knowing that a single correct node executed a request is enough for the client.

- If the client does not receive at least $f + 1$ **reply**-messages fast enough, it can start over by resending the request to initiate Algorithm 7.12 again. To prevent correct nodes that already executed the request from executing it a second time, clients can mark their requests with some kind of unique identifiers like a local timestamp. Correct nodes can then react to each request that is resent by a client as required by PBFT, and they can decide if they still need to execute a given request or have already done so before.

Lemma 7.18 (PBFT: Unique Sequence Numbers within View). *If a node gathers a prepared-certificate for (v, s, r), then no node can gather a prepared-certificate for (v, s, r') with $r' \neq r$.*

Proof. Assume two (not necessarily distinct) nodes gather prepared-certificates for (v, s, r) and (v, s, r'). Since a prepared-certificate contains $2f + 1$ messages, a correct node sent a **pre-prepare-** or **prepare**-message for each of (v, s, r) and (v, s, r') due to Lemma 7.9. A correct primary only sends a single **pre-prepare**-message for each (v, s), see Algorithm 7.12 Lines 2 and 3. A correct backup only sends a single **prepare**-message for each (v, s), see Algorithm 7.15 Lines 2 and 3. Thus, $r' = r$. $\square$

Remarks:

- Due to Lemma 7.18, once a node has a prepared-certificate for (v, s, r), no correct node will execute some $r' \neq r$ with sequence number s during view v because correct nodes wait for a prepared-certificate before executing a request (cf. Algorithm 7.17).

- However, that is not yet enough to make sure that no $r' \neq r$ will be executed by a correct node with sequence number s during some later view $v' > v$. How can we make sure that that does not happen?

7.4 PBFT: View Change Protocol

If the primary is faulty, the system has to perform a view change to move to the next primary so the system can make progress. Nodes use their faulty-timer (and only that!) to decide whether they consider the primary to be faulty (cf. Definition 7.13).

Remarks:

- During a view change, the protocol has to guarantee that requests that have already been executed by some correct nodes will not be executed with the different sequence numbers by other correct nodes.

- How can we guarantee that this happens?

Definition 7.19 (PBFT: View Change Protocol). *In the view change protocol, a node whose faulty-timer has expired enters the* *view change phase by running Algorithm 7.22. During the **new view phase** (which all nodes continually listen for), the primary of the next view runs Algorithm 7.23 while all other nodes run Algorithm 7.24.*

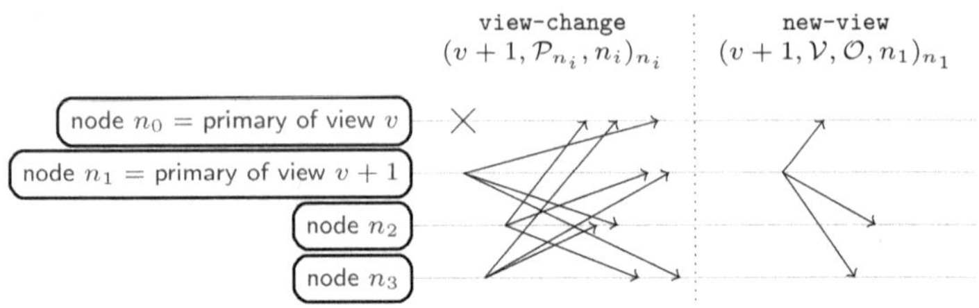

Figure 7.20: The view change protocol used in PBFT. Node n_0 is the primary of current view v, node n_1 the primary of view $v + 1$. Once backups consider n_0 to be faulty, they start the view change protocol (cf. Algorithms 7.22, 7.23, 7.24). The X signifies that n_0 is faulty.

Remarks:

- The idea behind the view change protocol is this: during the view change protocol, the new primary gathers prepared-certificates from $2f + 1$ nodes, so for every request that some correct node executed, the new primary will have at least one prepared-certificate.

- After gathering that information, the primary distributes it and tells all backups which requests need to be to executed with which sequence numbers.

- Backups can check whether the new primary makes the decisions required by the protocol, and if it does not, then the new primary must be byzantine and the backups can directly move to the next view change.

Definition 7.21 (New-View-Certificate). *$2f + 1$ **view-change-messages** for the same view v form a **new-view-certificate**.*

Algorithm 7.22 PBFT View Change Protocol: View Change Phase

Code for backup b in view v whose faulty-timer has expired:

1: stop accepting **pre-prepare**/**prepare**/**commit**-messages for v
2: let $\mathcal{P}_b$ be the set of all prepared-certificates that b has collected since the system was started
3: send **view-change**$(v + 1, \mathcal{P}_b, b)_b$ to all nodes

---

Algorithm 7.23 PBFT View Change Protocol: New View Phase - Primary

---

Code for primary p of view $v + 1$:

1: accept $2f + 1$ **view-change**-messages (including possibly p's own) in a set $\mathcal{V}$ (this is the *new-view-certificate*)
2: let $\mathcal{O}$ be a set of **pre-prepare**$(v + 1, s, r, p)_p$ for all pairs (s, r) where at least one prepared-certificate for (s, r) exists in $\mathcal{V}$
3: let $s^{\mathcal{V}}_{max}$ be the highest sequence number for which $\mathcal{O}$ contains a **pre-prepare**-message
4: add to $\mathcal{O}$ a message **pre-prepare**$(v + 1, s', \texttt{null}, p)_p$ for every sequence number $s' < s^{\mathcal{V}}_{max}$ for which $\mathcal{O}$ does not contain a **pre-prepare**-message
5: send **new-view**$(v + 1, \mathcal{V}, \mathcal{O}, p)_p$ to all nodes
6: start processing requests for view $v + 1$ according to Algorithm 7.12 starting from sequence number $s^{\mathcal{V}}_{max} + 1$

Remarks:

- It is possible that $\mathcal{V}$ contains a prepared-certificate for a sequence number s while it does not contain one for some sequence number $s' < s$. For each such sequence number s', we fill up $\mathcal{O}$ in Algorithm 7.23 Line 4 with **null**-requests, i.e. requests that backups understand to mean "do not do anything here".

Theorem 7.25 (PBFT:Unique Sequence Numbers Across Views). *Together, the PBFT agreement protocol and the PBFT view change protocol guarantee that if a correct node executes a request r in view v with sequence number s, then no correct node will execute any $r' \neq r$ with sequence number s in any view $v' \geq v$.*

Algorithm 7.24 PBFT View Change Protocol: New View Phase
- Backup

Code for backup b of view $v + 1$ if b's local view is $v' < v + 1$:

1: accept new-view$(v + 1, \mathcal{V}, \mathcal{O}, p)_p$
2: stop accepting pre-prepare-/prepare-/commit-messages for v
    // in case b has not run Algorithm 7.22 for $v+1$ yet
3: set local view to $v + 1$
4: **if** p is primary of $v + 1$ **then**
5:    **if** $\mathcal{O}$ was correctly constructed from $\mathcal{V}$ according to Algorithm 7.23 Lines 2 and 4 **then**
6:       respond to all pre-prepare-messages in $\mathcal{O}$ as in the agreement protocol, starting from Algorithm 7.15
7:       start accepting messages for view $v + 1$
8:    **else**
9:       trigger view change to $v + 2$ using Algorithm 7.22
10:   **end if**
11: **end if**

Proof. If no view change takes place, then Lemma 7.18 proves the statement. Therefore, assume that a view change takes place, and consider view $v' > v$.

We will show that if some correct node executed a request r with sequence number s during v, then a correct primary will send a pre-prepare-message matching (v', s, r) in the $\mathcal{O}$-component of the new-view$(v', \mathcal{V}, \mathcal{O}, p)$-message. This guarantees that no correct node will be able to collect a prepared-certificate for s and a different $r' \neq r$.

Consider the new-view-certificate $\mathcal{V}$ (see Algorithm 7.23 Line 1). If any correct node executed request r with sequence number s, then due to Algorithm 7.17 Line 3, there is a set R_1 of at least $2f + 1$ nodes that sent a commit-message matching (s, r), and thus the correct nodes in R_1 all collected a prepared-certificate in Algorithm 7.17 Line 1.

The new-view-certificate contains view-change-messages from a set R_2 of $2f + 1$ nodes. Thus according to Lemma 7.9, there is at least one correct node $c_r \in R_1 \cap R_2$ that both collected a prepared-certificate matching (s, r) and whose view-change-message is contained in $\mathcal{V}$.

Therefore, if some correct node executed r with sequence number s, then $\mathcal{V}$ contains a prepared-certificate matching (s, r) from c_r. Thus, if some correct node executed r with sequence number s, then due to Algorithm 7.23 Line 2, a correct primary p sends a new-view$(v', \mathcal{V}, \mathcal{O}, p)$-message where $\mathcal{O}$ contains a pre-prepare(v', s, r, p)-message.

Correct backups will enter view v' only if the new-view-message for v' contains a valid new-view-certificate $\mathcal{V}$ and if $\mathcal{O}$ was constructed correctly from $\mathcal{V}$, see Algorithm 7.24 Line 5. They will then respond to the messages in $\mathcal{O}$ before they start accepting other pre-prepare-messages for v' due to the order of Algorithm 7.24 Lines 6 and 7. Therefore, for the sequence numbers that appear in $\mathcal{O}$, correct backups will only send prepare-messages responding to the pre-prepare-messages found in $\mathcal{O}$ due to Algorithm 7.15 Lines 2 and 3. This guarantees that in v', for every sequence number s that appears in $\mathcal{O}$, backups can only collect prepared-certificates for the triple (v', s, r) that appears in $\mathcal{O}$.

Together with the above, this proves that if some correct node executed request r with sequence number s in v, then no node will be able to collect a prepared-certificate for some $r' \neq r$ with sequence number s in any view $v' \geq v$, and thus no correct node will execute r' with sequence number s. $\qquad\square$

Remarks:

- We have shown that PBFT protocol guarantees safety or nothing bad ever happens, i.e., the correct nodes never disagree on requests that were commited with the same sequence numbers. But, does PBFT also guarantee liveness, i.e., a legitimate client request is eventually committed and receives a reply.

- To prove liveness, we make an additional assumption that message delays are finite and bounded. With infinite message delays in an asynchronous system and even one faulty (byzantine) process, it is impossible to solve consensus with guaranteed termination [FLP85].

- A faulty new primary could delay the system indefinitely by never sending a new-view-message. To prevent this, as soon as a node sends its view-change-message for $v + 1$, it starts its faulty-timer and stops it once it accepts a new-view-message for $v + 1$. If the timer runs out before being stopped, the node triggers another view change.

- However, the timer doubles to trigger the next view change because the message delays might be larger. Eventually, the timer values are larger than the message delays and the messages are received before the timer expires.

- Since at most f consecutive primaries can be faulty, the system makes progress after at most $f + 1$ view changes.

- We described a simplified version of PBFT; any practically relevant variant makes adjustments to what we presented. The references found in the chapter notes can be consulted for details that we did not include.

Chapter Notes

PBFT is perhaps the central protocol for asynchronous byzantine state replication. The seminal first publication about it, of which we presented a simplified version, can be found in [CL$^+$99]. The canonical work about most versions of PBFT is Miguel Castro's PhD dissertation [Cas01]. Barbara Liskov was Miguel Castro's advisor, and show won a Turing award, partially because of her work on PBFT.

Notice that the sets $\mathcal{P}_b$ in Algorithm 7.22 grow with each view change as the system keeps running since they contain all prepared-certificates that nodes have collected so far. All variants of the protocol found in the literature introduce regular *checkpoints* where nodes agree that enough nodes executed all requests up to a certain sequence number so they can continuously garbage-collect prepared-certificates. We left this out for conciseness.

Remember that all messages are signed. Generating signatures is somewhat pricy, and variants of PBFT exist that use the cheaper, but less powerful Message Authentication Codes (MACs). These variants are more complicated because MACs only provide authentication between the two endpoints of a message and cannot prove to a third party who created a message. An extensive treatment of a variant that uses MACs can be found in [CL02].

Before PBFT, byzantine fault-tolerance was generally considered impractical, just something academics would be interested in. PBFT changed that as it showed that byzantine fault-tolerance can be practically feasible. As a result, numerous asynchronous byzantine state replication protocols were developed. Other well-known protocols are Q/U [AEMGG$^+$05], HQ [CML$^+$06], and Zyzzyva [KAD$^+$07]. An overview over the relevant literature can be found in [AGK$^+$15].

Bibliography

[AEMGG$^+$05] Michael Abd-El-Malek, Gregory R Ganger, Garth R Goodson, Michael K Reiter, and Jay J Wylie. Fault-scalable byzantine fault-tolerant services. In *ACM SIGOPS Operating Systems Review*, volume 39, pages 59–74. ACM, 2005.

[AGK$^+$15] Pierre-Louis Aublin, Rachid Guerraoui, Nikola Knežević, Vivien Quéma, and Marko Vukolić. The next 700 bft protocols. *ACM Transactions on Computer Systems (TOCS)*, 32(4):12, 2015.

[Cas01] Miguel Castro. *Practical Byzantine Fault Tolerance*. Ph.d., MIT, January 2001. Also as Technical Report MIT-LCS-TR-817.

[CL$^+$99] Miguel Castro, Barbara Liskov, et al. Practical byzantine fault tolerance. In *OSDI*, volume 99, pages 173–186, 1999.

[CL02] Miguel Castro and Barbara Liskov. Practical byzantine fault tolerance and proactive recovery. *ACM Transactions on Computer Systems (TOCS)*, 20(4):398–461, 2002.

[CML$^+$06] James Cowling, Daniel Myers, Barbara Liskov, Rodrigo Rodrigues, and Liuba Shrira. Hq replication: A hybrid quorum protocol for byzantine fault tolerance. In *Proceedings of the 7th symposium on Operating systems design and implementation*, pages 177–190. USENIX Association, 2006.

[FLP85] Michael J. Fischer, Nancy A. Lynch, and Mike Paterson. Impossibility of Distributed Consensus with One Faulty Process. *J. ACM*, 32(2):374–382, 1985.

[KAD$^+$07] Ramakrishna Kotla, Lorenzo Alvisi, Mike Dahlin, Allen Clement, and Edmund Wong. Zyzzyva: speculative byzantine fault tolerance. In *ACM SIGOPS Operating Systems Review*, volume 41, pages 45–58. ACM, 2007.

Chapter 8

Quorum Systems

What happens if a single server is no longer powerful enough to service all your customers? The obvious choice is to add more servers and to use the majority approach (e.g. Paxos, Chapter 2) to guarantee consistency. However, even if you buy one million servers, a client still has to access more than half of them per request! While you gain fault-tolerance, your efficiency can at most be doubled. Do we have to give up on consistency?

Let us take a step back: We used majorities because majority sets always overlap. But are majority sets the only sets that guarantee overlap? In this chapter we study the theory behind overlapping sets, known as quorum systems.

Definition 8.1 (quorum, quorum system). *Let $V = \{v_1, \ldots, v_n\}$ be a set of nodes. A **quorum** $Q \subseteq V$ is a subset of these nodes. A **quorum system** $\mathcal{S} \subset 2^V$ is a set of quorums s.t. every two quorums intersect, i.e., $Q_1 \cap Q_2 \neq \emptyset$ for all $Q_1, Q_2 \in \mathcal{S}$.*

Remarks:

- When a quorum system is being used, a client selects a quorum, acquires a lock (or ticket) on all nodes of the quorum, and when done releases all locks again. The idea is that no matter which quorum is chosen, its nodes will intersect with the nodes of every other quorum.

- What can happen if two quorums try to lock their nodes at the same time?

- A quorum system $\mathcal{S}$ is called **minimal** if $\forall Q_1, Q_2 \in \mathcal{S}$: $Q_1 \not\subset Q_2$.

- The simplest quorum system imaginable consists of just one quorum, which in turn just consists of one server. It is known as **Singleton**.

- In the **Majority** quorum system, every quorum has $\lfloor \frac{n}{2} \rfloor + 1$ nodes.

- Can you think of other simple quorum systems?

8.1   Load and Work

Definition 8.2 (access strategy). *An **access strategy** Z defines the probability $P_Z(Q)$ of accessing a quorum $Q \in \mathcal{S}$ s.t. $\sum_{Q \in \mathcal{S}} P_Z(Q) = 1$.*

Definition 8.3 (load).

- *The **load** of access strategy Z on a node v_i is $L_Z(v_i) = \sum_{Q \in \mathcal{S}; v_i \in Q} P_Z(Q)$.*

- *The **load** induced by access strategy Z on a quorum system $\mathcal{S}$ is the maximal load induced by Z on any node in $\mathcal{S}$, i.e., $L_Z(\mathcal{S}) = \max_{v_i \in \mathcal{S}} L_Z(v_i)$.*

- *The **load** of a quorum system $\mathcal{S}$ is $L(\mathcal{S}) = \min_Z L_Z(\mathcal{S})$.*

Definition 8.4 (work).

- *The **work** of a quorum $Q \in \mathcal{S}$ is the number of nodes in Q, $W(Q) = |Q|$.*

- *The **work** induced by access strategy Z on a quorum system $\mathcal{S}$ is the expected number of nodes accessed, i.e., $W_Z(\mathcal{S}) = \sum_{Q \in \mathcal{S}} P_Z(Q) \cdot W(Q)$.*

- *The **work** of a quorum system $\mathcal{S}$ is $W(\mathcal{S}) = \min_Z W_Z(\mathcal{S})$.*

Remarks:

- Note that you cannot choose different access strategies Z for work and load, you have to pick a single Z for both.

- We illustrate the above concepts with a small example. Let $V = \{v_1, v_2, v_3, v_4, v_5\}$ and $\mathcal{S} = \{Q_1, Q_2, Q_3, Q_4\}$, with $Q_1 = \{v_1, v_2\}$, $Q_2 = \{v_1, v_3, v_4\}$, $Q_3 = \{v_2, v_3, v_5\}$, $Q_4 = \{v_2, v_4, v_5\}$. If we choose the access strategy Z s.t. $P_Z(Q_1) = 1/2$ and $P_Z(Q_2) = P_Z(Q_3) = P_Z(Q_4) = 1/6$, then the node with the highest load is v_2 with $L_Z(v_2) = 1/2 + 1/6 + 1/6 = 5/6$, i.e., $L_Z(\mathcal{S}) = 5/6$. Regarding work, we have $W_Z(\mathcal{S}) = 1/2 \cdot 2 + 1/6 \cdot 3 + 1/6 \cdot 3 + 1/6 \cdot 3 = 15/6$.

- Can you come up with a better access strategy for $\mathcal{S}$?

- If every quorum Q in a quorum system $\mathcal{S}$ has the same number of elements, $\mathcal{S}$ is called *uniform*.

- What is the minimum load a quorum system can have?

Primary Copy vs. Majority		Singleton	Majority
How many nodes need to be accessed?	(Work)	1	$> n/2$
What is the load of the busiest node?	(Load)	1	$> 1/2$

Table 8.5: First comparison of the Singleton and Majority quorum systems. Note that the Singleton quorum system can be a good choice when the failure probability of every single node is $> 1/2$.

Theorem 8.6. *Let $\mathcal{S}$ be a quorum system. Then $L(\mathcal{S}) \geq 1/\sqrt{n}$ holds.*

Proof. Let $Q = \{v_1, \ldots, v_q\}$ be a quorum of minimal size in $\mathcal{S}$, with $|Q| = q$. Let Z be an access strategy for $\mathcal{S}$. Every other quorum in $\mathcal{S}$ intersects in at least one element with this quorum Q. Each time a quorum is accessed, at least one node in Q is accessed as well, yielding a lower bound of $L_Z(v_i) \geq 1/q$ for some $v_i \in Q$.

Furthermore, as Q is minimal, at least q nodes need to be accessed, yielding $W(\mathcal{S}) \geq q$. Thus, $L_Z(v_i) \geq q/n$ for some $v_i \in Q$, as each time q nodes are accessed, the load of the most accessed node is at least q/n.

Combining both ideas leads to $L_Z(\mathcal{S}) \geq \max(1/q, q/n) \Rightarrow L_Z(\mathcal{S}) \geq 1/\sqrt{n}$. Thus, $L(\mathcal{S}) \geq 1/\sqrt{n}$, as Z can be *any* access strategy. $\qquad\square$

Remarks:

- Can we achieve this load?

8.2 Grid Quorum Systems

Definition 8.7 (Basic Grid quorum system). *Assume $\sqrt{n} \in \mathbb{N}$, and arrange the n nodes in a square matrix with side length of $\sqrt{n}$, i.e., in a grid. The basic **Grid** quorum system consists of $\sqrt{n}$ quorums, with each containing the full row i and the full column i, for $1 \leq i \leq \sqrt{n}$.*

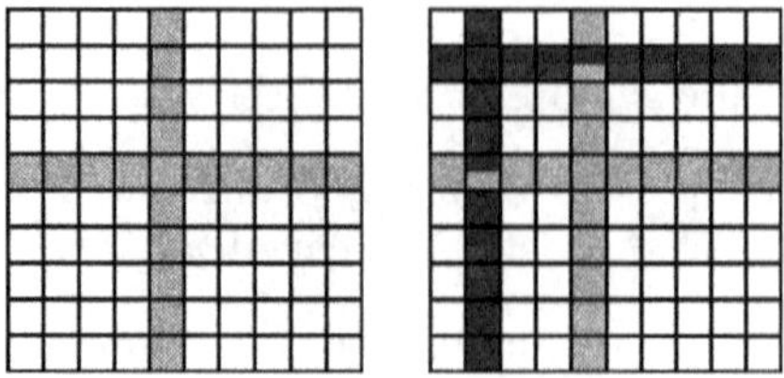

Figure 8.8: The basic version of the Grid quorum system, where each quorum Q_i with $1 \leq i \leq \sqrt{n}$ uses row i and column i. The size of each quorum is $2\sqrt{n} - 1$ and two quorums overlap in exactly two nodes. Thus, when the access strategy Z is uniform (i.e., the probability of each quorum is $1/\sqrt{n}$), the work is $2\sqrt{n} - 1$, and the load of every node is in $\Theta(1/\sqrt{n})$.

Remarks:

- Consider the right picture in Figure 8.8: The two quorums intersect in two nodes. If both quorums were to be accessed at the same time, it is not guaranteed that at least one quorum will lock all of its nodes, as they could enter a deadlock!

- In the case of just two quorums, one could solve this by letting the quorums just intersect in one node, see Figure 8.9. However, already with three quorums the same situation could occur again, progress is not guaranteed!

- However, by deviating from the "access all at once" strategy, we can guarantee progress if the nodes are totally ordered!

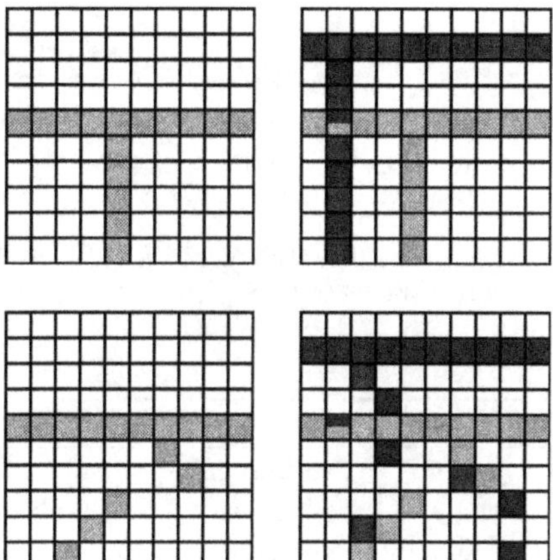

Figure 8.9: There are other ways to choose quorums in the grid s.t. pairwise different quorums only intersect in one node. The size of each quorum is between $\sqrt{n}$ and $2\sqrt{n} - 1$, i.e., the work is in $\Theta(\sqrt{n})$. When the access strategy Z is uniform, the load of every node is in $\Theta(1/\sqrt{n})$.

Algorithm 8.10 Sequential Locking Strategy for a Quorum Q

1: Attempt to lock the nodes one by one, ordered by their identifiers

2: Should a node be already locked, release all locks and start over

---

Theorem 8.11. *If each quorum is accessed by Algorithm 8.10, at least one quorum will obtain a lock for all of its nodes.*

Proof. We prove the theorem by contradiction. Assume no quorum can make progress, i.e., for every quorum we have: At least one of its nodes is locked by another quorum. Let v be the node with the highest identifier that is locked by some quorum Q. Observe that Q already locked all of its nodes with a smaller identifier than v, otherwise Q would have restarted. As all nodes with a higher identifier than v are not locked, Q either has locked all of its nodes or can make progress – a contradiction. As the set of nodes is finite, one quorum will eventually be able to lock all of its nodes. $\square$

Remarks:

- But now we are back to sequential accesses in a distributed system? Let's do it concurrently with the same idea, i.e., resolving conflicts by the ordering of the nodes. Then, a quorum that locked the highest identifier so far can always make progress!

Algorithm 8.12 Concurrent Locking Strategy for a Quorum Q

Invariant: Let $v_Q \in Q$ be the highest identifier of a node locked by Q s.t. all nodes $v_i \in Q$ with $v_i < v_Q$ are locked by Q as well. Should Q not have any lock, then v_Q is set to 0.

1: **repeat**
2:     Attempt to lock all nodes of the quorum Q
3:     **for each** node $v \in Q$ that was not able to be locked by Q **do**
4:         exchange v_Q and $v_{Q'}$ with the quorum Q' that locked v
5:         **if** $v_Q > v_{Q'}$ **then**
6:             Q' releases lock on v and Q acquires lock on v
7:         **end if**
8:     **end for**
9: **until** all nodes of the quorum Q are locked

Theorem 8.13. *If the nodes and quorums use Algorithm 8.12, at least one quorum will obtain a lock for all of its nodes.*

Proof. The proof is analogous to the proof of Theorem 8.11: Assume for contradiction that no quorum can make progress. However, at least the quorum with the highest v_Q can always make progress – a contradiction! As the set of nodes is finite, at least one quorum will eventually be able to acquire a lock on all of its nodes. $\qquad\square$

Remarks:

- What if a quorum locks all of its nodes and then crashes? Is the quorum system dead now? This issue can be prevented by, e.g., using leases instead of locks: leases have a timeout, i.e., a lock is released eventually.

8.3 Fault Tolerance

Definition 8.14 (resilience). *If any f nodes from a quorum system S can fail s.t. there is still a quorum $Q \in S$ without failed nodes, then S is f-**resilient***. *The largest such f is the **resilience** $R(S)$.*

Theorem 8.15. *Let S be a Grid quorum system where each of the n quorums consists of a full row and a full column. S has a resilience of $\sqrt{n} - 1$.*

Proof. If all $\sqrt{n}$ nodes on the diagonal of the grid fail, then every quorum will have at least one failed node. Should less than $\sqrt{n}$ nodes fail, then there is a row and a column without failed nodes. $\square$

Remarks:

- The Grid quorum system in Theorem 8.15 is different from the Basic Grid quorum system described in Definition 8.7. In each quorum in the Basic Grid quorum system the row and column index are identical, while in the Grid quorum system of Theorem 8.15 this is not the case.

Definition 8.16 (failure probability). *Assume that every node works with a fixed probability p (in the following we assume concrete values, e.g. $p > 1/2$). The **failure probability** $F_p(S)$ of a quorum system S is the probability that at least one node of every quorum fails.*

Remarks:

- The **asymptotic failure probability** is $F_p(S)$ for $n \to \infty$.

Facts 8.17. *A version of a **Chernoff bound** states the following: Let $x_1, \ldots, x_n$ be independent Bernoulli-distributed random variables with $Pr[x_i = 1] = p_i$ and $Pr[x_i = 0] = 1 - p_i = q_i$, then for $X := \sum_{i=1}^{n} x_i$ and $\mu := \mathbb{E}[X] = \sum_{i=1}^{n} p_i$ the following holds:*

$$\text{for all } 0 < \delta < 1\text{: } Pr[X \le (1 - \delta)\mu] \le e^{-\mu\delta^2/2} \, .$$

Theorem 8.18. *The asymptotic failure probability of the Majority quorum system is 0.*

Proof. In a Majority quorum system each quorum contains exactly $\lfloor \frac{n}{2} \rfloor + 1$ nodes and each subset of nodes with cardinality $\lfloor \frac{n}{2} \rfloor + 1$ forms a quorum. The Majority quorum system fails, if only $\lfloor \frac{n}{2} \rfloor$ nodes work. Otherwise there is at least one quorum available. In order to calculate the failure probability we define the following random variables:

$$x_i = \begin{cases} 1, & \text{if node } i \text{ works, happens with probability } p \\ 0, & \text{if node } i \text{ fails, happens with probability } q = 1 - p \end{cases}$$

and $X := \sum_{i=1}^{n} x_i$, with $\mu = np$,

whereas X corresponds to the number of working nodes. To estimate the probability that the number of working nodes is less than $\lfloor \frac{n}{2} \rfloor + 1$ we will make use of the Chernoff inequality from above. By setting $\delta = 1 - \frac{1}{2p}$ we obtain $F_P(\mathcal{S}) = Pr[X \leq \lfloor \frac{n}{2} \rfloor] \leq Pr[X \leq \frac{n}{2}] = Pr[X \leq (1 - \delta)\mu]$.

With $\delta = 1 - \frac{1}{2p}$ we have $0 < \delta \leq 1/2$ due to $1/2 < p \leq 1$. Thus, we can use the Chernoff bound and get $F_P(\mathcal{S}) \leq e^{-\mu\delta^2/2} \in e^{-\Omega(n)}$. $\qquad\square$

Theorem 8.19. *The asymptotic failure probability of the Grid quorum system is* 1.

Proof. Consider the $n = d \cdot d$ nodes to be arranged in a $d \times d$ grid. A quorum always contains one full row. In this estimation we will make use of the Bernoulli inequality which states that for all $n \in \mathbb{N}, x \geq -1 : (1 + x)^n \geq 1 + nx$.

The system fails, if in each row at least one node fails (which happens with probability $1 - p^d$ for a particular row, as all nodes work with probability p^d). Therefore we can bound the failure probability from below with:

$$F_p(\mathcal{S}) \geq Pr[\text{at least one failure per row}] = (1 - p^d)^d \geq 1 - dp^d \xrightarrow[n \to \infty]{} 1. \qquad\square$$

Remarks:

- Now we have a quorum system with optimal load (the Grid) and one with fault-tolerance (Majority), but what if we want both?

Definition 8.20 (B-Grid quorum system). *Consider* $n = dhr$ *nodes, arranged in a rectangular grid with $h \cdot r$ rows and d columns. Each group of r rows is a* band, *and r elements in a column restricted to a band are called a* mini-column. *A quorum consists of* *one mini-column in every band and one element from each mini-column of one band; thus every quorum has $d + hr - 1$ elements. The **B-Grid** quorum system consists of all such quorums.*

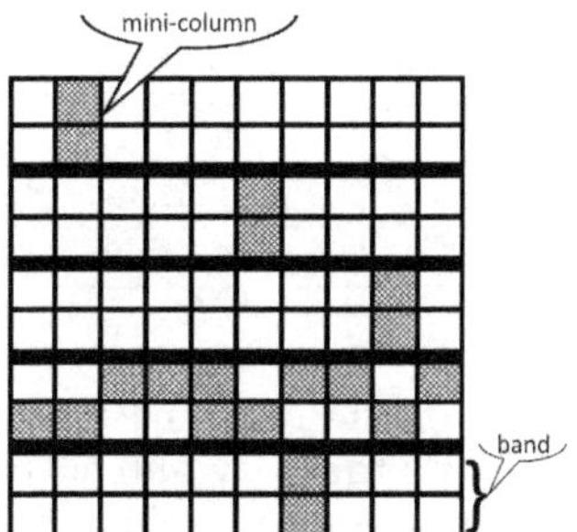

Figure 8.21: A B-Grid quorum system with $n = 100$ nodes, $d = 10$ columns, $h \cdot r = 10$ rows, $h = 5$ bands, and $r = 2$. The depicted quorum has a $d + hr - 1 = 10 + 5 \cdot 2 - 1 = 19$ nodes. If the access strategy Z is chosen uniformly, then we have a work of $d + hr - 1$ and a load of $\frac{d+hr-1}{n}$. By setting $d = \sqrt{n}$ and $r = \log n$, we obtain a work of $\Theta\left(\sqrt{n}\right)$ and a load of $\Theta\left(1/\sqrt{n}\right)$.

Theorem 8.22. *The asymptotic failure probability of the B-Grid quorum system is 0.*

Proof. Suppose $n = dhr$ and the elements are arranged in a grid with d columns and $h \cdot r$ rows. The B-Grid quorum system does fail if in each band a complete mini-column fails, because then it is not possible to choose a band where in each mini-column an element is still working. It also fails if in a band an element in each mini-column fails. Those events may not be independent of each other, but with the help of the union bound, we can upper bound the failure probability with the following equation:

$$F_p(\mathcal{S}) \leq Pr[\text{in every band a complete mini-column fails}]$$

$$+ \, Pr[\text{in a band at least one element of every m.-col. fails}]$$

$$\leq (d(1-p)^r)^h + h(1-p^r)^d$$

We use $d = \sqrt{n}, r = \ln d$, and $0 \leq (1-p) \leq 1/3$. Using $n^{\ln x} = x^{\ln n}$, we have $d(1-p)^r \leq d \cdot d^{\ln 1/3} \approx d^{-0.1}$, and hence for large enough d the whole first term is bounded from above by $d^{-0.1h} \ll 1/d^2 = 1/n$.

Regarding the second term, we have $p \geq 2/3$, and $h = d/\ln d < d$. Hence we can bound the term from above by $d(1 - d^{\ln 2/3})^d \approx d(1 - d^{-0.4})^d$. Using $(1 + t/n)^n \leq e^t$, we get (again, for large enough *d*) an upper bound of $d(1 - d^{-0.4})^d = d(1 - d^{0.6}/d)^d \leq d \cdot e^{-d^{0.6}} = d^{(-d^{0.6}/\ln d)+1} \ll d^{-2} = 1/n$. In total, we have $F_p(\mathcal{S}) \in O(1/n)$. $\square$

	Singleton	Majority	Grid	B-Grid*
Work	1	$> n/2$	$\Theta(\sqrt{n})$	$\Theta(\sqrt{n})$
Load	1	$> 1/2$	$\boldsymbol{\Theta(1/\sqrt{n})}$	$\boldsymbol{\Theta(1/\sqrt{n})}$
Resilience	0	$\boldsymbol{< n/2}$	$\Theta(\sqrt{n})$	$\Theta(\sqrt{n})$
F. Prob.**	$1 - p$	$\boldsymbol{\to 0}$	$\to 1$	$\boldsymbol{\to 0}$

Table 8.23: Overview of the different quorum systems regarding resilience, work, load, and their asymptotic failure probability. The best entries in each row are set in bold.

* Setting $d = \sqrt{n}$ and $r = \log n$
**Assuming prob. $q = (1 - p)$ is constant but significantly less than $1/2$

8.4　Byzantine Quorum Systems

While failed nodes are bad, they are still easy to deal with: just access another quorum where all nodes can respond! Byzantine nodes make life more difficult however, as they can pretend to be a regular node, i.e., one needs more sophisticated methods to deal with them. We need to ensure that the intersection of two quorums always contains a non-byzantine (correct) node and furthermore, the byzantine nodes should not be allowed to infiltrate every quorum. In this section we study three counter-measures of increasing strength, and their implications on the load of quorum systems.

Definition 8.24 (*f*-disseminating). *A quorum system $\mathcal{S}$ is f-**disseminating** if (1) the intersection of two different quorums always contains $f + 1$ nodes, and (2) for any set of f byzantine nodes, there is at least one quorum without byzantine nodes.*

Remarks:

- Thanks to (2), even with f byzantine nodes, the byzantine nodes cannot stop all quorums by just pretending to have crashed. At least one quorum will survive. We will also keep this assumption for the upcoming more advanced byzantine quorum systems.

- Byzantine nodes can also do something worse than crashing - they could falsify data! Nonetheless, due to (1), there is at least one non-byzantine node in every quorum intersection. If the data is self-verifying by, e.g., authentication, then this one node is enough.

- If the data is not self-verifying, then we need another mechanism.

Definition 8.25 (f-masking). *A quorum system S is f-**masking** if (1) the intersection of two different quorums always contains $2f + 1$ nodes, and (2) for any set of f byzantine nodes, there is at least one quorum without byzantine nodes.*

Remarks:

- Note that except for the second condition, an f-masking quorum system is the same as a $2f$-disseminating system. The idea is that the non-byzantine nodes (at least $f + 1$ can outvote the byzantine ones (at most f), but only if all non-byzantine nodes are up-to-date!

- This raises an issue not covered yet in this chapter. If we access some quorum and update its values, this change still has to be disseminated to the other nodes in the byzantine quorum system. Opaque quorum systems deal with this issue, which are discussed at the end of this section.

- f-disseminating quorum systems need more than $3f$ nodes and f-masking quorum systems need more than $4f$ nodes. Essentially, the quorums may not contain too many nodes, and the different intersection properties lead to the different bounds.

Theorem 8.26. *Let S be a f-disseminating quorum system. Then $L(S) \geq \sqrt{(f+1)/n}$ holds.*

Theorem 8.27. *Let S be a f-masking quorum system. Then $L(S) \geq \sqrt{(2f+1)/n}$ holds.*

Proofs of Theorems 8.26 and 8.27. The proofs follow the proof of Theorem 8.6, by observing that now not just one element is accessed from a minimal quorum, but $f+1$ or $2f+1$, respectively. $\square$

Definition 8.28 (*f*-masking Grid quorum system). *A **f-masking Grid** quorum system is constructed as the grid quorum system, but each quorum contains one full column and $f+1$ rows of nodes, with $2f + 1 \le \sqrt{n}$.*

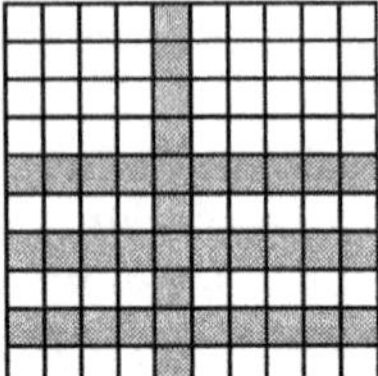

Figure 8.29: An example how to choose a quorum in the f-masking Grid with $f = 2$, i.e., $2+1 = 3$ rows. The load is in $\Theta(f/\sqrt{n})$ when the access strategy is chosen to be uniform. Two quorums overlap by their columns intersecting each other's rows, i.e., they overlap in at least $2f + 2$ nodes.

Remarks:

- The f-masking Grid nearly hits the lower bound for the load of f-masking quorum systems, but not quite. A small change and we will be optimal asymptotically.

Definition 8.30 (*M*-Grid quorum system). *The **M-Grid** quorum system is constructed as the grid quorum as well, but each quorum contains $\sqrt{f + 1}$ rows and $\sqrt{f + 1}$ columns of nodes, with $f \le \frac{\sqrt{n-1}}{2}$.*

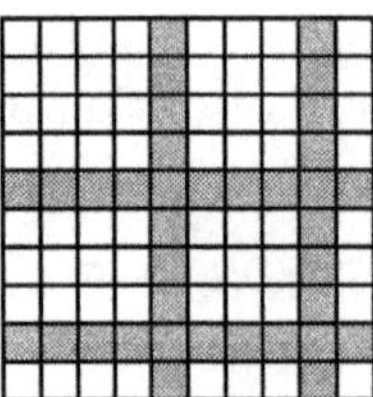

Figure 8.31: An example how to choose a quorum in the M-Grid with $f = 3$, i.e., 2 rows and 2 columns. The load is in $\Theta(\sqrt{f/n})$ when the access strategy is chosen to be uniform. Two quorums overlap with each row intersecting each other's column, i.e., $2\sqrt{f + 1}^2 = 2f + 2$ nodes.

Corollary 8.32. *The f-masking Grid quorum system and the M-Grid quorum system are f-masking quorum systems.*

Remarks:

- We achieved nearly the same load as without byzantine nodes! However, as mentioned earlier, what happens if we access a quorum that is not up-to-date, except for the intersection with an up-to-date quorum? Surely we can fix that as well without too much loss?

- This property will be handled in the last part of this chapter by *opaque* quorum systems. It will ensure that the number of correct up-to-date nodes accessed will be larger than the number of out-of-date nodes combined with the byzantine nodes in the quorum (cf. (8.33.1)).

Definition 8.33 (f-opaque quorum system). *A quorum system S is f-**opaque** if the following two properties hold for any set of f byzantine nodes F and any two different quorums Q_1, Q_2:*

$$|(Q_1 \cap Q_2) \setminus F| > |(Q_2 \cap F) \cup (Q_2 \setminus Q_1)| \qquad (8.33.1)$$

$$(F \cap Q) = \emptyset \text{ for some } Q \in S \qquad (8.33.2)$$

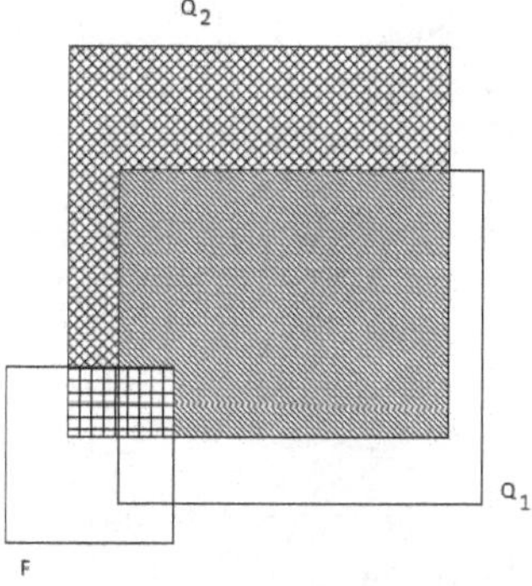

Figure 8.34: Intersection properties of an opaque quorum system. Equation (8.33.1) ensures that the set of non-byzantine nodes in the intersection of Q_1, Q_2 is larger than the set of out of date nodes, even if the byzantine nodes "team up" with those nodes. Thus, the correct up to date value can always be recognized by a majority voting.

Theorem 8.35. *Let $\mathcal{S}$ be a f-opaque quorum system. Then, $n > 5f$.*

Proof. Due to (8.33.2), there exists a quorum Q_1 with size at most $n - f$. With (8.33.1), $|Q_1| > f$ holds. Let F_1 be a set of f (byzantine) nodes $F_1 \subset Q_1$, and with (8.33.2), there exists a $Q_2 \subset V \setminus F_1$. Thus, $|Q_1 \cap Q_2| \leq n - 2f$. With (8.33.1), $|Q_1 \cap Q_2| > f$ holds. Thus, one could choose f (byzantine) nodes F_2 with $F_2 \subset (Q_1 \cap Q_2)$. Using (8.33.1) one can bound $n - 3f$ from below: $n - 3f > |(Q_2 \cap Q_1)| - |F_2| \geq |(Q_2 \cap Q_1) \cup (Q_1 \cap F_2)| \geq |F_1| + |F_2| = 2f$. $\qquad \square$

Remarks:

- One can extend the Majority quorum system to be f-opaque by setting the size of each quorum to contain $\lceil (2n + 2f)/3 \rceil$ nodes. Then its load is $1/n \lceil (2n + 2f)/3 \rceil \approx 2/3 + 2f/3n \geq 2/3$.

- Can we do much better? Sadly, no...

Theorem 8.36. *Let $\mathcal{S}$ be a f-opaque quorum system. Then $L(\mathcal{S}) \geq 1/2$ holds.*

Proof. Equation (8.33.1) implies that for $Q_1, Q_2 \in \mathcal{S}$, the intersection of both Q_1, Q_2 is at least half their size, i.e., $|(Q_1 \cap Q_2)| \geq |Q_1|/2$. Let $\mathcal{S}$ consist of quorums $Q_1, Q_2, \dots$. The load induced by an access strategy Z on Q_1 is:

$$\sum_{v \in Q_1} \sum_{v \in Q_i} L_Z(Q_i) \geq \sum_{Q_i} (|Q_1|/2)\, L_Z(Q_i) = |Q_1|/2 \ .$$

Using the pigeonhole principle, there must be at least one node in Q_1 with load of at least $1/2$. $\qquad \square$

Chapter Notes

Historically, a quorum is the minimum number of members of a deliberative body necessary to conduct the business of that group. Their use has inspired the introduction of quorum systems in computer science since the late 1970s/early 1980s. Early work focused on Majority quorum systems [Lam78, Gif79, Tho79], with the notion of minimality introduced shortly after [GB85]. The Grid quorum system was first considered in [Mae85], with the B-Grid being introduced in [NW94]. The latter article and [PW95] also initiated the study of load and resilience.

The f-masking Grid quorum system and opaque quorum systems are from [MR98], and the M-Grid quorum system was introduced in [MRW97]. Both papers also mark the start of the formal study of Byzantine quorum systems. The f-masking and the M-Grid have asymptotic failure probabilities of 1, more complex systems with better values can be found in these papers as well.

Quorum systems have also been extended to cope with nodes dynamically leaving and joining, see, e.g., the dynamic paths quorum system in [NW05].

For a further overview on quorum systems, we refer to the book by Vukolić [Vuk12] and the article by Merideth and Reiter [MR10].

Bibliography

[GB85] Hector Garcia-Molina and Daniel Barbará. How to assign votes in a distributed system. *J. ACM*, 32(4):841–860, 1985.

[Gif79] David K. Gifford. Weighted voting for replicated data. In Michael D. Schroeder and Anita K. Jones, editors, *Proceedings of the Seventh Symposium on Operating System Principles, SOSP 1979, Asilomar Conference Grounds, Pacific Grove, California, USA, 10-12, December 1979*, pages 150–162. ACM, 1979.

[Lam78] Leslie Lamport. The implementation of reliable distributed multiprocess systems. *Computer Networks*, 2:95–114, 1978.

[Mae85] Mamoru Maekawa. A square root N algorithm for mutual exclusion in decentralized systems. *ACM Trans. Comput. Syst.*, 3(2):145–159, 1985.

[MR98] Dahlia Malkhi and Michael K. Reiter. Byzantine quorum systems. *Distributed Computing*, 11(4):203–213, 1998.

[MR10] Michael G. Merideth and Michael K. Reiter. Selected results from the latest decade of quorum systems research. In Bernadette Charron-Bost, Fernando Pedone, and André Schiper, editors, *Replication: Theory and*

Practice, volume 5959 of *Lecture Notes in Computer Science*, pages 185–206. Springer, 2010.

[MRW97] Dahlia Malkhi, Michael K. Reiter, and Avishai Wool. The load and availability of byzantine quorum systems. In James E. Burns and Hagit Attiya, editors, *Proceedings of the Sixteenth Annual ACM Symposium on Principles of Distributed Computing, Santa Barbara, California, USA, August 21-24, 1997*, pages 249–257. ACM, 1997.

[NW94] Moni Naor and Avishai Wool. The load, capacity and availability of quorum systems. In *35th Annual Symposium on Foundations of Computer Science, Santa Fe, New Mexico, USA, 20-22 November 1994*, pages 214–225. IEEE Computer Society, 1994.

[NW05] Moni Naor and Udi Wieder. Scalable and dynamic quorum systems. *Distributed Computing*, 17(4):311–322, 2005.

[PW95] David Peleg and Avishai Wool. The availability of quorum systems. *Inf. Comput.*, 123(2):210–223, 1995.

[Tho79] Robert H. Thomas. A majority consensus approach to concurrency control for multiple copy databases. *ACM Trans. Database Syst.*, 4(2):180–209, 1979.

[Vuk12] Marko Vukolic. *Quorum Systems: With Applications to Storage and Consensus*. Synthesis Lectures on Distributed Computing Theory. Morgan & Claypool Publishers, 2012.

Part II

Permissionless Systems

Chapter 9

Eventual Consistency & Bitcoin

How would you implement an ATM? Does the following implementation work satisfactorily?

Algorithm 9.1 Naïve ATM

1: ATM makes withdrawal request to bank
2: ATM waits for response from bank
3: **if** balance of customer sufficient **then**
4:     ATM dispenses cash
5: **else**
6:     ATM displays error
7: **end if**

Remarks:

- A connection problem between the bank and the ATM may block Algorithm 9.1 in Line 2.

- A *network partition* is a failure where a network splits into at least two parts that cannot communicate with each other. Intuitively any non-trivial distributed system cannot proceed during a partition *and* maintain consistency. In the following we introduce the tradeoff between consistency, availability and partition tolerance.

- There are numerous causes for partitions to occur, e.g., physical disconnections, software errors, or incompatible protocol versions. From the point of view of a node in the system, a partition is similar to a period of sustained message loss.

9.1   Consistency, Availability and Partitions

Definition 9.2 (Consistency). *All nodes in the system agree on the current state of the system.*

Definition 9.3 (Availability). *The system is operational and instantly processing incoming requests.*

Definition 9.4 (Partition Tolerance). *Partition tolerance is the ability of a distributed system to continue operating correctly even in the presence of a network partition.*

Theorem 9.5 (CAP Theorem). *It is impossible for a distributed system to simultaneously provide Consistency, Availability and Partition Tolerance. A distributed system can satisfy any two of these but not all three.*

Proof. Assume two nodes, sharing some state. The nodes are in different partitions, i.e., they cannot communicate. Assume a request wants to update the state and contacts a node. The node may either: 1) update its local state, resulting in inconsistent states, or 2) not update its local state, i.e., the system is no longer available for updates. □

Algorithm 9.6 Partition tolerant and available ATM

1: **if** bank reachable **then**
2:     Synchronize local view of balances between ATM and bank
3:     **if** balance of customer insufficient **then**
4:         ATM displays error and aborts user interaction
5:     **end if**
6: **end if**
7: ATM dispenses cash
8: ATM logs withdrawal for synchronization

Remarks:

- Algorithm 9.6 is partition tolerant and available since it continues to process requests even when the bank is not reachable.

- The ATM's local view of the balances may diverge from the balances as seen by the bank, therefore consistency is no longer guaranteed.

- The algorithm will synchronize any changes it made to the local balances back to the bank once connectivity is re-established. This is known as eventual consistency.

Definition 9.7 (Eventual Consistency). *If no new updates to the shared state are issued, then eventually the system is in a quiescent state, i.e., no more messages need to be exchanged between nodes, and the shared state is consistent.*

Remarks:

- Eventual consistency is a form of *weak consistency.*

- Eventual consistency guarantees that the state is eventually agreed upon, but the nodes may disagree temporarily.

- During a partition, different updates may semantically conflict with each other. A *conflict resolution* mechanism is required to resolve the conflicts and allow the nodes to eventually agree on a common state.

- One example of eventual consistency is the Bitcoin cryptocurrency system.

9.2   Bitcoin

Definition 9.8 (Bitcoin Network). *The Bitcoin network is a randomly connected overlay network of a few thousand **nodes**, controlled by a variety of owners. All nodes perform the same operations, i.e., it is a homogenous network and without central control.*

Remarks:

- The lack of structure is intentional: it ensures that an attacker cannot strategically position itself in the network and manipulate the information exchange. Information is exchanged via a simple broadcasting protocol.

Definition 9.9 (Address). *Users may generate any number of private keys, from which a public key is then derived. An address is derived from a public key and may be used to identify the recipient of funds in Bitcoin. The private/public key pair is used to uniquely identify the owner of funds of an address.*

Remarks:

- The terms public key and address are often used interchangeably, since both are public information. The advantage of using an address is that its representation is shorter than the public key.

- It is hard to link addresses to the user that controls them, hence Bitcoin is often referred to as being *pseudonymous*.

- Not every user needs to run a fully validating node, and end-users will likely use a lightweight client that only temporarily connects to the network.

- The Bitcoin network collaboratively tracks the balance in bitcoins of each address.

- The address is composed of a network identifier byte, the hash of the public key and a checksum. It is commonly stored in base 58 encoding, a custom encoding similar to base 64 with some ambiguous symbols removed, e.g., lowercase letter "l" since it is similar to the number "1".

- The hashing algorithm produces addresses of size 20 bytes. This means that there are 2^{160} distinct addresses. It might be tempting to brute force a target address, however at one billion trials per second one still requires approximately 2^{45} years in expectation to find a matching private/public key pair. Due to the birthday paradox the odds improve if instead of brute forcing a single address we attempt to brute force any address. While the odds of a successful trial increase with the number of addresses, lookups become more costly.

Definition 9.10 (Output). *An output is a tuple consisting of an amount of bitcoins and a spending condition. Most commonly the spending condition requires a valid signature associated with the private key of an address.*

Remarks:

- Spending conditions are scripts that offer a variety of options. Apart from a single signature, they may include conditions that require the result of a simple computation, or the solution to a cryptographic puzzle.

- Outputs exist in two states: unspent and spent. Any output can be spent at most once. The address balance is the sum of bitcoin amounts in unspent outputs that are associated with the address.

- The set of unspent transaction outputs (UTXOs) and some additional global parameters are the shared state of Bitcoin. Every node in the Bitcoin network holds a complete replica of that state. Local replicas may temporarily diverge, but consistency is eventually re-established.

Definition 9.11 (Input). *An input is a tuple consisting of a reference to a previously created output and arguments (signature) to the spending condition, proving that the transaction creator has the permission to spend the referenced output.*

Definition 9.12 (Transaction). *A transaction is a data structure that describes the transfer of bitcoins from spenders to recipients. The transaction consists of a number of inputs and new outputs. The inputs result in the referenced outputs spent (removed from the UTXO), and the new outputs being added to the UTXO.*

Remarks:

- Inputs reference the output that is being spent by a (h, i)-tuple, where h is the hash of the transaction that created the output, and i specifies the index of the output in that transaction.

- Transactions are broadcast in the Bitcoin network and processed by every node that receives them.

Algorithm 9.13 Node Receives Transaction

1: Receive transaction t
2: **for each** input (h, i) in t **do**
3:    **if** output (h, i) is not in local UTXO **or** signature invalid **then**
4:       Drop t and stop
5:    **end if**
6: **end for**
7: **if** sum of values of inputs $<$ sum of values of new outputs **then**
8:    Drop t and stop
9: **end if**
10: **for each** input (h, i) in t **do**
11:    Remove (h, i) from local UTXO
12: **end for**
13: Append t to local history
14: Forward t to neighbors in the Bitcoin network

Remarks:

- Note that the effect of a transaction on the state is deterministic. In other words if all nodes receive the same set of transactions in the same order (Definition 2.8), then the state across nodes is consistent.

- The outputs of a transaction may assign less than the sum of inputs, in which case the difference is called the transaction *fee*. The fee is used to incentivize other participants in the system (see Definition 9.19)

- Notice that so far we only described a local acceptance policy. Nothing prevents nodes to locally accept different transactions that spend the same output.

- Transactions are in one of two states: unconfirmed or confirmed. Incoming transactions from the broadcast are unconfirmed and added to a pool of transactions called the *memory pool*.

Definition 9.14 (Doublespend). *A doublespend is a situation in which multiple transactions attempt to spend the same output. Only one transaction can be valid since outputs can only be spent once. When nodes accept different transactions in a doublespend, the shared state becomes inconsistent.*

Remarks:

- Doublespends may occur naturally, e.g., if outputs are co-owned by multiple users. However, often doublespends are intentional – we call these doublespend-attacks: In a transaction, an attacker pretends to transfer an output to a victim, only to doublespend the same output in another transaction back to itself.

- Doublespends can result in an inconsistent state since the validity of transactions depends on the order in which they arrive. If two conflicting transactions are seen by a node, the node considers the first to be valid, see Algorithm 9.13. The second transaction is invalid since it tries to spend an output that is already spent. The order in which transactions are seen, may not be the same for all nodes, hence the inconsistent state.

- If doublespends are not resolved, the shared state diverges. Therefore a conflict resolution mechanism is needed to decide which of the conflicting transactions is to be confirmed (accepted by everybody), to achieve eventual consistency.

Definition 9.15 (Proof-of-Work). *Proof-of-Work (PoW) is a mechanism that allows a party to prove to another party that a certain amount of computational resources has been utilized for a period of time. A function $\mathcal{F}_d(c, x) \rightarrow \{true, false\}$, where difficulty d is a positive number, while challenge c and nonce x are usually bit-strings, is called a Proof-of-Work function if it has following properties:*

1. *$\mathcal{F}_d(c, x)$ is fast to compute if d, c, and x are given.*

2. *For fixed parameters d and c, finding x such that $\mathcal{F}_d(c, x) = true$ is computationally difficult but feasible. The difficulty d is used to adjust the time to find such an x.*

Definition 9.16 (Bitcoin PoW function). *The Bitcoin PoW function is given by*

$$\mathcal{F}_d(c, x) \rightarrow \text{SHA256}(\text{SHA256}(c|x)) < \frac{2^{224}}{d}.$$

Remarks:

- This function concatenates the challenge c and nonce x, and hashes them twice using SHA256. The output of SHA256 is a cryptographic hash with a numeric value in $\{0, \ldots, 2^{256} - 1\}$ which is compared to a target value $\frac{2^{224}}{d}$, which gets smaller with increasing difficulty.

- SHA256 is a cryptographic hash function with pseudo-random output. No better algorithm is known to find a nonce x such that the function $\mathcal{F}_d(c, x)$ returns true than simply iterating over possible inputs. This is by design to make it difficult to find such an input, but simple to verify the validity once it has been found.

- If the PoW functions of all nodes had the same challenge, the fastest node would always win. However, as we will see in Definition 9.19, each node attempts to find a valid nonce for a node-specific challenge.

Definition 9.17 (Block). *A block is a data structure used to communicate incremental changes to the local state of a node. A block consists of a list of transactions, a reference to a previous block and a nonce. A block lists some transactions the block creator ("miner") has accepted to its memory pool since the previous block. A node finds and broadcasts a block when it finds a valid nonce for its PoW function.*

Algorithm 9.18 Node Finds Block

1: Nonce $x = 0$, challenge c, difficulty d, previous block b_{t-1}
2: **repeat**
3:    $x = x + 1$
4: **until** $\mathcal{F}_d(c, x) = true$
5: Broadcast block $b_t = (memory\ pool, b_{t-1}, x)$

Remarks:

- With their reference to a previous block, the blocks build a tree, rooted in the so called *genesis block*.

- The primary goal for using the PoW mechanism is to adjust the rate at which blocks are found in the network, giving the network time to synchronize on the latest block. Bitcoin sets the difficulty so that globally a block is created about every 10 minutes in expectation.

- Finding a block allows the finder to impose the transactions in its local memory pool to all other nodes. Upon receiving a block, all nodes roll back any local changes since the previous block and apply the new block's transactions.

- Transactions contained in a block are said to be *confirmed* by that block.

Definition 9.19 (Reward Transaction). *The first transaction in a block is called the reward transaction. The block's miner is rewarded for confirming transactions by allowing it to mint new coins. The reward transaction has a dummy input, and the sum of outputs is determined by a fixed subsidy plus the sum of the fees of transactions confirmed in the block.*

Remarks:

- A reward transaction is the sole exception to the rule that the sum of inputs must be at least the sum of outputs.

- The number of bitcoins that are minted by the reward transaction and assigned to the miner is determined by a subsidy schedule that is part of the protocol. Initially the subsidy was 50 bitcoins for every block, and it is being halved every 210,000 blocks, or 4 years in expectation. Due to the halving of the block reward, the total amount of bitcoins in circulation never exceeds 21 million bitcoins.

- It is expected that the cost of performing the PoW to find a block, in terms of energy and infrastructure, is close to the value of the reward the miner receives from the reward transaction in the block.

Definition 9.20 (Blockchain). *The longest path from the genesis block, i.e., root of the tree, to a leaf is called the blockchain. The blockchain acts as a consistent transaction history on which all nodes eventually agree.*

Remarks:

- The path length from the genesis block to block b is the height h_b.

- Only the longest path from the genesis block to a leaf is a valid transaction history, since branches may contradict each other because of doublespends.

- Since only transactions in the longest path are agreed upon, miners have an incentive to append their blocks to the longest chain, thus agreeing on the current state.

- The mining incentives quickly increased the difficulty of the PoW mechanism: initially miners used CPUs to mine blocks, but CPUs were quickly replaced by GPUs, FPGAs and even application specific integrated circuits (ASICs) as bitcoins appreciated. This results in an equilibrium today in which only the most cost efficient miners, in terms of hardware supply and electricity, make a profit in expectation.

- If multiple blocks are mined more or less concurrently, the system is said to have *forked*. Forks happen naturally because mining is a distributed random process and two new blocks may be found at roughly the same time.

Algorithm 9.21 Node Receives Block

1: Receive block b
2: For this node the current head is block b_{max} at height h_{max}
3: Connect block b in the tree as child of its parent p at height $h_b = h_p + 1$
4: **if** $h_b > h_{max}$ **then**
5: $\quad h_{max} = h_b$
6: $\quad b_{max} = b$
7: $\quad$ Compute UTXO for the path leading to b_{max}
8: $\quad$ Cleanup memory pool
9: **end if**

Remarks:

- Algorithm 9.21 describes how a node updates its local state upon receiving a block. Notice that, like Algorithm 9.13, this describes the local policy and may also result in node states diverging, i.e., by accepting different blocks at the same height as current head.

- Unlike extending the current path, switching paths may result in confirmed transactions no longer being confirmed, because the blocks in the new path do not include them. Switching paths is referred to as a *reorg*.

- Cleaning up the memory pool involves 1) removing transactions that were confirmed in a block in the current path, 2) removing transactions that conflict with confirmed transactions, and 3) adding transactions that were confirmed in the previous path, but are no longer confirmed in the current path.

- In order to avoid having to recompute the entire UTXO at every new block being added to the blockchain, all current implementations use data structures that store undo information about the operations applied by a block. This allows efficient switching of paths and updates of the head by moving along the path.

Theorem 9.22. *Forks are eventually resolved and all nodes eventually agree on which is the longest blockchain. The system therefore guarantees eventual consistency.*

Proof. In order for the fork to continue to exist, pairs of blocks need to be found in close succession, extending distinct branches, otherwise the nodes on the shorter branch would switch to the longer one. The probability of branches being extended almost simultaneously decreases exponentially with the length of the fork, hence there will eventually be a time when only one branch is being extended, becoming the longest branch. $\square$

9.3 Smart Contracts

Definition 9.23 (Smart Contract). *A smart contract is an agreement between two or more parties, encoded in such a way that the correct execution is guaranteed by the blockchain.*

Remarks:

- Contracts allow business logic to be encoded in Bitcoin transactions which mutually guarantee that an agreed upon action is performed. The blockchain acts as conflict mediator, should a party fail to honor an agreement.

- The use of scripts as spending conditions for outputs enables smart contracts. Scripts, together with some additional features such as timelocks, allow encoding complex conditions, specifying who may spend the funds associated with an output and when.

Definition 9.24 (Timelock). *Bitcoin provides a mechanism to make transactions invalid until some time in the future: **timelocks**. A transaction may specify a locktime: the earliest time, expressed in either a Unix timestamp or a blockchain height, at which it may be included in a block and therefore be confirmed.*

Remarks:

- Transactions with a timelock are not released into the network until the timelock expires. It is the responsibility of the node receiving the transaction to store it locally until the timelock expires and then release it into the network.

- Transactions with future timelocks are invalid. Blocks may not include transactions with timelocks that have not yet expired, i.e., they are mined before their expiry timestamp or in a lower block than specified. If a block includes an unexpired transaction it is invalid. Upon receiving invalid transactions or blocks, nodes discard them immediately and do not forward them to their peers.

- Timelocks can be used to replace or supersede transactions: a timelocked transaction t_1 can be replaced by another transaction t_0, spending some of the same outputs, if the replacing transaction t_0 has an earlier timelock and can be broadcast in the network before the replaced transaction t_1 becomes valid.

Definition 9.25 (Singlesig and Multisig Outputs). *When an output can be claimed by providing a single signature it is called a **singlesig output**. In contrast the script of **multisig outputs***

specifies a set of m public keys and requires k-of-m (with $k \leq m$) valid signatures from distinct matching public keys from that set in order to be valid.

Remarks:

- Most smart contracts begin with the creation of a 2-of-2 multisig output, requiring a signature from both parties. Once the transaction creating the multisig output is confirmed in the blockchain, both parties are guaranteed that the funds of that output cannot be spent unilaterally.

Algorithm 9.26 Parties A and B create a 2-of-2 multisig output o

---

1: B sends a list I_B of inputs with c_B coins to A
2: A selects its own inputs I_A with c_A coins
3: A creates transaction $t_s\{[I_A, I_B], [o = c_A + c_B \rightarrow (A, B)]\}$
4: A creates timelocked transaction $t_r\{[o], [c_A \rightarrow A, c_B \rightarrow B]\}$ and signs it
5: A sends t_s and t_r to B
6: B signs both t_s and t_r and sends them to A
7: A signs t_s and broadcasts it to the Bitcoin network

Remarks:

- t_s is called a *setup transaction* and is used to lock in funds into a shared account. If t_s is signed and broadcast immediately, one of the parties could not collaborate to spend the multisig output, and the funds become unspendable. To avoid a situation where the funds cannot be spent, the protocol also creates a timelocked *refund transaction* t_r which guarantees that, should the funds not be spent before the timelock expires, the funds are returned to the respective party. At no point in time one of the parties holds a fully signed setup transaction without the other party holding a fully signed refund transaction, guaranteeing that funds are eventually returned.

- Both transactions require the signature of both parties. In the case of the setup transaction because it has two inputs from A and B respectively which require individual signatures. In the case of the refund transaction the single input spending the multisig output requires both signatures being a 2-of-2 multisig output.

Algorithm 9.27 Simple Micropayment Channel from S to R with capacity c

---

1: $c_S = c$, $c_R = 0$
2: S and R use Algorithm 9.26 to set up output o with value c from S
3: Create settlement transaction $t_f\{[o], [c_S \to S, c_R \to R]\}$
4: **while** channel open **and** $c_R < c$ **do**
5:     In exchange for good with value δ
6:     $c_R = c_R + \delta$
7:     $c_S = c_S - \delta$
8:     Update t_f with outputs $[c_R \to R, c_S \to S]$
9:     S signs and sends t_f to R
10: **end while**
11: R signs last t_f and broadcasts it

Remarks:

- Algorithm 9.27 implements a Simple Micropayment Channel, a smart contract that is used for rapidly adjusting micropayments from a spender to a recipient. Only two transactions are ever broadcast and inserted into the blockchain: the setup transaction t_s and the last settlement transaction t_f. There may have been any number of updates to the settlement transaction, transferring ever more of the shared output to the recipient.

- The number of bitcoins c used to fund the channel is also the maximum total that may be transferred over the simple micropayment channel.

- At any time the recipient R is guaranteed to eventually receive the bitcoins, since she holds a fully signed settlement transaction, while the spender only has partially signed ones.

- The simple micropayment channel is intrinsically unidirectional. Since the recipient may choose any of the settlement transactions in the protocol, she will use the one with maximum payout for her. If we were to transfer bitcoins back, we would be reducing the amount paid out to the recipient, hence she would choose not to broadcast that transaction.

9.4   Weak Consistency

Eventual consistency is only one form of weak consistency. A number of different tradeoffs between partition tolerance and consistency exist in literature.

Definition 9.28 (Monotonic Read Consistency). *If a node u has seen a particular value of an object, any subsequent accesses of u will never return any older values.*

Remarks:

- Users are annoyed if they receive a notification about a comment on an online social network, but are unable to reply because the web interface does not show the same notification yet. In this case the notification acts as the first read operation, while looking up the comment on the web interface is the second read operation.

Definition 9.29 (Monotonic Write Consistency). *A write operation by a node on a data item is completed before any successive write operation by the same node (i.e., system guarantees to serialize writes by the same node).*

Remarks:

- The ATM must replay all operations in order, otherwise it might happen that an earlier operation overwrites the result of a later operation, resulting in an inconsistent final state.

Definition 9.30 (Read-Your-Write Consistency). *After a node u has updated a data item, any later reads from node u will never see an older value.*

Definition 9.31 (Causal Relation). *The following pairs of operations are said to be causally related:*

- *Two writes by the same node to different variables.*

- *A read followed by a write of the same node.*

- *A read that returns the value of a write from any node.*

- *Two operations that are transitively related according to the above conditions.*

Remarks:

- The first rule ensures that writes by a single node are seen in the same order. For example if a node writes a value in one variable and then signals that it has written the value by writing in another variable. Another node could then read the signalling variable but still read the old value from the first variable, if the two writes were not causally related.

Definition 9.32 (Causal Consistency). *A system provides causal consistency if operations that potentially are causally related are seen by every node of the system in the same order. Concurrent writes are not causally related, and may be seen in different orders by different nodes.*

Chapter Notes

The CAP theorem was first introduced by Fox and Brewer [FB99], although it is commonly attributed to a talk by Eric Brewer [Bre00]. It was later proven by Gilbert and Lynch [GL02] for the asynchronous model. Gilbert and Lynch also showed how to relax the consistency requirement in a partially synchronous system to achieve availability and partition tolerance.

Bitcoin was introduced in 2008 by Satoshi Nakamoto [Nak08]. Nakamoto is thought to be a pseudonym used by either a single person or a group of people; it is still unknown who invented Bitcoin, giving rise to speculation and conspiracy theories. Among the plausible theories are noted cryptographers Nick Szabo [Big13] and Hal Finney [Gre14]. The first Bitcoin client was published shortly after the paper and the first block was mined on January 3, 2009. The genesis block contained the headline of the release date's The Times issue *"The Times 03/Jan/2009 Chancellor on brink of second bailout for banks"*, which serves as proof that the genesis block has been indeed mined on that date, and that no one had mined before that date. The quote in the genesis block is also thought to be an ideological hint: Bitcoin was created in a climate of financial crisis, induced by rampant manipulation by the banking sector, and Bitcoin quickly grew in popularity in anarchic and libertarian circles. The original client is nowadays maintained by a group of independent core developers and remains the most used client in the Bitcoin network.

Central to Bitcoin is the resolution of conflicts due to double-spends, which is solved by waiting for transactions to be included in the blockchain. This however introduces large delays for the confirmation of payments which are undesirable in some scenarios in which an immediate confirmation is required. Karame et al. [KAC12] show that accepting unconfirmed transactions leads to a non-negligible probability of being defrauded as a result of a doublespending attack. This is facilitated by *information eclipsing* [DW13], i.e., that nodes do not forward conflicting transactions, hence the victim does not see both transactions of the doublespend. Bamert et al. [BDE$^+$13] showed that the odds of detecting a doublespending attack in real-time can be improved by connecting to a large sample of nodes and tracing the propagation of transactions in the network.

Bitcoin does not scale very well due to its reliance on confirmations in the blockchain. A copy of the entire transaction history is stored on every node in order to bootstrap joining nodes, which have to reconstruct the transaction history from the genesis block. Simple micropayment channels were introduced by Hearn and Spilman [HS12] and may be used to bundle multiple transfers between two parties but they are limited to transferring the funds locked into the channel once. Recently Duplex Micropayment Channels [DW15] and the Lightning Network [PD15] have been proposed to build bidirectional micropayment channels in which the funds can be transferred back and forth an arbitrary number of times, greatly increasing the flexibility of Bitcoin transfers and enabling a number of features, such as micropayments and routing payments between any two endpoints.

Bibliography

[BDE$^+$13] Tobias Bamert, Christian Decker, Lennart Elsen, Samuel Welten, and Roger Wattenhofer. Have a snack, pay with bitcoin. In *IEEE Internation Conference on Peer-to-Peer Computing (P2P)*, Trento, Italy, 2013.

[Big13] John Biggs. Who is the real satoshi nakamoto?

one researcher may have found the answer. http://on.tcrn.ch/l/R0vA, 2013.

[Bre00] Eric A. Brewer. Towards robust distributed systems. In *Symposium on Principles of Distributed Computing (PODC)*. ACM, 2000.

[DW13] Christian Decker and Roger Wattenhofer. Information propagation in the bitcoin network. In *IEEE International Conference on Peer-to-Peer Computing (P2P), Trento, Italy*, September 2013.

[DW15] Christian Decker and Roger Wattenhofer. A Fast and Scalable Payment Network with Bitcoin Duplex Micropayment Channels. In *Symposium on Stabilization, Safety, and Security of Distributed Systems (SSS)*, 2015.

[FB99] Armando Fox and Eric Brewer. Harvest, yield, and scalable tolerant systems. In *Hot Topics in Operating Systems*. IEEE, 1999.

[GL02] Seth Gilbert and Nancy Lynch. Brewer's conjecture and the feasibility of consistent, available, partition-tolerant web services. *SIGACT News*, 2002.

[Gre14] Andy Greenberg. Nakamoto's neighbor: My hunt for bitcoin's creator led to a paralyzed crypto genius. http://onforb.es/1rvyecq, 2014.

[HS12] Mike Hearn and Jeremy Spilman. Contract: Rapidly adjusting micro-payments. https://en.bitcoin.it/wiki/Contract, 2012. Last accessed on November 11, 2015.

[KAC12] G.O. Karame, E. Androulaki, and S. Capkun. Two Bitcoins at the Price of One? Double-Spending Attacks on Fast Payments in Bitcoin. In *Conference on Computer and Communication Security (CCS)*, 2012.

[Nak08] Satoshi Nakamoto. Bitcoin: A peer-to-peer electronic cash system. https://bitcoin.org/bitcoin.pdf, 2008.

[PD15] Joseph Poon and Thaddeus Dryja. The bitcoin lightning network. 2015.

Chapter 10

Inside Bitcoin

Bitcoin features various concepts that go beyond the blockchain centric discussion of Chapter 9. In this chapter we discuss some of Bitcoin's other interesting features.

10.1   Cryptographic Tools

The Bitcoin protocol limits its use of cryptographic tools to cryptographic hash functions such as SHA256 and RIPEMD160, Merkle trees, and the Elliptic Curve Digital Signature Algorithm.

Definition 10.1 (Cryptographic hash functions). *Cryptographic hash functions map an arbitrarily long input byte sequence to a fixed size output, commonly called **digest**, effectively fingerprinting the input.*

Remarks:

- Cryptographic hashes are designed such that it is computationally infeasible to recreate a valid input sequence.

- Ideal cryptographic hash functions are computationally inexpensive, and the output hash always changes when the input sequence is altered.

- Cryptographic hash functions are widely used in Bitcoin, e.g., the *id* of a transaction corresponds to the cryptographic hash of the transaction.

- Hash functions are a base component of other data structures used in Bitcoin, e.g. Merkle trees.

Definition 10.2 (Merkle Tree). *Merkle trees allow to combine multiple cryptographic hash input sequences in a hash tree.*

Remarks:

- A Merkle tree allows for a compact representation of a set of transactions, e.g., when the tree is built up from the transaction hashes, see Figure 10.3.

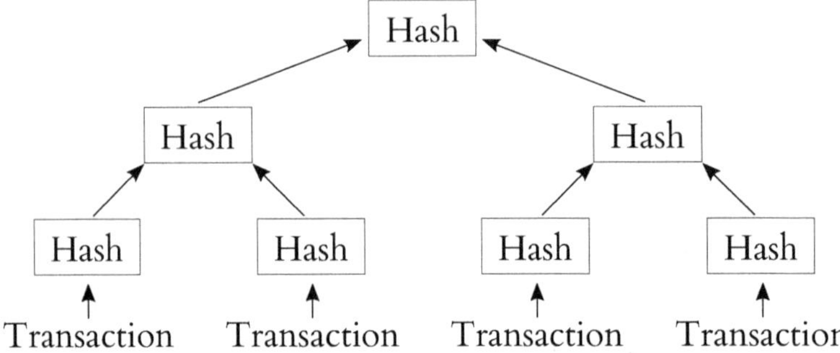

Figure 10.3: Merkle tree of transactions. The topmost hash is referred to as merkle root. It is a compact representation of the involved transactions.

10.2   Script & Message Formats

Definition 10.4 (Script). *Bitcoin uses a custom stack-based scripting language simply called Script in an attempt to allow different types of transactions.*

Remarks:

- Script's flexibility allows extending the functionality of transactions beyond the simple transfer of funds.

- Script is stack based, supports many functions (commonly referred to as opcodes) and either evaluates to true or false. Script supports dozens of different opcodes, ranging from simple comparison opcodes to cryptographic hash functions and signature verification.

- Because Script is supposed to be executed on any validating Bitcoin node, execution time is critical to prevent denial of service attacks. Therefore, many opcodes have been temporarily disabled. Consequently, Script is kept simple on purpose, and therefore does not support the same complexity as general purpose programming languages.

- An example Script program contains two constants (denoted by <...>) and one opcode (execution goes from the left to the right):

  `<signature> <publicKey> OP_CHECKSIG`.

  Constants are pushed by default on the stack, and upon execution, the stack contains

  `<signature> <publicKey>`.

  Then, `OP_CHECKSIG` is executed which verifies the `<signature>` under the provided `<publicKey>`. If the signature matches the provided public key, `OP_CHECKSIG` returns true, and in return, the script returns true.

Definition 10.5 (Transaction Format). *Transactions as introduced in Definition 9.12 must obey a certain format.*

Remarks:

- Table 10.6 summarizes the general format of a Bitcoin transaction.

- Tables 10.7 and 10.8 respectively describe the transaction input and output format.

Field	*Description*	*Size*
Version number	Version, currently 1	4 bytes
Input counter	positive integer	1 - 9 bytes
List of inputs	see Table regarding transaction inputs	Variable
Output counter	positive integer	1 - 9 bytes
List of outputs	see Table regarding transaction inputs	Variable
locktime	Block height or time when transaction is valid	4 bytes

Table 10.6: Transaction format inside a Bitcoin block.

Field	*Description*	*Size*
Previous transaction hash	Dependency	32 bytes
Previous transaction output index	Dependency index	4 bytes
Script length		1 - 9 bytes
ScriptSig	Input script	Variable
Sequence number	generally 0xFFFFFFFF	4 bytes

Table 10.7: Transaction input format inside a Bitcoin block.

Field	*Description*	*Size*
value	positive integer of Satoshis to be transferred	4 bytes
Script length		1 - 9 bytes
ScriptSig	Output script	Variable

Table 10.8: Transaction output format inside a Bitcoin block.

Definition 10.9 (Standard Transaction Types). *Bitcoin supports by default several standard transaction types.*

Remarks:

- Only standard transaction types are broadcasted and validated within the network. Transactions that do not match standard transaction types are generally discarded.

- Because transactions can have multiple outputs, the different output types can be combined within one transaction.

- Here are the standard transaction types:

- Pay To Public Key Hash (P2PKH): A P2PKH transaction output contains the following opcodes:

  ```
  OP_DUP OP_HASH160 <PubkeyHash> OP_EQUALVERIFY
  OP_CHECKSIG
  ```

  The corresponding input that would be eligible to spend the output, specifies the required signature and the full public key: `<Sig> <PubKey>`

- Pay To Script Hash (P2SH): A P2SH transaction output can only be redeemed by an input that provides a script, that hashes to the hash of the corresponding output. A P2SH output for example contains the following transaction output:

```
OP_HASH160 <Hash160(redeemScript)>
OP_EQUALVERIFY
```

The redeeming input consequently needs to provide a *redeemScript*, that hashes to the input's hash. Every standard Script can be used for this purpose:

```
<sig> <redeemScript>
```

P2SH allows to create a transaction where the responsibility for providing the redeem conditions of a transaction is pushed from the sender to the redeemer of the funds. Consequently the sender is not required to pay an excess in transaction fees, if the redeem script happens to be complex and thus big in terms of bytes. In practice P2SH outputs are heavily used for multi-signature (multisig) transactions, but multi-signatures can both be accomplished with m-of-n output scripts as well as P2SH.

- Multisig: A multi-signature (or commonly referred to as multisig) transaction, requires multiple signatures in order to be redeemable, c.g. Definition 9.25. Multisig transaction outputs are usually denoted as m-of-n, m being the minimum number of signatures that are required for the transaction output to be redeemable, out of the n possible signatures that correspond to the public keys defined in the transaction output. An example transaction output corresponds to:

```
<m> <A pubkey> [B pubkey] [C pubkey..] <n>
OP_CHECKMULTISIG
```

while the redeeming input follows this structure:

```
OP_0 <A signature> [B signature] [C signature..]
```

Definition 10.10 (Script Execution). *To validate a new transaction, the input (signature script) and the output of the previous transaction (pubkey script) are concatenated. Once concatenated, the script is executed according to the Script language. Constants, denoted by <..> are pushed on the stack, and opcodes execute their respective actions by taking into account the topmost stack value.*

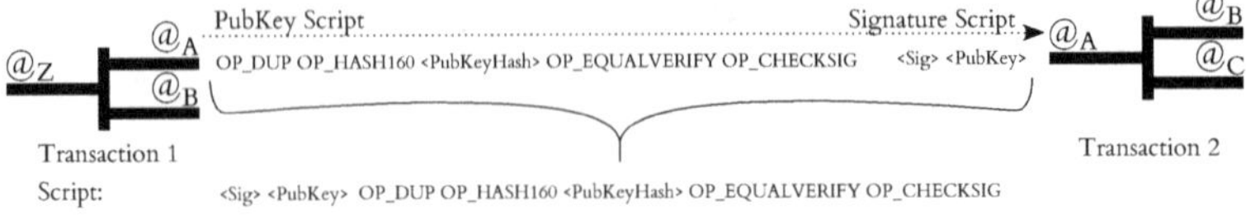

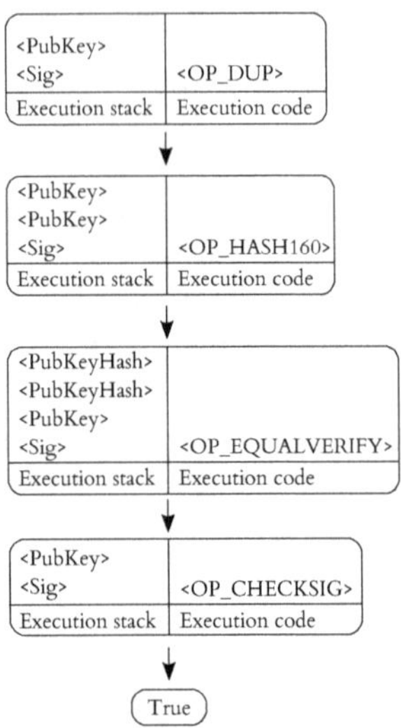

Figure 10.11: Script execution for a P2PKH transaction called Transaction 2: The output and input script are concatenated (Signature script first and then the PubKey script). In a first step, the two constants `<PubKey>` `<Sig>` are pushed onto the stack. Then `OP_DUP` duplicates the top-most stack value, `<PubKey>` in this case. The next opcode `OP_HASH160` hashes the `<PubKey>` and saves it as `<PubKeyHash>` on the stack. The constant `<PubKeyHash>` is pushed onto the stack and `OP_EQUALVERIFY` verifies if the two top-most stack elements are equal. If they are equal, they are removed from the stack, and the last opcode `OP_CHECKSIG` verifies if the public key on the stack (`<PubKey>`) matches the signature (`<Sig>`). If the signature is valid, the script returns true, meaning that the input of transaction 2 is allowed to spent the output 1 of Transaction 1.

Remarks:

- In Figure 10.11, we visualize the validation of a transaction.

Definition 10.12 (Block Format). *Blocks as introduced in Definition 9.17 must obey a certain format.*

Remarks:

- Each block header has a specific set of fields that we are listed in Table 10.13.

- The block itself contains the actual transactions.

Field	*Description*	*Size*
Version	Block version number	4 bytes
Hash of previous block	Hash of previous Block header	32 bytes
Merkle root hash	Transaction Merkle root hash	32 bytes
Time	Unix timestamp	4 bytes
Bits	Difficulty as in Algorithm 9.18	4 bytes
Nonce	PoW as in Algorithm 9.18	4 bytes

Table 10.13: Bitcoin block header format.

10.3 Players

The Bitcoin ecosystem emerged over the need to provide different services to different participating players depending on their available resources. We describe in the following the various players (also known as node types) and how they interoperate.

Definition 10.14 (Miner). *Miners perform the Proof-of-Work (Definition 9.15) to find and broadcast blocks in the Bitcoin network.*

Remarks:

- Miners must quickly retrieve information about the newest blocks, validate transactions that are included in new blocks, operate dedicated mining hardware to perform as many hash operations as possible, and efficiently spread found blocks to the whole network.

- As we discussed in Definition 9.19, every block provides a monetary reward.

- Because a block is found on average only every 10 minutes, it may take a long time until a miner receives a payout. Miners therefore typically organize themselves into groups of miners, commonly referred to as mining pools. Because of its higher overall hashing power, a mining pool has a higher chance to find a block, and mining pool members can consequently receive payouts more periodically than an independent miner.

Definition 10.15 (Full Node). *A full node is a node that (i) maintains the full copy of the blockchain, (ii) validates incoming transactions and blocks, and (iii) forwards transactions and blocks to its peer nodes.*

Remarks:

- In addition to providing validation services to the Bitcoin network, a full node might provide an open TCP port (Bitcoin uses the TCP port 8333), where other Bitcoin nodes can connect to.

Definition 10.16 (Lightweight Client). *A lightweight client does not maintain the full Bitcoin blockchain, but rather follows the co-called Simple Payment Verification (SPV) scheme.*

Remarks:

- The SPV scheme allows the lightweight client to verify that a transaction has been included in the blockchain, by only receiving the block headers. In order to find such transactions quickly, they often use so-called Bloom filters.

- Lightweight clients do not receive transactions that are irrelevant to their operation, do not need to perform transaction or block validation and consequently require significantly fewer resources to operate than full nodes or miners.

Definition 10.17 (Web Wallet). *A web wallet is an online wallet, hosted on a remote server and accessible through a website.*

Remarks:

- A full node installation takes a serious amount of disk space and requires several hours in order to download and index the current blockchain. Therefore, users started relying on centralised services that host the main Bitcoin functionalities, called web wallets.

- A web wallet is instantly functional, does not occupy hard disk space, is accessible anywhere and is consequently more convenient than a local Bitcoin client.

- However, a malicious web wallet operator could potentially have access to the funds of a user, and *(i)* steal or forward stolen Bitcoins, *(ii)* trade with non-used funds, or *(iii)* profile users.

Chapter Notes

While Bitcoin mostly focuses on the ability to provide a decentralized cryptocurrency, alternative PoW blockchains such as Ethereum [But14] allow executing smart contracts described in a Turing-complete programming language that run on top of the blockchain. For a comprehensive overview on cryptocurrencies, we refer to Bonneau et al. [BMC+15].

Several papers analyze double-spending attacks in Bitcoin, e.g., [Ros14]. Bamert et al. [BDE+13] compile countermeasures to detect double spending attacks. In [KAC12], Karame et al. investigate double-spending attacks of fast payments (payments that have not been confirmed in the blockchain) in Bitcoin, and show that double-spending of fast payments can be performed in spite of the measures recommended by Bitcoin developers. Barber et al. [BBSU12] analyze possible ways to enhance the resilience of Bitcoin against security threats.

Croman *et al.* [CDE+16] discuss the scalability limitations of Bitcoin, but do not quantify the security implications of smaller block intervals or bigger blocks on the security of the system. Several works [GKL15, CDE+16] analyse the security of Bitcoin's protocol in the synchronous network model.

Most security-related studies assume that nodes directly receive the information disseminated in the Bitcoin network. In [DW13], Decker et al. connect to a subset of the Bitcoin network, and measure the propagation delay of blocks. Miller et al. [MLP+15] try to discover Bitcoin's topology by exploiting, for instance, a 2-minute request timeout for transactions.

Open decentralized PoW blockchain's security relies on the assumption that most participating nodes receive all transaction and block information nearly simultaneously, i.e., there is a tight synchronization. Eclipse attacks aim to partition the network into 2 or more clusters, such that the synchronization is no longer possible. Heilman's et al. were the first to show eclipse attacks on Bitcoin [HKZG15]. The authors showed that by monopolizing the connections of nodes in the system (an expensive strategy), an adversary could perform selfish mining and abuse Bitcoin's consensus protocol.

A number of contributions focus on the privacy aspects of PoW blockchains. Although nodes transfer funds among pseudonyms (addresses), payments are linkable such that the origin of a payment is traceable at any time. Transaction prices and time of payment are also published and stored persistently in the blockchain.

Miers et al. introduced in [MGGR13] ZeroCoin, a cryptographic extension to Bitcoin that augments the protocol to prevent the tracing of coin expenditure. In [AK14], Androulaki and Karame proposed an extension of ZeroCoin to hide the transaction values and address balances in the system. In [Eli11], Elias investigates the legal aspects of privacy in Bitcoin. Reid and Harrigan [RH11] analyze the flow of Bitcoin transactions in a small part of Bitcoin log. In [AKC13], Androulaki et al. evaluate user privacy in Bitcoin and show that Bitcoin leaks considerable information about the profiles of users. More specifically, the authors show that in a typical university setting, even when users adopt privacy measures, profiles of almost 40% of the users are recoverable. In [RS13], Ron and Shamir analyze the behavior of Bitcoin users. In [OKH13], Ober et al. study the time-evolution properties of Bitcoin by analyzing its transaction graph. Decker et al. [DW14] investigate transaction malleability and the Mt. Gox incident. In [MPJ$^+$16], Meiklejohn et al. identify big players in the Bitcoin system by leveraging Heuristics I and II adapted from [KAR$^+$15, AKC13]. The authors perform transactions with big vendors such as Mt. Gox. and use our heuristics to identify clusters of addresses of such merchants. In [KKM14], the authors investigated the possibility of linking addresses of the same user by utilizing the network address information (IPs).

As far as we are aware, Mullin et al. [Mul83] were the first to propose an estimate of the false positive rate of Bloom filters.

In [CRJ10], Christensen et al. propose a novel technique for computing the false positive rate, which results in tighter estimates when compared to [Mul83].

In [BBL12], Bianchi et al. quantify the privacy properties of Bloom filters; their analysis, however, does not address the privacy provisions when the adversary has access to multiple Bloom filters originating from the same entity. In [NK09], Nojima et al., propose a cryptographically secure privacy-preserving Bloom-filtering protocol based on blind signatures; this proposal, however, incurs additional computational load on SPV nodes. Private Information Retrievals (e.g., [Ker12]) (PIRs) can also be used as an alternative to Bloom filters; PIR schemes, however, result in the non-negligible computational overhead on the nodes. For example, Bloom filters are used, e.g., to enhance the privacy of document search [BC07], design privacy-preserving record linkage [SBR09], or obfuscate the schemes of database tables from curious administrators [WA09].

In [BDOZ11], Babaioff et al. address the lack of incentives for Bitcoin users to include recently announced transactions in a block. Furthermore, in [Sye11], Syed et al. propose a user-friendly technique for managing Bitcoin wallets. In [MC13], Moore and Christin study the economic risks that investors face due to Bitcoin exchanges. Clark et al. [CE12] propose the use of the Bitcoin PoW to construct verifiable commitment schemes.

The Bitcoin protocol uses the following cryptographic concepts: SHA256 [NIS13] and RIPEMD160 [DBP96], Merkle trees [Mer82] and the Elliptic Curve Digital Signature Algorithm (ECDSA) [Kob87].

This chapter is based on a text by Arthur Gervais.

Bibliography

[AK14] Elli Androulaki and Ghassan Karame. Hiding transaction amounts and balances in bitcoin. In *Proceedings of International Conference on Trust & Trustworthy Computing (TRUST)*, 2014.

[AKC13] Elli Androulaki, Ghassan Karame, and Srdjan Capkun. Evaluating user privacy in bitcoin. In *Financial Cryptography*, 2013.

[BBL12] Giuseppe Bianchi, Lorenzo Bracciale, and Pierpaolo Loreti. Better than nothing privacy with bloom filters:

To what extent? In *Privacy in Statistical Databases*, pages 348–363. Springer, 2012.

[BBSU12] S. Barber, X. Boyen, E. Shi, and E. Uzun. Bitter to Better - How to Make Bitcoin a Better Currency. In *Proceedings of Financial Cryptography and Data Security*, 2012.

[BC07] Steven Michael Bellovin and William R Cheswick. Privacy-enhanced searches using encrypted bloom filters. 2007.

[BDE⁺13] Tobias Bamert, Christian Decker, Lennart Elsen, Samuel Welten, and Roger Wattenhofer. Have a snack, pay with bitcoin. In *IEEE Internation Conference on Peer-to-Peer Computing (P2P), Trento, Italy*, 2013.

[BDOZ11] M. Babaioff, S. Dobzinski, S. Oren, and A. Zohar. On Bitcoin and Red Balloons. 2011.

[BMC⁺15] Joseph Bonneau, Andrew Miller, Jeremy Clark, Arvind Narayanan, Joshua A. Kroll, and Edward W. Felten. SoK: Research Perspectives and Challenges for Bitcoin and Cryptocurrencies. In *2015 IEEE Symposium on Security and Privacy*, May 2015.

[But14] V. Buterin. A next-generation smart contract and decentralized application platform, 2014.

[CDE⁺16] Kyle Croman, Christian Decker, Ittay Eyal, Adem Efe Gencer, Ari Juels, Ahmed E. Kosba, Andrew Miller, Prateek Saxena, Elaine Shi, Emin Gün Sirer, Dawn Song, and Roger Wattenhofer. On scaling decentralized blockchains. In *Financial Cryptography and Data Security*, 2016.

[CE12] J. Clark and A. Essex. (Short Paper) CommitCoin: Carbon Dating Commitments with Bitcoin. In *Proceedings of Financial Cryptography and Data Security*, 2012.

[CRJ10] Ken Christensen, Allen Roginsky, and Miguel Jimeno. A new analysis of the false positive rate of a bloom filter. *Information Processing Letters*, 110(21):944–949, 2010.

[DBP96] Hans Dobbertin, Antoon Bosselaers, and Bart Preneel. RIPEMD-160: A strengthened version of RIPEMD. In *Fast Software Encryption, Third International Workshop, Cambridge, UK, February 21-23, 1996, Proceedings*, pages 71–82, 1996.

[DW13] Christian Decker and Roger Wattenhofer. Information propagation in the bitcoin network. In *IEEE International Conference on Peer-to-Peer Computing (P2P), Trento, Italy*, September 2013.

[DW14] Christian Decker and Roger Wattenhofer. Bitcoin transaction malleability and mtgox. In *Computer Security - ESORICS 2014 - 19th European Symposium on Research in Computer Security, Wroclaw, Poland, September 7-11, 2014. Proceedings, Part II*, pages 313–326, 2014.

[Eli11] Bitcoin: Tempering the Digital Ring of Gyges or Implausible Pecuniary Privacy, 2011. Available from `http://ssrn.com/abstract=1937769ordoi:10.2139/ssrn.1937769`.

[GKL15] Juan Garay, Aggelos Kiayias, and Nikos Leonardos. The bitcoin backbone protocol: Analysis and applications. In *Annual International Conference on the Theory and Applications of Cryptographic Techniques*, pages 281–310. Springer, 2015.

[HKZG15] E. Heilman, A. Kendler, A. Zohar, and S. Goldberg. Eclipse attacks on bitcoin's peer-to-peer network. 2015.

[KAC12] G.O. Karame, E. Androulaki, and S. Capkun. Two Bitcoins at the Price of One? Double-Spending Attacks on Fast Payments in Bitcoin. In *Conference on Computer and Communication Security (CCS)*, 2012.

[KAR+15] Ghassan O Karame, Elli Androulaki, Marc Roeschlin, Arthur Gervais, and Srdjan Čapkun. Misbehavior in bitcoin: a study of double-spending and accountability. *ACM Transactions on Information and System Security (TISSEC)*, 18(1):2, 2015.

[Ker12] Florian Kerschbaum. Outsourced private set intersection using homomorphic encryption. In *Proceedings of* the *7th ACM Symposium on Information, Computer and Communications Security*, pages 85–86. ACM, 2012.

[KKM14] Philip Koshy, Diana Koshy, and Patrick McDaniel. An analysis of anonymity in bitcoin using p2p network traffic. In *Proceedings of Financial Crypto 2014*, 2014. `http://fc14.ifca.ai/papers/fc14_submission_71.pdf`.

[Kob87] Neal Koblitz. Elliptic curve cryptosystems. *Mathematics of computation*, 48(177):203–209, 1987.

[MC13] Tyler Moore and Nicolas Christin. Beware the middleman: Empirical analysis of bitcoin-exchange risk. In *Financial Cryptography and Data Security*, pages 25–33, 2013.

[Mer82] R.C. Merkle. Method of providing digital signatures, January 5 1982. US Patent 4,309,569.

[MGGR13] Ian Miers, Christina Garman, Matthew Green, and Aviel D Rubin. Zerocoin: Anonymous distributed e-cash from bitcoin. In *Security and Privacy (SP), 2013 IEEE Symposium on*, pages 397–411. IEEE, 2013.

[MLP$^+$15] Andrew Miller, James Litton, Andrew Pachulski, Neal Gupta, Dave Levin, Neil Spring, and Bobby Bhattacharjee. Discovering bitcoin's public topology and influential nodes, 2015.

[MPJ$^+$16] Sarah Meiklejohn, Marjori Pomarole, Grant Jordan, Kirill Levchenko, Damon McCoy, Geoffrey M. Voelker, and Stefan Savage. A fistful of bitcoins: characterizing payments among men with no names. *Commun. ACM*, 59(4):86–93, 2016.

[Mul83] James K Mullin. A second look at bloom filters. *Communications of the ACM*, 26(8):570–571, 1983.

[NIS13] NIST. Sha 256, 2013. Available from: `https://web.archive.org/web/20130526224224/http://csrc.nist.gov/groups/STM/cavp/documents/shs/sha256-384-512.pdf`.

[NK09] Ryo Nojima and Youki Kadobayashi. Cryptographically secure bloom-filters. *Transactions on Data Privacy*, 2(2):131–139, 2009.

[OKH13] Micha Ober, Stefan Katzenbeisser, and Kay Hamacher. Structure and anonymity of the bitcoin transaction graph. *Future Internet*, 5(2):237–250, 2013.

[RH11] F. Reid and M. Harrigan. An Analysis of Anonymity in the Bitcoin System. 2011.

[Ros14] Meni Rosenfeld. Analysis of hashrate-based double spending. *arXiv preprint arXiv:1402.2009*, 2014.

[RS13] Dorit Ron and Adi Shamir. Quantitative analysis of the full bitcoin transaction graph. In *Financial Cryptography and Data Security*, pages 6–24, 2013. http://eprint.iacr.org/2012/584.pdf.

[SBR09] Rainer Schnell, Tobias Bachteler, and Jörg Reiher. Privacy-preserving record linkage using bloom filters. *BMC Medical Informatics and Decision Making*, 9(1):41, 2009.

[Sye11] Bitcoin Gateway, A Peer-to-peer Bitcoin Vault and Payment Network, 2011. Available from http://arimaa.com/bitcoin/.

[WA09] Chiemi Watanabe and Yuko Arai. Privacy-preserving queries for a das model using encrypted bloom filter. In *Database systems for advanced applications*, pages 491–495. Springer, 2009.

Chapter 11

Advanced Blockchain

In this chapter we study various advanced blockchain concepts, which are popular in research.

11.1 Selfish Mining

Satoshi Nakamoto suggested that it is rational to be altruistic, e.g., by always attaching newly found block to the longest chain. But is it true?

Definition 11.1 (Selfish Mining). *A selfish miner hopes to earn the reward of a larger share of blocks than its hardware would allow. The selfish miner achieves this by temporarily keeping newly found blocks secret.*

Remarks:

- If the selfish miner is more than two blocks ahead, the original research suggested to always answer a newly published block by releasing the oldest unpublished block. The idea is that honest miners will then split their mining power between these two blocks. However, what matters is how long it takes the honest miners to find the next block, to extend the public blockchain. This time does not change whether the honest miners split their efforts or not. Hence the case $d_p < d_s - 1$ is not needed in Algorithm 11.2.

- The concept of selfishness is introduced in Appendix 14.

161

Algorithm 11.2 Selfish Mining

1: Idea: Mine secretly, without immediately publishing newly found blocks
2: Let d_p be the depth of the public blockchain
3: Let d_s be the depth of the secretly mined blockchain
4: **if** a new block b_p is published, i.e., d_p has increased by 1 **then**
5:     **if** $d_p > d_s$ **then**
6:         Start mining on that newly published block b_p
7:     **else if** $d_p = d_s$ **then**
8:         Publish secretly mined block b_s
9:         Mine on b_s and publish newly found block immediately
10:     **else if** $d_p = d_s - 1$ **then**
11:         Publish both secretly mined blocks
12:     **end if**
13: **end if**

Theorem 11.3 (Selfish Mining). *It may be rational to mine selfishly, depending on two parameters α and γ, where α is the ratio of the mining power of the selfish miner, and γ is the share of the altruistic mining power the selfish miner can reach in the network if the selfish miner publishes a block right after seeing a newly published block. Precisely, the selfish miner share is*

$$\frac{\alpha(1-\alpha)^2(4\alpha + \gamma(1-2\alpha)) - \alpha^3}{1 - \alpha(1 + (2-\alpha)\alpha)}.$$

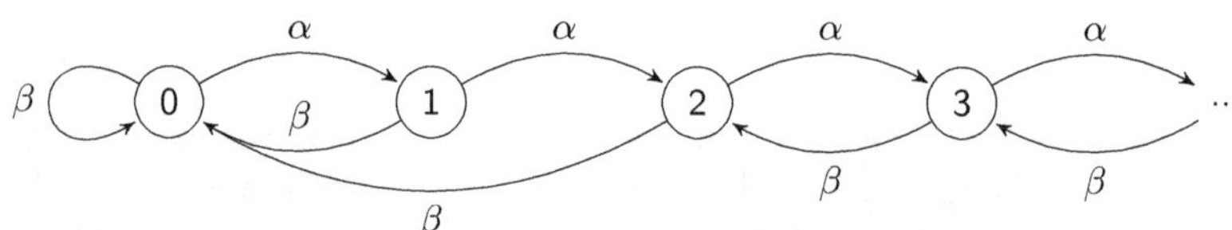

Figure 11.4: Each state of the Markov chain represents how many blocks the selfish miner is ahead, i.e., $d_s - d_p$. In each state, the selfish miner finds a block with probability α, and the honest miners find a block with probability $\beta = 1 - \alpha$. The interesting cases are the "irregular" β arrow from state 2 to state 0, and the β arrow from state 1 to state 0 as it will include three subcases.

Proof. We model the current state of the system with a Markov chain, see Figure 11.4. Appendix 16 will give an introduction to Markov chains.

We can solve the following Markov chain equations to figure out the probability of each state in the stationary distribution:

$$p_1 = \alpha p_0$$
$$\beta p_{i+1} = \alpha p_i, \text{ for all } i > 1$$
$$\text{and } 1 = \sum_i p_i.$$

Using $\rho = \alpha/\beta$, we express all terms of above sum with p_1:

$$1 = \frac{p_1}{\alpha} + p_1 \sum_{i \geq 0} \rho^i = \frac{p_1}{\alpha} + \frac{p_1}{1-\rho}, \text{ hence } p_1 = \frac{2\alpha^2 - \alpha}{\alpha^2 + \alpha - 1}.$$

Each state has an outgoing arrow with probability β. If this arrow is taken, one or two blocks (depending on the state) are attached that will eventually end up in the main chain of the blockchain. In state 0 (if arrow β is taken), the honest miners attach a block. In all states i with $i > 2$, the selfish miner eventually attaches a block. In state 2, the selfish miner directly attaches 2 blocks because of Line 11 in Algorithm 11.2.

State 1 in Line 8 is interesting. The selfish miner secretly was 1 block ahead, but now (after taking the β arrow) the honest miners are attaching a competing block. We have a race who attaches the next block, and where. There are three possibilities:

- Either the selfish miner manages to attach another block to its own block, giving 2 blocks to the selfish miner. This happens with probability α.

- Or the honest miners attach a block (with probability β) to their previous honest block (with probability $1 - \gamma$). This gives 2 blocks to the honest miners, with total probability $\beta(1 - \gamma)$.

- Or the honest miners attach a block to the selfish block, giving 1 block to each side, with probability $\beta\gamma$.

The blockchain process is just a biased random walk through these states. Since blocks are attached whenever we have an outgoing β arrow, the total number of blocks being attached per state is simply $1 + p_1 + p_2$ (all states attach a single block, except states 1 and 2 which attach 2 blocks each).

As argued above, of these blocks, $1 - p_0 + p_2 + \alpha p_1 - \beta(1 - \gamma)p_1$ are blocks by the selfish miner, i.e., the ratio of selfish blocks in the blockchain is

$$\frac{1 - p_0 + p_2 + \alpha p_1 - \beta(1 - \gamma)p_1}{1 + p_1 + p_2}.$$

$\square$

Remarks:

- If the miner is honest (altruistic), then a miner with computational share α should expect to find an α fraction of the blocks. For some values of α and γ the ratio of Theorem 11.3 is higher than α.

- In particular, if $\gamma = 0$ (the selfish miner only wins a race in Line 8 if it manages to mine 2 blocks in a row), the break even of selfish mining happens at $\alpha = 1/3$.

- If $\gamma = 1/2$ (the selfish miner learns about honest blocks very quickly and manages to convince half of the honest miners to mine on the selfish block instead of the slightly earlier published honest block), already $\alpha = 1/4$ is enough to have a higher share in expectation.

- And if $\gamma = 1$ (the selfish miner controls the network, and can hide any honest block until the selfish block is published) any $\alpha > 0$ justifies selfish mining.

11.2 DAG-Blockchain

Traditional Bitcoin-like blockchains require mining blocks sequentially. Sometimes effort is wasted if two blocks happen to be mined at roughly the same time, as one of these two blocks is going to become obsolete. DAG-blockchains (where DAG stands for directed acyclic graph) try to prevent such wasted blocks. They allow for faster block production, as forks are less of a problem.

Definition 11.5 (DAG-blockchain). *In a DAG-blockchain the genesis block does not reference other blocks. Every other block has at least one (and possibly multiple references) to previous blocks.*

Definition 11.6 (DAG Relations). *Block p is a dag-parent of block b if block b references (includes a hash) to p. Likewise b is a dag-child of p. Block a is a dag-ancestor of block b, if a is b's dag-parent, dag-grandparent (dag-parent of dag-parent), dag-grandgrandparent, and so on. Likewise b is a's dag-descendant.*

Theorem 11.7. *There are no cycles in a DAG-blockchain.*

Proof. A block b includes its dag-parents' hashes. These dag-parents themselves include the hashes of their dag-parents, etc. To get a cycle of references, some of b's dag-ancestors must include b's hash, which is cryptographically infeasible. $\square$

Definition 11.8 (Tree Relations). *We are going to implicitly mark some of the references in the DAG of blocks, such that these marked references form a tree, directed towards the genesis block. For every non-genesis block one edge to one of its dag-parents is marked. We use the prefix "tree" to denote these special relations. The marked edge is between tree-parent and tree-child. The tree also defines tree-ancestors and tree-descendants.*

Remarks:

- In other words, every tree-something is also a dag-something, but not necessarily vice versa.

- Blocks do not specify who is their tree-parent, or the order of their dag-parents. Instead, tree-parents are implicitly defined as follows.

Definition 11.9 (DAG Weight). *The weight of a dag-ancestor block a with respect to a block b is defined as the number of tree-descendants of a in the set of dag-ancestors of b. If two blocks a and a' have the same weight, we use the hashes of a and a' to break ties.*

Definition 11.10 (Parent Order). *Let x and y be any pair of dag-parents of b, and z be the lowest common tree-ancestor of x and y. x' and y' are the tree-children of z that are tree-ancestors of x and y respectively. If x' has a higher weight than y', then block b orders dag-parent x before y.*

Definition 11.11 (Tree-Parent). *The tree-parent of b is the first dag-parent in b's parent order.*

Remarks:

- Now we can totally order all the blocks in the DAG-Blockchain.

Algorithm 11.12 DAG-Blockchain Ordering

1: We totally order all dag-ancestors of block b as $<_b$ as follows:
2: Initialize $<_b$ as empty
3: **for** all dag-parents p of b, in their parent order **do**
4:     Compute $<_p$ (recursively)
5:     Remove from $<_p$ any blocks already included in $<_b$
6:     Append $<_p$ at the end of $<_b$
7: **end for**
8: Append block b at the end of $<_b$

Theorem 11.13. *Let p be the tree-parent of b. The order of blocks $<_b$ computed by Algorithm 11.12 extends the order $<_p$ by appending some blocks.*

Proof. Block p is the first dag-parent of b, so in the first iteration of the loop, we have $<_b\ =\ <_p$. Further modifications of $<_b$ consist only of appending more blocks to $<_b$, ending with block b itself.　□

Remarks:

- Note that b is appended to the order only after ordering all its dag-ancestors. The genesis block is the only block where the recursion will stop, so the genesis block is always first in the total order.

- By Theorem 11.13 tree-children extend the order of their tree-parent, so appending blocks to the DAG preserves the previous order and new blocks are appended at the end.

Definition 11.14 (Transaction Order). *Transactions in each block are ordered by the miner of the block. Since blocks themselves are ordered, all transactions are ordered. If two transactions contradict each other (e.g. they try to spend the same money twice), the first transaction in the total order is considered executed, while the second transaction is simply ignored (or possibly punished).*

11.3 Smart Contracts

Definition 11.15 (Ethereum). *Ethereum is a distributed state machine. Unlike Bitcoin, Ethereum promises to run arbitrary computer programs in a blockchain.*

Remarks:

- Like the Bitcoin network, Ethereum consists of nodes that are connected by a random virtual network. These nodes can join or leave the network arbitrarily. There is no central coordinator.

- Like in Bitcoin, users broadcast cryptographically signed transactions in the network. Nodes collate these transactions and decide on the ordering of transactions by putting them in a block on the Ethereum blockchain.

Definition 11.16 (Smart Contract). *Smart contracts are programs deployed on the Ethereum blockchain that have associated storage and can execute arbitrarily complex logic.*

Remarks:

- Smart Contracts are written in higher level programming languages like Solidity, Vyper, etc. and are compiled down to EVM (Ethereum Virtual Machine) bytecode, which is a Turing complete low level programming language.

- Smart contracts cannot be changed after deployment. But most smart contracts contain mutable storage, and this storage can be used to adapt the behavior of the smart contract. With this, many smart contracts can update to a new version.

Definition 11.17 (Account). *Ethereum knows two kinds of accounts. Externally Owned Accounts (EOAs) are controlled by individuals, with a secret key. Contract Accounts (CAs) are for smart contracts. CAs are not controlled by a user.*

Definition 11.18 (Ethereum Transaction). *An Ethereum transaction is sent by a user who controls an EOA to the Ethereum network. A transaction contains:*

- *Nonce: This "number only used once" is simply a counter that counts how many transactions the account of the sender of the transaction has already sent.*

- *160-bit address of the recipient.*

- *The transaction is signed by the user controlling the EOA.*

- *Value: The amount of Wei (the native currency of Ethereum) to transfer from the sender to the recipient.*

- *Data: Optional data field, which can be accessed by smart contracts.*

- *StartGas: A value representing the maximum amount of computation this transaction is allowed to use.*

- *GasPrice: How many Wei per unit of Gas the sender is paying. Miners will probably select transactions with a higher GasPrice, so a high GasPrice will make sure that the transaction is executed more quickly.*

Remarks:

- There are three types of transactions.

Definition 11.19 (Simple Transaction). *A simple transaction in Ethereum transfers some of the native currency, called Wei, from one EOA to another. Higher units of curency are called Szabo, Finney, and Ether, with 10^{18} Wei $= 10^6$ Szabo $= 10^3$ Finney $= 1$ Ether. The data field in a simple transaction is empty.*

Definition 11.20 (Smart Contract Creation Transaction). *A transaction whose recipient address field is set to 0 and whose data field is set to compiled EVM code is used to deploy that code as a smart contract on the Ethereum blockchain. The contract is considered deployed after it has been mined in a block and is included in the blockchain at a sufficient depth.*

Definition 11.21 (Smart Contract Execution Transaction). *A transaction that has a smart contract address in its recipient field and code to execute a specific function of that contract in its data field.*

Remarks:

- Smart Contracts can execute computations, store data, send Ether to other accounts or smart contracts, and invoke other smart contracts.

- Smart contracts can be programmed to self destruct. This is the only way to remove them again from the Ethereum blockchain.

- Each contract stores data in 3 separate entities: storage, memory, and stack. Of these, only the storage area is persistent between transactions. Storage is a key-value store of 256 bit words to 256 bit words. The storage data is persisted in the Ethereum blockchain, like the hard disk of a traditional computer. Memory and stack are for intermediate storage required while running a specific function, similar to RAM and registers of a traditional computer. The read/write gas costs of persistent storage is significantly higher than those of memory and stack.

Definition 11.22 (Gas). *Gas is the unit of an atomic computation, like swapping two variables. Complex operations use more than 1 Gas, e.g., ADDing two numbers costs 3 Gas.*

Remarks:

- As Ethereum contracts are programs (with loops, function calls, and recursions), end users need to pay more gas for more computations. In particular, smart contracts might call another smart contract as a subroutine, and StartGas must include enough gas to pay for all these function calls invoked by the transaction.

- The product of StartGas and GasPrice is the maximum cost of the entire transaction.

- Transactions are an all or nothing affair. If the entire transaction could not be finished within the StartGas limit, an Out-of-Gas exception is raised. The state of the blockchain is reverted back to its values before the transaction. The amount of gas consumed is not returned back to the sender.

Definition 11.23 (Block). *In Ethereum, like in Bitcoin, a block is a collection of transactions that is considered a part of the canonical history of transactions. Among other things, a block contains: pointers to parent and up to two uncles, the hash of the root node of a trie structure populated with each transaction of the block, the hash of the root node of the state trie (after transactions have been executed)*

Remarks:

- Ethereum allows blocks to not only have a parent, but also up to two "uncles" (childless blocks). In contrast to above description, blocks must specify the main parent.

- In Ethereum, new blocks are mined approximately every 15 seconds (as opposed to 10 minutes in Bitcoin). New blocks being generated in such rapid succession leads to a lot of childless blocks. Uncles have been introduced to not "waste" those blocks.

- In Ethereum, the original uncle-miners get 7/8 of the block reward. The miner who references these uncle blocks also gets a small reward. This reward depends on the height-difference of the uncle and the included parent. Also, to be included, the uncle and the current block should have a common ancestor not too far in the past.

11.4 Payment Hubs

How to we enable many parties to send payments to each other efficiently?

Definition 11.24 (Payment Hub). *Multiple parties can send payments to each other by means of a payment hub.*

Remarks:

- While we could always call the smart contract to transfer money between users that joined the hub, every smart contract call costs as it involves the blockchain. Rather, we want a frugal system with just few blockchain transactions.

Definition 11.25 (Smart Contract Hub). *A smart contract hub is a payment hub that is realized by a smart contract on a blockchain and an off-chain server. The smart contract and the server together enable off-chain payments between users that joined the hub.*

Algorithm 11.26 Smart Contract Hub

1: Users join the hub by depositing some native currency of the blockchain into the smart contract
2: Funds of all participants are maintained together as a fungible pool in the smart contract
3: Time is divided into epochs: in each epoch users can send each other payment transactions through the server
4: The server does the bookkeeping of who has paid how much to whom during the epoch
5: At the end of the epoch, the server aggregates all balances into a commitment, which is sent to the smart contract
6: Also at the end of the epoch, the server sends a proof to each user, informing about the current account balance
7: Each user can verify that its balance is correct; if not the user can call the smart contract with its proof to get its money back

---

Remarks:

- The smart contract lives forever, but the server can disappear anytime. If it does, nodes can show their recent balance proofs to the smart contract and withdraw their balances.

- The server can be scaled to in terms of latency and number of users. The smart contract does not need to scale as it only needs to just accept one commitment per epoch.

- In case the server disappears, the smart contract will be flooded with withdrawal requests, and could be subject to delays based on the delays of the underlying blockchain.

11.5 Proof-of-Stake

Almost all of the energy consumption of permissionless (everybody can participate) blockchains is wasted because of proof-of-work. Proof-of-stake avoids these wasteful computations, without going all the way to permissioned (the participating nodes are known a priori) systems such as Paxos or PBFT.

Definition 11.27 (Proof-of-stake). *Proof-of-work awards block rewards to the lucky miner that solved a cryptopuzzle. In contrast, proof-of-stake awards block rewards proportionally to the economic stake in the system.*

Remarks:

- Literally, "the rich get richer".

- Ethereum is expected to move to proof-of-stake eventually.

- There are multiple flavors of proof-of-stake algorithms.

Definition 11.28 (Chain based proof-of-stake). *Accounts hold lottery tickets according to their stake. The lottery is pseudo-random, in the sense that hash functions computed on the state of the blockchain will select which account is winning. The winning account can extend the longest chain by a block, and earn the block reward.*

Remarks:

- It gets tricky if the actual winner of the lottery does not produce a block in time, or some nodes do not see this block in time. This is why some suggested proof-of-stake systems add a voting phase (a la byzantine fault tolerance, see Chapter 4).

Definition 11.29 (BFT based proof-of-stake). *The lottery winner only gets to propose a block to be added to the blockchain. A committee then votes (yes, byzantine fault tolerance) whether to accept that block into the blockchain. If no agreement is reached, this process is repeated.*

Remarks:

- Proof-of-stake can be attacked in various ways. Let us discuss the two most prominent attacks.

- Most importantly, there is the "nothing at stake" attack: In blockchains, forks occur naturally. In proof-of-work, a fork is resolved because every miner has to choose which blockchain fork to extend, as it does not pay off to mine on a hopeless fork. Eventually, some chain will end up with more miners, and that chain is considered to be the real blockchain, whereas other (childless) blocks are just not being extended. In a proof-of-stake system, a user can trivially extend all prongs of a fork. As generating a block costs nothing, the miner has no incentive to not extend all the prongs of the fork. This results in a situation with more and more forks, and no canonical order of transactions. If there is a double-spend attack, there is no way to tell which blockchain is valid, as all blockchains are the same length (all miners are extending all forks). It can be argued that honest miners, who want to preserve the value of the network, will extend the first prong of the fork that they see. But that leaves room for a dishonest miner to double spend by moving their mining opportunity to the appropriate fork at the appropriate time.

- Long range attack: As there are no physical resources being used to produce blocks in a proof-of-stake system, nothing prevents a bad player from creating an alternate blockchain starting at the genesis block, and make it longer than the canonical blockchain. New nodes may have difficulties to determine which blockchain is the real established blockchain. In proof-of-work, long range attacks takes an enormous amount of computing power. In proof-of-stake systems, a new node has to check with trusted sources to know what the canonical blockchain is.

Chapter Notes

Eyal and Sirer introduced selfish mining in [ES14]. Similarly, Courtois and Bahack [CB14] study subversive mining strategies. In [NKMS15], Nayak et al. combine selfish mining and eclipse attacks. Sapirshtein et al. [SSZ15] devise optimal adversarial strategies for selfish mining in Bitcoin.

Vitalik Buterin introduced Ethereum in the 2013 whitepaper [eth13]. In 2014, Ethereum Foundation was created to create Ethereum's first implementation. An online crowd-sale was conducted to raise around 31,000 BTC (around USD 18 million at the time) for this. In this sense, Ethereum was the first ICO. Ethereum has also attempted to write a formal specification of its protocol in their yellow paper [Gav18]. This is in contrast to Bitcoin, which doesn't have a formal specification.

Bitcoin's blockchain forms as a chain, i.e., each block (except the genesis block) has a parent block. The longest chain with the highest difficulty is considered the main chain. GHOST [SZ15] is an alternative to the longest chain rule for establishing consensus in PoW based blockchains and aims to alleviate adverse impacts of stale blocks. Ethereum's blockchain structure is a variant of GHOST. Other systems based on DAGs have been proposed in [SLZ16], [SZ18], [LLX$^+$18], and [LSZ15].

Khalil and Gervais [KG18] introduced the notion of a payment hub that is a combination of a smart contract and an online server. Plasma [JP17] is another family of systems that uses a smart contract on the Ethereum blockchain and one or more off-chain operators to enable off-chain transactions.

Proof of Stake was first introduced in PPCoin [KN12]. The most well known Proof of Stake system is the one being implemented for Ethereum, which involves a transition phase from PoW to PoS [BG17], and finally, on to a more formally constructed PoS [VZ18]. More details are available in this article [Cho18] by Jon Choi.

Bibliography

[BG17] Vitalik Buterin and Virgil Griffith. Casper the friendly finality gadget. *CoRR*, abs/1710.09437, 2017.

[CB14] Nicolas T. Courtois and Lear Bahack. On subversive miner strategies and block withholding attack in bitcoin digital currency. *CoRR*, abs/1402.1718, 2014.

[Cho18] Jon Choi. Ethereum casper 101. 2018. Available from: https://medium.com/@jonchoi/ethereum-casper-101-7a851a4f1eb0.

[ES14] Ittay Eyal and Emin Gün Sirer. Majority is not enough: Bitcoin mining is vulnerable. In *Financial Cryptography and Data Security*, pages 436–454. Springer, 2014.

[eth13] A Next-Generation Smart Contract and Decentralized Application Platform, 2013. Available from: `https://github.com/ethereum/wiki/wiki/White-Paper`.

[Gav18] Gavin Wood. Ethereum: A Secure Decentralised Generalised Transaction Ledger, Byzantium Version, 2018. Available from: `https://ethereum.github.io/yellowpaper/paper.pdf`.

[JP17] Vitalik Buterin Joseph Poon. Plasma: Scalable autonomous smart contracts, 2017.

[KG18] Rami Khalil and Arthur Gervais. Nocust - a non-custodial 2nd-layer financial intermediary. Cryptology ePrint Archive, Report 2018/642, 2018. `https://eprint.iacr.org/2018/642`.

[KN12] Sunny King and Scott Nadal. Ppcoin: Peer-to-peer crypto-currency with proof-of-stake. *self-published paper, August*, 19, 2012.

[LLX+18] Chenxing Li, Peilun Li, Wei Xu, Fan Long, and Andrew Chi-Chih Yao. Scaling nakamoto consensus to thousands of transactions per second. *CoRR*, abs/1805.03870, 2018.

[LSZ15] Yoad Lewenberg, Yonatan Sompolinsky, and Aviv Zohar. Inclusive block chain protocols. In *Financial Cryptography and Data Security*, pages 528–547. Springer, 2015.

[NKMS15] Kartik Nayak, Srijan Kumar, Andrew Miller, and Elaine Shi. Stubborn mining: Generalizing selfish mining and combining with an eclipse attack. Technical report, IACR Cryptology ePrint Archive 2015, 2015.

[SLZ16] Yonatan Sompolinsky, Yoad Lewenberg, and Aviv Zohar. Spectre: A fast and scalable cryptocurrency protocol. Cryptology ePrint Archive, Report 2016/1159, 2016. `https://eprint.iacr.org/2016/1159`.

[SSZ15] Ayelet Sapirshtein, Yonatan Sompolinsky, and Aviv Zohar. Optimal selfish mining strategies in bitcoin. *arXiv preprint arXiv:1507.06183*, 2015.

[SZ15] Yonatan Sompolinsky and Aviv Zohar. Secure high-rate transaction processing in bitcoin. In *Financial Cryptography and Data Security*, pages 507–527. Springer, 2015.

[SZ18] Yonatan Sompolinsky and Aviv Zohar. Phantom: A scalable blockdag protocol. Cryptology ePrint Archive, Report 2018/104, 2018. `https://eprint.iacr.org/2018/104`.

[VZ18] Aditya Asgaonkar Georgios Piliouras Vlad Zamfir, Nate Rush. Introducing the "minimal cbc casper" family of consensus protocols. 2018. Available from: `https://github.com/cbc-casper/cbc-casper-paper/blob/master/cbc-casper-paper-draft.pdf`.

Chapter 12

Consistency & Logical Time

You submit a comment on your favorite social media platform using your phone. The comment is immediately visible on the phone, but not on your laptop. Is this level of consistency acceptable?

12.1   Consistency Models

Definition 12.1 (Object). *An **object** is a variable or a data structure storing information.*

Remarks:

- Object is a general term for any entity that can be modified, like a queue, stack, memory slot, file system, etc.

Definition 12.2 (Operation). *An **operation** f accesses or manipulates an object. The operation f starts at wall-clock time f_* and ends at wall-clock time $f_\dagger$.*

Remarks:

- The wall-clock time concept is borrowed from Appendix 15.

- An operation can be as simple as extracting an element from a data structure, but an operation may also be more complex, like fetching an element, modifying it and storing it again.

- If $f_\dagger < g_*$, we simply write $f < g$.

Definition 12.3 (Execution). *An **execution** E is a set of operations on one or multiple objects that are executed by a set of nodes.*

Definition 12.4 (Sequential Execution). *An execution restricted to a single node is a **sequential execution**. All operations are executed sequentially, which means that no two operations f and g are concurrent, i.e., we have $f < g$ or $g < f$.*

Definition 12.5 (Semantic Equivalence). *Two executions are **semantically equivalent** if they contain exactly the same operations. Moreover, each pair of corresponding operations has the same effect in both executions.*

Remarks:

- For example, when dealing with a stack object, corresponding `pop` operations in two different semantically equivalent executions must yield the same element of the stack.

- In general, the notion of semantic equivalence is non-trivial and dependent on the type of the object.

Definition 12.6 (Linearizability). *An execution E is called **linearizable** (or atomically consistent), if there is a sequence of operations (sequential execution) S such that:*

- *S is correct and semantically equivalent to E.*

- *Whenever $f < g$ for two operations f, g in E, then also $f < g$ in S.*

Definition 12.7. *A **linearization point** of operation f is some $f_\bullet \in [f_*, f_\dagger]$.*

Lemma 12.8. *An execution E is linearizable if and only if there exist linearization points such that the sequential execution S that results in ordering the operations according to those linearization points is semantically equivalent to E.*

Proof. Let f and g be two operations in E with $f_\dagger < g_*$. Then by definition of linearization points we also have $f_\bullet < g_\bullet$ and therefore $f < g$ in S. $\qquad\square$

Definition 12.9 (Sequential Consistency). *An execution E is called **sequentially consistent**, if there is a sequence of operations S such that:*

- *S is correct and semantically equivalent to E.*

- *Whenever $f < g$ for two operations f, g **on the same node** in E, then also $f < g$ in S.*

Lemma 12.10. *Every linearizable execution is also sequentially consistent, i.e., linearizability $\implies$ sequential consistency.*

Proof. Since linearizability (order of operations *on any* nodes must be respected) is stricter than sequential consistency (only order of operations *on the same node* must be respected), the lemma follows immediately. $\qquad\square$

Definition 12.11 (Quiescent Consistency). *An execution E is called **quiescently consistent**, if there is a sequence of operations S such that:*

- *S is correct and semantically equivalent to E.*

- *Let t be some quiescent point, i.e., for all operations f we have $f_\dagger < t$ or $f_* > t$. Then for every t and every pair of operations g, h with $g_\dagger < t$ and $h_* > t$ we also have $g < h$ in S.*

Lemma 12.12. *Every linearizable execution is also quiescently consistent, i.e., linearizability $\implies$ quiescent consistency.*

Proof. Let E be the original execution and S be the semantically equivalent sequential execution. Let t be a quiescent point and consider two operations g, h with $g_\dagger < t < h_*$. Then we have $g < h$ in S. This is also guaranteed by linearizability since $g_\dagger < t < h_*$ implies $g < h$. $\qquad\square$

Lemma 12.13. *Sequentially consistent and quiescent consistency do not imply one another.*

Proof. There are executions that are sequentially consistent but not quiescently consistent. An object initially has value 2. We apply two operations to this object: *inc* (increment the object by 1) and *double* (multiply the object by 2). Assume that *inc* < *double*, but *inc* and *double* are executed on different nodes. Then a result of 5 (first double, then inc) is sequentially consistent but not quiescently consistent.

There are executions that are quiescently consistent but not sequentially consistent. An object initially has value 2. Assume to have three operations on two nodes u and v. Node u calls first *inc* then *double*, node v calls *inc* once with $inc_*^v < inc_\dagger^u < double_*^u < inc_\dagger^v$. Since there is no quiescent point, quiescent consistency is okay with a sequential execution that doubles first, resulting in $((2 \cdot 2) + 1) + 1 = 6$. The sequential execution demands that $inc^u < double^u$, hence the result should be strictly larger than 6 (either 7 or 8). $\qquad\square$

Definition 12.14. *A system or an implementation is called **linearizable** if it ensures that every possible execution is linearizable. Analogous definitions exist for sequential and quiescent consistency.*

Remarks:

- In the introductory social media example, a linearizable implementation would have to make sure that the comment is immediately visible on any device, as the *read* operation starts after the *write* operation finishes. If the system is only sequentially consistent, the comment does not need to be immediately visible on every device.

Definition 12.15 (restricted execution). *Let E be an execution involving operations on multiple objects. For some object o we let the **restricted execution** $E|o$ be the execution E filtered to only contain operations involving object o.*

Definition 12.16. *A consistency model is called **composable** if the following holds: If for every object o the restricted execution $E|o$ is consistent, then also E is consistent.*

Remarks:

- Composability enables to implement, verify and execute multiple concurrent objects independently.

Lemma 12.17. *Sequential consistency is not composable.*

Proof. We consider an execution E with two nodes u and v, which operate on two objects x and y initially set to 0. The operations are as follows: u_1 reads $x = 1$, u_2 writes $y := 1$, v_1 reads $y = 1$, v_2 writes $x := 1$ with $u_1 < u_2$ on node u and $v_1 < v_2$ on node v. It is clear that $E|x$ as well as $E|y$ are sequentially consistent as the write operations may be before the respective read operations. In contrast, execution E is *not* sequentially consistent: Neither u_1 nor v_1 can possibly be the initial operation in any correct semantically equivalent sequential execution S, as that would imply reading 1 when the variable is still 0. $\square$

Theorem 12.18. *Linearizability is composable.*

Proof. Let E be an execution composed of multiple restricted executions $E|x$. For any object x there is a sequential execution $S|x$ that is semantically consistent to $E|x$ and in which the operations are ordered according to wall-clock-linearization points. Let S be the sequential execution ordered according to all linearization points of all executions $E|x$. S is semantically equivalent to E as $S|x$ is semantically equivalent to $E|x$ for all objects x and two object-disjoint executions cannot interfere. Furthermore, if $f_\dagger < g_*$ in E, then also $f_\bullet < g_\bullet$ in E and therefore also $f < g$ in S. $\square$

12.2 Logical Clocks

To capture dependencies between nodes in an implementation, we can use logical clocks. These are supposed to respect the so-called happened-before relation.

Definition 12.19. *Let S_u be a sequence of operations on some node u and define "$\rightarrow$" to be the **happened-before relation** on $E := S_1 \cup \cdots \cup S_n$ that satisfies the following three conditions:*

1. *If a local operation f occurs before operation g on the same node $(f < g)$, then $f \rightarrow g$.*

2. *If f is a send operation of one node, and g is the corresponding receive operation of another node, then $f \rightarrow g$.*

3. *If f, g, h are operations such that $f \to g$ and $g \to h$ then also $f \to h$.*

Remarks:

- If for two distinct operations f, g neither $f \to g$ nor $g \to f$, then we also say f and g are *independent* and write $f \sim g$. Sequential computations are characterized by $\to$ being a total order, whereas the computation is entirely concurrent if no operations f, g with $f \to g$ exist.

Definition 12.20 (Happened-before consistency). *An execution E is called **happened-before consistent**, if there is a sequence of operations S such that:*

- *S is correct and semantically equivalent to E.*

- *Whenever $f \to g$ for two operations f, g in E, then also $f < g$ in S.*

Lemma 12.21. *Happened-before consistency = sequential consistency.*

Proof. Both consistency models execute all operations of a single node in the sequential order. In addition, happened-before consistency also respects messages between nodes. However, messages are also ordered by sequential consistency because of semantic equivalence (a receive cannot be before the corresponding send). Finally, even though transitivity is defined more formally in happened-before consistency, also sequential consistency respects transitivity.

In addition, sequential consistency orders two operations o_u, o_v on two different nodes u, v if o_v can see a state change caused by o_u. Such a state change does not happen out of the blue, in practice some messages between u and v (maybe via "shared blackboard" or some other form of communication) will be involved to communicate the state change. $\square$

Definition 12.22 (Logical clock). *A logical clock is a family of functions c_u that map every operation $f \in E$ on node u to some logical time $c_u(f)$ such that the happened-before relation $\to$ is respected, i.e., for two operations g on node u and h on node v*

$$g \to h \implies c_u(g) < c_v(h).$$

Definition 12.23. *If it additionally holds that $c_u(g) < c_v(h) \implies g \to h$, then the clock is called a **strong logical clock**.*

Remarks:

- In algorithms we write c_u for the current logical time of node u.

- The simplest logical clock is the *Lamport clock*, given in Algorithm 12.24. Every message includes a timestamp, such that the receiving node may update its current logical time.

Algorithm 12.24 Lamport clock

1: (Code for node u)
2: Initialize $c_u := 0$.
3: Upon local operation: Increment current local time $c_u := c_u + 1$.

4: Upon send operation: Increment $c_u := c_u + 1$ and include c_u as T in message.
5: Upon receive operation: Extract T from message and update $c_u := \max(c_u, T) + 1$.

Theorem 12.25. *Lamport clocks are logical clocks.*

Proof. If for two operations f, g it holds that $f \to g$, then according to the definition three cases are possible.

1. If $f < g$ on the same node u, then $c_u(f) < c_u(g)$.

2. Let g be a receive operation on node v corresponding to some send operation f on another node u. We have $c_v(g) \geq T + 1 = c_u(f) + 1 > c_u(f)$.

3. Transitivity follows with $f \to g$ and $g \to h \Rightarrow g \to h$, and the first two cases.

$\square$

Remarks:

- Lamport logical clocks are not strong logical clocks, which means we cannot completely reconstruct $\rightarrow$ from the family of clocks c_u.

- To achieve a strong logical clock, nodes also have to gather information about other clocks in the system, i.e., node u needs to have a idea of node v's clock, for every u, v. This is what *vector clocks* in Algorithm 12.26 do: Each node u stores its knowledge about other node's logical clocks in an n-dimensional vector c_u.

Algorithm 12.26 Vector clocks

1: (Code for node u)
2: Initialize $c_u[v] := 0$ for all other nodes v.
3: Upon local operation: Increment current local time $c_u[u] := c_u[u] + 1$.
4: Upon send operation: Increment $c_u[u] := c_u[u] + 1$ and include the whole vector c_u as d in message.
5: Upon receive operation: Extract vector d from message and update $c_u[v] := \max(d[v], c_u[v])$ for all entries v. Increment $c_u[u] := c_u[u] + 1$.

Theorem 12.27. *Define $c_u < c_v$ if and only if $c_u[w] \leq c_v[w]$ for all entries w, and $c_u[x] < c_v[x]$ for at least one entry x. Then the vector clocks are strong logical clocks.*

Proof. We are given two operations f, g, with operation f on node u, and operation g on node v, possibly $v = u$.

If we have $f \rightarrow g$, then there must be a happened-before-path of operations and messages from f to g. According to Algorithm 12.26, $c_v(g)$ must include at least the values of the vector $c_u(f)$, and the value $c_v(g)[v] > c_u(f)[v]$.

If we do not have $f \rightarrow g$, then $c_v(g)[u]$ cannot know about $c_u(f)[u]$, and hence $c_v(g)[u] < c_u(f)[u]$, since $c_u(f)[u]$ was incremented when executing f on node u. $\qquad\square$

Remarks:

- Usually the number of interacting nodes is small compared to the overall number of nodes. Therefore we do not need to send the full length clock vector, but only a vector containing the entries of the nodes that are actually communicating. This optimization is the called the *differential technique.*

12.3 Consistent Snapshots

Definition 12.28 (cut). *A* **cut** *is some prefix of a distributed execution. More precisely, if a cut contains an operation f on some node u, then it also contains all the preceding operations of u. The set of last operations on every node included in the cut is called the* **frontier** *of the cut.*

Definition 12.29 (consistent snapshot). *A cut C is a* **consistent snapshot***, if for every operation g in C with $f \to g$, C also contains f.*

Remarks:

- In a consistent snapshot it is forbidden to see an effect without its cause.

- The number of possible consistent snapshots gives also information about the degree of concurrency of the system.

- One extreme is a sequential computation, where stopping one node halts the whole system. Let q_u be the number of operations on node $u \in \{1, \ldots, n\}$. Then the number of consistent snapshots (including the empty cut) in the sequential case is $\mu_s := 1 + q_1 + q_2 + \cdots + q_n$.

- One the other hand, in an entirely concurrent computation the nodes are not dependent on one another and therefore stopping one node does not impact others. The number of consistent snapshots in this case is $\mu_c := (1 + q_1) \cdot (1 + q_2) \cdots (1 + q_n)$.

Definition 12.30 (measure of concurrency). *The concurrency measure of an execution $E = (S_1, \ldots, S_n)$ is defined as the ratio*

$$m(E) := \frac{\mu - \mu_s}{\mu_c - \mu_s},$$

where μ denotes the number of consistent snapshot of E.

Remarks:

- This measure of concurrency is normalized to $[0, 1]$. F

- In order to evaluate the extent to which a computation is concurrent, we need to compute the number of consistent snapshots μ. This can be done via vector clocks.

- Imagine a bank having lots of accounts with transactions all over the world. The bank wants to make sure that at no point in time money gets created or destroyed. This is where consistent snapshots come in: They are supposed to capture the state of the system. Theoretically, we have already used snapshots when we discussed configurations in Definition 3.4:

Definition 12.31 (configuration). *We say that a system is fully defined (at any point during the execution) by its **configuration**. The configuration includes the state of every node, and all messages that are in transit (sent but not yet received).*

Remarks:

- One application of consistent snapshots is to check if certain invariants hold in a distributed setting. Other applications include distributed debugging or determining global states of a distributed system.

- In Algorithm 12.32 we assume that a node can record only its internal state and the messages it sends and receives. There is no common clock so it is not possible to just let each node record all information at precisely the same time.

Theorem 12.33. *Algorithm 12.32 collects a consistent snapshot.*

Algorithm 12.32 Distributed Snapshot Algorithm

1: Initiator: Save local state, send a snap message to all other nodes and collect incoming states and messages of all other nodes.
2: All other nodes:
3: Upon receiving a snap message for the first time: send own state (before message) to the initiator and propagate snap by adding snap tag to future messages.
4: If afterwards receiving a message m *without* snap tag: Forward m to the initiator.

Proof. Let C be the cut induced by the frontier of all states and messages forwarded to the initiator. For every node u, let t_u be the time when u gets the first snap message m (either by the initiator, or as a message tag). Then C contains all of u's operations before t_u, and none after t_u (also not the message m which arrives together with the tag at t_u).

Assume for the sake of contradiction we have operations f, g on nodes u, v respectively, with $f \to g$, $f \notin C$ and $g \in C$, hence $t_u \leq f$ and $g < t_v$. If $u = v$ we have $t_u \leq f < g < t_v = t_u$, which is a contradiction. On the other hand, if $u \neq v$: Since $t_u \leq f$ we know that all following send operations must have included the snap tag. Because of $f \to g$ we know there is a path of messages between f and g, all including the snap tag. So the snap tag must have been received by node v before or with operation g, hence $t_v \leq g$, which is a contradiction to $t_v > g$. $\qquad\square$

Remarks:

- It may of course happen that a node u sends a message m before receiving the first snap message at time t_u (hence not containing the snap tag), and this message m is only received by node v after t_v. Such a message m will be reported by v, and is as such included in the consistent snapshot (as a message that was *in transit* during the snapshot).

12.4 Distributed Tracing

Definition 12.34 (Microservice Architecture). *A **microservice architecture** refers to a system composed of loosely coupled ser-*

vices. These services communicate by various protocols and are either decentrally coordinated (also known as "choreography") or centrally ("orchestration").

Remarks:

- There is no exact definition for microservices. A rule of thumb is that you should be able to program a microservice from scratch within two weeks.

- Microservices are the architecture of choice to implement a cloud based distributed system, as they allow for different technology stacks, often also simplifying scalability issues.

- In contrast to a monolithic architecture, debugging and optimizing get trickier as it is difficult to detect which component exactly is causing problems.

- Due to the often heterogeneous technology, a uniform debugging framework is not feasible.

- Tracing enables tracking the set of services which participate in some task, and their interactions.

Definition 12.35 (Span). *A **span** s is a named and timed operation representing a contiguous sequence of operations on one node. A span s has a start time s_* and finish time $s_\dagger$.*

Remarks:

- Spans represent tasks, like a client submitting a request or a server processing this request. Spans often trigger several child spans or forwards the work to another service.

Definition 12.36 (Span Reference). *A span may causally depend on other spans. The two possible relations are **ChildOf** and **FollowsFrom** references. In a ChildOf reference, the parent span depends on the result of the child (the parents asks the child and the child answers), and therefore parent and child span must overlap. In FollowsFrom references parent spans do not depend in any way on the result of their child spans (the parent just invokes the child).*

Definition 12.37 (Trace). *A **trace** is a series-parallel directed acyclic graph representing the hierarchy of spans that are executed to serve some request. Edges are annotated by the type of the reference, either ChildOf or FollowsFrom.*

Remarks:

- The advantage of using an open source definition like opentracing is that it is easy to replace a specific tracing by another one. This mitigates the lock-in effect that is often experienced when using some specific technology.

- Algorithm 12.38 shows what is needed if you want to trace requests to your system.

Algorithm 12.38 Inter-Service Tracing

1: Upon requesting another service: Inject information of current trace and span (IDs or timing information) into the request header.
2: Upon receiving request from another service: Extract trace and span information from the request header and create new span as child span.

Remarks:

- All tracing information is collected and has to be sent to some tracing backend which stores the traces and usually provides a frontend to understand what is going on.

- Opentracing implementations are available for the most commonly used programming frameworks and can therefore be used for heterogeneous collections of microservices.

12.5 Mutual Exclusion

When multiple nodes compete for exclusive access to a shared resource, we need a protocol which coordinates the order in which the resource gets assigned to the nodes. The most obvious algorithm is letting a leader node organize everything:

Algorithm 12.39 Centralized Mutual Exclusion Algorithm

1: To access shared resource: Send request message to leader and wait for permission.
2: To release shared resource: Send release message to leader.

Remarks:

- An advantage of Algorithm 12.39 is its simplicity and low message overhead with 3 messages per access.

- An obvious disadvantage is that the leader is single point of failure and performance bottleneck. Assuming an asynchronous system, this protocol also does not achieve first come first serve fairness.

- To eliminate the single bottleneck we pass an access token from node to node. This token contains the time t of the earliest known outstanding request.

- We assume a ring of nodes, i.e., there is an order of the nodes given such that every node knows its successor and predecessor.

Algorithm 12.40 Token-Based Mutual Exclusion Algorithm

1: To access shared resource at time T_R: Wait for token containing time t of earliest known outstanding request.
2: Upon receiving token:
3: **if** $T_R = t$ **then**
4:     Hold token and access shared resource.
5: **else if** $T_R > t$ **then**
6:     Pass on token to next node.
7: **else if** $t = null$ or $T_R < t$ **then**
8:     Set $t = T_R$ and pass on token.
9: **end if**
10: To release access: Set $t = null$ and pass on token.

Remarks:

- Algorithm 12.40 achieves in-order fairness if all nodes stick to the rules.

- One issue is the breakdown if one node does not manage to pass on the token. In this case some new token has to be created and assigned to one of the remaining nodes.

- We can get rid of the token, if access to the token gets decided on a first come first serve basis with respect to logical clocks. This leads to Algorithm 12.41.

Algorithm 12.41 Distributed Mutual Exclusion Algorithm

1: To access shared resource: Send message to all nodes containing the node ID and the current timestamp.
2: Upon received request message: If access to the same resource is needed and the own timestamp is lower than timestamp in received message, **defer** response. Otherwise send back a response.
3: Upon responses **from all nodes** received: enter critical section. Afterwards send deferred responses.

Remarks:

- The algorithm guarantees mutual exclusion without deadlocks or starvation of a requesting process.

- The number of messages per entry is $2(n-1)$, where n is the number of nodes in the system: $(n-1)$ requests and $(n-1)$ responses.

- There is no single point of failure. Yet, whenever a node crashes, it will not reply with a response and the requesting node waits forever. Eeven worse, the requesting process cannot determine if the silence is due to the other process currently accessing the shared resource or crashing. Can we fix this? Indeed: Change step 2 in Algorithm 12.41 such that upon receiving request there will always be an answer, either Denied or OK. This way crashes will be detected.

Chapter Notes

In his seminal work, Leslie Lamport came up with the happened-before relation and gave the first logical clock algorithm [Lam78]. This paper also laid the foundation for the theory of logical clocks.

Fidge came some time later up with vector clocks [JF88]. An obvious drawback of vector clocks is the overhead caused by including the whole vector. Can we do better? In general, we cannot if we need strong logical clocks [CB91].

Lamport also introduced the algorithm for distributed snapshots, together with Chandy [CL85]. Besides this very basic algorithm, there exist several other algorithms, e.g., [LY87], [SK86].

Throughout the literature the definitions for, e.g., consistency or atomicity slightly differ. These concepts are studied in different communities, e.g., linearizability hails from the distributed systems community whereas the notion of serializability was first treated by the database community. As the two areas converged, the terminology got overloaded.

Our definitions for distributed tracing follow the OpenTracing API [1]. The opentracing API only gives high-level definitions of how a tracing system is supposed to work. Only the implementation specifies how it works internally.There are several systems that implement these generic definitions, like Uber's open source tracer called *Jaeger*, or *Zipkin*, which was first developed by Twitter. This technology is relevant for the growing number of companies that embrace a microservice architecture. Netflix for example has a growing number of over 1,000 microservices.

Bibliography

[CB91] Bernadette Charron-Bost. Concerning the size of logical clocks in distributed systems. *Inf. Process. Lett.*, 39(1):11–16, July 1991.

[CL85] K Chandy and Leslie Lamport. Distributed snapshots: Determining global states of distributed systems. 3:63–75, 02 1985.

[JF88] Colin J. Fidge. Timestamps in message-passing systems that preserve partial ordering. 10:56–66, 02 1988.

[Lam78] Leslie Lamport. Time, clocks, and the ordering of events in a distributed system. *Commun. ACM*, 21(7):558–565, jul 1978.

[LY87] Ten H. Lai and Tao H. Yang. On distributed snapshots. *Information Processing Letters*, 25(3):153 – 158, 1987.

---

[1] http://opentracing.io/documentation/

[SK86] Madalene Spezialetti and Phil Kearns. Efficient distributed snapshots. In *ICDCS*, pages 382–388. IEEE Computer Society, 1986.

Chapter 13

Distributed Storage

How do you store 1M movies, each with a size of about 1GB, on 1M nodes, each equipped with a 1TB disk? Simply store the movies on the nodes, arbitrarily, and memorize (with a global index) which movie is stored on which node. What if the set of movies or nodes changes over time, and you do not want to change your global index too often?

13.1 Consistent Hashing

Several variants of hashing will do the job, e.g. consistent hashing:

Algorithm 13.1 Consistent Hashing

1: Hash the unique file name of each movie x with a known set of hash functions $h_i(x) \rightarrow [0, 1)$, for $i = 1, \ldots, k$
2: Hash the unique name (e.g., IP address and port number) of each node with the same hash function $h(u) \rightarrow [0, 1)$
3: Store a copy of movie x on node u if $h_i(x) \approx h(u)$, for any i. More formally, store movie x on node u if

$$|h_i(x) - h(u)| = \min_v \{|h_i(x) - h(v)|\}, \text{ for any } i$$

Theorem 13.2 (Consistent Hashing). *In expectation, each node in Algorithm 13.1 stores km/n movies, where k is the number of hash functions, m the number of different movies and n the number of nodes.*

Proof. For a specific movie (out of m) and a specific hash function (out of k), all n nodes have the same probability $1/n$ to hash closest to the movie hash. By linearity of expectation, each node stores km/n movies in expectation if we also count duplicates of movies on a node. $\square$

Remarks:

- Let us do a back-of-the-envelope calculation. We have $m = 1\mathrm{M}$ movies, $n = 1\mathrm{M}$ nodes, each node has storage for $1\mathrm{TB}/1\mathrm{GB} = 1\mathrm{K}$ movies, i.e., we use $k = 1\mathrm{K}$ hash functions. Theorem 13.2 shows each node stores about 1K movies.

- Using the Chernoff bound below with $\mu = km/n = 1\mathrm{K}$, the probability that a node uses 10% more memory than expected is less than 1%.

Facts 13.3. *A version of a **Chernoff bound** states the following: Let $x_1, \ldots, x_n$ be independent Bernoulli-distributed random variables with $Pr[x_i = 1] = p_i$ and $Pr[x_i = 0] = 1 - p_i = q_i$, then for $X := \sum_{i=1}^{n} x_i$ and $\mu := \mathbb{E}[X] = \sum_{i=1}^{n} p_i$ the following holds:*

$$\text{for any } \delta > 0: \ Pr[X \geq (1+\delta)\mu] < \left(\frac{e^{\delta}}{(1+\delta)^{(1+\delta)}} \right)^{\mu}$$

Remarks:

- Instead of storing movies directly on nodes as in Algorithm 13.1, we can also store the movies on any nodes we like. The nodes of Algorithm 13.1 then simply store forward pointers to the actual movie locations.

- For better load balancing, we might also hash nodes multiple times.

- In this chapter we want to push unreliability to the extreme. What if the nodes are so unreliable that on average a node is only available for 1 hour? In other words, nodes exhibit a high *churn*, they constantly join and leave the distributed system.

- With such a high churn, hundreds or thousands of nodes will change every second. No single node can have an accurate picture of what other nodes are currently in the system. This is remarkably different to classic distributed systems, where a single unavailable node may already be a minor disaster: all the other nodes have to get a consistent view (Definition 7.5) of the system again. In high churn systems it is impossible to have a consistent view at any time.

- Instead, each node will just know about a small subset of 100 or less other nodes ("neighbors"). This way, nodes can withstand high churn situations.

- On the downside, nodes will not directly know which node is responsible for what movie. Instead, a node searching for a movie might have to ask a neighbor node, which in turn will recursively ask another neighbor node, until the correct node storing the movie (or a forward pointer to the movie) is found. The nodes of our distributed storage system form a virtual network, also called an *overlay network*.

13.2 Hypercubic Networks

In this section we present a few overlay topologies of general interest.

Definition 13.4 (Topology Properties). *Our virtual network should have the following properties:*

- *The network should be (somewhat)* **homogeneous***: no node should play a dominant role, no node should be a single point of failure.*

- *The nodes should have* **IDs***, and the IDs should span the universe $[0, 1)$, such that we can store data with hashing, as in Algorithm 13.1.*

- *Every node should have a small* **degree***, if possible polylogarithmic in n, the number of nodes. This will allow every* *node to maintain a persistent connection with each neighbor, which will help us to deal with churn.*

- *The network should have a small **diameter**, and routing should be easy. If a node does not have the information about a data item, then it should know which neighbor to ask. Within a few (polylogarithmic in n) hops, one should find the node that has the correct information.*

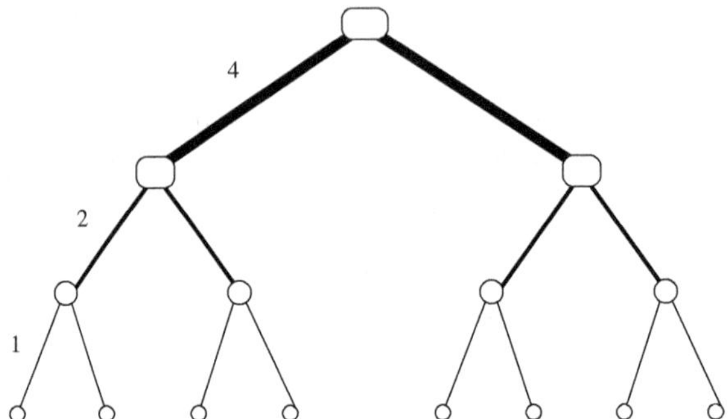

Figure 13.5: The structure of a fat tree.

Remarks:

- Some basic network topologies used in practice are trees, rings, grids or tori. Many other suggested networks are simply combinations or derivatives of these.

- The advantage of trees is that the routing is very easy: for every source-destination pair there is only one path. However, since the root of a tree is a bottleneck, trees are not homogeneous. Instead, so-called *fat trees* should be used. Fat trees have the property that every edge connecting a node v to its parent u has a capacity that is proportional to the number of leaves of the subtree rooted at v. See Figure 13.5 for a picture.

- Fat trees belong to a family of networks that require edges of non-uniform capacity to be efficient. Networks with edges of uniform capacity are easier to build. This is usually the case for grids and tori. Unless explicitly mentioned, we will treat all edges in the following to be of capacity 1.

Definition 13.6 (Torus, Mesh). *Let $m, d \in \mathbb{N}$. The (m,d)-**mesh** $M(m,d)$ is a graph with node set $V = [m]^d$ and edge set*

$$E = \left\{ \{(a_1, \ldots, a_d), (b_1, \ldots, b_d)\} \mid a_i, b_i \in [m], \sum_{i=1}^{d} |a_i - b_i| = 1 \right\},$$

*where $[m]$ means the set $\{0, \ldots, m-1\}$. The (m,d)-**torus** $T(m,d)$ is a graph that consists of an (m,d)-mesh and additionally wraparound edges from nodes $(a_1, \ldots, a_{i-1}, m-1, a_{i+1}, \ldots, a_d)$ to nodes $(a_1, \ldots, a_{i-1}, 0, a_{i+1}, \ldots, a_d)$ for all $i \in \{1, \ldots, d\}$ and all $a_j \in [m]$ with $j \neq i$. In other words, we take the expression $a_i - b_i$ in the sum modulo m prior to computing the absolute value. $M(m,1)$ is also called a **path**, $T(m,1)$ a **cycle**, and $M(2,d) = T(2,d)$ a d-**dimensional hypercube**. Figure 13.7 presents a linear array, a torus, and a hypercube.*

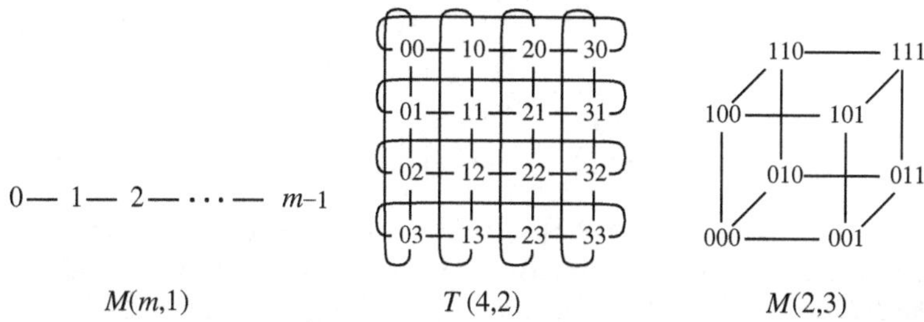

Figure 13.7: The structure of $M(m,1)$, $T(4,2)$, and $M(2,3)$.

Remarks:

- Routing on a mesh, torus, or hypercube is trivial. On a d-dimensional hypercube, to get from a source bitstring s to a target bitstring t one only needs to fix each "wrong" bit, one at a time; in other words, if the source and the target differ by k bits, there are $k!$ routes with k hops.

- As required by Definition 13.4, the d-bit IDs of the nodes need to be mapped to the universe $[0, 1)$. One way to do this is by interpreting an ID as the binary representation of the fractional part of a decimal number. For example, the ID **101** is mapped to $\mathbf{0.101_2}$ which has a decimal value of $\mathbf{0} \cdot 2^0 + \mathbf{1} \cdot 2^{-1} + \mathbf{0} \cdot 2^{-2} + \mathbf{1} \cdot 2^{-3} = \frac{5}{8}$.

- The Chord architecture is a close relative of the hypercube, basically a less rigid hypercube. The hypercube connects every node with an ID in $[0, 1)$ with every node in *exactly* distance 2^{-i}, $i = 1, 2, \ldots, d$ in $[0, 1)$. Chord instead connect nodes with *approximately* distance 2^{-i}.

- The hypercube has many derivatives, the so-called *hypercubic networks*. Among these are the butterfly, cube-connected-cycles, shuffle-exchange, and de Bruijn graph. We start with the butterfly, which is basically a "rolled out" hypercube.

Definition 13.8 (Butterfly). *Let $d \in \mathbb{N}$. The d-**dimensional butterfly** $BF(d)$ is a graph with node set $V = [d+1] \times [2]^d$ and an edge set $E = E_1 \cup E_2$ with*

$$E_1 = \{\{(i, \alpha), (i+1, \alpha)\} \mid i \in [d],\ \alpha \in [2]^d\}$$

and

$$E_2 \quad = \quad \{\{(i, \alpha), (i+1, \beta)\} \mid i \in [d],\ \alpha, \beta \in [2]^d, \alpha \oplus \beta = 2^i\}.$$

*A node set $\{(i, \alpha) \mid \alpha \in [2]^d\}$ is said to form **level** i of the butterfly. The d-**dimensional wrap-around butterfly** $W\text{-}BF(d)$ is defined by taking the $BF(d)$ and having $(d, \alpha) = (0, \alpha)$ for all $\alpha \in [2]^d$.*

Remarks:

- Figure 13.9 shows the 3-dimensional butterfly $BF(3)$. The $BF(d)$ has $(d+1)2^d$ nodes, $2d \cdot 2^d$ edges and degree 4. It is not difficult to check that combining the node sets $\{(i, \alpha) \mid i \in [d]\}$ for all $\alpha \in [2]^d$ into a single node results in the hypercube.

- Butterflies have the advantage of a constant node degree over hypercubes, whereas hypercubes feature more fault-tolerant routing.

- You may have seen butterfly-like structures before, e.g. sorting networks, communication switches, data center networks, fast fourier transform (FFT). The Benes network (telecommunication) is nothing but two back-to-back butterflies. The Clos network (data centers) is a close relative to Butterflies too. Actually, merging the 2^i nodes on level i that share the first $d - i$ bits into a single node, the Butterfly becomes a fat tree. Every year there are new applications for which hypercubic networks are the perfect solution!

- Next we define the cube-connected-cycles network. It only has a degree of 3 and it results from the hypercube by replacing the corners by cycles.

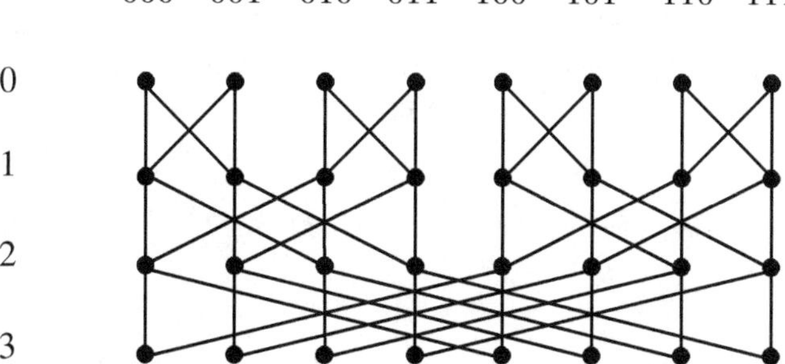

Figure 13.9: The structure of BF(3).

Definition 13.10 (Cube-Connected-Cycles). *Let $d \in \mathbb{N}$. The* ***cube-connected-cycles*** *network $CCC(d)$ is a graph with node set $V = \{(a, p) \mid a \in [2]^d, p \in [d]\}$ and edge set*

$$
\begin{aligned}
E \;=\; & \big\{\{(a, p), (a, (p + 1) \bmod d)\} \mid a \in [2]^d, p \in [d]\big\} \\
& \cup \big\{\{(a, p), (b, p)\} \mid a, b \in [2]^d, p \in [d], |a - b| = 2^p\big\}
\end{aligned}
$$

Remarks:

- Two possible representations of a CCC can be found in Figure 13.11.

- The shuffle-exchange is yet another way of transforming the hypercubic interconnection structure into a constant degree network.

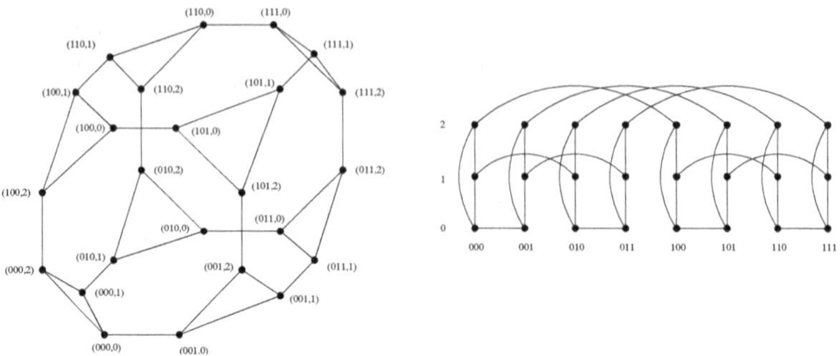

Figure 13.11: The structure of CCC(3).

Definition 13.12 (Shuffle-Exchange). *Let* $d \in \mathbb{N}$. *The d-dimensional **shuffle-exchange** $SE(d)$ is defined as an undirected graph with node set $V = [2]^d$ and an edge set $E = E_1 \cup E_2$ with*

$$E_1 = \left\{ \{(a_1, \ldots, a_d), (a_1, \ldots, \bar{a}_d)\} \mid (a_1, \ldots, a_d) \in [2]^d, \ \bar{a}_d = 1 - a_d \right\}$$

and

$$E_2 = \left\{ \{(a_1, \ldots, a_d), (a_d, a_1, \ldots, a_{d-1})\} \mid (a_1, \ldots, a_d) \in [2]^d \right\} \ .$$

Figure 13.13 shows the 3- and 4-dimensional shuffle-exchange graph.

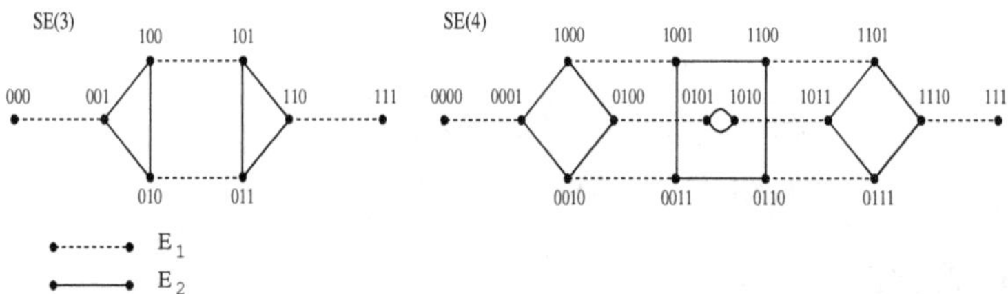

Figure 13.13: The structure of SE(3) and SE(4).

Definition 13.14 (DeBruijn). *The b-**ary DeBruijn graph of dimension** d $DB(b, d)$ is an undirected graph $G = (V, E)$ with* *node set $V = \{v \in [b]^d\}$ and edge set E that contains all edges $\{v, w\}$ with the property that $w \in \{(x, v_1, \ldots, v_{d-1}) : x \in [b]\}$, where $v = (v_1, \ldots, v_d)$.*

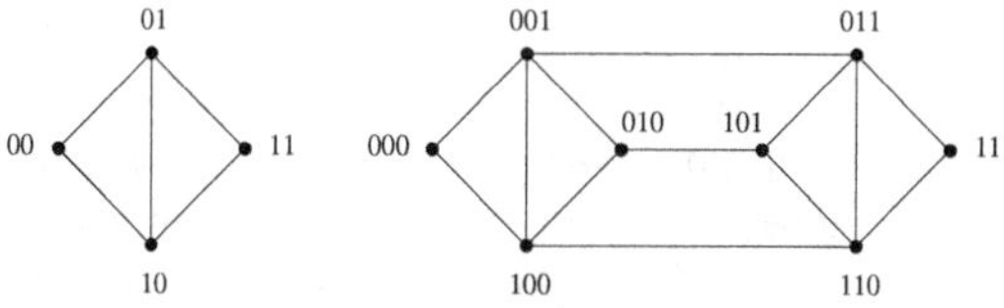

Figure 13.15: The structure of $DB(2, 2)$ and $DB(2, 3)$.

Remarks:

- Two examples of a DeBruijn graph can be found in Figure 13.15.

- There are some data structures which also qualify as hypercubic networks. An example of a hypercubic network is the skip list, the balanced binary search tree for the lazy programmer:

Definition 13.16 (Skip List). *The skip list is an ordinary ordered linked list of objects, augmented with additional forward links. The ordinary linked list is the level 0 of the skip list. In addition, every object is promoted to level 1 with probability 1/2. As for level 0, all level 1 objects are connected by a linked list. In general, every object on level i is promoted to the next level with probability 1/2. A special start-object points to the smallest/first object on each level.*

Remarks:

- Search, insert, and delete can be implemented in $\mathcal{O}(\log n)$ expected time in a skip list, simply by jumping from higher levels to lower ones when overshooting the searched position. Also, the amortized memory cost of each object is constant, as on average an object only has two forward links.

- The randomization can easily be discarded, by deterministically promoting a constant fraction of objects of level i to level $i + 1$, for all i. When inserting or deleting, object o simply checks whether its left and right level i neighbors are being promoted to level $i + 1$. If none of them is, promote object o itself. Essentially we establish a maximal independent set (MIS) on each level, hence at least every third and at most every second object is promoted.

- There are obvious variants of the skip list, e.g., the skip graph. Instead of promoting only half of the nodes to the next level, we always promote all the nodes, similarly to a balanced binary tree: All nodes are part of the root level of the binary tree. Half the nodes are promoted left, and half the nodes are promoted right, on each level. Hence on level i we have have 2^i lists (or, if we connect the last element again with the first: rings) of about $n/2^i$ objects. The skip graph features all the properties of Definition 13.4.

- More generally, how are degree and diameter of Definition 13.4 related? The following theorem gives a general lower bound.

Theorem 13.17. *Every graph of maximum degree $d > 2$ and size n must have a diameter of at least $\lceil (\log n)/(\log(d-1)) \rceil - 2$.*

Proof. Suppose we have a graph $G = (V, E)$ of maximum degree d and size n. Start from any node $v \in V$. In a first step at most d other nodes can be reached. In two steps at most $d \cdot (d - 1)$ additional nodes can be reached. Thus, in general, in at most r steps at most

$$1 + \sum_{i=0}^{r-1} d \cdot (d-1)^i = 1 + d \cdot \frac{(d-1)^r - 1}{(d-1) - 1} \leq \frac{d \cdot (d-1)^r}{d-2}$$

nodes (including v) can be reached. This has to be at least n to ensure that v can reach all other nodes in V within r steps. Hence,

$$(d-1)^r \geq \frac{(d-2) \cdot n}{d} \quad \Leftrightarrow \quad r \geq \log_{d-1}((d-2) \cdot n/d) .$$

Since $\log_{d-1}((d-2)/d) > -2$ for all $d > 2$, this is true only if $r \geq \lceil (\log n)/(\log(d-1)) \rceil - 2$. $\qquad \square$

Remarks:

- In other words, constant-degree hypercubic networks feature an asymptotically optimal diameter D.

- Other hypercubic graphs manage to have a different tradeoff between node degree d and diameter D. The pancake graph, for instance, minimizes the maximum of these with $\max(d, D) = \Theta(\log n / \log \log n)$. The ID of a node u in the pancake graph of dimension d is an arbitrary permutation of the numbers $1, 2, \ldots, d$. Two nodes u, v are connected by an edge if one can get the ID of node v by taking the ID of node u, and reversing (flipping) the first k (for $k = 1, \ldots, d$) numbers of u's ID. For example, in dimension $d = 4$, nodes $u = 2314$ and $v = 1324$ are neighbors.

- There are a few other interesting graph classes which are not hypercubic networks, but nevertheless seem to relate to the properties of Definition 13.4. Small-world graphs (a popular representations for social networks) also have small diameter, however, in contrast to hypercubic networks, they are not homogeneous and feature nodes with large degrees.

- Expander graphs (an expander graph is a sparse graph which has good connectivity properties, that is, from every not too large subset of nodes you are connected to an even larger set of nodes) are homogeneous, have a low degree and small diameter. However, expanders are often not routable.

13.3 DHT & Churn

Definition 13.18 (Distributed Hash Table (DHT)). *A **distributed hash table** (DHT) is a distributed data structure that implements a distributed storage. A DHT should support at least (i) a search (for a key) and (ii) an insert (key, object) operation, possibly also (iii) a delete (key) operation.*

Remarks:

- A DHT has many applications beyond storing movies, e.g., the Internet domain name system (DNS) is essentially a DHT.

- A DHT can be implemented as a hypercubic overlay network with nodes having identifiers such that they span the ID space $[0, 1)$.

- A hypercube can directly be used for a DHT. Just use a globally known set of hash functions h_i, mapping movies to bit strings with d bits.

- Other hypercubic structures may be a bit more intricate when using it as a DHT: The butterfly network, for instance, may directly use the $d + 1$ layers for replication, i.e., all the $d + 1$ nodes are responsible for the same ID.

- Other hypercubic networks, e.g. the pancake graph, might need a bit of twisting to find appropriate IDs.

- We assume that a joining node knows a node which already belongs to the system. This is known as the bootstrap problem. Typical solutions are: If a node has been connected with the DHT previously, just try some of these previous nodes. Or the node may ask some authority for a list of IP addresses (and ports) of nodes that are regularly part of the DHT.

- Many DHTs in the literature are analyzed against an adversary that can crash a fraction of random nodes. After crashing a few nodes the system is given sufficient time to recover again. However, this seems unrealistic. The scheme sketched in this section significantly differs from this in two major aspects.

- First, we assume that joins and leaves occur in a worst-case manner. We think of an adversary that can remove and add a bounded number of nodes; the adversary can choose which nodes to crash and how nodes join.

- Second, the adversary does not have to wait until the system is recovered before it crashes the next batch of nodes. Instead, the adversary can constantly crash nodes, while the system is trying to stay alive. Indeed, the system is *never fully repaired* but *always fully functional*. In particular, the system is resilient against an adversary that continuously attacks the "weakest part" of the system. The adversary could for example insert a crawler into the DHT, learn the topology of the system, and then repeatedly crash selected nodes, in an attempt to partition the DHT. The system counters such an adversary by continuously moving the remaining or newly joining nodes towards the areas under attack.

- Clearly, we cannot allow the adversary to have unbounded capabilities. In particular, in any constant time interval, the adversary can at most add and/or remove $O(\log n)$ nodes, n being the total number of nodes currently in the system. This model covers an adversary which repeatedly takes down nodes by a distributed denial of service attack, however only a logarithmic number of nodes at each point in time. The algorithm relies on messages being delivered timely, in at most constant time between any pair of operational nodes, i.e., the synchronous model. Using the trivial synchronizer this is not a problem. We only need bounded message delays in order to have a notion of time which is needed for the adversarial model. The duration of a round is then proportional to the propagation delay of the slowest message.

Algorithm 13.19 DHT

1: Given: a globally known set of hash functions h_i, and a hypercube (or any other hypercubic network)
2: Each hypercube virtual node ("hypernode") consists of $\Theta(\log n)$ nodes.
3: Nodes have connections to all other nodes of their hypernode and to nodes of their neighboring hypernodes.
4: Because of churn, some of the nodes have to change to another hypernode such that up to constant factors, all hypernodes own the same number of nodes at all times.
5: If the total number of nodes n grows or shrinks above or below a certain threshold, the dimension of the hypercube is increased or decreased by one, respectively.

Remarks:

- Having a logarithmic number of hypercube neighbors, each with a logarithmic number of nodes, means that each node has $\Theta(\log^2 n)$ neighbors. However, with some additional bells and whistles one can achieve $\Theta(\log n)$ neighbor nodes.

- The balancing of nodes among the hypernodes can be seen as a dynamic token distribution problem on the hypercube. Each hypernode has a certain number of tokens, the goal is to distribute the tokens along the edges of the graph such that all hypernodes end up with the same or almost the same number of tokens. While tokens are moved around, an adversary constantly inserts and deletes tokens. See also Figure 13.20.

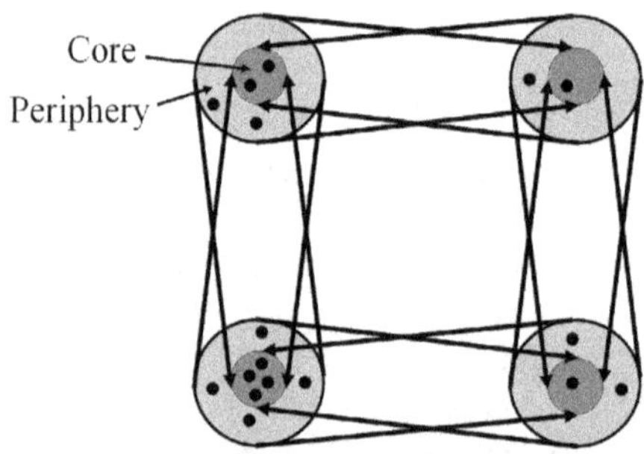

Figure 13.20: A simulated 2-dimensional hypercube with four hypernodes, each consisting of several nodes. Also, all the nodes are either in the core or in the periphery of a node. All nodes within the same hypernode are completely connected to each other, and additionally, all nodes of a hypernode are connected to the core nodes of the neighboring nodes. Only the core nodes store data items, while the peripheral nodes move between the nodes to balance biased adversarial churn.

- In summary, the storage system builds on two basic components: (i) an algorithm which performs the described dynamic token distribution and (ii) an information aggregation algorithm which is used to estimate the number of nodes in the system and to adapt the dimension of the hypercube accordingly:

Theorem 13.21 (DHT with Churn)**.** *We have a fully scalable, efficient distributed storage system which tolerates* $O(\log n)$ *worst-case joins and/or crashes per constant time interval. As in other storage systems, nodes have* $O(\log n)$ *overlay neighbors, and the usual operations (e.g., search, insert) take time* $O(\log n)$.

Remarks:

- Indeed, handling churn is only a minimal requirement to make a distributed storage system work. Advanced studies proposed more elaborate architectures which can also handle other security issues, e.g., privacy or Byzantine attacks.

Chapter Notes

The ideas behind distributed storage were laid during the peer-to-peer (P2P) file sharing hype around the year 2000, so a lot of the seminal research in this area is labeled P2P. The paper of Plaxton, Rajaraman, and Richa [PRR97] laid out a blueprint for many so-called structured P2P architecture proposals, such as Chord [SMK+01], CAN [RFH+01], Pastry [RD01], Viceroy [MNR02], Kademlia [MM02], Koorde [KK03], SkipGraph [AS03], SkipNet [HJS+03], or Tapestry [ZHS+04]. Also the paper of Plaxton et. al. was standing on the shoulders of giants. Some of its eminent precursors are: linear and consistent hashing [KLL+97], locating shared objects [AP90, AP91], compact routing [SK85, PU88], and even earlier: hypercubic networks, e.g. [AJ75, Wit81, GS81, BA84].

Furthermore, the techniques in use for prefix-based overlay structures are related to a proposal called LAND, a locality-aware distributed hash table proposed by Abraham et al. [AMD04].

More recently, a lot of P2P research focussed on security aspects, describing for instance attacks [LMSW06, SENB07, Lar07], and provable countermeasures [KSW05, AS09, BSS09]. Another topic currently garnering interest is using P2P to help distribute live streams of video content on a large scale [LMSW07]. There are several recommendable introductory books on P2P computing, e.g. [SW05, SG05, MS07, KW08, BYL08].

Bibliography

[AJ75] George A. Anderson and E. Douglas Jensen. Computer Interconnection Structures: Taxonomy, Characteristics, and Examples. *ACM Comput. Surv.*, 7(4):197–213, December 1975.

[AMD04] Ittai Abraham, Dahlia Malkhi, and Oren Dobzinski. LAND: stretch (1 + epsilon) locality-aware networks for DHTs. In *Proceedings of the fifteenth annual ACM-SIAM symposium on Discrete algorithms*, SODA '04, pages 550–559, Philadelphia, PA, USA, 2004. Society for Industrial and Applied Mathematics.

[AP90] Baruch Awerbuch and David Peleg. Efficient Distributed Construction of Sparse Covers. Technical report, The Weizmann Institute of Science, 1990.

[AP91] Baruch Awerbuch and David Peleg. Concurrent Online Tracking of Mobile Users. In *SIGCOMM*, pages 221–233, 1991.

[AS03] James Aspnes and Gauri Shah. Skip Graphs. In *SODA*, pages 384–393. ACM/SIAM, 2003.

[AS09] Baruch Awerbuch and Christian Scheideler. Towards a Scalable and Robust DHT. *Theory Comput. Syst.*, 45(2):234–260, 2009.

[BA84] L. N. Bhuyan and D. P. Agrawal. Generalized Hypercube and Hyperbus Structures for a Computer Network. *IEEE Trans. Comput.*, 33(4):323–333, April 1984.

[BSS09] Matthias Baumgart, Christian Scheideler, and Stefan Schmid. A DoS-resilient information system for dynamic data management. In *Proceedings of the twenty-first annual symposium on Parallelism in algorithms and architectures*, SPAA '09, pages 300–309, New York, NY, USA, 2009. ACM.

[BYL08] John Buford, Heather Yu, and Eng Keong Lua. *P2P Networking and Applications*. Morgan Kaufmann Publishers Inc., San Francisco, CA, USA, 2008.

[GS81] J.R. Goodman and C.H. Sequin. Hypertree: A Multiprocessor Interconnection Topology. *Computers, IEEE Transactions on*, C-30(12):923–933, dec. 1981.

[HJS⁺03] Nicholas J. A. Harvey, Michael B. Jones, Stefan Saroiu, Marvin Theimer, and Alec Wolman. SkipNet: a scalable overlay network with practical locality properties. In *Proceedings of the 4th conference on USENIX Symposium on Internet Technologies and Systems - Volume 4*, USITS'03, pages 9–9, Berkeley, CA, USA, 2003. USENIX Association.

[KK03] M. Frans Kaashoek and David R. Karger. Koorde: A Simple Degree-Optimal Distributed Hash Table. In M. Frans Kaashoek and Ion Stoica, editors, *IPTPS*, volume 2735 of *Lecture Notes in Computer Science*, pages 98–107. Springer, 2003.

[KLL⁺97] David R. Karger, Eric Lehman, Frank Thomson Leighton, Rina Panigrahy, Matthew S. Levine, and Daniel Lewin. Consistent Hashing and Random Trees: Distributed Caching Protocols for Relieving Hot Spots on the World Wide Web. In Frank Thomson Leighton and Peter W. Shor, editors, *STOC*, pages 654–663. ACM, 1997.

[KSW05] Fabian Kuhn, Stefan Schmid, and Roger Wattenhofer. A Self-Repairing Peer-to-Peer System Resilient to Dynamic Adversarial Churn. In *4th International Workshop on Peer-To-Peer Systems (IPTPS), Cornell University, Ithaca, New York, USA, Springer LNCS 3640*, February 2005.

[KW08] Javed I. Khan and Adam Wierzbicki. Introduction: Guest editors' introduction: Foundation of peer-to-peer computing. *Comput. Commun.*, 31(2):187–189, February 2008.

[Lar07] Erik Larkin. Storm Worm's virulence may change tactics. http://www.networkworld.com/news/2007/080207-black-hat-storm-worms-virulence.html, Agust 2007. Last accessed on June 11, 2012.

[LMSW06] Thomas Locher, Patrick Moor, Stefan Schmid, and Roger Wattenhofer. Free Riding in BitTorrent is Cheap. In *5th Workshop on Hot Topics in Networks (HotNets), Irvine, California, USA*, November 2006.

[LMSW07] Thomas Locher, Remo Meier, Stefan Schmid, and Roger Wattenhofer. Push-to-Pull Peer-to-Peer Live Streaming. In *21st International Symposium on Distributed Computing (DISC), Lemesos, Cyprus*, September 2007.

[MM02] Petar Maymounkov and David Mazières. Kademlia: A Peer-to-Peer Information System Based on the XOR Metric. In *Revised Papers from the First International Workshop on Peer-to-Peer Systems*, IPTPS '01, pages 53–65, London, UK, UK, 2002. Springer-Verlag.

[MNR02] Dahlia Malkhi, Moni Naor, and David Ratajczak. Viceroy: a scalable and dynamic emulation of the butterfly. In *Proceedings of the twenty-first annual symposium on Principles of distributed computing*, PODC '02, pages 183–192, New York, NY, USA, 2002. ACM.

[MS07] Peter Mahlmann and Christian Schindelhauer. *Peer-to-Peer Networks*. Springer, 2007.

[PRR97] C. Greg Plaxton, Rajmohan Rajaraman, and Andréa W. Richa. Accessing Nearby Copies of Replicated Objects in a Distributed Environment. In *SPAA*, pages 311–320, 1997.

[PU88] David Peleg and Eli Upfal. A tradeoff between space and efficiency for routing tables. In *Proceedings of the twentieth annual ACM symposium on Theory of computing*, STOC '88, pages 43–52, New York, NY, USA, 1988. ACM.

[RD01] Antony Rowstron and Peter Druschel. Pastry: Scalable, decentralized object location and routing for large-scale peer-to-peer systems. In *IFIP/ACM International Conference on Distributed Systems Platforms (Middleware)*, pages 329–350, November 2001.

[RFH⁺01] Sylvia Ratnasamy, Paul Francis, Mark Handley, Richard Karp, and Scott Shenker. A scalable content-addressable network. *SIGCOMM Comput. Commun. Rev.*, 31(4):161–172, August 2001.

[SENB07] Moritz Steiner, Taoufik En-Najjary, and Ernst W. Biersack. Exploiting KAD: possible uses and misuses. *SIGCOMM Comput. Commun. Rev.*, 37(5):65–70, October 2007.

[SG05] Ramesh Subramanian and Brian D. Goodman. *Peer to Peer Computing: The Evolution of a Disruptive Technology.* IGI Publishing, Hershey, PA, USA, 2005.

[SK85] Nicola Santoro and Ramez Khatib. Labelling and Implicit Routing in Networks. *Comput. J.*, 28(1):5–8, 1985.

[SMK⁺01] Ion Stoica, Robert Morris, David Karger, M. Frans Kaashoek, and Hari Balakrishnan. Chord: A scalable peer-to-peer lookup service for internet applications. *SIGCOMM Comput. Commun. Rev.*, 31(4):149–160, August 2001.

[SW05] Ralf Steinmetz and Klaus Wehrle, editors. *Peer-to-Peer Systems and Applications*, volume 3485 of *Lecture Notes in Computer Science*. Springer, 2005.

[Wit81] L. D. Wittie. Communication Structures for Large Networks of Microcomputers. *IEEE Trans. Comput.*, 30(4):264–273, April 1981.

[ZHS⁺04] Ben Y. Zhao, Ling Huang, Jeremy Stribling, Sean C. Rhea, Anthony D. Joseph, and John Kubiatowicz. Tapestry: a resilient global-scale overlay for service deployment. *IEEE Journal on Selected Areas in Communications*, 22(1):41–53, 2004.

Part III

Appendix

Chapter 14

Game Theory

"Game theory is a sort of umbrella or 'unified field' theory for the
rational side of social science, where 'social' is interpreted
broadly, to include human as well as non-human players
(computers, animals, plants)."

– Robert Aumann, 1987

14.1   Introduction

In this chapter we look at a distributed system from a different perspective. Nodes no longer have a common goal, but are *selfish*. The nodes are not byzantine (actively malicious), instead they try to benefit from a distributed system – possibly without contributing.

Game theory attempts to mathematically capture behavior in strategic situations, in which an individual's success depends on the choices of others.

Remarks:

- Examples of potentially selfish behavior are file sharing or TCP. If a packet is dropped, then most TCP implementations interpret this as a congested network and alleviate the problem by reducing the speed at which packets are sent. What if a selfish TCP implementation will not reduce its speed, but instead transmit each packet twice?

v \\ u		Player u	
		Cooperate	Defect
Player v	Cooperate	1 1	0 3
	Defect	3 0	2 2

Table 14.1: The prisoner's dilemma game as a matrix.

- We start with one of the most famous games to introduce some definitions and concepts of game theory.

14.2　Prisoner's Dilemma

A team of two prisoners (players u and v) are being questioned by the police. They are both held in solitary confinement and cannot talk to each other. The prosecutors offer a bargain to each prisoner: snitch on the other prisoner to reduce your prison sentence.

- If both of them stay silent (*cooperate*), both will be sentenced to one year of prison on a lesser charge.

- If both of them testify against their fellow prisoner (*defect*), the police has a stronger case and they will be sentenced to two years each.

- If player u defects and the player v cooperates, then player u will go free (snitching pays off) and player v will have to go to jail for three years; and vice versa.

- This two player game can be represented as a matrix, see Table 14.1.

Definition 14.2 (game). *A game requires at least two rational players, and each player can choose from at least two options (**strategies**). In every possible outcome (**strategy profile**) each player gets a certain payoff (or cost). The payoff of a player depends on the strategies of the other players.*

Definition 14.3 (social optimum). *A strategy profile is called social optimum (SO) if and only if it minimizes the sum of all costs (or maximizes payoff).*

Remarks:

- The social optimum for the prisoner's dilemma is when both players cooperate – the corresponding cost sum is 2.

Definition 14.4 (dominant strategy). *A strategy is dominant if a player is never worse off by playing this strategy. A dominant strategy profile is a strategy profile in which each player plays a dominant strategy.*

Remarks:

- The dominant strategy profile in the prisoner's dilemma is when both players defect – the corresponding cost sum is 4.

Definition 14.5 (Nash Equilibrium). *A Nash Equilibrium (NE) is a strategy profile in which no player can improve by unilaterally (the strategies of the other players do not change) changing its strategy.*

Remarks:

- A game can have multiple Nash Equilibria.

- In the prisoner's dilemma both players defecting is the only Nash Equilibrium.

- If every player plays a dominant strategy, then this is by definition a Nash Equilibrium.

- Nash Equilibria and dominant strategy profiles are so called solution concepts. They are used to analyze a game. There are more solution concepts, e.g. correlated equilibria or best response.

- The best response is the best strategy given a belief about the strategy of the other players. In this game the best response to both strategies of the other player is to defect. If one strategy is the best response to any strategy of the other players, it is a dominant strategy.

- If two players play the prisoner's dilemma repeatedly, it is called iterated prisoner's dilemma. It is a dominant strategy to always defect. To see this, consider the final game. Defecting is a dominant strategy. Thus, it is fixed what both players do in the last game. Now the penultimate game is the last game and by induction always defecting is a dominant strategy.

- Game theorists were invited to come up with a strategy for 200 iterations of the prisoner's dilemma to compete in a tournament. Each strategy had to play against every other strategy and accumulated points throughout the tournament. The simple Tit4Tat strategy (cooperate in the first game, then copy whatever the other player did in the previous game) won. One year later, after analyzing each strategy, another tournament (with new strategies) was held. Tit4Tat won again.

- We now look at a distributed system game.

14.3 Selfish Caching

Computers in a network want to access a file regularly. Each node $v \in V$, with V being the set of nodes and $n = |V|$, has a demand d_v for the file and wants to minimize the cost for accessing it. In order to access the file, node v can either cache the file locally which costs 1 or request the file from another node u which costs $c_{v \leftarrow u}$. If a node does not cache the file, the cost it incurs is the minimal cost to access the file remotely. Note that if no node caches the file, then every node incurs cost ∞. There is an example in Figure 14.6.

Remarks:

- We will sometimes depict this game as a graph. The cost $c_{v \leftarrow u}$ for node v to access the file from node u is equivalent to the length of the shortest path times the demand d_v.

- Note that in undirected graphs $c_{u \leftarrow v} > c_{v \leftarrow u}$ if and only if $d_u > d_v$. We assume that the graphs are undirected for the rest of the chapter.

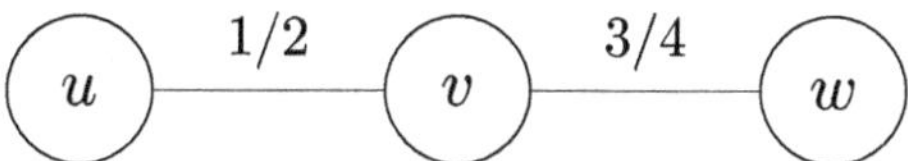

Figure 14.6: In this example we assume $d_u = d_v = d_w = 1$. Either the nodes u and w cache the file. Then neither of the three nodes has an incentive to change its behavior. The costs are 1, 1/2, and 1 for the nodes u, v, w, respectively. Alternatively, only node v caches the file. Again, neither of the three nodes has an incentive to change its behavior. The costs are 1/2, 1, and 3/4 for the nodes u, v, w, respectively.

Algorithm 14.7 Nash Equilibrium for Selfish Caching

1: $S = \{\}$ //set of nodes that cache the file
2: **repeat**
3:     Let v be a node with maximum demand d_v in set V
4:     $S = S \cup \{v\}, V = V \setminus \{v\}$
5:     Remove every node u from V with $c_{u \leftarrow v} \leq 1$
6: **until** $V = \{\}$

Theorem 14.8. *Algorithm 14.7 computes a Nash Equilibrium for Selfish Caching.*

Proof. Let u be a node that is not caching the file. Then there exists a node v for which $c_{u \leftarrow v} \leq 1$. Hence, node u has no incentive to cache.

Let u be a node that is caching the file. We now consider any other node v that is also caching the file. First, we consider the case where v cached the file before u did. Then it holds that $c_{u \leftarrow v} > 1$ by construction.

It could also be that v started caching the file after u did. Then it holds that $d_u \geq d_v$ and therefore $c_{u \leftarrow v} \geq c_{v \leftarrow u}$. Furthermore, we have $c_{v \leftarrow u} > 1$ by construction. Combining these implies that $c_{u \leftarrow v} \geq c_{v \leftarrow u} > 1$.

In either case, node u has no incentive to stop caching. $\qquad\square$

Definition 14.9 (Price of Anarchy). *Let NE_- denote the Nash Equilibrium with the highest cost (smallest payoff). The **Price of Anarchy** (PoA) is defined as*

$$PoA = \frac{\mathrm{cost}(NE_-)}{\mathrm{cost}(SO)}.$$

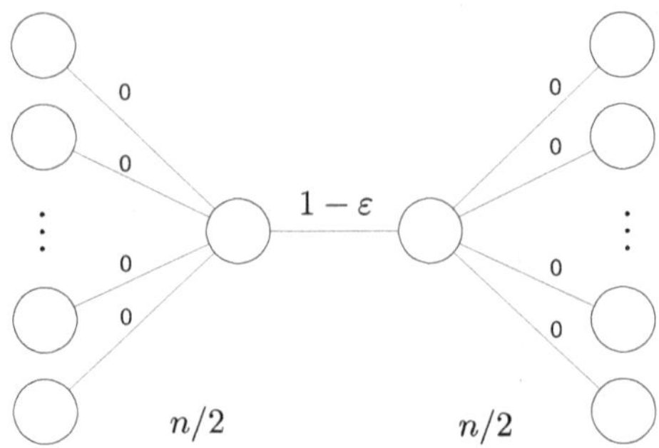

Figure 14.12: A network with a Price of Anarchy of $\Theta(n)$.

Definition 14.10 (Optimistic Price of Anarchy). *Let NE_+ denote the Nash Equilibrium with the smallest cost (highest payoff). The **Optimistic Price of Anarchy** (OPoA) is defined as*

$$OPoA = \frac{\text{cost}(NE_+)}{\text{cost}(SO)}.$$

Remarks:

- The Price of Anarchy measures how much a distributed system degrades because of selfish nodes.

- We have $PoA \geq OPoA \geq 1$.

Theorem 14.11. *The (Optimistic) Price of Anarchy of Selfish Caching can be $\Theta(n)$.*

Proof. Consider a network as depicted in Figure 14.12. Every node v has demand $d_v = 1$. Note that if any node caches the file, no other node has an incentive to cache the file as well since the cost to access the file is at most $1 - \varepsilon$. Without loss of generality, let us assume that a node v on the left caches the file, then it is cheaper for every node on the right to access the file remotely. Hence, the total cost of this solution is $1 + \frac{n}{2} \cdot (1 - \varepsilon)$. In the social optimum one node from the left and one node from the right cache the file. This reduces the cost to 2. Hence, the Price of Anarchy is

$$\frac{1 + \frac{n}{2} \cdot (1 - \varepsilon)}{2} \underset{\varepsilon \to 0}{=} \frac{1}{2} + \frac{n}{4} = \Theta(n). \qquad \square$$

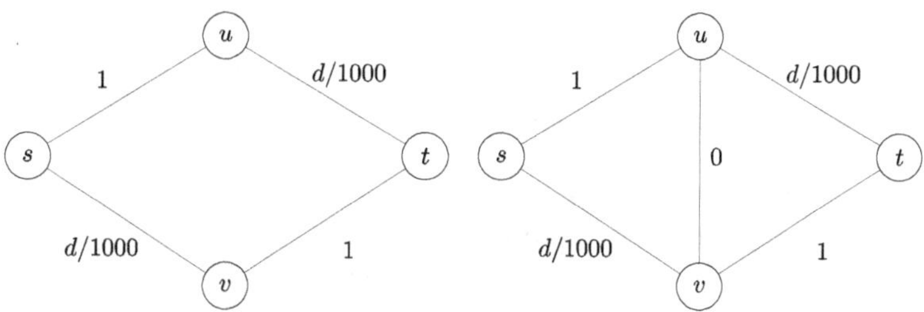

(a) The road network without the short-cut

(b) The road network with the shortcut

Figure 14.13: Braess' Paradox, where d denotes the number of drivers using an edge.

14.4 Braess' Paradox

Consider the graph in Figure 14.13, it models a road network. Let us assume that there are 1000 drivers (each in their own car) that want to travel from node s to node t. Traveling along the road from s to u (or v to t) always takes 1 hour. The travel time from s to v (or u to t) depends on the traffic and increases by $1/1000$ of an hour per car, i.e., when there are 500 cars driving, it takes 30 minutes to use this road.

Lemma 14.14. *Adding a super fast road (delay is 0) between u and v can increase the travel time from s to t.*

Proof. Since the drivers act rationally, they want to minimize the travel time. In the Nash Equilibrium, 500 drivers first drive to node u and then to t and 500 drivers first to node v and then to t. The travel time for each driver is $1 + 500 / 1000 = 1.5$.

To reduce congestion, a super fast road (delay is 0) is built between nodes u and v. This results in the following Nash Equilibrium: every driver now drives from s to v to u to t. The total cost is now $2 > 1.5$. $\qquad\square$

Remarks:

- There are physical systems which exhibit similar properties. Some famous ones employ a spring. YouTube has some fascinating videos about this. Simply search for "Braess Paradox Spring".

- We will now look at another famous game that will allow us to deepen our understanding of game theory.

14.5   Rock-Paper-Scissors

There are two players, u and v. Each player simultaneously chooses one of three options: rock, paper, or scissors. The rules are simple: paper beats rock, rock beats scissors, and scissors beat paper. A matrix representation of this game is in Table 14.15.

v u		Player u		
		Rock	Paper	Scissors
Player v	Rock	0 0	1 -1	-1 1
	Paper	-1 1	0 0	1 -1
	Scissors	1 -1	-1 1	0 0

Table 14.15: Rock-Paper-Scissors as a matrix.

Remarks:

- None of the three strategies is a Nash Equilibrium. Whatever player u chooses, player v can always switch her strategy such that she wins.

- This is highlighted in the best response concept. The best response to e.g. scissors is to play rock. The other player switches to paper. And so on.

- Is this a game without a Nash Equilibrium? John Nash answered this question in 1950. By choosing each strategy with a certain probability, we can obtain a so called mixed Nash Equilibrium. Indeed:

Theorem 14.16. *Every game has a mixed Nash Equilibrium.*

Remarks:

- The Nash Equilibrium of this game is if both players choose each strategy with probability 1/3. The expected payoff is 0.

- Any strategy (or mix of them) is a best response to a player choosing each strategy with probability 1/3.

- In a pure Nash Equilibrium, the strategies are chosen deterministically. Rock-Paper-Scissors does not have a pure Nash Equilibrium.

- Even though every game has a mixed Nash Equilibrium. Sometimes such an equilibrium is computationally difficult to compute. One should be cautious about economic assumptions such as "the market will always find the equilibrium".

- Unfortunately, game theory does not always model problems accurately. Many real world problems are too complex to be captured by a game. And as you may know, humans (not only politicians) are often not rational.

- In distributed systems, players can be servers, routers, etc. Game theory can tell us whether systems and protocols are prone to selfish behavior.

14.6   Mechanism Design

Whereas game theory analyzes existing systems, there is a related area that focuses on designing games – mechanism design. The task is to create a game where nodes have an incentive to behave "nicely".

Definition 14.17 (auction). *One good is sold to a group of bidders in an auction. Each bidder v_i has a secret value z_i for the good and tells his bid b_i to the auctioneer. The auctioneer sells the good to one bidder for a price p.*

Remarks:

- For simplicity, we assume that no two bids are the same, and that $b_1 > b_2 > b_3 > \ldots$

Definition 14.19 (truthful). *An auction is truthful if no player v_i can gain anything by not stating the truth, i.e., $b_i = z_i$.*

Algorithm 14.18 First Price Auction

1: every bidder v_i submits his bid b_i

2: the good is allocated to the highest bidder v_1 for the price $p = b_1$

Theorem 14.20. *A First Price Auction (Algorithm 14.18) is not truthful.*

Proof. Consider an auction with two bidders, with bids b_1 and b_2. By not stating the truth and decreasing his bid to $b_1 - \varepsilon > b_2$, player one could pay less and thus gain more. Thus, the first price auction is not truthful. $\square$

Algorithm 14.21 Second Price Auction

1: every bidder v_i submits his bid b_i

2: the good is allocated to the highest bidder v_1 for $p = b_2$

Theorem 14.22. *Truthful bidding is a dominant strategy in a Second Price Auction.*

Proof. Let z_i be the truthful value of node v_i and b_i his bid. Let $b_{\max} = \max_{j \neq i} b_j$ is the largest bid from other nodes but v_i. The payoff for node v_i is $z_i - b_{\max}$ if $b_i > b_{\max}$ and 0 else. Let us consider overbidding first, i.e., $b_i > z_i$:

- If $b_{\max} < z_i < b_i$, then both strategies win and yield the same payoff $(z_i - b_{\max})$.

- If $z_i < b_i < b_{\max}$, then both strategies lose and yield a payoff of 0.

- If $z_i < b_{\max} < b_i$, then overbidding wins the auction, but the payoff $(z_i - b_{\max})$ is negative. Truthful bidding loses and yields a payoff of 0.

Likewise underbidding, i.e. $b_i < z_i$:

- If $b_{\max} < b_i < z_i$, then both strategies win and yield the same payoff $(z_i - b_{\max})$.

- If $b_i < z_i < b_{\max}$, then both strategies lose and yield a payoff of 0.

- If $b_i < b_{\max} < z_i$, then truthful bidding wins and yields a positive payoff $(z_i - b_{\max})$. Underbidding loses and yields a payoff of 0.

Hence, truthful bidding is a dominant strategy for each node v_i. $\quad\square$

Remarks:

- Let us use this for Selfish Caching. We need to choose a node that is the first to cache the file. But how? By holding an auction. Every node says for which price it is willing to cache the file. We pay the node with the lowest offer and pay it the second lowest offer to ensure truthful offers.

- Since a mechanism designer can manipulate incentives, she can implement a strategy profile by making all the strategies in this profile dominant.

Theorem 14.23. *Any Nash Equilibrium of Selfish Caching can be implemented for free.*

Proof. If the mechanism designer wants the nodes from the caching set S of the Nash Equilibrium to cache, then she can offer the following deal to every node not in S: "If any node from set S does not cache the file, then I will ensure a positive payoff for you." Thus, all nodes not in S prefer not to cache since this is a dominant strategy for them. Consider now a node $v \in S$. Since S is a Nash Equilibrium, node v incurs cost of at least 1 if it does not cache the file. For nodes that incur cost of exactly 1, the mechanism designer can even issue a penalty if the node does not cache the file. Thus, every node $v \in S$ caches the file. $\quad\square$

Remarks:

- Mechanism design assumes that the players act rationally and want to maximize their payoff. In real-world distributed systems some players may be not selfish, but actively malicious (byzantine).

- What about P2P file sharing? To increase the overall experience, BitTorrent suggests that peers offer better upload speed to peers who upload more. This idea can be exploited. By always claiming to have nothing to trade yet, the BitThief client downloads without uploading. In addition to that, it connects to more peers than the standard client to increase its download speed.

- Many techniques have been proposed to limit such free riding behavior, e.g., tit-for-tat trading: I will only share something with you if you share something with me. To solve the bootstrap problem ("I don't have anything yet"), nodes receive files or pieces of files whose hash match their own hash for free. One can also imagine indirect trading. Peer u uploads to peer v, who uploads to peer w, who uploads to peer u. Finally, one could imagine using virtual currencies or a reputation system (a history of who uploaded what). Reputation systems suffer from collusion and Sybil attacks. If one node pretends to be many nodes who rate each other well, it will have a good reputation.

Chapter Notes

Game theory was started by a proof for mixed-strategy equilibria in two-person zero-sum games by John von Neumann [Neu28]. Later, von Neumann and Morgenstern introduced game theory to a wider audience [NM44]. In 1950 John Nash proved that every game has a mixed Nash Equilibrium [Nas50]. The Prisoner's Dilemma was first formalized by Flood and Dresher [Flo52]. The iterated prisoner's dilemma tournament was organized by Robert Axelrod [AH81]. The Price of Anarchy definition is from Koutsoupias and Papadimitriou [KP99]. This allowed the creation of the Selfish Caching Game [CCW$^+$04], which we used as a running example in this chapter. Braess' paradox was discovered by Dietrich Braess in 1968 [Bra68]. A generalized version of the second-price auction is the VCG auction, named after three successive papers from first Vickrey, then Clarke, and finally Groves [Vic61, Cla71, Gro73]. One popular example of selfishness in practice is BitThief – a BitTorrent client that successfully downloads without uploading [LMSW06]. Using game theory economists try to understand markets and predict crashes. Apart from John Nash, the Sveriges Riksbank Prize (Nobel Prize) in Economics has been awarded many times to game theorists. For example in 2007 Hurwicz, Maskin, and Myerson received the prize for "for having laid the foundations of mechanism design theory". There is a considerable amount of work on mixed adversarial models with byzantine, altruistic, and rational ("BAR") players, e.g., [AAC+05, ADGH06, MSW06]. Daskalakis et al. [DGP09] showed that computing a Nash Equilibrium may not be trivial.

Bibliography

[AAC+05] Amitanand S. Aiyer, Lorenzo Alvisi, Allen Clement, Michael Dahlin, Jean-Philippe Martin, and Carl Porth. BAR fault tolerance for cooperative services. In *Proceedings of the 20th ACM Symposium on Operating Systems Principles 2005, SOSP 2005, Brighton, UK, October 23-26, 2005*, pages 45–58, 2005.

[ADGH06] Ittai Abraham, Danny Dolev, Rica Gonen, and Joseph Y. Halpern. Distributed computing meets game theory: robust mechanisms for rational secret sharing and multiparty computation. In *Proceedings of the Twenty-Fifth Annual ACM Symposium on Principles of Distributed Computing, PODC 2006, Denver, CO, USA, July 23-26, 2006*, pages 53–62, 2006.

[AH81] Robert Axelrod and William Donald Hamilton. The evolution of cooperation. *Science*, 211(4489):1390–1396, 1981.

[Bra68] Dietrich Braess. Über ein paradoxon aus der verkehrsplanung. *Unternehmensforschung*, 12(1):258–268, 1968.

[CCW+04] Byung-Gon Chun, Kamalika Chaudhuri, Hoeteck Wee, Marco Barreno, Christos H Papadimitriou, and John Kubiatowicz. Selfish caching in distributed systems: a game-theoretic analysis. In *Proceedings of the twenty-third annual ACM symposium on Principles of distributed computing*, pages 21–30. ACM, 2004.

[Cla71] Edward H Clarke. Multipart pricing of public goods. *Public choice*, 11(1):17–33, 1971.

[DGP09] Constantinos Daskalakis, Paul W. Goldberg, and Christos H. Papadimitriou. The complexity of computing a nash equilibrium. *SIAM J. Comput.*, 39(1):195–259, 2009.

[Flo52] Merrill M Flood. Some experimental games. *Management Science*, 5(1):5–26, 1952.

[Gro73] Theodore Groves. Incentives in teams. *Econometrica: Journal of the Econometric Society*, pages 617–631, 1973.

[KP99] Elias Koutsoupias and Christos Papadimitriou. Worst-case equilibria. In *STACS 99*, pages 404–413. Springer, 1999.

[LMSW06] Thomas Locher, Patrick Moor, Stefan Schmid, and Roger Wattenhofer. Free Riding in BitTorrent is Cheap. In *5th Workshop on Hot Topics in Networks (HotNets), Irvine, California, USA*, November 2006.

[MSW06] Thomas Moscibroda, Stefan Schmid, and Roger Wattenhofer. When selfish meets evil: byzantine players in a virus inoculation game. In *Proceedings of the Twenty-Fifth Annual ACM Symposium on Principles of Distributed Computing, PODC 2006, Denver, CO, USA, July 23-26, 2006*, pages 35–44, 2006.

[Nas50] John F. Nash. Equilibrium points in n-person games. *Proc. Nat. Acad. Sci. USA*, 36(1):48–49, 1950.

[Neu28] John von Neumann. Zur Theorie der Gesellschaftsspiele. *Mathematische Annalen*, 100(1):295–320, 1928.

[NM44] John von Neumann and Oskar Morgenstern. *Theory of games and economic behavior*. Princeton university press, 1944.

[Vic61] William Vickrey. Counterspeculation, auctions, and competitive sealed tenders. *The Journal of finance*, 16(1):8–37, 1961.

Chapter 15

Time, Clocks & GPS

"A man with a clock knows what time it is – a man with two is never sure." (Segal's Law)

15.1   Time & Clocks

Definition 15.1 (Second). *A **second** is the time that passes during 9,192,631,770 oscillation cycles of a caesium-133 atom.*

Remarks:

- This definition is a bit simplified. The official definition is given by the *Bureau International des Poids et Mesures*.

- Historically, a second was defined as one in 86,400 parts of a day, dividing the day into 24 hours, 60 minutes and 60 seconds.

- Since the duration of a day depends on the unsteady rotation cycle of the Earth, the novel oscillation-based definition has been adopted. Leap seconds are used to keep time synchronized to Earth's rotation.

Definition 15.2 (Wall-Clock Time). *The **wall-clock time** t^* is the true time (a perfectly accurate clock would show).*

Definition 15.3 (Clock). *A **clock** is a device which tracks and indicates time.*

Remarks:

- A clock's time t is a function of the wall-clock time t^*, i.e., $t = f(t^*)$. Ideally, $t = t^*$, but in reality there are often errors.

Definition 15.4 (Clock Error). *The **clock error** or clock skew is the difference between two clocks, e.g., $t - t^*$ or $t - t'$. In practice the clock error is often modeled as $t = (1 + \delta)t^* + \xi(t^*)$.*

Remarks:

- The importance of accurate timekeeping and clock synchronization is reflected in the following statement by physicist Steven Jefferts: "We've learned that every time we build a better clock, somebody comes up with a use for it that you couldn't have foreseen."

Definition 15.5 (Drift). *The **drift** δ is the predictable clock error.*

Remarks:

- Drift is relatively constant over time, but may change with supply voltage, temperature and age of an oscillator.

- Stable clock sources, which offer a low drift, are generally preferred, but also more expensive, larger and more power hungry, which is why many consumer products feature inaccurate clocks.

Definition 15.6 (parts-per-million). *Clock drift is indicated in **parts-per-million (ppm)**. One ppm corresponds to a time error growth of one microsecond per second.*

Remarks:

- In PCs, the so-called *real-time clock* normally is a crystal oscillator with a maximum drift between 5 and 100 ppm.

- Applications in signal processing, for instance GPS, need more accurate clocks. Common drift values are 0.5 to 2 ppm.

Definition 15.7 (Jitter). *The **jitter** ξ is the unpredictable, random noise of the clock error.*

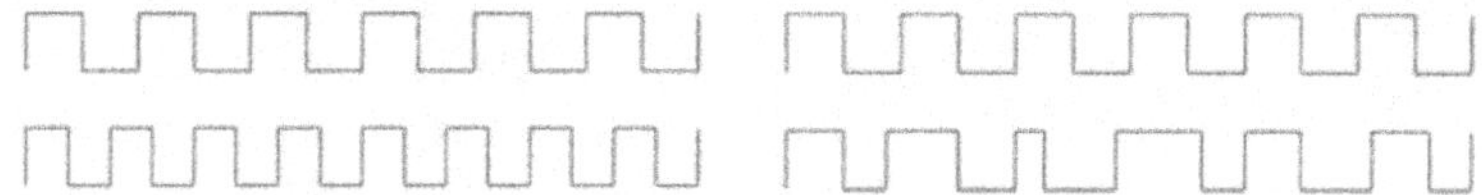

Figure 15.8: Drift (left) and Jitter (right). On top is a square wave, the wall-clock time t^*.

Remarks:

- In other words, jitter is the irregularity of the clock. Unlike drift, jitter can vary fast.

- Jitter captures all the errors that are not explained by drift. Figure 15.8 visualizes the concepts.

15.2 Clock Synchronization

Definition 15.9 (Clock Synchronization). *Clock synchronization is the process of matching multiple clocks (nodes) to have a common time.*

Remarks:

- A trade-off exists between synchronization accuracy, convergence time, and cost.

- Different clock synchronization variants may tolerate crashing, erroneous or byzantine nodes.

Algorithm 15.10 Network Time Protocol NTP

1: Two nodes, client u and server v

2: **while** true **do**
3:     Node u sends request to v at time t_u
4:     Node v receives request at time t_v
5:     Node v processes the request and replies at time t'_v
6:     Node u receives the response at time t'_u

7:     Propagation delay $\delta = \frac{(t'_u - t_u) - (t'_v - t_v)}{2}$ (assumption: symmetric)
8:     Clock skew $\theta = \frac{(t_v - (t_u + \delta)) - (t'_u - (t'_v + \delta))}{2} = \frac{(t_v - t_u) + (t'_v - t'_u)}{2}$
9:     Node u adjusts clock by $+\theta$
10:    Sleep before next synchronization
11: **end while**

Remarks:

- Many NTP servers are public, answering to UDP packets.

- The most accurate NTP servers derive their time from atomic clocks, synchronized to UTC. To reduce those server's load, a hierarchy of NTP servers is available in a forest (multiple trees) structure.

- The regular synchronization of NTP limits the maximum error despite unpredictable clock errors. Synchronizing clocks just once is only sufficient for a short time period.

Definition 15.11 (PTP). *The **Precision Time Protocol (PTP)** is a clock synchronization protocol similar to NTP, but which uses **medium access control (MAC)** layer timestamps.*

Remarks:

- MAC layer timestamping removes the unknown time delay incurred through messages passing through the software stack.

- PTP can achieve sub-microsecond accuracy in local networks.

Definition 15.12 (Global Synchronization). *Global synchronization establishes a common time between **any** two nodes in the system.*

Remarks:

- For example, email needs global timestamps. Also, event detection for power grid control and earthquake localization need global timestamps.

- Earthquake localization does not need real-time synchronization; it is sufficient if a common time can be reconstructed when needed, also known as "post factum" synchronization.

- NTP and PTP are both examples of clock synchronization algorithms that optimize for global synchronization.

- However, two nodes that constantly communicate may receive their timestamps through different paths of the NTP forest, and hence they may accumulate different errors. Because of the clock skew, a message sent by node u might arrive at node v with a timestamp in the future.

Algorithm 15.13 Local Time Synchronization

1: **while** true **do**
2:    Exchange current time with neighbors
3:    Adapt time to neighbors, e.g., to average or median
4:    Sleep before next synchronization
5: **end while**

Definition 15.14 (Local Synchronization). *Local synchronization establishes a common time between close-by (neighbor) nodes.*

Remarks:

- Local synchronization is the method of choice to establish *time-division multiple access (TDMA)* and coordination of wake-up and sleeping times in wireless networks. Only close-by nodes matter as far-away nodes will not interfere with their transmissions.

- Local synchronization is also relevant for precise event localization. For instance, using the speed of sound, measured sound arrival times from co-located sensors can be used to localize a shooter.

- While global synchronization algorithm such as NTP usually synchronize to an external time standard, local algorithms often just synchronize among themselves, i.e., the notion of time does not reflect any time standards.

- In wireless networks, one can simplify and improve synchronization.

Algorithm 15.15 Wireless Clock Synchronization with Known Delays

---

1: Given: transmitter s, receivers u, v, with known transmission delays d_u, d_v from transmitter s, respectively.

2: s sends signal at time t_s
3: u receives signal at time t_u
4: v receives signal at time t_v

5: $\Delta_u = t_u - (t_s + d_u)$
6: $\Delta_v = t_v - (t_s + d_v)$

7: Clock skew between u and v: $\theta = \Delta_v - \Delta_u = t_v - d_v + d_u - t_u$

15.3 Time Standards

time standards

Definition 15.16 (TAI). *The **International Atomic Time (TAI)** is a time standard derived from over 400 atomic clocks distributed worldwide.*

Remarks:

- Using a weighted average of all involved clocks, TAI is an order of magnitude more stable than the best clock.

- The involved clocks are synchronized using simultaneous observations of GPS or geostationary satellite transmissions using Algorithm 15.15.

- While a single satellite measurement has a time uncertainty on the order of nanoseconds, averaging over a month improves the accuracy by several orders of magnitude.

Definition 15.17 (Leap Second). *A leap second is an extra second added to a minute to make it irregularly 61 instead of 60 seconds long.*

Remarks:

- Time standards use leap seconds to compensate for the slowing of the Earth's rotation. In theory, also negative leap seconds can be used to make some minutes only 59 seconds long. But so far, this was never necessary.

- For easy implementation, not all time standards use leap seconds, for instance TAI and GPS time do not.

Definition 15.18 (UTC). *The **Coordinated Universal Time (UTC)** is a time standard based on TAI with leap seconds added at irregular intervals to keep it close to mean solar time at $0°$ longitude.*

Remarks:

- The global time standard *Greenwich Mean Time (GMT)* was already established in 1884. With the invention of caesium atomic clocks and the subsequent redefinition of the SI second, UTC replaced GMT in 1967.

- Before time standards existed, each city set their own time according to the local mean solar time, which is difficult to measure exactly. This was changed by the upcoming rail and communication networks.

- Different notations for time and date are in use. A standardized format for timestamps, mostly used for processing by computers, is the ISO 8601 standard. According to this standard, a UTC timestamp looks like this: `1712-02-30T07:39:52Z`. `T` separates the date and time parts while `Z` indicates the time zone with zero offset from UTC.

- Why UTC and not "CUT"? Because France insisted. Same for other abbreviations in this domain, e.g. TAI.

Definition 15.19 (Time Zone). *A **time zone** is a geographical region in which the same time offset from UTC is officially used.*

Remarks:

- Time zones serve to roughly synchronize noon with the sun reaching the day's highest apparent elevation angle.

- Some time zones' offset is not a whole number of hours, e.g. India.

15.4   Clock Sources

Definition 15.20 (Atomic Clock). *An **atomic clock** is a clock which keeps time by counting oscillations of atoms.*

Remarks:

- Atomic clocks are the most accurate clocks known. They can have a drift of only about one second in 150 million years, about 2e-10 ppm!

- Many atomic clocks are based on caesium atoms, which led to the current definition of a second. Others use hydrogen-1 or rubidium-87.

- In the future, atoms with higher frequency oscillations could yield even more accurate clocks.

- Atomic clocks are getting smaller and more energy efficient. Chip-scale atomic clocks (CSAC) are currently being produced for space applications and may eventually find their way into consumer electronics.

- Atomic clocks can serve as a fallback for GPS time in data centers.

Definition 15.21 (System Clock). *The **system clock** in a computer is an oscillator used to synchronize all components on the motherboard.*

Remarks:

- Usually, a quartz crystal oscillator with a frequency of some tens to hundreds MHz is used.

- Therefore, the system clock can achieve a precision of some ns!

- The *CPU clock* is usually a multiple of the system clock, generated from the system clock through a clock multiplier.

- To guarantee nominal operation of the computer, the system clock must have low jitter. Otherwise, some components might not get enough time to complete their operation before the next (early) clock pulse arrives.

- Drift however is not critical for system stability.

- Applications of the system clock include thread scheduling and ensuring smooth media playback.

- If a computer is shut down, the system clock is not running; it is reinitialized when starting the computer.

Definition 15.22 (RTC). *The **real-time clock (RTC)** in a computer is a battery backed oscillator which is running even if the computer is shut down or unplugged.*

Remarks:

- The RTC is read at system startup to initialize the system clock.

- This keeps the computer's time close to UTC even when the time cannot be synchronized over a network.

- RTCs are relatively inaccurate, with a common maximum drift of 5, 20 or even 100 ppm, depending on quality and temperature.

- In many cases, the RTC frequency is 32.768 kHz, which allows for simple timekeeping based on binary counter circuits because the frequency is exactly 2^{15} Hz.

Definition 15.23 (Radio Time Signal). *A **Radio Time Signal** is a time code transmitted via radio waves by a time signal station, referring to a time in a given standard such as UTC.*

Remarks:

- Time signal stations use atomic clocks to send as accurate time codes as possible.

- Radio-controlled clocks are an example application of radio signal time synchronization.

- In Europe, most radio-controlled clocks use the signal transmitted by the *DCF77* station near Frankfurt, Germany.

- Radio time signals can be received much farther than the horizon of the transmitter due to signal reflections at the ionosphere. DCF77 for instance has an official range of 2,000 km.

- The time synchronization accuracy when using radio time signals is limited by the propagation delay of the signal. For instance the delay Frankfurt-Zurich is about 1 ms.

Definition 15.24 (Power Line Clock). *A **power line clock** measures the oscillations from electric AC power lines, e.g. 50 Hz.*

Remarks:

- Clocks in kitchen ovens are usually driven by power line oscillations.

- AC power line oscillations drift about 10 ppm, which is remarkably stable.

- The magnetic field radiating from power lines is strong enough that power line clocks can work wirelessly.

- Power line clocks can be synchronized by matching the observed noisy power line oscillation patterns.

- Power line clocks operate with as little as a few ten µW.

Definition 15.25 (Sunlight Time Synchronization). *Sunlight time synchronization is a method of reconstructing global timestamps by correlating annual solar patterns from light sensors' length of day measurements.*

Remarks:

- Sunlight time synchronization is relatively inaccurate.

- Due to low data rates from length of day measurements, sunlight time synchronization is well-suited for long-time measurements with data storage and post-processing, requiring no communication at the time of measurement.

- Historically, sun and lunar observations were the first measurements used for time determination. Some clock towers still feature sun dials.

- ... but today, the most popular source of time is probably GPS!

15.5 GPS

Definition 15.26 (Global Positioning System). *The **Global Positioning System (GPS)** is a **Global Navigation Satellite System (GNSS)**, consisting of at least 24 satellites orbiting around the Earth, each continuously transmitting its position and time code.*

Remarks:

- Positioning is done in space and *time*!

- GPS provides position and time information to receivers anywhere on Earth where at least four satellite signals can be received.

- Line of sight (LOS) between satellite and receiver is advantageous. GPS works poorly indoors, or with reflections.

- Besides the US GPS, three other GNSS exist: the European Galileo, the Russian GLONASS and the Chinese BeiDou.

- GPS satellites orbit around Earth approximately 20,000 km above the surface, circling Earth twice a day. The signals take between 64 and 89 ms to reach Earth.

- The orbits are precisely determined by ground control stations, optimized for a high number of satellites being concurrently above the horizon at any place on Earth.

Algorithm 15.27 GPS Satellite

1: Given: Each satellite has a unique 1023 bit (± 1, see below) PRN sequence, plus some current navigation data D (also ± 1).

2: The code below is a bit simplified, concentrating on the digital aspects, ignoring that the data is sent on a carrier frequency of 1575.42 MHz.

3: **while** true **do**
4:   **for all** bits $D_i \in D$ **do**
5:     **for** $j = 0 \ldots 19$ **do**
6:       **for** $k = 0 \ldots 1022$ **do** {this loop takes exactly 1 ms}
7:         Send bit $PRN_k \cdot D_i$
8:       **end for**
9:     **end for**
10:   **end for**
11: **end while**

Definition 15.28 (PRN). *Pseudo-Random Noise (PRN) sequences are pseudo-random bit strings. Each GPS satellite uses a unique PRN sequence with a length of 1023 bits for its signal transmissions.*

Remarks:

- The GPS PRN sequences are so-called *Gold codes*, which have low cross-correlation with each other.

- To simplify our math (abstract from modulation), each PRN bit is either 1 or -1.

Definition 15.29 (Navigation Data). *Navigation Data is the data transmitted from satellites, which includes orbit parameters to determine satellite positions, timestamps of signal transmission,* *atmospheric delay estimations and status information of the satellites and GPS as a whole, such as the accuracy and validity of the data.*

Remarks:

- As seen in Algorithm 15.27 each bit is repeated 20 times for better robustness. Thus, the navigation data rate is only 50 bit/s.

- Due to this limited data rate, timestamps are sent every 6 seconds, satellite orbit parameters (function of the satellite position over time) only every 30 seconds. As a result, the latency of a first position estimate after turning on a receiver, which is called *time-to-first-fix (TTFF)*, can be high.

Definition 15.30 (Circular Cross-Correlation). *The **circular cross-correlation** is a similarity measure between two vectors of length N, **circularly** shifted by a given displacement d:*

$$cxcorr(\boldsymbol{a}, \boldsymbol{b}, d) = \sum_{i=0}^{N-1} a_i \cdot b_{i+d \bmod N}$$

Remarks:

- The two vectors are most similar at the displacement d where the sum (cross-correlation value) is maximum.

- The vector of cross-correlation values with all N displacements can efficiently be computed using a fast Fourier transform (FFT) in $\mathcal{O}(N \log N)$ instead of $\mathcal{O}(N^2)$ time.

Algorithm 15.31 Acquisition

1: Received 1 ms signal s with sampling rate $r \cdot 1,023$ kHz
2: Possible Doppler shifts F, e.g. {-10 kHz, -9.8 kHz, ..., +10 kHz}
3: Tensor $A = 0$: Satellite $\times$ carrier frequency $\times$ time

4: **for all** satellites i **do**
5:    $PRN'_i = PRN_i$ stretched with ratio r
6:   **for all** Doppler shifts $f \in F$ **do**
7:      Build modulated PRN''_i with PRN'_i and Doppler frequency f
8:      **for all** delays $d \in \{0, 1, \ldots, 1,023 \cdot r - 1\}$ **do**
9:        $A_i(f, d) = |cxcorr(s, \boldsymbol{PRN''_i}, d)|$
10:     **end for**
11:   **end for**
12:   Select d^* that maximizes $\max_d \max_f A_i(f, d)$
13:   Signal arrival time $r_i = d^* / (r \cdot 1,023$ kHz$)$
14: **end for**

Remarks:

- Multiple milliseconds of acquisition can be summed up to average out noise and therefore improve the arrival time detection probability.

Definition 15.32 (Acquisition). *Acquisition is the process in a GPS receiver that finds the visible satellite signals and detects the delays of the PRN sequences and the Doppler shifts of the signals.*

Remarks:

- The relative speed between satellite and receiver introduces a significant Doppler shift to the carrier frequency. In order to decode the signal, a frequency search for the Doppler shift is necessary.

- The nested loops make acquisition the computationally most intensive part of a GPS receiver.

Algorithm 15.33 Classic GPS Receiver

1: h: Unknown receiver *handset* position
2: θ: Unknown handset time offset to GPS system time
3: r_i: measured signal arrival time in *handset time system*
4: c: signal propagation speed (GPS: speed of light)

5: Perform Acquisition (Algorithm 15.31)
6: Track signals and decode navigation data
7: **for all** satellites i **do**
8:    Using navigation data, determine signal transmit time s_i and position p_i
9:    Measured satellite transmission delay $d_i = r_i - s_i$
10: **end for**
11: Solve the following system of equations for h and θ:
12: $||p_i - h||/c = d_i - \theta$, for all i

Remarks:

- GPS satellites carry precise atomic clocks, but the receiver is not synchronized with the satellites. The arrival times of the signals at the receiver are determined in the receiver's local time. Therefore, even though the satellite signals include transmit timestamps, the exact distance between satellites and receiver is unknown.

- In total, the positioning problem contains four unknown variables, three for the handset's spatial position and one for its time offset from the system time. Therefore, signals from at least four transmitters are needed to find the correct solution.

- Since the equations are quadratic (distance), with as many observations as variables, the system of equations has two solutions in principle. For GPS however, in practice one of the solutions is far from the Earth surface, so the correct solution can always be identified without a fifth satellite.

- More received signals help reducing the measurement noise and thus improving the accuracy.

- Since the positioning solution, which is also called position fix, includes the handset's time offset Δ, this establishes a global time for all handsets. Thus, GPS is useful for global time synchronization.

- For a handset with unknown position, GPS timing is more accurate than time synchronization with a single transmitter, like a time signal station (cf. Definition 15.23). With the latter, the unknown signal propagation delays cannot be accounted for.

Definition 15.34 (A-GPS). *An **Assisted GPS (A-GPS)** receiver fetches the satellite orbit parameters and other navigation data from the Internet, for instance via a cellular network.*

Remarks:

- A-GPS reduces the data transmission time, and thus the TTFF, from a maximum of 30 seconds per satellite to a maximum of 6 seconds.

- Smartphones regularly use A-GPS. However, coarse positioning is usually done based on nearby Wi-Fi base stations only, which saves energy compared to GPS.

- Another GPS improvement is *Differential GPS (DGPS)*: A receiver with a fixed location within a few kilometers of a mobile receiver compares the observed and actual satellite distances. This error is then subtracted at the mobile receiver. DGPS achieves accuracies in the order of 10 cm.

Definition 15.35 (Snapshot GPS Receiver). *A **snapshot receiver** is a GPS receiver that captures one or a few milliseconds of raw GPS signal for a position fix.*

Remarks:

- Snapshot receivers aim at the remaining latency that results from the transmission of timestamps from the satellites every six seconds.

- Since time changes continuously, timestamps cannot be fetched together with the satellite orbit parameters that are valid for two hours.

- Snapshot receiver can determine the ranges to the satellites modulo 1 ms, which corresponds to 300 km. An approximate time and location of the receiver is used to resolve these ambiguities without a timestamp from the satellite signals themselves.

Definition 15.36 (CTN). *Coarse Time Navigation (CTN) is a snapshot receiver positioning technique measuring sub-millisecond satellite ranges from correlation peaks, like conventional GPS receivers.*

Remarks:

- A CTN receiver determines the signal transmit times and satellite positions from its own approximate location by subtracting the signal propagation delay from the receive time. The receiver location and time is not exactly known, but since signals are transmitted exactly whole milliseconds, rounding to the nearest whole millisecond gives the signal transmit time.

- With only a few milliseconds of signal, noise cannot be averaged out well and may lead to wrong signal arrival time estimates. Such wrong measurements usually render the system of equations unsolvable, making positioning infeasible.

Algorithm 15.37 Collective Detection Receiver

1: Given: A raw 1 ms GPS sample s, a set H of location/time hypotheses
2: In addition, the receiver learned all navigation and atmospheric data

3: **for all** hypotheses $h \in H$ **do**
4:     Vector $r = 0$
5:     Set V = satellites that should be visible with hypothesis h
6:     **for all** satellites i in V **do**
7:         $r = r + r_i$, where r_i is expected signal of satellite i. The data of vector r_i incorporates all available information: distance and atmospheric delay between satellite and receiver, frequency shift because of Doppler shift due to satellite movement, current navigation data bit of satellite, etc.
8:     **end for**
9:     Probability $P_h = cxcorr(s, r, 0)$
10: **end for**
11: Solution: hypothesis $h \in H$ maximizing P_h

Definition 15.38 (Collective Detection). *Collective Detection (CD) is a maximum likelihood snapshot receiver localization method, which does not determine an arrival time for each satellite, but rather combine all the available information and take a decision only at the end of the computation.*

Remarks:

- CD can tolerate a few low quality satellite signals and is thus more robust than CTN.

- In essence, CD tests how well position hypotheses match the received signal. For large position and time uncertainties, the high number of hypotheses require a lot of computation power.

- CD can be sped up by a branch and bound approach, which reduces the computation per position fix to the order of one second even for uncertainties of 100 km and a minute.

15.6 Lower Bounds

In the *clock synchronization* problem, we are given a network (graph) with n nodes. The goal for each node is to have a (logical) clock such that the clock values are well synchronized, and close to real time. Each node is equipped with a hardware (system) clock, that ticks more or less in real time, i.e., the time between two pulses is arbitrary between $[1 - \epsilon, 1 + \epsilon]$, for a constant $\epsilon \ll 1$. We assume that messages sent over the edges of the graph have a delivery time between $[0, 1]$. In other words, we have a bounded but variable drift on the hardware clocks and an arbitrary jitter in the delivery times. The goal is to design a message-passing algorithm that ensures that the logical clock skew of adjacent nodes is as small as possible at all times.

Definition 15.39 (Local and Global Clock Skew). *In a network of nodes, the **local clock skew** is the skew between neighboring nodes, while the **global clock skew** is the maximum skew between any two nodes.*

Remarks:

- Of interest is also the *average global clock skew*, that is the average skew between any pair of nodes.

Theorem 15.40. *The global clock skew (Definition 15.12) is $\Omega(D)$, where D is the diameter of the network graph.*

Proof. For a node u, let t_u be the logical time of u and let $(u \to v)$ denote a message sent from u to a node v. Let $t(m)$ be the time delay of a message m and let u and v be neighboring nodes. First consider a case where the message delays between u and v are $1/2$. Then, all the messages sent by u and v at time t according to the clock of the sender arrive at time $t + 1/2$ according to the clock of the receiver.
  Then consider the following cases

- $t_u = t_v + 1/2$, $t(u \to v) = 1$, $t(v \to u) = 0$

- $t_u = t_v - 1/2$, $t(u \to v) = 0$, $t(v \to u) = 1$,

where the message delivery time is always fast for one node and slow for the other and the logical clocks are off by $1/2$. In both scenarios, the messages sent at time i according to the clock of the sender arrive at time $i + 1/2$ according to the logical clock of the receiver. Therefore, for nodes u and v, both cases with clock drift seem the same as the case with perfectly synchronized clocks. Furthermore, in a linked list of D nodes, the left- and rightmost nodes l, r cannot distinguish $t_l = t_r + D/2$ from $t_l = t_r - D/2$. $\quad\square$

Remarks:

- From Theorem 15.40, it directly follows that any reasonable clock synchronization algorithm must have a global skew of $\Omega(D)$.

- Many natural algorithms manage to achieve a global clock skew of $\mathcal{O}(D)$.

- As both message jitter and hardware clock drift are bounded by constants, it feels like we should be able to get a constant drift at least between neighboring nodes.

- Let us look at the following algorithm:

Algorithm 15.41 Local Clock Synchronization (at node v)

1: **repeat**
2:      **send** logical time t_v to all neighbors
3:      **if** Receive logical time t_u, where $t_u > t_v$, from any neighbor u **then**
4:          $t_v = t_u$
5:      **end if**
6: **until** done

Lemma 15.42. *The clock synchronization protocol of Algorithm 15.41 has a local skew of $\Omega(n)$.*

Proof. Let the graph be a linked list of D nodes. We denote the nodes by $v_1, v_2, \ldots, v_D$ from left to right and the logical clock of node v_i by t_i. Apart from the left-most node v_1 all hardware clocks run with speed 1 (real time). Node v_1 runs at maximum speed, i.e. the time between two pulses is not 1 but $1 - \epsilon$. Assume that initially all message delays are 1. After some time, node v_1 will start to speed up v_2, and after some more time v_2 will speed up v_3, and so on. At some point of time, we will have a clock skew of 1 between any two neighbors. In particular $t_1 = t_D + D - 1$.

Now we start playing around with the message delays. Let $t_1 = T$. First we set the delay between the v_1 and v_2 to 0. Now node v_2 immediately adjusts its logical clock to T. After this event (which is instantaneous in our model) we set the delay between v_2 and v_3 to 0, which results in v_3 setting its logical clock to T as well. We perform this successively to all pairs of nodes until v_{D-2} and v_{D-1}. Now node v_{D-1} sets its logical clock to T, which indicates that the difference between the logical clocks of v_{D-1} and v_D is $T - (T - (D-1)) = D - 1$. $\qquad\square$

Remarks:

- The introduced examples may seem cooked-up, but examples like this exist in all networks, and for all algorithms. Indeed, it was shown that any natural clock synchronization algorithm must have a bad local skew. In particular, a protocol that averages between all neighbors (like Algorithm 15.13) is even worse than Algorithm 15.41. An averaging algorithm has a clock skew of $\Omega(D^2)$ in the linked list, at all times.

- It was shown that the local clock skew is $\Theta(\log D)$, i.e., there is a protocol that achieves this bound, and there is a proof that no algorithm can be better than this bound!

- Note that these are worst-case bounds. In practice, clock drift and message delays may not be the worst possible, typically the speed of hardware clocks changes at a comparatively slow pace and the message transmission times follow a benign probability distribution. If we assume this, better protocols do exist, in theory as well as in practice.

Chapter Notes

Atomic clocks can be used as a GPS fallback for data center synchronization [CDE+13].

GPS has been such a technological breakthrough that even though it dates back to the 1970s, the new GNSS still use essentially the same techniques. Several people worked on snapshot GPS receivers, but the technique has not penetrated into commercial receivers yet. Liu et al. [LPH+12] presented a practical CTN receiver and reduced the solution space by eliminating solutions not lying on the ground. CD receivers are studied since at least

2011 [ABD$^+$11] and have recently been made practically feasible through branch and bound [BEW17]

It has been known for a long time that the global clock skew is $\Theta(D)$ [LL84, ST87]. The problem of synchronizing the clocks of nearby nodes was introduced by Fan and Lynch in [LF04]; they proved a surprising lower bound of $\Omega(\log D/\log\log D)$ for the local skew. The first algorithm providing a non-trivial local skew of $\mathcal{O}(\sqrt{D})$ was given in [LW06]. Later, matching upper and lower bounds of $\Theta(\log D)$ were given in [LLW10]. The problem has also been studied in a dynamic setting [KLO09, KLLO10] or when a fraction of nodes experience byzantine faults and the other nodes have to recover from faulty initial state (i.e., self-stabilizing) [DD06, DW04]. The self-stabilizing byzantine case has been solved with asymptotically optimal skew [KL18].

Clock synchronization is a well-studied problem in practice, for instance regarding the global clock skew in sensor networks, e.g. [EGE02, GKS03, MKSL04, PSJ04]. One more recent line of work is focussing on the problem of minimizing the local clock skew [BvRW07, SW09, LSW09, FW10, FZTS11].

Bibliography

[ABD$^+$11] Penina Axelrad, Ben K Bradley, James Donna, Megan Mitchell, and Shan Mohiuddin. Collective Detection and Direct Positioning Using Multiple GNSS Satellites. *Navigation*, 58(4):305–321, 2011.

[BEW17] Pascal Bissig, Manuel Eichelberger, and Roger Wattenhofer. Fast and Robust GPS Fix Using One Millisecond of Data. In *Information Processing in Sensor Networks (IPSN), 2017 16th ACM/IEEE International Conference on*, pages 223–234. IEEE, 2017.

[BvRW07] Nicolas Burri, Pascal von Rickenbach, and Roger Wattenhofer. Dozer: Ultra-Low Power Data Gathering in Sensor Networks. In *International Conference on Information Processing in Sensor Networks (IPSN), Cambridge, Massachusetts, USA*, April 2007.

[CDE$^+$13] James C Corbett, Jeffrey Dean, Michael Epstein, Andrew Fikes, Christopher Frost, Jeffrey John Furman, Sanjay Ghemawat, Andrey Gubarev, Christopher

Heiser, Peter Hochschild, et al. Spanner: Google's globally distributed database. *ACM Transactions on Computer Systems (TOCS)*, 31(3):8, 2013.

[DD06]   Ariel Daliot and Danny Dolev. Self-Stabilizing Byzantine Pulse Synchronization. *Computing Research Repository*, 2006.

[DW04]   Shlomi Dolev and Jennifer L. Welch. Self-stabilizing clock synchronization in the presence of Byzantine faults. September 2004.

[EGE02]   Jeremy Elson, Lewis Girod, and Deborah Estrin. Fine-grained Network Time Synchronization Using Reference Broadcasts. *ACM SIGOPS Operating Systems Review*, 36:147–163, 2002.

[FW10]   Roland Flury and Roger Wattenhofer. Slotted Programming for Sensor Networks. In *International Conference on Information Processing in Sensor Networks (IPSN), Stockholm, Sweden*, April 2010.

[FZTS11]   Federico Ferrari, Marco Zimmerling, Lothar Thiele, and Olga Saukh. Efficient Network Flooding and Time Synchronization with Glossy. In *Proceedings of the 10th International Conference on Information Processing in Sensor Networks (IPSN)*, pages 73–84, 2011.

[GKS03]   Saurabh Ganeriwal, Ram Kumar, and Mani B. Srivastava. Timing-sync Protocol for Sensor Networks. In *Proceedings of the 1st international conference on Embedded Networked Sensor Systems (SenSys)*, 2003.

[KL18]   Pankaj Khanchandani and Christoph Lenzen. Self-Stabilizing Byzantine Clock Synchronization with Optimal Precision. January 2018.

[KLLO10]   Fabian Kuhn, Christoph Lenzen, Thomas Locher, and Rotem Oshman. Optimal Gradient Clock Synchronization in Dynamic Networks. In *29th Symposium on Principles of Distributed Computing (PODC), Zurich, Switzerland*, July 2010.

[KLO09]   Fabian Kuhn, Thomas Locher, and Rotem Oshman. Gradient Clock Synchronization in Dynamic Networks.

In *21st ACM Symposium on Parallelism in Algorithms and Architectures (SPAA), Calgary, Canada*, August 2009.

[LF04] Nancy Lynch and Rui Fan. Gradient Clock Synchronization. In *Proceedings of the 23rd Annual ACM Symposium on Principles of Distributed Computing (PODC)*, 2004.

[LL84] Jennifer Lundelius and Nancy Lynch. An Upper and Lower Bound for Clock Synchronization. *Information and Control*, 62:190–204, 1984.

[LLW10] Christoph Lenzen, Thomas Locher, and Roger Wattenhofer. Tight Bounds for Clock Synchronization. In *Journal of the ACM, Volume 57, Number 2*, January 2010.

[LPH+12] Jie Liu, Bodhi Priyantha, Ted Hart, Heitor Ramos, Antonio A.F. Loureiro, and Qiang Wang. Energy Efficient GPS Sensing with Cloud Offloading. In *10th ACM Conference on Embedded Networked Sensor Systems (SenSys 2012)*. ACM, November 2012.

[LSW09] Christoph Lenzen, Philipp Sommer, and Roger Wattenhofer. Optimal Clock Synchronization in Networks. In *7th ACM Conference on Embedded Networked Sensor Systems (SenSys), Berkeley, California, USA*, November 2009.

[LW06] Thomas Locher and Roger Wattenhofer. Oblivious Gradient Clock Synchronization. In *20th International Symposium on Distributed Computing (DISC), Stockholm, Sweden*, September 2006.

[MKSL04] Miklós Maróti, Branislav Kusy, Gyula Simon, and Ákos Lédeczi. The Flooding Time Synchronization Protocol. In *Proceedings of the 2nd international Conference on Embedded Networked Sensor Systems*, SenSys '04, 2004.

[PSJ04] Santashil PalChaudhuri, Amit Kumar Saha, and David B. Johnson. Adaptive Clock Synchronization in Sensor Networks. In *Proceedings of the 3rd International Symposium on Information Processing in Sensor Networks*, IPSN '04, 2004.

[ST87] T. K. Srikanth and S. Toueg. Optimal Clock Synchronization. *Journal of the ACM*, 34:626–645, 1987.

[SW09] Philipp Sommer and Roger Wattenhofer. Gradient Clock Synchronization in Wireless Sensor Networks. In *8th ACM/IEEE International Conference on Information Processing in Sensor Networks (IPSN), San Francisco, USA*, April 2009.

Chapter 16

Markov Chains & PageRank

Let us try to predict the weather! How long until it is rainy the next time? What about the weather in ten days? What is the local "climate", i.e., the "average" weather?

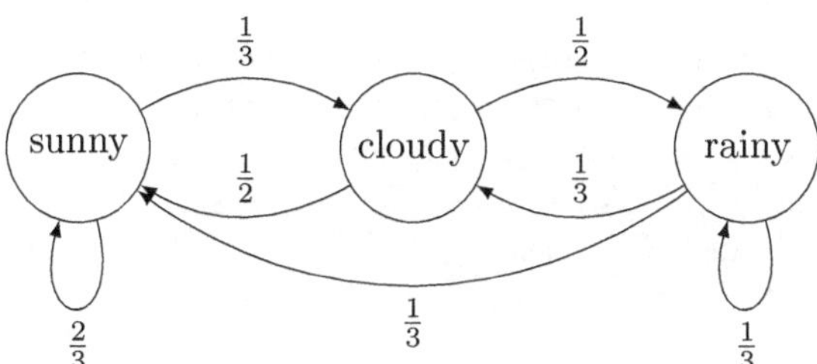

Figure 16.1: According to a self-proclaimed weather expert, the above graph models the weather in Zrich. On any given day, the weather is either *sunny*, *cloudy*, or *rainy*. The probability to have a cloudy day after a sunny day is $\frac{1}{3}$. In the context of Markov chains the nodes, in this case *sunny*, *rainy*, and *cloudy*, are called the *states* of the Markov chain.

Remarks:

- Figure 16.1 above is an example of a *Markov chain*—see the next section for a formal definition.

- If the weather is currently sunny, the predictions for the next few days according to the model from Figure 16.1 are:

Day	sunny	cloudy	rainy
0	1	0	0
1	$\frac{2}{3}$	$\frac{1}{3}$	0
2	0.611	0.222	0.167
3	0.574	0.259	0.167
4	0.568	0.247	0.185
$\vdots$	$\vdots$	$\vdots$	$\vdots$

16.1   Markov Chains

Markov chains are a tool for studying *stochastic processes* that evolve over time.

Definition 16.2 (Markov Chain). *Let S be a finite or countably infinite set of **states**. A **(discrete time) Markov chain** is a sequence of random variables $X_0, X_1, X_2, \ldots \in S$ that satisfies the Markov property (see below).*

Definition 16.3 (Markov Property). *A sequence (X_t) of random variables has the **Markov property** if for all t, the probability distribution for X_{t+1} depends only on X_t, but not on $X_{t-1}, \ldots, X_0$. More formally, for all $t \in \mathbb{N}_{>0}$ and $s_0, \ldots, s_{t+1} \in S$ it holds that $\Pr[X_{t+1} = s_{t+1} \mid X_0 = s_0, X_1 = s_1, \ldots, X_t = s_t] = \Pr[X_{t+1} = s_{t+1} \mid X_t = s_t]$.*

Remarks:

- A sequence of random variables is also called a *discrete time stochastic process*. Processes that satisfy the Markov property are also called *memoryless*.

- The probability distribution of X_0 does not depend on a previous state (since there is none). It is called the *initial distribution*, and we denote it by the vector $q_0 = (q_{0,s})_{s \in S}$ with the entries $\Pr[X_0 = s]$ for every state $s \in S$. If the first day is sunny, the initial distribution is $q_0 = (1, 0, 0)$.

Definition 16.4 (Time Homogeneous Markov Chains). *A Markov chain is* **time homogeneous** *if* $\Pr[X_{t+1} = s_{t+1} \mid X_t = s_t]$ *is independent of t, and in that case $p_{i,j} = \Pr[X_{t+1} = i \mid X_t = j]$ is well defined.*

Remarks:

- We will only consider time homogeneous Markov chains.

- Markov chains are often modeled using *directed* graphs, as in Figure 16.1. The states are represented as nodes, and an edge from state i to state j is weighted with probability $p_{i,j}$.

- Just like directed graphs, Markov chains can be written in matrix form (using the adjacency matrix). In this context, the matrix is called the *transition matrix*, and we denote it by P. For the example from Figure 16.1, the transition matrix is:

		to		
		sunny	cloudy	rainy
	sunny	$2/3$	$1/3$	0
from	cloudy	$1/2$	0	$1/2$
	rainy	$1/3$	$1/3$	$1/3$

- Let $q_t = (q_{t,i})_{i \in S}$ be the probability distribution on S for time t, i.e., $q_{t,i} = \Pr[X_t = i]$. The probability to be in state j at time $t + 1$ is $q_{t+1,j} = \sum_{i \in S} \Pr[X_t = i] \cdot \Pr[X_{t+1} = j \mid X_t = i] = \sum_{i \in S} q_{t,i} \cdot p_{i,j}$. This can be written as the vector-matrix-multiplication $q_{t+1} = q_t \cdot P$.

- The state distribution at time t is $q_t = q_0 \cdot P^t$. We denote by $p_{i,j}^{(t)}$ the entry at position i, j in P^t, i.e., the probability of reaching j from i in t steps.

- If we start a Markov chain in a single state (with probability 1), we do a random walk.

Definition 16.5 (Random Walk). *Let $G = (V, E)$ be a directed graph, and let $\omega : E \to [0, 1]$ be a weight function so that $\sum_{v:(u,v) \in E} \omega(u, v) = 1$ for all nodes u. Let $u \in V$ be the* **starting node**. *A* **weighted random walk on G starting at** u *is the following discrete Markov chain in discrete time. Beginning with*

*$X_0 = u$, in every step t, the node X_{t+1} is chosen according to the weights $\omega(X_t, v)$, where v are the neighbors of X_t. If G is undirected and unweighted, then X_{t+1} is chosen uniformly at random among X_t's neighbors and the random walk is called **simple**.*

Remarks:

- In Section 16.5 we will study some simple random walks.

- Now that we understand the definitions, we want to do some calculations. E.g., if it is sunny today, how long will it stay sunny?

16.2   Hitting Time & Arrival Probability

Definition 16.6 (Sojourn Time). *The **sojourn time** T_i of state i is the time the process stays in state i.*

Remarks:

- It holds that $\Pr[T_i = k] = p_{i,i}^{k-1} \cdot (1 - p_{i,i})$, i.e., T_i is *geometrically distributed*. For example $\mathbb{E}[T_{\text{sunny}}] = 3$.

- The sojourn time T_i does not depend on the time the process has spent in state i already (memoryless property). The geometric distribution is the only discrete distribution that is memoryless.

- If it is currently sunny, how long does it take until we see the first rainy day?

Definition 16.7 (Hitting Time & Arrival Probability). *Let i and j be two states. The **hitting time** $T_{i,j}$ is the random variable counting the number of steps until visiting j the first time when starting from state i, i.e., the value of $T_{i,j}$ is the smallest integer $t \geq 1$ for which $X_t = j$ under the condition that $X_0 = i$. The **expected hitting time** from i to j is the expected value $h_{i,j} = \mathbb{E}[T_{i,j}]$. The **arrival probability** from i to j is the probability $f_{i,j} = \Pr[T_{i,j} < \infty]$.*

Remarks:

- The time $c_{i,j} = h_{i,j} + h_{j,i}$ is referred to as the *commute time* between i and j.

- The following lemma states that the expected hitting time can be computed by solving a system of linear equations.

Lemma 16.8. *If $h_{i,j}$ exists for all $i, j \in S$, then the expected hitting times are*

$$h_{i,j} = 1 + \sum_{k \neq j} p_{i,k} h_{k,j} \,.$$

Proof. Plugging in the definition of $h_{i,j}$ and applying the law of total probability we get that

$$h_{i,j} = \mathbb{E}[T_{i,j}] = \sum_{k \in S} \mathbb{E}[T_{i,j} \mid X_1 = k] \cdot p_{i,k} \,.$$

Taking the jth term out, we obtain

$$h_{i,j} = \mathbb{E}[T_{i,j} \mid X_1 = j] \cdot p_{i,j} + \sum_{k \neq j} \mathbb{E}[T_{i,j} \mid X_1 = k] \cdot p_{i,k}$$

$$= 1 \cdot p_{i,j} + \sum_{k \neq j} (1 + \mathbb{E}[T_{k,j}]) \cdot p_{i,k} \,.$$

Since $p_{i,j}$ together with all the values $p_{i,k}$ sum up to 1, we can simplify to

$$h_{i,j} = 1 + \sum_{k \neq j} \mathbb{E}[T_{k,j}] \cdot p_{i,k} = 1 + \sum_{k \neq j} p_{i,k} h_{k,j} \,. \qquad \square$$

Remarks:

- On a sunny day it takes in expectation 8 days until it starts raining.

- Lemma 16.9 for the arrival probabilities can be established similarly to Lemma 16.8.

Lemma 16.9. *For all $i, j \in S$, the arrival probability is*

$$f_{i,j} = p_{i,j} + \sum_{k \neq j} p_{i,k} f_{k,j} \,.$$

16.3   Stationary Distribution & Ergodicity

What is the "climate" in Zrich? Often one is particularly interested in the long term behavior of Markov chains and random walks. The mathematical notion that captures a Markov chain's long term behavior is the *stationary distribution*, which we will introduce and study in the following.

Remarks:

- The entries in P^t contain the probability of entering a certain weather condition (state). What happens for large values of t? The matrix seems to converge!

$$P^{10} \approx \begin{pmatrix} 0.563 & 0.250 & 0.187 \\ 0.562 & 0.250 & 0.187 \\ 0.562 & 0.250 & 0.188 \end{pmatrix}$$

- No matter what the initial weather q_0 is, the product $q_0 \cdot P^t$ seems to approach $\tilde{q} \approx (0.563, 0.250, 0.187)$ as t grows. Moreover, if we multiply the vector $\tilde{q}$ with P we *almost* get $\tilde{q}$ again. In other words, $\tilde{q}$ is almost an eigenvector of P with eigenvalue 1.

Definition 16.10 (Stationary Distribution). *A distribution π over the states is called **stationary distribution** of the Markov chain with transition matrix P if $\pi = \pi \cdot P$.*

Remarks:

- Our weather Markov chain converges towards $\pi = (9/16, 4/16, 3/16)$, which is an eigenvector of P with eigenvalue 1. We conclude that in the long run, 9 out of 16 days are sunny in Zurich. The weather model appears to be not as accurate as the weather expert led us to believe ...

- Consider the sequence $q_i = q_{i-1} \cdot P$, where q_0 is the initial distribution. In general, this sequence does not necessarily converge as t grows. However, if it does converge to some distribution π, then it must hold that $\pi = \pi \cdot P$.

Lemma 16.11. *The transition matrix of every Markov chain has a left eigenvector with eigenvalue 1.*

Proof. Let P be the transition matrix of a Markov chain, and denote by $e = (1, \ldots, 1)^\top$ the all-ones vector. Because in P the entries in each row sum up to 1 (P is row stochastic), it holds that $Pe = e$. Denoting by I the identity matrix, it follows that $(P - I)e = 0$. In other words, e is an eigenvector with eigenvalue 0 for $(P - I)$, which implies that $(P - I)$ is singular, i.e., not invertible. Thus, also $(P - I)^\top$ is singular, and it follows that there is a vector $\pi \neq 0$ so that $0 = (P - I)^\top \pi = P^\top \pi - I\pi$. Transposing and rearranging we obtain that $\pi^\top P = \pi^\top$, as desired. $\qquad\square$

Remarks:

- Using Brouwer's fixed point theorem one can show that there is also a left eigenvector π that corresponds to a probability distribution.

- The stationary distribution is not necessarily unique, see Figure 16.12. The issue is that some states are not reachable from all other states.

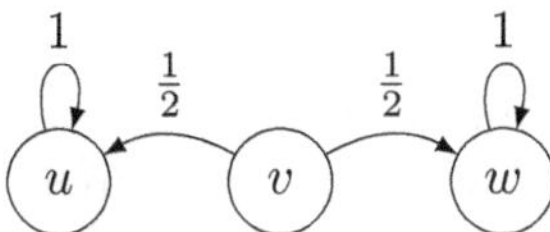

Figure 16.12: This Markov chain has infinitely many stationary distributions, for example $\pi_0 = (1, 0, 0)$, $\pi_1 = (0, 0, 1)$, and $\pi_{0.8} = (0.2, 0, 0.8)$. The states u and w are called *absorbing* states, since they are never left once they are entered.

Definition 16.13 (Irreducible Markov Chains). *A Markov chain is **irreducible** if all states are reachable from all other states. That is, if for all $i, j \in S$ there is some $t \in \mathbb{N}$, such that $p_{i,j}^{(t)} > 0$.*

Lemma 16.14. *In an irreducible Markov chain it holds that $h_{i,j} < \infty$ for all states i, j.*

Proof. Fix some state j, and observe that due to Definition 16.13 for every $s \in S$, there is some t_s so that $p_{s,j}^{(t_s)} > 0$. Denote by $t = \max\{t_s \mid s \in S\}$ the largest such value. State j can be reached from every state in at most t steps. We partition the random walk into *trials* of t successive steps. Within each trial, state j is reached with probability at least $p = \min\{p_{s,j}^{t_s} \mid s \in S\}$. The number of trials until the random walk reaches j is thus upper bounded by a geometric distribution with parameter p. It follows that at most $1/p$ trials are necessary to reach j, and we conclude that $h_{i,j} \leq t/p$ for any i. $\qquad\square$

Remarks:

- Similarly, it follows that $f_{i,j} = 1$ for all states i, j if the Markov chain is irreducible.

Lemma 16.15. *Every finite irreducible Markov chain has a unique stationary distribution π. The distribution is $\pi_j = \frac{1}{h_{j,j}}$ for all $j \in S$.*

Proof. Denote by P the transition matrix of an irreducible Markov chain. Let $\pi \neq 0$ be a left eigenvector of P with eigenvalue 1 as promised by Lemma 16.11. Denote further by $h_{i,j}$ the expected hitting times guaranteed by Lemma 16.14.

We first consider the case that $\sum_i \pi_i \neq 0$ and w.l.o.g. assume that $\sum_i \pi_i = 1$. Due to Lemma 16.8 it holds that for any $j \in S$,

$$\pi_i h_{i,j} = \pi_i \left(1 + \sum_{k \neq j} p_{i,k} h_{k,j}\right) \text{ for all } i \in S.$$

Since $\sum_i \pi_i = 1$, summing up those equations over all i yields

$$\pi_j h_{j,j} + \sum_{i \neq j} \pi_i h_{i,j} = 1 + \sum_i \pi_i \sum_{k \neq j} p_{i,k} h_{k,j}$$

$$= 1 + \sum_{k \neq j} h_{k,j} \sum_i \pi_i p_{i,k},$$

by switching the summation on the right hand side. Since π is an eigenvector with eigenvalue 1, it holds that $\sum_i \pi_i p_{i,k} = \pi_k$, and thus the equation becomes

$$\pi_j h_{j,j} + \sum_{i \neq j} \pi_i h_{i,j} = 1 + \sum_{k \neq j} h_{k,j} \pi_k \, .$$

Noting that all $h_{j,j} > 1$ we conclude that $\pi_j = 1/h_{j,j}$, as desired. In the remaining case where $\sum_i \pi_i = 0$, the equation turns into

$$\pi_j h_{j,j} + \sum_{i \neq j} \pi_i h_{i,j} = \sum_{k \neq j} h_{k,j} \pi_k \, ,$$

yielding that $\pi_j = 0$ for all j. This contradicts that π is an eigenvector. $\qquad\square$

Remarks:

- Irreducible Markov chains with an infinite number of states do not necessarily have a stationary distribution.

- Depending on the choice of the initial distribution, even an irreducible Markov chain does not necessarily converge towards its stationary distribution, see Figure 16.16.

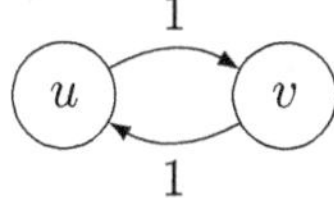

Figure 16.16: This Markov chain is irreducible, and has the unique stationary distribution $\pi = (0.5, 0.5)$. In this particular chain, each state can only be reached every other step, or in other words, both states have *period* 2. Therefore, the initial distribution is attained in every second step, and only $q_0 = \pi$ "converges" towards the stationary distribution.

Definition 16.17 (Aperiodic Markov Chains). *The **period** of a state $j \in S$ is the largest $\xi \in \mathbb{N}$ such that*

$$\{n \in \mathbb{N} \mid p_{j,j}^{(n)} > 0\} \subseteq \{i \cdot \xi \mid i \in \mathbb{N}\}$$

*A state with period $\xi = 1$ is called **aperiodic**, and the Markov chain is **aperiodic** if all its states are.*

Remarks:

- One can show that if the Markov chain is irreducible, then all states have the same period.

- A state j with $p_{j,j} > 0$ is trivially aperiodic.

- If $p_{j,j} = 0$, then one can check whether state j is aperiodic by testing, as illustrated in Figure 16.18, if the following holds: Does j lie on two directed cycles of lengths k and l (counting the edges in the chain) so that k and l are relatively prime, i.e., have a greatest common divisor of 1? Or, using the kth and l^{th} powers of P, are there relatively prime k and l such that both $p_{j,j}^{(k)}$ and $p_{j,j}^{(l)} > 0$?

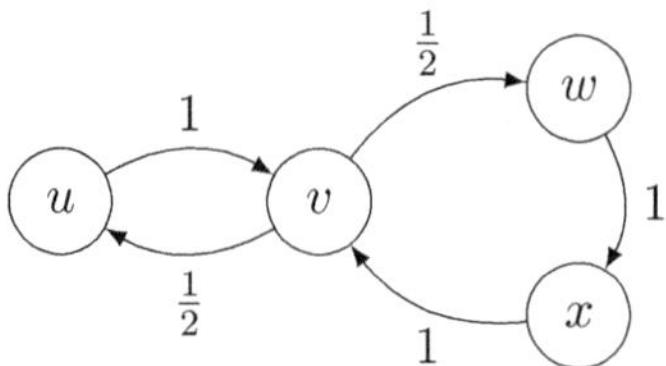

Figure 16.18: Starting at state v there is a cycle $v \to u \to v$ using 2 edges, and a cycle $v \to w \to x \to v$ using 3 edges. Because 2 and 3 are relatively prime, the state v is aperiodic.

Definition 16.19 (Ergodic Markov Chains). *If a finite Markov chain is irreducible and aperiodic, then it is called* ***ergodic***.

Theorem 16.20. *If a Markov chain is ergodic it holds that*

$$\lim_{t \to \infty} q_t = \pi,$$

where π is the unique stationary distribution of the chain.

Remarks:

- The theorem holds regardless of the initial distribution.

- The stationary distribution of ergodic Markov chains can thus be approximated efficiently, namely by successively multiplying a vector with a matrix instead of computing the powers of a matrix.

16.4 PageRank Algorithm

Google's PageRank algorithm is based on a Markov chain obtained from a variant of a random walk.

Remarks:

- Google provides search results that match the user's search terms. Under the hood Google maintains a ranking among websites to make sure "better" or "more important" websites appear early in the search results. Instead of solving the whole problem at once, this ranking is first established globally (independent of the search terms), and only later websites matching the search query are sorted according to some rank. In this section we focus on the ranking part.

- The first step to ranking websites is to crawl the web graph, i.e., a directed graph in which the nodes are websites, and an edge (u, v) indicates that website u contains a hyperlink to website v.

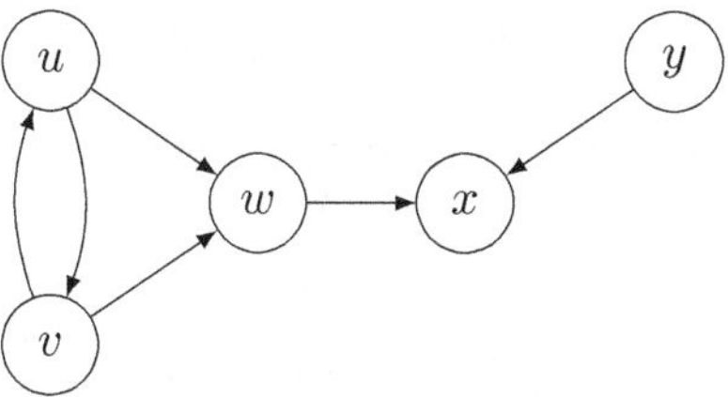

Figure 16.21: An example of a web graph with 5 websites. Website x does not link to any other website, i.e., x is a *sink*.

- A naïve approach is to rank the sites by the number of incoming hyperlinks. In the example from Figure 16.21 this yields the same rank for websites w and x. One could, however, argue that the link from w to x means that x is more important than w.

- Google's idea is to model a *random surfer* who follows hyperlinks in the web graph, i.e., performs a simple random walk. After sufficiently many steps, the websites can be ranked by how many times they were visited. The intuition is that websites are visited more often if they are

- linked by many other sites, which should be a good measure of how important a website is.

- Since the walk is directed, the random surfer can get stuck in sinks (nodes with no outgoing edges). To fix this issue, a random website is chosen for the next step whenever the random surfer reaches a sink.

- Let us denote the *random surfer matrix* describing this simple random walk by W.

- Simulating the simple random walk described by W to find a stationary distribution is not feasible: There are over 1 billion websites—meaning that a lot of steps have to be simulated to get a good estimation of the stationary distribution. Using our knowledge about Markov chains we can simulate many random walks at once by repeatedly multiplying some initial distribution q_0 with W.

- There is no guarantee that this process converges to a stationary distribution. We know that this can be fixed by making the Markov chain ergodic.

- One way to make a Markov chain ergodic is to insert an edge between every two nodes.

Definition 16.22 (Google Matrix). *Let W be a random surfer matrix, and let $\alpha \in (0,1)$ be a constant. Denote further by R the matrix in which all entries are $1/n$. The following matrix M is called the **Google Matrix**:*

$$M = \alpha \cdot W + (1 - \alpha) \cdot R.$$

Remarks:

- The intuition behind R is that in every step, with probability $1-\alpha$, the random surfer "gets bored" by the current website and surfs to a new random site.

- While the R-component in M ensures that the Markov chain converges, it also changes the stationary distribution. To ensure the impact is not too large, α should be chosen close to 1. A typical value for α is 0.85.

- The rate at which the process converges depends on the magnitude of M's second largest eigenvalue. One can show that for M the second largest eigenvalue is at most α, and that the error decreases by a factor of α in each step.

- In the example from Figure 16.21, the page ranks are

Website	Rank
x	0.384615
w	0.230769
u	0.153846
v	0.153846
y	0.0769231

- This initial version of the PageRank algorithm worked well at the time it was invented. However, it can be (and has been) fooled. Consider the following example.

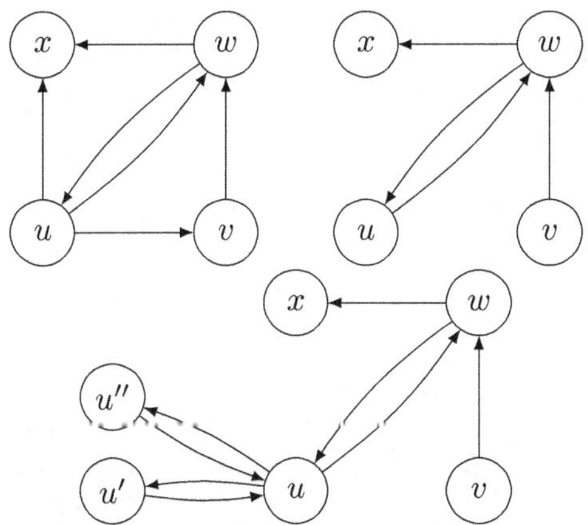

Figure 16.23: Website u wants to improve its PageRank, which is ≈ 0.23 in the initial setting on the left. First, all outgoing links to websites that do not link back are removed. The PageRank improves to ≈ 0.27. In a *Sybil attack* (right) the owner of u creates fake websites u' and u'' whose purpose is to exchange links with u. Moreover, the new websites increase the probability to visit u after a sink. Now, website u is the highest ranked site in the network with a rank of ≈ 0.41.

- Attacks where a single party pretends to be more than one individual are called *Sybil Attacks*.

- It is unknown how exactly Google ranks websites today, and specifically how the engineers at Google mitigate the effects of attacks.

- A different kind of attack on Google is *Google bombing*. This attack relies on the fact that the search terms for which a website v is considered relevant also take the *anchor text* of hyperlinks to website v into account. If, for instance, many websites link to `http://www.ethz.ch` using the anchor text "Smartest People Alive", then a search query for smart people might end up presenting ETH's website.

16.5   Simple Random Walks

In this section, all random walks are considered to be simple. This means that the edges are undirected, and the node for the next step is chosen uniformly at random among the current node's neighbors.

Lemma 16.24. *Let G be a graph with m edges. The stationary distribution π of any simple random walk on G is*

$$\pi_u = \frac{\deg(u)}{2m}.$$

Proof. The Markov chain underlying the random walk is irreducible, with Lemma 16.15 it has a unique stationary distribution. We first verify that π from above satisfies the equation $\pi = \pi \cdot P$ from Definition 16.10:

$$\pi_u = \sum_{v \in N(u)} \pi_v \cdot p_{v,u} = \sum_{v \in N(u)} \frac{\deg(v)}{2m} \cdot \frac{1}{\deg(v)} = \frac{\deg(u)}{2m},$$

for some arbitrary node $u \in V$. Since $\sum_{v \in V} \deg(v) = 2m$, π is a distribution. This proves that π is the unique stationary distribution. $\qquad\square$

Remarks:

- It follows from Lemma 16.15 that for a simple random walk, $h_{u,u}$ is $2m/\deg(u)$.

- The *cover time* $\mathrm{cov}(v)$ is the expected number of steps until all nodes in G were visited at least once, starting at v.

- One could use the following Markov chain to compute the cover time of a simple random walk on the graph $G = (V, E)$. The set of states is $\{(v, I) \mid v \in V$ and $I \in 2^V\} \cup \{t\}$, where v denotes the current state, I denotes the visited states, and t is an additional sink state. The probabilities $p_{(v,I),(w,I \cup \{w\})}$ are 0 if either $I = V$ or $\{v, w\} \notin E$, and $1/\deg(v)$ else (if $\{v, w\} \in E$). Additionally, each state (v, V) has an edge to the sink t with $p_{(v,V),t} = 1$. Then, the cover time is $\mathrm{cov}(v) = h_{(v,\{v\}),t} - 1$.

Lemma 16.25. *Let $G = (V, E)$ be a graph with n nodes and m edges. It holds that* $\mathrm{cov}(s) < 4m(n-1)$ *for any starting node $s \in V$.*

Proof. Let $\{u, v\} \in E$ be an edge. It holds that

$$\frac{2m}{\delta(u)} = h_{u,u} = \frac{1}{\delta(u)} \sum_{w \in N(u)} (h_{w,u} + 1),$$

and thus it must be true that $h_{u,v} < 2m$. Next, observe that it is possible to traverse all nodes in G by using no more than $2n - 2$ edges, e.g., by traversing a spanning tree rooted at s. Since $h_{u,v} < 2m$ holds for every edge $\{u, v\}$ used in the traversal, it follows that $\mathrm{cov}(s) < (2n - 2) \cdot 2m = 4m(n - 1)$, as desired. $\square$

Remarks:

- Consider the resistor network obtained from G by replacing every edge with a 1Ω resistor. Let u and v be two nodes in the resistor network. It can be shown that the commute time $c_{u,v} = 2m \cdot R(u, v)$, where $R(u, v)$ denotes the effective resistance between u and v.

- Foster's Theorem states that for every connected graph $G = (V, E)$ with n nodes,

$$\sum_{(u,v) \in E} R(u, v) = n - 1,$$

i.e., that adding/removing an edge in G reduces/increases the effective resistance, respectively.

Chapter Notes

Historic background on the development of Markov chains can be found in [BLN04]. The short version is that in a 1902 paper [Nek02], the theologist Pavel Alekseevich Nekrasov, in his effort to establish free will on a mathematical basis, (falsely) postulated that independence of events is necessary for the law of large numbers. Markov, being an atheist and considering Nekrasov's reasoning an "abuse of mathematics", set out to prove him wrong.

In 1906, Markov published his first findings on chains of pairwise dependent random variables [Mar06]. This work already includes a variant of Theorem 16.20, thus disproving Nekrasov's claim. Markov also studied the notion of irreducibility [Mar08], proving that for irreducible Markov chains 1 is a single eigenvalue and the largest by magnitude. Today, Markov's ideas are widely applied in, e.g., physics, chemistry, and economics.

Markov chains are the basis for queueing theory, an important transport layer concept. Another application in computer science is the PageRank algorithm [PBMW99]. The bound on the Google matrix' second eigenvalue is from [HK03]. Sybil attacks were originally studied in the context of peer to peer systems [Dou02], and PageRank's sensitivity to such attacks was investigated in [CF06].

The connection from random walks to resistor networks is investigated in depth in [DS06]. By associating a word with each state, random walks can be used to generate random text [SKA05]. More than 120 "scientific" papers were generated using such methods [LL13] and later withdrawn by the publishers.

Bibliography

[BLN04] Gely P. Basharin, Amy N. Langville, and Valeriy A. Naumov. The life and work of a.a. markov. *Linear Algebra and its Applications*, 386:3 – 26, 2004.

[CF06] Alice Cheng and Eric Friedman. Manipulability of pagerank under sybil strategies, 2006.

[Dou02] John R. Douceur. The sybil attack. In *Peer-to-Peer Systems*, volume 2429 of *LNCS*, pages 251–260. Springer Berlin Heidelberg, 2002.

[DS06] Peter G. Doyle and J. Laurie Snell. Random walks and electric networks. `http://math.dartmouth.edu/~doyle/docs/walks/walks.pdf`, July 2006. Originally published 1984. Website accessed Sep. 23, 2015.

[HK03] Taher Haveliwala and Sepandar Kamvar. The second eigenvalue of the google matrix. Technical Report 2003-20, Stanford InfoLab, 2003.

[LL13] Cyril Labb and Dominique Labb. Duplicate and fake publications in the scientific literature: How many SCIgen papers in computer science? *Scientometrics*, 94(1):379–396, 2013.

[Mar06] Andrey Andreyevich Markov. Rasprostranenie zakona bol'shih chisel na velichiny, zavisyaschie drug ot druga. *Izvestiya Fiziko-matematicheskogo obschestva pri Kazanskom universitete*, 2-ya seriya 15 (94):135–156, 1906. (Extension of the law of large numbers to random variables dependent on each other).

[Mar08] Andrey Andreyevich Markov. Rasprostranenie predel'nyh teorem ischisleniya veroyatnostej na summu velichin svyazannyh v cep'. *Zapiski Akademii Nauk po Fiziko-matematicheskomu otdeleniyu*, VIII seriya 25 (3), 1908. (Extension of the limit theorems of probability theory to a sum of variables connected in a chain).

[Nek02] Pavel Alekseevich Nekrasov. The philosophy and logic of science of mass phenomena in human activity, Moscow 1902. In Russian.

[PBMW99] Lawrence Page, Sergey Brin, Rajeev Motwani, and Terry Winograd. The pagerank citation ranking: Bringing order to the web. Technical Report 1999-66, Stanford InfoLab, November 1999.

[SKA05] Jeremy Stribling, Max Krohn, and Dan Aguayo. SCIgen - an automatic CS paper generator. `https://pdos.csail.mit.edu/archive/scigen/`, 2005. Website accessed Sep. 23, 2015.

Index

CPSIA information can be obtained
at www.ICGtesting.com
Printed in the USA
BVHW041716010721
610989BV00009B/54

ST. PAUL
Apostle and Martyr

ST. PAUL
Apostle and Martyr

by Igino Giordani

TRANSLATED FROM THE ITALIAN
BY
MOTHER CLELIA MARANZANA
AND
MOTHER MARY PAULA WILLIAMSON

*Religious of Our Lady of the Retreat
in the Cenacle*

WITH FOREWORD BY
RICHARD CARDINAL CUSHING

ST. PAUL EDITIONS

NIHIL OBSTAT

Edward G. Murray, D.D.
Censor Librorum

IMPRIMATUR

✝*Richard Cardinal Cushing*

Cum permissu superiorum

The rights for translation and publication of this book were granted October 29, 1943, by the Right Reverend Monsignor Francesco Lardone, D.D. of the Catholic University of America, Washington, D.C. who represents the interests of Igino Giordani in the United States.

ISBN 0-8198-0138-0 cloth
     0-8198-0139-9 paper

Library of Congress Catalog Card Number: 61–11836

Printed in U.S.A. by the Daughters of St. Paul
50 St. Paul's Ave., Boston, MA 02130

The Daughters of St. Paul are an international congregation of religious women serving the Church with the communications media.

We wish to acknowledge the gracious courtesy of the Rev. John F. X. Murphy S.J. for his kind criticism and examination of the manuscript. Also our gratitude to Mrs. Sarah Judge and Miss Eileen O'Connor for their stenographic help.

The Translators

FOREWORD

The clouds of controversy have hung like a low-lying mist over thousands of volumes that analyze the life, the writing, the theology, the sociology of St. Paul. Jews, Gentiles, Christians, neo-pagans—all have made him their own. Oratory, rhetoric, and exegesis have been able to strike off subtleties, over-nice distinctions, and "smart sayings" like a shower of sparks from the solid substance of Paul's personality. But the essence of that glowing flame which illumined the Gospel of Christ with such blinding flashes of light can be caught in its completeness in one simple word. By a happy choice the author of this unpretentious volume has built his simple, direct, and scholarly picture upon this word: Apostle.

With deep scholarship and scientific research he has laid a realistic foundation for his rich assembly of facts. But the greatest value of this work is neither research nor scholarship: it is the delicate and sensitive appreciation of the supernatural in the life of St. Paul. In the midst of Greek intellectualism, Hebrew exclusivism, and Roman imperialism, St. Paul drove straight as an arrow to the heart of truth. Theology was his chief pre-occupation. In all his driving restlessness, in all his endless "racing" through the civilized world of his day, he had only one concern: to spread the knowledge of the Kingdom of God.

And consider the means he took! He met every issue head-on, without compromise. Impatiently, fearlessly, quickly, he tore away hypocrisy, smugness, selfishness. The brilliance of his thought, the richness and imagery of his language, the deftness and speed of his strategy, have tended to give him a place in history with the suave, the polished, the learned, the sophisticated of this world. It is convenient to forget what manner of man he really was: this man whose whole personality can only be contained in the word "Apostle." Time has tended to obscure his ruggedness of character, the simplicity of his life, his innate humility. It is refreshing to read here the homely details of his trade of tent-making, of his poor, worn and roughened hands, too rough to make any but the crudest of marks with the stylus. Modern apostles, tortured with the neurotic tendencies of a world worn out with its own labor-saving inventions, might well gain new strength and hope from this realistic picture of an aged tradesman carding his goats'-hair by the dim light of an oil lamp, while he dictates messages of hope and courage to his infant communities in distant lands. Sensitive souls, hurt by the rivalries that creep in even among the servants of God, are brought face to face, in this straight-forward account, with Paul's tireless affection for his own people in the face of their fickleness, their defection to other more "showy" teachers, their constant reversion to racial pride and arrogance.

We need the example of St. Paul today. While he labored quietly in prison, ceaselessly giving individual interviews and endless personal exhortations, writing numberless letters, untangling perpetual misunderstandings, taking into the new Christian community slaves and unimportant people without distinction, the old community of pagan pomp and power was about to fall dramatically into desuetude. The measure of its colossalism was the measure of its emptiness. We, too, have seen mass and size and material strength mistaken for symbols of greatness. In the very act of subduing these hostile forces we, too, have expanded, extended our energies, stretched out our resources. Without the wisdom of St. Paul we could end as empty of real life as our foes.

What was the essence of that wisdom? The knowledge that comes with love. St. Paul convinced his hearers, not because of dexterity in turning a phrase, nor agility in dialectic, but because he *knew* in his own life, the divine charity he sought to explain to others. Every line of this straightforward and sincere account of St. Paul drives this home. It is a rich and moving pageant of the cultural and social life of the Roman Empire, of Hellenistic civilization, of Hebrew ritual. And because it is so very rich and varied, so authentic and detailed in its historical perspective, it gives all the more power to the picture of the nervous, wiry little Jew who was aflame with the love of Christ. He stands out in strong, clear outline against all the confusions and dissensions of his day. Here is the St. Paul of the Catholic Apostolate. The final picture of his death sums up his whole life. He is strong, unmoved by fear, joyful in the thought of his reunion with Christ. The author gives us an unforgettable picture of a great and noble soul meeting a supreme and final testing.

In the midst of Roman decadence St. Paul was the spearhead of a great movement for renewed social life. The basis of that life was supernatural, its external marks at first hidden and obscure. But it was the basis of the great new civilization of the Western world. The modern world needs just such an Apostolate. It cries out for social and spiritual renewal. But that renewal cannot come if religion is contained and enclosed only within the individual person. Unless it flows over into abundant and ever-increasing works for neighbors, it is not social, it is not divine. This story of St. Paul should inspire the modern day-laborer, the housewife, the intellectual, the business man, the politician, the statesman. For, as St. Paul preached so tirelessly, the Kingdom of God is for all men: for all races, for all classes, for all nations. To quicken the consciousness of the reality of this Kingdom is a great work indeed.

With every blessing, I am

Devotedly yours,

Archbishop of Boston

TRANSLATOR'S NOTE

This life of St. Paul was written by Igino Giordani, at present connected officially with the Vatican library, and well known for years in his native land, Italy, as a teacher, journalist and *littérateur*.

He is personally known to the present Roman Pontiff as well as to his predecessor, and has entered, with their approval, into the field of Catholic Action.

This enthusiasm of his shows itself unmistakably in the "Life of St. Paul" we have translated. Repeatedly the reader will observe that Giordani takes occasion, from the example of St. Paul, to show how the most ordinary things of life can be pressed into the service of the Apostolate of Christ. Consequently not merely the theologian and the priest, but the humblest layman and laywoman, can gain consolation from this book.

Although based upon profound and exact research, the book is so written as to invite the attention of the simplest reader.

As much as possible, we have tried to keep the author's style and expressions, even at the risk of being too literal. Whatever faults or defects may appear, they are ours.

All direct quotations from the Old Testament are from the Douay version of the Bible. Those from the New Testament are from the American revised edition of 1941. Where Giordani has not used a direct quotation, but merely given the sense of St. Paul's words, we have left the author's expression.

MOTHER CLELIA MARANZANA
MOTHER MARY PAULA WILLIAMSON
Religious of Our Lady of the Cenacle

Boston, Massachusetts

AUTHOR'S NOTE

In this biography the author has tried to place before us a man, living and magnetic, still vital to millions of his co-religionists. We have endeavored to place him before the eyes of many who have never seen him; or at least have only seen him from afar. We have pictured him as an inveterate traveller for the Gospel and have re-created the atmosphere of the period in which he walked the earth preaching his Gospel.

To present Paul as a living person does not imply that his story becomes a romance or a work robbed of truth by fantasy. Quite the contrary. (Paul is too great a figure of history to destroy his personality by fictionizing him, except for one of depraved taste). The events of his life do make a romance far more beautiful than that of any literary invention.

Because it was our intention to produce a work easily read and enjoyable, recreational in the Pauline sense, there has been no attempt at a show of profound erudition; nevertheless, it has taken much serious research and study to produce it. Plenty of it.

Each statement is based upon research and rests, as it were, upon a solid foundation of critical and biographical data.

St. Paul has been studied in his own writings, and in the Acts of the Apostles, and also in his labors of bringing the Gentiles into the Church—a great work, to which he gave the best part of himself. In our modern civilization we are all his children; more especially perhaps at the present time.

The author realizes what might happen to a book of this kind, written in a seemingly casual style without much exterior show of learning. There are other books considered scientifically profound and critically exegetical, but they only reduce Paul to a collection, as it were, of anatomical parts. And the Gospel of Jesus Crucified preached by him becomes in their hands a mass of theosophic-philosophies, Afro-Asiatic or Greek-Roman.

In this way, the religion expounded by this great Apostle is reduced to a mixture labelled "Pauline Doctrines" which can neither be understood nor assimilated. The Apostle himself, the great Martyr for Christ, remains a genius indeed, but the victim of hallucination, or an impostor of road-side philosophy, or a restless rabbi.

These would indeed be romances, but very sad, regrettable and ugly ones—a rough and stony story. In such books about St. Paul, ignorance would unconsciously caricature him, and it would be difficult to separate truth from alleged facts.

It may truthfully be said that there are many biographies of St. Paul in circulation, and therefore, this one is not needed; whereas, precisely because there are so many, one more will do no harm. The more so because this one does not present any so-called original views, nor does it aim at filling any pretended gap. Such a thing might be expected where "a searching and analyzing instinct in religious matters" had succeeded in reducing Christianity to a kind of "corpus vile," on which experiments could be made and a hypothesis deduced.

In such studies, personal preconceptions are often preferred to real facts. An author is often looked upon with pity if he has not discovered in each Pauline Epistle one or two new ideas. The Paul of this book is the St. Paul of the Church, a member of the family with which he was identified.

The impulse to write this life sprang above all from the marvellous words of Christ to St. Paul, summoning him to an Apostolate which would mean for him great suffering. This association of the Apostolate with suffering is complementary; both are exercises of heroism every day in Paul's life. The life of faith means a good fight. And finally, the long, laborious march of the Apostolate was to end in Martyrdom.

The words, St. Paul, Apostle, Martyr, inscribed upon his tomb, have always been rich in meaning and significance for the author;

so much so, that he determined to study most closely and thoroughly all the various phases in the life of the Apostle to the Gentiles. This is the reason this particular biography has nothing in common with the other more artistic works; they have in themselves their own raisons d'être.

No one can approach St. Paul, whose soul is a firebrand, without feeling the flame. In order to understand him and to draw profit from knowing him, one must be inflamed with the same passion that Paul experienced in all he did; nor should one fear to be aroused from a calm and static way of life.

The author has had a practical purpose in view, and in it lies the justification, in what for him seems like a daring deed. It is to inspire some readers who have not yet done so, to study for themselves, and in the letters themselves, St. Paul.

These documents of the Christian Revolution have, in large measure, helped to form Christianity through the centuries. They have transmitted to posterity the doctrines and the Spirit of Jesus. This seems a modest scope, and yet it is a most ambitious one.

Finally, the author thanks his friend, Reverend Giuseppe Riciotti, for the weary labor he took upon himself in the midst of his many occupations, of reading the proof of this book with the rare intelligence that is his.

IGINO GIORDANI

Rome,
Feast of SST. Peter and Paul

CONTENTS

CONTENTS

CHAPTER IV

THE THIRD VOYAGE, A.D. 54–58

CHAPTER V

THE CHURCH AND THE MYSTICAL BODY

CHAPTER VI

ROME AND JERUSALEM, A.D. 57–58

CHAPTER VII

PAUL IN CHAINS AT ROME

CONTENTS

CONTENTS

THE PERSECUTOR BECOMES AN APOSTLE

Saul in Jerusalem

Small of stature, slender and all nerves, Saul at ten years of age showed a lively disposition for a study of the Sacred Books. A Jewish boy, educated according to the prevailing system for intellectual discipline, usually began to read the Sacred Scriptures at five years of age. At ten he studied the Law; at thirteen the Commandments. At fifteen the wisdom of the Rabbis was unfolded to him; at eighteen it was the custom to marry.

Saul, not yet having reached this marriageable age, his father, a loyal Roman as well as a most devoted Hebrew, resolved to send his son from Tarsus to Jerusalem. Here, at the great Temple, the Law was explained and interpreted to Jewish youth by the most famous Rabbis of the time. At Jerusalem and at the Temple the ancient moral laws were less influenced by the current Greek thought which was speculative and compromising.

The Jewish community at Tarsus, situated on the shores of the river Cydnus, maintained very good schools at or near the Synagogue. However jealously the Jews guarded their traditions and customs, they saw day by day the thought of the pagan world invading their own thought, a pagan world that barred them out of society on every side.

Tarsus, a proud city, the rival of Athens and Alexandria in culture, was rich in her memories of the sensuous Cleopatra and Sardanapalus. The temples were filled with idols and the streets with sophists. Jewish youth were sorely tempted by the seductions of the gay city's life. Even the Greek language itself seemed to weaken the native vigor of the Jewish teaching.

There was no scarcity of learned teachers. Nestorius, who had been a Master to Marcellus on the Palatine, was now directing the higher schools of thought at Tarsus. As these schools were centers of idolatry, Saul could not attend them.

This boy with a vigorous intelligence and a keen mind had, like his father only more so, taken seriously the Precepts of the Law and the faith of his ancestors. It was most expedient, therefore, that he should complete his education at Jerusalem. Saul was a Hebrew of the tribe of Benjamin, a sincere follower of the Pharisees. He knew the Hebrew language as well as the Greek. He practiced a manual trade and would be a burden to no one, not even to his relatives who dwelt in the Holy City.

Saul, then in the twelfth year of his age, came to the city that was to saturate him with the glorious history of the Chosen People. There was the High Priest Caiaphas, Pilate the Procurator, the Temple and the Tower of Antonia where they respectively dwelt. These two buildings stood facing each other, high above the strange assortment of little houses that pressed one against the other, straggling up the hill with narrow, stony lanes intersecting them.

In the Temple the boy was probably questioned by the Rabbi. Perhaps he was the same Rabbi who had listened with astonishment some years before to a boy from Galilee called Jesus. By his ardor and alertness, Saul must have astounded the most illustrious Rabbi, Gamaliel, the nephew of Hillel and member of the Sanhedrin. Saul entered his school and was a frequent visitor at his home. He sat with the other pupils on a rug and, like them, he folded his arms about his knees as he listened attentively to the interpretation of the Bible. He followed the Hebrew text which the Master read from one of the parchment scrolls.

At school his knowledge became more accurate and more clear, aided as it was by the sacred atmosphere where no idol was to be seen. The Temple, the very heart of Judaism, dominated all. Every-where palaces, streets and wells were records of national glories, like so many finger prints left by the one true God upon his own holy city.

What sort of gods were these idols? They were devilish illusions. Their false divinity was a destructive influence so that even the Gentiles, who were sinners according to Hebrew morals, had done away entirely with any idea of the true God. The Promised One, ex-pected by His people, the Messiah, would come to destroy the idols of the pagans, possess the Gentile peoples and establish everywhere the worship of the Most High God. Saul's soul was filled with this hope, as were the souls of all good Jews.

During the long nights the thought of this great expectation lighted his soul as by a flame of fire. Into this land, promised by God to the Hebrews, a host of strangers had come to dwell, like a hawk which has settled itself into the nest of a dove. For generations the children of Abraham and Isaac had been dispersed throughout the Empire of Assyria and Arabia, like so much pollen scattered about by the Spirit of God to fructify these lands. Millions of pagan idolators lived like people asleep, under the hallucination of foolish doctrines and the practice of loathsome rites. They hedged in or tore asunder the families of the Israelites.

The Hebrew people were despised, vanquished, and saturated with bitterness. They struggled to keep pure their idea of God and clung to the ceremonies of their worship as God had commanded and taught Moses on Mt. Sinai. They continued to hold to their faith with a tenacity made sharper by a sorrow which too easily turned to hatred.

Many Jews suffered from these conditions. Many became stiff with pride and looked upon the mass of pagans as packs of unclean dogs. Even Jews in rags, physical outcasts, would thrill with pride while reading and repeating the prophecies. They hailed with longing and desire the defeat of idolatry, when the descendants of King David should triumphantly re-establish the primacy of the Chosen People.

Saul saw all this, and in the depths of his soul made his own plans for conquest. He vibrated like an arrow about to be shot from the bow.

Meanwhile he studied with Gamaliel. We do not know how long he attended the classes. At eighteen he had not married, either at Jerusalem or at Tarsus, a rare thing among his compatriots. In all probability he was again living in Jerusalem when the Son of Man came to the Holy City to conclude the message of His Gospel by His crucifixion.

In Tarsus Saul must have heard enough about the coming event to make him detest Christ as a heretic, One who was especially opposed to his own sect of the Pharisees, and Who, like so many others, had proclaimed Himself the Messiah.

Later on, when he was about twenty years of age, Saul returned to Jerusalem, drawn there by religion and other interests. He had reason to detest Christ still more. There, right in the city of Judea, in the very shadow of the Temple, he found the followers of the Crucified, at the very time when it behooved the Jews to prepare for the imminent coming of the Messiah by purifying their doctrines and preparing their minds.

A group of these deserters and heretics were whispering from door to door in semi-clandestine gatherings that the Messiah had come and had died. Worse still, He had died on that instrument of death so accursed in the sacred writings of the Jews—the Cross. This Messiah was none other than the detested Galilean.

A Messiah who had come and gone, overcoming no enemy, without re-establishing the Kingdom of Judah, Who had not revived from east to west the former beauty of worship for the true God: to believe such absurdity was to break down the resistance of the Jewish people and to compromise their hope of a millennium.

When Saul met them in the porticoes of the Temple or when he saw them talking near the Synagogue, the Pharisee in him blazed up and he thought it an urgent and holy work to destroy those various groups of deserters.

Saul, returning to Jerusalem to seek there the purity of the Law, found instead a people who had infected its purity with new ideas. Coming again to the capital of the Hebrew people to enjoy there the integrity of his race, he found that his own people were mingling with the Gentiles. It was claimed that they, through love, had taken into the very confines of the Temple of God those who were not Israelites but pagans. The natural structure of Judaism was falling apart; its legal integrity was being corrupted, a veritable landslide was threatening to destroy all that protected the Laws of Moses.

At once, in his impetuous faith, the young Saul was ready to spring to his feet in defense. When meeting these Jews he would fix on them his flaming eyes as if to reduce them to ashes. So Saul did not cease asking the elders of the Sanhedrin, who were rather fearful and hesitant, to act energetically and cut out this defilement with the sword.

The Sanhedrin was the supreme assembly, both religious and administrative, of the Jewish people, but the Romans had taken from them the use of the right to inflict the death penalty. Nevertheless at times when there was a vacancy in the office of Procurator, or when they succeeded in winning the favor of Roman authority, the Sanhedrin again used the right of the sword.

Had the Elders been as daring as Saul of Tarsus wished they were, they would have proceeded with vigor against the deserters as against dogs. But threats were not enough.

When it was intimated to the stubborn Peter and the deluded John that they should not mention the name of their dead teacher (Saul would not deign to pronounce it), what had been the result? Nothing. Peter under his bushy hair had resisted like a bull. His mouth, shut tight in defiance, only opened to say, "We must obey God rather than man." This was provocative.

And he had dared to add to this heretical profession of faith, "The

God of our Fathers has raised from the dead Jesus whom you killed, hanging Him on a tree." [1] Saul, remembering this, clenched his fists, and his face grew purple with rage.

The Stoning of Stephen

On the other hand, Peter's firmness had made an impression on the mind of Gamaliel. His was a meek spirit, and he was venerated universally for his wisdom and mildness. When he stood up and said, "Do not touch these men; if theirs is a human work, it will fall of itself; if divine, you cannot destroy it," they listened to his words.

Saul would not have acted thus. He revered Gamaliel but judged him to be weak, good for other times and other affairs. Saul was asking for energetic action—so that a new courage should renew the spirit of the people and initiate the Messianic era. One day when some of the most fiery of the Jews had laid hands on Stephen and led him to the Sanhedrin, Saul was in their midst.

Stephen was young like Saul. He, too, was of Jewish blood though Greek by birth. He, too, looked to the future with inspired and steady eyes; and he thought of a peace that was to be carefully guarded but not won by the sword. He was, as they said, a Deacon; that is, he was appointed to serve his companions in the faith. He gave them both bread and the words of life; faith and works belong together.

The young Stephen had acquired a certain popularity that the Sanhedrin feared. They thought it an opportune time to get rid of him, and for this cause witnesses were easily found. These accused him of saying that Jesus the Nazarene, Whom he followed, would destroy the Temple and change all the rites of Moses. This was the worst of crimes and the greatest shame a Jew could commit against Jews.

In the mob that pushed its way into the Sanhedrin to assist at the examination, Saul wedged himself into the front row. Light flashed

[1] Acts 5:30.

from his eyes as Stephen stood erect before the High Priest Caiaphas, the same who had condemned Jesus. In the presence of the clamoring mob Stephen began to speak, recalling to the minds of his listeners the glories of the great personages in the Covenants of Circumcision. So far the old faith and the new faith were blending; but here was the abrupt turn, the changing of national Judaism into the universal spirituality of Christ.

Stephen unfolded before their eyes and their consciences the memory of the Prophets. How they and their forefathers had killed these just ones and even the greatest—the All—Just One, Jesus. Here, in Jerusalem, in the shedding of His Human and Divine Blood, the great rupture had taken place. Hearing this spoken with such boldness by a mere youth, the High Priest, his face angry beneath his headband of gold, the Pharisees pale with emotion, and the bearded Scribes seated on their stools stiff with pride, gnashed their teeth.

Stephen, though sick at heart, stared into their faces, then turned his eyes to heaven. He said he saw the heavens opened and the glory of God revealed, and the Son of Man on the right hand of the Father. The crowd rose in fury and dashed outside, dragging the accused with them. The younger ones, in their rage, attempted to snatch Stephen from the guards, striking him with their fists. Less than ever did they want, or fear, a regular trial for the condemned, since at that moment the stern Pilate was away in Rome.

Young Saul, the most uncompromising exponent and belligerent champion for the very letter of the Law, carried away with zeal, leapt into the midst of the shouting band. When they arrived outside the city, he took his stand on a heap of rocks, inciting the others as self-appointed leader.

That mixed crowd of Scribes, Sadducees, and beggars, was an exciting spectacle. The witnesses responsible for the false testimony and consequently for the murder, turned to Saul and entrusted their cloaks to his keeping, sure that they would be safe.

"Take this, Saul! Here, guard this, Saul!"

Saul with the heap of odorous phylacteries, headgear and cloaks at his feet, standing erect and aflame with the indignation of the Prophets, represented well the revolutionary youth, intolerant for the Law. The slopes outside Jerusalem were full of stones and with these they stoned the Nazarene as they would stone a dog.

Saul saw Stephen sink to the ground with a look of peace on his face, in sharp contrast to the fury of his murderers; and he heard him call on Jesus. Always that Jesus, Who had caused the destruction of Jewish traditions and ceremonies. That name rang in Saul's ears louder than the shouts of those who did the stoning.

This stoning took place under Tiberius, probably in the year 36, five or six years after the crucifixion of Jesus. With it the red story of martyrdom began, a continuation of the Crucifixion even up to the present time.

Saul had not taken part in the stoning but he had consented to the deed by keeping guard over the garments of those who did. He shared in it, not only through personal responsibility but also through a corporate one, since he was the most eloquent promoter of the war waged against the new sect. Now that the persecution had begun with the stoning of Stephen, Saul put himself at the head of the persecutors. He always followed an idea without swerving. Either he would exterminate those deserters from the faith of the Fathers or else they must renounce the new religion. His choice made, he went straight forward.

Saul solicited and obtained full power from the Sanhedrin, for they could not resist the stimulating eloquence of that youth filled with the spirit of the Prophets. He began by seizing the Nazarenes all over Palestine, in the cities and villages, in the countryside and along the seashore. Men and women were taken and put into prison like herds of swine. Others were compelled to take flight beyond the confines of Judea.

Saul's fanatic ardor increased with every persecution, so much so that soon he imagined he had freed his country from this pest. He had passed through the land like a fiery column, erect and thundering. He had purified the house of his forefathers. His faith had been turned into action; and his life was wholly sworn to the service of his Jewish religion. Henceforward those who rejected the Law were no longer seen about the Temple. The land of Judea was restored to the integrity of the Mosaic tradition.

The name of Jesus was heard no more. It was urgent that this name should be blotted out even beyond Palestine. The Rabbis had added it to the list of the traitors. In a short time Saul had pushed himself into prominence, taking by assault the honors of the Jewish profession and surpassing all the other young men of his own age.

In the light of his success Saul obtained from the High Priest, who at that time was Jonathan, credentials to the Synagogues of Damascus in order to fill his net there also. Nationalism and ritualism in Judea had found a civil arm of defense, an arm controlled by an intrepid faith.

The Meeting with Jesus

Saul, with all the air of a conqueror, started for Damascus with quick, bold intent. He was accompanied by an armed escort and provided with money. He passed through Palestine and on all sides he saw the results of his purifying activity. The Ancients and the people applauded and sent their blessings after him.

All the ardor of the Seers of Israel burned in his heart. He loved the glory of God, and believed it to be one and the same as the glory of his people. Being zealously religious, he understood that a good Jew was bound to devote himself entirely to the cause of the Most High, so that God's glory might never be dimmed by compromise.

If Saul loved glory it was only God's glory. As idolatry pressed in on all sides, Saul felt an urgent need of protecting the integrity of the religious spirit by a rigid exercise of the Mosaic Law. His soul was a rare one. Knowing that all he had came from God, he surrendered all to God's service.

Like every son of Israel he had been taught a trade. From the days of his boyhood he had worked with his hands, weaving tents from goat's hair. In Jerusalem he supported himself. He provided for his simple food, his poor lodging, and the oil for the lamp that enabled him to read at night in the Hebrew and Greek books of the Sacred Covenant. His ardent soul was absorbed in their spiritual wealth. He read even to the point of wearing out his eyes which became red and watery. During the day, as he combed goat's hair and sewed on the tents of rough cloth, he pondered over the words of the Prophets.

Now as he travelled on horseback to Damascus, the prophetic words from the past urged him forward, pressing him on. Hatred of Jesus rose up before him like a phantom, beckoning him on to the capital of Syria whose queer assortment of little houses lay flat in the scorching noonday sun.

Saul paid no attention to that. Like a hound, he tracked his prey, determined to clear away from Hebraism this nest of apostasy. He was planning to travel this road again on the return journey, with a cortege of men and women in chains whom he would goad forward with the whip. He advanced eagerly, his eyes darting about in an effort to locate some of the Synagogues he knew, while the sun beat down upon Damascus in a white glare of heat.

Of a sudden, from east to west, as if the ball of the sun had burst asunder, with a rumbling sound a wall of dazzling white light stretched before him. It was such a sudden and powerful flare that Saul's eyes, accustomed as they were to the glare of Syria, could not endure it, and he fell from his horse. His companions quickly dismounted to lift him up, but they drew back when Saul rose to his knees and was heard speaking to an invisible being. When he fell, he heard a voice in that flash of light saying, "Saul, Saul, why persecutest thou me?"

Saul, crushed and helpless, raised his eyes and saw a person in the center of that radiant brightness, but the brilliant white light burned the pupils of his eyes, and filled them with red shadows, like a flood of blood. Trembling, he asked, "Who art thou, Lord?" In the evidence of the blinding miracle, he could not doubt but that this was a Divine Being. And the Being answered, "I am that Jesus whom thou persecutest."

The reply was a new outburst of light for the youth kneeling in the dust of the road, plunged into the darkness that succeeded such great brilliance and glory. He had known of Jesus, but believed Him to be an enemy of God. Now Jesus presented Himself to Saul with unmistakable signs of divinity. Saul understood, in a confused way, that in every follower of His, in each and all of those men and women Saul had put in chains, he had chained and persecuted Jesus. This first idea, like a new light, was an arrow piercing his mind. Bent in the dust under this overwhelming revelation, he heard again that voice strong but gentle, speaking to him, "It is hard for thee to kick against the goad." Truly, it was hard.

Everything about him seemed to be crumbling; his boldness as well as his strength were shattered. Lying in the dust, all his Pharisaical self-assurance rebelled and struggled, until his love for the Most High God overcame his pride, and surrendering, he moaned:

"Lord, what wilt Thou have me do?"

In his usual decisive way, and ruled by God's power, he at once put himself at the service of Jesus, and called Him Lord. And the Lord commanded, "Arise, enter the city, and there it will be told thee what thou must do."

The red glare that seemed to pierce him from every side began to fade out, darkness swallowed him up, and he felt utterly alone. His companions who had seen no one, did not understand, and it was only when he tried to rise that they ran to him. The daring youth was now as helpless as an old man, an utterly ruined old man without power or strength. He groped for the light, and tried to open his eyes; then he realized that his sight was completely gone in that brilliant, glowing glare. The pupils of his eyes were burned as if by lightning.

The Call

Saul with bent head and body took the road to the city, silent as one returning from a great defeat. He who was the leader of the company was now led by the hand like one of the many blind who went about in Jerusalem begging on the great feast days. Instead of the bold envoy of the Sanhedrin, a weak and helpless blind man was led to Damascus, eager to hide himself from view. They took him to the home of one of his co-religionists named Judas, who lived in the street called Straight. There they left him in his blindness and his mental torment. For three days he refused to taste either food or drink, and lay in a heap of misery, wrapped in his racking thoughts and trembling in his fearful darkness.

His fright had been great, but his surprise was even greater. All that he had ever lived for, everything in his life was now turned topsy-turvy; his pride as a learned Pharisee, one who pretended to discriminate between truth and falsehood, to distinguish between the just and the wicked, the pure and the impure, all was now dispersed like a breath of air. All his plans for Judaism had collapsed around him and had only made his darkness more intense. On the contrary, those ragged Nazarenes whom he had judged to be traitors to his nation, were on the side of truth and justice. They were identified (and this thought pierced him) with the Lord Jesus.

Jesus of Nazareth! He had, until now, thought him an impostor who had died a few years previously, put to death by the express order of the religious and civil authorities. And now that condemned One was God, the Son of God. All Saul's past education, his passions and youthful ideals, reacted against this revelation. His flesh and all his ambitions fought and clashed throughout his whole being until he was exhausted. Everything seemed to say to Saul that it must be an illusion.

Blindness shrouded him from everything, even from himself. Out of that darkness came the meaning of what had happened. In his mind he saw Gamaliel so indulgent. He saw again Stephen dying. From the inmost soul of Saul there came a new realization, a new warmth which made him turn to Jesus, to Jesus the Christ. He felt himself born again for the second time. Out of a complete annihilation there came forth a new and different person. Are these the illusions of a defeated one? he asked himself.

Lying on his mat, curled up in a miserable heap against the white-washed wall, Saul writhed and moaned. At one moment he felt that God was with him more than ever before; at the next, he was plunged into desolation and felt himself utterly forsaken. To his friends, who urged him to take some food and to drink a little milk or wine, he could only answer with moans. He wished he could disappear in his humiliation, sink and lose himself in his darkness.

On the third day, at the moment when his blindness seemed most to crush his spirit, he turned to the Lord in deep humility. At that moment he saw faintly the figure of a man whom he did not know coming towards him, who touched his eyes as if to take away the veil that blotted out his sight. Saul waited motionless and breathless, not understanding the meaning of this vision. After a while someone came to tell him that a certain Ananias wished to see him. Saul did not know the man, and no doubt wished he had not come to disturb him, but the stranger had already entered. Coming near he laid his hands on Saul's head with great tenderness, and then on his eyes, calling him, "brother."

"Brother Saul, the Lord Who has appeared to you on the way, has sent me, in order that you might see, and be filled with the Holy Ghost."

Saul, who had raised himself and had turned his face towards the voice, felt something like scales falling from his eyes. Now he could see!! And the first thing he saw was that brotherly face. Then he asked eagerly, "Do you know Jesus? Then I am pardoned? Then the Lord has not abandoned me?"

"Far from it!" answered Ananias. "The Lord told me in a vision to seek you; and when I remarked that you were a persecutor, He revealed to me that He had chosen you for an Apostle among the Gentiles and the children of Israel. He is calling you to bear much suffering for His name's sake. You are for the Lord, a vessel of election."

Although Saul had lived for three days in the very midst of divine activity, at this news of his vocation he was still more amazed. He had been a persecutor, now God was calling him to suffer persecution for a great cause. God had chosen him from among his people to announce the truth to Israel and to others—even to *all* people. For such a cause he would have to suffer much. The reward of his Apostolate would be suffering; but this did not frighten Saul.

He knew that whosoever gives himself to God must brave the anger of those who are against God. His character was too well molded on that of the Prophets, too well formed by the traditions of his people, to be concerned with suffering. He was ready for all things, knowing that if God were with him, he, a poor Hebrew, would be able to do all things for God.

The fiery youth had now become a most docile pupil. He got up at the request of Ananias and was baptized, receiving the Holy Ghost. From that moment he belonged entirely to the Son of God Who had died and had risen again, to the Son of God Who had appeared to him in His power and His splendor. The miracle had been a great one, but only because a persecutor like Saul needed such a miracle to transform him into a "Servant of Jesus Christ."

Since he had come to Damascus with letters from the Synagogues, back to the Synagogues he would go. Verily, the old Saul was dead—it was the new Apostle who there presented himself. His companions of the journey were stupefied, and waited for an explanation for this most extraordinary fact; and he gave it to them. Rising to his feet in the midst of the brethren, he told them about the apparition of Jesus.

"I had come to persecute Him and to blaspheme Him; but now I have seen His power. He is the Lord, the Son of God. Be baptized, if you wish to be saved. Jesus is the Christ."

The Jews could not believe their ears. Was not this man the exterminator of all who had invoked that name in Jerusalem and in all of Palestine? A stir of emotion and anxiety ran through the Synagogues. Some believed, recognizing Saul's accent of sincerity, others rebelled, not wishing to abandon the faith of the Scribes and the Priests. They considered plans for killing him. Meanwhile Saul, having now given public testimony to Christ, withdrew into the desert.

In the Desert

Saul was a deeply religious man. Just as formerly it was characteristic of him to be completely carried away by ardor and zeal in all his undertakings, so now he was as completely dominated by grace. To grace he surrendered himself without heeding the demands of flesh or blood. That he might listen only to the voice of the Holy Spirit, he withdrew into the desert beyond Damascus, into a country vaguely called Arabia.

That complete transformation, the revolution he had experienced in his soul, had been so swift and moving that he needed quiet and seclusion to take account of himself. He knew God would speak to him during his nights spent in prayer and in the days spent in fasting. He wanted to make his new adjustment, and what could be better than to go into the seclusion of the great desert? The fathers of Israel had done this in their great hours of anxiety, either for what concerned their own personal problems, or in the great crises of their people. Already hermits were dwelling in caves and listening in silence to the voice of God coming gently to them from the bosom of time and from the vast universe.

Therefore Saul went forth seeking solitude in this barren region scorched by the sun. His departure was quite different from his coming to Damascus. Before he had come as a ruler, led on by irrational passions; now he was the vanquished one, but free with the freedom of God. For many years he had sought the voice of God in the sermons of the Rabbis, in the ceremonies of Jewish worship, and in his persecuting zeal. Now he had found it. Like Moses he had seen God, Whose Voice, more enlightening than the column of fire, led the way before him.

It was no more he who lived but the Spirit of God living in him. It filled him day and night with the knowledge that he now possessed

Jesus the Christ, the long expected One Who had come. At night the stars spoke to him of God's laws, and the teachings of the Divine Master became more intense, more clear as they penetrated his heart one by one.

They were the treasures and the riches of the Gospel. In this new spiritual construction, the Law and the Prophets took on new meanings and purposes. Saul no longer saw the history of the Hebrew people as an escape from the rest of humanity. Now through them there would be a great diffusion of truth among all peoples. He saw the Messianic Kingdom of God becoming complete, not as the dominion of one people over others but as a Kingdom of God for all people. All are brothers one to another. His conscience, his soul, his spiritual perceptions grew deeper and wider.

The glory of God became in his soul a new flame of great light. He felt a vast hunger for souls, far beyond the confines of Israel, even to the very ends of the world. He yearned to bring all people to the feet of Christ, and while as yet he could only yearn for this, he placed himself there.

As the new life of the spirit grew inwardly in Saul, he punished his body in expiation for the sufferings he had inflicted on others, on the Christian Community, the Church, which he had come to recognize as the Mystical Christ. This revelation was becoming clearer and more precious to him every day. He relived in spirit the scourges he had made others suffer through a hatred for Christ. They tormented him now in his own flesh, since he was himself a member of that same Body which he had once endeavored to tear to pieces. And he wept for love of Christ.

The center of his former life had been the Law, with its ceremonies and denials. Now in the new economy of Christ, all these appeared fruitless and useless fatigue, merely external exercises. This new life had Christ as its center and love as its expression. In the heat of this love, the old hatred against the Gentiles was vanishing, and in its place there was born a sense of brotherhood towards all God's children, whether circumcised or uncircumcised.

Both had gone astray, both were deserving of God's love, both had to be led back to the Father, through the Son, and by the indwelling of the Holy Spirit. In the apparition of Ananias Saul had been called by the Lord, "a vessel of election." Behold, his spirit was being filled with grace and wisdom from on high, to complete and supplement his old nature already richly endowed with intelligence and capacity for physical endurance.

Saul had had a thorough education in the Greek-Roman culture. He was born in a Greek world, and his education was perfected in Jerusalem, the Holy City. He had varied and outstanding qualities with which to testify before the Jews, before the pagans, the learned and the unlearned of the working classes. The grace of God gave a new power to all these qualities, and the doctrines of Christ blended them all into one. He was a vessel filled with divine and human gifts.

After two years Saul returned from the desert and knew himself to be not only a disciple but also an Apostle. We can find no evidence that he had been instructed in the doctrines of Christ by other Christians. On the contrary, all testimony affirms repeatedly that he became a Christian and an Apostle by a direct revelation from Jesus Himself. Christians, in the person of Ananias, had stepped in but only to bring him into the Church.

Jesus, Who had personally taught Saul in a most unusual manner, had not supplanted the Church in order to do this; and Saul realized it. For this reason no one more than Saul loved the Church and praised it. Having been made an Apostle not by men but by Jesus Christ and by God his Father, and seeing in his conversion and vocation one of the greatest privileges ever bestowed upon man born of woman, he knew how honored he was and how gloriously chosen.

The Visit to Peter—A.D. 38

When Saul returned to Damascus his formation as an Apostle was full and complete. Jesus had taught him the Gospel and revealed it to him. He had filled his heart with a fiery zeal for spreading it abroad. Only direct teaching could give a man the key to such profound mysteries. Only such an extraordinary infusion of grace could have molded a man of Saul's size into an instrument of such might and power for preaching the faith. Some doubted then as now any intervention from on high. The same is true now as it was then, only those doubt who fear the action of God.

In Damascus, the new Saul, while remaining the same old Saul, gave himself completely to preaching that Jesus is the Christ, and this he did for four years. Those who refused to accept this revolutionary announcement tried to rid themselves of the announcer by killing him, as had been done to the importunate Prophets, to John the Baptist, to Jesus and to Stephen. They watched for Saul at the gates of the city as hounds watch for their prey. They hated him as much as they had loved him, probably even more so, since he personified the most dangerous desertion from the ancient faith and customs of Israel. The minister of King Aretas not only allowed them to do so, he even gave them some assistance that he might gain their favor and at the same time free himself from this source of disorder.

When the Christians of Damascus discovered the plot, they consulted among themselves how they might save the Apostle. They hid him for a time in their houses among those narrow crooked streets that looked like stairs, up and down which all the city people crawled like ants. Guards were set at all the gates of the city but, shrewd as ever, the Brethren eluded the vigilance of the government.

One night, perhaps a foggy one, they let Saul down from the wall in a basket. He was small of stature and very thin on account of his fasts, so it was small effort to lower him down among the bushes and stones. Once down, he turned with a salute to the Brethren, and went on his way with cautious, quick step down the slopes thick with trees that extended to the sea, and took the road to Jerusalem.

Saul knew now that the search for him in the cause of Christ had begun. The same search he had practiced against others for the sake of Christ. He was gathering from men the first fruits of suffering in the great Apostolate.

But why did Saul go to Jerusalem where he had no friends, and where his work was not needed? He explained the reason to the Galatians. It was to see Peter. He wanted to know the Head of the Church, who stood in the place of Jesus Christ, to receive from him some sort of ecclesiastical investiture. This, his first going up to Jerusalem, might be called his first visit *"ad limina."*

In Jerusalem, the attitude of the Christian converts as well as of the Jews not yet converted was one of diffidence and reserve towards him. The Christians doubted his change, and the unconverted reproached him with apostasy; knowing that he was daring and strong, they all feared him.

Only one disciple with open-minded intelligence and courageous energy could overcome his reluctance, stretch out his hand to the new Brother and introduce him to the Community. This disciple was Barnabas. Barnabas then presented Saul to the other Apostles, Peter, and James the "brother of the Lord." Then Peter welcomed him to his house where Saul stayed for fifteen days. The Chief of the Apostles gave the new recruit the full ecclesiastical recognition of his Apostolate. So much so that Saul, commissioned by the Lord and approved by the Church, undertook at once in Jerusalem the work for which he now lived: the Apostolate of Christ.

The daily program consisted of a sermon and discussion with Jews and pagans, with Semites and Greeks, without distinction. Since Saul spoke Aramaic fluently as well as Greek, he could dispute with citizens and with foreigners. No one could remain indifferent to an incendiary eloquence and logic as compact and clear as that of Saul. He whose soul was fed on the Scriptures, was now armed with an irresistible reasoning and especially with a burning love for Christ. Those who did not believe him turned against him and, as usual, conspired to do away with him, a custom, it seems, of those thinking they are in the right when they are really in the wrong.

This time the Christian brethren again intervened, wishing to spare his life and to protect the Church in Jerusalem from a fresh persecution, since it was now enjoying a period of peace following upon Saul's conversion. They therefore thought it necessary to send him away from the Holy City. The argument of saving his person from persecution was not sufficient to bend the will of Saul, so he asked the Lord what to do. One day while he was in the Temple, he was ravished in spirit. Jesus again appeared to him and said, "Hasten to leave Jerusalem, because these here will not receive your testimony of Me."

Saul was conscious of his past failings and wanted to make reparation; and he was not forgetful of his part in Stephen's martyrdom. "Lord, they know that I threw into prison, and scourged in the Synagogues, those who believe in You. And when the blood of Stephen, your martyr, was being shed, I assisted and approved. Nay, I even kept guard over the garments of the murderers." But the Lord insisted. "Go, I will send you to a people far away."

One might say that Saul felt himself to be the one most responsible for the killing of the Proto-martyr, and therefore bound to make reparation by continuing Stephen's work cut short by the stoning. It seemed as if Stephen, when dying, had passed into Saul's hands the torch of his own intrepid eloquence.

Saul was a Pharisee, and loved with a special affection Jerusalem and his own people. Determined as he was to make expiation, he was nevertheless docile to the Master and to the Apostles. Towards them he felt so much the more humble, in that he had been the more guilty in the years of his ignorance.

When he was informed of the plotting schemes of the Jews (or more correctly of the proselyte Greeks, who were far more fanatic than the born Israelites) he obeyed the Church. He withdrew from the mission to the people nearest his heart, so that he might seek others farther away and make them his new brothers in Christ. He went to Caesarea and from there he boarded a sailing ship which coasted the shores of Phoenicia and Syria. Finally, he arrived at Tarsus in Cilicia, his native city.

This seemed to be his calling: to bring the Gospel to men, and yet to be pursued by men from city to city. He carried with him the burning torch of the Gospel. All the defenders of Traditionalism of the Old Order, and of Materialism (dressed up, as it were, in religious rites and ceremonies) seemed to hurl themselves at him as if to suffocate him.

He remained a few years at Tarsus, perhaps as a stranger, until the year 43. His relations and friends who knew his impetuous but sincere nature, may have believed him, but the majority turned their backs on him. Their fellow-citizen, now become so talkative, was only a scatterbrain. To the pagans he appeared merely as one of the sophists, who went lecturing along the Mediterranean coast with illogical and inconclusive discourses.

Saul had become one with Christ, and the charity of Christ burned in his veins. If unresponsive men repulsed him, he strengthened himself by waiting, and prayed without ceasing in his untiring demand for more strength. And perhaps it was in this period of mystical union with God, in a transport of love, that he was caught up (in the body, or without the body?—he could never say) beyond the visible heaven to the Throne of God.

To complement the teaching he had already received, words were addressed to him which he never felt able to repeat or reveal. Only once, in a moment of expansiveness, and to reassure the Corinthians of his divine mission, he made an allusion to them in a letter. So that he might not feel any pride over this mystical experience and that he might give to God alone the credit for these revelations, an incurable malady of the flesh afflicted him like an angel of Satan sent to buffet him.

He asked the Lord three times to be rid of it, but the Lord said to him, "My grace is sufficient for you, for power is made perfect in infirmity." "Gladly," said Paul, "will I glory in my infirmities that the power of Christ may dwell in me." [2] Therefore, these infirmities were never wanting to him. As for his great Apostolic labor, he waited confidently, leaving all to God.

Saul was dynamic as few other men have ever been. This continuous waiting upon God's will and for His directions in all things kept Saul in unceasing communication with the Eternal and runs through all his life. This living in constant expectancy with God is proper to souls intensely religious. They have found the way of communication with God, a way closed for the majority of souls by the thick hedges of materialism.

This waiting on God was not a loss of time for Saul, but an accumulation of energy and an interior study of the Gospel which, drop by drop, penetrated his whole being. He matured in this retirement, and waited, until one day he saw again under a full beard the honest countenance of Barnabas, the Apostle of courageous speech. Barnabas now invited him to another field of labor. Saul did not hesitate but went with him to Antioch in Syria.

Antioch, the gilded city, spread her bath houses and temples along the River Orontes in profuse abundance. It was the second city of the Empire in importance and was meant to be the metropolis of Asia. Seleucia of Perea, only a few miles distant from the sea, served as its port. Antioch was rich in traffic and in its shining marble monuments. Syrians, Greeks, Jews, Romans and other races moved about in the streets and formed a crowd, gay and voluble. They were exposed to unhealthy idolatries that united an oriental sensuality with a Greek refinement. They were intent on getting rich and enjoying life; by nature, they were easily excited, and as easily checked. Since they were apt to turn from frivolity to more serious moods, men of ascetic and religious life were produced.

The seed of Christ had been brought among them by the disciples whom the persecution of Saul—in which Stephen had fallen—had

---

[2] 2 Cor. 12:9.

scattered, and also by other disciples from Cyprus and Cyrene. The former disciples, scattered by Saul's persecution, were still imbued with Jewish exclusiveness and had limited their efforts in conversions to Jews only. Those others from Cyrene and Cyprus, probably after the example of Peter who had baptized the centurion Cornelius, had announced Christ to these pagans also.

So promising a center of evangelization had been formed that the Head of the Church at Jerusalem had sent the courageous Barnabas to see it and to provide for it. Barnabas had seen that, for the movements of the Apostolate, Antioch was a vital point. A worker of exceptional resources was needed; Barnabas remembered Saul and sought him out.

Securing lodgings for themselves in the midst of that mixed gathering, they worked together for a year, converting a large number. So many that the people began to distinguish the followers of Christ from the other Jews and to call them *Christians* for the first time, a Greek name with a Latin ending which in the popular mind meant a party—the party of Christ. This was a sign that the doctrine and life of the disciples appeared, even outwardly, ruled by Christ as the Head.

In the course of that year there came from Jerusalem a Brother named Agabus who foretold a great famine. It was in A.D. 44 or 45. The famine came, and the poor in the badly organized country of Palestine suffered most. Then the Christians in Antioch put together as much of their substance as each could spare, and sent it to the Ancients of Judea, delegating the two Apostles, Barnabas and Saul, to bring it.

After fulfilling their task as distributors of bread as well as distributors of the word of the Gospel, the two Apostles returned to Antioch. Meanwhile, in Palestine, probably with the intention of distracting the people from the thought of their misery, Herod Agrippa, a worthy descendant of Herod the Great, began to feed his brutal passions with murders rather than to feed the hungry with bread.

First, he caused the Apostle James, brother of John, son of Thunder, to be killed. Then, seeing that this pleased the Jews, he had Peter taken and put in prison; but angels came to set him free again. He was not the only Apostle who should pass from a prison cell to the great capital of Rome.

CHAPTER II

THE FIRST VOYAGE
A.D. 45-49

Saul Becomes Paul

Up to now Saul had been the companion and co-worker of Barnabas. He served the Church at Antioch; fasted with Barnabas, Simon called Niger, Lucius of Cyrene, and Manahen, the half brother of Herod the Tetrarch. One day the leaders and teachers of the Church, inspired by the Holy Spirit, sent Saul and Barnabas on a special mission.

It was probably in the year 46, or at the end of 45. The two, sent from Antioch, came to Seleucia and from there they sailed for the Isle of Cyprus which the poets say was dear to the Goddess Venus. Saul the Pharisee would have chosen to stay away from the licentious city, but Saul the Christian went there purposely to fight licentiousness. Landing at Salamis, the capital, they preached the word of Jesus, helped by John Mark a cousin of Barnabas and the future author of the second Gospel.

From Salamis, climbing the mountains into the interior of the country, these three tried to approach the prisoners who worked in the copper mines, and to announce to them their true freedom in Christ. Always preaching, they pushed on as far as Paphos, the residence of the Proconsul Sergius Paulus. He was a pagan official who was interested in religious matters.

In that age of much political polytheism the myths, which were older than the contemporary idol worship, had lost all meaning for the people. Philosophers and wise men, as well as women of inquisitive minds, turned to the oriental cults in order to draw from fountains that seemed to possess more life. In this way, they were often deceived by false sophists. Sergius Paulus, a prudent man, had just then taken into his household a magician by name Bar-Jesus, who naturally resented his master listening to the Apostles.

One day Saul the most resolute of the three openly faced Bar-Jesus. Saul, his eyes shining with the light of the Spirit of God scrutinized the Magician and said, "O full of all guile and of all deceit, child of the Devil, enemy of all justice, thou ceasest not to pervert the right ways of the Lord. And now behold, the hand of the Lord is upon you, and you shall be blind for a time." [1]

As Saul spoke he remembered another man who in that same way had been punished for his interior blindness. At his words, darkness and a mist suddenly fell on the eyes of the impostor. He stretched out his hands, tottering and seeking a support. That episode changed the heart of Sergius Paulus, who believed and was, as it seems, the first person of rank to embrace the new faith. It is also believed that on his account Saul changed his name to Paul. Was it according to a custom common in the Empire that Saul adopted the name of his illustrious convert? Or did Saul use the two names before, one for the Jewish world, and one for the Roman world? We do not know.

The change was a slight one; in Greek it was easy to pass from Saulus to Paulus. At any rate, St. Luke, who narrates the miracle, begins at the moment of this meeting of Saul with the false Jewish prophet, to give to the Apostle the new name: "Saul, who was also called Paul." [2] In the Latin world Paul was more acceptable than Saul. Even today the Hebrews frequently use the names more common among the people with whom they live, neglecting their Hebrew names.

From Paphos, Paul and Barnabas, sailing along the coasts of Asia, landed at Pamphylia and turned towards Perge. At Perge John Mark left the little band in order to return to Jerusalem, to the great disappointment of Paul who would never admit that any Apostolic

[1] Acts 13:10, 11.
[2] Acts 13:9.

work should be left unfinished. But John Mark, the cousin of Barnabas, was still very young and perhaps felt the need of returning home to his mother after a voyage that had been rough and full of hardships.

Once Paul had started an enterprise he never turned back; human motives and considerations had no more value for him since he had heard the divine call. With Barnabas he proceeded into the interior of Pisidia, which was still half barbarian, only recently subdued by the Romans. It was very difficult to penetrate into the country; there were no roads, and brigands infested the trails along which one could travel only on muleback. Only with the greatest fatigue were they able to reach Antioch in Pisidia. According to their constant rule they decided to carry the Gospel to the Jewish colony first; so on the Sabbath they went to the Synagogue.

Someone, probably the Master of the Synagogue, took the scroll from the archivist and read a few texts from the Law and the Prophets. Then, to show deference to guests, as was their custom, the Elders asked the two strangers if they had a word of exhortation for the people.

Paul spoke. Evidently he was the more eloquent of the two. When a son of Israel spoke to a group of his own race, although not known to him personally, he usually began by recalling a passage from the history of Israel, and then made a brief summary of it. This was a way to secure their attention and was also a profession of religious loyalty and of national unity. And so Paul told of God's choice and exaltation of the Jewish people, of their emigration from Egypt, of the rule under the Judges, and then as far as King David, the great glory of Israel.

The name of David should have offered a starting point to the orator for the exhortation that was expected, running somewhat in this manner: "Children of Israel, take courage because a descendant of King David will return to the throne and will banish from Judea the idolatrous stranger, and then he will destroy the Gentiles from the face of the earth."

Instead, the discourse of Paul, a Pharisee of the Pharisees, took an unforeseen turn. "From the descendants of David," he said, "God has raised up one for the salvation of Israel, Jesus. Jesus was not accepted and was put to death, as it had been foretold by the Prophets. But He rose again from the dead, and unlike David, He did not know corruption. In what does this salvation consist that He brought to you? Be it known therefore, to you men, children of the stock of Abraham, that through Him forgiveness of sins is preached to you; and from all things by which you could not be justified in the Law of Moses. Everyone who believes in Him is justified." [3]

To believe in Jesus . . . the insufficiency of the Mosaic Law for justification, . . . a deliverance from sin. The people of Antioch, whose hearts were forever yearning for the hills of Judea, were stunned as they listened. The accents of Paul were convincing, his argument rigorous, his eyes burning as with a flame—but what he asked was too new, too daring. They had been expecting a liberation from the enemy for years and years, and now instead a liberation from sin was announced. In place of a new Kingdom of Israel, the justification of the Crucified was given.

For the sake of courtesy, the Elders of the Synagogue invited the two Apostles to return the following Sabbath and to continue the discourse. These Jews could not bring themselves to make any decision, nor yet to accept their teaching. To break away from the old customs, from the past, even from the commonplace, is for most people too great an effort. However, several of the Jews and some of the pagans who feared God (called proselytes), followed the Apostles and had themselves instructed in the Gospel.

Meanwhile the news spread, and the following Sabbath almost the entire city was jammed into the Synagogue. Such a crowd angered the most zealous among the Jews. They began to contradict Paul's discourse. Because of their behavior, Paul and Barnabas spoke up

---

[3] Acts 13:16–42.

fearlessly, "It behoved us to bring the Gospel of God to you first, oh Jews, but since you refuse it, we turn to the Gentiles. And this too, has been foreseen and told by the Prophets." [4]

In fact, the Gentiles, more simple, more docile, were glad to receive the tidings of salvation. Conversions took place in all that region. Paul and Barnabas, untiring sowers of the Gospel, entered into that great mass of idolaters with courage and zeal, gathering many to the faith.

This so infuriated the chief leaders of the large colony, that they stirred up religious women of rank against the Apostles, since women are more easily enkindled by religious motives and are more demonstrative. It was thought that if the women succeeded in provoking a tumult, the men would then intervene. All would go in a body to the city magistrates and demand to be rid of these agents of disorder. Then the magistrates, merely to have peace, would waste no time in investigating theological bickerings but would banish the strangers so unworthy of the hospitality given them.

The Iconians and the Lystrians

The Apostles were not easily discouraged. They knew now by experience, and Paul knew by the prophecies, that in proportion as they were true Apostles they would suffer persecutions. The Apostolate would be a hard battle and that implied wounds. So they started on another march through hard ways and byways. When tired, they sat in the shade of a tree or hut, ate some fruit and quenched their thirst at a brook. The Apostolate also meant continual walking.

Retracing their steps eastward, they came to Iconium, which had only lately become a Roman colony; here they stayed for some time, receiving many converts from among the Jews and Gentiles. When Paul heard that the people were plotting to stone them to death

[4] Acts 13:46.

(Paul felt a clutch at his heart remembering the inspired Stephen), they pushed on towards the interior of Lycaonia.

Their plan was to carry the Gospel to the pagans if the Jews did not want it; to carry it to a second city if the first refused it. If persecutors interrupted the work in one place, they were to resume it elsewhere. It was a never-ending competition with opposition. Paul had the patience of a weaver, now busy in weaving a divine canvas with human threads.

At Lystra in Lycaonia things were even worse. Paul cured a cripple and this made such a commotion that the crowds thought the gods had returned to earth. He had come to preach about the true God, and the people of Lystra, superstitious and ignorant, mistook him for Mercury since he was always the first to speak, and Barnabas for Jupiter because he had a beautiful beard and an imposing personality. Pushing their mistake to a concrete expression, they dragged the priest of Jupiter from the temple, led out the sacred bulls from their stalls, festooned with garlands and flowers, in order to offer a sacrifice to the Apostles in all due form.

This was the exact opposite of their mission. The Apostles wanted to put an end to idolatry and, behold, they themselves were mistaken for gods. Had they not preached that the idols stood for falsehood, ignorance and deviltry? Frightened and indignant, Barnabas and Paul tore their garments, dashing in among the people, trying to bring them back to their senses. By dint of shouting and preaching to these insane people that they must be converted from these vain things, the Apostles avoided the holocaust of the bulls. They now experienced how fickle a mob can be when not controlled by some social bond, whether civil or religious; a combination of such forces can be guided by a man of conscience towards a noble end, or degraded by a demigod into an instrument of destruction.

At that time some men who had arrived from Antioch and Iconium, seeing what was done, excited the mob against the two messengers of the Gospel. Paul was dragged outside the city wall, stoned and left lying on the ground as dead. As he fell under the pelting stones, perhaps he repeated Stephen's prayer and was glad to expiate the sin of his youth. However, the hour of his martyrdom had not yet come, and when the disciples ran to his rescue, he stood up, bruised and wounded, and returned with them to the city. The following day with Barnabas, he took the road to Derbe; it was not rest he sought but another place of labor.

However stubborn enemies, were in pursuing him, he was even more persistent in changing from place to place. Identical with the materialists of every age who limit their ideas to a mortal body, these men believed they could be rid of Christianity by killing the leaders. Caiaphas had attempted this with Jesus, the Sanhedrin with Stephen, and Herod Agrippa with James. The Apostles, their descendants, professed that speech cannot be chained. It moves about as God's breath which cannot be intercepted.

Paul and Barnabas went on their way, passing through the cities they had previously evangelized. The sufferings they had endured gave them a new prestige and added courage. They exhorted all to stand firm in the faith; because, said they, it is only through many tribulations that one can enter the Kingdom of God. It was not a very appealing program for those who made all value consist in the things of the body and in the goods of this world. It did allure heroic souls, awakening in them a quality of endurance, detachment, and a spirituality so much the loftier because of the swift drop into popular materialism, which was a kind of moral whirlwind begotten of the pressure of religious superstition, economic misery, and political paralysis.

These journeys of the Apostles did not last longer than three years. Perhaps John Mark, still too young, had been afraid to venture into such distant and unknown lands. Such a thought Paul could never admit. Every land, no matter how distant, was his and it was near. Wherever people were, there were souls to whom it behooved him to reveal that Jesus is the Christ.

The new converts were not left alone to themselves. In every city they formed a Community called the Church. The Greek word was characteristic; it was applied to people officially united in an assembly. At the head of each Church were placed some older men called presbyters or priests; and one of them, probably the most venerable and wise, had local authority over the rest. Paul kept for himself, in a large measure, the supreme guidance and authority. These Communities were not isolated, they were blended together so that they formed one great Church whose heads were then residing in Jerusalem.

From this grew the desire and the obligation on the part of the Apostles to return to Jerusalem after three or four years of work, to give a report, and thus to make the bonds with the center stronger and more complete. It was a new and stunning thing, this gathering together of all people of every class and nationality into an organism whose head was Christ and in whose soul breathed the Spirit of God.

The two Apostles crossed the region of Pisidia, and entered again into Pamphylia where they saw the Christians of Perge. Then they proceeded down the coast to the port of Attalia, from whence they sailed for Antioch in Syria. There in the year A.D. 49 Paul concluded his first missionary round in the same place where he had begun it.

The Question of Catholicity

Antioch, with its medley of races, could appreciate the importance of the Gospel and its influence on the pagan people of Asia Minor. This capital of Syria was for several years the center from which Christianity radiated along the shores of the Mediterranean Sea and throughout all Asia. At the same time, the city linked the new field of conquest with the larger center at Jerusalem, so long as Jerusalem controlled the direction of the movement of Christianity.

The resolute advance towards universality, which to the Jews was a most serious break in their national exclusiveness, was being accomplished especially at Antioch. The adoption of all men as children of God, Jews and Gentiles, without distinction, was still to the majority of people incomprehensible.

It was especially those who came from the sect of the Pharisees who were alarmed at learning what Peter had done, and what was being done on a larger scale by Paul and Barnabas and those of the Church in Antioch towards this new "mark" of universality of the Church.

They became fearful and kept themselves aloof, hiding from notice. They were willing to admit some Gentiles to the Community of the Saints, as they called those who were justified by faith in Christ, but only after the Gentiles had been circumcised. This rite linked them with Mosaism and incorporated them into the Jewish people. In other words, they admitted pagans into Christianity only after they had first become Jews.

They said there was no salvation without circumcision; no one ought to be baptized who had not passed through the rites of the Law of Moses. Such a pretense made the Redemption of Christ null and void.

While salvation came from the Blood of Jesus Christ shed on the Cross and through faith in Him on the part of the baptized, they placed it in man's bloodshed in the exterior rite.

Facing a possible dissension, which could generate a schism because of the gravity of its nature, Paul, an ex-Pharisee himself, wished to settle the matter once for all. He recognized a central authority, and in agreement with Barnabas and with the Church at Antioch, as well as with the opponents, that is, the Judaizers, he left the decision of the matter to the other Apostles and to the Ancients at Jerusalem.

Paul wished to go back to the source. Dissensions on points of view can always arise; therefore a central authority capable of distinguishing and deciding is necessary. It is not possible that the living Church and the virtue of Charity can flourish if dissensions, like so many infections, are not promptly ended. There were as yet no written rules, but this was no hindrance to anyone since there was the living Church which acted as the witness of Christ, in the light of the Holy Spirit.

These two Apostles of the Gentiles in Asia who, be it noted, were both circumcised, started for Jerusalem, moving along the coast of Phoenicia and crossing Samaria. Such was the devotion of their flock towards the Apostles that the community of the faithful in Antioch accompanied them part of the way. In every center they found other communities which received them with joy and festivity, listening with wonder to the news of their conquests among the pagans, the expansion of the Kingdom of God beyond the limits of the Kingdom of Israel—and marvelled at it all.

The First Council-
-A.D. 49 or 50

Almost five years had passed since the last visit of Paul and Barnabas to the Holy City. They were not returning with a yearning homesickness to the Temple again nor to recall the memories of their forefathers; it was, above all else, to see Peter the pillar of the Church, the relatives of Jesus, and the place of the Crucifixion. They were bringing back their Apostolic harvest and had many things to say about the countries they had visited and the communities they had established.

In Paul's eyes, seared by the sun, tears welled up when he saw from afar the towers of the city of the Prophets. Against the sky shone the pinnacles of the Temple, white with a shimmer of gold, a huge heap of marble on a gray hill. When the news of their arrival spread, a large number of the faithful came to meet them and to accompany them to the Apostles and Ancients of the whole Church. There amid tears they exchanged the brotherly embrace.

Those who had remained in Jerusalem saw again with joy the vigorous Barnabas, and were proud of that living miracle Paul, who from a persecutor had become the most intrepid and persuasive minister of the Gospel. Truly his work and his presence were a living exponent of the Gospel and a continual miracle of divine power.

At the time of the arrival of the two Evangelizers there had come up from Antioch a few followers of the Mosaic party, entrusted with the charge of speaking for the Jews.

It was probably a few days later that the Apostles and Elders came together to examine the difficulty that had been submitted to their judgment by Paul and Barnabas on the one hand, and the Christian-Jews on the other. The opinion of the latter was well known and no one was surprised at it. Many of the Christians who were first Jews still observed the Mosaic practices, and James, called the Just, the "brother of Jesus," was, in the eyes of the whole city, a model of such strict observance. It was, however, a different thing to impose these Mosaic practices on those who came from paganism, and to make Christianity first pass through Judaism.

This meeting was what is commonly called the First Council of the Universal Church. In it the Apostles who had followed Jesus from the beginning were present with those who had joined them after His resurrection.

Peter opened the session and put the question directly and clearly, acting as the Head appointed by Jesus Himself to rule the Church.

He began by recalling his own personal experience, the invitation addressed to him from the beginning by the Lord to evangelize the Gentiles in order that they too might believe; because with God there is no difference between Jew and pagan who have both been purified through faith. It is by this faith that one can be saved through the grace of our Lord Jesus Christ. He who accepts it, is, by this very act, emancipated from the Mosaic Law. It was, then, an outright tempting of God to pretend to impose a yoke on the disciples which neither the Fathers nor their ancestors had been able to carry; nor should the Christians, converted from Judaism, have it imposed upon them.

In a few words Peter had stated the problem and solved the difficulty. He even said that it had been solved from the beginning, by himself, in the fact that the first converted Gentiles had received the Holy Spirit like the others. These had not passed through the Jewish rites which are not considered a necessary yoke. Peter's thought was the same which Paul had used in his polemics against those who favored Jewish practices.

After Peter had finished, Paul and Barnabas spoke, and they reported about their mission in pagan lands and the miracles that had strengthened their teaching all along the way.

Finally James rose to speak. His piety, which had won for him the name of "Just," the fact that he was related to Jesus Christ, his strict asceticism that made him avoid the use of meat and wine, the great esteem that all Jews had for him and, finally, the dignity of being the head of the Church at Jerusalem, gave to his words great worth and prestige.

He confirmed with testimony from the Scriptures what Peter had affirmed, showing that the extension of Christianity in the direction of universality realized the Messianic prophecies concerning the spiritual kingdom of Christ, as David had foretold. He also gave as his opinion that convert Gentiles should not be disturbed in their faith.

Man of prudence as he was, and having at heart the welfare of the converts from Judaism (lest too deep a divergence of life between the two groups might grow into a real separation), he asked the Jews to accept the decision that circumcision and Mosaic practices be not imposed on the newcomers but he did ask those from paganism to make some sacrifices in favor of their older brethren.

They could abstain from meat sacrificed to idols, from fornication, from strangled animals, and from blood. There were Jews in all cities, and this slight concession towards their centuries-old customs would have disposed them favorably towards the Gospel. At any rate it would lessen the differences in the exterior conduct of the two groups.

The advice of James was consequently accepted. This solution of the problem definitely saved the principle that salvation comes through faith in the Lord Christ by showing that Christianity is not an appendage of Judaism and that the new economy of the New Covenant had begun with the Risen Jesus.

The decision of the Church which was that of the Holy Spirit (the Church being a visible assembly of the faithful gathered around their head, who decides under the inspiration of the Holy Spirit), was stated in a letter. The bearers of this epistle were the two Elders, much esteemed, Jude Barsabas and Silas. With the bearers of the letter Paul and Barnabas returned to Antioch, where the answer was received with reverence and satisfaction. It had the same value as the direct teaching of Jesus of which it was an explanation demanded by circumstances.

Paul and Peter in Antioch

It is not credible that all in the Judaizing party were silenced by the Apostolic answer. To believe this would be to ignore the persistency of error, especially among the fanatics. Paul was destined continually to meet these along his way.

A little later in Antioch itself, the very city where those clashes were apt to take place, a regrettable incident happened to him. While Paul and Barnabas were working there Peter, of whom that city kept most lively memories, arrived unexpectedly. He had previously come here on his first flight from Jerusalem and had gathered together a community of the faithful converted from the Synagogue, so that he could be considered the founder of this first Church and its first Bishop.

By a stipulated agreement, Peter concerned himself more especially with the faithful of the Circumcision, while Paul busied himself more with those of the Uncircumcision. Surrounded by Jews and pressed by the agitation resulting from the answer received from Jerusalem, especially by some of the more fanatical of the Judaizing party who came from the Church there, Peter, meek though impetuous, thought it best to keep aloof from the Brethren converted from paganism, at least as long as the fanatical representatives were present. He did this in order not to irritate feelings and to give time a chance to heal the divergencies. His reason for doing so could not have been pointless, especially in view of the fact that it was he who had first broken the national exclusiveness and that he had always, in this very city of Antioch, eaten with converted Gentiles. Furthermore, Barnabas himself a man of serious character and an Apostle to the Gentiles like Paul, had followed Peter's example.

Paul perceived the danger of this conduct from which a schism could so easily spring. It would result in two separate communities, one of the Jews and the other of the Gentiles, so that the unity and universality, essential to the meaning of the Gospel, might be broken. Paul disapproved of aloofness on the part of the chief of the Apostles, deeming it the more dangerous precisely because it came from him, Cephas the foundation stone of the Church. In a general gathering, the two groups being present and headed by Peter and Paul respectively, Paul reproached his Superior and colleague in the Apostolate.

"Why are you, being a Jew, and in the past, living in the manner of the converted Gentiles, today forcing the Gentiles to follow the practices of the Jews?"

We can understand from the subsequent unfolding of the Apostle's story that Peter found the observation of Brother Paul just and right, and that he no longer considered himself obliged to use the old precautions in favor of the Jews.

But this episode has been the source of two divergent evangelical traditions: one Petrine, the other Pauline. It has also been an occasion for denying the infallibility of Peter. It has not, however, been sufficiently noted that there was no question of a different interpretation of the Gospel, but only of a particular line of conduct, in a particular context, at a particular time.

If there was error, as Tertullian says, it was an error in conduct, not in doctrine; in tactics, and not in faith. Paul himself had indulged in some Mosaic practices when he had Timothy circumcised, and he submitted to the Nazarite vow himself to please James and the brethren in Jerusalem.

CHAPTER III

THE SECOND VOYAGE.

A.D. 51-53

Paul's Visit to the Christian Community of Asia

Paul had hardly arrived in Antioch when he thought of starting again on a new journey. The Blood of Christ ran in his veins, the Charity of Christ urged him on. He could not understand how anyone could be inactive with that fire of love burning within, a fire of love that was meant to embrace the whole world. There was need of spreading it; everywhere there were souls. The Apostolate is an extension of love—love for God, and love for men. It impels the Apostle to go out in search of brothers, as many as he can find.

Jude had gone back to Jerusalem but Silas had remained with Paul and, with his prophetic inspiration, was comforting the community. Then Peter had come, and so there was reason to be assured of the life of that great Church. Therefore Paul proposed to Barnabas that they visit again the Brethren in the cities where they had formerly preached, to see how they stood in the faith and to confirm them, knowing how men's weakness needs to be continually strengthened.

Barnabas consented but wanted to take with him his cousin, John Mark. Paul, remembering how Mark had left them in Pamphylia and fearing lest he might not be able to endure the fatigue, begged Barnabas not to include him as a companion. Since they did not agree on this point, they parted. Barnabas, taking Mark with him, sailed for Cyprus: Paul took Silas and penetrated into Syria. Paul and Barnabas were both of strong temperaments, both born to govern, and the Lord disposed that each should be at the head of a mission. Thus was the harvest made greater.

It is easy to imagine the consolation of Paul at seeing again those whom he had led into the life of grace. And their joy was great in seeing again the Apostle who had been made so directly by Christ. They never tired of reading in those eyes the shining traces of the vision of the Risen Lord.

Moving along the coasts of Cilicia, it is almost certain that he stopped at Tarsus, a city which had special interest for him, and visited the Church there. From Tarsus through the narrow pass of Taurus and through the Cilician Gate, he went to Derbe; from there to Lystra, then to Iconium and on to Antioch in Pisidia. Everywhere he rejoiced to see the growth of those centers established in the first visit with Barnabas and to walk again in those places that had witnessed their first sufferings.

Everywhere he added to the Gospel, already preached there, the further teachings of the Apostles and of the Elders. The faithful learned that side by side with the precepts given directly by Jesus there were also those of the Authority which He had ordained, to teach, to unfold, and to protect His own divine laws.

In Lystra some of the women had preceded their husbands in receiving Christ. One of them, Eunice by name, helped by her most pious mother Lois, has brought up her son Timothy in a wonderful manner, in the true spirit of Christian piety. Perhaps the two women had been converted by Paul on his first mission. Now he saw them again, and saw the young man Timothy. Paul questioned him and was well pleased with him. Timothy was heart and soul for Christ, so much so that Paul thought he might be an excellent bearer of the Gospel to the Jews. Although Timothy had a Jewish mother, he was still uncircumcised because of his Greek father. Since this might prove an impediment to Timothy's apostolate among the Israelites, Paul circumcised him, considering this act only an act of expediency.

The parents of Timothy knew Paul well. They knew he loved the young man as a son, begotten by him in the faith, and as a younger brother in Christ. Therefore they entrusted the boy to Paul, acknowledging that, having now received Christ, all they had was due to Him, even their son. Timothy, by his generous spirit in dedicating himself to the service of Christ and in serving Paul, was worthy to become the disciple of predilection. He had not the same character as Paul; he was rather gentle and shy while Paul was resolute and impetuous; but in the faith he was Paul's companion and kinsman.

With his companions, Paul wished to go to other centers in Asia Minor, possibly to Ephesus. A divine revelation forbade Paul to proclaim the Gospel in Asia,[1] so he changed his route and turned northwest. He entered Phrygia, the land of religious turmoil in which had germinated rites of an obscure and diseased mysticism. From Phrygia, probably passing through Pessinus, he penetrated into Galatia, a mountainous district, at that time the very frontier of the Roman Empire, where the most important center, Ancyra, was more like a fortress than a city.

It is most certain that Paul went there and spoke to the people, so uncouth and changeable, still so untouched by aesthetic and refined Greek thought. He climbed the long narrow streets filled with soldiers which extended up to the public square. Here stood the newly erected temple dedicated to Rome and Augustus.

Paul must have paused to read on its walls the long inscription which gave the list of the honors and achievements of the "Divine Augustus" in Greek and in Latin. Surely he must have glanced at all those titles, those offices of rank, those records of conquered provinces, those victories and, like a good Roman citizen, felt pleased that peace was assured to so many different people. Under conditions of peace Paul saw a preparation for the Christian message which needed freedom in order to spread. He saw and admired in that earthly power the power of God Himself, of whom the Roman Emperor was only an instrument, honored by God with authority to rule over

---

[1] Asia here, means specifically the Roman political province of which Ephesus was the capital, and was the great peninsula commonly known as Asia Minor.

men and thus prepare the way for Christ. And Paul prayed that the minds of rulers would be enlightened by the principles of true religion and that they might not fall into the foolish and useless expedient of persecution.

The Galatians received Paul as an angel; they were enthusiastic over his message and, with a spontaneous impulse, they would have plucked out their own eyes to bestow them upon Paul who suffered so much from his eyes especially in that climate.

Having preached the Gospel and established some promising Churches, the Evangelists passed on to Mysia, and from there they intended to go into Bithynia but the Holy Ghost held them back. Then crossing that region rapidly, they descended to Troas on the Aegean Sea near the mouth of the Propontis. On the plains they saw many ruins of old Troy partly buried in the soil, and before them on the opposite side the shores of Europe awaiting them.

God revealed to Paul in a vision at night that he should pass over to Europe. A Macedonian appeared before him and said, "Come over to us and help us." Paul did not hesitate and at once made ready to cross the Aegean Sea. He was taking the route that led to the center of philosophical and religious controversy of the Greeks, a place near the very heart of the Empire.

Preaching at Philippi

At this point a third disciple joins Paul and Silas: Luke, the narrator of the Acts of the Apostles, and especially of the history of Paul. He enters the narrative without any introduction, when the verb is changed from the third person plural to the first person; he enters humbly, and without any ostentation. Perhaps he was at Troas as a physician, and an authority on matters pertaining to the sea. Perhaps it was the preaching of Paul that had converted him from paganism to Christianity. It is certain, however, that he learned from Paul that total abandonment of himself and of earthly things was needed in order to give himself to God and to the Apostolate.

Paul knew the value of such a helper, who was proficient in medical science, who knew the Greek world, who spoke and wrote in a correct and precise style. Luke would serve excellently in Greece. So they boarded a ship at Troas and sailed towards the mountainous island of Samothrace, and near its shores, where there was a wealth of tiny bays, they spent the night.

Surely at the sight of the shady mountains, Luke must have discoursed with Paul and his companions of myths connected with all those bays and inlets, the stories of Poseidon who, according to Homer, had climbed one of those peaks in order to watch the battles between the Greeks and the Trojans going on in the plain below. There were the fables of the Cabiri, in whose honor periodical rites were celebrated which were regular orgies. As Paul listened, he was filled with indignation at such degraded concepts and ideas of God. His desire to reveal Christ to a world so unconscious of Him became more ardent and consuming.

Taking off early the following morning, they soon touched at Neapolis, a small city that was used as a port for Philippi. From thence they started on the Egnatian Way that linked the Aegean Sea with the Adriatic, through the beautiful Roman road, and soon reached Philippi.

This Roman colony had become the principal city of the region since the victory of Octavius. Philippi was a sort of advance post on the way to Asia for the Roman world, in the midst of Hellenism. The city enjoyed the *"jus italicum,"* the freedom of an Italian city. It was not merely a provincial town, its citizens were Romans by right.

The people of Philippi were far more Latin than Greek, very religious, honest, hard workers and little spoiled by the quibbles and dreams of the sophists. There was no longer much traffic since the old gold mines were nearly exhausted, and for this reason the Israelites in Philippi were not a very important group. Indeed, there was not even a synagogue, its substitute was only a modest enclosure open to the sky. This mere shelter was on the bank of the Gangites River, at the foot of the hill on which the city was compactly built.

On the Sabbath, the three Apostles went there, and sitting on the ground in oriental fashion, they began a conversation with some women assembled there.

Wherever a person endowed with reason could be found, Paul was sure to start discoursing and turning the talk towards the point he always had at heart. One of these women was Lydia from Thyatira who became a convert. She was a seller of purple dye, a very lucrative business at that time. Although not a Jewess, she was "God fearing" and frequented the Jewish gatherings. Hers was an ardent and open mind, so without delay she begged to be baptized, and then with affectionate insistence, she implored the Apostle and his companions to lodge in her house. And behold, a house that was a business establishment became in a short time a Church.

Once more the first conquest of St. Paul in Europe was a woman; it was to be the same in several other places. There is in women a greater sensibility to religious influences, a quicker intuition of spiritual mysteries, and a more zealous care of their souls, even in the midst of pressing occupations. Maternity keeps a woman in more direct contact with the source of creation, and the home keeps her in more intimate contact with her own soul.

Following upon Lydia's conversion, the Apostles had to deal with another woman of quite a different social class. She was a slave, a fortune teller, and she brought her masters great profits by her forecastings. The "Pythoness," having seen and heard the three Evangelists, ran after them crying, "These men are servants of the Most High God; they preach unto you the way of salvation." [2] She did this for many days, until Paul, filled with indignation, commanded the spirit that possessed her to leave in the name of Jesus Christ.

The spirit went and with it went the power of divination. The slave girl must have rejoiced at her liberation, but not so her masters, who saw their gains go up in smoke. In their anger they seized Paul and Silas and brought them to the praetors, the *"duumviri,"* or municipal authority of the colony. The owners of the slave girl accused the

[2] Acts 16:17.

Apostles not of expelling a spirit but of being Jews and of going about preaching usages that were not "Roman." Luke and Timothy were no doubt away on some matter concerning the Apostolate, or perhaps on account of their rank as mere helpers, they were not disturbed by the magistrates and people.

Paul and Silas in Prison

If Paul had been accused merely of having stopped a source of gain, the praetors would have shrugged their shoulders, but the owners of the diviner were shrewd. They appealed to anti-Semitic feeling with which even then many were affected, and also to Roman patriotism which might be menaced by these foreign usages.

Many various yet similar adversaries of the Gospel have ever since made use of the same high-sounding phrases; and from a certain pagan point of view their accusations are not so absurd. Christianity was demolishing the idols, the gods of the Empire, and was doing so in those years when the Emperors were trying to make the gods of Rome and the gods of Caesar a bond of unity in order to control the different people now subjugated under Roman law.

The law spoke with clarity. It was not permissible to introduce new deities without the authorization of the Senate. It was treason against the Imperial Majesty, even more than an offense against religion, to reject the national cult, at the summit of which stood Rome and the Emperor. The *"duumviri"* had little time to ponder over these considerations with the mob in tumult; but the tumult was sufficient motive for the local magistrates to intervene.

Rome wanted nothing so much as order, and whoever disturbed order was a criminal. Behold, here were Paul and Silas, who by their discourses were provoking disorder. There was no doubt about it. In fact, before their arrival all things had been running as smooth as oil.

By such falsification as converting a religious controversy into a civic matter, the magistrates and people found as many pretexts then as they do now for the persecution of Christians. The Christians were followers of a Deity above all nationality, above all political systems, universal and for all. To pagan political thought, universality had always seemed treason. So Paul and Silas were roughly stripped of their garments, cruelly flogged, and thrown into prison. The jailkeeper, who had been warned and was frightened, put them in chains. He threw them into the darkest, lowest cell, a kind of black well, into which dripped all the dampness and mud of that loathsome underground place.

The Apostolate brings calumnies and rods to those who are engaged in it until martyrdom puts an end to it all. Others would have been discouraged, but Paul and Silas understood the purpose of these things; and in those scourges and chains they saw an imitation of the Master, whose preaching had been crowned with scourging and had ended on the Cross. Therefore, in the darkness, in the middle of the night, they sang hymns to God.

The prisoners above and around them did not at first understand where the song was coming from. At that hour of the night those who could sleep, slept, and those who could not, groaned; they could not comprehend how anyone in chains, in that dungeon, could find either physical strength or moral courage to sing hymns. That singing was prayer, and when one prays even a dungeon becomes a temple of God. Heaven answered their prayers.

At midnight a terrible earthquake shook the foundations of the building, broke the doors off their hinges and loosened the chains and fetters of the prisoners. The keeper, suddenly awakened and full of fear at seeing the doors thrown down, believed the prisoners had fled. According to Roman law, the jailers were responsible for each prisoner; if any one of these escaped, the jailer paid for the desertion with his life. It was no joke and no light matter.

The keeper of the prisoners from Philippi, knowing this, in desperation drew out his sword to kill himself but Paul, perceiving it, called to him, "Do not do yourself any harm, we are all here." That cry must have stupefied the poor man even more than the earthquake itself. He sought for a light, jumped into the pit where Paul and Silas had been thrown and, trembling with fear, fell at their feet. He now had supernatural proof that the two were not malefactors. The mob had hurled its rage against them at the instigation of the weak praetors. These prisoners were messengers from Heaven. They brought salvation, as the jailer had heard it whispered of them.

He drew them out of the pit and asked humbly, "Sirs, what must I do to be saved?" "You must believe in Jesus; that He is the Lord," the Apostles replied. A thing very simple, and yet for most men so difficult because it means a radical change of spirit and of the intellect; its effects are felt even in the flesh.

The jailer believed, took the two prisoners to a decent room, washed the wounds that covered their bodies all spattered with blood: and he and his family were baptized. Then he invited them to his house where he refreshed them with food amidst the great rejoicing of his whole household.

In a few hours a series of miracles had taken place. An eruption of light had released them from that dark dungeon and revealed the supernatural character of the Apostolate of the two Evangelists, and baptism had been given to a number of persons. The prison had become a Church and the jailer no longer trembled with fear.

The Roman Citizen

The *"duumviri"* were the petty magistrates of this colony and they had appropriated to themselves the title of praetors. It was not long before they realized that a mistake had been made and that they were responsible for this injustice by acting without regard to proper procedure. All this they had done merely to satisfy a shouting and excited mob. Probably the influential Lydia had brought her own authority and that of her friends to bear on the matter.

In the morning the magistrates sent some lictors to the prison with orders to free the two prisoners. Perhaps a person other than Paul would have been glad to get away without saying anything in order to avoid further trouble and to forget the whole matter. On the contrary, Paul had a very keen interest in all civic affairs and a sensitive conscience towards them. He respected the civil laws and wanted to see them respected. Being a Jew by blood, a Christian by religion, he was a Roman by legal right. He knew, too, that to duties there are also correlative rights and that the protection of one must not imperil the existence of the other.

Paul and Silas were Roman citizens; that is, they enjoyed a privilege not common to the Asiatics and still less so to the Jews, since Rome granted citizenship sparingly and even parsimoniously. The Philippians, who enjoyed the *"jus italicum,"* fully understood the value of Roman citizenship by which an Asiatic was made equal to a Roman citizen, and like him enjoyed all civil rights. This meant an exemption from corporal punishment and the right of appeal to the Emperor from a criminal tribunal. Paul had inherited from his father his *"jus civitatis,"* which clearly indicated that his father must have been particularly deserving in his services to the Roman commonwealth.

Now if Paul was proud and resolute as an Apostle of Christ, he was equally proud and resolute as a citizen of Rome. He knew the value of his privilege and he was going to use it. Therefore he said to the lictors, "How is it, that we who are Roman citizens have been scourged in public, and without a trial thrown into prison? And now the magistrates would dismiss us secretly? Not at all; let them come in person and set us free."

Paul demanded reparation, and he was right. The people would have a greater esteem both for the Apostles and for their message of the Gospel. As far as lay in his power he tried to convince the magistrates of the futility of trying to get rid of Christianity by scourges, a weak expedient indeed.

Roman law was invoked in their defense. It served that purpose quite often. The accusers had also invoked the Roman law against the Apostles.

In any case the Apostles did not seek to be above the common law, neither did they want to take a place below it. And though they were willing to bear all humiliations for Christ, for the dignity due their office as Evangelists as well as for the message of the Gospel of which they were the bearers, they demanded respect, at least outward respect.

Paul's attitude obtained the desired result. The *"duumviri,"* when they heard that they were dealing with Roman citizens, were alarmed and frightened. Their own sentence would have been heavy indeed if these prisoners reversed matters and denounced them, since it was formally forbidden to scourge Roman citizens.

Therefore they came in person and humbly asked Paul and Silas to pardon them; and leading them out of the prison, they begged the two to leave the city. The two Apostles had pity on the poor wretches. They had no desire to avenge themselves, only to teach these praetors to be law-abiding citizens and to respect all future missionaries.

Paul and Silas returned to the home of Lydia where they saw the other brethren. These gave them such cordial and sincere proofs of their affection that the heart of the Apostle ever afterwards turned to them with longing and love. When they had consoled the disciples, the two Evangelists left Philippi; and so this mission also was a success having ended in a jail.

At Thessalonica

From Philippi the two once more took the Roman road which bordered the sea, crossing Amphipolis and Apollonia, the Salonica of today. It was the largest city and the capital of Macedonia; its port was alive with trade and commerce. For this reason no doubt, it was crowded with Jews. They had established a synagogue there, the center of religion and of the race, like a kind of advanced outpost in pagan lands.

The two Evangelists took lodgings at the house of a Jew who had changed the original form of his name from Jesus to the Greek Jason. On the Sabbath, following the directions given them as well as the yearnings of their Israelite hearts, they wended their way to the

Synagogue. The Jews of Thessalonica were in the habit of doing this every week for the purpose of keeping alive in their hearts the hope of the Messiah Whose coming they believed to be near at hand.

At this assembly Paul announced that Christ had come, had been crucified, and was risen from the dead according to the prophecies. He stood before them with the Sacred Books in his hands to prove his statements. For three consecutive Sabbaths he went there. Meanwhile, through the week he preached to the Gentiles and made a number of converts. It is worth noting that among these converts were many ladies of rank, both by birth and social position.

These numerous conversions are easily understood when we realize that the period was one when the old state mythologies had lost their religious content and were merely patriotic symbols. Many sensitive minds were turning to Asia and the East, eagerly seeking a faith in something above the sensible and the material. People were embracing Egyptian and Asiatic cults, hoping to find in them a purification of life and the salvation for which their souls yearned.

A few Greeks, drawn by such sentiments, had become proselytes of Judaism; that is, a kind of Jew without circumcision, professing belief in one God and following the moral precepts of the Scriptures.

Many generous souls received Christianity with transports of joy and enthusiasm when they realized it was pure spiritual truth without materialistic or political entanglements and that in it all the prophecies of Israel had been divinely fulfilled. Women found in it special causes for attraction; above all, the strict morality that protected women from being exploited by men. Christianity exalted all household and domestic duties; it stressed the dignity and worth of the mother, of the sister, of the daughter, the unmarried woman, and of the widow. It inculcated discipline, order and authority in the home, and in the whole of life; it contributed greatly to the establishment of peace: all conditions most precious to the feminine mind.

Paul preached with enthusiasm; not the enthusiasm of one advocating a private and human cause but a universal and divine one.

He gave all he had and asked for nothing. Although he had a right to be supported by the converts to whom he gave his service so freely, he refused to be a charge or a burden to anyone, preferring to live by the labor of his own hands. He was the servant of each and all; always working with one intention, to fashion souls in "a way of life" worthy of God; building lives of sanctity. Surely this was a most fatiguing labor.

The conservatives, alarmed at Paul's influence and success, had recourse to the usual expedient, always sure and effective. They went to the public square, where the loafers, vagabonds, and dregs of the people idled away their time, and hired a few dozens of these to start a tumult and riot in front of the house of Jason where the Apostles had their lodging.

Here the hired rioters put on a noisy scene but, since the Apostles were absent, they seized Jason and some Christians who were with him, dragging them all before the city magistrates. The charge was that these men were traitors and that the fatherland was in danger.

They then accused Paul and his Christian companions of provoking disorder in the city. (In reality, the case was exactly the opposite.) The Apostles were further accused of acting against Caesar's decrees.

The magistrates of a large city like Thessalonica were not so easily deceived. They questioned Jason, made him pay a heavy fine and sent him home with his followers. The faithful, nevertheless, sent Paul and Silas away in a hurry and by night, towards Beroea. They knew the stubbornness of the anti-Christian men and did not feel too sure of the safety of the missioners. And so ended that tumult, the first in a series directed against the Christians. They were to be so serious that Antoninus Pius would have to intervene to put a stop to them.

However, Paul and Silas had lighted a fire in that pagan port, a fire which continued to burn and blaze long after their departure. Works were now added to faith. Missioners were sent through Macedonia and Achaia; and all the initial groups of believers the Apostles had established developed rapidly. Later, when the test came, they resisted persecutions, so that the fame of that Church reached the Aegean and the provinces beyond.

At Beroea the success of the Apostles was even greater both within and without the Synagogue. The adversaries in Thessalonica, hearing of it, started to repeat the riot, using the same provocations. Once again the Brethren induced Paul to take the road by the sea, leaving behind Silas and Timothy; promising to send these two collaborators in the Apostolate to him as soon as possible.

Paul at Athens

Paul's visit to Athens is one of the most thrilling in all the history of his spiritual labors. Here took place one of his intense contests in the realm of the spirit. If Paul had found in Athens a Socrates or a Plato, the discussions between the two would have been supremely interesting. Exponents of the highest revelation and the most clear-minded speculation would thus have met; perhaps, when they came to know each other more thoroughly their respective systems might have been fused into one. This was done later when Christian wisdom began to gather and incorporate into itself as its own the purest product of all ancient thought.

At that time there were no longer any great teachers at Athens; only their inferior imitators called the "Epigoni." They endeavored to pass on the doctrines of the great philosophers Zeno and Epicurus, adding to these their own lesser speculations. They dissected and rearranged the old doctrines instead of improving on them by new thought and thus giving these ancient theories new life. The Athenians lived on boasting and recounting their memories of a history long past, instead of on independent creative thought and activity. Athens was far more an open-air museum than a philosophical school in the Arts and Sciences.

Facing the wide blue sea stood the Acropolis with its gilded pinnacles. The great peristyles of colonnades, which circled the walls of rose-colored marble, glistened and shone in the sun. All this recalled to the Greeks their military glories in the remote past; their lost political influence, once so active and far-reaching, now quite empty and spent. All their elaborate ethical thought during that political regime was now congealed on parchment. The new generations of men lived on a lucrative income and cared little for the ancient wisdom now crystallized in their scholastic anthologies.

The Roman Empire had respected Athens, keeping the city as a collection of marble beauty, an ornament to the Imperial Crown and a proof of Rome's power in subjugating a people of such creative genius and Hellenic culture. For administrative purposes the province was called Achaia.

The Athenians, knowing this, had become sceptical and corroded by superstition, as a conquered and fallen people are wont to be when they refuse to resign themselves to their condition. Christianity was not for them. Christianity demands simple souls, dissatisfied souls, restless souls, but not indifferent souls. These Athenians were defeated, apathetic men. Could the Crucifix ever ascend and crown the Parthenon?

In Athens Paul saw many idols, beautiful and lascivious in form. They were everywhere, on the open plains as well as on the slopes to the Agora, the spacious marketplace; on up the hill of Mars as far as the Acropolis from whose summit there was a sweeping view of the open sea. It was from this height that the Greeks had watched the flight of the Persian armies. The whole scene was one of smug complacency. Under the clear blue skies, hopes and aspirations ascended as if shooting from the soil, only to return to it. From earth, not from heaven, a new ideology would germinate and bear fruit.

Through the ascending streets, at the open forum, in the porticoes, the Stoics, Epicureans and Sophists wandered aimlessly about. They were a petulant and fierce intellectual aristocracy and even more ar-

rogant in speech. Paul cleverly assailed them with questions and
started many animated and lively discussions.

In those days the customary disputation revealed a new accent when
it came from the lips of Greek or Semite who continued their discourse under the porches. They had the vocabulary and speech of
worldly wisdom, Paul had the Word of Wisdom Itself. They were
tricky and wrangling, Paul was tenacious, tactful and persuasive.
They did not understand him, nor did he understand them. In the
eyes of the Greeks who were slaves to words and to a lengthy vocabulary, Paul was merely a seller of curious and strange oriental
fables.

The Greek deities were the products of fancy and imagination.
Consequently, the idea of a personal God, Who had descended from
heaven to become man, had no meaning whatsoever for them. Wisdom had given place to sophistry: truth to scepticism.

The activity the Greeks loved best was to hold long dialogues and
discussions, to listen to learned speeches, and to wander from one
speaker to another. They were no different from the intellectually
curious of today who spend their time running to concerts and lectures. So they invited Paul to expound his doctrines in some open
place where all could hear him.

They chose the esplanade of the Areopagus, on the Hill of Mars,
the famous tribunal where the cases for murder and bloodshed were
tried. Paul ascended to the Areopagus by the steep stairlike street
that led upwards beyond the great Agora. He mounted the last
flight of steps and found himself on a sort of wide terrace. This lay
between the altar of Athene and the great white stone bench on
which the accused and their accusers were wont to sit during a trial.

Although he had little hope of success in convincing these people,
he would leave no effort untried to make Christ known to them. It
would be worth while to talk about Him, even should no one believe.

The scene was a unique one. The little Jew standing on a step of
the tribunal, or perhaps on the pedestal of a statue, or even on the

capital of some overturned column. These were commonly used when the listeners wished to hear some person of renown.

Spread out before him and all around him, Paul saw a multitude of apathetic Greeks, reserved and sophisticated. A crowd of boys had climbed on some projections in order to see and hear, while others squatted on the pedestals of the statues of ancient orators. These, too, had once spoken in this place.

Near by rose the tall slender columns surrounding the vestibules of the Acropolis. Bordering their quadrilateral sides, covered with beautiful Pentelic marble, rose the colonnade of the temple upon which stood the trophies and statues of the gods, scintillating against a brilliant sun. The natural and material beauty of the place was made concrete in forms of art as yet unsurpassed.

Here was realized an ideal of life without strong emotions, lived in carefree idleness, divided in equal measure between the service of the country and one's own personal pleasures. The scene before Paul seemed in its very outlook to reject with horror, as something sordid and terrifying, any idea of a life of pain, accepted with self-denial in order to live again the sufferings of the Son of Man crucified.

At the foot of the hill the city stretched out before him, a panorama of arches, chimneys, and small houses. Athens, the great city that had nourished, and was still nourishing with her thought, the choicest part of the civilized world. There it lay, with its porticoes and stone figures of Hermes spread over the barren plains as far as Phaleron and Peiraeus on the one side, and towards the slopes of the sharp-pointed Lycabettus on the other. These slopes were crowded with snow-white temples scattered over a green and golden landscape.

On all sides were the souvenirs of a glorious history, monuments with their long inscriptions and chronicles of triumph. On all this the hearts of his listeners were centered when Paul, facing a huge bust of the great orator Demosthenes, revealed to them the knowledge of a God not made of gold or stone, but a pure Spirit. Then he graciously gave the title of "ignorant" to these people who thought they possessed the most sacred learning of all antiquity.

The little Semite, wrapped in his poor tunic, spoke in the only way one could speak to such a public gathering. He used their own language in a clear and elegant manner, beginning with their own ideas. He said that in all the aspects of their life he had found them very religious, even to the point of having erected an altar to the "Unknown God." No doubt in speaking thus he was somewhat ironical, for it seemed singular that in a city where idols were numbered by the thousands and where the genealogies of the gods filled interminable columns, one god was left out of count through ignorance. That unknown god in this city of so much culture gave Paul his happy beginning.

"Then," said Paul, "the God you honor, without knowing Him, I reveal to you!" The Athenians were startled into attention while at the same time they were scornful.

"He is a God, Creator of the universe (the readers of Plato could understand this). He being the Lord of heaven and earth, does not dwell in temples made by hands. He has made all the peoples on the earth from one single man, determining the time and place of their dwelling. God would induce all nations to seek Him, and to find Him. God is in us. As your own poet, Aratus, has said, 'We are also His offspring.'" Paul went on to say that idolatry, which imprisons the concept of God in statues made by hands, is therefore the product of ignorance. Ignorance must be done away with without delay. God had declared this word to them, that all men should amend their lives, in expectation of the judgment, which would be rendered by a Man chosen by Him, and Whom He would raise from the dead.[3]

This was the summary of Paul's discourse, in which neither the name of Christ nor of the Scriptures was mentioned; for the Athenians would not have understood either one. The audacity of the little barbarian Jew did not displease the descendants of Pericles, accustomed as they were to listening to all kinds of innovators and exponents of religious cults from the East.

---

[3] Acts 17:16–34.

But when they heard of the resurrection of the dead, they shrugged their shoulders in contempt, persuaded that this was utterly impossible, something that could not be done, and some said mockingly, "We will hear you another time!" Others laughed in his face.

Nevertheless, they were cultured and refined people, who made no disorder, nor did they in any way persecute the Apostle. These Athenians were accustomed to giving full liberty of speech to any doctrine, esteeming all intellectual exercise as a superior activity.

Certainly then, as afterwards, the dogma regarding the resurrection of the body remained the greatest obstacle for the Greeks. They were afflicted with idealism and strove to exclude from the purely intellectual all things of the exterior world and of the senses. The flesh, therefore, was looked upon as so much corruption. For this same reason, they found it hard to accept the dogma of the Incarnation, and tried to weaken its meaning with their idealism. However, some more serious-minded and sincere were impressed by the inspired conviction of Paul. They were persons in whom all sense of the human had not become atrophied by Greek culture and, receiving Paul's instructions, they believed.

There was among the converts a judge of the Areopagus named Dionysius who, according to Christian legends, was the first Bishop of Athens and author of several mystical writings; and there was a woman named Damaris.

There had been no persecution and therefore there was not much fruit. But Paul's discourse was not useless. It became a model for Christian Apologists, especially for the Greeks during the Empire period, for contacting and convincing the learned. It was a model of moderation and skill in taking advantage of the doctrines held by the intellectuals.

It was not easy, nor has it ever been, to gain converts from the intellectual classes who are always smug and conservative. However, it is only by discussions with them that Christian principles can reach

Three worlds witnessed the Great Apostle's labors: the Hebrew world centered about Jerusalem (above), toward which every Jewish heart yearned; the Hellenic world symbolized in the Parthenon at Athens (centered); and the Roman world (below) whose crumbling ruins are stately reminders of bygone glory.

The Island of Malta, where Paul was shipwrecked while sailing to Rome in the winter of 60 A.D.

(Right)—The statue of the Doctor of the Gentiles in the Church of St. Paul, Malta. The Maltese profess a centuries-old devotion to the Apostle Paul, having received from him the gift of Faith which they have steadfastly preserved down through the ages.

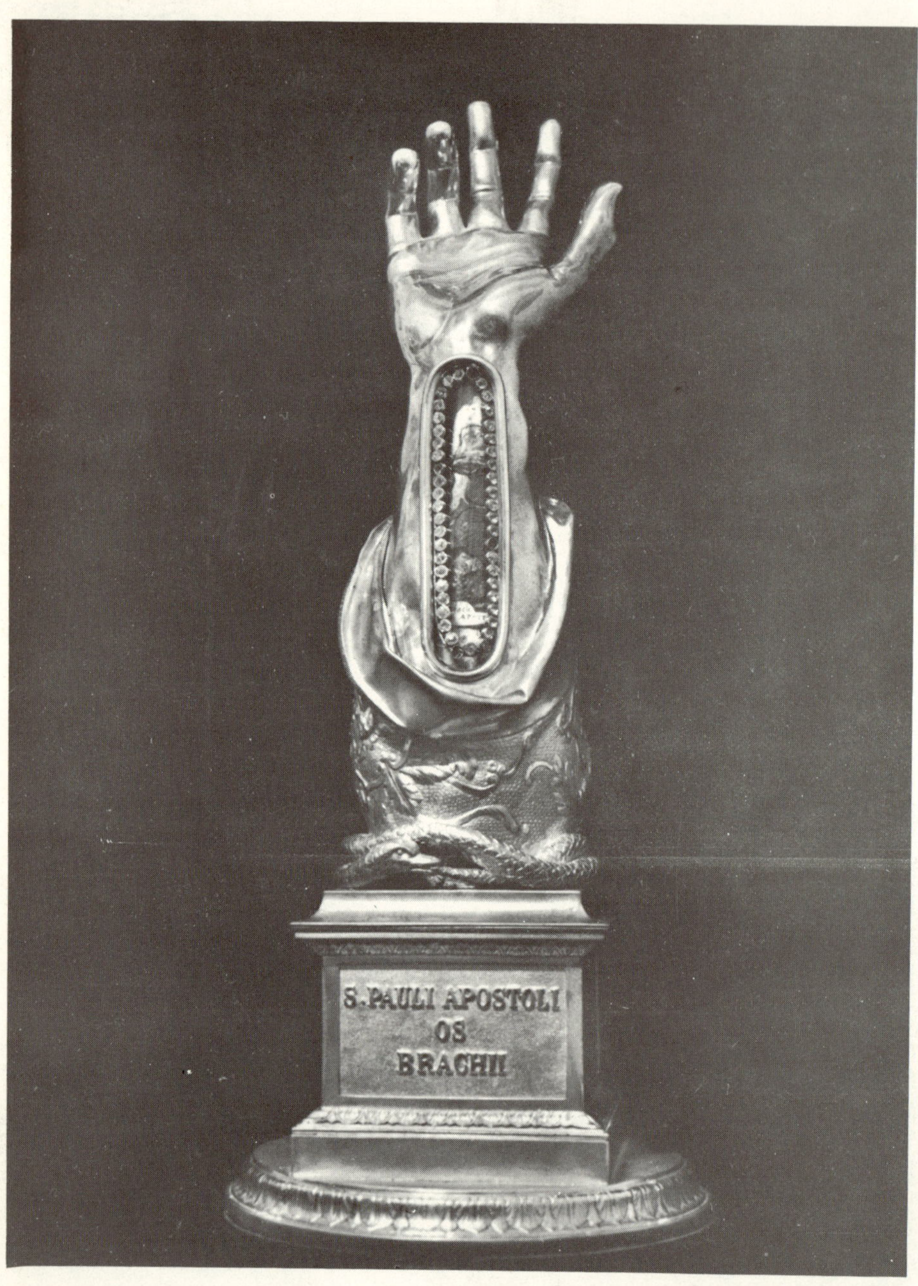

The relics of the arm of St. Paul venerated in the Church of St. Paul, Malta. Paul worked many miracles during his stay on the island of Malta. He cured the governor's father and after that "all the sick of the island came to him and were cured" (Acts 28:9).

The ruins of the Basilica of St. John in Syracuse (above) presently stand over the catacombs of St. John (below) where Paul celebrated the Eucharistic Sacrifice during the three days his ship was in port at Syracuse. The arrows point to the entrance to the Catacombs from the basilica and to the location of the altar in the crypt.

The facade of the Cathedral of Syracuse before which stand the statues of
the Apostles Peter and Paul.

(Right) The statue of the Doctor of the Gentiles in front of the Cathedral.

Paul preaching to the faithful of Syracuse in the c

St. Martius built beneath the Basilica of St. John.

The Miracle of the Burning Pillar — In wrapt attention the Syracuse faithful listened to Paul's ardent words ringing through the crypt. Unnoticed by all except the Apostle, the solitary torch illuminating the crypt flickered feebly and slowly burnt itself out. Wishing to continue his discourse, Paul paused momentarily. He turned toward a pillar in the crypt and miraculously caused it to burst into flame. Conserved in the Cathedral of Syracuse, the remains of this pillar are a reminder of the wonders God wrought through His Vessel of Election.

After a few more days at sea, Paul landed at Puteoli. The gates of Rome were at hand! Rome—symbol and center of the pagan world; the hope of Christ and Christianity; the focal point of Paul's flaming desire.

(Left) Notified by the brethren in Puteoli of Paul's arrival, the Roman Christians warmly greeted the Traveler of Christ at the market of Appius. Today there remains of the ancient market town only the stone erected during the reigns of Nerva and Trajan.

(Below and right) The historic Appian Way, "the Queen of Highways," trodden by the Apostle Paul en route from Naples to Rome.

The ancient gate of St. Sebastian through which the Great Apostle first entered the Holy City of Rome nineteen centuries ago.

(Right) Paul—the Prisoner *of* Christ, a Prisoner *for* Christ. The Apostle looked upon himself as the conquest, the prisoner of Christ Jesus, held fast by bonds stronger than the chains he wore entering Rome. Yet again the Prisoner of Christ was to return to Rome. He would embrace martyrdom and unite himself forever with Him Who was his Supreme Love from the instant they met on the road to Damascus.

ME
S
A
PERSEQVERIS EGO SVM
QVEM TV PERSEQVERIS
STIMVLVM CALCITRARE

Paul was the shepherd ever ready to give his life for his sheep. No one understood better than he the value of the souls redeemed by the Blood of Christ, and the sublime doctrine that whoever labors for souls must add to the chalice of the Redemption drops of his own blood. Thus it was that the Apostle would often repeat, "I have been crucified with Christ."

the supreme authority of the State insofar as they provoke a philosophical and theological reaction in the world of culture. To this effort Paul gave a real impulse and direction.

From that time on he refused to have anything to do with professors or philosophers; on the contrary, he spoke of them with no little severity. The meeting at Athens had taught Paul that intellectual pride is opposed to charity and that the wisdom which descends from God is superior to the natural wisdom that ascends from man. Henceforth he did not try to present Christianity from the standpoint of reason. He stated it clearly and briefly, in all its startling crudeness, as a religion of One condemned to death, Who died by crucifixion.

Before leaving Athens for Corinth, Paul probably reviewed his labors in the capital of Greece, and his mind saw with clarity and precision what he afterwards put down in writing—the conflict between the knowledge that puffs up and the charity that builds up.

When the proud intellectual loses sight of all that he does not know, resting complacent and satisfied in the little he does know, he shrouds himself and blinds himself in his small world. The larger world of men outside himself has no interest for him and charity finds him cold. The follower of Christ, on the contrary forgets himself in the loving service of others.

To Corinth

Between two seas lay the city of Corinth, which Spurius Mummius had destroyed and Caesar had rebuilt, peopling it chiefly with his Roman war veterans. It had, because of its unique position like a bridge between Italy and the oriental provinces, taken on a vigorous development. Corinth was the chief city of Achaia, with six hundred thousand inhabitants, two-thirds of whom were slaves.

The city received its life from Rome and in this respect differed from Athens, the city which was pompously vegetating, winding itself around the old dry trunk of its memories. On the contrary, Corinth pulsated with traffic, carried on between the small banks and the Baths, the theaters and the temples, at the foot of the Acro-Corinthus. The great rock fortress was crowned with the beautiful temple of Aphrodite, circled with rows of marble columns. In this temple prostitution was practiced accompanied with all the theories and rites of a morbid oriental mysticism. Corinth, the city of Venus, in the midst of commercial prosperity and political importance, was famous for its luxury and for its pleasure devotees from East and West.

In Corinth an atmosphere of sin surrounded men's minds. On the other hand, there was less boasting and self-conceit than among the Athenians. And if the number of philosophers and argumentative persons encountered at every street crossing was excessive, the number of artisans and small shop keepers was even greater. The Corinthians were a corrupt people, but they were not hardened in their sin; they were foolish and fickle, but disposed to accept the hand held out to help them.

Here, in the dim evening light shining on the marbles everywhere, in the midst of an intense moving throng of people, the shrill sound of many voices, there entered on foot (those feet that had traversed so many miles, in so many countries), a little Jew, unknown to all, named Paul. The boys saw in him one more pilgrim; the dock laborers saw in him one more seeker of adventure.

Hospitality was more generously given in the old Roman times than it is today, since poverty was greater. Paul found lodging in the house of a Jew whose name was Aquila. Perhaps Paul recognized him as a Jew by his manner of dress or by the type of features common to their race, and more probably he met him in some tent-maker's shop where Paul went seeking work. When two Jews met, especially in a foreign land, they were, or were expected to be, like brothers to each other. The duty of giving mutual assistance was inculcated by the Scriptures and sprang naturally from racial solidarity.

Aquila was born in Pontus, but he had gone to Rome on business. Lately he had had to leave Rome because of the decree published by Claudius expelling the Jews. This expulsion was caused by the serious riots and tumults that continually arose in a certain district concerning one "Chrestus," that is, Christ.

Aquila was a pious Jew, who had perhaps believed in Christ during his stay in Rome, and with his wife Priscilla, an intelligent and sensible woman, managed a promising business of manufacturing tents. This was the trade Paul followed and he may have offered his help and been engaged to work for them. The tents were of goat's hair, woven in the Cilician manner, much appreciated and sought after because of their durability. Consequently, a good weaver could always find work and a fair pay.

The great Apostle, like Christ his Master, enhanced the value of work by his example. On the Sabbath, being the Lord's day, he went to the Synagogue and accomplished another work for the Lord. When Silas and Timothy finally arrived, Paul gave himself up altogether to preaching.

Paul was no longer working by the day, so he left Aquila's house and moved to that of a certain Titus, called "the Just," who was not a Jew but belonged to that class of Gentile sympathizers whom they called "God-fearing." The house of Titus was next to the Synagogue, and this was favorable to Paul's conversations with the head of the Synagogue, Crispus, whom he subsequently won for Christ.

The Apostle had thought of leaving Corinth, but the Lord told him in a vision not to do so. "And one night the Lord said to Paul in a vision, 'Do not fear, but speak and do not keep silence; because I am with thee, and no one shall attack thee or injure thee, for I have many people in this city.' " [4]

The divine order bound him more closely to that center of fickle and lascivious people, where it was truly seen that publicans and harlots are often better disposed toward the Gospel than the Pharisees and the doctors. Paul left a portion of his heart there. The vision had again insisted that the Apostolate should be fearless and insistent, making use of speech without ceasing. So Paul spoke by day and by night, in the houses and in the streets, in Greek and in Aramaic, and when this was not enough he wrote and dictated. His word was hammering consciences and reforming them.

Speech is the essential means of evangelization. Faith comes by hearing and it is not produced by material promises nor insidious allurements. Speech is a projection of reason, a divine instrument of thought. In the Divine Nature, the Logos or Divine Wisdom is the Word of the Father. Speech is the most direct way of communication between the Eternal and man. It is the channel of spirituality and contemplation.

Therefore the champions of material force, opposed to the force of reason, always begin by taking away the power of speech from the Apostolate, and Paul had to experience this and to suffer for it. But the divine admonition had said more: that the building of the Kingdom of God among men is a work of courage. Fear not, if men attack, God defends. It is a work of persevering labor and fatigue without pause or rest, stone upon stone, word upon word. The Christian is never to lose courage, never grow weary.

Paul was the personification of that program. They bound him and he spoke; they stoned him and he discussed; they shut him up in

---

[4] Acts 18:9, 10.

prison and he wrote. He was travelling and he converted his companions; they brought him to the tribunal and he announced Christ to the judges; they presented him before kings and great people and he reminded them of the Last Judgment.

First Letter to the Thessalonians- -A.D. 51-52

Corinth was a large city, and it was necessary to labor at all hours in order to form a Community of Saints out of that gathering of merchants, craftsmen, housekeepers and harlots. Paul worked vigorously, making himself all things to all men, assisted by Silas and Timothy. He went to the small towns and villages of Achaia, as far as Illyria on the Adriatic Sea. At the same time he cared for the Churches scattered on either side of the sea. He sent directions and counsels by means of the faithful who went that way; perhaps for that purpose; and in more important cases, he dictated letters.

No doubt the two Epistles we still possess were written from Corinth, one at the end of the year 51 or at the beginning of 52. The other in the year 53 to the faithful of Thessalonica, where the Apostle had received a most affectionate welcome; and where in a short time many Greeks, noble ladies, and also some Jews had received Baptism. Timothy had visited the city, having been sent there by Paul.

On his return Timothy brought some consoling accounts. The Church at Thessalonica had become a center for the diffusion of the Gospel and for the collection of alms destined for the poor of Jerusalem. This Church had in a short time reached such religious maturity as to equal the old Apostolic Churches of Judea. Later they stood the test, suffering much at the hands of fellow citizens. Suffering was the confirmation as well as the result of good Christian conduct; therefore we are destined to suffer.

The Apostle reminded the Thessalonians of this in his first letter. He dictated it in the name of Silas or, as the Latin version puts it, Sylvanus, and of Timothy, his two brave collaborators, always hiding in Paul's shadow for the love of Christ. Paul recalled to the Thessalonians his fatherly love towards them; and that they, the faithful, were his glory and his joy. Such is the language of a father towards his sons. He desired to see them again, and to perfect them in the faith, as they also longed to see him, but Satan was opposing this through his enemies.

Meanwhile Paul pleaded with them to follow more closely the precepts he had given them. All the Apostles used to leave certain precepts and doctrines to be practiced in the Churches where they had preached or taught. These gradually formed the deposit of Tradition, to which Christianity had recourse before any documents were written. Documents could not reach everywhere, and in some places the faithful did not know how to read.

The usual precept left by Paul as the expression of God's Will for his spiritual children could be summed up in one word: sanctification. God has called us to it and we are not to neglect it; to do so is to offend God, not man. Sanctification is an unceasing work. It demands an assiduous acceptance of the Will of God, and also a continual feeding of the flame of love. Sanctification takes hold of the spirit, and the soul and the body.

In Paul's words, we repeatedly find this three-fold division, which corresponds to three classes of men: the spiritual, the human, and the carnal. The carnal are those who live for the instincts of the flesh. The human are those who follow the dictates of the natural or rational part of the soul. The spiritual are those supernaturally illumined by the Holy Spirit.

In this instance the Apostle wants to say that the whole person, spirit, intellect and body, must all concur in sanctification. The whole man must be invested with sanctity, within and without, all that is visible in man as well as all that is invisible. If the Christians at Thessalonica had had this totality always present in their minds, certain bad Christians there would not have invented an idea of the separation of body and soul in the work of sanctification, as if one could be sanctified independently of the other.

Sanctification must first take care of the body by mastering it in chastity and honorable conduct towards other men, in order to lessen concupiscence. After that sanctity is to manifest itself in acts of a social character; for example the Thessalonians, who were given to commerce, must be honest in their business dealings, since God Who is Judge, watches over such things also.

In a city where traffic and commerce abounded, far too many people had become a prey to the fever of gain and profit. Paul exhorted them to be ambitious only in living quietly; attending to their own business; to work with their own hands, so as to be independent and to keep their dignity. Here the Apostle made use of his wisdom as a Pharisee. He was an expert in his understanding of the Law and in the customs of industrious Jewish people. Paul described the first Christian communities as quiet colonies, made up of honest workmen and bound together by a mutual and growing charity.

Christian life, in order to become holy, either individually or corporately, demands ecclesiastical discipline. This begins with a certain respect for those who preside over the Church and instruct in the Gospel. It establishes Christian unity, or solidarity, among the brethren. The result of such a life is joy; Paul had no use for long sad faces. This was the moral portion of the letter and the rest has to do with Paul's theology.

The Thessalonians were disturbed by eschatological anxieties, being perplexed about the condition of those "who sleep," that is of the dead who die before the second coming of Christ. They feared that the departed ones might not participate in triumphal glory with the same fullness as those that should be living at the moment of Christ's coming.

Paul reassured them. When the Lord shall come from Heaven, after the Archangel has announced Him, the resurrection of those who died in Christ will take place. Then these, together with those still living, shall be taken by flight above the clouds to meet the Lord. It cannot be known now when this shall happen because the Lord will come suddenly and unexpectedly, like a thief in the night. Therefore, it is necessary to be ready at every moment, living every second of one's life with Christ, in faith, hope and charity. This is the only thing that matters. We should not be preoccupied about the second coming except to be ready for it, ready by our manner of living and, above all, by a holy life.

The letter ends with a request for prayers. This circulation of religious charity which ascends from man to God, binds all the faithful in a single current of love. Then Paul salutes all the brethren with a holy kiss.

Second Letter to the Thessalonians- -A.D. 53

The second Epistle was written some time later. As always and everywhere there had entered among the good Thessalonians some fanatics and exploiters; presumptuous men who wanted to substitute or insert their own Utopian views into the Apostolic Tradition. They were heretics and instigators of confusion, always ready to compromise. Faith is faith because it accepts God's views and not man's own private views. Faith is objective truth that God has revealed, and man must accept it thus; but too often man, instead of becoming Godlike and adhering to God, presumes to make God conform to his ideas. He seeks to substitute his own changeable notions for the immutable idea of God.

Perhaps this mania did not appear for the first time in Macedonia; it has reappeared many times since, times without number. Everywhere Jesus had taught His doctrines with authority and they were definite. He taught the whole of objective truth. And yet, even among some of His followers there were those who sought to substitute their own interpretations for His, under the pretext of seeking the truth; as if truth had not been taught, or was still hidden and had yet to be found. For belief, was substituted inquiry; for faith, knowledge; for the Mind of God, the intelligence of man.

In Thessalonica the second coming of Christ, or the "Parousia," as it was called, was the special point on which imaginations were working. A tendency to speculative analysis was always strong among the Greeks. For them it was an easy turn, a light deviation in their fantastic imaginations. A tendency to literary fraud was not such a rare thing in those times; so someone under Paul's name had circulated an apocryphal letter, spreading the conviction that the Parousia was imminent, and therefore it was useless to bother about the things of this world.

This was an attempt to insert, in the Christian order, a social anarchy inspired by an ideal of idleness; a human weakness to enjoy the things of life by levelling all study of eschatology. In fact these innovators were sliding easily enough into all the evils which idleness produces, under the pretext of waiting (between one gossip and the next) for the tremendous burst of light in the heavens, in the midst of which Christ the King should come.

It was an interpretation very pseudo-mystical, many times repeated in our own time. While seeking to attend to spiritual matters and to the mysteries of the Last Day, temporal things were neglected, especially the constant, steady labor for one's livelihood and the responsibilities which exist in life. They are the hair shirt for many of us in the work of our sanctification for eternity.

The Apostle must have been petrified to hear such tales. He could not imagine that a truth so clear, could in so short a time have become so obscure and full of so many errors and deviations. With what patience and ardor he warned his Christians against such seducers. The coming of Christ would not take place until after the great Apostasy, and the coming into the world of the "man of sin, the son of perdition" (Antichrist), who would invade the temple of God and seek to usurp the adoration due to God.

This Antichrist would endeavor to invade the consciences of men; and in fact, the mystery of his wickedness was already at work. Even now, there were attempts to usurp divine titles, to gain control of consciences, but his attack upon men was already opposed by another force, by One Whom the Thessalonians already knew.

What was this Power, and Who was this Person who blocked the coming of the Antichrist? The tradition of the Thessalonians is interrupted on this point, and has not passed the instruction on to us. Ancient and modern writers have tried to fill in this gap with their own conjectures, but without success. The larger number have thought it to be the Roman Empire; but since the Roman Empire is no longer in existence, we must think of some Power still existing. Therefore the hypothesis is that St. Paul had in mind the Church.

Antichrist, supported by Satan, will surround himself with all the signs of a false and counterfeit divinity; power and prodigies of deceit that will be gratifying to all those who have not adhered to the truth.

"Resist then, my brethren, and keep the Traditions that you have received, either by my word or by my letter"; [5] that is, by the spoken word or by writing. Writing, as it is clear in this instance, serves only to remind one of what has been said orally; and there would have been no writing had there been no reason to remind them of that.

The closing of the letter is characteristic of Paul. Paul did not write, he only dictated; this made false interpretations possible, and already there had been a favorable chance for such interpretations. Therefore in this second letter Paul adds a salutation with his own fist. His writing was large and heavy, quite proper to the calloused hand of a craftsman and also of one who suffered from weak eyes. His signature was thus easily recognized, it served as a seal. Hereafter he would in this way sign the letters he dictated.

The Return to Syria

The Apostle worked for a year and six months in Corinth, probably between the end of the year 51 and the beginning of 53, teaching all classes and kinds of people, as St. Luke records. Paul wanted to reach everyone because salvation was a matter that concerned all, and no one escaped him. His task was to evangelize. When conversions took place, Paul left the baptizing to the "presbyters" or priests; however, in the case of influential persons, he made an exception and

[5] 2 Cor. 2:14.

baptized Crispus the Ruler of the Synagogue, Caius his own host, (in whose house he lodged) and the family of Stephanas.

As usual the attempt to denounce him to the tribunal as an innovator who led the people to embrace a cult contrary to the Roman law could not fail.

It seems that not long before Paul's arrival there had come to Corinth the new proconsul, the governor of Achaia. This province had recently been returned to the jurisdiction of the Roman Senate by Claudius. The name of the new proconsul was L. Julius Gallio, brother of the philosopher Seneca, a man belonging to a wealthy family, of refined and cultured upbringing, meek even unto weakness.

Gallio was too shrewd not to read the conniving behind this noisy patriotic clamor. With that sense of superiority and calm poise proper to the ruling classes educated in the Roman fashion, Gallio answered that if it were a question of ordinary crime he could intervene, but since they were dealing with "words and names" belonging to the Jewish law he would not enter into their quarrel.

The Roman law and the Christian religion were in agreement as long as the principle affirmed by Paul and Gallio was carried out. The principle was that magistrates should act only in cases where the common law was violated and not in matters of religion. It was only when politics meddled with the science of theology that persecutions broke out.

The plans of these mean Jews who wished to enjoy the spectacle of seeing Paul flogged were therefore foiled, so they took their revenge on the chief ruler of the Synagogue, Sosthenes, holding him responsible for their discomfiture and they overwhelmed him with blows. Gallio, grand lord that he was and Roman philosopher, did not stir himself. In his heart, like the other Romans, he may have despised that mob. No doubt he raised his eyes towards the Temple of Aphrodite, the smiling symbol of beauty and self-satisfaction.

Paul continued on his way. He, too, had in his heart an ideal of beauty and of joy which were not the special possession of a privileged class or race, and which would not be destroyed, either by good or evil fortune. A time would come when both the rich proconsul and the poor Apostle would fall under the melancholy and insane despotism of the Emperor Nero. Then the former was not ashamed to clasp the tyrant's knees in full view of the Senate, forsaking both his dignity and his philosophy; while the poor Apostle went to his martyrdom in great tranquillity of soul, and never retracted one iota of his doctrines. That was the difference.

Now that a flourishing Church had been started in the city, Paul thought of those who lived farther away and so he resumed his travels. After taking leave of the brethren brought by him into the life of the Spirit and made part of the Mystical Body of Christ, he boarded a ship going to Syria.

There were with him his first friends and hosts of Corinth—Aquila and Priscilla, always faithful and resolved to make even their business affairs serve the Gospel. They had already given themselves and their goods to the service of Christ and His Church.

At Cenchrae Paul took a Nazarite's Vow. This consisted in letting one's hair grow, in abstaining from wine, and from touching dead bodies. This Vow was to be completed with a sacrifice offered in the Temple. The Vow was a renewed bond, though merely external and reverential, between the new religion and the old, between Christianity and Mosaism.

At last Paul reached Ephesus, called "the eye of Asia," the luxurious and elegant capital of the Roman province and the seat of the Proconsul. This city was another rendezvous for Greeks and Asiatics.

On his arrival, Paul's attention was not attracted to the temples and industries but to the great mass of idolaters to whom it was urgent that he should reveal the new Way of Life, the Gospel. But for the moment he could not do much as he had to go up to Jerusalem to see the other Apostles.

While waiting for a ship to sail from Caesarea to Palestine, he left his companions for a few days and held discussions in the Synagogues. When they besought him to stay longer, he promised to return to them, saying, "I will come back to you, God willing."

From Caesarea he went up to Jerusalem, fulfilled his Nazarite Vow, paid his dues, had his hair cut and thus everyone could see what a good Israelite he was by his respect for the Temple. At the same time he saw the older Apostles again, and so his second round trip brought him once more to the Mother Church. Like a good servant, he returned at the end of each enterprise to the older brethren, to the center of authority. After giving a full account of his missions and embracing them all, he descended as he had done before to Antioch.

CHAPTER IV

THE THIRD VOYAGE

A.D. 54-58

The Sojourn in Ephesus

Like the two preceding journeys, this one also, after a short pause, began at Antioch. Again Paul's itinerary was by land. He revisited the places of his first and most successful missions, confirming the brethren in the faith. These missions were like small Christian colonies in strange, if not adverse, lands, and they needed communication with the Mother Church to strengthen the bonds of union. These bonds the itinerant Apostle supplied. In this same capacity, he visited Galatia and Phrygia. Then, turning westward, he came again to Ephesus, as he had promised. It was the year 54; the year in which Claudius had been poisoned by Agrippina in order to substitute her son Nero as ruler of the Empire.

For some time there had been working in Ephesus a Jew by the name of Apollos (a diminutive of Apollonius), a native of Alexandria, the center of Hellenic culture, where there flourished a school of Jewish modernists trying to make the most of Greek thought. In this metropolis a few years before, a Jew named Philo had attempted a curious and ingenious infusion of Platonism with Mosaism. Here, at a still earlier period, a version of the Sacred Scriptures had been translated into Greek. This translation was called the Septuagint. Apollos was an intelligent man, very learned in the Scriptures and animated by a lively religious zeal. Perhaps he had frequented Philo's school.

Had he known John the Baptist and received baptism from him?

It is certain he knew only the baptism of John from whom or from whose disciples he had gained his first knowledge of Jesus. Jesus he was proclaiming. Apollos was a fervent but incomplete Christian, since he had not yet received true Christian baptism. In the Synagogue where he spoke and which served as a meeting place for the followers of Jesus, there came to hear him one day, among others, Aquila and Priscilla. It may be remembered they had remained at Ephesus. They quickly perceived what was missing in the ardent speaker's discourses so, taking him home with them, they taught him the complete doctrine of Christ as they had learned it from Paul.

Thus even a housekeeper and a day laborer can, and ought to, proclaim the Kingdom of God. After baptism, they inspired and infused, into the mind of their catechumen, the mind of Paul. At once Apollos was sent to the brethren at Achaia with letters and strong recommendations from his hosts and teachers, who were much esteemed by the Greek Christians.

Apollos, with his rare intellectual gifts and pleasing personality, engaged in discussions with the Jews as Paul had done; and he clearly became outstanding by the superiority of his Biblical knowledge, and most convincing because of his sincere faith. He proved to them incontrovertibly that the Messiah had come, and that Jesus was the Messiah they had looked for—and no other.

When Paul finally reached Ephesus, he found a dozen or more imperfect Christians waiting for him. They had been baptized by Apollos, but only in the baptism of John—a baptism that lacked the name of Jesus as proclaimed by the Precursor, and lacked also the grace of the Holy Spirit. Paul explained to them the deficiency in their conversion since they had not yet received the Holy Ghost. He taught them that Jesus was the Christ. Baptizing them in the name of the Lord Jesus and, laying his hands upon them, he made the Spirit of God descend upon them.

For three full months Paul frequented the Synagogue and spread the word of Christ, continually discoursing on the Gospel. Seated on the ground, on the bare floor, or on mats, those bearded Jews began to argue and dispute over Paul's words, seeking to disprove his statements by quoting the Scriptures, the source and strength of their faith.

Paul compared text with text, confronting them with the teachings and deeds of Jesus, never growing tired or weary. Some refused to yield so he separated his disciples from the rest of the community, and left the Synagogue.   He called his own together in the school belonging to a man named Tyrannus.

Thus the differences between Judaism and Christianity became more clearly defined, and the separation between the two deepened and widened. Henceforth for the next two years, those Greeks and Jews who wished to hear Paul, found him in the school of Tyrannus. This was the first Christian school for catechetical instruction ever opened. It was held not only on the Sabbath but every day in the week.

Paul, the teacher, never let a day pass without Apostolic labor. He confirmed his teaching by many miracles so astounding that people stole the towels and aprons of the tent-maker and, touching the sick with them, these recovered or were cured. Those exegetes who would reduce Christianity exclusively to a body of doctrines, miss or neglect this channel of miraculous and spiritual activity which is an inseparable concomitance of grace, by which the body of doctrine is both strengthened and vivified. Whoever fails to notice this wonder-working activity will not understand the full meaning of Christianity nor the secret of Paul's astounding success in the Apostolate.

The Ephesians made another discovery: that the aprons which Paul used for work, and the towels with which he mopped his brow, when applied to the possessed, expelled demons. Those possessed by demons were certainly more numerous before Christianity when souls were more ignorant of God and were deprived of His grace. Also, at this time, souls were exposed to greater danger in being robbed of grace by the spirits of evil. Under the action of grace in Baptism and in all the other Sacraments, the phenomenon of diabolical possession became gradually more rare in the life of the Church.

From then on, the action of Satan was exercised under cover, deep in the strata of the spiritual life. Today, with faith dying out in so many souls, and with the repudiation of Christ in so many countries, we see the number of souls possessed by Satan increased. Men are going mad in the very midst of Christianity and accomplishing deeds that normally are inconceivable: deeds that appear to be, and that are, diabolical.

Later in the West the Church appointed special ministers, called exorcists, for expelling demons; but even among the Jews there were those who threatened the devils. It is a curious fact that even at this time, some Jews, take for example the seven sons of Sceva, a high priest, began using the name of Jesus in their threats towards the devils, having noticed the power of this name in Christian exorcisms. Later it is noticed that the name of Jesus recurs often among the gnostics as well as among the Jews.

One day the seven sons of Sceva were trying to expel a demon from a possessed man, saying to him, "I command you through the Jesus, whom Paul preaches." [1] And the demon replied, "Jesus I know and Paul I know, but who are you?" At that moment the demoniac leaped upon them, struck them with blows and so badly injured them that they escaped from him naked, covered with wounds.

This incident became known and served to spread abroad still more widely the names of Jesus and of Paul. A sort of sacred terror seemed to invade all minds, and as a result many pagans and Jews were converted. Under this action of the fear of God, the name of Jesus was magnified, and the people ran to the Apostles and the brethren, confessing their use of magical arts and deeds and practices. Quite a number of them were given to practicing occult sciences and magic. All over the East, and particularly in Ephesus, soothsayers and fortune-tellers were going about. Through their incantations and

---

[1] Acts 19:13–17.

strange hypnotic utterances, they tried to obtain from the gods numberless petitions for money and health, together with secret revenges, and success in their unholy love affairs.

Paul's preaching and miracles had struck at the very center of superstition in all its many forms by unveiling the reality of the one true God. Those who were in good faith, mended their ways at once and brought their manuals and books of sorcery to lay at the feet of the Apostles who gathered them in a heap and burned them publicly. The Jews, always shrewd appraisers, valued the books that were burned at fifty thousand pieces of silver, or $40,000, a large sum in those days and in the poor economy of the old world.

The Judaizers in Galatia

Paul had been informed of other abuses and contaminations among his Christians in Galatia, and on more dangerous grounds. There for some time attempts had been made to dissolve and weaken the essential character of Christianity. While he was at Ephesus at the end of the year 54, Paul heard that in Galatia the Christians were lending a willing ear to some of the Judaizers who had recently come from Jerusalem.

The Galatians, cramped as they were in the mountainous regions of northern Asia Minor around the center of Ancyra, were farmers, simple, excitable, impetuous, and men easily deceived. It had been repeatedly proclaimed that Paul was, after all, an Apostle of inferior rank and not to be compared with the Twelve, and that consequently these Christians should practice the Mosaic Law as they themselves were doing. Furthermore, the Judaizers said that Paul was teaching them to neglect Mosaism and had no authority to do so. He was acting contrary to the Covenant established between God and Abraham, the father prototype of all true believers.

They did not fail to remind Paul that when it suited him he, like all the rest, practiced the Mosaic observances. They said that Paul had had Timothy circumcised and had himself recently fulfilled a Nazarite's Vow and had completed it by offering a sacrifice in the Temple at Jerusalem.

So, with anguish of heart, Paul learned the news that with his wheat of true doctrine, the cockle of error had been sown; that another gospel had been superimposed on the Gospel of Christ—and he was justly indignant. The pagans moved him to pity but the false Christians moved him to anger. As in other circumstances, he was facing a new problem in his enemies: the universality of salvation, and the gratuitous gift of Grace.

Paul would have hastened thither as fast as he could to caution those dear sons, but since he could not move to come to their aid, he wrote. His circular letter to them was full of anger, and at the same time full of affection. "Oh, foolish Galatians," he calls them. First of all he sets about to vindicate the divine origin of his Apostolate, the source of his teaching authority, and a guarantee that his doctrines were orthodox.

The neophytes of Galatia had rapidly passed from one form of the Gospel to another, as if there could be two different gospels, thus missing the most essential condition of truth, that it is always one, not two or three. And they missed another essential and fundamental duty, to guard the truth and pass it on to others unsmirched by error. They must guard it so well that even if Paul himself, or an angel from heaven, came to announce a different doctrine as truth, each should be anathematized.

The Gospel Paul had given them was derived from a direct revelation of Jesus Christ. It had been confirmed first by Peter, then by all the heads of the Mother Church, and his work had been approved by Peter, James and John, the "pillars" of the Church. This Gospel does not admit Mosaism, although Paul, due to his Pharisaical origin and his zeal for the Law, might have inclined towards the observances of Moses. Christ and His Church would always be the source, the sanction and the guarantee of a Gospel that is true. Any other one is false.

The Gospel is an announcement of freedom from the Mosaic Law, and the "false brethren" are those who wished to impose circumcision and the practice of Jewish rites, to re-establish the servitude of the Mosaic Law, as if these were necessary to salvation while in reality they were of an utterly indifferent nature. Salvation comes by faith in Christ and from no one else. Here is all the theology of salvation.

In order to understand the insistence with which Paul separates the new Christian religion from the old Mosaic religion (a liberation that was to reach a complete and systematic exposition in his letter to the Romans), we must remember that the conviction was then growing and sharpening that works could give justification and that the Jews should accumulate them as much as possible, even with the persistence of a miser. In the Syrian Apocalypse of Baruch it was taught that justification is in the observance of the Law; thus salvation is secured by means of works. The Law had, in their eyes, an intrinsic virtue by which it appeared capable, of itself, to justify man.

In such a system God had little or nothing to do. He was reduced to a meticulous accountant or bookkeeper, bound to give to each a reward in proportion to his legal works. Salvation would come from the Law that gave it, and from man who observed this Law, not from God. The Pharisee in the Gospel story did not ask favors from God; he made up the balance sheet of his own actions. On the contrary, Paul taught the Galatians, "Man is not justified by the works of the Law, but by faith in Jesus Christ." Here is the great difference; and here is the truth.

The Law had served the Hebrew people to reach Christ but, having fulfilled this task, it served no more. In having Christ, the purpose of the Law ceased; it was abrogated, it was dead; and the faithful were dead to the Law with the death of Christ. He alone, has given us salvation. He who would add to Christ's giving, the obligation of the Law, would thereby consider Christ's giving as insufficient, and attribute to the Law the merit of salvation. If this were so, if justification descended from the Law, the death of Christ would have been useless. On the contrary, that death was our life; and therefore, a return to Mosaism was equivalent to abandoning the spirit for the flesh, the interior life for exterior observances, life for death.

The Law had a great value, but it was a passing one. It served only for a definite period of time in the history of the Jewish people. The example of Abraham, father of all the faithful, could not be invoked in favor of legal practices, because Abraham was justified by faith not by circumcision and still less by the Law. The Law did not exist in his time; so that those who have faith are the true children of Abraham. And this had been foretold by the Lord when He gave to the great Patriarch the Promise, "In thee all nations shall be blessed." Now, therefore, all those who believe like Abraham share in the blessings given in him to all his posterity.

It must be either the Law or faith; either the old man or the new man; either the observer or the believer. We would say: either remain with your ancient past which is dead, or accept the Christian revolution, the beginning of a new life.

The Law does not liberate from sin. On the contrary, it gives a consciousness of sin. It places sin before God and the conscience, as sin; therefore it is a source of remorse and not of justification. He who remains under the Law, remains under the curse that menaces all sinners; and the numberless sinners balanced the weight of sin until Jesus Christ took upon Himself all our transgressions and expiated them on the Cross. Then our sins were annulled by His Sacrifice; and thus was realized the blessing promised to Abraham for those who believe and not for those who observe only the Law.

The Galatians might ask, "To what purpose then is the Law?" The ex-Pharisee answers, marking out its limits with pleasing but sharply defined lines. The Law had been given four centuries after the Promise was made to Abraham on account of men's sins, on condition that it should last until the coming of that seed, Christ, in Whom the Promise should be fulfilled. Then Jesus Christ would unite to Himself all those who have faith in Him, and who, like Paul, are by Baptism nailed with Christ to the Cross. They no longer live in themselves but rather Christ lives in them.

"You are all the sons of God, by faith in Christ Jesus; for as many of you as have been baptized in Christ, have put on Christ. There is neither Jew nor Greek, there is neither slave nor free, male and female. For you are all one in Christ Jesus." [2]

Thus the beginning of the new economy makes everything consist in the universality of grace, of faith and of the sonship of God.

Away with separation, taught Paul. Limitation means servitude; it is a principle of death, because it decomposes life and arrests its movements. The Law is like the slave (the pedagogue), who always accompanies and instructs the child of wealthy families as long as he is a minor, and until he comes of age. The Law had fulfilled its task of leading humanity, still an infant, to Christ. [3]

This done, it is now like the pedagogue, who when the master's son has reached the age of maturity, loses his appearance of authority and returns to obscurity. He himself is now subject to the son who is no longer a minor. Christ having come, men have come of age. They no longer need tutors. They are free; adopted sons of God; and because they are sons, then heirs also of Him. They are now under the New Testament which is one of freedom, promulgated in the heavenly Jerusalem, while the Old Testament, given to a people enslaved, was promulgated on Mount Sinai.

These two Testaments are prefigured in Abraham's two sons. One, Isaac born of Sarah the free woman, was himself free. The other Ismael, born of the slave Agar, was a slave. The first was generated in virtue of the Promise, the latter generated carnally. The Christians, like Isaac, are children of the Promise, and therefore persecuted by the son of the flesh as Isaac was persecuted by Ismael.

[2] Gal. 3:26–29.

[3] Gal. 3:25.

The Galatians before Baptism did not follow the Mosaic Law, but were, even so, slaves; slaves of idolatry. To go back now from Baptism to the Law, to the Jewish feasts and ceremonies, to the complicated rites (those primeval rudiments of men's religious life), is to return to slavery, renouncing the liberty of the children of God. And all the work of Paul towards their conversion would have been wasted.

It may seem strange and surprising that Christians should renounce the simple, emancipating dogma of faith in Christ for a complicated system of ablutions, practices and rites, in which the spirit is hindered and smothered as if by a blanket filled with irritating bristles. It is the same surprise one would feel in seeing a slave preferring prison to liberty because liberty calls for responsibility and activity. While on the contrary it is believed that all this ceremonial servitude, although it limits the spirit, at the same time encourages a man to resist moral laziness and cowardice.

There are still people who see more value in a hundred exterior, mechanical acts than in one interior act of faith; more value in the repetition of a hundred formulas of devotion than in the exercise of one act of virtue. In its substance liberty is hard work from which sloth runs away.

Having developed his dogmatic argument, Paul gives expression to his affection for the Galatians; his love is that of a mother for her little children. Mark well, he says, "mother" rather than "father," because the word includes the idea of the priestly maternity of the Apostle, who generates sons in the Mystical Body of the Church, forming them in Christ, as the Word was formed in Mary in His Humanity.

In virtue of the rights which such a mystical generation gives him, Paul pleads with them not to submit to circumcision; otherwise Christ would be of no profit to them. As many as submit to circumcision become slaves to the Law and are obliged to observe all its precepts (and these are as many as six hundred and thirteen, if one counts them). Paul knows well that he is persecuted for this struggle . Nevertheless, his bitter trials could never make him turn back.

In all probability, not a few of the Galatians had lent an ear to the Judaizers only to avoid quarrelling with them and in order "not to suffer persecution for the Cross of Christ." He who renounces the catholicity of the faith and is contented with exterior ritual makes void the scandal of the Cross; so do they who hide the new faith in the security of an ancient people whose customs are approved by civil law; so do those who circumscribe spirituality within the confines of a state, of a caste, of a people. In this way persecution can be avoided, but Christian religion is emptied of charity and its most essential quality is lost.

In Galatia, no doubt, the newness of Christianity began to produce reactions among the people and suspicion among the authorities. Judaism was both national and racial, while as yet Christianity was neither. Those who submitted to circumcision became members of Judaism, and since this was a recognized religion and united the Jews in a race protected by law, they spared themselves many worries and even worse.

Paul suffered and the Church has always suffered for this same reason, both from pagans and Jews; and also from the apostasy and desertion of Christians for the same cause. In other words, they withdrew from the infinite freedom of the spirit to confine themselves to the limitations of the flesh.

But, it could be objected, if all legal observances were abolished, then when a person is once baptized and has received the faith which is sufficient, is there nothing more to be done? Indeed there is. There is a whole series of interior observances of the spirit to practice, according to the precept of love (the new Law), by which one's neighbor is loved as one's self. The Law of Moses is put aside, and the Law of Christ takes its place.

Liberty does not mean abolition of all law. That would be anarchy. Liberty is the atmosphere in which love acts, and it produces good works. When the commandment of love is put into action, it is evident at once how much there is to be done. Neither does liberty mean an unbridled use of the senses. "He who sows in the flesh, of the flesh, he will reap corruption; he who sows in the Spirit, of the Spirit, will reap life everlasting." [4]

In the new Life of the Spirit, eternal life is found; in the old life of the Law, eternal death is found; in the former is gathered the Israel of God, in the latter the Israel of the flesh.

"See what kind of letter I have written you with my own hand," says the Apostle in closing. "And be not troublesome to me, for I bear in my body the stigmata of the Lord Jesus." And these marks (scars of contradictions, and of stones thrown at his poor flesh) testify to the goodness and truth of his Gospel. If it were not genuine, he would have suffered in vain. It would have been enough, in order to escape persecutions, merely to change the Gospel.

It can easily be imagined how this flaming letter was carried to the mountainous villages of Galatia, and read and commented on in the meetings of those mountaineers. It must have raised a storm of reactions and protests against the sowers of cockle. And they learned that it was not enough to receive the faith, it must be defended in its integrity against the temptations of those who wanted to subsitute for the titles of the Spirit, the mania of matter; for the dogma of Christ, the quarrelsome opinions of men; for unity, factions and divisions; for universality, particularisms.

The effect the letter produced was deep. Later the Apostle was able to organize in Galatia a collection of alms for the poor of Jerusalem, the new Christian way of charity, in order to unite the Christians who came from paganism with those who came from Judaism.

---

[4] Gal. 6:8.

Divisions in Corinth

In the same manner that Paul had written to the Galatians, he wrote to the other Churches he had founded; sending his letters or directions by trustworthy persons while day by day he built up the Church at Ephesus. During part of the day, and even at night, he worked in the shop of Aquila, carding and weaving those coarse, rough threads of goat's hair which cut his fingers and calloused the palms of his hands. For this reason they were not fit to hold the stylus used for letter-writing. Then in the more convenient hours he taught groups of Christians in the school-room of Tyrannus, or went from door to door, from shop to shop, to visit the brethren. Faith is built, that is, Christ is built in souls, not only by explanations of the Scriptures, by Christian example and by writings, but also by the work of individual instruction. So Paul labored, taking a modest offering to some lodging of the poor; giving good counsel in a time of doubt and perplexity. In a word, he gave all the manifestations of that charity which is the greatest wealth men can possess because it is something divine.

Thus several years passed by. Notwithstanding the eloquence Paul used, and the miracles God wrought, it was not an easy thing, and it never has been easy, to form sanctity in consciences molded to pagan habits or in intelligences obscured by prejudices bred of abnormal philosophies and theosophies with their consequent mysteries.

At the same time he taught the distant communities, especially those of Gentile origin (and here was his preferred field of action), to increase their personal sanctity and to promote the Apostolate. And, in fact, the word of the Gospel was circulating and spreading under his influence; first, around those centers most important for the conquests of Christ, as they were equally important for Caesar; secondly, in smaller centers united to the larger ones. This became the first ecclesiastical system for the Church's authoritative administration and pastoral direction.

It was a truly heroic period, one in which Paul built his spiritual edifice with daring and tenacious intensity. It was heroic in a true Christian sense, for Paul's announcement of the Gospel seemed to be an extension of courage such as were symbolised by the Pentelican marble memorials. These stood outlined against the deep blue Aegean Sea under a smiling iridescent sky. Paul's announcement seemed like a shadow cast upon them, like an eruption of ignorance, which the Greeks could only tolerate through a spirit of frivolous indifference.

Of course that little Jew who emerged from a carder's shop to discuss his mysteries was taken for a fanatic, one who had renounced life and had become a social outcast. Those who amused themselves with philosophical skill turned up their noses at him; those who lounged around and within the Temple of Artemis laughed at those ideas of asceticism so ridiculous for people who sang the amorous verses of Hypponax.

In the eyes of his enemies, he was either an intruder or a thief; as for him, he felt his condition most keenly. He seemed to be a stranger upon earth, journeying alone to a fatherland to which most men gave little thought. How his soul suffered from the spectacle of exulting idolatry in this evil city—the loose manners of men and women so ostentatiously displayed even on the streets. Very often also his stomach was racked with hunger. At every street crossing he was insulted; youngsters would throw rotten fruit at him as at a maniac, or some idle loafer would prick him with cutting jokes. All the while his heart groaned for news, worrisome as it would be, from those distant Churches where he knew the party of Judaizers were defaming him. The Ephesians were calling him a man down and out, an ambitious and illiterate man. He was forever building up while, at the same time, numberless, invisible hands seemed always trying to tear down his work of construction. This was the payment on the part of the world for Evangelization, and the world had plenty of reasons for not wanting it.

On a certain day a most serious fear came to Paul concerning the Church at Corinth, consecrated by him in the faith through so many sacrifices. The Corinthians were a fickle people, surrounded by all the attractions and seductions of a seaport through which passed all sorts and kinds of people, philosophers and superstitious necromancers. It seems that in Corinth the Christians had greatly relaxed and had returned to their old pagan ways of living as soon as the Apostle had left them. Fortunately, Apollos, as it may be remembered, besides knowing the Scriptures, had an attractive manner of speaking, and since he came from a Hellenistic environment, he knew and shared their taste for a refined and eloquent expression of thought. Apollos had made a sensation.

To many of the Corinthians, his rhetorical and pleasing manner of presenting Christianity was more acceptable than the bluntness of the Apostle Paul. Paul was apt to be both timid and abrupt. He cared only for teaching Christ crucified, without indulging in rhetorical eloquence. Apollos knew how to dress up the truths of Christianity with subtle quotations and brilliant considerations.

Two currents in thought and leadership began to be noticeable in the Christian communities. In the meantime the corruption for which Corinth was notable began to seep in among the Christians to such an extent that Apollos was unable to call them to order. In those days the word corruption was interchangeable with the word Corinth, so greatly was the city famous for its immorality. Apollos left the city and went to Paul to whom he related everything. Paul felt a clutch at his heart. Without losing any time, he wrote the Corinthian Christians a strong letter, commanding the faithful ones to have nothing to do with the fornicators. That letter has not reached us; this and many other Apostolic documents have been lost. If they had all been lost, however, faith would not have been lost; before these letters were written, there was the Church, and the Church is Christ.

Paul's intervention by letter, if it helped to put a stop to the familiar associations with fornicators, also stirred up some resistance to authority and sharpened party strife. Many pagans regarded fornication as being as blameless as eating or drinking. Therefore some of the Corinthian Christians resented these associations with fornicators while others did not. Personal preferences began to be accentuated: some remained attached to Paul, others to Apollos, and in the meantime, the emissaries of the Judaizers, who always opposed Paul, had arrived. They claimed that Peter was a true Apostle and set a better example, since he, unlike Paul, recognized the authority of the Jewish Law and the Mosaic practices.

In this way a number of factions had arisen in the Church in Corinth, and each took for a leader one of the Apostles or teachers. They spoke of the party of Cephas, of that of Paul, or of Apollos; and also, of a party, not very clearly defined, of Christ. This last was composed of persons who esteemed themselves superior to others. Even in very recent times there have been groups of Christians who wished to separate and differentiate themselves from the rest on the pretense of preserving unity. They have continued to call themselves Christians, the party of Christ par excellence. So as not to seem to detach themselves, they elevated themselves above the others, unaware that in this way they were also cut off from the Body of Christ, the Church.

Prevailing Greek customs favored discords in matters of doctrine. The Greeks loved to group themselves around various teachers for the mere pleasure of arguing. This characteristic had brought about such deadly moral weakness that the Christians had tolerated in their midst a man who lived sinfully with his stepmother. And then there were irregularities of another kind. Christians, quarrelling with Christians, brought their grievances before the pagan magistrates for vengeful satisfactions—believers brought before unbelievers to be judged. All this was giving a very poor illustration of the mutual love and charity they should bear towards one another, and of the dignity proper to the redeemed who were destined to judge the world. (In this as in other prerogatives of Christ they were to share).

There appeared again during the "Agape" that old sense of exclusiveness, those distinctions based on economic differences and conditions, with a marked indifference towards the poor, all of which Apostolic charity condemned. There were other disorders which proved how easily and how rapidly the orthodoxy and purity of the faith was dying without the Apostle.

With romantic fantasy we may imagine the first Christian communities as gatherings of saints; on the contrary, they were gatherings of sinners, just as in our own day. Sanctity is a work requiring fatiguing and assiduous labor, for individuals as well as for the Apostle. Paul was wholly occupied with it and kept on repairing its ruin wherever it collapsed. One can imagine how he suffered when two servants of a noble lady in Corinth, Chloe by name—either sent by her or coming to Ephesus on business—told Paul what was happening at Corinth.

In his anguish and distress, he immediately sent to Corinth the person in whom he had the greatest confidence, a man formed by him after his own heart, the young Timothy. Paul planned to entrust to Timothy the mission of renewing, in that frivolous community, the memory and the integrity of his teaching. Perhaps at the same time Timothy made another long tour of the Churches in Macedonia (Paul was always carrying on several things together), to organize a collection for the poor in Jerusalem.

In the meantime, three other informants arrived at Ephesus, three trustworthy persons from the same Church of Corinth: Stephanas, whose family deserved much praise for their help in the Apostolate in that city; Fortunatus and Achaicus. They were the bearers of a letter from the Christian Community, or at least from some of the more faithfully devoted ones. The letter contained questions concerning various problems of a theological, moral, and disciplinary order—problems that revealed the difficulties of life for a Christian Community in a pagan society.

Paul wished more than ever to go personally to re-establish order; but for the moment he could not leave. He asked Apollos to go for him, but the latter, knowing well the difficulties of the situation, refused. There was nothing left for Paul to do, but to write a second letter—and a wonderful letter it was. He had to dictate it, which proves how much he loved these children of the Church and, at the same time, how proud he was of these men, led by him into the Christian life.

CHAPTER V

THE CHURCH AND THE MYSTICAL BODY

The Gospel and Sophism

It was in the spring of the year 57 that Paul dictated his last letter to the Corinthians and attacked all the evils of schism, immorality and pagan customs from which they were suffering. Always the outstanding advocate and martyr for unity and catholicity, Paul first of all stigmatizes the divisions among them and implores the faithful to be of one mind, to say the same things in doctrine, to have one spirit, and to be always of one sentiment. . . . It is almost certain that even in Corinth where sophists and others addicted to lofty speculations, intellectual tricksters, faddists in the use of words, were so numerous, there were some who must have distinguished the difference between unity and uniformity, and they must have injured unity on the pretext of turning away from division.

Paul was on fire with indignation and alarm. "Each of you is saying, I am of Paul, I am of Apollos, I am of Cephas, and I am of Christ. Is Christ torn to pieces? Was Paul, perhaps, crucified for you? He who tears the Church tears Christ. The schismatic and the heretic is a crucifier; and even worse; although, alas! (sadly does the writer remark it) there must needs be heresies, so that the truth may appear: as Judas was necessary, so that Christ might redeem us with His Blood."[1]

Corinth was a Greek city, at that time the capital, and displayed some air of culture. There were many men devoted to syllogisms while lecturers prospered; many who had no political ambitions or

[1] 1 Cor. 1:10–13.

activity spent their energies in splitting in four the thread of some concept; reasoning merely for the love of it, and discoursing in an elaborate diction but without any force of spirit or sincerity for truth. So-called philosophy, espoused to rhetoric, was a profession and a pastime. It brought in money and some glory. It gathered under its wings a caste both quarrelsome and proud.

The sophists, the orators and lovers of distinction, had mingled with, and penetrated into the life of the Christians. In the midst of the faithful these took pleasure in trying to remake the simple evangelical doctrine: showing a more or less open contempt for the uncultured Apostle who alternated his Apostolate with coarse manual work. So the aristocracy of intellectualism, like a fungus growth, sprouted in the midst of the simple souls of the faithful. The parasite of sophistry was climbing up the trunk of the vine of Christ. A disease of the intelligence was developing, in which fantasy was mistaken for speculation and a false pretense of knowledge was substituted for faith.

In this way a new enemy was presenting itself to the Apostle, the intelligentsia of rationalism, which stood like a stone wall to shut out the spirit. Since the wall was thick and solid (he had experienced it at Athens), Paul did not attempt to walk around it but assailed it directly in front with vehement blows, without compromise, crudely exposing the contrasts of intellectualism to the simple doctrine of the Gospel.

To the pseudo-philosophers and the distillers of the Gospel the message of the Cross was foolishness; Christianity would end either in prison or on the gibbet. These great intellectuals were trying to rectify this but only succeeded in destroying it by their syllogisms. Alas! they only lost their way. "Has not God made the wisdom of the world foolishness?" the Apostle asked impetuously. God, Who was identified with a Wisdom far removed from that of the schools and the marketplaces.

The Christian revolution destroyed many of the opinions then in vogue about culture and subordinated culture to sanctity. Paul held high, not academic decorations, but the naked arms of a Cross. He made men see that salvation is not made known by fine speakers nor by the most learned rhetoricians, but by modest, humble workers enlightened by God; and because there are such, they are in themselves the most convincing confutation of wisdom in high places. In other words there existed this apparent absurdity: the so-called ignorant were the really wise; and the so-called wise were the really ignorant. The wisdom of the world is ignorance to God.

The Corinthians were still carnal men, hardly beginning to know or understand the true doctrine; they were like infants fed at the breast with milk: that is, with the first rudiments in the science of God, namely, theology. The fullness of theology is possessed by spiritual men, who on that account may be called perfect. These have progressed in their knowledge of the mysteries, and in the practice of virtue, for the achievement of which they needed the Spirit of God and not the wisdom of the world.

To understand the things of God, one needs the Spirit of God. To understand Christianity, one needs the sense of Christ; but the "carnal" man stops at appearances, at the bodily senses; and the merely intellectual man stops at philology, at history, at human philosophy, going no further, and so these men never catch the knowledge of the Spirit. They remain in a different and limited order of things.

To study the things of God with the Spirit of God is a great good. To study with the spirit of the world is useless labor, if one wishes to attain a knowledge of the things of God. Therefore a poor old coal vender in Rome may possess more of the wisdom of God than a "Pasteur" who knows only the science of the world. The worldly wise do not reach Christ. These leaders in the world, who attend only to earthly science, such as Caiaphas, Pilate, Herod, and other magistrates—such as these condemn the Lord of Glory.

From the very first, Paul stood in opposition to those who sought to make a philosophy out of religion, as the tendency of the time was to make philosophy into a religion. Paul took his position against worldly science, not because it was science but as a pretended revelation of the mysteries of God that can be reached only by faith; and finally, he opposed those first symptoms of a criticism that would substitute Paulism for Paul, and the message of Christ for a professorial thesis.

In such a world, the Gospel proceeded by paradoxes, breaking down the systems of thought no less than the systems of caste. The Jews asked for miracles; the Gentiles wanted doctrine; and the Christians preached Christ crucified, a horror for the formalism of the one and the aestheticism of the latter, because the cross was the instrument of death, a punishment most degrading and most horrible.

Medical science has explained the awful complex of pain in the human body, by crucifixion, thought out and devised by a cruelty which is always the science of a godless world. Neither the Jews nor the Gentiles could reconcile the idea of the Redemption with that horrible instrument of death reserved for the scum of society. Even its name (which Cicero remarks) was never to be uttered, much less thought, and the majority of Roman citizens were careful never to see or hear this word, reserved for slaves and highway brigands. On this infamous cross Christ had taken the place of a thief, Barabbas.

Such a fact did violence to the ancient way of thinking and to the consciences of men. And yet it was this very fact that Paul presented to them, and he even exalted it in the presence of the most learned men of the period. Paul remembered the rhetoricians of Athens, the professors of Tarsus, who all day long sat under the porticoes or lounged along the banks of the Cydnus, talking about some fragment of an ancient image or some remnant of etymology.

Paul, always so direct and precise, could not accept their empty activity of words and ideas, through which a simple truth was rendered unrecognizable by dint of stretching, pulling apart, and dissecting. He had a just intuition of the havoc which the learned would make of the Gospel (from the beginning, even to the present times), and of the preaching that would be called "Pauline." It was for Paul a sort of crucifixion at the hands of the learned professors and exegetes.

He saw already that at Corinth they had substituted Paulism, Petrism, and Apollonism for Christianity. For this reason he insisted on recalling to them that God chooses the foolish to confound the worldly wise, and the weak to confound the strong. The new Christian life ascends from below, works from the interior to the exterior, and has to do with all those things of the spirit which the world despises but which are of fundamental importance in the work of the Church. This is so, that all may see that the Church's work is the work of God, Who does not need the power of men, or their worldly wealth, or their nobility of blood.

Christianity is a revolution that takes place in the depths of the souls of men, and which brings about an essential human and social revolution. In this new system of cause and effect, men in rags, the weak, the rejected of society can become, if God chooses them and if they are willing, co-partners with God in a divine task. They are the outposts in the battles of the Eternal.

They will constitute the aristocracy in the Kingdom of God, to which the noble, the rich and the great of the earth can also belong, if they become inwardly humble, poor in spirit, and servants of Christ. The learned of this world must make themselves foolish in order to become wise. They must put away the pride that has entangled them as if caught in the midst of thorns. All glory must return to God through Christ, Who is true Wisdom. Therefore he who will glory let him glory in the Lord.

It is easy to understand what all this leads to. If all glory belongs to the Lord, then men have no reason to be proud, to believe themselves superior to their brethren; he who believes himself superior separates himself from them.

Sublime reasoning power is not necessary to an Apostle. It is out of place in the Apostolate because the art of employing words makes void the efficacy of the Cross of Christ. The voice and the words of the Holy Spirit are most suitable for a true Apostle of Christ. All he needs is the wisdom of Christ, and Christ crucified. The Apostle has this wisdom and he has the mind of Christ, both being the gift of God. In Corinth Paul had planted, Apollos watered, but He Who gave the increase was God. Such a restoration of merit to God as being the only One to Whom it is rightfully due had a tendency to bring about a certain relaxation and was also an incentive to sloth.

Some men said that if all is done by Christ, then men, even in relation to the work of the Church, have nothing to do. This is not so, says the Apostle, who meets the objections of the sophists as soon as they are born. The voice and words of the Holy Spirit are the same today as then and will be the same tomorrow. God acts, but we must act in union with Him. Men are not mere spectators of God's work; they are helpers and auxiliaries in the construction of His Church, co-workers with God.

Consequently, those who have been reduced to nothing in human evaluation, now become men whose lives have a divine value. As mere men, they were nothing; as Apostles, they are raised near to God. This sublime and admirable association with God in His divine activities, which is a communication of the divine nature, is a gift from God. He rewards us in proportion to the contribution and co-operation each one gives to Him.

Moral Teachings

Paul hammered all these truths into the Corinthians in brief and concise phrases. They diminished considerably the inflated pride to which the Corinthians were always easily inclined. As a people they were rather vain and thought themselves strong and honorable; their ears were full of pompous phrases. So much the more so now that the old vigor of Hellenistic intellectualism was nearing its end.

But many of the old human traits still lived and the old leaven fermented in their ranks. Once more Paul spoke of himself, giving them the example of a man who had completely lost himself in Christ; who sought only the glory of God. He was careless and wasteful of the judgments of men, whose salvation (the one and only matter of essential value) depended, not on men, but on the judgment of God.

In a realistic manner, vigorous and ironical, he pulls the Corinthians down from their mountain of pride and makes them sit in the depths of their nothingness. He contrasts their vain glory, sustained by elaborate discourses, to the sufferings of the Apostles, who, to save souls, had become the refuse of the world and the dregs of all mankind. And while he exhorts them, he also threatens them. In his next visit he will use his authority against them and will judge them not on their words but on their actions. This is a sign that it was not an easy matter in those days to impose the new Christian values and standards on men. The Corinthians, having heard Apollos, an orator naturally more brilliant and erudite, were in danger of putting form above substance and of placing the authority of the Apostle above that of the Church.

It was also a sign that the Church was acting as a visible society, in which the Apostle Paul ruled with an authority that came to him not from below, that is, from those who composed the Church, but from God through Christ. We now behold him exercising this authority in a concrete case. The foundations of morality among the Christians were endangered by tolerating the presence of an incestuous man in their midst, a thing the pagans would not tolerate. The Apostle, present with them in spirit, gave a terrifying example of his divine authority, of the power of the Church spiritually assembled for the deliberation of this very matter: he expelled the sinner from the Community of the Christians in Corinth.

The excommunication was the more terrible in that it abandoned the sinner to Satan to be tormented in the flesh, so that, through suffering physical pain, his soul might be saved; and being deprived of the Sacraments, detached from the life of the Mystical Body, he had less resistance against the Prince of Evil, who could more easily take possession of him and obsess him. In this way Satan could completely destroy him.

In dealing with the case of this man, it is clear that the Apostle had to do much of his pastoral work in Christian formation by letter. In the first letter, now lost, he had written, "Have nothing to do with fornicators." Some critics have given these words too extensive and abnormal a meaning; they should be understood in the same sense as the rest of Paul's teaching. Some, however, understood fornicators to mean a class which comprised all sinners and all pagans. By doing this they reduced the Church to an exclusive life, to an enclosed circle, drawing odium to itself and closing the door on all charity. If contact with the pagans was forbidden, all chance of converting would be lost. It would be a return to Pharisaical sectarianism, and to caste. "If you act like that," explains the Apostle, "you will have to leave the world altogether." "But now I write to you not to associate with one who is called a brother, if he is immoral, or covetous, or an idolater, or evil-tongued, or a drunkard, or greedy; with such a one not even to take food." This was to prevent evil from fermenting within the Community of the saints.

The quarrelsome Corinthians, even after Baptism, dragged their brethren before a pagan tribunal, when Christian love should have softened the spirit of contention, or at any rate the dispute should have been settled by some of their own wiser brethren. In themselves, the disputes were such trifles that the most ordinary of the brethren could have settled them. Brothers—members of the same family, the Church—cannot oppose one another without harming the whole body as well as themselves.

Corinth was a busy market center and a lucrative meeting place for merchants from the East and the West; there were also those who came to provide amusements, such as the mimics, trick-players, and dancers. It was not surprising then if some Christians, not yet sufficiently imbued with the Spirit of the Gospel, were caught by the allurements of the place; especially at night when the city of Aphrodite became a place of adultery and banquets.

The worst of it all was that they tried to justify their sin according to Christian doctrine. Some thought that when a person was baptised and his soul purified, his body might be allowed to become soiled; and that it was the spirit and not the body that must be kept pure. "All is licit," they were saying. In this way they were accepting again the principle of division and not of unity. This amounted to an attack on the principle of Catholicity which includes body and soul, heaven and earth, time and eternity. The Corinthians were not the first ones to try that convenient deception by means of which the currents of Persian dualism were spread around by soldiers and merchants from the Orient.

The danger was a serious one. It wounded Christian morality on the one hand, while Mosaism wounded it on the other hand, and both aimed at rendering null and void the Incarnation and the death of the Lord, that is, the Redemption that had taken place in His Flesh. St. Paul reminds us that the body also shares in the work of sanctification. It has been created by the Lord, consequently it is sacred and through the Lord it is made a Temple of the Holy Spirit. It was bought at a great price, the price of Blood, and is destined by Christ to be glorified in the Resurrection. The body is a member of Christ, to Whom it is united sacramentally, and it must not be united to a harlot by sin.

Thus Paul in a few bold strokes, enumerates some of the works of the New Law; lifts to a high spiritual level, severe but pure, that body of flesh which, as an evil thing, far too many dragged through halls and houses of ill fame. He makes of it an instrument for the glorification of God and the Apostolate. The body becomes a "Christopher," that is, a Christ-bearer.

Problems of the Corinthians

So much for the preface. Now Paul passes to the questions put to him by the Corinthians in the letter they had sent. The first question concerned matters relating to marriage and the state of virginity.

The Apostle stresses the duties of the conjugal state; the necessity for unity, and the indissolubility of the marriage bond. He also exalts the advantages of celibacy as being more perfect and more pleasing to God when observed in religious life. This gives him the opportunity of recalling to their minds the relative value of the things of this world and eternal things, for the things of this world pass away so quickly.

The second question concerned the use of meats sacrificed to idols. The Corinthians boasted of knowing all about this matter. They said that since idols were vain things, represented merely by words, the meats offered to them could not be contaminated. The Apostle replied that those who attribute to idols power and reality had contaminated their consciences; and also they must have recognized the bad influence that their example would have upon the weaker brethren, who, not knowing how to discriminate, might receive scandal and fall into sin.

Besides the reason (that of giving scandal) there was the great obligation of charity. Here was a reason that touched the very essence and substance of God, since offerings made to idols were given to a power that usurped the rights of Divinity. It was, then, a way of offering tribute to the devils, and in this, Paul was but repeating what the prophets had taught before him. He who eats of the victim, enters into communion with the one to whom the offering was made; you cannot drink the Chalice of the Lord, and also the chalice of the demon; you cannot participate in the Eucharistic banquet, and also in the idolatrous banquets.

Paul's answer, unfolding gradually, moving from a rational concession to a theological condemnation, breaks down the tendency towards syncretism and the weakness of indifferentism; he opposes to these the observances of the decrees of the Council at Jerusalem. He strikes at the very root of the cult of idolatry, and separates the true religion from the false. Some modern exegetes have accused Paul of making use of idolatrous mysteries. This is not true; from the very beginning, he condemns them, and puts a problem before the syncretists: choose either idolatry or the Cross of Christ.

It would have been difficult for Christians living in a pagan city, surrounded by friends and relatives who were pagans, to abstain altogether from the banquets of the idolaters. The Apostle is understanding and practical; where the banquet is not a religious rite, but only an occasion for food, he leaves the Christians quite free to mingle with the pagans on a social plane. "If you are invited to eat in pagan homes, you may go and eat what is put before you without too much examination; but if you are told beforehand that there is meat that has been offered to idols, then, having regard for the consciences of others, abstain from taking it." Thus in the end charity solves this and all such problems.

The third question concerned gossip started by the Mosaists and some of the superficial brethren, to the effect that Paul asked to be served and supported by the Community, and that sometimes he lived like a Jew, and at other times like the pagans. The accusations implied that he lived on the substance of the Christians like a parasite and that his manner of living was illogical. This placed him in great contrast to the other Apostles, for it could be recognized that they were the true Apostles and that he was not. It can easily be seen that the Judaizers everywhere were trying to uproot his authority, and to undo his work by the old scheme of throwing discredit on it and by defaming him. One can readily understand how criticism and contention must have abounded in the conversations of many of the first disciples.

Paul sweeps away all this gossip and idle talk. "Am I not an Apostle like the others?" he dryly replies. "Have I not seen the Lord Jesus Christ? And if I am not an Apostle like the others, at least I am for you Corinthians." So much for the first point.

Now for the second point which concerned his board and lodging. It is obvious that he who preaches the Gospel has the right to live by the Gospel; the minister has a right to live by his ministry, as every laborer lives from the fruits of his labor. It is a right of strict justice which Moses had established and Christ had confirmed. And yet Paul had not made use of the right, preferring to work with his own hands and to earn his own living. He had in this way kept himself independent of all. This was another one of those aspects of freedom of which he was the herald; freedom from sin, freedom from the Mosaic legalities, and freedom from man, in order that he might the better serve God and his brethren.

It was by this spirit of independence that he could become a Jew with the Jews, to gain those of his own nation to Christ. He practiced the Law, although he did not deem its observances necessary; he disregarded the Law with those who had no Law; he was weak with the weak, all things to all, and solely for the sake of the Gospel in order to have a part in it. In his mission Paul was like one striving for a prize in the Isthmian games held in Corinth, but he was not running at random, not as one merely beating the air.

Church Gatherings in Corinth

Paul was obliged to establish a few rules of a disciplinary character for the gatherings of the Christians of the Church in Corinth. Some disorders had occurred which were due to a wrong interpretation of these rules. The Gospel had brought about an entirely new emancipation, an equality before God for the souls of men and women. It had pulled down those philosophical and political systems which had made women the slaves of men. Some women, understanding themselves to be now equal with men, pretended to aspire to the same offices in the church assemblies and even adopted the manners of the other sex, as if a mannish manner gave women equality with men. This only resulted in more disorder. No, moral equality does not change the social order which the Law of God has established in the order of nature.

In the social level of life each needs the other. Man is the head, and not the woman; neither does man exist without woman, nor woman exist without man. Masculine dignity and decorum requires that a man appear in the assemblies with uncovered head. A woman, because she is subject to man who is head of the family, holds a lesser place in the social order of government and should appear with her head veiled. It will be the men and not the women who will teach, prophesy, recite hymns and prayers in the Church. Women should be silent, and if more instruction is needed let the husband give it at home. "It is not becoming for a woman to speak in Church," said St. Paul. It would give rise to gossip, envies and jealousies, and cause religion to become fantastic and sentimental.

Another disorder had been introduced into the evening meal which preceded the celebration of the Eucharist. As always it was due to the prevailing selfishness in human nature. That meal was meant to be a manifestation of charity and a preparation, through charity, for the Divine Supper of the Lord. It was an imitation of the Last Supper in the Cenacle and was called the "Agape" meaning "love." The faithful brought and shared in common the bread, wine and other things they had, so that the poor could benefit by the offerings of the rich. All was to be done in Christian love and affection.

Instead, the very opposite was happening; each one, forgetting the precept of charity, sat down before his own basket and ate alone and aloof, so that those who had plenty were satisfied while the poor were left alone to look on. The meaning and purpose of the Agape was lost; supernatural solidarity had died with a full stomach. The Agape, since it consisted in sharing a meal in common, made a bond of union which was more perfectly realized later in Holy Communion. Once it lost that character, it became a profanation of the Eucharist and showed contempt for others in the Church of God. Such conduct was an expression of an overflowing egotism and was, therefore, a contrast to the Eucharistic Communion which unites souls in Christ.

To cut short such abuses and to mortify the egotists, Paul could think of no better way than to relate once more the story of the institution of the Divine Eucharist, the very heart of the Church. "For I received from the Lord (what I also delivered to you), that the Lord

Jesus, on the night in which He was betrayed, took bread, and giving thanks broke it, and said, 'This is My Body which shall be given up for you; do this in remembrance of Me.' In like manner also the cup, after He had supped, saying, 'This chalice is the New Testament in My Blood; do this as often as you drink it, in remembrance of me.'" In fact, continues St. Paul, "For as often as you shall eat this bread, and drink this cup, you proclaim the death of the Lord, until He comes." Therefore whoever eats this bread or drinks the cup of the Lord unworthily will be guilty of the Body and the Blood of the Lord. Let every man make himself worthy, and then let him eat of that Bread and drink of that Chalice, for he who eats and drinks unworthily, eats and drinks his own judgment, not distinguishing the Body and Blood of the Lord from ordinary food.

Behold the Divine Eucharistic meal, the new Sacrifice which will announce the death of Christ until the end of time; behold the New Alliance between heaven and earth sealed by this Bread and Chalice which are Christ Himself, true God and true Man. By feeding on this Bread and drinking of this Chalice, man is "Christified" and "Deified," and the Blood of the Lord runs in his poor veins, giving him Life. But if this sacred food is consumed unworthily, the divine virtue does not act, and the guilty Christian falls into spiritual anemia and lethargy. "This is why many among you are infirm and weak, and many sleep." The Eucharist is the sacrament of unity and the miracle of love; and the Corinthians, who had violated both unity and charity by their dissensions and selfishness, were greatly in need of receiving It worthily.

Finally, in order to give further rules regarding the meetings, Paul recalls to their knowledge that all the gifts and graces, from that of the gift of tongues to that of curing diseases, from prophecy to miracles, are all given by one and the same Spirit of God Who confers them on each one according as He pleases. Therefore there must be no rivalry; the various gifts must work harmoniously in the life of the Body of Christ.

He who speaks, cannot pretend to be using a language which

neither he nor the brethren can understand, for such a gift would have only a sterile effect in the Church and edification would be lost; it would be equally useless from the viewpoint of charity, in whose light every act is to be judged. A gift that does not serve others, that has no social function in the ecclesiastical society of the Church is worth very little. He who speaks with divers tongues may edify himself but he does not help to edify or build up the Church. If there is to be diversity of unknown tongues someone will be required to interpret them, to translate them for the use and enlightenment of the Church and Community. Therefore, the gift of prophecy is preferable, because it requires neither interpretation nor translation, and it edifies.

More than one Corinthian Christian would have liked to possess all the Gifts en bloc, or at least the most showy ones; and no doubt all wanted to be Apostles, Prophets, Healers, Speakers of Tongues, and Interpreters; a beautiful ambition, but not at all possible. In the Church, all could not be Apostles or Prophets and so on, just as in the human body all the members cannot be eyes, or all ears, or all mouth. There is, however, a more excellent way which the Apostle recommends, a way which is open to all, through which all can reach to a high degree in the royal way of Christianity. The Apostle then unveils its vivifying beauty with the ardor of an inspired poet, observing how completely every form of decadence among the Corinthians springs from the utter want of the regenerating spirit. This regenerating spirit is charity, outside of which all values are lost; whereas, all the Gifts live by it, and converge towards it.

"If I should speak with the tongues of men and angels, but have not charity, I have become as sounding brass or a tinkling cymbal. And if I have prophecy and know all mysteries and all knowledge, and if I have all faith so as to remove mountains, yet do not have charity, I am nothing. And if I distribute all my goods to feed the poor, and if I deliver my body to be burned, yet do not have charity, it profits me nothing.

"Charity is patient, is kind; charity does not envy, is not pretentious, is not puffed up, is not ambitious, is not self-seeking, is not provoked; thinks no evil, does not rejoice over wickedness, but rejoices with the truth; bears with all things, believes all things, hopes all things, endures all things. Charity never fails, whereas prophecies will disappear, and tongues will cease, and knowledge will be destroyed. For we know partially, and we prophesy in part; but when that which is perfect has come, that which is imperfect will be done away with.

"We see now through a mirror in an obscure manner, but then face to face. Now I know in part, but then I shall know even as I have been known. So there abide faith, hope and charity, these three; but the greatest of these is charity."

It is a theological exposition. And yet it sounds like a glorious lyric; to such a point was dogma aflame with the Light of Life in Paul's soul.

Finally there was the matter of the resurrection of the dead which the Corinthians shrank from accepting. Their reluctance was a relic of Hellenic spiritualism in which an exaggerated contempt for the body went so far as to regard sins of impurity as of no consequence; therefore, according to their way of thinking, there could be no resurrection of the flesh.

On the contrary, says St. Paul in his letter, Christ is risen, and so men will rise again. One resurrection is the guarantee of the other. If Christ were not risen, then faith would be useless, the Apostolate would be in vain, Christ's suffering of no avail. There would be no Redemption, and sin would still be as closely knit into the consciences of men as a slab riveted onto a tomb. Also, virtue would be useless; all would fall a prey to death, and the pagan would be right in singing, "Let us eat and drink today, for tomorrow we die." If the dead do not rise, then neither is Christ risen; but all men will rise as the Man Christ rose. As all are dead in Adam, so all will be reborn again in Christ.

No one rises who has not first died. The manner resembles the process of the seed which, in order to bring forth fruit, must first die in the earth. It is sown a corruptible body and it rises an incorruptible body; ignoble and helpless, it rises glorious and strong; first animal and then spiritual. The last enemy to be vanquished will be death, which wounds us with the sting of sin.

Paul closes his letter by recommending a collection for the Church at Jerusalem and suggests the way to conduct it. That letter sprang from his great intellect and from his affections; it was inspired by his love for Christ. As he dictated it, he seemed to tear it word for word from his heart; deeply moved, with the tears falling from his tired eyes, he pondered on those accusations made against him, those sad deflections, so much impurity. Now he had explained everything by way of morals and theology; he had caressed them, and he had threatened them, in order to rebuild their Christian life.

The letter gives us a fundamental teaching on Christ and the Church, "the fulness of Christ." It is a letter Christo-centric in substance, because all is centered in Christ; all is seen under the aspect of Christ, for Christ is all in all. It is Christ Who instituted the Eucharist; Christ Who is the Head of the Church in His Mystical Body. It teaches that one's neighbor is not to be offended or scandalized, since Christ died for him. Christ being in all men makes them all sacred, and it is He Who determines our duties towards our fellow men.

To offend the brethren is to attack the work of Christ and to offend Christ; therefore, he who sins against the brethren sins against Christ. The great duty for all men is that of charity. Since Baptism makes us all one in the Body of Christ, for a brother to sin against a brother is really to sin against oneself; it is an act of spiritual suicide. "If any man does not love our Lord Jesus Christ, let him be anathema." [2]

Paul had spoken of the Church and had enumerated those great theological truths concerning it, so beautiful and so glorious; he had pointed out the admirable applications of those truths in social life; then at the close, he adds in his own hand a final salutation in Christ to the brethren. It was like the last touch the workman gives to a work which has been both arduous and difficult. He felt that he had reached

[2] 1 Cor. 16:21.

the end of a hard mission and that he had fought it on hard grounds. In his salutations he unites the Churches of Asia to those in Achaia, which in his own heart, as in the heart of Christ, form but one in love. "My love is with you all in Christ Jesus. Amen." [3]

The Flight from Ephesus

Paul sealed the letter, then entrusted it with many recommendations to the brethren who were to take it and later read it to the Community at Corinth. In it he told them that he expected to come soon in person to see them. Meanwhile Timothy had returned, but he brought with him no news of peace. Then Paul, greatly alarmed, found a ship going by way of Achaia and departed at once for Corinth. There he quickly gathered the Community together and expressed his disappointment in them, in accents severe and clear. This visit was a favor done to them but it was made with great sadness of heart. The fact is, that while he was reproving the gossipers and the fornicators, one of the group jumped up and insulted the Apostle. It made a tremendous impression on Paul as well as on the Community.

He returned immediately to Ephesus with an aching heart but not at all resigned to losing all the fruit of his preaching. He wrote, so it seems, a third letter which is now lost. Some exegetes think they have recognized part of its contents in the second canonical letter to the Corinthians. He confided this letter to Titus, a man of authority and meekness, esteemed by all, and charged him with the task of bringing back discipline into that torn and divided Community.

Meanwhile things were reaching a climax at Ephesus. Ephesus had been like a wide-open door to the Gospel, but a coalition of enemies and adversaries had been making inroads into this guileless and over-tolerant group of Christians. There had been an energetic purification from superstitious incrustations, a purification which renders souls precious in the sight of God. This had been a menace to the industry of the bookmakers, and to trade in general. It menaced the gains of

[3] 1 Cor. 16:24.

those who provided parchments, papyrus, and the stylus, because the bonfire of the magic tablets was still remembered. In other words, the new religion had begun to overthrow economic interests. On this account there were many reactions in the pagan world, where the denial of their myths, since few believed in them, was tolerated so long as the source of profits was not in any way molested. This had recently happened at Philippi when Paul, by expelling the demon from the slave-Pythoness, had met with vengeance from her masters, deprived of their gains by her divinations.

A similar reaction now took place at Ephesus, only on a larger scale. In the shop of a silversmith there were made and sold small reproductions of the temple of Diana. People came from Asia and from Europe to ask favors of the goddess who, it was believed, fell from the skies for no other reason than to grant favors to her clients. She was, then, very famous throughout the whole East. This idol was enclosed in a temple whose construction had consumed two centuries, and was considered one of the world's seven wonders. One night, in the year 356 before Christ, a maniac of immortal infamy, named Erostratus, had set fire to it. This was the night Alexander the Great was born. The edifice was rebuilt, more elegant and beautiful than before, with marbles and by artists from Greece.

This temple of shining marbles rested on one hundred and twenty-eight columns. The site was a beautiful one on the banks of the river Selinus. In its immense enclosure, which gave the right of sanctuary, the rites of idolatrous cults were carried on. Carnivals, fairs, and banquets were held in the porticoes under the direction of the temple priests called "megabyzos," surrounded by diviners, singers, priestesses and numerous slaves. The one hundred and fifty thousand inhabitants of Ephesus considered the Artemision (the temple of Diana) as the golden heart of the city, on account of the pilgrimages, the traffic, and gifts coming from people who flocked there from all parts of the world, east and west.

Now it happened that a silversmith, named Demetrius, had started a large industry for making reproductions of the Artemision. These little reproductions were sold around the temple to pilgrims, who bought them to take home as souvenirs of their visit to the goddess; and they were also specimens of a fascinating art. Since Paul's preaching waged war against those who exercised superstitious and magical arts, it likewise threatened souvenir industry. Idols, being images made by hands, were now regarded as vain things, only an idea; these little temples and statues of the goddess were becoming useless. The industry was imperilled.

Demetrius was an astute man, the forerunner of the manufacturer of the industrial period of today, so he had an intuition for saving his business. He would show it up in the seducing light of civic honor, and he concentrated first on the temple of Diana. He would excite a class reaction, then color it with the pretext of religion and authority. After building up his plan in his own mind first, he called a committee composed of his workers and spoke to them in burning words. "This Paul goes about saying that the images we are making are not gods." And he pointed with outstretched hand to the numerous images and statues lining his shelves which were now threatened with loss of honor. "Since this Paul is persuading a great multitude of people, there is danger that the number of our customers may diminish, and we be left without bread."

The mass of his listeners began to be stirred, and a threatening murmur ran through the crowd. They pictured themselves without employment, in misery and insecurity. Demetrius had no difficulty in convincing those directly interested. That being done, he thought of other people, and continued, "This is not all, nor the worst of it. Our city is famous for the temple of Diana, the great goddess. If the preaching of this little Jew continues, there is a possibility that the great temple will fall into discredit, and the goddess, now adored by all Asia, even by the whole world, will be stripped of her royal majesty."

Moreover, for motives of political shrewdness, the statue of the Emperor had been raised near the statue of the goddess, thus assuring the goddess from heaven the protection of the god on Earth. If Rome protected the Ephesian Artemis, their business would be secure. The mass of the workers understood at once, and grew excited, quite beyond control. The danger spread rapidly; besides the interests of the industry, it touched authority, superstition, and undermined local glory and prestige. The crowd was not excited by merely hearing that the silversmiths were threatened with unemployment; in that case, the Asiatic pagans would have only shrugged their shoulders and turned away, and the magistrates would have silenced them with harshness.

The cry that went up was that a great danger threatened Diana of the Ephesians. The Ephesians, not understanding very clearly just what was the matter, became excited—it never took much to heat them up—so that the narrow streets were packed with people. The excitement mounted when it was learned that it concerned Paul and his companions. For some time, there had been fermenting some resentment against them by the conservatives, the idolatrous priests of the temple, many pious pagans, and the Jews themselves. All these accumulated rancors and fears now became united into one, and exploded; for the Asiatic mind is easily set on fire.

It appears that Paul was taken and beaten to a pitiful condition; but Aquila and Priscilla, risking their lives for him, and with the help of other brethren, saved him from lynching. The mob then turned on two of Paul's companions from Macedonia, Caius and Aristarchus. These were dragged to the theater to be judged. The people constituted themselves a high court and, having filled the various tiers of the immense amphitheater, they howled and shouted, exciting themselves by their own cries.

Paul, who knew no fear, wanted to run to the theater to present himself to the people. He would have been glad of a chance to make his thoughts known to such an exceptional gathering. The disciples and some of the public functionaries, called Asiarchs, and who were friendly towards him, induced Paul to remain in the house. Meanwhile, the uncontrolled riot and noise continued at the theater. The silversmiths were breathlessly running up the steps to the platform, while the larger part of the spectators were still waiting for someone to explain to them what had happened. "Great is Diana of the Ephesians!" the artisans cried with all their might; but voices began to tire, and people began to yawn.

The anti-Christian mob tried to take advantage of the situation and turn the confusion against the Christians. They sent up a certain Alexander who had some facility in speaking, in order to explain that all the trouble came from the Christians.

But the Ephesians, drowned out his voice with their shouting, and would not let him speak.   "Great is Diana of the Ephesians!" they cried.

Demetrius was not able to control the tumult he had initiated. In such circumstances a clever demagogue could have driven the multitude into any excess, but probably Demetrius feared that phantom of Roman authority which did not tolerate disorders, and which punished with heavy severity those who instigated them. Finally, when the fury had subsided a little on the one hand, and the annoyance of the people on the other hand had increased, an official of the city, whose business it was to convoke and direct the assemblies of the people, obtained a partial silence in that bedlam, and made a short speech. He was tactful and wise, knowing the humors of a mob and how to control them.

"Great is Diana of the Ephesians! Well, we know that. Who doubts it? No one. Why make so much noise about it? The two men you have taken have committed no sacrilege, nor have they pronounced any blasphemy against our great goddess. I know this. There is Demetrius, who with his men, had some complaints to make. Why does he not make them in the proper place, before the tribunals? If their industry is in danger, and the returns are lower, that is their affair; what have we to do with private business? The public assembly treats of public questions; in legal sessions, and not by private convocation. Remember, dear Ephesians, that having come here in such a large crowd you risk being accused of sedition."

He did not say how implacable Rome was with those cities accused of sedition, but let them understand this by his silence. Rome punished with frightful severity, as some Asiatic cities had experienced. If it were convicted of sedition, the city of Ephesus could be reduced to a miserable village, and its citizens massacred or put in prison. And most assuredly, it would not be the great Diana who would shelter them from the anger of Caesar and of Rome, the super-gods.

The Ephesians did not need many explanations; they understood at once and, as they had been set on fire for nothing, they cooled off as easily. At a sign from the town clerk, they filed down the narrow stone steps, down through the tiers of the amphitheater, happy that nothing worse had befallen them. Once more the strong legal system of Rome had saved the Apostle of the Gentiles. Although Paul had not been dragged to the amphitheater, what he had suffered that day lay heavy on his heart and mind. He could not remain in Ephesus; what had been so narrowly avoided this day might not be avoided another time. Probably it was the brethren and the friendly Asiarchs who begged him to seek safety elsewhere.

The Cross of the Apostolate

Paul, like a defeated man, had to leave Ephesus by stealth. The wide door, that had opened so easily in the city of Artemis, was now closing behind him. A few of the brethren, timid through fear, accompanied him a part of the way outside the city walls, down the narrow street which made a short cut to the sea. The Apostle took leave of them, never wishing to be a burden to anyone. He turned to give a last glance at the city walls; the tiny figure raised itself a little among the boxwood and sycamores; the eyes of the brethren beheld him for the last time.

They saw how pale he was from strong emotions, many bruises and loss of blood. Paul, bent over on his staff and with the cold calm of one who had had much experience in travelling, started on his way. He did not, as on other occasions, raise his head as if to measure and to take possession of the distance that lay before him; on the contrary, he bent it deeper under the anguish that tormented his soul. Fatigue made his knees cave in under him, while the whole exterior man seemed to be collapsing under his torn tunic. He did not notice the stars that trembled over the opposite hill as they faded in the early morning light, and dark thoughts of a stormy night accompanied him.

The Church he had brought forth in Ephesus with so much pain, was now dispersed. From Galatia and Achaia disheartening news was arriving. The persecutors were growing in numbers, friends were becoming fewer. Leaving the school of Tyrannus, he felt lost. His whole work seemed to be crumbling; pagans, Jews, and heretics corroded it, at the same time seeking to demolish it and reduce it to dust. As he walked the long distance to Troas, all his Apostolic work seemed doomed to failure; he felt so alone, so useless, that for a moment he wished he could die. His whole humanity rebelled under the weight of a struggle that was becoming harder and more exhausting with the years as his poor health wore him down.

Among the brethren, not a few criticized him for his zealous labors in the Apostolate, saying with the wisdom of lazy cowards, "It serves you right; you have brought it on yourself." Then, the authorities were annoyed at the disturbances he was causing everywhere.

The departure from Ephesus was Paul's "Garden of Olives," and he too felt abandoned. If the desolation was intense, it was not for long; grace slowly flowed back into his weary heart, bringing new energy, and the unconquered will resumed control of his acts.

For some time he had thought of making a long tour, from Asia to Macedonia, from there to Corinth, and then of concluding this third circle with a visit to the Mother Church at Jerusalem. There he could make a report of his work and bring the offerings for the poor. Afterwards, having been comforted by the companionship of the other Apostles, he would begin from there a fourth journey which should carry him directly to Rome.

"I must see Rome," he had said to himself. An Apostle whose work was to create new centers of the Gospel could not help but long to visit Rome, the greatest and most famous city of the Empire. Paul already knew those other humble and great announcers of the Gospel message, beginning with Peter who had arrived there to scatter the word. Aquila and Priscilla were returning to Rome after having risked their lives for him. He would find them there, these co-workers in Christ, together with many other brethren, and afterwards he would return to Jerusalem.

Taking the northern route, we do not know whether it was by land or by sea, he travelled towards Troas, where he had promised to meet Titus. His heavy heart made him feel unequal to going again to Corinth. The community was still restless, and his own heavy-heartedness would most likely be misconstrued and misunderstood by his adversaries and by the weaker brethren. He was already wondering about the effect of his last letter to them, in which he had spoken with severity, no doubt causing sadness to many. Consequently, he preferred to know through a trusted disciple the effect of his visit by letter.

Since he had started from Ephesus against his will and much sooner than he had planned, he arrived too soon at the meeting place. Titus, his dear brother in Christ, was not yet there. Then the impatient Paul, having greeted the community of the place, who had received him with filial devotion, decided to go and meet Titus in Macedonia.

He took ship, and there in Macedonia he found Timothy, far more a son to him than a disciple. With Erasmus, Timothy had substituted for Paul in Macedonia. Paul again saw the Christians of Philippi and those in nearby centers; and from their affection, he drew new hopes and great comfort. Those who welcomed him found him aged, but richer in heavenly mysteries and filled with human sweetness.

They listened to him with joy and eagerness, and although poor themselves, they begged to take part in the collection that he was organizing for the poor Christians in Jerusalem. Then accompanying him for a part of the way, they left him with great reluctance. This man had seen with his own eyes the physical glory of Jesus in Heaven, and perhaps had ascended bodily into Heaven. He had been an instrument of many miracles and had passed through unheard-of tribulations for the love of God and the brethren.

Paul had noticed among the well-known faces many new ones, for the communities, like so many vigorous plants, were growing. Probably in Philippi he met Titus, and one can imagine with what anxiety he drew him aside to hear the news of those at Corinth. He had waited for Titus with much anguish of soul from battles within and from fears without. As he talked, his eager anxiety seemed to pass into the soul of his brother and disciple. The news was good; peace and serenity flooded his soul once more. He had been associated with the sufferings of Christ, and behold, Christ was now renewing his strength.

The majority of the Corinthians had let themselves be persuaded by a man as prudent and venerated as Titus and, yielding to the inspired vehemence of Paul's letter, they had recognized how well grounded were his remonstrances. They repented with real sorrow for all that had happened. Since they repented, Paul had no longer any reason to regret having written to them in such a way. Their tears were now his joy; a sorrow pleasing to God brings salvation. Titus, who was received by them at first with fear and trembling, now rejoiced; and Paul felt more drawn to those souls whom he loved so much, since they were so ready to acknowledge their faults and their falls.

He began to prepare for his third visit to the Corinthians by another letter. It is one of his most ardent and personal letters and in it he reveals himself and his work in a full light. In the preceding letters he had denounced the serious fault of impurity existing in the Church at Corinth, he had laid down rules for discipline, and given pastoral directions. The letters were meant to recall his spiritual sons, fickle and turbulent by nature but also docile, to a better Christian living. As a consequence the work of sanctification had gained in their midst.

However, there still existed among them the petulant and irritating Mosaists and other false Apostles so important in their own eyes. These continued to speak ill of Paul, making his own words an excuse to accuse him of contradiction. They said that when writing he was daring and grave, but when speaking in person he was timorous and colorless; in his writings he gave the impression of great determination, when speaking he was rude and abrupt. All their values were formed on the basis of external appearances. They liked full faces, beards well trimmed and pomaded, an eloquence accompanied by graceful gestures, and a discourse difficult to understand. And then some continued to criticise Paul's teaching of universalism, saying that in this he pretended to be different from the other Apostles; also that they were the real Apostles while he usurped the attributes and titles of an Apostle. Finally, at best, Paul was in their opinion an Apostle of lesser rank than the others. In this way the Judaizers tried to propagate the Mosaic observances.

Second Letter to the Corinthians

Paul wrote this time to clear the place, if it could be done, of those false Apostles and deceitful workers; to defend the orthodoxy of his Gospel and the authenticity and dignity of his own Apostleship. Therefore his letter may be defined as his apologia. And such it was. Personally, Paul considers himself to be nothing, but God made him an Apostle, that is, a minister of the Gospel, an ambassador of God and a co-worker with Christ. God had clothed his nothingness with divine dignity. This Paul defends with just pride, since the evidences are found in the results obtained, so that in praising his own works he is praising the work of God. He does this, not for his own advantage, but for the edification of the brethren, his children.

When Paul is the object of harmful accusations, he considers only one fact—that the prestige of the Apostolate is compromised, and in defending himself, he is defending Christ in Whom he lives. Paul is humble. He calls himself foolish; he considers himself the refuse of the world; he knows only ragged apparel, beatings, sickness, hasty flights, and narrow escapes from death, such as he experienced at Ephesus. All of these afflictions remind him still more of his nothingness. The consciousness of this did not make him less sensitive to the whisperings of his enemies; his spirit is never one of helpless inhibition to injuries, which usually invites more injuries and throws a shadow on the work done as a full dedication to Christ. Paul invariably makes the value of truth stand out, even if it concerns his own person, and this also throws into relief the dignity of the Son of God which reflects back to God the Father.

Clothed and reclothed, as it were, with Christ, Paul has the noble independence of Christ; being an Apostle, he identifies himself with the Church and its work. He will not let the first be defamed without dragging the second into discredit. He is tender with the humble, gentle with the penitent, but he is terrible as the Prophets of old, striking out as with a whip against the defamers and sowers of cockle. He loves the Gospel and will never allow it to be degraded. He lives humbly according to Christ, and will allow no stain on his own conduct. If he has endured beatings and imprisonments, it is that others may not fear to suffer thus. He claims the merit of having suffered for Christ so that he might be associated with the sufferings of Christ in His Passion. He would never tolerate any equality between himself as an Apostle and those who were not but claimed to be. He has done his work at the risk of his life, while they have only talked and handed on to others the fatigues and labors of the Apostolate.

If there are evil speakers among the ministers of God, Paul is more a minister than they. He can give a frightful list of floggings received, shipwrecks, stonings, dangers of all kinds by land and by sea, hunger and thirst, cold and nakedness. If they glory in divine gifts (this is not expedient), then Paul can tell of greater privileges. He can tell of the unique experience which happened to him fourteen years ago when he had been taken up, perhaps in the body, to the third heaven, where he had heard words of eternal significance spoken to him—words he could never afterwards reveal. Because he is so weak he may not glory, inasmuch as all the gifts which God manifested through him are indeed, given to him for the glory of God alone. They belong to Another; they represent the power of Christ, and this must be respected always.

It is with such sentiments that he writes, in conjunction with Timothy, to the Church in Corinth and to all the Greek Christians in general. He praises the Corinthians for having repented and for the obedience they now show towards the authority of the Church. He even asks them to be indulgent with the man who insulted him, not to push him to despair and thus to leave him in the hands of Satan. He admonishes them to correct the other crooked and relaxed ways that had crept in if they do not want him to use his authority against them when he comes.

Although the Apostle has no ordinary weapons at his disposal, he has divine strength and such a knowledge of the divine message that he can overthrow all the subtleties imagined by the half-Christianized rhetoricians. Paul aims at bringing the human intelligence into obedience to Christ and thus making human knowledge, the result of man's intelligence, something akin to the Divine Mind of God.

The Church is not an anarchical gathering; the freedom of God does not mean a lack of discipline among men and license among women, as some have pretended to interpret them.

They even reproached Paul for not going directly from Ephesus to Corinth, without passing through Macedonia as he had probably announced as his intention in his preceding letter, now lost. So they accused him of being changeable, of always saying yes, and then no. If he had changed his mind, it was from motives of charity towards the Corinthians. It was to avoid bringing to them an atmosphere of sadness for a second time; when on the contrary, he wished always to be a bearer of joy. The Gospel is good tidings, because it brings liberty of spirit. Sadness, as well as the fault that produces it, must not be allowed to last; it must be merely a pause in darkness, followed by peace when God floods the soul with light.

Paul's adversaries, like the scoundrels of all times, tried to strike him where calumny works successfully; they accused him of thrusting himself on the Church for his maintenance, and of being an exploiter of other people's work. Paul, in ironical and burning sentences that sting like the strokes of a whip, silences such wickedness. He recalls to their minds once more that, although he had a right to be supported in his Apostolate, yet he had never been a burden to anyone. He had worked with his own hands; and only when his Apostolic occupations had taken all his time or did not allow him to attend to manual labor and he had found himself in need, only then did he accept a contribution sent him with so much affection by his dear children in Macedonia. He had never been a burden to the Corinthians.

The Christians of Macedonia were poorer than those of Achaia, and far poorer than those of Corinth, a city of great resources. The example of others, especially of the Macedonians, spoken of with so much feeling, must have had a sting for those who did not help, except to spread the accusations of a mercenary and pharisaic spirit, poisoning the work of an Evangelizer. The Corinthians had not received less than the other Churches; the one and only difference was that Paul had not been a burden to them.

At all times, false Apostles are to be found among the true Apostles; there are true brethren and false brethren who fulfill Satan's functions towards the Mystical Body of Christ. "This is not to be marvelled at," says St. Paul, the founder of so many Christian Communities. "I did take from other Churches stipends with which to serve you. Now that I am coming to you for the third time, I will do the same, because I seek the brethren and not the brethren's goods."

As Paul acted, so did Titus and the other companion whom Paul had sent. Paul, who never asked for anything for himself, could be a beggar for others; especially for the poor in Jerusalem. In this way, he was giving the Corinthians a chance to practice charity, and to make up for the humiliation they felt in seeing how personally disinterested the Apostle had always been. The collection would be taken by persons highly esteemed in all the Churches; Titus and two well-known companions, perhaps Luke and Timothy.

Some confusion still persisted in regard to the conduct of Christians at the pagan banquets and feasts. In his first letter, Paul had allowed a certain freedom, but since it had been badly interpreted, some continued to be scandalized by the banquets, others were scandalized by taking part in them, seeing the danger of greater laxity. To differentiate more clearly the Christian religion from the pagan cults, Paul suggested that they reject all contact with idolatry. He resigned himself reluctantly to the necessity of allowing the Christians to be a group apart. They must be like pilgrims on their way to another land, provided they kept the faith and customs in their way of life.

There can be no possible relation between Christ and Belial, between light and darkness, between God (Whose temples the Christians are) and idols enclosed in houses of stone. The Judaizers had received a stern blow through the other letters Paul wrote but these old enemies had not disappeared. Mean and stupid, they still wished to rivet the chains of the Mosaic Law to the liberty of Christ. All day long, these observers, worshippers of the letter, with an angry finger on the list enumerated the numberless practices of the Law which must be observed. They did not understand that the Old Covenant had ended with the coming of the Messiah, with Whom a New Alliance had been initiated, not based on a written paper but on the Holy Spirit. The first is slavery, the second, liberty; the letter kills but the Spirit gives life. Those worshippers of the Mosaic legalities were the forerunners of the modern and tortuous philosophers and vivisecting exegetes who, even today, twist and obstruct the flow of meaning in a text.

CHAPTER VI

ROME AND JERUSALEM,

A.D. 57-58

The Universal Reconciliation

When the letter was written Paul gave it to others to deliver and to read, while he waited to let the desired effects be produced. He wished to repress all arguments, criticisms, boastings, immorality, and at the same time to revive them in joy, peace and solidarity. The letter contained praises and reproaches, for he who gave both was like a father, a teacher and a judge. And if a brusque change of tone surprises us moderns, it did not surprise the groups to whom the various parts of the letter were addressed.

After having prepared the ground for his visit, the Apostle goes to Corinth, whether by land or by sea we do not know. His letter, full of strong but affectionate words, had deeply stirred the Corinthians and calmed their quarrels. The greater number had finally returned to the meetings, no longer casting evil glances at each other nor attacking one another in contradictory interpretations of the same doctrines; nor did each one sit down to eat his own supper while his neighbor yawned with hunger. With order restored and mutual concord re-established, they gave each other the kiss of peace. The charity of Christ burned in their hearts, spreading its rays among them. At least it was so for the moment, although a generation later Pope Clement of Rome had to intervene and, as Paul had done, write them a letter, striving to bring back a unity which had been torn asunder by factions.

Once again Paul took possession of their souls, and with Apostolic authority he sat among them to instruct and to govern, excommunicating the impenitent, judging all altercations on the depositions of two or three witnesses.

He remained three months in Corinth. And as was his custom, he took care not only of those Churches near by but also of those farther away. All those he knew and those he did not know were near and known to him in Christ; he loved each and all. His solicitude extended also to the Romans. Corinth had continual military and commercial relationships with Rome, and the Christians had from the first constant relations with the Church in Rome. When Claudius had expelled the Jews from Rome, a few of them had settled in that Greek city, Corinth; among others there were Aquila and Priscilla, two persons with the souls of Apostles. Many Christian brethren, whom Paul knew, passed through Corinth on their way to Rome.

It was probably during his stay in Corinth, while at the house of his host Gaius (a very old tradition says that later Gaius became the Bishop of Thessalonica), that Paul dictated to the scribe Tertius a grand letter to the Church at Rome, the first of the Canonical Epistles. He entrusted it to the deaconess Phoebe, who was going to the capital of the Empire. Paul longed to go to Rome and, according to a plan previously made, he hoped to go west from there, as far as Spain, and even to Britain. However, he could not do so at this time; so consequently, "with some daring," he wrote.

He longed to make contact with that flourishing and exemplary Church of the Gentiles (he, the Apostle of the Gentiles), and this even in view of further travel. In Rome he would be comforted by the company of that Christian Community, and he hoped he could obtain some companions for his mission in the other parts of the Empire.

Paul was never the man to work in a field ploughed by others. Perhaps Christianity had been announced first in Rome by Jewish pilgrims returning from Jerusalem; and the Church, according to a tradition that has never changed, had been begun there by Peter. Peter had probably arrived there after fleeing from the Holy City during the persecution of Herod Agrippa. The Christian Community of Rome had grown enormously large. On account of Peter's Episcopacy, the pre-eminence of the city, and the strength of faith among the Christians, Rome was already known throughout the whole world. She was also fulfilling a function as center for the other Christian Communities scattered throughout the Empire. Consequently, Paul had no special question to solve with the Romans, but he felt that he was as much an Apostle to them as to the other Churches. So he wrote on a subject of great reality to them, and of immense importance, being certain that from Rome it would spread throughout the Empire.

Rome was the crucible of all races, which she drew and blended together under the impulse of a political concept of universality which aimed at embracing all people in one common law. This idea of universality could, then, be understood in Rome better than in any other city, and Rome could make the Christian universality its own. To minds educated in the Roman fashion, the dogma of the universal vocation of all men, Jews and pagans, to salvation through Christ, was more easily understood.

So Paul develops a theme thoroughly Roman, but of a "Romanism" free from temporal confines and earthly interest, transfigured by religion, and in a full sense universal. The Church, evolved from the earthly Jerusalem, was now becoming concrete in the heavenly Jerusalem; it was changing the Rome of arches and walls into a center of Mystical "Romanism."

The Apostolate of Christ yearns to embrace all men; and Paul had already told the Corinthians of his keen desire to go beyond the confines of the East. As an Apostle, he felt himself a debtor to all peoples: to men of all kinds, to the wise and foolish, the cultured and the uncultured. Evangelization of the world to Christ is an extension of love; it knows no barriers of caste or of blood, of intelligence or of wealth, it annuls all divisions and constructs a universal family composed of the children of God.

It was with this intention that Christ destroyed the walls of division between the pagans and the Jews, to make of the two but one people.

Paul (that universal soul) inserted deeply the dogma of Catholicity in the Church at Rome, which made of Jews and Gentiles a united people, the new Israel, that is, a spiritual kingdom and not a racial one.

In Original Sin, both one and the other were the same; although this was a negative unity (sin being a negation), because sin is death and ruin; therefore, both needed Redemption. The pagans were not exempt from guilt in not knowing and in not obeying God, even though they did not have the prophets and the Law, because God, inasmuch as He can be known, had manifested Himself to them also.

Invisible in His Essence, He had made Himself visible in His creation; and if His Law was not written on stone, it was engraved on men's hearts—the natural law, to which the conscience gives testimony. Therefore, the pagans had no excuse for pride in themselves in respect to the Jews, nor had the Jews such pride over the pagans; both were on the same level in regard to sin.

"Was the Mosaic Law useless?" To this objection, raised against his doctrine, Paul replies, "No, indeed." And he explains that the Law was to lead to the Gospel and that it ended in the coming of Christ Who was the object of the Scriptures. The Law was not useless, since it predisposed the Jews to the faith; and it was not evil, even if it gave the knowledge of sin. It could not give the Grace which liberates us from sin. Besides, the Hebrew people, keeping the Scriptures with faith in the true God, deserved the right of priority in the plan of Evangelization for all men.

Christ, Who is at the very apex of the Old Testament, re-established the universality of the Sonship of God by means of the universality of the salvation brought by Him. And having detached the Prophets and the Scriptures from being the possession of a single people, He gave them to all people. There is no distinction of persons with God. This is the dominating note of Paul's preaching and the basis of the anti-Jewish discussions. "There is no distinction between the Jew and the Greek. One God is Lord of all, Who justifies all; the circumcised through faith, the uncircumcised through faith. Circumcision divides, but faith unites."

How does this universal reconciliation of all men with God, and of men among themselves, come to pass? By means of the Redemption. Sin divided, because sin is death; the Cross has reunited, because by the Cross came life. In Christ the justice of God has manifested itself; it no longer needs the Mosaic Law. And this is witnessed to by the Prophets and by the Law itself.

Salvation, procured for us by the Blood of Christ, is given to him who believes in Christ. The condition of Justification (that is, the act by which God makes us just, and admits us to salvation) is that we believe in God; but we must remember that justification is a gratuitous gift, it is a gift of grace.

The Mosaic legalists clung to Abraham as to their father to whom the promises had been made. "But Abraham," replies the Apostle, "prefigured our state; for he was justified because he believed; that is, he had faith. And thus, before receiving circumcision, his faith being accepted for justice, he became the father of the uncircumcised; afterwards, he became the father of the circumcised." The promise of this universal sonship had been made to him in virtue of his faith. As by a single man (Adam) sin entered the world, and with sin came death; so also, by one man (Christ) came justification, which is life returned to the world.

Faith and Works

Paul preaches with great flashes of light, both divine and human. At that time, as well as afterwards, especially in the sixteenth century, men were tempted to reject works, and to be contented with faith alone; trying to separate faith from works. Already, this danger had appeared at Corinth. There was a little of it everywhere, since later the Apostle James was obliged to intervene against such falsifiers of the Gospel. These falsifiers knew how to make use of Paul's doctrines, although wrongly understood. If faith is sufficient, they said, or "faith alone," as Luther put it later, then works are useless, even deadly.

"God forbid," answered the Apostle. We must practice good works, and we must sanctify the body also. We were freed from the works of the Mosaic Law, but not freed from works of faith—that is, from the moral obligations contained in the Mosaic Law. Although emancipated from Mosaic rites, we are still servants of Justice, with obligations to cleave to the good, shrink from evil, and practice the Commandments of God, all of which can be summed up in the precept of Evangelical Love.

We must love the brethren and all men, practice unity in the Church, hospitality and peace, renounce vengeance, feed the enemy if he is hungry, give him to drink if he is thirsty, not render evil for evil but render good for evil, and in this way overcome evil with good.

Among all these duties for doing good there are the *civic* obligations on all for doing good. These are obedience to proper authority, respect to superiors, and the paying of one's tribute to the tax collectors. Paul taught this to the Romans at the very time when anti-Roman factions, in Palestine and among the Jews of the Dispersion, were preaching revolt against Roman authority. Thus, in every aspect of life, the Christian must be an exemplary person, in obedience, in patience, in purity, and in all manner of honorable conduct. He should be a stranger to drunkenness, self-indulgence, dishonesty, envy, in order to strip himself of all concupiscence, and to put on Christ.

Sanctification, for the Christian, does not mean something inert and dead; it is something *living* which costs him sacrifice and blood; it is the fruit of an interior and exterior activity of every moment of his time.

Paul proclaims the end of the Law of Moses, of the law of the flesh, of sin, of death, and for these he substitutes the Law of the Holy Spirit, the Law of Grace, and the Law of Life. For all that, he does not say that he has abandoned the people of his own race and nation; he is not a deserter as some were whispering. No, Paul loves his people, he is proud of belonging to them, and he tells the Gentiles so, who might be tempted to despise the sons of Israel. This love for his own people fills his soul with continual anguish, so ardent is his desire for them to become converted to Christ, and for this he continually prays. In order that this may become true, he goes so far as to say that although he had become one with Christ, he would, for the sake of his brothers according to blood, be cut away from Christ.

It is the Israelites who have been enriched with the highest gifts and with divine titles; they are the children of God by adoption, to them belongs the glory of the First Covenant, of the first Law, the worship and promise of God. They are the Israelite fathers from whom Christ is born according to the flesh.

Even if they do not all become converted, the word of God is not made void; for all born of Israel are not all true Israelites. God chooses whom He wills, and calls to the Promise him who believes, for this is a mercy of the Lord, and not a right belonging to men.

The Jews had always been the chosen people of God; and the prophets, who came of their race, are the roots of a mighty tree, which is the Church.

The Jews are the natural branches; but the obstinate have been cut off and, in their stead, have been grafted as wild branches, the Gentiles. These should remember that they are sprung from the one root, the Hebrew Prophets, and that if they go astray through their pride, they too will be cut off and God will graft again, in place of these severed branches, the Jews who do believe. In this way Paul holds in check the nascent pride of the brethren converted from paganism, who might be tempted to prefer themselves to those converted from Judaism on account of their more prompt acceptance of the Gospel. In this way he also removes obstacles to a full flow of charity and to the expansion of universality.

If a portion of Israel did blind itself, this blindness served for a light to the Gentiles; but in the end, the Israelites, sanctified already by belonging first to the roots of the Prophets, and loved because of their fathers, will obtain mercy for their sin of disobedience of today—and will be converted.

In the pastoral part of his letter, which aimed at making a Christian a model of Christ, Paul imagined (or perhaps, he knew through information easily enough obtained) that there was trouble in Rome also over the use of meats and wine. The rigorists abstained from them, either because of asceticism or because of a hankering after Mosaism—on account of their scruples, Paul calls them *weak*—while others ate everything. We should remember that Paul did not make much of food, it is an exterior thing, connected with the works of the Law; while he made much more of the things of the Spirit. He was, however, considerate of the scrupulous and did not want them scandalized; he understood all, sympathized with all, and wished that in this matter, mutual tolerance might be practiced. "Let each one follow his own judgment," he says, "and let him who eats meat, and him who eats vegetables, do it for the Lord." Thus a thing in itself so indifferent (for there is nothing impure in itself, and the Kingdom of God does not consist in food and drink, but in justice and peace and joy in the Holy Spirit) becomes an exercise of charity towards men and towards God. There are means of sanctification in all things for all men (evil excluded—which is a negation), and food may furnish a means for building up sanctity.

The important point is not to despise or to judge a brother; this would be a cause of separation, and separation is a breach in unity. Only in unity can charity be realized. This is always a sure criterion for conduct: to hold to what contributes to peace, acting for the sake of mutual edification; and therefore not to scandalize anyone because of food.

In closing Paul becomes extraordinarily emotional. On the one hand, the persistent idea of carrying the Gospel to Spain attracts him; on the other hand, he is tormented by the presentiment that in an imminent journey to Jerusalem he may become the victim of the unbelievers in Judea—and so he asks the prayers of the Romans. And thus in the exchange of prayers, by which the Church of Rome was invited to overcome the anti-Christian action in Jerusalem, universality in charity is kept alive.

After that, descending in a natural manner from his lofty speculations on grace and on predestination, his recommendations in morals, the Apostle speaks of his fellow laborers. First of all, Sister Phoebe, the deaconess, "who serves the Church at Cenchrae" and who is the bearer of the letter to Rome. He sends no less than twenty-five salutations to the Brethren individually, and by name; who were well-known to him; to Aquila and Priscilla, to whom all the Churches of the Gentiles were grateful for the heroic devotion with which they assisted Paul at Corinth, still more so at Ephesus; to Epaenetus and Mary who had suffered much for the growth of the Church at Rome; to kinsmen and fellow prisoners, Andronicus and Junias; to the

household living in the confiscated property of Narcissus, whom
Agrippina had put to death three years previously; to men and
women who had borne fatigues and labors for the Lord. He has a
word of religious praise for each one; doubly precious when coming
from the mouth of the Apostle to the Gentiles. He also sends salutations to his co-workers; there is from one side of the sea to the other
an air of intimacy among those who love Christ, and in Paul they are
drawn near together. These messages of friendship seal the grave and
serene character of the letter, in which appears the perfect equilibrium
of Paul's gifts: intelligence, sympathy, leadership, and a genius for
organization.

The Meeting at Miletus

While Paul was endeavoring to enlighten and instruct the various
Churches in Asia and Europe in sanctity, he was organizing the collection, which was a social expression of sanctity. In the year 57,
towards the end of May, he had fled from Ephesus, crossing Macedonia and Achaia during the summer and fall; and he wintered for
three months at Corinth. This was in February or March of the year
58, when the return of spring made navigation possible once more.
Paul had given up the idea of going to Rome, so he decided to sail
for Syria in order to go to the Holy City.

This is what the most fanatical of his enemies were expecting
him to do. They now made up their minds to do away with this
dangerous enemy of Mosaism.

Paul and his friends, who knew well their schemes, foiled such
plots by changing their itinerary. Neither Luke nor Paul records a
single word of condemnation about this and other attempts on their
lives; they were returning good for evil.

Then Paul retraced his steps towards his trusted Macedonians, with a little escort composed of Sopater, son of Phyrrhus, who had come from Beroea, Aristarchus and Secundus from Thessalonica, Gaius and Timothy who had joined him at Derbe, and the two Asiatics, Tychicus and Trophimus.

At Philippi, the little caravan divided into two; Tychicus and Trophimus went ahead to Troas: Paul and Luke (who had rejoined the Apostle) perhaps with other Jews, remained till after the solemn celebration of the Passover which lasted seven days in the middle of the month of Nisan. After five days they reached Troas and remained there a week.

There was a fine community at Troas. The meeting hall was a spacious room lighted by many lamps, probably in the house of a wealthy brother. The building must have been more than ordinarily high, since the room was on the third floor. On the last evening of their stay, which was the first day of the week—for the Christians this had taken the place of the Jewish Sabbath—the Brethren were gathered to celebrate the Eucharistic rite of the "Breaking of the Bread," or *fractio panis.*

The ceremony was, as usual, accompanied by a sermon. Paul was obliged to leave the next morning, and having a presentiment that he might never see again those children whom he had generated to the life of Christ, he abandoned himself to the flow of his confidences and exhortations. He had so many truths to unfold to them and to re-awaken, so many instructive facts to relate, that he prolonged his sermon until after midnight. If some stenographer could have left us his words, as well as many other discourses, our New Testament literature would be so much the richer, but the first Christians did not think of writing. To learn and to transmit what they had learned was all that they had at heart. This transmission was part of the Tradition. Only later, when new needs arose and in order to reach the Brethren who were far away, and to help in the preaching, were any collections of words, spoken by the Apostles, written and circulated.

Paul and the other Apostles found themselves at times obliged to write letters, when unable to visit in person. Writing was one of the first means used for propagating Christianity, but it was not the only or the principal one. The body of doctrines confided to the Church or, precisely, to the Apostles and to persons delegated by them, were transmitted as a sacred deposit, the Holy Spirit continuously assisting them. The Church lived and taught long before her teaching was put into writing, for faith comes through hearing; that is, from her oral authority.

Then Paul, notwithstanding the fact that he must start soon or that it was late, and unmindful of fatigue, continued his discourse. He was wholly absorbed in answering questions and explaining new aspects of the mysteries revealed to him. The brethren were listening with loving and lively attention, which served as a motive for him to continue. But a boy by the name of Eutychus, who was sitting on a window sill in order to listen more comfortably, was overcome by sleep. He fell out of the window, head downwards from the third floor, and was killed. A cry was raised. The brethren ran down to the street to lift him up, but the fall had been a violent one and he was dead. Paul ran out also and, bending over the boy, clasped him to his breast like a father. "Do not grieve, he is alive," he said to the parents and friends.

Those people knew that Eutychus was dead; that he had died instantly, having struck his head on a stone; they also knew Paul, and all were astounded as they gazed at him. When Paul released the boy from his arms, he returned him to his parents alive, resuscitated, sound. Death's interruption had been brief. They all went back into the hospitable home and resumed the sacred rite. Paul broke the Eucharistic Bread; he ate of It and gave It to the rest to eat. He spoke again until dawn, when he took leave of them all and went on his way. Eutychus was taken home amid universal rejoicing.

No doubt this time also, in order to escape the men sent to kill him, Paul turned his steps towards Assos, a city of Mysia, one day's journey from Troas. Luke and the others of the party went by sea. This separation was in order to elude their enemies. At Assos, Paul boarded a ship, and with his companions landed at the near-by isle of Mitylene, where they spent the night. Then continuing by sea, they arrived at Chios the following day. (This island claimed to be the birthplace of the poet Homer.) The next day they landed at Samos, the birthplace of Pythagoras, where the temple of Hera seemed to stretch out its marble arms to receive them. After another day, they came to Miletus in Asia.

Thus they had gone beyond Ephesus, not wishing to be detained by the brethren there, for Paul wanted to be in Jerusalem for the Feast of Pentecost. However, he would not go farther without leaving a remembrance to the Churches of Asia Minor, dear to him on account of so many sacrifices. Therefore, from Miletus, he called the "Presbyters" or priests, the Ancients of the Church of Ephesus, and probably those from the neighboring Churches, and addressed to them a sad discourse of farewell. Since all his work had been pursued by the calumnies of adversaries, he briefly recalled how, amid tears and snares, he had announced to them the Gospel, both in private and in public, to the Jews and to the Gentiles, faith in Jesus Christ our Lord.

Now he was going to Jerusalem, led by the Holy Spirit as though he were led in chains, and knowing through the same Spirit that other chains and tribulations awaited him there. This meant, that for the success of the Apostolate, sufferings and prison were needed; and especially in Jerusalem, where Jesus had suffered unto death. Knowing this, Paul did not fear for himself. "I fear none of these, nor do I count my life more precious than myself, if only I may accomplish my course and the ministry that I received from the Lord Jesus, to bear witness to the Gospel of the grace of God." [1]

In his farewell discourse, he summed up the program of his Apostolate with expressions, so typical of his language: life is more valuable than himself, but not more valuable than his soul, his real self.

[1] Acts 20:24–25.

And the mission, called in Greek a "marathon" or race, had indeed been a race for him, running without pause from one end of the Near East to the other.

He was a man; and he groaned at the thought that he might never again see these children of the Gospel. He grieved even more in thinking of those who had listened to his word but had not heeded it. So taking the Christians present before him as witnesses, he affirmed that he had omitted nothing in order to gain each and all for Christ. Consequently, he was exonerated from the responsibility for the loss of the obstinate. Thus Paul taught that it is an Apostle's duty to reach all men, to reveal to them the grace of God; and only after having tried all possible ways is he exonerated from further responsibility.

He also taught the necessity for a special and divine organ, or divinely constituted body of pastors (in his time sometimes called Priests and sometimes called Bishops), for the communication of the grace of God; for ruling the Church, and as mediators between God and humanity; for the defense of orthodoxy and unity. "Therefore," he concludes, "take heed to yourselves and to the whole flock in which the Holy Spirit has placed you as bishops, to rule the Church of God, which He purchased with His own Blood. I know that after my departure fierce wolves will get in among you, and will not spare the flock. And from among your own selves men will rise speaking perverse things, to draw away the disciples after them. Watch, therefore, and remember that for three years night and day I did not cease with tears to admonish every one of you." [2]

Paul was sobbing as he said this; his emaciated face expressing the anguish he felt by the horror he foresaw in the future. Poor Apostle! Intrepid for himself, he feared for human weakness; and enlightened by revelation from heaven and his experiences in the past, he read the future of the Church of God, torn by heretics from within far more than by aggression from without, those dispensers of private interpretations, those deformers who were to arise from the very bosom of the priesthood and who would be capable of tearing Chris-

[2] Acts 20:28–32.

tianity limb from limb, as it were, and of drawing disciples after themselves. Perhaps in the very group before him, some such innovator would be found—as later on so many appeared, even though they had seen Paul in person and had read these very words which were spoken with tears streaming from his suffering but luminous eyes.

Heresy is pitiless; it looks after its own vanity, and cares very little for the tears of the Apostles. At the vision of dismemberment—a real tearing of the flesh of the Mystical Body of Christ, caused by heretics and similar to the action of rapacious wolves—Paul's heart was wrung with grief. He was going where he would soon be put in chains. It was the tragedy of the Church and not his own tragedy that pierced his soul, as he was saying farewell—a farewell which was like a testament between himself and his children of the Church. It was this same anguish that tormented the souls of all those who succeeded the Apostles when similar separations occurred and heretics left the Church.

"And now I commend you to God and to the word of His Grace, who is able to build up and to give the inheritance among all the sanctified. I have coveted no one's silver or gold or apparel. You yourselves know that these hands of mine have provided for my needs and those of my companions. In all things I have shown you that by so toiling you ought to help the weak and remember the word of the Lord Jesus, that He Himself said, 'It is more blessed to give than to receive.'" [3]

At the mention of Jesus, he knelt down to pray, for prayer completes and surpasses speech. In the good administration of the Church he had given an example in his own person of poverty, of work and, therefore, of independence. In the work of the Holy Spirit, the danger begins when we start to accept for ourselves gold or silver, or anything else; when instead of giving, which is to conquer, we receive, which is being conquered. When instead of serving the Church, we enrich ourselves, like a slimy leech which draws blood, as it were, from her virginal Body under the pretext of wealth. The exploiters of the

---

[3] Acts 20:32–36.

Church, through avarice, are enemies along with the heretics who torture her Creeds. The Apostle, thinking of all this, sees the future, and his heart bleeds.

He had taken up collections but these were for the poor; for himself he had taken nothing from anyone; on the contrary, he had helped everyone else, although he had the right to live by his ministry, a work more fatiguing but far more precious than any other.

In all these admonitions and memories, they saw shadows of the past cast over the future, gathering about the gray head of this indefatigable stimulator in the spiritual life. All this must have pressed on their hearts and brought tears to the eyes of these Ancients of Asia as they foresaw the future so heavy with dangers. The inheritance of the Christian is the Cross!

They all fell on their knees, weeping. When the Apostle rose and was about to leave, they all gathered about him, clasping him to their hearts and kissing him, for they feared they should never see him again. Their father was leaving them forever, was leaving for a prison, at the end of which, most likely, stood a gibbet. Up to this time, he had broken for them the bread of the Gospel, but now he was going from them, never to return, leaving them to continue his work, a work of supreme responsibility. It would be so easy to bend under persecution or to be deceived by vanity. In bidding Paul farewell, each one was conscious of all he had received from him, in counsel, in help, in wise admonitions, in deeds of love—and no one knew how to be resigned to his loss.

The eyes of all were fixed on the rugged features of that face, the humble lines of that figure, as if to fix them forever in their souls. They accompanied him to the ship; standing on the shore they waved farewell with tears, until the ship, cutting loose from the pier, was lost to sight in the fogs of the Aegean Sea. Then they slowly went home, bent with grief and feeling like orphans.

The Prediction of Agabus

On board the ship, Paul sat on his bundles under the cover of an awning, and all that was human in him wept for the dear Ephesians from whom he was now separated, for thought of the trials that lay ahead of him, and for the future of the Church. The boat sailed straight to the island of Cos, which spread itself out on the blue waters like a peacock, or like a huge basket of leaves, in the midst of which blossomed, like a white tulip, the marble temple of Aesculapius. The following day they touched at Rhodes, the island of roses; at the entrance of its port stood the colossal statue of the Sun God, one of the world's seven wonders.

Then, bending their course towards the east, moving along the coast of Lycia, they stopped at Patara. Paul scarcely noticed the marvels of nature augmented by the marvels of art; from the depths of his soul came the thought and the vision of the city of God, with its many Christian centers, its martyrs, its crosses, down through the centuries of the future.

At Patara, the ship unloaded its cargo and turned back. Paul, and the brethren with him, took another small sailing vessel which was going to Phoenicia. They followed the left coast of the island of Cyprus, dear to the heart of the vigorous Barnabas and, passing by the coast of Syria, they came to Phoenicia, disembarking in the ample port of Tyre. This famous Phoenician city, "daughter of the sea," reminded Paul of the vehement prophecy of Isaias, indignant over the devotion of Mammon to this great harlot. Now a Community of Christians flourished in the old colony of Sidon. Paul went to meet them, and stayed with them seven days while the boat took on a new cargo.

On the last day, after having pleaded in vain with Paul not to ascend to Jerusalem, the Christians of Tyre accompanied him to the port with their women and children. It was like a tearful family

PICTORIAL LIFE OF
ST. PAUL, APOSTLE AND MARTYR

REPRODUCED FROM THE FRESCOES IN THE
BASILICA OF ST. PAUL OUTSIDE THE WALLS, ROME

Coghetti

The Condemnation of St. Stephen

Ardent pharisee that he was, Saul viewed the teachings
of Jesus of Nazareth as an attempt to overthrow the Hebrew
Religion. He rejoiced when one of the leading propagators of
this doctrine, the Levite Stephen, was summoned before the
Sanhedrin. Stephen was not silenced by the Sanhedrin's awesome
presence but cried out, "You always oppose the Holy Spirit!"

Gagliardi

St. Stephen Is Stoned

Though too young to actively participate in St. Stephen's stoning, Saul was present at the scene, approving the punishment inflicted on the traitor to the Law and encouraging the persecutors whose garments he guarded. Stephen's final prayer —"Lord, lay not this sin to their charge"—was offered even for Saul.

Camuccini

The Conversion of Saul

Saul's entire being was fired with a desire to annihilate the followers of the Nazarene. With letters of recommendation from the High Priest he set out from Jerusalem for Damascus, intending to make the city's Christians his prisoners. At midday, struck suddenly by a great bolt of light, Saul was jolted from his mount and fell prostrate in the dust. "Saul, Saul! Why do you persecute Me? . . ." A voice pierced the air and Saul's very soul.

Podesti

Ananias Is Sent to Saul

Numb and sightless, Saul rose from the ground and was led by the hand to Damascus. When commanded by the Lord to seek a man from Tarsus named Saul, Ananias hesitated. "Lord, I have heard from many about this man...." "Go," Christ reassured him, "for this man is a chosen vessel to Me, to carry My name among nations and kings.... For I will show him how much he must suffer for My name."

Saul's Baptism

"Brother Saul," said Ananias, "the Lord Jesus has sent me that you may regain your sight and be filled with the Holy Spirit." Immediately there fell from Saul's eyes something like scales. He recovered his sight, arose and was baptized.

De Sanctis

Saul Preaches in Damascus

After a sojourn in Arabia, Saul returned to Damascus, dedicating himself to spreading the truths that Christ revealed to him. The people of Damascus questioned one another, "Is this not he who used to make havoc in Jerusalem of those who called upon the name of Jesus?"

De Sanctis

The Flight from Damascus

In Damascus Saul was now considered a traitor, and a plot to assassinate him was formed. Discovering the plot, the Christians lowered Saul under cover of night over the city wall in a basket. Alone but safe, Saul directed his steps toward Jerusalem.

Dies

Saul Visits Jerusalem

Three years did not erase the memory of the devastation wrought by Saul in the Church. Thus the Christians of Jerusalem fled his company. But Barnabas bore witness to Saul before the Apostles who received him in their midst and allowed him to preach. One day while he prayed in the Temple Christ appeared to Saul and commanded him to leave Jerusalem. "Go, for to the Gentiles far away will I send you."

Saul's Ecstasy

Saul returned to Tarsus and prayerfully prepared himself for the great mission that God had entrusted to him. In the year 43 A.D.—whether in the body or out of it, he did not know—Saul beheld the vision of God in heaven. Saul's mind and heart were penetrated with that light and joy of things divine which God reserves for them that love Him.

The Consecration of Saul and Barnabas

Barnabas traveled to Tarsus in search of Saul during 44 A.D. and brought him to Antioch where he labored a year making conversions. One day while the prophets and teachers were praying and fasting, the Holy Spirit said, "Set apart for me Saul and Barnabas unto the work to which I have called them." Thus Saul and Barnabas were consecrated bishops and prepared to spread the Church to other lands.

Mariani

Saul at Paphos

The Holy Spirit now directed Saul's steps. Saul, Barnabas and John Mark landed on Cyprus in 45 A.D., and preached the Gospel throughout the whole island. A diabolical sorcerer, Bar Jesus by name, attempted to influence Sergius Paulus, the governor of Cyprus, and turn him away from Christianity. Filled with the Holy Spirit, Saul fixed his gaze on the magician and cried out, "Behold, the hand of the Lord is upon you, and you shall be blind!" The sightless Bar Jesus groped about in terror for someone to lead him away. Sergius Paulus believed and was baptized. Henceforth Saul was known by his Roman name, Paul.

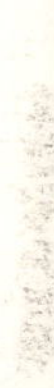

Mariani

Paul and Barnabas at Lystra

Paul and Barnabas carried the Gospel as far as Pisidian Antioch and Iconium. The people of Iconium being stirred up against them, the apostles hastened to Lystra. While preaching at Lystra, Paul's eyes rested on a man crippled from birth. With a loud voice the Apostle addressed him, "Stand upright on your feet!" The man rose up. Seeing the miracle the crowds believed Paul and Barnabas to be Mercury and Jove and prepared to offer sacrifice. Tearing their garments the apostles rushed into the crowd shouting, "Why are you doing this? We are not gods but mortals like you! We are preaching that you may turn from these foolish things to the true God."

Mariani

The Stoning of Paul at Lystra

Paul and Barnabas made numerous converts at Lystra. All too soon, however, non-believers arrived from Antioch to turn the populace against the apostles. Paul was stoned. Believing him dead, the crowd dragged his broken, bleeding body outside the city. His disciples gathered about Paul and brought him back to the city where they ministered to his wounds. Soon afterwards Saul and Barnabas departed for Derbe.

Consoni

Paul at Jerusalem—The First Church Council

Retracing their steps, Paul and Barnabas returned to Antioch and then proceeded to Jerusalem to submit their labors to the approval of the Apostles. A question had arisen as to whether or not Gentile converts were bound by the Mosaic Law of Circumcision. Peter addressed the gathering at Jerusalem, "Brethren, God has made no distinction between us and the Gentiles, having given us both the Holy Spirit. Why then do you now try to test God by putting on the neck of the disciples a yoke that neither our fathers nor we have been able to bear?"

Coghetti

Paul's Vision at Troas

Accompanied by Silas, Paul undertook his second missionary journey in 50 A.D. Perils of every sort beset his path, but he confronted them all for love of Christ. Reaching Troas, Paul one night had a vision of a Macedonian who appealed to him, saying, "Come over into Macedonia and help us." Certain that God had summoned him to preach the Gospel there, Paul immediately prepared to sail for Macedonia.

Coghetti

Paul Cures a Possessed Girl

Paul disembarked at Philippi. The Lord touched the heart of a certain woman there named Lydia, a seller of purple, who heard Paul's preaching. She was baptized with her entire household. As the apostles were going to their place of prayer one day, a possessed girl cried after them, "These men are servants of the most high God and proclaim to you the way of salvation!" The girl repeated this for many days until Paul "being very much grieved, turned and said to the spirit, 'I order you in the Name of Jesus Christ to go out of her,' and it went out that very moment."

Paul and Silas Are Scourged

The possessed girl's masters, now deprived of the profits gained from her divining powers, seized Paul and Silas and dragged them before the city magistrates, accusing them of disturbing the peace. Sensing the fury of the angered populace, the magistrates had the apostles scourged and cast into prison.

Sereni

The Jailer's Conversion

In the stillness of the night, despite the agony of their scourged flesh, Paul and Silas joined their voices in hymns praising God. Suddenly the foundations of the prison were shaken by a tremendous earthquake. Cell doors flew open; manacles dropped from hands and feet. The terrified jailer was about to commit suicide when Paul cried out, "Do not harm yourself, we are all here." Trembling he cast himself at Paul's feet and begged, "Sir, what must I do to be saved?" "Believe in the Lord Jesus," responded Paul.

Paul Preaches in the Areopagus

The following day Paul and Silas were released and left Philippi. They paused briefly in Thessalonica and Beroea and soon arrived in Athens. There Paul spoke to the members of the Jewish Synagogue and disputed with a number of the philosophers with which Athens abounded. Standing in the midst of the Areopagus Paul proclaimed: "Men of Athens, you adore the unknown God. He is the God that I proclaim. We are His offspring and He will judge the world with justice by a Man Whom He has appointed, and Whom He has guaranteed to all by raising Him from the dead."

Aquila and Priscilla

Corinth, a turbulent seaport city, also received the Gospel from the lips of the Apostle Paul. He was received into the home of Aquila and his wife Priscilla who had recently been driven from Rome by an edict of the Emperor Claudius. Paul remained long at Corinth for Christ told him in a vision, "Do not fear, but speak and do not keep silence; because I am with you, and no one shall attack you or injure you for I have many people in this city." During his stay at Corinth Paul composed two epistles to the faithful of Thessalonica.

The Ephesians Burn Their Books of Magic

Paul returned again to Antioch after his second missionary journey. After a brief sojourn there the Apostle began his third missionary journey in 53 A.D. For three years he labored in Ephesus, the key city of Asia Minor, preaching and performing such astounding miracles that the Faith spread through all of Asia. Some Ephesians attempted to imitate Paul's power over the devil with black magic, but the demons overpowered the exorcists, thrashing them mercilessly. Thoroughly frightened, many collected their books of occult knowledge and burned them publicly.

Carta

Paul Restores Eutychus to Life

After addressing two epistles to the church at Corinth, Paul
hastened there to personally heal a breach daily widening between the faithful. Returning to Troas, he instructed the faithful far into the night. A young boy named Eutychus, seated
on a window ledge was overcome by sleep and fell three stories
to the ground, dying instantly. Paul went down, laid himself
upon him and embraced him saying, "Do not be alarmed, life
is still in him." He then returned to the upper chamber, consecrated the Eucharist and discoursed until daybreak with the
faithful who were overjoyed at having Eutychus restored to
them.

Sozzi

Farewell to the Ephesians

Hastening to be in Jerusalem for Pentecost, Paul paused at Miletus and summoned the elders of nearby Ephesus to bid them a last farewell. Paul opened his heart to his beloved bishops. "Compelled by the Spirit, I am going to Jerusalem. . . . In every city I am warned by the Holy Spirit that imprisonment and persecution await me. You shall never again see my face. Take heed to yourselves and to the whole flock in which the Holy Spirit has placed you as bishops to rule the Church of God which He has purchased with His own Blood."

Bompiani

Agabus Prophesies Paul's Imprisonment

At Caesarea, Paul's proximate capture was foretold. Agabus, a prophet from Judea, took Paul's girdle and bound his own hands and feet saying, "The man whose girdle this is will thus be bound at Jerusalem and delivered to the Gentiles." When begged not to go on to Jerusalem Paul responded, "What do you mean by weeping and breaking my heart? For I am ready not only to be bound but even to die at Jerusalem for the name of the Lord Jesus."

Grandi

Paul Is Driven from the Temple

The brethren of Jerusalem received Paul joyously and invited him to join four young men bound by a Nazarite vow to prove to the multitude his fidelity to the Law of Moses. After purifying himself, Paul entered the Temple. However some days later, a group of enemies seeing Paul in the Temple seized him, shouting, "Men of Israel, help! This is the man who teaches everywhere against the Law of Moses!" In a wild tumult Paul was taken and dragged from the Temple. The tribune, Claudius Lysias, summoned his soldiers and rushed to the Temple courtyard. He bound Paul in chains and ordered him to be imprisoned in the fortress.

Paul Addresses the People of Jerusalem

As they were about to enter the fortress Paul asked the tribune, "May I speak to the people?" Facing the populace Paul began, "I was brought up in this city, and instructed according to the Law of our fathers. I was zealous for the Law ... and persecuted Christianity even unto the death. ... As I was on my way approaching Damascus suddenly there shone about me a great light from heaven and I heard a voice saying to me 'Saul, Saul, why do you persecute Me?' 'Who are you Lord?' 'I am Jesus of Nazareth Whom you are persecuting.' I was baptized and then returned to Jerusalem but the Lord bid me leave saying 'Go, for to the Gentiles far away will I send you'." At these words the angry tumult broke anew.

Paul Proclaims Himself a Roman Citizen

The tribune ordered Paul into the fortress to be scourged and tortured until he gave the reason why the Jews had risen up against him. Turning to the centurion, the Apostle demanded, "Is it legal for you to scourge a Roman and without trial?" The centurion immediately reported to Lysias that his prisoner was a Roman citizen. Frightened, Lysias hastened to the scene and with his own hands loosed Paul from his bonds.

Paul's Vision at Jerusalem

The next day, the tribune ordered the Sanhedrin to assemble and brought his prisoner before them. Paul spoke his own brilliant defense and set the members of the Sanhedrin at odds among themselves. Such a violent dispute broke out that Paul was again in danger of being torn to pieces. He returned to the fortress. The following night Christ comforted him and said, "Be steadfast; for just as you have borne witness to Me in Jerusalem, bear witness in Rome also."

Paul before Felix at Caesarea

Meanwhile forty men vowed neither to eat nor drink until they murdered Paul. Warned of the plot by Paul's nephew, Lysias conducted his prisoner by night to Caesarea, escorted by soldiers, lancers and cavalry. The tribune wrote to Felix, governor of Caesarea, "This man is a Roman citizen accused about questions of the Mosaic Law. As there was a plot to ambush and murder him, I am sending him to you." Paul was comparatively free in Caesarea and was often summoned to preach Christ's doctrine before Felix.

Scaccioni

Paul Is Shipwrecked

Festus succeeded Felix as governor. Before him Paul declared, "I am innocent of all which I have been accused. I appeal to Caesar!" "To Caesar you shall go," returned the governor who some days later consigned Paul and a group of prisoners to the centurion Julius. They set sail for Asia Minor and at Alexandria boarded a ship for Italy. Off the coast of Crete the ship was caught in a violent storm that tossed it about for fourteen days. Paul exhorted his companions, "Be of good cheer. Last night an angel of the Lord said to me, 'Do not be afraid, Paul; you must stand before Caesar; and behold, God has granted you all who are sailing with you.'"

Paul Is Bitten by a Viper

The fourteenth night the ship ran aground off the coast of
Malta. Stuck fast, with waves battering the stern to pieces,
the passengers jumped overboard and swam toward the shore.
Native islanders built a fire and aided the shipwrecked travelers. As Paul laid a bundle of firewood on the flames a viper
slid from the pile and fastened itself to his hand. The Maltese
thought this a sign of vengeance from on high. When Paul
shook the viper off unharmed the natives gazed upon him in
mute astonishment, believing him a god.

Consoni

The Cure of the Governor's Father

Publius, governor of Malta, received the travelers kindly
and entertained them three days. His father was ill with fever.
Paul went to him, and "after praying and laying his hands on
him he healed him. After this all the sick of the island came
and were cured." Thus by his miracles did Paul demonstrate
the divinity of the doctrine he preached.

Paul's Meeting with the Christians of Rome

When good weather returned, the passengers continued their voyage, setting out for Syracuse and from thence to Rome, the city to which Paul had ever desired to bring the Word of Christ. It was the year 61 A.D. A moving surprise awaited Paul at the Market of Appius. The Roman Christians had hurried there to greet the valiant Champion of Christ, whose untiring zeal and sublime doctrine they were well aware of through the epistle he addressed to them three years previously.

Paul Preaching at Rome

While in the city of the Caesars Paul lived in a private
house attended by a single guard. There he received all those
who sought him. He preached the kingdom of God and taught
the truths concerning our redemption as accomplished by Jesus
Christ.

Reliquary in the Basilica of St. Paul

The Chains of St. Paul

Chains might bind Paul's wrists but they could not bind the Word of God which he had the duty and honor to propagate among the Gentiles. Where the sound of his voice could no longer penetrate he sent his written word. Thus from Rome he encouraged the Colossians, Ephesians and the faithful Philippians. After two years in custody, the Roman tribunal declared Paul innocent and he was released.

Coghetti

In the Mamertine Prison

Once again Paul returned to the East, revisiting the Christian communities. Hunted by Nero's troops he was taken prisoner, perhaps at Troas, and brought again to Rome. Tradition tells us that both the Apostles Peter and Paul were confined in the Mamertine Prison. Together they continued to labor for the conversion of the Romans notwithstanding Nero's lengthy persecution of the followers of Christ.

The Last Earthly Embrace of the Two Apostles
Peter and Paul were united by Christ in the apostolate and in glorious martyrdom. The last earthly embrace of the two Apostles was followed shortly by their heavenly reunion. Peter quickly reached the Vatican hill and Paul the site of his martyrdom on the Ostian Way.

Paul's Martyrdom

As a citizen of Rome, death could be inflicted on Paul in no other way than by the sword. After being scourged the great Apostle inclined his venerable head. A Roman sword severed it from his body and the earth was purpled by his glorious blood. Triumphantly the Church sings, "Rejoice, O Rome, for you have been consecrated by the glorious blood of the Princes of the Apostles."

Camuccini

St. Paul in Glory

The soul of Paul—the man for whom to live was Christ;
passionately loved by his followers and bitterly hated by his
enemies—gloriously entered Paradise. Over the tumult of
centuries his exhortation rings clear, "Remember my chains
—those chains I bore for Christ's Gospel. Conserve your entire
being, body and soul, without blemish, that Christ may be
glorified in you."

cortege, weeping over the dangers that awaited him, which they too knew by a revelation of the Holy Spirit. When they came outside the city, they all knelt on the shore and prayed together, placing in God's hands His cause which men were hindering through satanic wiles. When Paul and his companions went on board the ship, the Christians lingered on the shore with broken hearts, knowing that they would never see him again.

The ship stopped at Ptolemais which was near, and where the Apostle was able to spend the day with the Community there. On the following day, still moving within sight of the shore, they stopped at Caesarea, the city that Herod the Great had built in honor of Augustus. Paul rejoiced at seeing it once more, and yet he was sad. Caesarea, with its large administration buildings, was a fortified port, the military and political capital of Judea. With what proud ostentation it exhibited to the eyes of pilgrims, the temples, the baths, the theaters, the great prisons constructed by that King, half Jew, under whom Christ was born. Like its founder, it was an ambiguous city; a mixture of Greek marbles and Semitic shops of antiques; with a population of Jews and Syrians, always fighting among themselves. There was much in the city that was very modern, superadded to a place of the utmost antiquity. Caesarea (in Greek called Sebaste) marked the time when Palestine passed into the possession of Rome.

As soon as Paul landed there he sought the brethren. There was one among them of extraordinary authority and renown for his work of Evangelization, the Deacon Philip, one of the seven who had been chosen in Jerusalem in the first days of the Church. He had four daughters, all virgins, all endowed with the gift of prophecy. It was a great consolation for these co-workers of Christ to see one another, to hear the news about the diffusion of the Gospel, which seemed to spread like a conflagration over the face of the earth.

Paul told about the work in the Aegean centers. Philip told about the progress made in other parts of the interior of Asia. After a few days there came from Judea a prophet by name of Agabus. Standing before Paul in the presence of all the brethren, under the impulse of a rather lugubrious inspiration, he took hold of Paul's girdle and wound it about his own hands and feet. He prophesied that in this manner Paul would be bound by the Jews in Jerusalem, and then delivered into the hands of the pagans. The prophet predicted this under the illumination of the Holy Spirit, and those listening were filled with consternation but, looking on Paul's face, they saw not the slightest emotion portrayed.

When Agabus had finished speaking, Paul's companions as well as the Christians gathered at Caesarea begged him not to go to Jerusalem. Why put one's self into the enemies' hands? Why risk going to prison? But Paul only shook his head and asked them to say no more. "What do you mean by weeping and breaking my heart? For I am ready not only to be bound but even to die at Jerusalem for the name of the Lord Jesus."

The hatred of his enemies was directed against Jesus; His very name was detested and it was considered a crime to pronounce it. Later on, the Christians would be persecuted for that name, which the Sanhedrin and the Pharisees wished to eliminate from the lips of everyone. The accent of Paul was that of a man who knows; whose will is irrevocably set; as for the brethren, they had to be resigned to God's Will through their tears. When the time came for him to start, some of them accompanied him as far as Jerusalem. Among them was a certain Mnason, an old disciple from Cyprus, who was to give hospitality to the Apostle in the Holy City.

Paul and his friends started on their way. They crossed Samaria, all in blossom, walking over the hills of Judea, where spring had awakened to new life trees and shrubs. The sky smiled down upon little houses, and the gay scene was a contrast to the sad group. Paul saw none of these things. He could only trace the story of the Evangelization as they neared the place of the Crucifixion. The desire to imitate the Master, in His bloody offering, distilled into his soul a joy mixed with trepidation in the consciousness of his unworthiness and lowliness.

The sky was already studded with stars, and the soft air was filled with the bleating of sheep, when, after a two-days' walk he entered the city which had killed Christ and the Prophets before Him. Paul entered as a conqueror, and yet as one already judged.

His entrance into the city marks the beginning of the third and last stage of Paul's life, that of imprisonment and death. Nevertheless, he resigned himself into the hands of God. Weeping with emotion, Paul saw again the city of his forefathers, to which he was returning after an absence of nearly seven years, with all the homesickness of a son who, although hated, was unconquerably faithful.

PAUL IN CHAINS AT ROME

The Arrest in Jerusalem

Paul arrived in Jerusalem in May, A.D. 58, just one year after his flight from Ephesus. In Jerusalem those political passions were already fermenting and ready to burst into flames, passions that would bring such terrible butchery on the nation in 69 and the destruction of the city in 70. The little person, Paul, was entering an atmosphere red hot against him. He represented universalism in a period of the most intense national particularism.

After the death of Herod Agrippa in 44, Judea lost her complete independence and was forced under the direct domination of Rome. Roman control was exercised through procurators. These functionaries descended upon the province and, for the most part, aimed at amassing a fortune during their short and uncertain term of office. They were unscrupulous of either the rights or dignity of individuals in acquiring their booty.

At that time the Procurator of Judea, Samaria, Galilee, and Perea was a freedman, Antonius Felix, brother of Pallas, the favorite of Agrippina. Felix's power at court had increased when his mistress, in 54, had poisoned her husband Claudius, and had substituted for him on the throne, her son, Nero. Felix, who was an ex-slave, governed in a slave's way, although he had chosen his wives from among royalty. In Judea he hunted down whole bands of brigands, and crucified them. He had not, however, uprooted the bad plant from which, by way of reaction, there came forth the Sicarii, the worst form of brigandage.

These had not hesitated to kill even the High Priest Jonathan. No doubt this was done by order of the same Felix, who, when there was need, did not hesitate to use the Sicarii, or even to do the deed himself. In fact, the Sicarii fanatics cared less about robbing than they did about spreading terrorism in order to clear the country of Roman domination and of the Jews who supported it. Therefore, it was above all during the Feasts when, lost in the crowds with their short daggers hidden under their cloaks, they assassinated their adversaries—the national enemies of Rome—thus pushing the political fanaticism of zealots to the use of murder.

The terrorism of the Sicarii had, on the one hand, spread suspicion and fear among the people and, on the other, had excited the ambition of adventurers. Among these, there was a false Egyptian prophet who had incited many thousands of rash followers in all kinds of reckless daring. With these followers he had prepared a march upon Jerusalem from the desert, to overcome the Romans and to establish his own regime there.

Such plots were irritating Jewish nationalism, already strong and fierce, and were spreading suspicion and menace on all who seemed to deviate in the slightest degree from Jewish customs and usages. Paul was looked upon as one of these. Reports that he was destroying the race and its religion had come from merchants, even from some of the faithful, who had migrated from new Christian centers in the Aegean archipelago and in Asia Minor. Such reports had filled the souls of the priests, Pharisees, Zealots and the rigorists with resentment.

During the first few days, they had not recognized Paul in the narrow streets nor under the Temple's porticoes. He was so broken with age and fatigue that he looked like another person. More than twenty years had passed since the time he had come to Jerusalem for orders to persecute the Christians, so those of the younger generation had never seen him. Furthermore, the city was full of Jews who had come from all parts of the Empire and beyond, to celebrate the Feast of Tabernacles, so it was not easy among so many different faces and so many different languages, to identify Paul.

The brethren of the Church received him with joy, and the day following his arrival, they took him to see James, the brother of the Lord. The other Apostles were away at the time, travelling about, either within or without the Empire. The Ancients were present, and asked Paul to tell of his success in his missions to the pagans. As he spoke, there passed in vision across their amazed minds, those files of young brothers from Syria, Asia, Illyria, Achaia, and Macedonia; and they gave thanks to God.

In their turn, the Ancients reported the talk spread about by some of the Judaizers and other Jews of the Dispersion, according to which he was accused of teaching the baptized Jews to abandon entirely the Laws of Moses. This rumor had caused trouble among the brethren, who with James at their head, had continued to practice all the rites of Judaism. Perhaps the rumor was an erroneous interpretation of Paul's doctrine about the uselessness of legal works towards justification which can be achieved only through faith in Jesus Christ. Or, more exactly, it was derived from Paul's constant opposition to circumcising baptized Gentiles and obliging them to adopt legal practices.

For such reasons as these, the Ancients suggested that Paul give some public proof of his attachment to Mosaism by joining four other Jews who had made a Nazarite vow, and by paying the expenses of their sacrifice which had to be offered in order to conclude the vow. Paul was always a Jew with the Jews, and even if he did not attribute any value to the Mosaic ritual for salvation, he nevertheless understood the feelings of reverence with which it had always been regarded and practiced by the Israelites. He was always ready to make a sacrifice of externals in order not to scandalize the brethren, so he gladly agreed. He had his head shaved along with the other Jews and, after purifying himself, entered the Temple with them to pronounce the vow.

All went well and pleased the brethren. Paul was pleased, too, to give them this sign of good will; ready, as he always was, to make himself all things to all men, practicing even the Mosaic rites for edification's sake. But on the last day of the festive week Paul was recognized by some who espied him in the Temple and cried out, "He contaminates the Temple, introducing pagans therein!" This cry was the equivalent of the other one, "Great is Diana of the Ephesians!" And it contained enough inflammable material to set the crowd on fire. The crowd ran, the doors of the Temple were slammed shut, and the Apostle was taken.

It was a calumny. They had seen Paul in the company of Trophimus, a Christian from Ephesus, and pretended that the laws (which were carved in three different languages on the columns of the Temple) had been violated when Paul had brought an uncircumcised person into the Sacred Precincts. This was the immediate pretext. Once they had hold of the Apostle, his real crime was revealed in their excited conversation: he had left Judaism and was preaching a new Law.

In their rage they would have lynched him if Claudius Lysias, the tribune of the cohort, had not been notified and at once intervened. He came running with a force of soldiers and centurions. When they saw that armed force, the fanatical Jews refrained from killing the Apostle, knowing that Roman authority did not tolerate disorders in the Temple courts. The prompt intervention of the tribune need not surprise us since the tower of Antonia, where the garrison was quartered, was near the Temple and was joined to it by a flight of steps. Also in those days Roman authority watched very attentively all the moves of the people in whom the passions of a deeply anti-Roman nationalism were apt to break out into tumult. Flavius Josephus tells us that, on the days of the great feasts, the Roman cohorts were lined up near the Temple porticoes in order to intervene quickly when seditions arose among the crowds.

When the tribune advanced, the aggressors, moved backwards, The Roman officer took the Apostle and consigned him to the centurions to be bound with two chains, thinking that if he provoked all that pandemonium he must be someone very worthless. Turning to the crowd, he asked, "Who is this man? What has he done?" The crowd answered as only persons drawn together by irrational impulses could answer. Some shouted one thing, some shouted another. Neither the authorities nor the action of the tribune could put order into the minds or cries of the excited crowd who really did not know of what they were accusing Paul.

Then the tribune ordered Paul taken to the fortress. The fanatical mob, emboldened by the sight of the chains and seeing their prey, whom they had vowed to lynch, taken from them, dashed in among the soldiers and began beating Paul with their fists, while from all sides they howled, "Kill him! Kill him!" They would have torn him to pieces if the legionaries had not carried him up the steps of the fortress to safety.

The Roman Citizen

In all the noisy confusion the only one who kept calm was the victim. When they came near the entrance to the fortress, Paul made a sign to the tribune and asked:

"May I speak to thee?"

"How? Dost thou speak Greek?" answered Lysias in surprise. "Art thou the Egyptian who caused four thousand Sicarii to revolt?"

Josephus Flavius, who often exaggerates, says that the Egyptian, by pretending to be a prophet, had gathered thirty thousand men. Someone in that bedlam must have shouted his name.

"I am not an Egyptian," answered Paul. "I am a Jew, a citizen of Tarsus, a well-known city of Cilicia. I beg thee, let me speak to the people."

It took courage for a man in his condition to speak to that mob of demoniacs. But Paul was an Apostle as well as a Jew. He loved with a special love the souls of his compatriots even if they had turned against him. Standing at the head of the flight of stairs, bound with chains, he made a sign with his hand. Small of stature but raised higher by the steps, standing in the midst of the soldiers with their gleaming arms, although in chains, he seemed to dominate the scene. His proud calm was amazing. As the voices died out little by little, like a tempest subsiding, and silence ensued, Paul addressed them as "brothers and fathers" in the Aramaic language. He told the story of his conversion; how he had come to the Holy City from Cilicia to study the Law at the feet of Gamaliel; how for zeal for the Law, he had persecuted "that doctrine unto death," when one day there had appeared to him in a ray of light, Jesus the Nazarene. He told the story in all its details, how he had lost his sight, and how he had re-covered it again; how, having come to Jerusalem, he had received in the Temple (the very Temple in which they were now standing) the command from the Lord Jesus to "go unto the Gentiles afar off, for so I send thee."

Behold the evil deed confessed by the doer himself! This was the point in question: he was demolishing the partition between Israel and other nations. The crowd had listened to the series of miraculous happenings told in such accents of sincerity, but the mention of privileges extended beyond the limits of the Chosen People, of a universality that abolished their exclusiveness, making no distinction between the pure and the impure, between the just and the unjust, were inflammable statements, and the crowd took fire again. They began to shout, "Kill him! Kill him! Away with such a one! He is not fit to live!" Then they began throwing dust in the air, and pull-ing off their outer garments, which is the oriental way of showing anger.

The tribune had understood nothing of the discourse. But seeing again that sea of congested, angry faces, of open mouths, dust and rags, he felt impelled to put an end to the disorder. He was annoyed with his prisoner for creating another riot, so he ordered him away with the command, "Take him into the fortress, and scourge him before the interrogation takes place." Such an order must have satis-fied the people. It was also the easiest and most immediate thing for a military tribune to do in all the excitement of the moment.

The tribune knew—and the crowd knew—that six years before, another tribune named Celeris, found guilty of giving a decision against the Jews in a quarrel with the Samaritans, had been consigned by order of the Emperor to the same Jews, dragged about the city and, in the end, beheaded. So the poor man in the riotous fury and pressure of the moment gave the order for scourging. Flogging was always part of the ordinary procedure in the inquiries of the Roman tribunal when it was dealing with subjects of conquered peoples.

Paul, who knew something of Roman procedure, as he was being tied with straps for the flogging, turned to the centurion and asked, "Is it lawful for you to scourge a Roman citizen not yet condemned?"

A Roman citizen! The centurion opened his eyes wide, and running to the tribune, exclaimed, "Tribune, what are you about to do? This man is a Roman citizen!"

"A Roman citizen?" said the tribune. Much surprised, therefore, he ran to the prisoner.

"Tell me, sir, art thou a Roman?"

"Yes, in very truth," answered Paul.

"I obtained my citizenship at a high price," said the officer, shaking his head.

"And I was born so," replied Paul.

There was, then, a sort of superiority on the part of Paul. Roman citizenship conferred immunity from torture; so much so, that the tribune feared at having tied a Roman citizen to the column for scourging. He had Paul unbound immediately.

They stood facing each other, the tribune and the prisoner; and lo! the majesty of Rome came between them, a powerful and commanding reality, and the officer bowed, trembling before the prisoner. For several years now Rome's adherence to justice and right had protected Paul from the will of the people, about to proceed against him led by instinct and passion and to do away with him.

Each time this had happened, Paul must have appreciated a legal system that made a way for the expansion of the Gospel regardless of the hatred of private persons as well as of public anger. In the meantime the tribune was still puzzled, not knowing yet whom he was dealing with nor the crime of the accused. Since the case concerned a Jew, he would have preferred letting the Sanhedrin take care of it, but Roman authority forbade, and at this time Roman authority was very watchful and strict. However, on the following day, relieved of his chains, Paul was brought before the Sanhedrin which was convoked especially for the purpose.

A Pharisee Among Pharisees

The Sanhedrin was the supreme tribunal, religious and civil, of the Hebrew people. It was composed of seventy-two members from various classes and parties, with a prevalence of Pharisees and Sadducees. It was presided over by the Supreme High Priest, who at that time was the haughty Ananias, son of Zebedee. He had been installed in his place of dignity ten years before by the little King Herod of Chalcis.

Paul would always have to suffer from his desire to bring salvation to his people and from being repulsed by them. He now stood looking at the members of the tribunal and fixed his eyes on them. Although appearing before them in the garb of the accused, he had every right to address those in the seats of the judges in familiar terms:

"Brethren, fellow-men, fathers, I have behaved with a right conscience before God till this day."

Ananias ordered one of the servants to strike the bold speaker on the mouth. The witnesses to the scene do not say whether this was actually done or not, but Paul was not one who would allow an offence to be committed against him as an Apostle who had a right conscience. Neither would he tolerate irregularities in the procedure according to law, therefore, he addressed the High Priest:

"God will strike thee, thou whitened wall. How is it that thou sittest to judge according to the Law, and dost violate the Law in ordering them to strike me?"

None of those standing there had ever heard such an answer from a Jew to a Jewish High Priest, and they remarked that in speaking thus, Paul lacked respect for the Prince of the Priests. Paul excused himself bitterly and ironically:

"Brethren, I did not know he was the Prince of the Priests." No doubt he meant, "How could I suppose such a man filled a place of such high dignity?"

Minds were aflame. The outburst of passion on the previous day in the square was boiling up again inside the palace; no way was presented for settling the problem. It was sheer loss of time for the Apostle to free himself from the grasp of the Sanhedrin by affirming that his mission to the Gentiles was by divine command. The very name of Jesus would have exposed him to the worst effects of anger, and his advocating a religious universality would have united all the various parties against him. Paul, though always genial and kind, knew all the shades of doctrines and factions in Judaism. So he suddenly threw into the midst of that gathering the apple of discord, thus giving Lysias and all present the unique spectacle of seeing the contention between the accusers and the judges.

"Brethren," said Paul, "I am a Pharisee, and the son of Pharisees. Behold, I am dragged here to be judged for our hope in God and the resurrection of the dead."

Hearing this, the Pharisees, who believed in the survival of the soul and in the resurrection of the dead, turned against the Sadducees, who were materialists and denied both the one and the other. Another of the many disputes between the two groups was now started in the Sanhedrin under the very eyes of the tribune.

Paul alone was unmoved and calm. He stood looking at the storm he had brought on. Some of the extreme Pharisees were shouting that perhaps he was innocent, or perhaps in him spoke an angel, or some other spirit. The Sadducees, acting like wild beasts, attempted, by hurling all manner of charges against him, to do away with him on the spot. With flaming eyes these representatives of the dominating class rallied to the defence of their national privileges. To them this man Paul represented subversion and extinction. Oh, that they were able to annihilate him!

Lysias, seeing the danger and fearing that the prisoner might be torn to pieces, gave orders for the soldiers to take Paul into the fortress for safety. Once more Paul had foiled the snares of his adversaries. Once again Roman power had saved him. During the night the Lord appeared to him and said, "Be of good heart; for just as you have borne witness to Me in Jerusalem, you shall bear witness to Me in Rome also."

Paul went to sleep under the Master's smile, thinking of the imperial city to which the primacy of Jerusalem was being transferred.

The Jews rejected the authority of Rome and thereby thrust the Apostolate of Christianity upon Rome. The Catholicity of Christianity frightened them, as it has frightened many people. The assembly of the Sanhedrin, brought about by that little man, had ended in an explosion. Many minds among those assembled there were exasperated at the outcome. A group of more than forty men (perhaps Sicarii or Zealots) bound themselves by a religious vow neither to eat nor drink until they had killed Paul. They went to the High Priest and proposed to him that he induce the tribune to take the prisoner before the Sanhedrin again under the pretext of further examination. They would kill him on the way there or back.

Someone, probably one of the Pharisees and a member of the Sanhedrin, hearing of the conspiracy, secretly warned Paul's relatives. One of Paul's sisters sent her son, a mere boy, to put his uncle on his guard. The youngster succeeded in entering the fortress and he told Paul all he knew about the plot. Paul called one of the centurions and begged him to take the courageous nephew to the tribune, as he had important matters to reveal to him. The boy, alert and daring, must have made a good impression, because he was soon taken into the presence of the tribune.

"The prisoner Paul called me and asked me to bring this young man to thee, for he has something to say to thee," said the centurion.

"What new thing is this?" thought the officer as he took the boy by the hand and led him apart. "Well, what hast thou to tell me?"

The boy must have had some of his uncle's intelligence; so he told of the plot that was to be carried out the next day. "I understand," said the tribune, dismissing the lad. "Hold your peace, and leave the whole matter to me."

Since the contest between legality and anarchy was intense, the officer made a quick decision. He ordered two centurions to prepare an escort of seventy horsemen, two hundred lancers, and a horse for Paul. In the evening, when the city was silent and dark, he sent Paul, thus escorted, on his way to Caesarea, seat of the procurator.

Perhaps Luke also went with Paul since he is the historian of this mission. It is he who quotes the letter of introduction, written by the tribune to his superior. It was a letter of bureaucratic flavor in which the case of the prisoner was briefly stated. A warning was given that the alleged accusations concerned some bickerings about the Mosaic Law. While no ordinary crime was laid to his charge, no mention either was made of the tribune's preparations for the scourging.

At Herod's Praetorium in Caesarea

The strength of the escort was justified by the fear Lysias had of a surprise attack by the Jews, which would have seriously involved him had there been any suspicion or accusation against him for bribery or for dishonesty. Sending the prisoner to his superior freed him from all further imputation.

At early dawn the escort reached Antipatris. The whole escort, having walked all night, remained there; the lancers returned to Jerusalem, and the cavalry continued on to Caesarea.

On their arrival in Caesarea, the letter was delivered and the prisoner handed over to authority. Felix read the letter, questioned the prisoner and, hearing that he was from Cilicia (Cilicia, Crete, and Cappadocia—all C's of bad reputation), postponed the interrogation until the arrival of the accusers. In the meantime, Paul was well guarded in the proconsul's palace, called "Herod's Praetorium" after the name of the builder.

We may well imagine the shame and rage of the conspirators when they discovered their victim had escaped. When they complained to Lysias, he shrugged his shoulders and told them to carry their accusations to Felix at Caesarea; and this they had to do.

After five days (to be exact, the date was May 23, A.D. 58) the High Priest came in person. No doubt this was intended to impress Felix. He was accompanied by a commission of the principal Elders from the Sanhedrin, and he brought along a famous lawyer named Tertullus. It was the duty of this man to present the case before the presiding authority, the accused being present.

Like a real professional, Tertullus prefaced his exposition with a speech full of suave praise for the peaceful and vigilant administration of Felix. This was open hypocrisy, for everyone knew with what vulgar avarice Felix held his charge, intent on extracting all the money possible from his oppressed territory. By contrast, the orator classified Paul as a "pestilent" man. And this came to be the common way the Christians were referred to—as a "pest" in the mouths of their adversaries. Paul was accused of being an "instigator of disorders" among the Jews all over the world (the clients of Tertullus had informed him of the complaints made by the various Synagogues). And it was alleged that Paul was "one of the leaders in the Sect of the Nazarenes." (From a Jewish standpoint this was true.) Another charge was that he was the "author of an attempt to defile the Temple." (This was false since it was only an attempt and not an accomplished fact.)

Paul was accustomed to polemics and was well trained in logic and dialetics. He speedily refuted each accusation, beginning with the last and most important.

"No one found me disputing in the Temple, or gathering people together in any part of the city. I came here only twelve days ago. As for the doctrines of these, called the Sect of the Nazarene, I serve the God of our Fathers and follow the Law and the Prophets as they do also; and I believe in the resurrection of the dead, both for the just and the unjust. If I came to Jerusalem, it was to bring help to my people and to fulfill a vow; which is quite a different thing from plotting tumults. If any of the Jews from Asia, who recognized me, had anything of which to accuse me, they should have come here. Neither in the Sanhedrin did they find anything to reproach me with, except that allusion of mine to the resurrection of the dead."

Paul's argument was conclusive and clever. He refuted all the accusations. Among them the capital one, in the eyes of a Roman magistrate, was that of having provoked disorders and promoting seditions. Always an Apostle, Paul was also exercising his Apostolate in announcing Christ, even before the tribunal. Hesitating between two expedients, Felix knew no better course than to suspend the hearing, alleging that he wanted to hear Lysias and to seek more information about the doctrines of that sect which Paul had mentioned.

He sent Paul back to prison, but with orders that he be treated better and given a certain freedom for his friends from outside to see him and serve him. If Felix had been of a different moral make-up, he would have set Paul free; but he feared to exasperate the Jews and, avaricious as he was, he hoped to receive some money for the deliverance of the prisoner. Nevertheless, it must be said, that with all the venality and with all the possibility of receiving bribes with greater facility from the accusers, he did not lend himself to their designs. Roman legality curbed, in some measure at least, the evil tendencies of bad functionaries. On the other hand, Felix knew, as Paul had recalled in the preamble of his defense, the mind of the Jews after so many years in office and just how much account should be taken of their accusations.

Still hoping to receive money from Paul, he kept him in prison two years. Luke relates nothing of this except the short discourse begun by the Apostle before the governor and his wife Drusilla a few days after his transfer to Caesarea. Drusilla was the daughter of Agrippa I. She was divorced from King Aziz of Emessa and was married to the freedman of Antonius and Agrippina. Dissolute, superstitious and frivolous, she wanted to know and see the man for whose murder forty fanatics had pledged themselves to die of hunger. When questioned about his doctrines, the Apostle began to speak of justice, of chastity, and of the future judgment. It is evident that Paul yearned to convert the proconsul and to exercise his Apostolate even in prison, but Felix, at the mere sound of those words which he had never heard before, became alarmed and said, "For the present go thy way; but when I get an opportunity, I will send for thee."

Paul could have asked that a collection be taken among the brethren and some money given to that rapacious functionary, thus obtaining a liberty useful to the Apostolate. But he preferred prison to bribery, trusting securely in the Lord's promise that he was destined to go to Rome. In short, he let God act; and on his part, he applied himself to suffer well. This he knew was a most profitable means of collaboration with the divine plan in the exercise of his Apostolate; especially since Felix had allowed him to have visitors.

There were times when Felix did send for Paul and converse with him. He fell under the influence of that spirit so full of faith and the richness of that great intelligence. Felix was superstitious, corrupt and ignorant; and so he could not make up his mind to accept the truth expounded by his prisoner; he recognized this truth through a weak remnant of light left in his conscience which had survived all his crimes. Contact with people completely turned towards the Messianic hope and towards the life of the soul, weighed him down with fear and filled his soul with terror and remorse.

The Appeal to Caesar

The governor, Felix, had been hard on the Jews; and they, on their part, had not tried to lighten his task. We may be sure that the majority of the people yearned to be allowed to work in peace; but the various parties, headed by evil doers, were bent on raising tumults in Caesarea. This state of things the procurator, Procius Festus, had tried to remedy when he succeeded Felix in the year 60. Festus was an honest and energetic man who turned his efforts towards improving the administration of the country. Three days after taking over his charge in Caesarea, he went to Jerusalem. There a deputation of high priests and leaders of the people, in all the glamour of their white robes, decorated with the insignia of their rank, came asking that in the urgent interests of the state, a process be conducted against Paul in Jerusalem.

Festus knew how to proceed. "If you have any accusation against this man, come to Caesarea." And to Caesarea he betook himself after eight or ten days.

The morning after his arrival there, he held a hearing. The Jews, who had come in large numbers, renewed their accusations, and Paul replied to them, point by point. "I have done nothing against the Jewish Law, or against the Temple, or against Caesar," he said. Festus would have liked to show some favor to the leaders of the Jews from whom he had received great exterior signs of deference, although their real aim he did not know. He had not had sufficient opportunity in dealing with them so he proposed to the prisoner, "Wouldst thou come to Jerusalem to be judged by me on the spot?"

Notice, it was not an order, simply a proposal. Paul, whose mind was always alert, saw the danger of a return to Jerusalem: the conspirators could kill him, and the procurator might leave the sentence to the Sanhedrin.

"No," he answered, "I stand at Caesar's tribunal; here must I be judged. I have done nothing against the Jews, thou well knowest. If I have done anything worthy of death, I do not refuse to be put to death; but if none of their accusations are true, no one can give me over to them solely to please them."

The reasoning was clear and convincing; but Paul, not knowing very well the mind of the new magistrate, feared lest Jewish pressure might induce Festus to remove him to Jerusalem. Therefore, to cut the matter short, he added, "I appeal to Caesar."

By appealing to Caesar, a right of every Roman citizen, Paul freed himself from the fluctuations of local justice and from the snares of the Jews at Jerusalem. At the same time, he was now taking the road to Rome, whither the Lord had called him.

Festus, having listened to the opinions of his counsellors, proceeded to carry out the appeal. So he made preparations for sending the accused to Caesar's tribunal, which was Nero's. Even Nero could be used in God's designs. Once more, the leaders of Judaism had to return to the city, foiled.

After a few days two personages came to Caesarea to gain some favor from the new magistrate; they were King Agrippa II and Bernice, the brother and sister of Drusilla, who had wished to see and hear Paul. These two also, at the invitation of Festus, wished to have this pleasure and to hear the accused speak of a certain Jesus Who had died, but Who (so said the Procurator) Paul declared to be alive.

Agrippa and Bernice came to the audience hall which was decorated for the occasion with all the tinsel of oriental royalty. Formality was as important for them as morality was negligible; (it was said that they lived in sin). The Ancients of the city accompanied the royal guests, curious to see the unusual spectacle. Unconsciously, the imposing audience paid homage to the importance of Christ's message and to the merit of His Apostle.

Festus introduced the accused. "This is the man whose death Judea demands, but whom I judge to be innocent. Since he has appealed to Augustus, I shall send him to Rome; but I do not know what to write to my lord concerning him." The lord was not God but the Emperor; or rather, the Emperor was a god, in the mind of the good Roman official. As imperial power was gradually decaying inwardly, it was becoming more and more inflated outwardly, even to self-deification. In the statement, clear and concise, with which Festus presented Paul, he made the person of this little man stand out in bold relief; Paul was the man whose death a whole nation was demanding, considering him a national danger. Indeed, there was reason. The universality Paul announced would be the end of Judaism. Through faith in Christ the Law of Moses became a dead thing; and with it went the whole system of the civic and religious ideology of Judaism which had been built upon the Law of Moses.

The words of so important a person as Festus sounded clearly in the silence that pervaded the hall. Paul spoke, as he always did, as an Apostle, and addressed the King directly. Agrippa was a Jew, tetrarch of a Jewish province. Consequently he could understand the ideas in these separating influences better than could Festus, who had referred to "a certain Jesus." Moreover, since his disorderly moral life showed him to be a worthy descendant of Herod the Great, Paul felt this to be an added reason for trying to convert him.

Then there were all those persons surrounding him; Paul knew that such an occasion for announcing Christ should not be lost. He explained that the principal accusation against him was his hope in eternal life, the promise given to the fathers which he held in common with all true Hebrew people. He made no mention of the profanation of the Temple alleged against him, for that was evidently only a pretext. Neither did he speak of the universality of his teaching, that the Gospel was to be shared with the pagans also, because this was a positive command of the Risen Christ. If one believed in the Risen Christ then all else was clear, explained and justified. It was for this purpose that Paul told of the vision on the way to Damascus where he was going, as a principal agent of the persecution, to put in chains the followers of Jesus.

It was Jesus, appearing to him in a light more powerful than the sun itself, Who had assigned to him his mission among the Gentiles, in which he would not fail. It was for this reason he had taught the truths of the prophets and of Moses to the pagans as well as to the Jews; it was the prophets who had foretold the sufferings and resurrection of Christ. Paul's graphic account, his vibrating accents and decisive gestures, must have made a lively impression on the Jews. What he said must have seemed foolish to Festus who, as a good pagan, understood nothing of the prophets and could form no idea of the resurrection; so much so that, at this point, he interrupted.

"Paul, thou art mad; thy great learning hath turned thy head." It was not the first time that Paul had heard the doctrine of Christ defined as madness by pagan lips; but without losing his composure, and with a note of sadness in his voice, he replied, "I am not mad, excellent Festus, but I speak words of sober truth." This tranquil reply, which Paul directed to the pagan Festus, who knew only about arms and government, thus of no power higher than the Emperor, continues to be addressed to all pagans having no concept of the supernatural. Because these are steeped in the things of sense and matter, they continue to profess that Paul had lost his reason.

Paul shook his head, now quite gray and, turning again to the Jewish King who could understand him, said: "Do you, O King, believe in the Prophets? I know that you believe." And he wanted to say, "If you believe in the Prophets, you must believe also in the Messias predicted by them." Agrippa understood the import of the questions. "You *almost persuade* me to become a Christian." "I would to God," answered the Apostle, "that not only you, but as many as hear me would become what I am, without these chains."

There was much delicacy in that wish; the vigorous master of polemics revealed himself tender and tactful in dealing with souls. These alone had real value for him, and for their salvation no sacrifice was too great, not even that of God Himself. On the whole the discourse made a favorable impression on Agrippa and Bernice. Festus thought Paul a little unbalanced, but not guilty. The three admitted that they found no fault in him; on the contrary, Agrippa even said, "This man might have been set at liberty, if he had not appealed to Caesar."

It is paradoxical, from a human point of view, that the message of Life should be brought by a man in chains; it is also paradoxical that pagan Rome, thinking that she is transporting a prisoner, is in reality transporting a great spiritual Firebrand. No one really knows the man he passes on the road; that man may be a genius or a dullard, a saint or a criminal. Certainly Julius, the centurion of the Augustan cohort stationed at Caesarea, who accompanied Paul with other prisoners to Rome, would never have imagined the greatness of the man hidden under the poor tunic who was his prisoner. Neither could he anticipate the flood of books that would be written about the thoughts that throbbed behind that brow, beneath which were set two poor eyes.

Shipwreck

Paul's companion was the trusty Luke who jotted down every detail because he was, at least partially, conscious of their immense historical value. Aristarchus, the faithful Thessalonian, was also with them; for Paul's cause and for the Gospel, he had been arrested at Ephesus. No doubt others wanted to go but could not; Paul drew as many sympathizers among the friends of Jesus as he repelled those who were His enemies.

A ship going to Adrumythium, loaded with goods and prisoners, started from Caesarea. After a day's sail the ship anchored at Sidon in Phoenicia where Julius, a good-natured man, allowed the Apostle to visit the brethren of the city and take some rest there.

It seems that the first night at sea was not so pleasant; in fact, a wind was blowing from the west and this was not favorable to navigation. From Sidon they continued along the coast of Cyprus, leaving Cilicia and Pamphylia on the north; they touched at Myra in Lycia, the city that was to become famous through the bishop, Saint Nicholas. At Myra they changed vessels and took a ship coming from Alexandria which, after moving along the coast of Asia Minor and having laboriously reached Cnidus, entered the Aegean Sea, fighting contrary winds. They neared Crete not far from Salmone, and veered to the south to a place called "Good Havens," near the city of Lasaea, where they landed.

The prisoners, crowded into the narrow ships, must have suffered much on an open sea swept by winds, deprived as they were of all convenience in their narrow quarters. The time of the great fast had passed, called "Yom Kippur" (the great Expiation), which fell between the latter part of September and the early part of October at the time of the autumn equinox. The sea was heavy with tempest, and navigation was unsafe. The mariners shook their heads, doubting if they should cross the great expanse of open sea which lay between Crete and Malta, with no possibility of stopping for protection.

Paul knew the sea. He had already suffered shipwreck three times; therefore he counselled the men to wait at Good Havens if they wanted to save the cargo, passengers and crew, two hundred and seventy-six persons in all. The centurion thought he could trust the pilot and the owner of the ship rather than a man who was a nobody and knew nothing of navigation. So he held to the plan, accepted by the majority, of pushing on towards the extreme western point of Crete, and then of casting anchor at the port of Phoenis to winter there. Since the wind was still mild, coming from the south, they moved along the shores of the island.

Hardly had they left the bay than a mighty wind, called the Euroaquilo, a "northeaster," seized the ship and drew it out on the high sea, sucking it into the vortex. In the midst of the howling wind and the frightful noise of the waves that swept the boat near the tiny island called Cauda, the mariners could only with great effort hold on to the lifeboat, in order to throw a rope around the keel of the ship so that it might resist the assault of the winds and waves. The storm was coming from the north towards the south and threatened to drive the ship on the quicksands of the Syrtis in Africa. The sailors, to diminish the resistance, furled the sails and abandoned themselves to whatever might happen.

The storm raged all day and all night, tossing the ship about on the waves like a straw, so that the men expected to be engulfed any moment. The ship was leaking, so they threw the cargo overboard to lighten it. The third day they did the same with the tackle of the ship; but the storm continued for several more days. They did not know where they were being carried, as the sun did not shine during the day, nor was a star to be seen at night. The sea wolves (mariners) economically ruined by the loss of their merchandise and of the rigging, began to lose courage and resistance; they refused to eat, fatalistically waiting for the final catastrophe. When all human hope seemed at an end, the insignificant prisoner of Christ, standing on his feet as best he could in that violent heaving and rolling, dragged himself into the midst of the crew to give them courage.

"Men, you should indeed have listened to me and not have sailed from Crete, thus sparing yourselves this disaster and loss. And now I beg you to be of good cheer, for there will be no loss of life among you, but only of the ship. For last night an angel of the God I belong to and serve, stood by me, saying, 'Do not be afraid, Paul; thou must stand before Caesar; and behold, God has granted thee all who are sailing with thee.' So, men, be of good cheer; for I have faith in God that it will be as it has been told me. But we are to reach a certain island."

Even on the brink of death, Paul continued his Apostolate; he gave back to those unfortunates the hope of physical life and announced to them Eternal Life in the God Who was saving them. Some of them may have remembered it afterwards. In that dramatic moment, God reminded Paul of his mission to Rome and, for the sake of the mission, He made a gift of the lives of those men who were so near to death. It was so important a matter that Paul should reach the city. God used the sedition of Jerusalem and the tempests of the Mediterranean to transport this "vessel of election" to Rome. It was a complicated mystery which involved the rejection of the Gospel by the Jews and the acceptance of the Gospel by the Gentiles. In this great drama, heaven and earth, men and elements all took part. Perhaps Paul's thoughts were revolving about this powerful evidence of God's Providence, while the wind and rain beat on his forehead and his hollow cheeks.

For fourteen days the ship had been a prey to the waves which had driven it wandering across the Ionian Sea (called at that time the Sea of Adria) until, on the fourteenth night, the crew had the impression that they were nearing land. They took a sounding of the sea and found the depth to be only twenty fathoms; they sounded again after a short distance and found the depth to be only fifteen fathoms. There was great fear that the wind would drive the ship against the rocks and, to avoid this, they threw out four anchors at the stern in order to hold the ship steady, and waited for dawn.

The mariners had such fear of a crash against the rocks that on the pretext of throwing out an anchor from the bow of the ship, they lowered the lifeboat with the intention of getting away, deserting the ship and the passengers. As usual it was Paul who discovered the plot, and once more proved that he had not lost his head like the majority of his companions. He notified the centurion and the military escort. "Be on your guard, because if these men do not remain on the ship, there is no rescue for you." At this warning the soldiers cut the rope of the lifeboat, which fell loose on the waves and was lost.

At the first rays of light Paul went again to those poor men to encourage them and to rouse them from the sad state of apathy into which fear and suffering had plunged them, and he begged them to take some food. Because of nausea and despair, they had been fasting during the fourteen days, expecting the end. Again he reassured them that not so much as a hair of their heads should perish. It must have been an astounding sight to see that little Jew, so careless about himself, taking care of each upset stomach, encouraging each desperate soul, and giving to them all revived hope.

He, following the example of the Lord Jesus, gave even to the simple act of eating the ceremony of thanksgiving. In the presence of them all he took some bread, gave thanks to the Lord, broke it and began to eat. The men were encouraged and they too began to eat bread. Afterwards, in order to lighten the ship still more, they threw the whole cargo of wheat into the sea.

When day dawned they saw before them a shore line which they did not recognize; nevertheless, having spied a bay with a beach they planned to steer the ship towards it. Lifting the anchors and loosening the rudder, they unfurled the sails, maneuvering against the wind. Notwithstanding all their efforts, the bow struck a sandbar and remained fast, while the fury of the waves, beating on the ship, soon demolished it, piece by piece.

The wreck was complete. The captain probably called out, "Let each one save himself who can." The land could be seen not so far away, but the churning waves and a cold rain made rescue work dangerous. The soldiers, who were responsible for the prisoners, thought they would free themselves of all blame by hastily killing their charges; since, if the prisoners escaped, their punishment would have been death. The centurion, who was a man with some heart, and who had, during the terrible crossing, come to know by experience Paul's superior gifts of mind, in order to save Paul, prevented the soldiers from touching the prisoners. He commanded these latter to swim and to try to reach the land. Those who could swim did so, he saved others by planks or on the shoulders of the men of the rascally crew. It was as Paul had foretold: all were saved and all reached the land.

The Island of Malta, and on to Rome

They landed on the island of Malta. Thus the island came to know the Gospel and its Apostle by means of a shipwreck. This island was far distant from the continent. Navigation was difficult and Malta had no particular importance of its own, the inhabitants being poor fishermen and farmers who led a miserable life. They were good simple people and hospitable. When they saw the struggling survivors of the disaster, they brought to them all the help they could provide. First of all, the inhabitants lighted a fire to warm the mariners, for they were drenched by the rain and the sea, and numb with cold.

All through the frightful adventure, the Apostle had shown a marked superiority of spirit, but not the least shadow of pride had ever entered his mind. His whole being was completely given to the service of God, and in no lesser measure it was given to the service of his brethren. He was among the first to help gather bundles of branches to feed the fire. It happened that as he dropped one of his bundles on the flames, a viper jumped out and clung to one of Paul's hands.

When the islanders saw the reptile hanging from his fist, being superstitious, they exclaimed, "Surely this man is a murderer, for though he has escaped the sea, justice does not let him live." They saw that Paul was a prisoner, and being attacked by a viper, he must, at the very least—so they thought—be an assassin. The natural sense of justice in these people (and it is in many such) was translated into a deduction of rough simplicity.

They stood looking at Paul, expecting to see him swell and fall dead under the quick action of the poison that spared no one. On the contrary, Paul shook off the viper into the fire and remained standing there peacefully warming himself. Then, seeing that he was not dying, they thought he must be a god. The truth is, that Paul, even in the rain, with drenched clothes, always had the Apostolate in mind, and he knew that nothing could make a greater impression on these simple people than a miracle. So it is clear that even vipers can be of service in the work of Evangelization.

Just as Jesus would have done, Paul helped the poor islanders with miraculous deeds and by curing diseases. Since he observed no class distinctions, he also worked a miracle of cure for the father of the richest man on the island.

This man was a certain Publius who gave honorable hospitality to Paul and his companions for three days. Many gifts and attentions came from other people also whom he had benefited. The cold north wind having now been succeeded by a warm wind from the south, they made ready to depart. A ship was found which had wintered on the island. The good folk provided them with all necessary things, and thus Paul's presence among them proved to be a blessing to the very last. The departure took place, it seems, in February of the year 61.

The ship was from Alexandria, and sailed under the protecting sign of Castor and Pollux, patrons of navigation. It stopped three days at Syracuse, then moving along the eastern coast of Sicily, came to Reggio in the Straits; in two days more, the wind being favorable, they came to Puteoli.

At this place there was a flourishing community of Christians who welcomed Paul and his companions with much affection, begging them to stay a week. They knew of some of Paul's letters, and had heard so much of his bold enterprises in the Apostolate that it seemed like a dream to be able to listen to him for seven whole days. And he experienced once more the solidarity in the Mystical Body of Christ, the Church.

In some way the news from Puteoli [1] reached Rome; and when Paul and his escort were on the road thither, groups of the faithful came to meet him as far as the Forum of Appius, on the majestic Appian Way, forty miles from the city. Perhaps they were Christians converted by Peter, and anxious to know this other giant of the Apostolate. Their faith was known throughout all Christian Communities, and Paul yielded himself with serenity to their affection, thanking God that he could see their faces and experience the brotherhood of Christ in such a distant place.

The Forum of Appius was a post relay station and, like all such places, a slum, full of a filthy conglomeration of taverns and narrow streets where stagnant water spread its dampness into the miserable houses. From these streets came the noise of the discordant voices of drunken cart-drivers, stable-keepers and soldiers.

The kindly brethren gave him the sense of feeling at home with them, as they accompanied Paul on his walk, that peculiar step of the prisoner bound with chains. They moved slowly along the stony consular way to the conquest of the city. The chains, old age, and the tribulations he had suffered, made his steps painful but never lessened his determination to go on. A centurion, four or five legionaries, a group of poor laborers accompanying a prisoner and surrounded by other prisoners, made up the cortege. It was so common a sight that women in their houses, or men on muleback, seldom bothered to look as they passed by.

It was along this beautiful highway, paved with huge black slabs of stone, running in a direct line from Terracina to Rome, that the

[1] The modern town of Puzzuoli.

triumphant legions came, the consuls, and the emperors, to receive the honors of a triumph at Rome, while behind them came the pack animals loaded with their booty, and the prisoners with hands and feet in chains, their backs bare to show the marks of the floggings.

The Appian Way was the queen among all highways and became more sumptuous as it neared the city of Rome. It stretched for miles between two rows of cypress trees, and prepared the eye for the great sight of the city itself, the center of the world. Along its length, among the cypress, were those white marble monuments, gleaming in the sun, with their inscription lists telling of victories and glorious achievements; the names and titles of notable persons; now and then statues of idols and busts of ancestors, as if these last were to witness the passing pageant of life from some window in Eternity. It was a road that made one think of Rome and of death.

As all great people do, the Romans cared for the bodies of the dead and preserved their memory by putting their last resting places along her beautiful highways, under the transparent arch of the sky among the flowers and greenery in order to have her dead remembered. Round mausoleums of red bricks or sheathed in marble rose up like fortresses with ramparts and towers, real houses of death—or, shall we say, resistance to death? Before Christ came, the world was obsessed by a fear of death. It was conscious of sin for which death is the price; but that little man in chains was the bearer of tidings of liberation. He would proclaim a definite victory over death.

All around and beyond there stretched an expanse of bleak plain, broken here and there by marshes; on the left, in the distance, the sea; on the right, the plain ended in groves of willows, clumps of ferns at the foot of the Lepini [2] mountains whose villages and temples could be seen in the distance. Stagnant water, full of croaking frogs, invaded broken places in the consular road so that travellers had to wade through the water almost to their knees.

Where the Appian Way began to descend for a level stretch, if Paul had stopped for a few minutes to look and admire (the escort

---

[2] Lepini—a continuation of the Appenines.

would never refuse a request to gaze upon such delightful and superb beauty), he would have seen the road ahead ascending a hill and ending at its top in a slender spire piercing the blue sky, narrowed in by a mortuary chapel on one side and on the other by a solitary pine. Paul's ardent mind imagined that it continued even to the Heavenly Sion, to which end all his travels had been leading him for years and years—the place of his eternal meeting with his Master and Saviour.

When he turned his eyes to the right or the left as he walked, Paul shook his head sadly that people could be so vain or so foolish as to wall up ashes and lifeless bodies within stones or columns of stones. When the resurrection of the dead takes place, these stone ramparts will break open as easily as the pomegranates whose green stems could be seen among the hedges. After the same manner as the pomegranates open, so the graves will open at the resurrection, and future men will blossom forth as new creatures ready for reward or punishment. The spectacle of that imperial road and funereal way revealed a reverence for the human body. Such reverence illumined by the light of the Gospel and made complete by faith, would have transformed the body into a temple of the Holy Spirit! The body would be like a chalice to receive the Blood of the Son of God. It would be an edifice from which would flash out the perfections of the Eternal Builder, God Himself.

And behold, some of the faithful came to meet him the following day at the "Three Taverns." They had started the day before and had walked all night in order to welcome him there. St. Luke relates that when Paul saw them he thanked the Lord and was filled with new joy and courage. He realized how far the Word of God had travelled, and that in Rome also a fruitful work was being done. He entered the city through the Capena Gate, walking between the soldiers and the faithful; in the eyes of the Roman Institution, he was an accused; in the eyes of the Roman Church, he was a conqueror.

At Rome, where the Christian Community was composed mostly of converted pagans, Paul was already known for his Apostolate among the Gentiles and for his letter to that Church. He also had personal friends and relatives who lived in Rome. The Jews frequently travelled from one business center to another. Perhaps some of these who knew him came to greet him at the gateway of the city. Paul must have been deeply moved to tears at seeing and meeting all these brethren, known or unknown to him, but in whom the devotion to the Gospel was solid and upright against all the influences of heresy. With transports of joy he thanked God, that being now in their midst, he had reached one of the principal goals of his travels.

If Paul's arrival had chanced to be on a sunny day with the limpid blue sky of a Roman spring smiling down upon him, he must have been dazzled as he lifted his eyes, full of keen interest in the spectacle of life before him. There were the unending stretches of little houses closely packed together, the narrow streets crowded with people and with the din of labor; the imposing marble monuments (looking so strong and secure), and the high palaces that crowned the hills.

As the cortege neared the center of the city, Paul found himself in the midst of a curious crowd of magistrates in cap and gown; of soldiers in shining armor. Then they reached the *miliarium aureum,* the gilded column erected by Augustus from which point radiated Roman roads to all parts of Italy. Paul must have been filled with admiration and surprise at the evidence of so much power and with the outward show of wealth. Any ordinary man coming from the rural districts would have felt small and insignificant in the midst of the great amphitheaters, the great basilicas and arches of the Forum, the comings and goings of gilded chariots, luxurious litters with their numerous escorts; and an ordinary prisoner would have felt his last bit of courage oozing away. On the contrary, Paul admired all those marvels of human achievement and saw in them the genius of God. If he felt his own nothingness more keenly, he was also keenly conscious of the power of the Lord Whom he served and for Whom he wore those chains.

He never doubted but that the city would be won for Christ—but won only through bloodshed and persecutions. The barrier of idolatry would fall, and the whole Empire become a realm of Christian justice. The prisoner Paul had high ambitions. He knew Christ could—and that He would—make that great metropolis the center of His Kingdom upon earth.

Certainly by temperament and because of the nature of the Gospel message, Paul would prefer Rome to Athens. The monuments of Rome testified that her subjugation of nations had been by force and by power, but Athens only bewildered men to no purpose by her monuments to human intellectuality. Paul found in the Romans far more spontaneity and more sincerity.

So the strange procession, tired from its long march, traversed the dingy streets crowded with artisans, laborers, slaves and idlers, which gave the thickly populated city an oriental aspect. In the midst of noisy voices Paul went up the street between the Quirinal and the Esquiline hills, towards the Praetorian Camp. And there finally, he halted in a prison.

CHAPTER VIII

PAUL IN ROME.

A.D. 61-63

In the Praetorium

Peter the fisherman and Paul the tentmaker are in Rome to conquer the city for Christ. In paradoxical contrast to these two is the sovereign Nero who ruled the world from Rome. At that time the Caesar in purple and the two barbarians [1] in their poor tunics were personages in a most powerful drama, out of which the new Christian Romanism would unfold.

If Nero in his chariot had chanced to pass by and had turned his eyes towards those two orientals,[2] bent with age and poorly dressed, he would have felt the nausea that these insignificant people from the East usually gave him. They were crowding into the slums of the city, and this annoyed him. If Poppaea Sabina, a mistress of Nero, had passed by in her perfumed litter, with five hundred she-asses at the head of her cortege, and had chanced to cast her beautiful eyes (which the celebrated poets of the times sang of in their verses), at these two bearded faces, especially at Paul with his sore eyes, she, too, might have felt the need of her bottles of perfume and directed her gaze to some vision less repulsive.

As they walked along the stone-paved imperial road, their poverty and simplicity clashed in every way with Nero's pride and exaggerated vanity. The marble monuments and military show on all sides helped to feed his pride and testified to the greatness of Rome's sov-

---

[1] Barbarian is a loose term used to denote anyone who was neither Greek nor Roman.
[2] Oriental here refers to people from the East, which included Palestine.

ereign. Nero was the comedian Emperor, who considered the Empire a stage and his subjects a coerced and applauding audience. His vanity and pomp were increasing from year to year, fed by his weak oratory and his mediocre poems; his stentorian exhibitions of singing alternated with his periods of bloodshed. In the year 59, he had had his own mother, who had placed him on the throne as Emperor, assassinated in the midst of orgies and intrigues.

Meanwhile, the influence of counsellors whom she had given him, Burrhus Africanus a soldier, and Seneca a pagan philosopher, was diminishing through the evil plans of the freedman Tigellinus, a man without scruples, who made use of Nero's prevailing sense of fear and his weakness for hypocritical praise. Divine Providence thus ruled that salvation should come to Rome in the hour of her greatest depravity: that is, in the hour of her greatest spiritual need. And so the two Apostles were sent to oppose Nero. The Apostles, exponents of spiritual things, were brought into opposition with the blind exponents of brute force; but because of that very fact, viewed from Eternity and in the light of history revealed by the centuries, they were victorious.

In this Babylon, as Peter called it, Paul had arrived to ask justice of Nero, the most wicked of men. Because Rome was the most needy city, the Fatherhood of God had assigned to her the Princes of the Apostles, who outwardly had nothing princely about them. So it happened that Paul was consigned to the prefect of the Praetorium who was Burrhus Africanus.

The extraordinary qualities of the Apostle Paul had won for him the admiration of Julian the centurion; and the report of Festus presented him as one accused only of bickerings concerning the Jewish religion. For this reason the prefect assigned him to a private house where, guarded by a soldier, Paul could have a certain amount of liberty to go about the city and to receive friends and acquaintances. There he settled down as well as he could with the assistance of the faithful of Rome. It can easily be imagined with what eagerness many of his old co-workers came to kiss his chains; friends like Aquila and Priscilla, who had come from Ephesus to Rome; Ampliatus and Stachys, and his relatives; many others came who had heard his letter at the meetings. The more his letter was read, the more riches it revealed.

Peter was missing, absent, no doubt, because of the duties of his Apostolate which called him here and there. Paul, who never thought of himself at any time, turned at once to his Apostolate. First he called a meeting of the heads of the eight or nine Synagogues scattered about Rome. It was always his conviction that he must announce the Gospel to the sons of Israel first; to his own people his heart always turned with affection.

The Elders came and Paul addressed them in a humble and affectionate discourse. "Brethren, although I have done nothing against the people or against the Law or the customs of our fathers, yet I was handed over as a prisoner in chains to the Romans at Jerusalem."

Paul concluded, "Not that I had any charge to bring against my nation. This then, is why I asked to see you and speak with you. For it is because of the hope of Israel that I am wearing this chain." The hope of Israel was the Messiah; and Paul could have revealed the Messiah to them. The members of the Synagogues prudently answered, "We ourselves have received no letters about you from Judea, and no one of the brethren upon arrival has reported or spoken any evil of you. But we want to hear from you later what your views are; for as regards this sect, we know that everywhere it is the subject of opposition."

The Apostle spent the entire day speaking to them about Moses and the Prophets, proving that the one and the others meant Jesus Who is the Messiah. The Jews did not accept Paul's message, nor did they agree among themselves on this vital point of their whole faith.

As usual Paul, having done his duty, admonished them, "Well did the Holy Spirit speak through Isaias the prophet to our fathers, saying:

" 'Go to this people and say:
With the ear you will hear and will not understand;
And seeing you will see and will not perceive.
For the heart of this people has become gross,
And with their ears they have been hard of hearing,
And their eyes they have shut;
Lest perhaps they should see with their eyes,
and hear with their ears,
and understand with their heart,
and turn back,
and I should heal them.'

"Be it know to you therefore that this salvation of God has been sent to the Gentiles, and they will listen to it."

Some believed, agreeing that in the Crucified and Risen Christ all their faith in the promises had been fulfilled. Others could not be persuaded, and they went away talking the matter over, down the dark, narrow streets and into the little houses so poorly lighted by a lantern. These hovels composed the poor part of Rome built of bricks.

Neronian justice moved slowly. Nero was bored at the tribunals; he preferred to be at the races or at those performances where he could show himself off and win some applause which, in his vanity, he never recognized as insincere and a sham. Compared with these personal satisfactions, the cases of the prisoners awaiting justice lost all their importance.

Also, the reports from Palestine were late in coming. Now that their worst enemy was out of the way, the Sadducees and other leaders forgot about Paul for a while; they were absorbed by other local political intrigues. So Paul remained for two years in his little house under the *"custodia militaris,"* a chain fastened to his right wrist with the other end fastened to the left arm of the soldier who had charge of him. Paul was fettered, but his speech was not.

His little dwelling was open day and night; whoever wished could enter freely to hear him tell of the Kingdom of God. The Word of God went forth from a prison in regal fashion. Paul's chains only enhanced the Apostolate with new luster and glow; within the Praetorium the officers and guards knew that he bore them for Christ; consequently they learned who Christ was, and more than one embraced the Gospel.

Outside the Praetorium, many brethren, seeing the courage and patience with which Paul served the Lord, gained new confidence, overcoming their fear and excessive prudence in announcing Christ to a pagan world. Also within Caesar's household, Paul gained new friends among the slaves and freedmen; or rather, he gained new friends for Christ. Later, these would render him special service in distant churches. As always, even among the carriers of the Gospel message, there arose not so much heresies as petty rivalries which could amount to small divisions. (Who knows? Narrow and ill-intentioned minds may have found pretexts for rivalry even in the presence of Simon Peter or of Paul of Tarsus?) And the Apostle who wanted unity grieved at this.

His great heart was filled with sympathy for everyone and, with his far-sighted intelligence, which looked ahead into the future, he was pleased that in any way, through pretext or through loyalty, Christ should be announced. Christ must come before all else.

Although he was so absorbed in the work of constructing the Kingdom of God, the Church, he took personal care of the Churches he had started, sending letters to them and receiving messengers. Timothy worked with him, also Clement and others. Aristarchus was such a close companion that he was considered a prisoner. Then there was Mark, the cousin of Barnabas, to whom Paul now gave his full esteem since Mark had proved himself faithful and active in the Apostolate; and there was Jesus, called the "Just," and Luke his "most dear physician," and Demas, who later left him. These and others not only comforted him and helped him but were used by him as secretaries and messengers of confidence. From that narrow cell there came and went a perfect stream of workers with the message of the Gospel, while Christians came to visit him from all parts of Italy, Greece, Macedonia and Asia. They came to seek comfort in his presence, to hear his teaching, and to seek counsel. Few periods in Paul's life were as intensely active as this one was when his prison cell was converted into a small ecclesiastical court.

Those of the Praetorium saw all this and while they did not understand many of these things they merely shook their heads; perhaps others admired, while some grumbled. We may be very sure that some of the soldiers appointed to watch him became his sons in Christ, and the chain that bound one to the other was also the symbol of the unity in the Mystical Body of Christ, the Church.

There was a continual coming and going of humble people, who most of the time walked close to the walls, not daring to stare at the sumptuous palaces or at the trophies of a hundred victorious wars. The small, unimportant people of Rome lived then as now on state aid, persuaded that the labors and glories of their ancestors had won for them—their helpless descendants—the right to a pension, a provision of bread, and admission to the public games. They cared nothing at all for these seekers after Eternity and only saw in them a fanatic and illegal sect which sought to capture the good faith of miserable officials and men of arms, as so many other Asiatic superstitious cults had done. Those who knew something about the Christians did not spare their contempt for these insignificant little Jews who disagreed with the Synagogues, and they turned away from them in disgust.

Their worming in and out of their poor dwellings, Peter living at one end of the city and Paul at the other, served to let them pass more or less unobserved by official Rome. The square legions that entered the city with measured step through the great marble gates, carrying their signs of glory and power, meant much more to Rome. Seneca himself with his clear and penetrating mind would never have thought that those poor humble, human lives carried in them the elements of a glory and power that would transport the name of Rome much farther and higher than the legionaries had ever done, transfiguring the earthly symbols of glory into values above matter and changing the fear of Rome's power into a love for Rome.

Some civilians of a suspicious disposition saw revolutionary tendencies in those little groups that gathered apart, who did not accept the gods of the fatherland, of Caesar and of Rome; they could not believe that the Christians were not revolutionaries aiming at the acquisition of territories and at imperial changes.

And thus the two worlds, the new one humble and ascending, the old one bold and descending, were outwardly and for the moment intermingling, while the inner life of men was becoming irreparably different.

The Philippians Remember Paul

Little was needed for the prisoner's maintenance. Paul knew how to be contented in abundance or in indigence, and the faithful of Rome as well as the affectionate Macedonians provided for his needs. The Philippians, who had shown themselves so devoted to Paul from the beginning, sent him one of their most active and well deserving personalities in the Church, the generous Epaphroditus, who brought messages and gifts.

So Paul had the joy of experiencing how much he was still loved and, above all, followed by the Philippians, although the Judaizers had come down to them with their petulant opposition towards a spirituality that was for all men without limitations, while they, on the contrary, were willing to place the limits of salvation within their own race.

The presence of Epaphroditus reminded the Apostle of their common labor in spreading the Gospel and of his precious collaboration and fellowship in the struggle, so that his companionship rejoiced Paul greatly. This generous brother became seriously ill in Rome, causing great alarm to Paul and to the community of Philippi who feared to lose him. Paul gave him a care that was paternal; God had pity upon him and Epaphroditus, restoring the sick man to health.

Then Paul sent him back to the Church of Philippi, which was anxiously awaiting news, entrusting to him a letter steeped with affection, a letter which was rendered more precious because of his prestige as a prisoner. Paul wrote the letter in his own name, and in the name of Timothy, his "son," who had given himself up to the service of the Apostle as to a father.

Timothy was well known in Macedonia and in Achaia and seemed destined to substitute for the Apostle in many emergencies, for no one knew and shared Paul's sentiments so much as he did. At the present moment Paul needed Timothy to assist him in the developments of his own lawsuit, but as soon as things were settled, Paul promised to send him back to Philippi for the good of his children there.

Paul poured out his heart in his letter, telling his far-away children of the consolations and of the sufferings in his imprisonment, although these could in no way shake his faith. He had spoken to them so much about faith, and now in this trial he knew he would not be confounded and that Christ was honored in all his sufferings in the flesh. Thus, in his physical body, outwardly oppressed because of the Gospel, in reality a glorification was being realized, a "magnification" of Christ. The body, consecrated by sufferings endured for the Gospel, became in life or in death an instrument for the work of the Apostolate; if he died, he gained the glory of being with Christ forever. He, the Apostle, did not know which to choose: service for the brethren, or to labor for his own personal eternal profit. Such uncertainty shows that the Apostolate is self-dedication to the cause of Christ; it is the whole person given to Christ. On account of such a dedication, death and heaven on the one hand, sufferings and the labors of the Apostolate on the other, balance each other, both being one thing, *Christ.*

"For me to live is Christ, to die is gain."

Against the presumption of the circumcised Christians, Paul recalls to their minds in a few words the uselessness of the works of the Law, since salvation comes now through faith; therefore, true circumcision is that of the *spirit.* Well could he say this because he was himself circumcised, a Pharisee, an Israelite of the tribe of Benjamin, and formerly a persecutor of the Church; consequently he was more competent to speak on the subject of works according to the flesh than those who were half-Christian and half Mosaists.

These tore the Gospel to pieces; and in place of their works of discord, the prisoner of Christ recommends to the faithful unity in thoughts and sentiments based on humility and consequently bringing peace and joy. Persecution must never frighten them. Persecution brings harm to those who wage it but it brings great advantages to those who suffer it: through persecution the gift of faith is exercised and also the gift of suffering for Christ. Thus in sanctifying themselves, the Philippians become the light of the world and the glory of the Apostle who had made them what they were in the sight of God.

The conclusion of his letter is full of affectionate sadness, although he recommends joy to his children. In his solitude and in his chains he feels keenly the vanity and emptiness of the things of this world, while his soul is filled with an ardent longing for the heavenly life. He feels the futility of earthly cares, of doctrinal bickerings, of the works of the flesh, even of food and drink. Already he perceives his imminent meeting with the Lord and the decline of his life; stripped, as he is, of the world, he possesses all in Him Who has given him strength to bear all. Christ is all; all else is secondary, useless, and even harmful. The one thing of importance is to prepare one's self by a life humble, chaste and full of Apostolic activity.

Therefore Paul recommends Syntyche and Evodia to give up the individual and particular opinions that separated them and to be united in the love of Jesus. What are all these doctrinal discussions in the face of the unity of the Mystical Body? He asks a fellow laborer, a relative perhaps, to help him in this enterprise of promoting concord and unity. And he says all this without any shadow of reproach because these disciples at Philippi have always been so faithful, first in working with him in the Apostolate, secondly in sending him gifts, and now in sharing his sufferings; so he has no complaint to make.

On the contrary, he has every reason to rejoice, since that Christian Community followed so well in his footsteps. In his salutations, he includes the disciples—the Saints of Rome and, in particular, the stewards of the imperial household who serve Nero with the heart of Christ.

The Fugitive Slave

It was well known throughout Christendom that no one ever entered the Apostle's miserable dwelling in vain. Besides the two greatest of the Apostles in Rome, Peter and Paul, there was also the attraction of the marvelous city and the imperial court. It is then quite possible that small groups of pilgrims from Europe and Asia arrived to see Rome, but the greatest attraction Rome held for the Christians was the two Apostles. A fugitive slave, knowing this, fled to Paul for protection and salvation, the slave Onesimus.

In the ancient world, a runaway slave was only a wandering dog. Anyone had the right (if not the duty) to stone him or to put a rope about his neck. He was an outlaw, against whom customs and the law were most severe; so much so, that when taken to prison, he could be crucified or tortured at the will of his master, or made a slave to serve the one who found him.

Onesimus was a pagan slave who had run away from a Christian master, Philemon of Colossae. Paul had never visited Colossae in his travels through Phrygia, but he had sent some competent missionaries, among them the trusted Epaphras. A flourishing Church had been organized which claimed to be indebted to Paul and was most devoted to him. The same is to be said of the neighboring Church in Laodicea. When the Christians heard that Paul was a prisoner in Rome, the two Churches sent Epaphras as the representative head of the Communities, to see him and to give him an account of themselves.

Before Epaphras, who was perhaps the bishop, got there, the slave Onesimus arrived in Rome with his burden of odium and fear. The instinct that urged him to seek salvation urged him to seek Paul's hovel. The entreaties of friends or of any others would be of little use with his master, and the law would be merciless on his poor flesh. Paul had all control over a Christian, and so, in the whole Empire, the slave trusted no one but the prisoner Paul.

Paul received Onesimus with ready and lavish tenderness. All his prophetic vehemence vanished when there was a question of some poor creature, broken by misery and trodden down by ignorance. He gave eager and intense care full of pity to the poor slave and treated him as a son just returned to his father. He gave him lodging, food and peace; while, at the same time, he took care to cleanse his conscience. Paul instructed him, baptized him, and the slave—outcast in the ancient society, only a tool for work in the pagan social order, this object of the Roman citizen's right—now received one of the greatest privileges that can come to a Christian: that of being born again in Christ by Paul himself—and Paul in chains for Christ.

Having been made a Christian, Onesimus was transformed into a brother equal to Philemon, the rich master of Colossae, with whom through baptism, he now shared in the organic unity of the Mystical Body of Christ, the Church. Paul, the Apostle, would wish to keep him with himself, to aid him in his numerous duties, but Paul, the Roman citizen, would not act against the Roman law, and above all, seek to profit in any way by his friend Philemon of Colossae without first consulting him. Therefore Paul deemed it more opportune to send Onesimus back to his master with a commendatory letter in which he presented the slave as a Christian, as Paul's own son;

in fact, as though he were Paul himself. Paul used all his rights as a spiritual superior with authority towards Philemon, a subordinate Christian, so that all resentments and the question of rights should be put aside. The master is asked to receive the slave into his household under new relationships. In the letter, short and pithy, Paul offers to make good all the damage caused by Onesimus in his flight, although the master is reminded that he is debtor to Paul for his own eternal life.

The Apostle, always so affectionate with everybody, becomes more tender with emotion and anxiety for this servant whom the law considered merely a "thing" (*res*), an instrument, a tool, a bit of domestic cattle. With his own hand Paul writes the letter of recommendation, although his arm was painful and heavy from the chain tied to his wrist. To give the letter more efficacy, and to make the outcome more sure, he sends the slave back with Tychicus, the bearer of the great letters to the Churches of Asia.

The letter of recommendation was well received and kept as a treasure of unique value by the wealthy master. It was circulated among the Churches and has reached us, while many other letters, more precious from a theological and disciplinary viewpoint, have been lost. It has softened the lot of many servants and taught masters their relationship of brotherhood with those under them.

In this letter we see Paul, a prisoner, giving orders with an authority superior to that of a consul in his charge, because it is not supported by any coercive power. We see a Society with its organs and functions, acting on the minutest details of life; molding life's conditions in the very bosom of imperial society. This was something the Roman State could not tolerate, since it never allowed the right of associations or unions, and did not recognize any form of unity except the one centered in the Emperor.

The Contaminations of the First Gnostics

Epaphras had now arrived from proconsular Asia. He was, so it seems, the founder and evangelizer of the Churches of Colossae,

Laodicea, and Hierapolis, one of the most intelligent persons and one whom Paul trusted and made use of in extending the Apostolate in those distant places where he could not go. Paul eagerly desired that the evangelization should reach to the ends of the earth; he, servant of the Gospel and of souls, considered Epaphras a fellow-servant, vowed like himself to the service of Christ in souls.

Epaphras informed him of the last attempts made by false teachers and prophets to introduce a compromise with Judaism and an upstart gnostic sophistry. In Hellenic Asia, especially, there were many currents of false mysticism, contamination from ideologies and cloudy speculations, which were dignified by the name of mystico-philosophy. These were permeating everywhere. The Roman State made use of these various gods and the beliefs of various peoples to build up a pyramidal hierarchy with Caesar at the apex; the same effort was being made to blend all religious philosophy with idolatry, mystical interpretations, and the superstitions of Egypt and Asia. It was not surprising, therefore, if efforts were made to draw Christianity into that mixture, and especially so in Phrygia, a land that was fertile in dreamers, visionaries and muddy mysticism.

Consequently, many Christians began to fear, in Christianity, a moral-religious revolution; and there were many social reasons which gave rise to worries and persecutions. An avalanche of reaction was imminently threatening the faithful. Some sought to submerge Christianity in Judaism, even in Mithraism, or to distill it into some gnostic philosophy. In other words, they were disposed to annul the simplicity of the Gospel in order to save their own lives. Many of the contaminations of those days, as they are also at the present time, mean simply this: Christianity is highly dangerous when it is whole and one, as they say in Greek, *Catholic*. When mutilated and broken apart into fragments, it is harmless, or practically so.

At this time, the Judaizers had brought in some strange doctrines concerning the angels; they filled the universe with celestial creatures whose power was superior even to that of Christ. These were doctrines germinated from the apocryphal Jewish literature; from Persian influences, from some special books of the Essenes (Jewish monks) and, above all, from the studious efforts of Philo of Alexandria who tried to transfer Plato's ideas to the heaven of Moses, transforming all into divine powers.

The primitive gnosticism of Simon Magus, against which Simon Peter had protested, attributed the creation of the world to the work of the angels, grouped into many complicated hierarchies. In this way the first vague mixture of doctrines and myths began, which later was systematized by Valentinus and other Gnostics. Thus was perpetrated a usurpation of attributes which Paul, with his keen vision, foresaw would end in sacrilegious destruction of the great concept of Jesus Christ; it was another destruction of the Redemption through His Blood, as the first had been. In fact, the Gnostics who succeeded Valentinus, while taking God from among men, substituted a fantastic genealogy of intermediary beings for God, in this way annulling the work of the only Mediator, Christ. They ended by attributing Redemption to the angels or Aeons, of whom one was Jesus.

It was a vague and complicated heresy, and took root especially in Asia, where later the author of the Apocalypse was to condemn it. "And I, John, am he who heard and saw these things. And when I heard and saw, I fell down to worship at the feet of the angel who showed me these things. And he said to me, Thou must not do that. I am a fellow creature of thine, and of thy brethren the prophets, and of those who keep the words of this book. Worship God."

It was not, then, the prison that hindered the Gospel so much as heresy, which like corrosives was decomposing it by eating into it. In the last year of his life Paul was faced with the problem of this and other contaminations of the Gospel in many parts of Asia where heresies were propagated from large centers like Ephesus. Many simple Christians allowed themselves to be deceived by "fables and unending genealogies." A specious attempt was made to overthrow the "mystery of God the Father and His Son Jesus Christ" with the products of fantasy, wrongly called philosophy.

There was real reason for discouragement. Paul had already warned the priests at Miletus; but his faith knew no surrender. With a flaming zeal, he dictated three letters; one to the Laodiceans, one (an encyclical) to the Ephesians and near-by Churches, and one to the Colossians, entrusting them to Tychicus who faithfully delivered them. The letter to the Church of Laodicea has been lost; it may be the same as that addressed to the Ephesians, like the one for the Colossians, and to all those who had never seen his "face in the flesh." One can tell by these letters how closely the Apostle followed their doings and how much he knew about them.

In the letter to the Colossians (written in his own name and that of Timothy), Paul attacked the "cult of the angels." He begins by re-etablishing the fundamental doctrines of Christianity: the mystery of the God-Christ, Head of the Church, His Body; the first-born of all creatures; Creator of the world, of angels and of men, and therefore superior to them. He reconciled by His Blood heaven and earth; the fullness of all things, the beginning and the end, the Exemplary Cause; and by His death on the Cross, the Saviour of all men. This is the "mystery" to which the faith of all believers corresponds, and it is an essential condition for salvation.

In this idea of the absolute and universal primacy of Christ is true knowledge and the spiritual intelligence that makes men "perfect."

The other science that seems to be ashamed of Redemption through the Blood of Christ, the universal reconciliation achieved by means of a body of flesh which passed through death, is vain and empty speech; it does not even touch the "mystery" of Christ which is the depository of all knowledge.

The Church in which Christ lives is also a body, His Body, to Whose Life the faithful bring their contributions of sufferings and sacrifices, and they fulfill those things that were wanting in the sufferings of Christ. In His Body dwells the plenitude of the Divinity, (one may say that Divinity has taken flesh in Him); and since the Church is His Mystical Body, one may deduce that in the Church Divinity is embodied.

Now these eternal attributes of Christ, His vital Power and our faith in Him were attacked with the most subtile human reasonings by those who favored a new moon, and the Sabbath, and food and drink; those who, while pretending to construct a religion more elevated and spiritual, were in reality substituting the works of the flesh for the eternal spirit. In the past all such things were meant to foreshadow the reality—Christ Who was to come.

Those works were of no avail in the New Dispensations. We had been set free from the entanglements of flesh and blood, and from race. There is no more Greek or Jew, circumcised or uncircumcised, barbarian, or learned freemen, or slave. Christ is all in all. This is the revolution of joy, while the false teachers and philosophers are the extinguishers of light. They limit horizons, mummify peoples into corpses. One must be deaf to their arguments and live in sanctity; in the true spirit of liberty in God, singing hymns to Him in the heart to hush all those enticements that would enslave the spirit.

As for news of himself, the Apostle has charged Tychicus, his fellow prisoner, and Onesimus "his most dear and faithful brother" (no longer a fugitive and unfaithful slave) to give all details. In the conclusion, there are many salutations which show how familiarly the workers in the Gospel were known to each other in those distant communities. Salutations were sent to the Colossians from Aristarchus, a companion in prison through love for Paul, and Mark, the cousin of Barnabas; also Jesus, called the "Justus," and Epaphras the "slave of Jesus," Luke and Demas.

A special greeting was sent to Nymphas, a Christian in whose house a "church" used to convene; and the deacon Archippus was admonished to fulfill faithfully his ministry received from the Lord. At the end Paul signs his own personal salutations in his own hand. He is so human, he begs them to remember his chains: an Apostolic warning more eloquent than words.

The Letter to the Ephesians

Tychicus was charged with the delivery of a letter to the Ephesian Christian Community. He was to land at Ephesus and from there proceed to Colossae, Laodicea and Hierapolis to have Paul's messages read in the Churches. Paul had expressed the desire that the letter destined for the Colossians should be read in Laodicea also, and then exchanged. In both places the needs and dangers were the same, and his love for both was equally abundant. The letter to the Ephesians was in the same tenor, only more elaborate since it was sent to a Church, or probably, on account of its encyclical character, to many Churches, so full of Hellenic culture and therefore exposed to more dangers. They were made up of so many divergent elements. The Church of Ephesus had been generated in Christ by Paul, and at the risk of his life. He still bore on his body the scars of his "struggle with wild beasts," and the thought of that city was often in his mind.

This time Paul writes in his own hand only, because the care of those disciples, as well as their Christian formation, depended wholly upon him. It is for them that he reviews the Mystery of the Redemption through the Blood of Christ, and of their predestination as adopted sons of God, Who gives the "spirit of wisdom" which is one and the same as the "Spiritual Wisdom" by which He is known. Before their spiritual vision Paul reviews all the titles of the Redeemer, Who sits at the right hand of God the Father; above all the choirs of Angels, above all Principalities and Powers, Virtues and Dominations; above all and any title that could ever be conferred.

Christ has made sinners to live again; that is, those who were dead under the power and sway of the devil, the "prince of the powers of the air." Christ is now our peace and our life. This life is realized in the Church; and Paul, with many variations, brings before the eyes of his distant readers the ecclesiastical actuality in which they are reborn through Baptism. Christ is the Head of the Church which is His Body and contains the fullness of plenitude of Him. Thanks to such an incorporation, the Ephesians who believed, being dead to sin, are restored with Christ, made to live in Christ by the wonderful effects of grace.

Grace, a gift of God, has lifted them from paganism (where they lacked even the hope of the Redeemer) to this new life in Christ and with Christ. Paul is deeply moved when he speaks of the prodigious gift of God which has demolished the partition that separated the Gentiles from the Israelites; grace has been won for them by the Blood of Christ. The Gentiles are now an important part of His Spiritual Kingdom. All that had separated them from the Jews, and had been the cause of discord, was now dissolved, and both people are reconciled into the Body, the Church. The Gentiles are no more strangers but fellow citizens with all the saints; they were once in darkness, and are now full of light. They were lost, and now they are a part of the Church, the new Temple of the Lord built on the foundations of the prophets and Apostles, having as corner-stone Christ Jesus Himself.

All this has been obtained through the Crucifixion, in which all enmities have been crucified with Christ. The Cross unifies all, and stands as the meeting point. This general reunion of humanity, formerly torn into two parts, flashes before one in the brief sentences of the Apostle to the Gentiles as he recalls it to the minds of the Ephesians. They lived in a city which was both a meeting point and a separating point of the two groups, Gentiles and Jews.

Paul is himself moved by this loving miracle of a universal reconstruction, of a unity and plenitude in which all divisions and exclusiveness, all differences and ignorances are removed and annulled. He kneels down to pray that God may dwell in their hearts by faith, so that, understanding this love of Christ, "the love of the knowledge of Christ," they may be made perfect in the fullness of God.

The Cross unifies the Hebrews and the pagans; it makes of them a new organism which lives by charity, by faith, and by hope; and not by death, or by the works of the flesh.

God wishes men to be an imitator of Him, and consequently aim at living in unity, peace and concord. "One Lord, one faith, one Baptism, one God and Father of us all." And the many different missions, or chrisms as Paul calls them, must not be a cause of dissension or rivalry, but a means for co-operation in the upbuilding of unity which culminates in Christ and through Christ. Unity is a Divine Gift from God, therefore it is very essential to the life of faith.

From this molding of each class into one body only, whose Head is Christ, from this theological actuality, there develops an immediate series of social obligations. When this consciousness of being members one of another has been clarified in the faithful, their relations cannot be other than those of perfect charity and fraternity.

The order of charity must reign not only in the spirit of each Christian, or within the Church, but in all situations and circumstances; whence will follow a series of obligations towards all classes of people with whom one has social contact: duties of works and of words. The influence of charity will be possible only when one is remodelled in a personal, intimate way according to Christ in purity, truth, and charity. It is the practice of these obligations towards one's self, towards other men, towards God, that makes Christian life such a continual warfare.

Certainly Paul never thought that Christian life could be limited within domestic walls, or within the bosom of the Church. Christianity is a life that embraces all the hours of the day, all the thoughts of the mind, all the actions of the body; it concerns the individual, and the whole collective order of men. Unity will be perfect when all are brought back to Christ, not only the Gentiles and Jews, but all men and women; the soul with the body, doctrines and works, earth with heaven.

This synthesis came with the Blood from Christ's Body, and is realized anew and unceasingly in His Mystical Body which is the Church. The new man is entirely new, not only in an interior way, for Christianity contains in itself all and sums up the entire circle of life; it excludes nothing but sin, that is death.

In concluding his letter, Paul the prisoner recommends courage and perseverance in the struggle against the powers of this world, which are the spirits of darkness, and all the evil forces allied with them. With this thought in mind Paul alludes especially to the infernal Powers of Hell. He sees the signs of their persecutions upon earth and exhorts each person to prepare himself to resist by practicing virtue, prayer, and good works.

CHAPTER IX

PAUL AND SENECA

A Comparison

Into Paul's prison cell there came daily many brethren from Rome and elsewhere. They flocked to him as to one who gave out a great flame of sanctity; and if his letters thrill us and inspire us after nineteen centuries, what must his spoken word have done to those who listened to him? We can well imagine that his spoken word had still greater life and power accompanied, as it was, with his expressive gestures, so indicative of a life burning with zeal and an influence strengthened by his chains and the stigmata. No one could see those eyes, which had looked at Christ in all His majestic glory and which had contemplated heaven for a short time, without being struck by their wonderful light.

Perhaps Seneca also had passed into that hovel; he liked to glean wisdom from the inferior classes of people; or perhaps some of Caesar's servants, who frequented Paul's company, took the Apostle to Seneca's palace. The philosopher was a friend of Burrhus, the prefect of the Praetorium, also a Stoic and the official on whom Paul depended. Perhaps Seneca and Burrhus talked together about the barbarian sophist who was propagating the knowledge of a God-Crucified, even at the cost of chains.

On the other hand, Paul was known in Corinth to Gallio, the Proconsul and brother of Seneca, who, returning to Rome, may have given witness in favor of the prisoner and, more probable still, may have spoken of him to his brother, the philosopher. According to an imaginary writing, friendship existed between the most illustrious philosopher of Rome in Nero's time and the great Apostle.

The philosophy of that period was largely Stoicism, in which in the past a few exegetes have pretended to see some analogy to Christianity. Not so long ago some imagined they saw a dependence of the Gospel on the Stoic philosophy; or, as it was said, Paul borrowed from Seneca (more rarely, Seneca from Paul). Seneca and Paul, were, however, the two greatest exponents at that time of the two highest systems of thought and life.

Now in fact there could be no such dependence of the Gospel upon Stoicism because, especially during the period of his imprisonment, Paul had occasion many times to experience the harm done by a philosophy that presumed to circumscribe the divine within the confines of the human and to set itself up as a religion. Notwithstanding all appearances, Paul was at the opposite pole from Seneca, and he remained there. The Christian is what his theology makes him: the Stoic is what physiology makes him.

The difference between Christianity and Stoicism being reduced to this, it is easily seen and understood why Seneca was never like St. Paul. In other words, the Christian system of thought and life came down to earth from heaven. St. Paul received his Gospel through a revelation bestowed on him by Christ; he was caught up into the third heaven where he received an ineffable infusion of divine knowledge which he could never reveal. The Stoic—and Seneca is a Stoic, although on many points he may seem like one of us with many broad views—ascends from earth. He *ascends,* and makes a vigorous effort to climb to heaven. In fact he can reach the highest peaks of human wisdom where the air is purer, so clear that it seems spiritualized, but these heights are still earthly heights over which the sky bends as an arch; not detached, but leaning on the world and a part of the whole physical system, an arch that does not separate the two worlds but marks the division of two compartments of matter. The Stoic does not leave nature. He ignores the transcending world of the spirit, and therefore limits himself to a small and poor zone, that same zone from which the Apostolic soul continually frees itself.

Paul looks downward from the supernatural, and Seneca looks upward from the natural. Seneca, Epictetus, Marcus Aurelius, no less than the Greek and Roman precursors of Stoicism, belong to the old world of mythology in which gods germinated from the forests and the seas. Paul is the herald of a revolution which destroys gates and locks, draws man out into the open regions of the Infinite, away from earth in which he is enslaved, remaking him free as a son of God, thanks to the unique and recent miracle of Christ Who made Himself a servant and the Son of Man.

Near the beginning of the fourth century a falsifier composed an epistolary correspondence between the philosopher Seneca, teacher of Nero, the Emperor, and the Apostle of Christ the King. For a long time, that epistolary writing was supposed to be authentic and probable, limited as it was to short notes of courtesy which were rather insipid; this much did Stoicism seem to resemble Christianity.

Thus within the span of three hundred years, a romancer (none too accurate) could imagine a correspondence, based on a spiritual harmony believed to exist between a pagan idealist and a neo-scholastic, due to a deception over an analogy of words; for both used the common vocabulary of the times in which they lived. Seneca spoke of God, of providence, of virtues; and in Paul's writings such words are found as faith, belief, hope, salvation, sacrament, humility, to absolve, and others; but their similarity is all external. The difference between the two systems is infinite. Stoicism is monism, immanence; divinity is a part of the world, being immanent in it, and ending naturally in a materialistic pantheism. Christianity is a dualism in which divinity and humanity act together; it is immanence and transcendency of spirit and matter.

The Stoic lacks the supernatural life; he lacks a theology, which is considered by him beyond the rational and natural world, and therefore non-subsistent. This is why at Athens, both Stoics and Epicureans with one accord shrugged their shoulders, and asked, "What is this babbler trying to say?"[1] In Rome a century later, Epictetus, a slave, and Marcus Aurelius, the Emperor, expressed the same con-

[1] Acts 17:18.

tempt for the evangelical doctrines and practice. For Paul, God is a Person, a pure Spirit, the Creator of the world: for the Stoic, God is an indistinct vague soul of the world. He is the world (matter) although of a superior nature, the active element in matter itself.

In the Stoic hypothesis of God (which marks a step backward from the Platonic and Aristotelian philosophy), the world is both the beginning and the end; it is for men and gods a prison house, a cage, where death alone is the end of all things, and where, for the sake of justice or fair play, everything must periodically turn to ashes in order to give life to a new world developing.

It was an iron destiny, an inexorable linking-up of causes and effects which held men and gods chained and bound. From this determinism flowed all the most powerful and remote fatalistic doctrines of the East and the West, solidified into the Stoic system. At every moment Stoicism, having obtained a place in Roman civilization, was preparing to enroll the ruling classes and the Emperors themselves, wishing to display among them and their political system the end of liberty as if it had become exhausted after a race through the centuries.

Against this hard construction of an inaccessible approach, there came as a shock the announcement of the Redemption, that is, a liberation by which men are set free from the ancient idea of servitude. Stoicism, the fruit of despair, is conservative; Christianity, the generator of hope, is revolutionary. It is not without reason that Marcus Aurelius, the most cruel of all the Antonines, stood out so fiercely against Christianity and the Christians.

Therefore the prose of Seneca and the prose of Paul do not represent two systems of thought that influence each other, they are two currents of thought that cross each other. If in later years Christianity has, according to its character of constructive revolution, gathered into itself the most beautiful and best of moral aspirations in Stoicism, it is not surprising. Had it not done this by collecting the best of Judaism and, as it appears, utilized even Platonic ideas and Aristotelian logic? It is characteristic of Christianity to transform all that it touches. Once Christianized, Stoicism is no longer Stoicism; it loses its basis, because it accepts hope and is open to liberty. Much of its vocabulary may seem to remain but it, too, is transfigured by Christ.

The Saint and the Savant

St. Paul had been molded in the East, in a Pharisaic school very remote from Roman Stoicism. When he became an Apostle, he acquired a definite disdain for all merely human knowledge. He is a man who is never weary of speaking wherever he goes, although not in the "magnificence of words," lest the Cross of Christ which he preaches be made void and empty of all meaning. The Cross is to the Stoic the gibbet for deserters, while on the contrary dialetics is to him a virtue.

Worldly knowledge disdains the Cross, considering it as unnecessary and foolish, but the world has never known God by the way of Wisdom. Paul recalls this to the learned, when to the Greeks who seek wisdom he preaches Christ crucified, "a scandal to the Jews, and foolishness to the Gentiles." What seems to be foolishness to men is more often wisdom to God. The learned man was to the Stoic what the saint is to the Christian.

Seneca said, "Whether we be constrained by the inexorable law of destiny, whether all be disposed by the divine will of Providence, whether chance moves human events without any determined order, our philosophy must always defend us."

The word Paul preaches goes to the lowly folk whom philosophy does not reach. Celsus and the other erudites will despise Christianity as being the religion of laborers and the ignorant, artisans and the illiterate.

To the wise Stoic who believes himself to be happy, rich, a demigod, the depository of truth and justice, Paul opposes the Hebrew teachings that God alone is true and pure, and men are unjust and liars. The Stoic ignores all supernatural faith, since he accepts no other light than that of human reason. Paul, on the contrary, asserts the necessity of faith, by which the just man lives and which is the beginning of all Christian life. When Paul wrote to the Romans he exalted faith in contrast to the vanity of subtle reasonings with which the wise men of the pagans filled their foolish hearts. It is for this reason they fell into idolatry and depravity of nature.

To the Ephesians Paul had set forth the Christian doctrines as an antithesis to pagan doctrine, in the same relationship as light is to darkness. "O Timothy, guard the trust and keep free from profane novelties in speech and the contradictions of so-called knowledge, which some have professed, and have fallen away from the faith." [2]

A still greater difference remains between Stoicism and all other systems of philosophy not Christian. This difference lies hidden in the person of Jesus Christ and, above all, in His death, which Paul asserts is the necessary and absolute principle of the spiritual life, of the reconciliation with God, and of salvation. The dogma of an Incarnate God, of a God-Man Who expiates sin for all men, Who rises from the tomb, could not enter the mind of any philosopher of the old classic period of the world.

The new man, in Paul's mind, is united to Christ as the branch is united to the vine; just as each member of the human body is united to the head. It is a vital and living union which neither tribulations, persecutions, angels or demons can sever. It is in Christ we live; we are enveloped in the love of Christ, which motivates us in all we do; to live is Christ. "With Christ I am nailed to the Cross. It is now no longer I that live, but Christ lives in me." [3] This love of Christ surpasses all worldly knowledge; therefore, Stoicism, having only human reason for its vital principle, is natural philosophy only. Christianity, whose vital principle is love of God, is true religion and has for a Founder, not a proud philosopher like Zeno, but a Priest, a great High Priest, at the same time made a Victim for His people.

For Paul Christ and the doctrines of Christ are his very life; for him to live *is Christ*. Therefore any discord or contradiction between

[2] I Tim. 6:20, 21.
[3] Gal. 2:20.

what is taught and what is practiced in the moral theology of Christianity is an impossibility. Paul, having set the example in himself, can justly propose to others the imitation of himself. This was quite a different matter for Seneca who, with all his noble sentiments and noble thoughts, esteemed men of doubtful reputation (like the libertines); who made an excuse for patricide, who lived in luxury and sin, and who never thought of translating into action any social morals.

On this point at least, Epictetus and Marcus Aurelius would have made more progress; they were nearer to the Cross. In their time Christian preaching had expanded, and they had seen the example of many followers of Christ. The reaction to so much preaching and teaching could not but have had an influence.

Christian Theology and Fatalism

From the Stoic theogony (cosmogony) sprang the doctrine of soul and body. The Stoic believes that the soul dies with the body since both are made of matter; that is to say, they are two phases of the same substance, one being more subtle, the other more dense. In the same manner as the soul is to the body, the life of the world is to the world itself. The Stoic deifies the soul, supposing it to be a small part of the great cosmic soul which is God; while at the same time he regards the body as something vile, being both matter and mortal.

Some Stoics attributed to the soul of the learned a survival, a contradictory and confused notion which subjected the soul to a sort of Pythagorean metamorphosis; but this survival will not last beyond the universal conflagration when all the world will finally be reduced to ashes. The Stoic feels proud of this soul so deified, while in the same measure he despises the body which, in the mind of Seneca and others like him, he regards as a chain, a prison, a burden, a beast, a weight, or a veil.

For Seneca the body is flesh; it is the same for St. Paul, but what a difference in value for each in the identical and same expression.

Paul claims that since the Redemption and Justification took place in the flesh of Christ, then every man must become a saint both in his flesh and in his soul in order to rise in the Resurrection in the flesh. He must make his body a temple of the Holy Spirit in order that it may co-operate in an active manner for his eternal salvation and even become a holy sacrifice, living, acceptable to God.

St. Paul rehabilitating the flesh with Christ, Who is God living in the flesh, withdraws it from vice, to which Stoic contempt abandons it as being an inferior thing. St. Paul demands that both soul and body become sanctified and kept holy, without blame. Still deeper is the difference between the Stoic and the Christian concerning the final destiny of the body since, like so many pagans, the Stoic does not admit (he has no conception of) the resurrection of the body. He rebels against this more than against any other dogma of the new religion. On the contrary, Paul gives the most explicit and fervent affirmations for the complete reconstruction of the whole man and promises for him a triumphant sense of peace and joy.

Seneca, following the dialectics of a different system, which identify the soul with God, writes, "It is not necessary to lift the hands to heaven, or to solicit the keeper of the temple to let us hear the idol speak, as if we had thus more possibility of being heard, God is near thee, with thee, within thee." [4] This last phrase has a Christian savor (Paul had said something similar that day in the Areopagus), but the substance is pagan, because it springs from pantheistic monism. Where the ego is, there is God.

Providence is praised by Seneca and Epictetus, who speak of God with the love of a Christian; but it is a providence identified with an inexorable destiny, with the soul of material things. It is, in other words, helplessness in the face of which man is alone, an exile in the midst of the world and without hope either in the gods or in men. It is for this reason that the counsels of Marcus Aurelius are full of the accents of sadness; he makes a dramatic appeal to detach one's self from all, to stand unresisting against all, but to hope for nothing.

[4] Epistle 41:1.

Of course, one must imitate the gods, propitiate them with gifts and practice goodness; but to follow the gods means simply to follow nature. It is not said that one must love the gods and still less fear them; therefore prayer dies out in this form of worship.

In fact the Stoic does not admit any idea of worship; this would be utterly vain according to the logic of the system, but it can be tolerated for the sake of opportunism and politics. "The wise man will observe the acts of the cult prescribed by the laws, although he knows that they are not pleasing to the gods." [5] Such opportunism must have horrified St. Paul, who tries to relight the fire of the prophets against every idolatrous cult which he considers as an "usurper of the dignity and honour due to God alone." St. Paul preaches adoration in spirit, nor do we need images made by hands; he exhorts us to pray without ceasing or weariness and to be in the arms of God the Father at every moment.

The Stoic is self-sufficient; he does not need God because God is sufficient in Himself, and only in Himself. The Stoic is proud, self-satisfied, and therefore he will kill himself rather than submit to the force of pain or misfortune from which he cannot escape. He misses the supernatural secret of resignation, of humble acceptance of suffering from God's hands; sufferings used for the upbuilding of the Mystical Body of Christ, according to the doctrine of Paul. The Stoic misses hope which is the expectation of a better world and a better life without end. It is from this eternal life that there flashes back a reflection of divine joy which shines on all in the life of the Christian.

So the Christian is always optimistic because he hopes in God; he knows he is always in God's care, as a son is in the care of a good father. The pagan becomes desperate; even when he laughs, it is to hide his despair. In the midst of his tribulations, Paul can send exhortations of joy, intimate joy which is not noisy laughter, "Rejoice in the Lord always, again I say rejoice." And he says this while he is in chains.

[5] Seneca—Frag. 38.

In contrast to this, there drips a cold light from the heartless Heimarmene (inexorable fate) that chills, and from the eschatology of experience there comes a faint reflex of a red glare that frightens. The Epicurean avoids both by deafening himself with the moral slogan, "Make the most of today, for tomorrow we die." The Stoic is more courageous and bends before the determinism of destiny, and when he can yield no more he breaks apart his own existence; it is because he trusts in himself that he cannot accept misfortune in any form.

Paul in his afflictions often feels the burdens of life, but he rises from the dust and goes on because he has confidence in God and not in himself. It is God Who rose from the dead, it is God Who raises us from the dead. Paul knows that the life of Christ is manifested in our mortal flesh through suffering; he is pleased with infirmity and anguish because when he is in weakness, then he is strong. The most heroic remedy for the Stoic, and the one practiced by Seneca against evil, whether personal or social, is suicide. Every vein of the body, every tree, every well and river is to the Stoic a way to liberation through death. "We are not anyone's possession when death is in our possession," professes the great teacher of Nero. It may sound like an heroic suggestion; it is in fact a coward's flight.

The Christian resists; Paul, annoyed, sick, imprisoned, never gives way but understands life as warfare. Therefore under the waves of Nero's tyranny, Seneca kills himself, and Paul allows himself to be killed; the first becomes an accomplice to the crime, the second throws on the tyrant the entire guilt of the crime. Therefore the hero of Stoicism is Cato, a suicide: and the hero of Christianity is Christ Crucified. In the doctrine of the Porch, he is wise who lives according to nature, conscious that if he does not do so freely, he is coerced to do it; in truth, he is not free.

Seneca says, "He who gives way is led by another; he who rebels is dragged by destiny. This means that freedom does not exist, nor can there be any responsibility to our actions." And so the most severe moral law of paganism ends by doing away altogether with morals. If there is no such thing as liberty, it follows that the Redemption, which means being redeemed from servitude, can have no meaning. The only real liberation would consist in yielding to the demands of nature, and to evil. To the Stoic, it is an evil to live in necessity but there is no necessity of living in necessity; and so it is a closed circle which death alone can break.

To the Christian death is the beginning of life. If circumstances are unavoidable, one can make a virtue of necessity; this is the Christian way. To the Stoic, virtue is a reward in itself; and since there is neither reward or punishment for works done out of necessity, the Stoic avoids both. Humanity is driven like a herd of cattle under the whip of the blind-folded Heimarmene,[6] who herself cannot help doing what she does. "No wisdom can uproot the natural vices, either of body or soul," says Seneca in his letters. And it is an illusion to fatigue oneself in trying to correct humanity.

Then from the viewpoint of the doctrines of the Porch (the porch in which the Stoic lectures were given), the warm and loving pressure that Paul uses in transforming those Romans, Corinthians, Jews and pagans into a chaste people, into a Church, members of the Body of Christ, must all be an illusion. Only a handful of philosophers, conscious of their own impotence, seek to procure for themselves some degree of liberty by not resisting the force of destiny. All they really have is the freedom of moving about in a prison, at the beck of the jailer, and resigning themselves to the universal servitude of all men. These few wise men follow destiny like dogs tied to a cart; if they do not follow they are dragged through the mire of life.

How little they know of what the Redemption has accomplished in setting them free, as St. Paul is never tired of repeating over and over again; glorying in the liberty which belongs to the sons of God. No wonder he was continually fighting those false brethren who set

[6] Absolute Fate.

snares to oppose the liberty Jesus Christ would give and who want to bring all back again to servitude. We are redeemed, therefore no longer slaves or servants, but sons and heirs of God.

The Redemption, with which Christ has bought back humanity from the bondage of sin, can in no way be grafted onto the Stoic system. If the world is God, then man, who is a small particle of the world, is no better than, or different from God; at least man is as good as God by nature, according to the Stoic. "He is mistaken who believes that defects come from us, nature has generated us sound and free," writes Seneca. In the logic of Seneca, defects come later and are added to the nature of man.

Paul starts from the proved truth of Original Sin, and rises to the concept of liberation through the expiation of sin by the new Adam. In such a liberation, the freedom of the will remains, as also the responsibility; and with it comes the divine sanction of man's works. "Since we must all appear before the tribunal of Christ, every man will receive the reward of those things done in the body, according as he has done good or evil." [7] Virtue is not only its own reward, it is also the true and greatest good for all people. Virtue becomes a means for bringing about this good and glorifies Him Who created us. It is the only criterion for evaluating our earthly experiences.

In truth, the Stoic makes an heroic effort to realize an interior liberty, but it is an effort of supreme pride by which he pulls himself out of the crowd and shuts himself up, as it were, in a tower that resembles a mausoleum. He lives in such a state of impassability that even in the face of death he does not lose his composure. Such a sentiment is the exact opposite of St. Paul who was "all things to all men" through charity.

Out of charity Paul went from country to country seeking souls, utterly careless of himself, reaching out to others with his whole being. Charity, of which the ex-Pharisee of Tarsus was the most powerful exponent, radiates from him as from a center; while Ataraxia, the Greek symbol for a calm and peaceful state, distilled

[7] 2 Cor. 5:10.

from Stoic wisdom, is ego-centric. Charity is like a house opened at the four cardinal points, a welcome to all those outside who suffer. The Stoic is in a house with all the bolts and locks of windows and doors shut tight against a brother's pain and misery.

The basis for each is different. Charity is born of humility, which requires a stripping of self in order to be a docile creature in the hands of God: the calm of the Stoic is born of pride, which rejects God's help, and leans on its own strength. Paul feared God and sought to serve Him in other men. The Stoic fears neither God nor other men, he feels himself to be a god. He professes with Seneca that God is outside suffering, and the Stoic is above it.

Politics

In civic matters Stoicism had a great outlook; the widest yet for intelligences of the ancient world and time. Since man is a part of nature, and nature is the world, and the world is God, it follows that man is at home in any part of the world. Marcus Aurelius and Epictetus may say, with the author of the Letters to Diognetus and Tertullian, that their fatherland is the world. For the Christian, the world is more exactly a place of exile, "since here we have no abiding city; but we seek one that is above." For the Stoic the world is a dwelling place, both the beginning and the end of life. In this respect, Stoicism does not differ greatly from paganism, for both the world was a place wherein to dwell. The Christian, moved by a supernatural power, regards it as a place through which one passes.

To begin with, the Stoic admits that there is such a thing as a universal citizenship to which all men belong, and that all are ruled by the same natural laws. Such a concept served as a means of loosening the grip of Roman imperialism on municipal and regional narrowness and of launching out for a spiritual conquest of the world as of something that belonged to Stoicism. It supported the Roman's wise policy which allowed much autonomy to the provinces and united many nations into one people.

For a certain period such a conception could be favorable to Christianity, and it was. But in practice, the Stoic mutilated its cosmopolitanism with extreme political conservatism for which it submitted its own ideas, if not through conviction at least for convention's sake, to usages and laws. Consequently its universality ended wherever the legions of Rome arrived.

Such cosmopolitanism was an earthly fact. Christianity included all this and more; it rapidly surpassed it in the idea of the Mystical Body of Christ, in which the oneness of the sons of God acquires full vigor and supernatural life. It knows no limits of space, or race, or time; there is no more Jew or Greek, slave or free, male or female, but all are one in Jesus Christ.

In the order of classes, Stoic universality ended in a circle much more restricted, that of the aristocracy of intellectualism. Seneca proposed, in theory (and here his mind expanded in some beautiful ideals) one must be "joyful with one's friends, and meek with one's enemies," in virtue of the common citizenship of all people in the only fatherhood that is the world. In reality, he would not have cared, either materially or spiritually, for slaves or for the disinherited. As for goods or fortune, he tried to dispose himself to bear poverty, and saw that in this there could be a certain condition of liberty. He pondered over the condition of riches, and found it preferable. He said it was important to make a wise use of money, keeping control of it, but to avoid being dominated by it. His motive in everything was for acquiring a peace of soul. The Christian could, in a large measure, adopt much of this point of view, these valuations, but his greatest disposition was for the acquiring of his eternal salvation.

Paul was in agreement with Seneca when he said, "I know how to be in need, and how to abound"; but the principle underlying it was different. "I can do all things in Him Who strengthens me." Paul's principle was outside him, and above him.

Human society is, for the Christian, based on supernatural virtues: while for the Stoic, he is leaning on natural virtues; he is overcome by them, or they are overcome by his lower instincts. We have mentioned a few characteristics; they suffice, perhaps, to show, and also to define, the difference between the Catholic announcement brought by Paul to the people of Asia and Europe, and the aristocratic rationalism of Seneca and the other Stoics. These, when they became conscious of Christianity, gave such a judgment of the new religion that it brought on a most tragic reaction. They said it was a revolution; and as such they fought against it with fire and sword.

CHAPTER X

THE MARTYRDOM OF PAUL

His Last Voyages, A.D. 63-66

The justice of Rome under Nero was not more speedy than it had been under Felix at Caesarea; and the distance from the center (Jerusalem) from whence the accusations had started, did not favor its progress. Bureaucracy was slow; and the Emperor used no more energy in doing the little he had to do as supreme judge than was obligatory. Two years were thus employed in discussing Paul's cause.

It is not known if the accusers from Jerusalem ever presented themselves at Caesar's tribunal or not. In Jerusalem political passions had become stronger, the clash between factions harder, and the tyranny of the governors more provoking. It seems probable, then, that the Sanhedrin sent no representatives directly from Jerusalem, but perhaps some from the Roman Synagogues were appointed to appear. The report from Festus had been favorable to Paul and, according to Roman Law, the dogmatic differences within the Hebrew religion (the tolerated religion of a conquered people) were not considered material for the penal law. Therefore the innocence of Paul had been recognized by sentences of the tribunal, and he was set free at the beginning of the year 63.

The Roman Community, through the influence of the brethren installed in the imperial palace, had promoted the steady course of the lawsuit and its decision. They now rejoiced, for during the two years (especially on account of Peter's absence), Paul had been the prop in the work of evangelization and of Christian life in the city. When Paul wanted to leave for Spain, they provided him with the means and men to accompany him. Luke, alas, does not inform us, or at least we do not have his notes on this voyage in which, according to his custom, Paul would have referred to the Synagogues and Hellenistic colonies.

His Roman companions introduced him to the Latin groups with whom it is most likely Paul spoke Latin. He was a Roman citizen; and all persons of culture knew both the Greek and Roman languages since they were in continual intercourse with Greeks and Latins. Paul had, no doubt, while in Rome perfected his Latin. He belonged to a race that easily acquired a knowledge of several languages, something necessary for traffic in an Empire which was officially versatile in the practice of many dialects.

Clement of Rome, later Bishop of Rome about the year 90, speaks of Peter and Paul in his letters to the Corinthians as "the good Apostles." He refers to them as persons well known in the Roman Community, and hints at Paul's voyage to the extreme west. The term "west" commonly meant Spain, although it could also mean Britain. If he had the means to do so, most assuredly the Apostle would never miss the opportunity of announcing Christ to the most remote confines of the Empire. "He taught justice to the whole world," wrote St. Clement, who knew it from personal knowledge. That had been the constant ambition of Paul.

From the west he returned to Rome; recalled there perhaps by the calamities which befell the great Church, of which he knew himself to be a co-founder with Peter. In July of the year 64, a conflagration starting near the Circus Maximus, which was packed with small shops and stores at the foot of the Palatine hill, spread rapidly, aided by the wind, and devoured ten of the fourteen regions of Rome. Tacitus says that it is not known whether the fire was started by accident, or was one of the crimes of Nero. Enormous crowds of people without homes, shelter, or goods, gathered under the Palatine palace, and with cries and tears poured imprecations on Nero, calling him an incendiary and a matricide. This was the beginning of a revolt.

The frightened Emperor, accepting the suggestion given him by some Jews, or perhaps yielding to some scheme of Poppea his wife, threw the blame on the Christians, now well known and hated by the common people who were ready to impute to them a series of other crimes. The advice worked successfully. A large number of Christians were arrested and condemned to death; not so much for the crime of having started the fire as for the accusation of hating mankind. Since they detested the idols, and kept apart from the pagans, they appeared to be a sect given to inhuman and anti-Roman hatred.

To distract the attention of the homeless people and to satisfy his fondness for glamorous performances, Nero made use of their death for a theatrical display in his own gardens opened to the public, now, the Vatican hill. Christian men and women were covered with the skins of wild animals, nailed to crosses, and used as burning torches along the avenues, while the imperial assassin in golden attire mingled with the crowds celebrating the games of the Circus. The butchery, which continued by day and by night, took place chiefly in the Circus Maximus. This was an enormous oval enclosed by the imperial gardens, at one end of which rose an obelisk, now standing in the square of St. Peter—a mute witness to the bloody triumph of the Christian martyrs and of the peaceful glory of their successors.

In Rome, therefore, took place the second great contact of Christianity with the polytheistic state. The first had been in Jerusalem with Jesus Christ Himself. Paul, as well as Peter, if he were absent, must have hurried to Rome to comfort the afflicted Community. The attention of the people was temporarily diverted by the bloodshed and by the games in the Circus, so that the persecution seemed to be a formal condemnation of the Christian religion which had worked so much havoc in Rome and had even spread to the provinces.

From Rome, Paul started travelling again to visit his Hellenic Churches. This last circuit was like a race. It was an urgent matter that he avoid the old enemies and adversaries and return quickly, for the time was short. He followed a bloody trail.

He visited Ephesus again, and perhaps saw the Christians of Colossae and Laodicea. In the city of Aphrodite from which he had previously fled under the idolatrous uprising, he left his most trusted disciple, the one who most resembled him, the beloved Timothy. Then reascending the coast to Troas, where he was the guest of Carpus, he took ship for Macedonia. There he embraced those cherished brethren of Philippi and afterwards those of Thessalonica. From Macedonia he wrote a letter of encouragement and counsel to Timothy who, on account of his youth and naturally timorous temperament and the simplicity of his faith, felt the burden of the Community he had to shepherd.

Now that persecution made faith a great risk, many of the learned were inclined to dissolve the Gospel into ambiguous formulas and high-sounding speech; it was the old snare for compromise. After his rapid inspection of the Churches in Macedonia, Paul passed into Achaia, and the Corinthians had the joy of contemplating once more that countenance, now lined with deep wrinkles and crowned with the white hair of an old father. He had hardly arrived when he had to leave again.

It is probable that from Corinth, he took ship for Crete with Titus for a companion. It was in this island he had stopped five or six years before in his chains on his voyage to Rome. Here he had sowed the good seed of the Gospel and had organized a Christian Community. He did not stay long this time, and the impression he took away with him was not a happy one.   Paul left with them his "son in Christ"—Titus, his companion and confidant, especially in the missions of this third itinerary.

Returning to Corinth, he went to Nicopolis, the "City of Victory" in Epirus; from Nicopolis, he wrote a concise letter of directions to advise Titus and to encourage him, promising to send Artemas and Tychicus to replace him; and they would spend the winter with him in that city. While Paul waited for Titus, he evangelized Illyria. This was before the approach of winter and before his return to Asia, as he had planned.

At Troas, he had left some clothes and some books, but before he could get them, he was obliged to cut short all his projects and start at once for Rome. Was he arrested at Corinth, or was it at Nicopolis, together with Timothy who had rejoined him? Had he taken Titus with him also to Rome? It may be. St. Clement of Rome recalls that before Paul's death the Apostle had been in chains seven times.

It is also probable that in order to avoid being arrested, he had hastily taken the road to Rome. St. Dionysius, who was bishop of Corinth a century later, where the fact must have been well known, says that Peter and Paul were reunited in Corinth and together preached the Gospel there once more, and from there started for Italy.

In their eyes the great Church of Rome was more venerable than ever, now that an immense multitude of her children had so imitated Christ and confessed [1] Him in the midst of torments and death. In this center of the civilized world the most overwhelming proof of fidelity to Christ had been given, and it had been successful. That city was now a most precious Temple for them. Many Christians were languishing in prisons, others were hiding in hovels in the suburbs and in caverns on the outskirts of the city. The unusual spectacle, a revolutionary spectacle of such endurance, if it had sharpened hatred on the one side, had caused admiration on the other, and this was the most favorable disposition for receiving the Gospel. And so there much good was being done.

Paul arrived in Rome. We do not know whether he was set free after the first interrogation or allowed to go about during the sessions of the tribunal. This we do know, that he still worked. He was burning with charity and with pity for the sufferings he witnessed. New centers of the faith continued to be organized; he continued to admonish, without losing the goodwill of those who

---

[1] Martyrdom meant "witnessing" or "confessing" Christ.

trusted in him because he trusted all in Christ. His body was worn out by fatigue, by sufferings, and by sickness, but he only seemed to grow the stronger, his physical energies increasing with a faith that seemed to devour him. Not even in the midst of persecutions was his ministry allowed any time of peace or tranquillity by the inventions of new-fangled preachers and distorters of the Gospel.

The Christian Life

During the years that followed Paul's first imprisonment in Rome and while he was engaged in his Apostolic journeys, he had not neglected to dictate various letters when occasion offered. We mention one addressed to Timothy and another written to Titus. In his great letters to the different Churches and Christian Communities, he had fought with prophetic vigor against the intrusion of the Mosaic observances as a necessary condition for salvation within Christianity. He had spoken clearly; and his condemnation was aimed at the material and carnal aspects of practices which, by means of ablutions, discriminations in food, and physical macerations, pretended to supplant a faith in Christ which already included suffering the ills and afflictions of life. For such faith, there is no substitute in seeking salvation, because salvation is solely a gift from God in relation to man's acts.

Abraham was justified through faith, taught St. Paul; also through works, urged St. James. According to both, faith and works acted together, becoming something concrete in form. It was a great work for Abraham to offer his son Isaac on the altar of sacrifice; only faith could have done it. "What will it profit, my brethren, if a man says he has faith but does not have works? Can faith save him?" Then comes the conclusive sentence, "So faith too, unless it has works is dead in itself." [2]

Some time later, Peter, also writing from Rome to the Churches of Asia Minor, had insisted on the doing of good works. He considered it a condition *"sine qua non"* for being acceptable to God; for confuting the evil accusations aimed at the Christians from all sides, which, because it spread beyond the limits of nationality, was therefore doubly suspected by the pagans.

Persecution was imminent; there were hundreds of indications of it. The conflagration at Rome had set fire to a heap of prejudices al-

[2] St. James 2:14, 18.

ready amassed in the course of years. Nothing could prevent persecution except the spectacle of an irreprehensible, honest and blameless life; if it was necessary to face persecution, it ought to be done with a clean conscience.

At the end of his career, when writing to those same Churches, Peter had denounced the false teachers who had given themselves up to a sinful life, and called them "fountains without water, clouds driven by the wind," and like dogs returned to their vomit. He had referred to the letters of his "most dear brother Paul" and went on to say that there were some things difficult to understand, that the ignorant and the unstable would misinterpret, as they did with the rest of the Scriptures, but to their own destruction.

So also the Apostle Jude, brother of St. James the Less, in the year 64 had written a concise and vehement letter against the false Apostles who intruded on the ranks of the faithful, perverting the life of grace into a worldly life of luxury and giving out abnormal and twisted theories on the cult of the angels. They praised "someone," probably Paul, for his "self-interested aims," in order to draw from his letters a sterile doctrine and an unworthy practice. This generated divisions, insulted the hierarchy, and blasphemed the majesty of the Lord.

All this fermentation of sensuality and false knowledge prevailed in Asia Minor, a restless land influenced by Hellenism because it was in constant contact with Athens and Alexandria. Paul shared the anxiety of James and Peter and of Jude; (later John would also react to this unrest by his burning and scathing words in the Apocalypse). With the other Apostles then, Paul fought the errors and abuses produced by a superficial and artificial exegesis of his own doctrines. Foreseeing that from this there would arise the greatest schism in the Community of Christ, he explained in a series of letters the duties of Christian life and practice, together with the theology he had preached.

Such letters are: the one to the Hebrews, both of those to Timothy, and the one to Titus. The last three, specifically called Pastorals, are a guide in the practical Christian life. They give a number of counsels for the sanctification of the individual as well as for the discipline of social relations within and without the Church. They are catalogues of Christian virtue, animated and inspired by apostolic ardor; rules useful for good bishops, for good priests, and for all the faithful under their care.

Particular attention is given to women whom Paul wishes to see adorned with good works and not with costly garments and jewels. The outlines for an orderly and chaste life are given in the fulfillment of the mission, or state of life, assigned to each. The protection of the one and only Gospel which has been taught is the theme of his first letter to Timothy who had been left in charge of the Church at Ephesus. This was now assailed by the innovators who tried to overthrow dogma in order to get rid of morals.

Paul's Legacy to the Hebrews

Paul loved his own people with the human love of blood relationship; he loved them because of the divine love God had shown them in the special privileges He had granted the Hebrew race. From them had sprung the Prophets and the Apostles who were the foundation of the Christian Church, of whose blood the Man-God Christ had been born, Redeemer of both Jews and pagans: Jews first, and after them the pagans.

Nothing sufficed to reduce the ardor of this son of Israel nor the duty of the Apostle who, in order to convert Jews to Christ, would have made himself anathema to all. During these last months in Rome, foreseeing the end, he disposed of his few belongings and wrote his last letters as a testament. He remembered again the Christians from Judaism, and with them, all the Jews. He left to them the doctrine of the wonderful unfolding of the Old Testament into the

New Testament, of the march of the Prophets down the centuries, and of the people of God turning towards Christ as towards the Eternal Priest, giving testimony of all from the Scriptures which was a last blow to Mosaism.

He had already spoken and written much to define the position of the new converts from paganism to the New Religion. Now he wished to specify in a definite manner the position of the Hebrews towards Christianity, so he composed to this effect a kind of superior catechism, which should crown and complete the elementary teaching they had followed until then. He now provided "solid food" as befitted perfect men instead of the "milk of babes" they had been given. Therefore he used a more unusual vocabulary, or perhaps he entrusted his thoughts to a more cultured disciple in order that he might give them in more careful form, blending all his Scriptural knowledge into the glowing light of his illumined faith in Christ.

It was a solemn testament which, because it dealt with a superior doctrine, he wished to see written with worthy precision and clarity. The truth is that the understanding of this writing demands a knowledge exercised in the science of God; without this, it remains abstruse and without meaning.

The persecution of heresy and of blood was raging. Paul took those beaten and defeated Christians who were beginning to waver in their faith and good works and to keep themselves aloof from the meetings in the Churches and, with a daring gesture, he transferred them to a higher plane. On the supernatural level, the sins with which Christ was being crucified afresh appeared as small and miserable, while the greatness of their vocation as Christians seemed more evident and glorious and powerful. At the same time, he comforted them for the misfortunes that had befallen their Communities; and this thought from him, the Apostle to the Gentiles, spoke of his great heart that could hold within itself the entire universal Church.

Perhaps some of the other Apostles to the Israelites were dead, or else far away. The success of the zealous Nationalists constituted an increasing menace for the followers of Christ; so much so that in the year 66 they had to flee from Jerusalem to Pella. The little Christian Community there, converted from Judaism, was being severely tried by the persecutions of their co-nationalists and by the pagans. They had paid for their fidelity to Jesus Christ by the confiscation of their property, insults and prison.

If some of them, through fear, had returned to Judaism, the greater number had preferred the Gospel's riches to stolen goods, and accepted peace of conscience in exchange for the wounds caused by calumny. So they upheld one another by a supernatural solidarity and unity. Paul was right in encouraging them to reconstruct in their minds the ideal and realization of the fact that they were redeemed men and the consciousness of being in the right relationship with the prophets of old.

First of all, he dealt a blow to the current worship of the angels, reducing it to the just place where it belonged. The angels are a part of God's creation through Christ, Who, therefore, is infinitely superior to them, as He is superior to Moses because Moses was also created by Him, and chosen by Him as His own minister. The angels were the heralds of the Old Testament as the prophets were, and the Lord Himself is the herald of the New Testament.

This makes the New Covenant between God and His creatures far superior because it is a great Reality; whereas the Old Covenant was only by promise a preparation for the New Covenant. It was well to remind the neophytes of this who, under the pressure of the Roman and Jewish persecutions, could be tempted to return to the former religion of their forefathers. This could be legally licit for them, but not spiritually so.

The Jews possessed the Scriptures and understood them, so the Apostle quotes numerous passages to prove the supereminence of Christ. The Scriptures described the voluntary humiliations and sufferings of the Lord; Who, superior as He was to the angels, made Himself inferior to them in order to make Himself the equal of all

Under house arrest for two years during his first Roman imprisonment, Paul never ceased to work for souls. Through his labors Christ's word penetrated as far as Caesar's palace and the praetorian barracks.

The Word of God is not bound! Paul was taken captive and imprisoned at Rome a second time, about 66 A. D., during Nero's persecution. Though confined to a dark narrow cell, the Apostle preached the Gospel to his every visitor. Lacking visitors, he addressed the doctrines of Christ to his pagan jailers and even they were conquered by his forceful words and burning love of Christ.

SS. Peter and Paul in Prison. Jesus Christ had chosen two Christbearers: Peter, His Vicar on earth, the Universal Pastor of His Church and Paul, Vessel of Election, the Apostle of the Nations. United by charity they prepared the ground in the center of the civilized world for Christ's Church and sealed its foundations with their martyrs' blood.

The Mamertine Prison, where according to pious tradition Peter and Paul passed the last days of their Roman imprisonment awaiting martyrdom under Nero. The plaque at left reads: This is the column to which the Apostles Peter and Paul were bound. They converted the prison wardens, SS. Processus and Martinian, Martyrs, and forty-seven others, baptizing them with the waters that gushed miraculously forth from the fountain on the right.

Paul's entire life was a testimony of fidelity to Christ. His strength in overcoming without discouragement or bitterness the numberless trials and tribulations that confronted him lay in his unbounded love for Christ and souls. Only love can accomplish what Paul accomplished and suffer what he suffered—only love that is stronger than death.

Paul's final testimony for Christ—Martyrdom. "I have fought the good fight, I have finished the course, I have kept the faith. For the rest there is laid up for me a crown of justice, which the Lord, the Just Judge, will give to me in that day; yet not to me only, but also to those who love His coming."

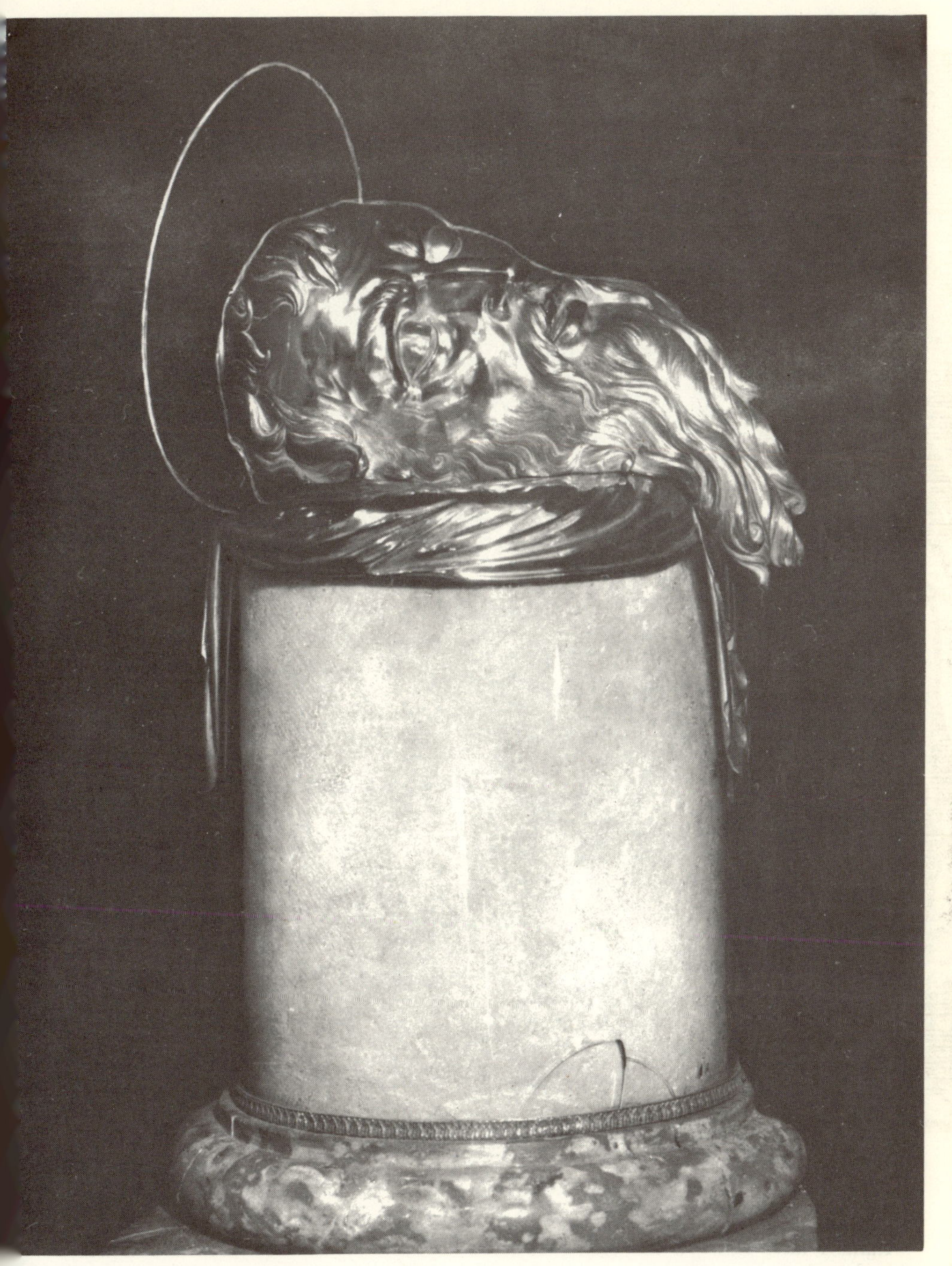

St. Paul's beheading pillar.

The interior of the Basilica of St. Paul Outside the Walls, Rom

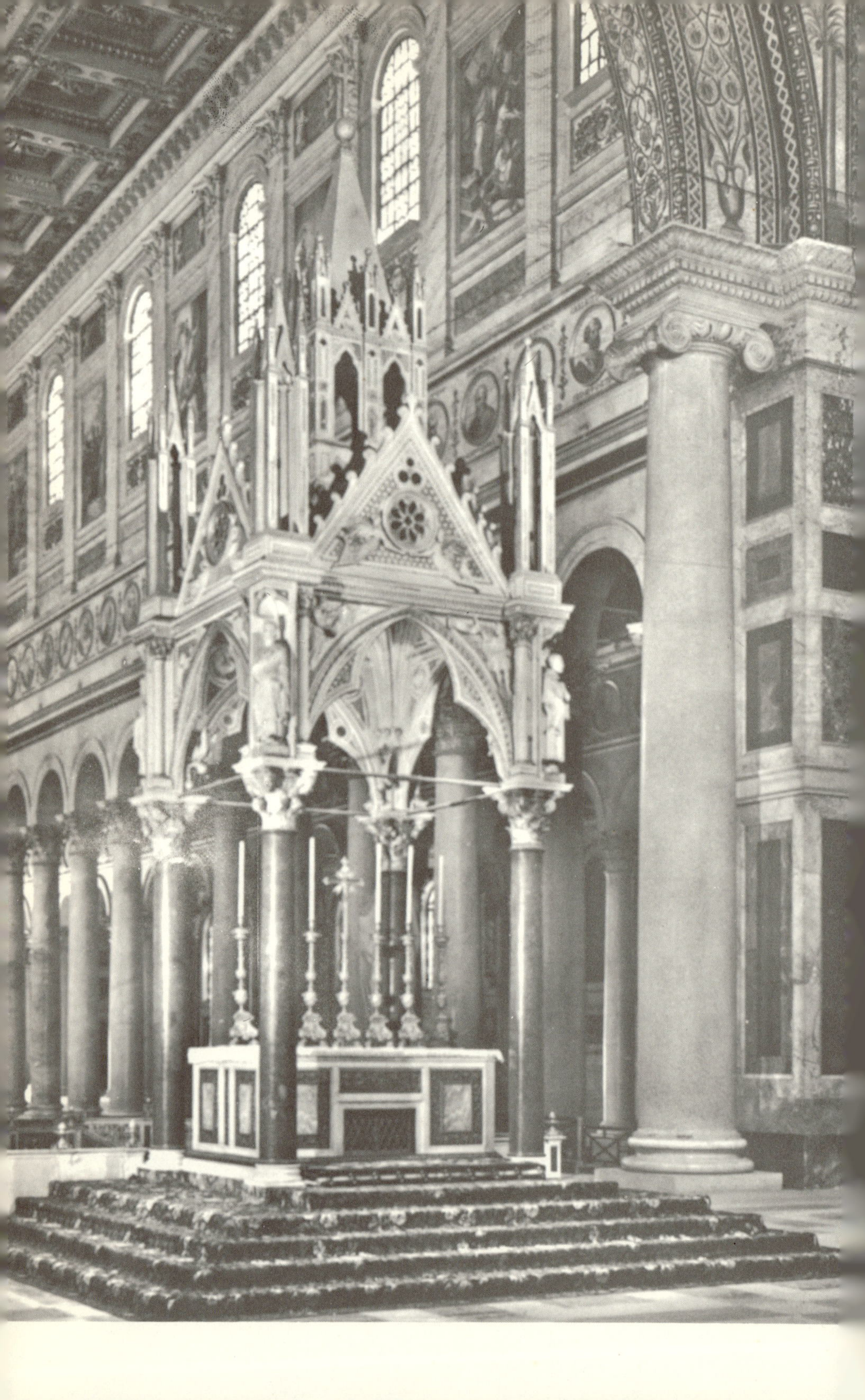

(Above) The facade of the Basilica of St. Paul decorated with a resplendent mosaic and facing on a spacious court.

(Left) The papal altar of the Basilica beneath which lies the tomb of the Great Apostle inscribed: *Paul, Apostle and Martyr.*

The magnificent cloister walk of the Basilica of St. Paul.

Three Fountains. An ancient tradition narrates that three fountains miraculously gushed forth from the earth over which the Apostle's decapitated head rolled.

Like Christ, Paul too was "a sign of contradiction." In vain does one search the history of Christianity for another soul so gifted. At one and the same time Paul was a mystic and man of action, theologian and missionary, founder and organizer, orator, pastor, catechist and director of souls; he was fierce yet humble, audacious yet timid, severe yet affectionate, vehement yet gentle, generous and prudent yet strong and impetuous; and it is through the Pauline Epistles that one comes into direct, personal contact with this astounding genius.

(Above) The Temple of St. Paul, Alba, North Italy, cradle of the "Pauline Family". The main altar is dominated by an impressive statue of the Apostle of the Nations.

It has been said that if St. Paul were to return to this world he would adapt every modern means to spread Christ's Gospel. Thus it is that through his powerful intercession before Almighty God there has arisen in the Church the "Pauline Family" of seven Religious Congregations founded by the Very Rev. James Alberione, S.S.P., S.T.D., which consecrate to the apostolate every means modern science, technology and skill present for the diffusion of Christ's Word.

Across the world's five continents the "Pauline Family" represents the image, spirit and heritage of the Great Apostle, and ceaselessly strives toward new conquests for the Kingdom of God. "I strain forward that I may lay hold of that for which Christ has laid hold of me."

men by becoming Incarnate. This He did in order to be of the same flesh and blood as all men. And since these lay under the servitude of Satan, under the threat of death, He, their Creator, died for them. Christ's death annulled death and overthrew the deadly empire of the devil. By His Incarnation, Christ entered into fellowship with us; by His Sacrifice on the Cross, we enter into fellowship with Him. In this lies our immense dignity as Christians.

In spontaneously offering His Blood in expiation for the sins of men, Christ acted as the Great High Priest. He is a Pontiff Who shares our temptations and our infirmities, sin excepted. Consequently, He is a High Priest Who can have compassion on us, and when He ascended into Heaven, He took compassion with Him to the very throne of God. A Priest is one whom God chooses from among men to minister to other men in the things of religion; to offer gifts and expiatory sacrifices and through whom God exercises pity and compassion and mercy towards those who err.

Christ received this priestly dignity and power from God; and on account of the perfect obedience with which He received it, He was made the Eternal High Priest forever, according to the order of Melchisedech. In the order of priesthood, like that of Melchisedech, the office is not a carnal nor exclusive one, as it was in the priesthood of Aaron (fallen with all the Levitical order on account of its weakness and uselessness), but is spiritual and eternal.

Abraham, who represents the laity, is towards the Law what the spiritual priesthood of Melchisedech is towards the Levitical order. Abraham was blessed by Melchisedech. Abraham represents the Christian people, as Melchisdech represents Christ, the Eternal Pontiff, Who gives a justice which the Mosaic Law could not give.

The priesthood of the Levites only lasted as long as they lived; that of Jesus will last forever. Only He can save eternally, ever living to make intercession for us. His sacrifice is not that of immolated animals, or of food, or of drink offered every morning for the sins of the Levites first and then for the people afterwards. He had no sin;

and it was enough that He should offer Himself but once, thereby forming a second covenant, which was necessary since the first one was imperfect.

The priesthood of Christ, which is unending, does away with the old rites that are now useless and powerless. In the same manner faith in Christ does away with the Law of Moses. The old Order is concluded, finished; the new Era has begun, to last until the end of time. The New Covenant is initiated, of which Jesus Christ is the Immortal Mediator with God for the salvation of all men.

The Jewish High Priest who offered only bread and wine to God was an anticipation, a shadow of Christ's Priesthood, which is not concerned with earthly goods, but with eternal ones. It is exercised, not in a temple made with hands, but in an Eternal See in Heaven, where Jesus has entered, having immolated His own Body, and where He remains. The Jewish High Priest went into the Holy of Holies one day a year to intercede for his people, Jesus is eternally in the Presence of God to intercede for us. The blood of goats and bulls cleansed the flesh; the Immaculate Blood of Christ cleanses consciences. In the Old Covenant, men acted for other men who were like themselves, corruptible and sinners, and therefore this order could not last. In the New Covenant, because it is new, it makes the other old. A Holy Priest acts for men, with a definite and absolute ministry.

A testament has value only on the death of the testator; the New Covenant between God and men drew its value from the death of Jesus. As the Old was inaugurated with blood (the blood of goats), so the New was sealed with Blood, the Blood of the God-Man. "For without the shedding of Blood, there is no remission of sins." It is the offering of that Blood, made once and forever, which sanctifies us and opens the way into the Eternal Sanctuary of Heaven.

If He has sanctified us, His people, in His Blood, we should, on our part, be willing to shed our blood for Him; not being ashamed of His Blood (and of the Church) but willingly and gladly "bear reproaches." He who profanes this Blood, in which he has been sanctified, offends the Holy Spirit and dissipates Grace. He, who once knew the truth (and this is a terrible thing to contemplate), will fall into the hands of the living God, Who will condemn him to the eternal fires of Hell. We must resist evil. The trial is short, but hard; and the judgment is near. Faith is indispensable. Without faith we cannot please God. Dante says, "Faith is hope of things created, and the substance of things that appear not." In this Dante has translated and borrowed from St. Paul.

The whole dramatic existence of the Hebrew people had been lived on faith. They had believed in the midst of all their deportations and wanderings, massacres and oppressions. Abel had lived by faith; Henoch was translated because of his faith. Noah was told of the deluge to come and was saved. Abraham left his native country on faith, and Sarah bore him a son by faith. Isaac blessed Jacob, and Moses faced the Kings of Egypt; while all the Prophets, Judges, Kings and Martyrs acted by faith. Their faith rested in a Promise; that is, in Christ Who was to come, for He is the "author and perfecter of our faith, Jesus Christ."

How much greater our faith ought to be, now that the Promise is no more to come but has been realized for our salvation? With charity, faith and good works, let us have peace, chastity, hospitality, frequenting the meetings where love is increased and multiplied by reciprocal help and comfort. So much the more so as the day approaches when persecution may strike us down in death and bring us speedily to the judgment of God.

In his great letter to the Hebrew people, Paul had revealed Christ in Heaven, explaining by Scripture His functions as a High Priest, which gave a new and immense significance to the aspirations and to the rites of the Hebrew people. He imparts to those poor brethren a new courage and strength. They were so discouraged and cast down in spirit, robbed, calumniated, and many of them had been put to death; so utterly beaten and prostrated, they wondered if the Lord had forgotten them. "No," says St. Paul, "you have forgotten the exhortation that is addressed to you as sons, saying:

> " 'My son, neglect not the discipline of the Lord,
> neither be thou weary when thou art rebuked by him.
> " 'For whom the Lord loves, he chastises;
> and he scourges every son whom he receives.' " [3]

God will act towards them as a father acts towards his children.

Paul reminds them of the sacrifices they have already made so courageously when, on account of their being baptized, that is to say, "illuminated," they have to suffer reproaches, prison, spoliations. How heroically they have borne all these, he says, because of faith and hope in better things to come. "Resist" is the watchword. At the same time they are to oppose the flood of evil with good deeds; to oppose war with peace, fornication with chastity, the politics of the state with faith in the immovable Kingdom of God. They are to exchange the unstable city here below for the future city above which is Heaven. "Therefore, since we receive a kingdom that cannot be shaken, we have grace, through which we may offer pleasing service to God with fear and reverence. For our God is a consuming fire." [4] The children of Israel had experienced this. Faith is a fire that shall consume the enemies of God, but the just who reverence and fear Him have no cause to fear men. Jesus Christ is the same, yesterday and today, yes, and forever.

Paul recommends unity and solidarity, assisting one's neighbor and strangers, prisoners, and the suffering, to be always in reverent submission to the hierarchy of the Church, our guide. He tells them to pray for the Apostle who is far away, but who has a desire to return and see them again and to share all the tribulations of his brethren in the land of their fathers.

[3] Heb. 12:5–7.
[4] Heb. 12:28, 29.

The Mystery of Persecution

In St. Paul's Epistle to the Hebrews, which is the letter on the "Blood of Christ," the idea of persecution dominates. A rain of blood continues to issue from the wounds of the Mystical Christ, a continuation and part of the Sacrifice of Jesus Christ, the first-born of the brethren. Paul, like an affectionate father, now old and infirm, wishes to be wherever anyone is suffering, and everywhere someone is suffering.

He worked in one place, and yearned to go somewhere else; he suffered in Rome, and wanted to go to Jerusalem to endure more pains. His heart was continually on a voyage, or on a journey towards his Father's house. The desire for the fatherland of Heaven must have become even more pressing since the demons of Hell had been let loose on the earth. Anyone else would have been overcome, but not the Apostle. Christianity was passing through a period of laxity and perhaps of delusion following upon the bright hopes of the first announcement.

Instead of the expected parousia, or manifestation of Christ's second coming which would be in great glory and majesty and which was expected from day to day, there were the caprices of the mad Nero, a matricide and incendiary, usurping the titles belonging to the divinity of God. This mad Emperor set fire to the Churches of God, dispersing the Christians.

Heresy had cropped out here and there and had infiltrated itself, encouraged by the laxity of those who twisted the law of liberty into the law of license. In Palestine, the Sicarii and the Pharisees fought against the exhausted Communities of the faithful, already tormented beyond endurance by the Mosaists who had demolished a "column" of the Church in the person of James the Apostle.

Humanly speaking, Christianity seemed about to collapse. There were many superficial persons who looked only at the outside, the material facts, and still more, those who thought that the end of

Christianity was at hand. The neophytes, whose faith was brief and limited, saw in their fidelity to the Crucified a career that ended in prison; while officials of higher rank, the learned, and the ruling classes, together with the lesser peoples, heaped contempt upon the Church. They regarded the Christians as carriers of pestilence which must soon be gotten rid of.

The Apostle Paul never weakened; he had received the spirit of strength and not of fear; he was a fighter, and believed the life of faith to be a good fight all the way through. Knowing the eternal value of faith, he was not so much afflicted by persecutions as he was by the insidious novelties, heretical intrusions, parties and divisions that turned the fickle people of Asia against him. There were two petulant teachers, Phigelus and Hermogenes, who led a group of false Mosaist doctors; and the two other innovators, Hymeneus and Philetus. There were innumerable other controversalists saying that the Resurrection had already taken place, and thus, the deposit of faith and doctrines entrusted by Paul to the Churches of Asia was laid waste. These were mere tendencies, but Paul foresaw the results.

The old mania of these orientals for discussing, analyzing, making fine distinctions, sophisticating, on the one hand, and for listening to beautiful phrases, bright remarks, clever answers, on the other hand, would soon bury the great deposit of revealed truth under oratorical rubbish. In place of Christ and the Apostles, equivocal masters would be welcomed by the false gnostics and by the authors of myths.

While Paul grieved over this state of affairs, the Roman police, who for three years had hounded and pursued the Christians and above all their leaders, now laid hands on him and on Peter, the two greatest of the Apostles. They were finally ensnared in an ambush brought about by espionage, and for the seventh time Paul wore prison chains for the sake of Jesus Christ, and also for the reason that the Christians were accused of infamous deeds. He was thrown among the criminals in a filthy prison in Rome where the contaminated air was stifling.

The law of Nero, following upon the conflagration, forbade the very existence of Christians. Any person who was a Christian, and persisted in being one, was considered guilty. When discovered, he was subjected to a law suit and then put to death. The pagan state at that time, and for a long time afterwards, thought that to get rid of Christianity, it was enough to kill off the Christians.

As so often happens among men, when Paul was arrested, many of the disciples abandoned him to save their own lives. They shut themselves up in houses, they dispersed to the fields, keeping hidden as best they could. They did as Peter had done in the praetorium of Jerusalem, they denied Paul. When Paul was questioned for the first time, not a single witness appeared to speak in his favor or for the Christians arrested with him. On the contrary, a disciple named Alexander and his companion Hymeneus, once excommunicated from the Church and handed over to Satan because of their defection from the faith, now came forward to avenge themselves, first by venally betraying him to the authorities, and afterwards by making false accusations.

They contradicted Paul in the court when he rose to defend his own deeds and those of the other true Christians with his usual warm and vehement logic. Nevertheless, the inspired defense of the Apostle made an impression and once more he was "set free from the mouth of the lions."

He even succeeded in establishing some relations with people outside the prison; besides seeing Luke quite often, and Eubulus. He saw Pudens and Linus who would succeed Peter as bishop of Rome; Claudia and other faithful ones among the brethren. He received a visit from Onesiphorus, a Christian of Ephesus who had been very generous towards him in that city. It was through him Paul had sent his second letter to Timothy. After Timothy had been dismissed from prison, he was sent again to Asia to fill the Apostle's place in a world grown more antagonistic than ever against the Gospel.

Even then Paul did not bother himself about his chains; his concern was for that youth (Timothy), in poor health and carrying a heavy burden; therefore, he wrote him a letter full of help and encouragement. "For God has not given us the spirit of fear, but of power and of love and of prudence."[5] The mature calm that radiates from this letter, written in prison, only adds to its power. Faith, when openly attacked by Satan's agents who are armed with the iron power of this world, demands strength for martyrdom; that is, "bearing witness." Christian life is a battle, and the Christian must be a soldier for Christ.

The Apostolate was now taking on a new form. Spreading the Word would follow the shedding of blood, as it did with Christ; and Paul knew well that his sufferings were a collaboration with the Gospel and an immense service to the brethren. There is no other way. He who wants to live religiously in Christ must suffer persecution, and the prisoner repeats this as a well-known truth vitally related to the Gospel.

If the Churches were emptied by the police and by the executioners; if the bishops and priests and deacons were bound in chains, there would yet be salvation, since the Word of God, like a two-edged sword, penetrates as far as the joining of the soul with the body and cannot be chained. In its opinion, the formidable mechanism of the Roman state became impotent. Christ would be faithful to him who was faithful to Christ.

The follower of Christ, above all the one who had the duty of directing others, as Timothy had, must hold the Word of God tenaciously and preach it insistently, in time and out of time, reprehending, admonishing, supplicating, exhorting with patience the truth of doctrine. The essential matter was to *hold* and *maintain* the *deposit of doctrine,* and thereby to merit God's grace. Timothy, young and impetuous like all Asiatics, had been disputing warmly with the innovators, but Paul counseled him not to do so, for it was useless as far as truth was concerned and harmful to peace. Paul told him

[5] 2 Tim. 1:7.

to ignore them; to resist the enemies from outside, recalling the truth to their minds. This had been Paul's way in the Apostolate and it had borne much good fruit. Timothy must learn to dwell on the Scriptures by long meditations and prayer and to remember that fidelity to Christ always provoked persecution.

Paul's great concern was to leave a worthy disciple to carry on the work, one well prepared and one who would follow his own example in the Apostolic life. The Church would soon pass into other hands, and the deposit of truth would be entrusted to others also. As for himself, he had no hope of liberation; Paul knew no one would be spared who professed Christianity. He was offering himself in death as a sacrifice to God. He felt that now the end of his life's drama was at hand, and he kept his serenity of soul. He had given proof of his strength before, and he could say in summarizing all the events of his life, "I have fought the good fight, I have finished my course, I have kept the faith." It seemed as if he had chiselled this epitaph for himself.

Nevertheless he still hoped to see Timothy once more, and to give him by word of mouth many recommendations, as one who would be his heir. The procedure of the Roman law was slow. Paul wished that Timothy would make haste and come, bringing Mark with him and the cloak he had left in the home of Carpus at Troas. He needed the cloak as it was often cold in the damp prison, and he also asked that the sacred books be brought him, especially those written on parchment. He could enjoy these in his hours of solitude; to repeat the prophecies and feel again the joy he always experienced in seeing them realized in Christ—the joy ever old and ever new in realizing that Christ had chosen him as His minister.

Paul, being of an active temperament, suffered in solitude. Demas of Thessalonica had been with him, hoping to make Paul's contacts with the outer world, but facing the danger of being drawn into the trial, one day he fled back to Thessalonica. Another faithful disciple, Crescens, had gone to Galatia; Titus was in Dalmatia; Tychicus had been sent to Ephesus; Erastus had remained in Corinth. Trophimus was sick at Miletus, only Luke was with him.

Those names, passing through the mind of the prisoner, recalled so many conquests as well as many defections. To their list in his salutations, Paul included the ever faithful Priscilla and her husband Aquila; this exemplary married couple were as active in the cause of the Gospel as they were in their daily occupations and ordinary business.

The Crown,
A.D. 67

The second process of the Roman law was also long. This is not surprising, even following after the promulgation of Nero's laws which condemned all Christians without any examination at all. Paul was a Roman citizen, therefore he must be treated according to the most meticulous procedure. He was also a Jew; consequently he was to be dealt with according to the Roman regulations concerning the Jewish laws. In the minds of the magistrates, the distinction between Hebraism and Christianity was not very clear. Paul, who exalted Christ as the Flower and Fruit of Hebraism, did not help them any in clarifying their ideas.

His compact and logical dialectics embarrassed them. His personal prestige weakened their will to persecute him, while his friends in the imperial palace put continual obstacles in the way of Nero's justice. Besides, there was the hope of obtaining information regarding the ramifications of the Christian Communities in Rome as well as throughout the Empire. So Peter and Paul were detained in prison a longer time in order to question them. At all events, by their dignity, by their faith, and by their sufferings the two Apostles glorified Christ in their flesh, and all who saw them or heard them must have been edified and impressed.

Finally, a sentence was passed which ended abruptly all the questionings and applied briefly but simply the dispositions of Nero's decree. When taken before the magistrates, Paul was asked whether in the horror of his prison he had become wiser and was ready to deny Christ and thereby gain a few more months or years of existence among men? Paul, serene and firm, confessed his love for Christ, to Him he belonged; and he wept for joy to be able to give this last testimony for Christ.

The judgment hall was crowded with pagans and Jews, who were anxious to see the famous organizer of Churches, the father of the martyrs, himself to be a martyr now. Peter was passing through the same process, but because of his status as a barbarian (as the Jews from outside Rome were called) he was tortured.

Worn out by so much walking in the service of the Gospel, Peter abandoned himself to the sweet embrace of his Master and to his return to the One he so ardently loved. Now Peter understood how painful had been the abandonment in the garden, in the praetorium, and what the solitude on the Cross must have been for Christ. Tradition has it that the two Apostles were put to death on the same day.

It could well be true, as one sentence could have condemned both. They were the two leaders of the Christian Communities, a fact that could easily be proved by spies. And they were condemned for the same crime. However, death could not be inflicted in the same manner because Paul was a Roman citizen while Peter was not; Paul was to be beheaded, Peter was to be crucified.

The Chief of the Apostles, older, with white hair and beard, followed his executioners to the Vatican hill, where the soil was already stained with the blood of martyrs. He was crucified, conformably to the Lord's prediction, "When thou shalt be old, thou shalt stretch forth thy hand, and another shall gird thee and lead thee whither thou wouldst not; signifying by what manner of death he should glorify God." [6] Through humility, Peter would not in his death imitate his Master and asked to be crucified head down, as if he wished to be a holocaust at the feet of Christ. Pious Christians buried

[6] St. John 21:18, 19.

that glorious body in the same place where it fell and there, even today, it glorifies the Lord Jesus Christ.

Paul was led out to a country place called "Aquae Salviae" which means "healing waters," three miles from Rome, not far from the road to Ostia. That venerable old man whose white head was still more bent by the sufferings endured in prison, walking in the midst of a company of soldiers, the lictor preceding them, was an object of curiosity to the spectators and the butt of jokes from idlers. Years and sufferings had still more reduced his height, and the prison had bent his whole person. Now and then, he raised that intelligent countenance as if to inhale the fresh air, and as if undertaking another voyage.

Only on his mouth was there stamped an expression of deep sadness; a sadness which came from a homesickness for his Master, together with a sense of pity for those he was leaving behind. These had not yet heard the Gospel word; and he thought of the ruin wrought by persecution which seemed to be all about him. A great mass of thought burned in those tired eyes peering from beneath an ample forehead, showing the effects of sufferings so patiently endured. He thought of the sufferings he had seen others bear, and felt the consciousness of more to come. His lips moved faintly as he murmured his prayer. The end was near; the fight was coming to an end. The expectancy of Christ awaited him and his eyes shone with vision and ecstasy. They were taking him to his execution, and he was marching his last mile to Paradise.

A few faithful disciples with broken hearts followed from a distance, with the servants of the household of Lucina, a rich Christian convert, in whom some recognize the penitent Pomponia Graecina whom Tacitus mentions. Three miles from the city the cortege turned off the Ostian road and in a short time reached the Aquae Salviae. There, near a pine tree that glorious head was detached by a single stroke of the sword, the head which had given so much glorious thought to all mankind.

The matron Lucina requested the body that she might bury it. It was a request which the Roman law readily granted. A number of Christians and servants, in a sad procession, carried the body to the estate of Lucina on the Ostian road, about a mile from the city. It was buried there, and became the place for many pilgrimages of the Christians until persecutions made it advisable to remove it, along with the body of St. Peter, to a place more secure on the Appian Way called "Ad Catacumbas," The Catacombs.

When peace returned, the two relics were taken from the place called "The Memoria Apostolorum" and brought back to their first burying place on the Ostian Way and the Vatican hill. Over them the Emperor Constantine constructed two basilicas to consecrate their supernatural royalty. Now Rome had, after Romulus and Remus, two new Patrons and Founders, and because of them Rome has become the capital of a new Empire.

On the tomb of Paul was written an epitaph with Roman brevity: "Paulo, Apostolo, Mart" (Paul, Apostle and Martyr). The Church blossomed from those two tombs as from a fountain of life, surrounding the city built on seven hills with a new glory. St. John Chrysostom who loved it, saw in those tombs the most solemn titles of majesty. He delighted to imagine a vision on the Resurrection day when Paul and Peter together should rise to meet the Lord, interpreting the sentiment of all Christianity.

The two Apostles in Rome are like two lamps shining above the whole world. And so did Venantius Fortunatus think of them when he sang:

Gates of Heaven; two lamps for the great world.
Paul thunders with the Word,
Peter flashes from the Rock;
The first opens Heaven with his Doctrine,
The other with the Keys;
Paul shows the way that leads there,
Peter unlocks the door of Heaven.
They stand against the enemy as two armed fortresses;
Towers of faith, whom the city, head of the world contains.

In life they were united. They still live together in the hearts of all the faithful. Like the humble Christians hiding in the underground passages of the Catacombs of St. Sebastian, we will ever invoke them:

"Petre et Paule petite";
"Peter and Paul pray for us!"

Heresy has tried to divide them in order to divide the integrity of the Gospel and to rob Rome of her glory, but the Universal Church on every 29th of June acclaims their birthday: that of their death on earth, by singing a thrilling song to Rome,

O happy Rome, thou of Two Princes
Art consecrated by the glorious
Blood.
Purpled by their blood,
Thou dost surpass all the beauties
Of the world.

CHAPTER XI

PAUL'S CHARACTER

His Faith

The judges and lictors who brought about the death of that old man, dragging himself along on feet so tired and worn from walking thousands of miles through the years, could never have imagined the greatness they had cut down by their decision and their deed of execution. Never had a more glorious spirit passed through Rome. There is in his work the genius of a great conqueror; an Alexander of the Greeks, a Caesar of the Romans. There is in his thought and considerations a depth and richness that resembles the divine Plato but excels him. There is in his manner a tenderness, an enamored fantasy that likens him to Virgil. In his relations to the Eternal God he reminds us of the prophets of old. In his relations to the earthly city of Rome he showed the wisdom of the ancient Consuls. In his relations with all social classes, he surpasses in penetration and tact the greatest masters of Greece and Rome.

The influence exercised by him has been so varied and so vast that whole libraries have been written to explain him; and after centuries his writings have lost nothing of their efficacy. Some have been impressed by his notions of civil law, others by his ideas of sociology. Some have seen in him the support of the Roman Empire and also the creator of medieval society; and a pillar of the Holy Roman Empire. If the Church considers him her most brilliant light in dogma and ethics, heretics also pretend to have him for their doctor.

Paul interests the man of letters and the theologian, the artist, and the sociologist. He is still all things to all men in the most amazing manner. Every sentence of his has generated conversions, every step of his has brought forth Apostles. Cornelius a Lapide, at the beginning of his famous Commentaries, condensed into eight points the admirable qualities of the little man of Tarsus. His nature and temperament; his vocation and grace; his wisdom; his heroic virtues; the efficacy and fruit of his evangelization; his glorious martyrdom; the miracles; and his fame and glory.

Paul is one of the most complete men in recorded history, in whose formation, grace and nature, Judaism and Christianity combined to make of him a universal person. Such a man was needed to defend the universality of Christianity with superhuman vigor and strength. He was a Hebrew and he was a Greek; an agent and, perhaps, a member of the Sanhedrin; a citizen of Rome; an artisan and a student of the Scriptures; a most active man, and also a mystic. He satisfies the learned and the ignorant, the rich and the poor.

He was at ease in Athens among the monuments, and in Galatia among the mountains. He was timid and at the same time authoritative; prudent and yet intrepid; humble and full of just dignity as having been chosen by God. Verily, he was a "vessel of election."

All these qualities blended in him in a perfect synthesis, like a seven-branch candlestick which throws out but one light. He had but one great quality—he was an APOSTLE.

After Christ and the Blessed Virgin Mary, Paul was, perhaps, the most complete person. There was fused in him dogmatic speculation with pastoral practice, an absorbing love for Christ translated into a self-surrendering love for men, a fiery style in the rough handwriting proper to the hand of a tent-maker. He was a man who could speak equally well to a group of philosophers or to a gathering of tanners. He gave into the power of Satan the incestuous man, and the Syncretists; and he could turn his attention to so small a matter as advising a bit of wine for Timothy. In him was united the most sublime mystic with the minutest details in organized activity. He put as much heart into developing the doctrine of the Priesthood of Christ as in writing a commendatory letter for a fugitive slave.

Paul's life was a full one. He gave himself wholly to Christ, allowing Christ to possess him totally, and he was intent on the service of Christ day and night. On he marched, climbing mountains, crossing plains, sailing over seas; resolute and indomitable, seeing Christ in all things, dead to all things else.

"Are they Hebrews? So am I! Are they Israelites? So am I! Are they the offspring of Abraham? So am I! Are they ministers of Christ? I—to speak as a fool—am more: in many more labors, in prisons more frequently, in lashes above measure, often exposed to death. From the Jews five times I received forty lashes less one. Thrice I was scourged, once I was stoned, thrice I suffered shipwreck, a night and a day I was adrift on the sea; in journeyings often, in perils from floods, in perils from robbers, in perils from my own nation, in perils from the Gentiles, in perils in the city, in perils from the wilderness, in perils in the sea, in perils from false brethren; in labor and hardships, in many sleepless nights, in hunger and thirst, in fastings often, in cold and nakedness. Besides those outer things, there is my daily pressing anxiety, the care of all the Churches! Who is weak, and I am not weak? Who is made to stumble, and I am not inflamed? If I must boast, I will boast of the things that concern my weakness." [1]

He said all this before he went up to Jerusalem, where he was so ill-treated and arrested; before his imprisonment in Caesarea and in Rome, the shipwreck at Malta, and before Nero's persecution. It sounds like the story of an adventurer; instead, it is merely a synopsis of his Apostolate. It is the story of heroic adventure, in which men and angels play their part, the demons from hell and Christ in Heaven.

Very often Paul had to consider how to earn his living and how to help those who were poorer than himself. He was tormented by an

[1] 2 Cor. 11:22–31.

illness which he described as a sting in the flesh, but yet he never stopped. A mediocre man might have spent his time in taking care of his health, consulting physicians and talking about remedies. Paul conquered his weakness of the flesh by the power of his spirit. He illuminated the path of the ignorant; fought like a lion in propagating the Kingdom of Christ and in combatting its enemies.

He was a pastor and a teacher; a friend and a guide. He could be severe and he could be most gracious; awe-inspiring and meek. He had understanding for all, and he had compassion for all; on fire only against fornicators of the flesh and falsifiers of the truth.

Everyone could have recourse to him with his varied tastes, humors, failings, and could always find in him their complement and their strength. To the pro-Jews, he was indulgent in regard to their scruples about food. To the pagans, he praised the light of their rational consciences. To the strong, he taught pity; to the weak, fortitude. Pharisee as he was, he became the Apostle to the Gentiles. With the Jews, he was Jewish; with those who were outside the Law, he was as if he had no Law, becoming as he said, all things to all in order to save all. Since he impersonated the spirit of Christ Who is the Redeemer of all, nothing escaped him and no one was a stranger to him. He chose to suffer all things and to sympathize with all men.

He knew how to face the most opposing conditions; to be in abundance or in want; being able to do all in Him Who gave him strength. He was in Asia and thought of those in Macedonia; he was in Achaia and thought of those in Rome and in Ephesus; he was in Italy and thought of his children in Spain and Illyricum.

Possessing a love that was universal, he considered himself a debtor to all. He offered himself as a holocaust to the Lord and for the benefit of the brethren. His life seemed to be consumed in giving life to others. In this, he was a faithful imitator of the Lord. The holocaust was complete; the persecutions of the enemies of the Church, the misunderstandings of friends and the want of confidence from his own people. There were apostasies and divisions among the

Christians; the small annoying circumstances which overflow from the carnal works and influences of the times, seemed to mount up in an ascending scale. Then there were the frequent explosions of Satan against that magnanimous spirit of Paul who labored to spread the Gospel with such lavish generosity.

Paul emptied himself so completely of self; one might say, even of his flesh and blood. He loved his own people for their place in God's plan of the Redemption. He had dismissed for himself all titles, honors and prestige; his place in the Sanhedrin, all wealth, and a career. However, he did not hesitate to proclaim his dignity as an Apostle, and in this respect esteemed himself inferior to none. He regarded himself as the refuse of the world, as an abortive: and at the same time, he offered himself to his children as a model to imitate. And all this because it was not he that was living but Christ living in him; and because everything in him served the Gospel of Christ. He wished to increase the flame of Divine Love and threw into it everything both human or divine, of knowledge or experience, even of his very life.

Because Paul, like Apollos, like everything else, belongs to the souls who are to be conquered for Christ, they belong to Christ and Christ to God. Paul is always so conscious of his total dedication and he expresses it in one of those beautiful effusions of affection. "Let us conduct ourselves in all circumstances as God's ministers, in much patience; in tribulations, in hardships, in distresses; in stripes, in imprisonments, in tumults; in labors, in sleepless nights, in fastings; in innocence, in knowledge, in long-suffering; in kindness, in the Holy Spirit, in unaffected love; in the word of truth, in the power of God; with the armor of justice on the right hand and on the left; in honor and dishonor, in evil report and good report; as deceivers and yet truthful, as unknown yet well-known, as dying and behold, we live, as chastised but not killed, as sorrowful yet always rejoicing, as poor yet enriching many, as having nothing yet possessing all things." [2]

[2] 2 Cor. 6:4-11.

They could beat him, stone him, and nearly tear him to pieces in their attempt to lynch him, but as soon as he left their hands, he calmly adjusted his tunic, wiped the blood and sweat from his face, and began to speak to the first person he met, not of himself, but of Christ. All his marching, tramping, walking was a continual search for souls.

The many sides of Paul's personality projected themselves in many different aspects and in various places and times. He is humble and he can be sarcastic; he is tender and also terrible. When in anguish, he recommends joyfulness. He passes from the dizzy heights of mysticism to scorching invectives. "What is your wish?" he writes to the Corinthians. "Shall I come to you with a rod, or in love and in the spirit of meekness?" He draws from his interior life the most varied sentiments in order to arouse, to teach, and to convince.

Very supple in his ways of presenting the Gospel, Paul used a different method for the learned ones of the Areopagus than he did for the mountaineers of Epirus. How readily he adapts himself to souls to win them for Christ. He was flexible enough in all that was unessential such as food, the Nazarite vow, and circumcision, but he was most uncompromising for truth. He made no mystery that the substance of his teaching is Christ Crucified, and consequently he repudiated all legal formalism and rationalistic paganism. Because Paul is God's minister, and His co-worker, he is the servant of Christ. This service must be rendered in the form of service to souls.

This man, small of stature and infirm in health, has a powerful strength, the greatest that any man can have because it is the strength of God. In this strength every resistance can be overcome; every intelligence bends before it. All machinations are dispelled and all personal weakness overcome. The Apostle knows, when there is need, how to demolish in his followers the slavish idolatry of physical force with its deceitful appearances, substituting for these, true greatness which is that of the spirit. Of this he was himself a great example and one that revolutionized the ideas of men. He had a miserable physique, but it was inhabited by an imperial soul.

His wonderful success in both East and West cannot be explained in human terms. It was certainly due to the grace of God; but a grace that Paul welcomed in its fullness, without any opposing resistance. He gave up everything, career, interests, affections, and allowed himself to be filled and molded by grace. So that in him two forces were always acting, God, Who made the approach to him, and Paul, who in return, went to meet God. And having found God, he abandoned himself to God with all his strength and power. Such a collaboration produced miracles at every turn.

The Apostle

Paul is a voice that speaks only for the Gospel; his person is a means for Evangelization. Having given himself to Christ, he sees only the glory of Christ: Christ and souls. To put it more concisely, souls are to be conquered for the glory of Christ. Paul, giving the whole of himself, gives the whole of the Gospel; his mouth is open wide to declare it, his heart is dilated with Christ. Just as he had identified himself with Christ, so also the souls he has generated in the Gospel become identified with him. Evangelization means for him generating souls for Christ and therefore he must keep in touch with these, spurring them on further to Christ. He loves them, he directs and corrects them as though they were sons, even little children, whom he must nourish with the milk of the Gospel.

"We are frank with you, O Corinthians; our heart is wide open to you. In us there is no lack of room for you, but in your heart there is no room for us." [3] As a father is proud of his sons, so the Corinthians are his glory, his title of nobility before God. He understands the immense responsibility contracted with his election to the Apostolate; and therefore, he fights, and weeps and writes and travels, bears chains, makes tents, all in order to present to God on the day of Judgment an Apostolate complete, unspoiled, and unwasted.

[3] 2 Cor. 6:11–14.

It may be said that the gift he made of himself to his disciples was heroically full and disinterested and won souls for him no less than the force of his arguments, the eloquence of his words, or the endurance of his sufferings. The simple Galatians, for example, would have willingly plucked out their own eyes to bestow them on him. It is very true also that those same Galatians would have done as much for false Apostles. It is, then, with a sorrowing heart that he wrote what must have filled his readers with contrition, "My little children whom I carry in my bosom until Christ be formed in you." He feels himself a father to them; even more, he is both father and mother.

The Apostle, since he concurs with God for the building up of the Mystical Body of Christ, regards his work as similar to the maternity of Mary who gave life to Christ. As such, he belongs entirely to his sons, since "the children are not for the parents, but the parents for the children." Therefore he says to the Corinthians, "But I most gladly spend and am spent myself for your souls, even though, loving you more, I be loved less." [4]

Because in love—and the Apostolate is first of all love—what we give is of more value than what we receive. Paul loves his children even jealously and with zeal in the Lord. It was Christ in Person Who made him an Apostle. It is by the Will of God he is chosen an Apostle of Jesus Christ; selected, called to that mission by the Father of our Lord Jesus Christ. As such he esteems himself an Apostle, and bears this title along with Peter and James and John and the rest of the Eleven. He is inferior in nothing to those who are the great Apostles called the "pillars" of the Church. Although of himself he is nothing, he remembers with sorrow that he once persecuted the Church of God. Because Paul knows who has chosen him, he expects in his Apostolate the fruit of miracles and virtues.

The Judaizers and other rivals denied his rights to his titles but he vindicates them strongly. He writes these titles at the beginning of all his great Epistles and defends them against all detractors. He has

[4] 2 Cor. 12:15.

seen Jesus Christ: and now he sees the evidence in the fruit of his labors. The Churches he founded set the seal on his Apostolate. Although his visible relations with Jesus were less continuous and were shorter than those of the other Apostles, he compensates for this by a greater intensity of work, and by what amounts to a *hunger* for Christ in order to see Him grow in His Church.

All his personal action is directed towards the Gentiles. There is, between him and Peter, a kind of understanding in the field of preaching; Peter went to the dispersed Jews, and Paul to the Gentiles; thus he became known as the "teacher of the Gentiles." For this function he was well suited. Although a member of the Israelite people, he belonged by birth to the Hellenic community, and he was a Roman citizen. It was part of the universality of the Christian message to cultivate an interest in any social group without distinction; Peter in fact spread the Gospel in Antioch and in Rome among both the Jews and pagans; Paul preached repeatedly in the Synagogues of Rome.

Paul was the docile and powerful instrument in calling the pagans to the Church of God, the new Israel, and the greatest glory of his Apostolate is in this. It cost him much, even his own blood. To a Pharisee, universality meant a cutting loose from the past, a revolt against his own people, a real tearing of the flesh, and he felt this keenly. Nevertheless, he imposed his mission on the doubters and the stubborn rejectors. He finally introduced the Gentiles into the Church and in this way opened the Kingdom of God to the pagans.

Through Paul, more than through any other person, Christ levelled the dividing wall between the Monotheists and the Polytheists, between the circumcised and the uncircumcised. If God Himself had called Paul to be an Apostle, he could be nothing else but an Apostle. He could be tormented, imprisoned, calumniated, but he must be an Apostle: he could not refuse to announce Christ. "I do all things for the sake of the Gospel, that I may be a partaker thereof." He would rather be in chains, on a ship adrift at the mercy of the waves, in a city obsessed by pride and dissolute by evil living, than not to be an Apostle.

If he is not ashamed of the Gospel, even under the blast of scorn or scourging, neither does he glory in his success as an Evangelizer; to preach was for him a necessity. "Woe to me if I do not evangelize," he says.

Suffering for the Apostolate

The teaching of Paul, as we find it in his letters and in the writings of St. Luke, is contained for the most part in the question that Jesus addressed to him from the cloud of light on the road to Damascus. "Paul, why persecutest thou Me?" That question had enlightened the Pharisee, so blind in the depths of his soul, unveiling for him the great reality that Christ and the Christian are all one. This common identity had impressed him and left its stamp on all his doctrine.

Once this was clear to Paul, he knew that as a Christian he was one with Christ. Grace and will made this union so strong that never again was it Paul who lived, but Christ living in him. Starting from this first premise, that the Christian is another Christ, an *"alter Christus,"* then the Apostolate became a spiritual effusion which nothing could stop, an exuberant activity and the very life of the new man. Henceforth, he acts as in Christ with Whom he has become one body.

The Apostolate has its counterpart in heaven. On God's part, it is a Kingdom; on earth, man's part is to suffer. In a certain sense, the measure of the Apostolate, given any man, is in equal measure to the suffering it occasions. Better still, the Apostolate is carried out both by teaching and suffering; the latter completes and confirms the former just as Jesus concluded His Evangelization with His death on the Cross. Paul learned this also at the moment his vocation was made known to him; and for this cause the persecutor became the persecuted.

Paul had no fear of suffering. Since he must reproduce Christ in himself, it was not surprising that he should repeat Christ's sufferings. After receiving the Holy Spirit, he was entirely given to Christ from that moment, and consequently to the Apostolate. The Apostolate which each one of us accomplishes is in due proportion to our love of Christ; and the Apostolate each one omits is in due proportion to the love of self.

Paul was never ashamed of the Gospel; neither before the Sanhedrin, nor before the princes of Palestine, nor before the skeptics of Greece. In order to preach Christ, he traversed the Empire from Palestine to Spain, from Galatia to Rome; without rest or pause; speaking and disputing, day and night, with those who wished to hear, and even with those who did not. His spirit possessed endless patience and it was a devouring fire. His preaching accompanied the labor of his hands, and the prodigies from God's hands increased.

As long as Paul lived he spoke. Faith must be released in speech as the sparks fly from the flint; for this, he spoke in the public squares and in the Synagogues; and when he could not speak he wrote. Everywhere his voice was heard: in the royal courts, in the prisons, on land and on sea, to the Jews and to the idolaters. A sacred fire burned within him; and like his Master he wished to set the world on fire with Divine Love. So he took up and prolonged the work of Christ upon earth. He ceased to speak only when they severed his head from his body. The Apostle is always an Apostle; he does not waste an hour, or a quarter of an hour; he does not miss an occasion that may be of value to a soul. If he does not convert, at least he arouses interest.

With these sentiments to urge him on in his work, death appears to Paul as the crown for a well-won fight, a very good fight, like the goal in a competitive race. It was also, for him, a race from one place to another for the purpose of reaching other groups, to fly from snares of his enemies, and this he had to do constantly. In his Apostolate Paul dies daily; like the seed thrown into the ground, if it does not die, it does not produce. It is by his death that he will give life to others.

Paul went wandering for Christ. For the sake of Christ he preferred the maledictions of his own people to a career in the Sanhedrin. He was a new spectacle to the world, to men and to angels. He suffered hunger, thirst and nakedness; he was struck on the face, and he was homeless. His soul received bitterness in proportion as it gave out the Gospel, but this never caused him to lose courage. By his good deeds he annulled the effects of evil; he opposed imprecations with blessings, persecutions with patience. He became the refuse of the world that he might more perfectly imitate Christ. Since the dignity of an Apostle is the greatest of all dignities, he humbled himself the more, into the very dust.

Paul lives the life of Christ crucified; in Christ he dies, yearning to be dissolved and to be with Him. Christ gives not only the gift of faith but the gift of suffering. The life of the Christian is an exercise of faith and of pain; that is, of warfare, for in persecution the Christian is a soldier who must fight; indeed, he is to resist and defeat the prince of this world, Satan with all his satellites.

More especially is the Apostolate an uninterrupted term of suffering, and Paul suffers. He draws from his pain joy for others, and joy for himself; he glories in his pains because they are not suffered in vain. They supplement what is wanting in the sufferings of Christ, and for the benefit of the Mystical Body which is the Church.

Thus if any man is saved through faith, he is associated in a sense with the work of Redemption, fruit of the sufferings of Christ. Therefore man must be associated with suffering. If the Mystical Body, the Church, suffers, it is Christ Who suffers; and the Christian who willingly accepts suffering helps to accumulate for the Church the fruits of the Passion of Christ.

Christ and the Apostle

Paul the Apostle preaches Christ and Christ crucified. He is always vigilant that his objective doctrine may never be supplanted by the subjective opinions of men. Faith is a condition for salvation and for unity. By faith men are saved, by grace they are united to Christ, by doctrine they are part of the organization of the Church.

All that Paul does, all that he teaches, he does as another Christ. He is engaged in an intense drama with Christ for the center: Christocentric. As for himself, Paul wishes to be only an exemplar for Christ. If he asks his own disciples that they, too, become imitators of him, Paul, it is because he has become an imitator of Christ. In imitating Paul, his disciples had before their eyes a reproduction of Christ Himself. This was of immense importance, because, while many of them were not able to follow his profound doctrine, wholly Christocentric, they could understand, without too much effort, what it meant to see Christ living in Paul. It has been the same ever since; Christian people wish to see in their pastors so many copies of Christ; to see the living doctrine which is faith in action.

The heart of Paul is the heart of Christ; the word of Paul is the word Christ speaks through him. Paul was buried with the Lord in baptism, and with Him rose again, changed, a new man and an Apostle. He carries Christ to others, and gives himself wholly to the life of Christ.

If this is the sentiment of the Apostle, it can readily be imagined that his doctrine and the whole range of his theology is centered in the Person of Jesus Christ. Christ is the Mediator Who brings man close to God, earth close to Heaven, Who reunites humanity with divinity, the flesh with the spirit, the past with the future. Christ recapitulates in Himself in all things; He is the great High Priest, He is the Saviour and the Redeemer Who, in destroying sin, has vanquished death, bringing life back to the world. He is the source from which flows all the past and all the future; both meet in Him.

Redemption was accomplished through the shedding of Blood, the Blood of Christ. The Church is the result of that Blood; all the Sacraments draw their efficacy from that Blood, and by that Blood we live. Christ is the High Priest in a sanctuary not made by hands, offering to God in expiation for man's sins, His own Divine Blood, since He is both Priest and Victim. For this saving task He had humbled Himself, even to becoming man and embracing the whole state of man, sin excepted. Christ is, as it were, burdened with sin in order to destroy it by letting Himself be crucified; to bury it by allowing Himself to be buried.

This divine operation has wrought the great miracle of re-establishing a universal reconciliation of all things; whether on earth or in heaven. In the midst thereof, sin (the principle of disintegration) had entered like a flash of lightning, cleaving asunder what was human from what was divine, producing dissensions and divisions among men.

By sin, the bonds between the Eternal God and man had been severed; the Blood of Christ, poured upon the world, had re-established them. It has destroyed enmities, demolished the wall that divided the Jews from the Gentiles; and in place of war caused by sin, He has given His peace among men.

The fountain of Blood pouring from those Five Wounds and that Divine Head, still flows from the Chalice of blessing and benediction which communicates to us the Blood of Christ. The Bread which is broken for us communicates to us the Body of Christ. And the Eucharistic Bread of which all eat, is One and the same Body of Christ. In this Body all are made one in Christ, and It is also the Body which all compose, the Church.

The Church is the Body of Christ; theologians would say more specifically, the Mystical Body of Christ. The Eucharist is the spiritual food and drink which slakes our thirst for divinity, which remolds those who are baptized into the living organism of the Body Whose Head is Christ. It is Christ Who confers on this Body, the Church, His gifts of eternity and incorruptibility.

The greatest of all revolutions is seen in the new Christian society and universal unity actuated by Him. Hebraism is abolished, the differences between peoples annulled; all men are restored to a reconquered level of liberty; freed from the chains of legalism and the Law, from idolatry and innumerable defects. There are no longer Greeks or Jews, circumcised or uncircumcised, slaves or free; but all belong to Christ Who is all in all. He is in all things and in all men; that is, all men and all things are unified in the one and only Christ, forming with Him the Head of a single Organism: the Catholic Church.

It is a universal, and at the same time, an individual revolution, because it embraces the whole of humanity at all times, and concerns every individual creature. The individual person, once baptized, dies to his state of sin, to the "old man," and becomes another, a new divine creature. Faith in Christ is an impulse to a continual renewal, an inexhaustible rebirth, so that, in the Church, her life is always new and always eternally young. It is a revolution that begins again at each moment, with each creature.

The Eschatology of Paul is the doctrine of the supreme dissolving of the universe under the power of Christ. The epilogue of those days when, after the last domination the enemy of Christ is vanquished, sin and death are destroyed forever, the Kingdom of Life everlasting (with the resurrection of the body) will make the Just to reign with Christ since they are co-heirs with Him for all Eternity. For this purpose Christ, the Son of God, already sits at the right hand of the Father in Heaven. He shall return in glory and power to destroy all His enemies, to make Himself known as King of kings, Lord of lords. He is over all, angels and men, heaven and earth. There is no greatness or glory above His.

The Church and the Apostle

Paul's theological doctrines moved abreast with his Christological doctrines. There is Christ and there is the Church. Christ has founded a society, the Church; it is a living organism of which He is the Head, a Head completed by the members, both constituting the Body. Christ lives and operates in the Church; Redemption is being indefinitely carried on there. The Church is the Mystical Christ, the total Christ; and Paul loves the Church just as he loves Christ, with Whom he sees it identified. It is in the Church Paul sees realized that recapitulation which the revolution of the Cross has brought about.

There are those incipient gnostic contaminations which aim at annulling this Society, reducing it to a mere aggregation of spirits, making it an *invisible entity,* and thinking in this way to elevate it to something of higher worth. In the new order the Incarnation demands that bodies be where souls are; that the external be an expression of the internal; that charity and justice be concrete and visible in the brotherhood of men.

Therefore we see from the very start the Apostle cultivating the sanctity of his converts by frequenting the assemblies of the Christians and learning the doctrine. The Church is becoming something definite and particular, a distinct institution, both human and divine; and this in the midst of a world pagan and Jewish.

This visibility is a proof of its sanctity. This organization which the Apostles, bishops, priests, deacons, teachers, all serve, is a guarantee of its unity and orthodoxy. In its ministry of baptism, in the Eucharist, and in its counsels, all become co-sharers in Christ. They take up collections by which the poor share in the goods of the rich. This Body, the Church, exercises an authority that renders justice in private dissensions and differences, and since it has Divine Power to bind or loosen, it can also abandon an unrepentant sinner to Satan.

Finally, the Church which is the whole Christ, is Theandric; it is as human and divine as the Man-God. The Church, like Christ, is both flesh and spirit; and thus it can fulfill the mission of Christ in uniting humanity and divinity. It cannot help being one, as Christ is One.

As the Eucharist on which we are all fed is One and the same, so all who partake of it in Holy Communion are made one in Christ. All receive the same vital Substance, all form one Body in Christ.

The Church is this Body of Christ Which continues to pour His

Divine Blood out upon men, in spite of the fact that men on their part continue to pour sin over the world. And since the soul of the Church is the Holy Spirit, and her Head is Christ, her blood is the Blood of Christ, she possesses incorruptibility and distributes Divinity. Strong in this unity, the baptized with their divinely given gifts, special to each in vocation or in duty, work together harmoniously as with one heart, enriching the Body with life and vitality. They all serve this Body of which they are members by serving Christ and other souls.

The Christian is not an isolated person and cannot be an individualist because, being baptized, he is vitally ingrafted into an organism which is both human and divine. In many incisive and descriptive ways Paul never wearies of explaining to his disciples, who had been brought up in the idea of atomic individualism or in the exclusiveness of sects, that they are a part of a vital and living organism. This organism, the Church, is a universal Body that comprehends in itself heaven and earth, breaking down all barriers of individualism and exclusivism. The consequences of this teaching were far-reaching. The first duty of Christians was to preserve this solidarity among themselves by sharing responsibilities. Each must be united to each, and each to all, working for the good of Christian brethren, and thus making Christ realized continually in the world.

The Holy Spirit Which animates all Christians is One, but different ministries are entrusted to each for the service of all. One person may be given the gift of doctrine, another the gift of miracles, another of prophecy, another the discernment of spirits; but all these gifts are carried on by one and the same Holy Spirit, Who distributes to each as He wills.

"For as the body is one and has many members, and all the members of the body, many as they are, form one body, so also is it with Christ. For in one Spirit we were all baptized into one body, whether Jews or Gentiles, whether slaves or free; and we were all given to drink of one Spirit. For the body is not one member, but many. If the foot says, 'Because I am not a hand, I am not of the body,' is it therefore not of the body? And if the ear says, 'Because I am not an eye, I am not of the body,' is it therefore not of the body?

"If the whole body were an eye, where would be the hearing? If the whole body were hearing, where would be the smelling? But as it is, God has set the members, each of them, in the body as he willed. Now if they were all one member, where would the body be? But as it is, there are indeed many members, yet but one body. And the eye cannot say to the hand, 'I do not need thy help'; nor again the head to the feet, 'I have no need of you.' Nay, much rather, those that seem the more feeble members of the body are more necessary; and those that we think the less honorable members of the body, we surround with more abundant honor, and our uncomely parts receive a more abundant comeliness, whereas our comely parts have no need of it. But God has so tempered the body together in due portion as to give more abundant honor where it was lacking; that there may be no disunion in the body, but that the members may have care for one another. And if one member suffers anything, all the members suffer with it, or if one member glories, all the members rejoice with it.

"Now you are the body of Christ, member for member. And God indeed has placed some in the Church, first apostles, secondly prophets, thirdly teachers; after that miracles, then gifts of healing, services of help, power of administration, and the speaking of various tongues. Are all apostles? Are all prophets? Are all teachers? Are all workers of miracles? Do all have the gift of healing? Do all speak with tongues? Do all interpret? Yet strive after the greater gifts." [5]

There is one gift all may possess and which is above all other gifts in value and importance, and that is charity. Paul, who is filled with the Spirit of Christ, intones the most sublime hymn to charity. Charity is both heat and life in the Body of Christ. Charity can be described as the cement which binds together all social life in the world. The more there is of charity, the better society is fused into one. It is the bond of perfection; the more it unifies, the more it perfects. We are as

[5] I Cor. 12:12–31.

perfect as we are united in the Church, and the more we adhere to the Church, the nearer we come to Christ. To live in the Church and with the Church and of the Church is an unceasing transformation into Christ.

The Romans especially had a clearer conception of what Paul meant by the "body," although their idea was a juridical one. Paul teaches that we are members of a single body and also belong to one another. The Church is a perfect society organized in multiplicity and unity. Her ministers, apostles, bishops, priests, deacons, prophets, and assemblies of the faithful are all under one head.

The Church is a perfect society in still another sense; it is a true state, *"sui generis"* whose See is in Heaven and, as such, Paul calls it the "Heavenly Jerusalem" in his letter to the Hebrews. Its members are called "citizens of heaven" fellow-citizens with the Saints, all are one family of God.

"But you have come to Mount Sion, and to the city of the living God, the heavenly Jerusalem, and to the company of many thousands of angels, and to the Church of the firstborn who are enrolled in the heavens, and to God, the judge of all, and to the spirits of the just made perfect." [6]

In its unity and its stability, Paul compares the Church to an edifice constructed on the foundation of the Apostles and Prophets, whose corner-stone is Jesus Christ Himself. This edifice rises like a great temple of the Lord, a house of the living God, the pillar and ground of truth. The component parts of the Church are, on the one hand, the just and, on the other hand, the sinners. They resemble vessels of gold, of silver, of wood, or of clay for use in a home. The Lord and Master of the home knows what belongs to Him.

In regard to all that preceded the Cross, the Church is likened to a tree; always a shady olive tree, a favorite simile of the Hebrews. The Chosen People of the Promise are the natural branches, and the pagans are the wild branches grafted into the tree. Faith in Jesus Christ has made all equal, made all into one family.

[6] Heb. 12:22–24.

An organism so complex and so united, a society so vast and of such solidarity, must have its laws and its doctrines. These are found in Tradition and Scripture. It must have a hierarchy and organs for action; these are the bishops, the priests, and the deacons. All these must faithfully transmit the teaching received from the Apostles who in their turn received it from Christ.

Orthodoxy consists in a faithful, uninterrupted transmission of truth from those who have the authority to rule, just as any inheritance is handed on from father to son. It is with scrupulous fidelity that the teachings of Christ are thus transmitted. Those in authority, entrusted with this transmission, must be on their guard against spurious doctrines and innovations put forward by false teachers. St. Paul calls these false leaders "dogs." They are false workmen who do not labor for the building up of the Church but for the destruction of the edifice. Therefore bishops, priests, and deacons must be not only irreprehensible and blameless in their personal lives, but they must also be sure and true in the doctrines they teach.

In the first sowing of the Gospel it is evident that the hierarchy is still in the process of formation; however, particular deference is shown Peter, and the spirit of discipline is already established. The bishops and priests ordained by the Apostle Peter, by the imposition of his hands, are venerated and obeyed by the Communities since they represent the Apostle himself.

CHAPTER XII

THE WORKS OF ST. PAUL

Sanctification

The sanctity of the faithful within the ecclesiastical society of the Church is in no way pantheistic. It is the sanctity of Christ which fills the whole, rather than that of the individual members. In his letter to the Romans Paul defines in vigorous terms the principle of unity in the whole body and the harmony that must bind members to members. He teaches also that each one will be required to give a personal and individual account of himself to God. Each member of the ecclesiastical society, the Church, shares in the responsibility of the whole and he must make his own personal contribution of sanctity to the collective life of the Church.

Therefore, no person is an isolated one, lost in the crowd. There is union in the society, but the individual is not submerged in it; there is solidarity, but not the destruction of liberty, so newly won for each one by Christ Who died for each. Each member can exert an influence for good inasmuch as he contributes to the work of the whole. For this reason, the Apostle unfolds the meaning of dogma and morals. Customs and habits must be the fruit of faith. What we do follows what we believe; body and soul must work together, testifying each to each, so that a person's sensible exterior must be a faithful reflex of the invisible interior.

The end is God; the means, man in human flesh working out his own salvation in the field of life's experiences, and all this in the society of the Church on earth. Christ has redeemed us; He has given us His grace to render us just and to sanctify us. To accomplish this plan in its fullest measure Paul gives many detailed rules of life. The essence of all he explains is the central idea that the Christian must empty himself of self and be filled with Christ.

Paul describes this as meaning that Christ must be formed in us; it is building up Christ in the individual. The true Christian is one in whom Christ has been formed. When this is done, good works, holy works radiate easily and spontaneously. Whether such a Christian eats or sleeps, he lives with Christ, lives in Christ, lives for Christ. His life becomes Christ and whatever he is doing, it is all for the glory of God.

His body, filled with Christ, glorifies Christ, and his whole existence, through Christ, glorifies God. Everything for the Christian, eating, drinking, his labor—whether he is an artist, a professional man, or a slave—all conspire to glorify God. This is the purpose for which he exists and it becomes the rule of his life.

The relation of the Christian to Christ is a blood relationship, for the Blood of Christ molds believers into one body and unites them to one another. For this reason they have constant duties to one another, obligations in which charity is translated into action, and which builds up the solidarity of the whole. One for all, and all for one, is the principle charity inspires. In this way each member helps the others and assists in the edification of the whole body.

This is a most difficult work and can only be accomplished by the destruction of selfishness, which, being constantly pruned as constantly puts out new branches. Every time he spoke and in the letters he wrote, Paul had to recall this necessity for mutual help and mutual duties among the Christians. It is a lesson so easily forgotten. The duties of one Christian towards another spring from three essential virtues, faith, hope and charity; they are the links which bind Christian to Christian, and make them brothers.

These three virtues, which the theologians call theological, are explicitly praised and explained by St. Paul. In his polemics for the Jews, Paul emphasizes faith because the Jews stressed the works of the Law; in his polemics for the pagans he emphasizes charity as they were strongly inclined to egoism.

Faith is essential to salvation; we are made just by our faith in Jesus Christ. There is no other means for salvation; therefore, the just man lives by faith. The rabbis of the period multiplied the many ways for observing the Law and believed that performing these numerous works, such as ablutions, incisions, gestures, and steps, produced the *right* to justification. Later on the Rabbi Akiba wrote, "All has been examined (that is, all of these works), free will has been given, the world will be judged in goodness and all depends on the quantity of works."

If such a criterion of values should be transferred to the new religion of Christianity, then salvation would not be a gift of God but a conquest made by man. It would require recompense from God due to man, as a salary is paid for services rendered. Jesus Christ would have become man in vain and His death for men would have neither value nor meaning.

Paul combats vigorously, with vehemence of sentiment and thought, this presumption by which man takes the place of Christ and legal practices usurp the place of the Divine Redemption. The ex-Pharisee understood very well that if the right relation between faith and works was not solidly and firmly established in the new economy, one would slide backwards from Christianity to rabbinical doctrines, from the New Covenant to the Old, from Christ back to Moses, and the Cross would be made void.

But let us understand one another. From the beginning Paul's polemics, launched against the works of the Law, provoked misunderstanding among the ill-intentioned, who were ready to pretend a misinterpretation of the belief that salvation came only with faith. And as for works, one could do as one pleased. More than one Christian has made an effort to believe that Christ could be formed in a body subject to sin. This strange paradoxical concept made its appearance in Paul's lifetime and has reappeared since his death.

It is true that faith alone saves us, and that God makes us this gift of salvation, purchased by the Blood of Christ, but it is also true that faith operates through charity. Faith must be living and active, and not a dead weight. The activity of faith is a movement towards God inspired by charity.

Charity towards God consists in forming Christ in us, and its effects are two-fold: we are sanctified and we assist in the sanctification of our brothers by helping them to bear their burdens in life. Paul calls this "fulfilling the law of Christ." Where there is faith, there is charity. Of all the virtues, charity is the greatest because it shows itself in works and in rendering service to others.

The Law of Christ replaces the Law of Moses; the latter is the shadow and prefigures the former. The Mosaic Law imposed carnal works and was only intended to awaken the conscience to a sense of sin, and thus prepare for the new Law of Christ in Whom the works of the spirit would break asunder the bonds of the Old. The New Law binds us closely to the necessity for virtue, and the practice of virtue leads to sanctification. "All Scripture is inspired by God and useful for teaching, for reproving, for correcting, for instructing in justice; that the man of God may be perfect, equipped for every good work." [1]

The New Covenant sets us free from the legal works of Mosaism but not from the good works due to God; the former became superfluous and dead, the latter are living, useful, and necessary. To live in Christ, incisions in the flesh are of no avail, but it is indispensable that we make incisions in the spirit by cutting out concupiscence. The love of Christ and the love of men urges the Christian to a dynamic activity.

Such a dynamic work is the preoccupation of the Christian by day and by night; so much so, that the religion of Christ is not a static condition but a *doing*. It is an activity interior and exterior, and without pause.

The first duty of a Christian is his own sanctification; to model his own life on Christ, crucifying the flesh with its vices and concupiscences. When the body has become chaste it is offered to God as a

---

[1] 2 Tim. 3:16, 17.

living sacrifice, a holy victim which is pleasing to Him. This is the worship due to God from a rational creature. Modelling his life on Christ the Christian goes about doing good. "And in doing good let us not grow tired; for in due time we shall reap if we do not relax. Therefore, while we have time, let us do good to all men, but especially to those who are of the household of faith. What things a man shall sow, that he shall reap." [2]

Here follows a lesson for the Galatians explaining the gratuitous aspects of the gift of salvation. A rich man gives a reward to exemplary citizens. He does not cease to be the donor of the gifts gratuitously given simply because he is giving his gifts to worthy people; nor does the fact that they are worthy people give them the *right* to possess the gifts or to merit them. This is true in our relation to God. Man on his part does good works; this is pleasing to God and what He desires. God wills it so, and in this way man co-operates with God.

Jesus Christ is the foundation for every personal life as well as for Christian society. Men build on Him and God will give the recompense. In serving God man does not acquire a right to a recompense, but his service pleases God Who can reward it. Through man's collaboration with God and by means of good works, he exercises his free will. Man can, therefore, accept or refuse to serve God. If he has faith, but refuses to serve God, his faith becomes inert, weak, listless, whereas the exercise of faith must be "a good fight" in order to carry away the prize of "eternal life" to which we are called by God.

The Christian must be rich in good works. This is his spiritual wealth, which he acquires by both faith and good works. St. Paul admonishes his children to abhor evil, and to cling to the good. "Let us consider how to unite one another to charity and good works." [3]

Such is the complete thought of St. Paul. He stresses details that are proper to the circumstances of life according to the particular class of people he is instructing.

[2] Gal. 6:9, 10.
[3] Heb. 10:24.

The Social Doctrines

Good works are insisted upon and urged so constantly by St. Paul that he has become the teacher of pastoral life. He is the most complete exponent of social doctrines found in the New Testament. "Doing good" is a principle he applied to every class of people in the whole range of human society; all must practice doing good, not only in relation to God but also in relation to one's neighbor. The Christian is one who does so, and his charity has two aspects: towards God his Creator, and towards man God's creature. The Christian is baptized, therefore every act of his must be a Christian act, whether he is asleep, or awake, at work, at commerce, at home, or in the forum, and especially when he is in the assemblies of the Church.

Paul's sociology describes what a man must be in order to be a saint, and what a saint must do when he enters into contact with other men. He must then become an exponent of sanctity in human society, he must be *sanctity in action*.

Here again he starts with God towards Whom all actions lead, since He is their beginning and last end. In Heaven (God's Kingdom) there is a perfect hierarchy of order and of love. Human society is intended to be modelled on this same regime; to be an image of Heaven just as man himself is an image of God.

The first of all our social duties is towards the faithful. There must be deference towards superiors, docility towards one's teachers, contributions to the material maintenance of the ministers and pastors of the Church, and obligations in the ceremonies, meetings, and assemblies of the Church. There is the duty to preserve peace among the faithful in order to avoid disputes and divisions. Such humility is needed so that each one will consider himself less than the others, and the servant of all since he is the servant of Christ. Each must aim to work in such a way that he is working less for himself than he is for his brethren. Thus the life of the Church becomes peace, harmony, and disinterestedness.

The social virtue par excellence is charity copied from Jesus Christ Who became the universal servant of all men. Man honors his neighbor when he considers himself his neighbor's servant. All responsibilities, offices, duties, and tasks are done successfully and well when inspired by this ideal of service. It excludes self-love, self-interest, radical egoism, exploitations, and it prevents friction. Because of charity, mutual help and support is freely given; therefore St. Paul says, "Charity is patient (does not murmur or complain), and is kind. Charity does not envy, is not pretentious, is not puffed up, is not ambitious (that is, for self), is not self-seeking, is not provoked to anger; thinks no evil, does not rejoice over wickedness, but rejoices with the truth; bears with all things, believes all things, hopes all things, endures all things." [4]

Such sentiments make brothers compassionate towards one another. They can rejoice with those who are rejoicing, and weep with those who are in sorrow, making the feelings of others their own. This must be done without simulation for, being members one of another, there must be nothing false or untrue entering into the relationships of the members of Christ. A Christian "does not rejoice over wickedness, but rejoices with the truth" writes St. Paul to his children in Corinth. Anything in the nature of untruth destroys unity in the Church and proves harmful to those who spread it.

A Christian must be as sincere and truthful towards his brother as he must be towards himself. In this manner God is glorified in all men's relations with one another. The spirit must be sincere without any shadow of sin, as becomes the saints. Therefore, impurity, obscenity, scurrility are not even to be mentioned, neither foolish talk, but let there be a spirit of joy among Christians. Paul knew how easy it was, for the sake of amusement, to fall into the snare of telling unbecoming jokes or tales in the company of others. Books, public amusements, the theatres, songs and popular legends favored such looseness of morals. All these influence thoughts, and thoughts are spoken in words, and words express a person's inward spirit.

[4] 1 Cor. 13:4–9.

In all our social relations there must be justice and charity. To each one must be given his just due according to Roman custom, but when one gives what is one's own in a larger measure, this would be charity according to the Christian custom. We are to remember that honor and loyalty are due those in authority as heads of the state—all governors and magistrates—remembering that according to Jewish wisdom Roman authority is from God, and he who exercises it, is the minister of God. Therefore, to obey the representative of rightful authority is an act of virtue.

Even towards Nero who persecuted him, Paul—and Peter also—following in their Master's footsteps, set the example of loyalty and obedience to duly constituted authority and power by their promptness in paying the taxes and tributes exacted of the people. Paul's civic loyalty was always great. His admonitions prove his own carefulness since the whole matter of taxes and tributes demanded by the Roman government were occasions for numerous revolts and migrations of the Jews in order to escape paying them.

The exaction of taxes in the time of Nero—and Paul was writing from Rome at that time—had emptied whole villages in Egypt of their male population. Women and children were often persecuted and judged guilty because they were not able to ransom the men who, in their misery, had fled from home. In Judea this had provoked a storm of resentment and not a few revolts.

The whole Christian Law can be summed up in the commandment, "Love thy neighbor as thyself." This is something positive while it also includes the negative commands of the Old Law. "Thou shalt not kill, thou shalt not steal, etc.," all have the same force, but are far surpassed by something greater. In abstaining from doing evil, one is *obliged* to do good, to exercise charity according to the new precept. Charity is the great flame of the Christian revolution. Love is now the debt due to all men.

Love must draw us out of our selfishness and our exclusiveness, and put into common use all spiritual and material goods. This aim will bring about a better balance and prevent those excessive differences in social life, such as immense wealth or intense poverty. Charity alone will draw society towards a relative equality. He who has, must give to him who has not. The first obligation in spiritual and economic solidarity will be to aid the poorer brothers in their needs. At that time, the first in destitution and in need of aid were the Christians at Jerusalem.

The vice St. Paul abhors most is avarice. He regards the avaricious as idolaters who put gold in the place of the living God. Together with the impure, these shall have no place in the inheritance of Christ and of God. Avarice is like a barrier of metal opposing the free flow of charity. If an avaricious man enters into the society of the faithful, they are to send him away and not even consent to eat with him. There may be some necessity, however, of dealing with him, because all contact with such persons cannot be avoided as long as one is in this world. No intimacy must be allowed, even if such a one were baptized, because his works make null and void his baptismal promises and the obligations of faith. Paul knows very well that when the spirit of a man is absorbed in the accumulation of money, Mammon becomes his god, and virtue is only hypocrisy.

In themselves, riches are indifferent things. All things are good in their origin since they were created by God; it is in their *use* that they become good or evil. Therefore riches are not condemned, but it is deceitful to trust in them, and they are intended to be used in making one rich in good works.

The purpose of man's existence is not in becoming rich in the goods of this world; he came into this world with nothing, and he leaves it with nothing. He should be contented with what is necessary; if he yields to the desire of enriching himself, he falls into the snares of the devil, who eventually strangles him with useless and harmful desires. "The root of all evil is avarice," [5] and in this revealed wisdom of Paul, he confirms the best expression of rational wisdom in all antiquity.

Like riches, the action of eating is in itself an indifferent thing be-

[5] 1 Tim. 6:10.

cause all food is in itself good. This is a courageous truth for a Jew to admit, since one of the obstacles to the assimilation or amalgamation of the Jews with other peoples, was exactly this discrimination of foods, pure or impure, drinks allowed and drinks forbidden. It is rather the use and not the measure that gives food and drink their ethical or moral value. It is the spirit with which one eats or drinks that gives value to the act. The measure is necessary, but it must be placed on him who eats rather than on what is eaten.

This concept explains why the Apostle Paul, who is always so indifferent to the use of meat, abstains from meats in order not to give scandal. For this reason he willingly practices severe fasts for the sake of penance and prayer.

The fruit of our labor is to be used for ourselves and for those who have less than we, and so Paul weaves tents to support himself and others in need of his help. The beautiful saying of Jesus, omitted by the Evangelists, is gathered up and treasured for us by Paul, "It is better to give than to receive."

Work is the common way (if not the most fortunate way) to earn one's living as well as to gain profit. Work is a means to an end. It is a common and most necessary social function in life, a bond of union among men. It was St. Paul's ideal (which he exemplified in himself) that all men should work in order to have the wherewithal to live, although this ideal had in it no hint of speculation upon labor or of being an instrument for greed. On the other hand Paul had no use for parasites. "He who does not work should not eat," he declares.

This aphorism has been taken up and wrongly used by many labor movements that are based on production. Paul regarded work as necessary but as something that had only a transitory value: a value as a means and not as an end. The end will always remain the same; it is above production, beyond earthly life for eternal values only.

Therefore labor must not receive a super-evaluation. It must not seek a recompense far above and beyond its just due, because this is only another form of idolatry and tends to brutalize the nature of a man. The Apostle visualizes a society where no one is idle, in which he who can work shares with him who cannot work. Paul would never have his Christians a burden to anyone, least of all to the pagans or the Jews. He desired each Christian community to become a source of help rather than a reservoir of affluence.

The poor, the infirm, the sick, pilgrims, prisoners, the homeless, all must be assisted. Deacons and deaconesses were appointed to take care of the sick and the hungry. These latter were to be widows of mature years, who had been married only once and who had no families to support. The Church provided for their maintenance and they assisted the priests in the service of the women.

It is clearly discernible that the Church is becoming something different from its pagan surroundings, and from the Roman state. The Church now claims autonomy in her obligations in life, since these are in relation to her Head, Jesus Christ, and not from the state or from Caesar. The fact is that although the environment was pagan, this differentiation became more apparent, which gave the Christian communities an air of aloofness.

Paul, as well as Peter and all the ancient ecclesiastical writers, always reacted against any rigorous tendency that would isolate the Christians from other people. Peace being the most essential factor in the whole program of Christianity, the faithful must always shun what would separate them from others and especially must guard against any dissensions among themselves. It is a sin to quarrel, a violation of charity and of unity.

If there are differences between Christians they are not to take their law-suits before the pagan courts. It is not right, according to St. Paul, that the unjustified (the unbaptized) should judge the saints; on the contrary, the saints shall have a part with Christ in judging the world.

It is more logical, observes St. Paul, not without a certain irony, to reduce these bickerings and foolish controversies to their proper level and worth by carrying them before the most ignorant of the brethren; or again, before the wisest among them.

The Family

The first necessity for the Christian is his own personal and individual sanctification. He must labor for his formation in Christ by the exercise of Christian virtue. Then the disciple of Christ brings to the family group, which is a small social unit, concord, purity, and unity, that there the full Christian ideal may be realized. Chastity is one of the most sublime virtues, which Paul himself chose, and he set the example of celibacy for his most heroic followers. Chastity requires strength of character, it is, therefore, for the few rather than for the many.

Matrimony is a great sacrament. Paul would see it honored and kept inviolate. He compares the union of a man with his wife to the union of Christ with His Church. God is the prototype of fatherhood, just as the Church, His Bride, is the prototype of motherhood. Christ is the symbol of the husband and the head of the woman just as Christ is the Head of His Church. The unity of the two who marry goes so far as to make them one flesh, which reflects the unity between Christ and His Church. The submission of the wife to her husband is modelled upon that of the Church to Christ. It is more than a question of symbols and models. The same relations are taken from the supernatural plane and extended to the natural plane in order to bring about a supernatural result. Love is elevated to the divine; matrimony becomes a sublime mode of collaboration with the work of the Creator in building His Church.

St. Paul expresses it thus: "Let wives be subject to their husbands as to the Lord; because a husband is head of the wife as Christ is Head of the Church, being Himself a saviour of the body. But just as the Church is subject to Christ, so also let wives be to their husbands in all things.

"Husbands, love your wives, just as Christ also loved the Church, and delivered himself up for her, that He might sanctify her, cleansing her in the bath of water by means of the word.

"Even thus ought husbands also to love their wives as their own bodies. He who loves his own wife, loves himself. For no one ever hated his own flesh; on the contrary he nourishes and cherishes it, as Christ also does the Church (because we are members of his body, made from his flesh and from his bones).

"For this reason a man shall leave his father and mother, and shall cleave to his wife; and the two shall become one flesh.

"This is a great mystery—I mean in reference to Christ and to the Church. However, let each one of you also love his wife just as he loves himself; and let the wife respect her husband." [6]

This changing and purifying of the concept of matrimony is all the more appreciated when we remember that it was a living fact in the midst of a pagan society where matrimonial dissolution was the common thing and to break the marriage contract an easy thing to do.

Matrimony modelled upon the example of Christ and His Church was taught to a society which had for its models the adulterous gods on Mt. Olympus and on the Palatine Hill. Matrimony which makes of two people one flesh is to be an indissoluble union.

In the early Christian society it frequently happened that one of the two married persons was a pagan. If the pagan was satisfied to live with the Christian partner, it was well not to loosen the bond of the contract; the baptized one, sanctified by grace, might help to sanctify the other. If, however, the unbeliever wished to be separated from the Christian, the Christian should consent so that his faith would run no risk of being lost. The Christian would then be free to marry again if fulfilling a true matrimony in Christ, and this is what is known as the Pauline privilege.

In Christian matrimony the husband belongs to the wife and the wife to the husband; each is obliged to observe fidelity to the other. For either one the sin of adultery is very grave. The head of the family is the man who must love his wife without being bitter towards her. Such a husband must have been highly desirable in a society where a woman was considered a costly ornament or merely an ani-

[6] Eph. 5:22–33.

mal to be exploited. In every respect, in the estimate of the judicial Roman courts or in pagan society, she was kept down on a level far inferior to men. Upholding the family hierarchy, St. Paul pronounces man and woman completely equal in the sight of God; both have souls, and if they possess grace there is no difference between the two.

In the discipline of the Church, the woman retains her inferior place and is not allowed to speak in the assemblies of the Christians or at their ceremonies in public worship. She has the right to receive great love from her husband, and for her there will be great merit and grace in all the sacrifices demanded by motherhood. St. Paul writes thus: "Yet women will be saved by childbearing, if they continue in faith and love and holiness with modesty." [7]

In the peace of conjugal life children are associated with and linked with their parents through the grace of Baptism and through their bonds in the Mystical Body, over and above the natural ties of blood. They must obey their parents in all things with reverence and respect in order to please God. Parents have authority over their children and must educate and train them properly.

Slavery still existed, and Paul was not a social agitator. To abolish slavery at that time would have been as ill-advised as to abolish the use of the machine today in our own technical age. The social condition that already existed was Christianized. The slave was made a brother by the bond of grace and equal to his master as regards the value of his soul. In the Christian concept he ceases to be a slave (that is, a commodity, or utensil, as the pagans regarded the slave). As a Christian the slave has acquired a new dignity, that of a son of God. He, too, has been redeemed by the Blood of Christ. His rank in the Church will be according to virtue and not according to his social class or station.

Even slavery can serve to advance one's sanctification. The servant can make of his obedience an act of virtue and a way of serving our Lord Jesus Christ. Masters can practice virtue by guarding against injustice and aggression since they will be required to give an account

[7] 1 Tim. 2:15.

of the use they make of their authority received from God, Who makes no distinction of persons. By treating servants with equity they prove themselves worthy servants of their common Master. In such a system, new spiritual values, standards and doctrines, slavery (if it remains a lawful social institution) is morally annulled and shorn of its odium.

The Originality of St. Paul

When Paul expounded his Christian ideas he must have seemed like a madman in the eyes of his contemporaries who knew only the wisdom of the old civilization. He was so regarded by the state officials and the intelligentsia of his times. In fact, his system, as compared with the ideals and standards of the pre-Christian world, must have sounded like the ravings of a barbarian.

If some modern critics had considered the positive effects and results of his preaching in a world both pagan and conservative, they would have spared themselves their paradoxical and contradictory thesis that the great Apostle borrowed from, or was dependent upon, the pagan and oriental mystical philosophies of his times. The Evangelical announcement sounded so new—and it was so extremely original—to the Jews, Greeks and Romans, that as soon as they understood a little of its meaning, they at once tried to crush it and to banish it by persecution. This truth is all the more remarkable since it took place in the Roman Empire, the most intolerant institution of antiquity in its philosophies and laws.

Paul's message was one of charity, peace and liberty. After the first moments of surprise and astonishment had passed, the exponents of the ancient way of thinking gathered together to suppress him and his message, as they had done with all the other announcers of Christ.

Paul said that each person should remain in the state of life to which each had been called by Christ Jesus. This meant leaving the social structure of the old order intact. Philosophers, rabbis, magistrates, and slaves called *"hieroduli,"* dedicated to the worship of the pagan deities, soon perceived that Christ and His Apostle would leave intact only the outer shell of life; the essence of the traditional spirit would be emptied and changed. They saw in the new message a revolution, all the more dangerous since it came in the guise of peace, of patience and of harmony. A revolution, beginning with the interior spirit and moving outwards, modified politics, philosophy, economy, castes and classes; literally turned all things in the world upside down.

In Paul's vocabulary one finds all the terms and expressions used in his times by people of culture. His vocabulary was everybody's vocabulary. He put a new meaning in his words that made them penetrate into the thoughts of society like a flame of fire. He gave them a new sense so radically different and they received a power so dynamic that it brought them to the point of explosion. From Christ is born a new man. With a new interior spirit a different spiritual order is evolved so that even the exterior is new. In Christ all things of the old order seem to be killed and buried, to be born again spiritually but different.

The Christian keeps his name, his outward features, but he is not the same because he takes his place within a system whose center and aim and inspiration are different. The orbit is changed. The central axis is not fixed by earthly values and worldly prestige but is centered on Christ; taking its motion and direction from another world. The heart of man and the heart of society were lighted with the fire of a supernatural love. Above the Empire of Caesar the Kingdom of God was rising.

It may be said that Paul is not Mark, nor is he Peter. That is true; just as Peter is not John, and John is not Luke, because each is himself, and not another person. Every Christian lives Christianity with his own temperament, with the intelligence and individual gifts with which the Holy Spirit has particularly endowed him. This means that Christianity does not destroy personality but gives it a new power. Such an objection is therefore archaic and superficial; it belongs to the age of those contemporaries of Paul who thought that they had discovered that his Gospel was different from that of the other Apostles.

In answering these and their successors, Paul is careful to repeat that his Gospel is that of Christ, and nothing more. The same may be said of the other Apostles. The style of his exposition is different. Among Christians there have always been contemplatives, or active persons, melancholy or cheerful, severe or serene people; St. John of the Cross is not St. Thomas More, and St. Catherine of Siena is not Mother Cabrini. Each personality gives to faith a particular tone, a coloring all its own; but faith is one and the same. The functions of faith all tend to the same point or end, but they are not all uniform.

The Gospel in the person of Paul passes through a great love like a burning lava which gives to his expressions an intense heat. His tone, so full of originality, can be either a roaring tempest or a caressing breeze. The particular relief in which he places some aspects of the Gospel, the special manner in which he presents them, according to his own mind, or to the listeners and readers to whom he is addressing himself, and the exercise of his own intellectual faculties, fuses all into a pliable and ready instrument for Evangelization. This is the originality of St. Paul.

The particular points of his evangelical preachings can be summed up in this way: there is one God, Father and Lord of all, Jesus Christ His Son, and the Holy Spirit. Christ is all and in all, the center of life. He is the Redeemer by His own Blood, the Head and foundation of His Church, the model for all Christians to imitate. Christ was put to death on the Cross, and with Him, Who was without sin, sin was put to death, likewise all enmities and differences. These He took upon Himself through Love.

From the Sacrifice of the Cross a new cycle begins. It is eternal; it restores life and destroys death. The faithful are called into the society of Jesus Christ, which is His Body, the Church, and to the eternal city of the Saints. Christ in His Church is the column and foundation of truth, one and indivisible.

Salvation comes by faith; it is a gift of Christ. He is both priest and victim, and reconciles us to God. The understanding of divine things comes through the light of grace and the authority of a teaching Church. Exploration into profane wisdom is useless in understanding the mysteries of Christ.

The criterion of truth is found in Tradition, which is the faithful transmission of all that has been taught by the Apostles. Every change or alteration in this deposit of truth in Tradition is to be spurned.

With baptism, the old man (that is, the old nature), is put away; the new man (that is, the new spiritual nature) is put on. "All is made new," says St. Paul. Before God there are no privileged men, nor any rejected men; there is neither Jew nor Greek, slave nor free. We who before were equal in sin are now made equal by grace.

The universality and unity of the Church is now known and understood. The Mosaic Law and paganism, two forms of servitude, have come to an end. Men have come to a new liberty. Charity is the agent and principle of reform in social life. It is a gift granted to all and used through man's free will. The body has become the temple of the Holy Spirit. Man knows an interior life; in this he is transformed into Christ by grace. Putting on Christ is his own sanctity, and the edification of his neighbor.

Paul the Writer

These are St. Paul's teachings of Christian doctrines: rapid, concise, and very essential. Paul is never lost in details or unnecessary words; he keeps strictly to primary truths. His teaching does not expand systematically, but is distributed briefly throughout his writings and discourses as inspiration or circumstances demand.

The principal truths are comprehensible to all, both the learned and the unlearned, although at times they are enveloped in profound thought. Salvation is not an intellectual work; it is a gift of the grace of God to which man responds through faith. Did Paul make use of philosophy, or politics, or history? With what words, comparisons, methods, and spirit did he present Christ? We answer that he subordinated all men and all things to the one purpose of converting them to Christ.

Paul possessed a general culture that was balanced and sound. He never thought of exhibiting it for its own self, or for boasting. Philosophy, as such, never inspired him, and he had a natural loathing for it. In fact, he had just reason for being diffident, since the fashion of the day was to reduce intellectual thought to mere verbosity, and rhetoric to a matter of purely technical and euphonic verbiage.

He did not care to lean on human resources; he made himself all things to all men. It was his love for the Gospel that inspired those warm, clear-cut phrases in which he pours out a thought, a thought too vibrating to be contained in a common vocabulary. Paul and the other writers of the New Testament initiate a new literature which is not preoccupied with style but with souls; or better still, with the one and only person who counts—Jesus Christ.

It is a literature born of the rejection of a literature. Paul's preaching was not founded on rules of rhetoric. He used no elegance of speech nor subtlety of argument. He knew nothing of style, nor did he want to know anything; therefore he is truly a great writer.

In the same manner he is a great speaker. His strength lay in the things he said, and in the faith that inspired him to say them even though he felt himself timid and fearful. The spoken word was only a means to an end. In his speech, he is not like a single flower that can be contemplated by itself. Paul was always inflammable material; he threw in himself and all that was his to feed the flame of love burning in his soul for Christ.

His art, unconscious but powerful, is a form, a product of the Apostolate. Some have tried with subtle analysis to single out the origin of his vocabulary. Did it come from the Septuagint? From the Sophists, or the Jewish manuscripts, or rolls? They give no answers.

Paul is an artist by instinct. He collects his words from ordinary speech, makes an intuitive choice guided by his moral sensibilities and avoids vulgar expressions. Therefore, he is neither studied nor commonplace; his high concept and exquisite feeling uplift ordinary words and give them sublime and richer meanings. The phrase is carried on by an urgent thought from a supernatural source and carries away the language as though unable to contain it, so that the period cannot check it. His thought is like water that bursts the dike by its pressure.

This is a phenomenon that the Stylists would like to call an *anacoluthon,* that is, a construction without sequence but which does express strong emotion. It is a current in which his love for Christ and for souls tends to break the outward envelope of words. This explains his numerous parentheses, his repetition of thought; it is like something obscure laboring to clarify itself. At the same time there is a continual crescendo of significance in the terms he uses and in the necessity for coining new ones. This necessity is proper to the genius who will invariably use an ordinary expression in a new way or employ common words to convey extraordinary meanings.

This creation of new words is not a conscious intellectual operation, it is a spontaneous outburst of his burning love. It is not surprising then if his most characteristic and most vigorous words are those molded to express the dogma nearest his heart and the one most difficult for his converts among the Gentiles to accept; their fellowship with Christ. They are incorporated into Christ. They have a partnership in His sufferings as they have in His grace and inheritance. There was no word in the whole range of Hellenistic culture to express the degrees of this "oneness," co-suffering, co-crucifixion, co-burial, and co-resurrection, or of this supernatural life to be lived in society. Paul had to use ingenuity, even with effort, to give some idea of it.

For such a use the worn instrument becomes original, like a new language at the service of a new thought—at its service, but never dominating it. This would be at times most inconvenient and would be misunderstood; which did happen and still happens. Paul feared this so he labored to make clear his thought within the phrase by twisting and reshaping it as if it were iron melting in a flame, so that he, the artisan, seems to sweat over his exertions. There is no end to his supplementary explanations and marginal notes. He gathers his thoughts and he strikes, so that they seem to spring like sparks from every side of the anvil.

His thought moves forward in a firm, straight, clear course, notwithstanding the evident effort of dragging the burden of an impoverished tongue. He lifts it continually into the light of a sun that melts all metals. His diction is also an effort and reads like a drama. If one fails to pick up his thought or to embrace its synthesis, one risks misunderstanding him, as has often happened. Once Peter had to intervene, to put the reader on his guard, and to explain the meaning.

It is possible to find some Pauline constructions in the Greek versions of the Bible, in the parchments, or in contemporary writers, but his style is not understood unless the ardent Paul, and no one else, is reflected therein. Wilamowitz-Moellendorff calls him a classic of Hellenism; this could be true, if by this is meant that Paul knew how to make language a docile and lucid instrument for expressing his thought. His thought and his speech pour forth in one and the same burning flow, they cannot be separated. Paul would have regarded it as hypocrisy, quite like the use of cosmetics; and he had too much respect and reverence for the Gospel to present it under any deforming make-up.

The parallelisms found in his letters classify him neither with the Semites nor the Greeks. They are a necessity for that lively consciousness he feels between the opprobrium of the Cross and the viewpoint of the ancient civilization. He uses a dualism of phrases to clarify the antithesis and to develop the contrast between the two orders, the old and the new; between the letter and the spirit; between the flesh and the soul; between the Church and the world.

Apropos of the various aspects of truth which are found in the fourteen letters of St. Paul still in our possession, someone has spoken of an "evolving Pauline thought." It cannot be denied that Paul did progress and develop spiritually as well as intellectually. It seems, however, more logical to say that Christian communities were continually evolving and perfecting themselves in the new life and doctrine, so that Paul had, continually through the years, to lift the tone of his dictation as well as of his theme. He frequently had to examine his former teachings in order to present them under a new aspect.

Thus he never repeats, even when he presents the same argument. Who knows how many other images, considerations, or discoveries he may have given his listeners, already strengthened by the Eucharist in the Churches at Corinth, at Ephesus, and at Rome?

And so every letter has its own particular tone, content and purpose. Each is an added wealth; each opens a new series, or passes on in some inaccessible depths of mystery from which a beauty radiates with its own attractions; each is a masterpiece in itself.

What variety and nobility of thought follow from one expression to another, from wrath to prayer, from a catechesis to an exhortation, from a rigid consideration to an effusion of heart. "Salute his mother and mine." What tenderness of expression in this. It is like a jewel set in his letter to the Romans: a letter which is a strong obelisk of Christian theology.

Paul dictated his letters but certainly not with idle hands. He handled his tools, and at the same time he explored the whole Mosaic economy. While carding he was pondering on the effects his words would have on the Christian Communities. He foresaw the objections that were likely to arise and in spirit he entered into all their anxieties.

All this gives a particular movement to his Epistles in which the erudite have pretended to see a likeness to the prevailing diatribes in vogue among the Stoics and Cynics. If there are any likenesses, certainly Paul did not seek them. He made use of all the material at his disposal but he did it in his own way.

When he spoke of Christ, to Whom his thoughts turned incessantly —for his thoughts were always Christ-centered—perhaps he let his arms fall on the rough weaving while he raised his eyes to seek on the bare walls the dazzling features of Christ's Face. His eyes would fill with tears, and yet shine with a light reflected from that first radiant vision on the road below Damascus.

No doubt his emotions became so strong that he had to stop and resume his dictation on the morrow, thus giving a brusque turn to the thread of his reasoning or to the fullness of his sentiment. When he had finished dictating he took the stylus from the hand of the brother, his amanuensis, and engraved on the tablet, or wrote on the parchment, a few words in which he seemed to place a shred of his heart.

A spectacle just as wonderful as to witness one of his miracles was to see Paul in his room working by the light of a lantern while he recalled numberless visions of heaven and earth, of God and the demons. Within those four walls, so poor and bare a place, could be seen a spectacle of superhuman greatness under the tunic of an infirm workman.

Thus there came to light those letters so fit to set the world on fire; nor were they to be hidden in archives along with the epistles of Cicero and Seneca. They were composed in their first draft, dictated spontaneously as Paul's mind suggested. It is evident that they were often interrupted and then resumed, as they contain all the irregularities that try the patience of the ornate writers.

Readers of the prevailing Greek literature, accustomed to anthologies and old books revised, suddenly discovered a new tone, elevated and animated, such as they once found in the writings of Aesculapius and Plato; and the new supernatural, spiritual flavor thrilled them. There was vigor of concept, close logic, an inspiration that carried them away into other and new regions of thought. The richness of phraseology, clear-cut expressions, swept away their resistance or softness, and conquered their spirit.

Paul's words possess a power that dominates us even today. They are unspoiled by nineteen centuries of grinding by philological exegetes, historical and theological.

In everything and in every way Paul centers all in Christ, even the style of his writing. He is so absorbed inwardly in the contemplation of his Redeemer that in his discourses or in his writing there is hardly ever a reference to nature or to the world about him.

The preaching of Jesus is beautifully ornamented with vines, trees, towers, flowers, flocks, while the blue lakes mirror the blue skies crossed by a flight of birds. Surely Paul must have seen some wonderful countries in his travels. He saw many historical monuments, spent many a night in a tempest on the sea, and threaded his way through the various gatherings of people in many different cities. But he lived only in a world crowded with the things of the spirit, within the movements of an intelligence which was like a luminous night. Nature did not impress Paul, he lived too much under the arch of supernature; in a spiritual world above the material world.

This complete reversal of values takes place also in the realm of culture. In a sense, Paul holds that it is impossible to reach God by the aid of natural or human reason alone, without the gift of faith. Here, too, Christianity is at the opposite pole of the world; those volunteers who wore themselves out trying to establish a symbiosis, a living together of two opposite orders, did not know what they were doing.

For this reason Paul is polemical in his Epistles. Christ has given His message with divine calm and strength. Paul defends it against falsifiers, detractors, and adversaries. He can soar like an eagle and as swiftly descend upon the enemies of Christ. He speaks his doctrine with cutting phrase as though he would tear it apart with claws.

Paul knew that the intellectuals of his day sought philosophy for its own sake. It opened up careers and it summed up all culture. Paul never indulged in the fashion of the period. In the city of Athens, the center of this culture, he did not speak on philosophy but on theology. His speech to the Athenians was largely a failure. Intellectualism is always rather restrictive to faith.

Paul stood out, as always, against the attempts to rationalize the clear and simple Christian teaching—the Personality of God in Christ, the Redemption by Christ, and the resurrection of the dead; which doctrines the Rationalists attempted to dissolve into vapors.

When speaking to the Corinthians—the Greeks were frivolous and more easily caught by brilliant oratorical discourses—Paul contrasts the prevailing wisdom which the world esteems great with the foolishness of the Cross. That which, in the eyes of the Rationalists—incapable of seeing beyond the senses—seemed to be contrary to philosophy, was for Paul true wisdom; or, as the Greek apologists would say, true philosophy. Christ, Incarnate Wisdom, came to confound the wisdom and the strength of this world; it is the lover of Christ who surpasses all science.

Finally Paul advocates only one culture: the Christian religion. This was all that was necessary and it was sufficient for the Apostolate. He never compromised or mutilated truth. He presented the opposite view with precision and thus established clearly the originality of the Christian message; the contrast, as he remarked to the Corinthians, between the word of the Cross and the wisdom of the world. Faith is not a product for human consideration, a matter which might be settled by a commission of professors; it is a spirit coming from God; it is a supernatural gift.

A saint can convert more sinners than a university professor of theology, especially if the professor is not animated by the Spirit of God. We are never to forget that in preaching, and in writing too, he who plants as well as he who waters, are nothing; God alone gives the increase. God alone converts. We must have humility, or rather, the greatness to be docile instruments in His hands.

In conclusion, Paul is the example of a perfect teacher. He is essential in substance, uncompromising in dogma, and pleasing in secondary matters. He is varied in exposition and always confirms his words by his own life. The power and efficacy of his words lies in the fact that his listeners always saw them lived out in Paul. Paul was burning with love for Christ and from Paul they understood Who Christ was. Like Thecla in the Apocryphal "Acts of Paul," who beheld the Apostle of the Gentiles in the mirror of his own prose, they saw, not Paul, but Jesus Christ with Whom Paul had identified himself so perfectly.

Also available from St. Paul Editions:

Africa or Death!
Rev. A.G. Mondini, FSCJ

Heroic life of the dedicated missionary, Bishop Comboni, Founder of the Verona Fathers. His motto—"Africa or Death!" 336 pages
cloth $5.00 — BI0010

Africa's Twelve Apostles
Rev. H. Russell, S.M.A.

The story of how Catholicism has been planted in Africa since the middle of the last century pulsates with heroism and warmth, with humor and surprise. The author portrays the lives of twelve outstanding men who pioneered much of this progress and left their impact on the African missions. 426 pages
cloth $6.95; paper $5.50 — BI0025

Autobiography of St. John Neumann, C.SS.R.
Translation, Introduction, Commentary and Epilogue by Alfred C. Rush, CSSR

"This autobiography is important for the insight it gives us into the character of Bishop Neumann, of Philadelphia, into Neumann as a person...how he faced life, how he coped with difficulties, disappointments and setbacks....

"The life of John Neumann remains a challenge to all of us...to manifest to all the world our loyalty to Jesus Christ and His Church." —John Cardinal Krol
118 pages
cloth $3.50; paper $2.50 — ST0010

Doctor Luke, Beloved Physician
Msgr. Leo Gregory Fink

A vibrant presentation of the Christ-like personality of the great physician of early Christian times. 216 pages
cloth $4.00; paper $2.75 — ST0040

Every Man's Challenge
Daughters of St. Paul

The warm and dynamic personalities of 38 saints are captured in brief inspiring profiles. Their lives confirm Christ's message: sanctity is "everyman's challenge."
345 pages
cloth $5.00 — ST0050

Families That Followed the Lord
Martin P. Harney, SJ

This book contains the lives of over one hundred fifty brother and sister saints of various nationalities, places, and times. This account of fraternal and religious loyalty, which blends the best of what is human and divine, cannot fail to touch and inspire the reader of today. 145
145 pages
cloth $3.95; paper $2.95 — ST0060

The Great Blackrobe
Jean Pitrone

The thrilling experiences of Father DeSmet, the Jesuit missionary to the Indians of America's great Northwest.
cloth $4.00; paper $3.00 — BI0110

Hero of Molokai

Rev. Omer Englebert

Gripping story of Father Damien, apostle of the lepers—filled with thrills, pathos and intense human interest. Illustrated. 364 pages
cloth $4.00; paper $3.00 — BI0120

In Praise of St. Paul

St. John Chrysostom

Translated by Halton, Ph.D. The sermons contained in this volume testify to the saint's knowledge of St. Paul's writings as well as to his deep admiration of Paul's many virtues. 128 pages
cloth $2.00 — SP0300

James Alberione: A Marvel of Our Times

Fr. Stephen Lamera, SSP

The first life in English of the Servant of God and Founder of five Religious Congregations of Priests, Brothers and Sisters and of three Secular Institutes for Priests, men and women. In the person and work of Father Alberione the prophetic and apostolic charism of St. Paul lives again. A strong personality and moral giant whose ideas were original, he was possessed of a temperament which brought things to a realization in a way that few others could. He is in a certain way another St. Paul for today. Incarnated in this modern apostle is the zeal of St. Paul for all peoples. For him, every "technical" means was "elevated to being an apostolate." "His religious were to be perfect apostles and perfect professionals, for the 'purpose of doing good' and of 'leading others to do good' in order to reach everyone where they were to be reached: not only in churches, but in the family, at work, on the highways, in entertainments, everywhere; through the films, radio, television, with books, newspapers, records, cassettes, comic books, with any other means of progress of the mass means of communication; that all means might be pulpits to make the voice of the Divine Master heard in every environment."

Readers will discover with great joy, be deeply and irresistibly attracted to, and come to love dearly, this great and most humble priest through whom God chose to do such wonders for mankind, a noble-souled priest who wrote to the Holy Father words which he lived in unswerving and total fidelity: *"Our joy is that of living attached to you, Holy Father, to obey you in everything, to be completely yours till the last breath."* 186 pages
cloth $4.00; paper $3.00 — BI0150

Joseph, the Just Man

Rosalie Marie Levy

A complete biography, supplemented with accounts of favors granted and selections of special prayers. 285 pages
cloth $4.00; paper $3.00 — ST0100

Joseph: The Man Closest to Jesus

Francis L. Filas, SJ

Never before has all this wealth of intensely interesting and little-known facts about St. Joseph been compiled into a single book. This can truly be called a "little Summa" of St. Joseph, as the only survey existing in any language of the complete life, theology, and devotional history of St. Joseph. 682 pages
cloth $7.75 — ST0110

The Legacy of St. Patrick

Martin P. Harney, SJ

The legacy of St. Patrick, which he would bequeath to his

brethren and their descendants, was his own holy idealism. It can be found in his two writings, the Confession of St. Patrick and the Letters to the Soldiers of Coroticus.

A thoughtful perusal of the Confession and of the Letter will reward the reader with a true and an intimate knowledge of St. Patrick. 148 pages
cloth $3.50; paper $2.25 — ST0120

The Man in Chains, St. Paul

Rosalie Marie Levy

An intriguing life of one of the world's greatest heroes and saints—the Apostle Paul.
225 pages
cloth $4.00; paper $3.00 — ST0150

Meditation Notes on Paul the Apostle, Model of the Spiritual Life

Rev. James Alberione, SSP, STD

These writings of Father James Alberione, Founder of the Pauline Family, were discovered after his death in November, 1971. They are meditation notes and resolutions made during a course of spiritual exercises. The theme is St. Paul and the priest. Every priest and spiritual guide can find in these pages a great wealth of material. 100 pages
cloth $2.00 — SP0420

Moments of Decision

Daughters of St. Paul

Profiles of 28 saints from many backgrounds and states in life. Portrayed with warmth and vitality, their lives teach us to use our "moments of decision" for Christ and His people. 315 pages
cloth $5.00; paper $4.00 — ST0170

Month with St. Paul

Rev. James Alberione, SSP, STD
Rev. Timothy Giaccardo, SSP

This book of 31 inspiring meditations will bear frequent rereading and be of great spiritual help for priests, religious and for the laity. It is a true guide and consoler for those who are seeking spiritual happiness and perfection. 232 pages
paper $2.25 — SP0445

Mother Cabrini

Daughters of St. Paul

Animated story of the labors of the first American-citizen saint, whose greatest happiness lay in caring for the orphans, the sick and the destitute, and saving souls in a new land. 223 pages
cloth $3.50; paper $2.50 — ST0180

Mother Seton—wife, mother, educator, foundress, saint

Daughters of St. Paul

This fast-paced life of "an authentic daughter of America" (Pope John's term) is completed by selections from Mother Seton's own writings—Spiritual Gems—that permit us to glimpse the deep spirituality of the first American-born saint. 140 pages
cloth $3.95 — ST0160

The Personality of St. Paul

Cornelius a Lapide, SJ

The author, with the sensitivity of an artist, depicts in detail the inestimable virtues of this great apostle. 153 pages
cloth $3.50; paper $2.25 — SP0530

Saint and Thought for Everyday

Profiles by Daughters of St. Paul
Thoughts by Rev. James Alberione, SSP, STD

Brief sketches of lives of the saints for all year are presented according to the new calendar of saints.

Challenging daily thoughts by the renowned author Fr. James Alberione are arranged so as to assist us in our growth to full stature in Christ. 311 pages
cloth $3.95; paper $2.95 — ST0190

St. Catherine of Siena

Igino Giordani

The 14th century was one of the most turbulent in the history of Christianity. A semi-literate Italian woman dominated that century with her prodigious temporal activity. Readers are deeply led into the recesses of Catherine's mysticism— an outstanding life of a recently proclaimed Doctor of the Church. 258 pages
cloth $8.00; paper $7.00 — ST0220

St. Francis de Sales and His Friends

Maurice Henry-Couannier

In selecting the most significant features of his life the author has discovered that St. Francis is probably best understood through his friends and friendships and against the background of the people he knew and loved, for in a very special way he deserves to be called the Saint of Friendship. 414 pages
cloth $5.00 — ST0230

St. Francis of Assisi

Msgr. Leon Cristiani

Msgr. Leon Cristiani's life of St. Francis offers the reader facts, authentic traditions, revered texts and a hope to foster in the reader a deep love and admiration for the saint whose fruitful life he tells. 164 pages
cloth $4.95; paper $3.95 — ST0240

St. Joan of Arc, Virgin— Soldier

Msgr. Leon Cristiani

The author scrupulously strives to present the simple, naked, historical truth about the life and times of Joan of Arc. He also outlines the supernatural in Joan's life in all its clarity. 160 pages
cloth $3.95; paper $2.95 — ST0260

St. Pius X, Pope

Most Rev. Jan Olav Smit

Journey through the boyhood, priesthood, papacy and sainthood of this remarkable man— warm, lovable, humorous— capable of leading the people of God with extraordinary wisdom— the influence of which we still feel in the Church today. 184 pages
cloth $4.00; paper $3.00 — ST0320

St. Teresa of Avila

Giorgio Papasogli

It took the author a year's visit to Spain, exhaustive research and an intensive study of all the existing material before he was ready to write. The result was an entirely new biography of one of the most written-about women in the world. 410 pages
cloth $5.00 — ST0330

The Story of Monica and Her Son Augustine

Msgr. Leon Cristiani

The stirring story of a woman's faith and steadfastness in prayer that won the conversion of her wayward son. 176 pages
cloth $3.95; paper $2.95 — ST0380

Three Ways of Love

Frances Parkinson Keyes

The world-famous author here captures the romance, the tragedy and the history of three great women: St. Agnes, whose

name has become synonymous with courage; St. Frances of Rome, a mother and the protectress of the poor and sick; and St. Catherine of Siena, the famous ambassadress and stateswoman. 304 pages
cloth $6.00; paper $5.00 — ST0390

The Village Priest Who Fought God's Battles
St. John Mary Vianney

Msgr. Leon Cristiani

The lovable Cure of Ars, patron of all diocesan priests, is widely known for his battles with the devil and his victory over the power of evil. Here he comes alive in his ministry of prayer, penance and apostolic zeal. But first we meet the man who fought his own spiritual battles—a great source of inspiration and courage in our own war against evil.
172 pages
cloth $4.00; paper $3.00 — ST0400

A Woman for Our Time

S. Lucarini

The Servant of God, Mother Thecla Merlo. "This biography of Mother Thecla Merlo, first Superior General of the Daughters of St. Paul, comes from the pen of one who is not a member of the Pauline Family, but who was able to look in from outside, choosing and making use of the words, impressions and judgments of a wide range of people." 254 pages
cloth $3.95 — BI0250

Woman of Faith

Daughters of St. Paul

Profile of the Servant of God, Mother Thecla Merlo, Co-foundress of the Daughters of St. Paul. An illuminating discovery of how Christian involvement in our modern world goes hand in hand with the perfection of charity and love of God. 226 pages
cloth $3.00 — BI0260

Please order from any of the addresses on the following page, specifying title and item number.

Daughters of St. Paul

IN MASSACHUSETTS
   50 St. Paul's Ave. Jamaica Plain, Boston, MA 02130;
      617-522-8911; 617-522-0875;
   172 Tremont Street, Boston, MA 02111; **617-426-5464;**
      617-426-4230
IN NEW YORK
   78 Fort Place, Staten Island, NY 10301; **212-447-5071**
   59 East 43rd Street, New York, NY 10017; **212-986-7580**
   7 State Street, New York, NY 10004; **212-447-5071**
   625 East 187th Street, Bronx, NY 10458; **212-584-0440**
   525 Main Street, Buffalo, NY 14203; **716-847-6044**
IN NEW JERSEY
   Hudson Mall — Route 440 and Communipaw Ave.,
      Jersey City, NJ 07304; **201-433-7740**
IN CONNECTICUT
   202 Fairfield Ave., Bridgeport, CT 06604; **203-335-9913**
IN OHIO
   2105 Ontario St. (at Prospect Ave.), Cleveland, OH 44115; **216-621-9427**
   25 E. Eighth Street, Cincinnati, OH 45202; **513-721-4838**
IN PENNSYLVANIA
   1719 Chestnut Street, Philadelphia, PA 19103; **215-568-2638**
IN FLORIDA
   2700 Biscayne Blvd., Miami, FL 33137; **305-573-1618**
IN LOUISIANA
   4403 Veterans Memorial Blvd., Metairie, LA 70002; **504-887-7631;**
      504-887-0113
   1800 South Acadian Thruway, P.O. Box 2028, Baton Rouge, LA 70821
      504-343-4057; 504-343-3814
IN MISSOURI
   1001 Pine Street (at North 10th), St. Louis, MO 63101; **314-621-0346;**
      314-231-1034
IN ILLINOIS
   172 North Michigan Ave., Chicago, IL 60601; **312-346-4228;**
      312-346-3240
IN TEXAS
   114 Main Plaza, San Antonio, TX 78205; **512-224-8101**
IN CALIFORNIA
   1570 Fifth Avenue, San Diego, CA 92101; **714-232-1442**
   46 Geary Street, San Francisco, CA 94108; **415-781-5180**
IN HAWAII
   1143 Bishop Street, Honolulu, HI 96813; **808-521-2731**
IN ALASKA
   750 West 5th Avenue, Anchorage AK 99501; **907-272-8183**
IN CANADA
   3022 Dufferin Street, Toronto 395, Ontario, Canada
IN ENGLAND
   128, Notting Hill Gate, London W11 3QG, England
   133 Corporation Street, Birmingham B4 6PH, England
   5A-7 Royal Exchange Square, Glasgow G1 3AH, England
   82 Bold Street, Liverpool L1 4HR, England
IN AUSTRALIA
   58 Abbotsford Rd., Homebush, N.S.W., Sydney 2140, Australia